THE DOWN HOME GUIDE TO THE BLUES

Frank Scott
and the Staff of *Down Home Music*

a cappella books

Library of Congress Cataloging-in-Publication Data

Scott, Frank, 1942–
    The Down Home guide to the blues / by Frank Scott and the staff of
Down Home Music.
       p.   cm.
    Summary: A discographical guide to more than 3,000 blues and gospel
LPs, CDs, and cassettes with information on the featured artists, and the
quality and availability of the recordings.
    ISBN 1-55652-130-8 : $14.95
    1. Blues (Music)—Discography. 2. Gospel music—Discography.
[1. Blues (music)—Discography. 2. Gospel music—Discography.]
I. Down Home Music (Firm) II. Title.
ML 156.4.B6S26   1990
016.781643'026'6—dc20
                                        90-37638
                                        CIP
                                        AC MN

a cappella books
an imprint of Chicago Review Press

Editorial offices:
PO Box 380
Pennington, NJ 08534

Business/Sales offices:
814 N. Franklin St.
Chicago, IL 60610

Cover photograph: B. B. King in performance by Marc PoKempner

Cover design: Fran Lee
Editorial coordinator: Richard Carlin

Introduction

This book is a little different from most blues books. Rather than a history or critical analysis of the music, it is a mail order catalog rendered as a book, but a catalog with a difference. When Chris Strachwitz and I turned the Down Home Music retail store into a mail order operation in 1978, we decided to issue a regular newsletter that would not only list all new releases we received but also would provide very brief critical reviews of the releases. Although we did not exclusively carry blues, that was, and still is, a substantial part of our business.

Over the years these reviews have been gathered into catalogs. What you have here is the latest incarnation of our blues catalog. Since we wanted our stock of blues recordings to be as complete as possible, this catalog is the most comprehensive listing of currently available recordings in existence. Listed here is information on some 3,500 blues recordings issued on record, cassette, and compact disc.

The last few years have seen a terrific growth in interest in the blues, with several contemporary blues performers, most notably Robert Cray, entering the pop mainstream, and vintage recordings gaining a new respectability. As a result, sales of vintage reissues have reached new heights; the recent comprehensive reissue of the great Delta blues singer Robert Johnson sold enough copies that it reached the top 100 in the pop charts and gained a gold record in the process—this from recordings more than 50 years old!

The growth to prominence of the compact disc as the preferred sound recording medium has been both a boon and a curse for music lovers. The arrival of this high-quality sound medium has encouraged companies to delve into their vaults to issue vintage recordings that had been languishing there for many years and use new technology to make them sound better than ever before. On the negative side, since the music business is driven by the marketplace, companies are dropping LPs from their catalogs at an ever-increasing pace without making compact discs available to replace them. By the time this book is in your hands, many records listed may be out of print! However, the diligent collector may still be able to track down these items, which are often discarded by record companies at a bargain price.

Since the listings here have grown over a period of 12 years and a number of people have been involved in providing reviews, the book may seem occasionally lopsided. Older recordings sometimes have briefer reviews than more recent issues. This does not necessarily mean that the newer recording is of greater merit; the earlier releases were listed when time constraints on reviewers permitted only shorter reviews. In subsequent editions of the book, we will attempt to redress this balance. Although there is a lively scene in white blues bands with quite a few recordings available, there are only limited listings here of what we feel are the most interesting or significant of these recordings. This reflects my musical preferences and those of most of our reviewers, and we make no apologies for the fact.

With so many recordings available, this listing may be intimidating to the new blues listener, so we have provided a guide for the beginning listener by indicating some 100 essential recordings. These are not necessarily the 100 best or most comprehensive recordings of given artists, but those we feel would give the beginning listener a good cross-section of the music and provide a starting point from which to build a well-balanced collection.

The mini-reviews in this book are the work of several people—besides my own contributions the reviewers include Myles Boisen, Al Ennis, Ray Funk, John McCord, Gary Mollica, Opal Louis Nations, Randy Pitts, Peter Rossman, and Russ Schoenwetter. Since the listings reflect more than 12 years of work, I may have missed someone—so please accept my apologies.

These are exciting times for lovers of this wonderful African-American art form, with more recordings available than ever before. We hope we can share some of our excitement and enthusiasm with you in the listings here.

Frank Scott
El Cerrito, California, April 1991

How to Use This Book

The Down Home Guide to the Blues is the most comprehensive listing of in-print records, cassettes, and CDs of blues music. We have not limited ourselves solely to country and urban blues stylists; some other musical styles that you will find in these pages include Cajun and Zydeco, early jazz, boogie woogie, jump and swing, R&B and early rock, vaudeville and hokum, blues-rock, and saxophone honkers.

The book is divided into two parts: the first part gives listings by artist and forms the heart of the book; the second part is a listing of anthologies, divided into prewar and postwar sections. Within these sections, there are further divisions by geographic area (Chicago, New York, West Coast, and so on) or style (boogie-woogie piano, jug bands, and so on).

Artists are alphabetized by last name. Artists who recorded under stage names such as "Muddy Waters" or "Little Walter" are alphabetized by the first letter in the pseudonym (Muddy Waters under "M," for example). After all, Muddy wasn't Mr. Waters!

Under each artist, records are organized alphabetically by label, and within each label numerically by catalog number. This means the listings are not chronological.

The symbols "(c)" or "(d)" following a record album number indicate that the recording is also available on cassette (c) or compact disc (d). Cassette only and CD only issues are listed at the end of the LP list for each artist or category. When a CD has been issued of an album on a different label, or if it has a different catalog number, it is listed directly below the original label information for the LP.

Although information is given on sidemen and song selection for many records, the listings are not meant to give full discographical information.

Finally, we have limited ourselves to recordings that are currently in-print, although we draw on labels from around the world. However, in today's rapidly changing world, where LPs are disappearing quickly and being replaced by cassettes and CDs, it is possible that some of these titles may soon disappear to reappear in different configurations. Also due to the vagaries of small label finance, record companies come and go, while the bigger companies have been known to drop entire series (or renumber and recatalog records) without much concern for continuity. You will want to consult with us for label information. All of the recordings in this book are available from Down Home Music Mail Order, located at 6921 Stockton Avenue, El Cerrito, CA 94530, (415) 525-1494. Write or call for our latest update. The Down Home Music retail store is located at 10341 San Pablo Avenue in El Cerrito. For a complete catalog of hundreds of CDs, cassettes, LPs, and videos, write to ARHOOLIE CATALOG, 10341 San Pablo Avenue, El Cerrito, CA 94530.

We have used the following abbreviations throughout the text to indicate musical instrumentation:

acst (acoustic)	org (organ)
alto sax (alto saxophone)	perc (percussion)
b (bass)	pno (piano)
bar sax (baritone sax)	rubd (rubboard)
clr (clarinet)	tam (tambourine)
cnt (cornet)	ten sax (tenor sax)
drm (drums)	trb (trombone)
elec (electric)	tpt (trumpet)
fdl (fiddle)	vcl (vocal)
gtr (guitar)	vibes (vibraphone)
hca (harmonica/harp)	vln (violin)
kybds (keyboards)	washbd (washboard)
mdln (mandolin)	

JOHNNY ACE

Popular blues/ballad singer from Memphis who died Christmas Eve 1954 while playing Russian Roulette. In the early 50s, he was a member of the Beale Streeters with B. B. King and Roscoe Gordon. He set off on a short-lived but highly successful solo career in 1952, when he signed with Don Robey's Duke label, from which the following record comes.

MCA 27014 (c,d) **Johnny Ace Memorial Album**
Originally issued as Duke 40, it features his biggest hits. My Song/Pledging My Love/The Clock/Saving My Love For You.

RAY AGEE

After many years of obscurity, this brilliant West Coast singer and songwriter is finally getting some of the attention he deserves. Agee is an outstanding singer with a mellow soulful style that, at times, brings to mind Charles Brown and Bobby Bland, but Agee is very much a unique stylist. His songs are striking, brilliantly crafted works. During his lengthy recording career, he recorded for some 30 different labels.

Diving Duck 4301 **Tin Pan Alley**
Excellent set of reissues from the 60s. Fine soul-based singing with excellent and mostly unknown bands, some featuring the superb guitar of Johnny Heartsman. Tin Pan Alley/It's A Helluva Thing/'Til Death Do Us Part/Love Is A Cold Shot/The Gamble/Tough Competition.

Mr. R&B 105 **Black Night Is Gone**
Seventeen of Agee's early recordings cut between 1951–57. On these recordings, Agee was accompanied by top West Coast sessionmen like J. D. Nicholson, Wilbur Reynolds, Chuck Norris, and Maxwell Davis. Sound quality and packaging are first rate.

Mr. R&B 1003 **I'm Not Looking Back**
Covers the period 1955–71, with most tracks coming from the mid-60s, when Ray was at his peak. This period produced some lovely slow, soulful blues sides with Ray accompanied by fine West Coast bands. There are some great guitarists featured here, including the superb Johnny Heartsman and, surprisingly, white country-swing guitarist Jimmy Rivers!

DAVE ALEXANDER

Fine West Coast-based singer and blues and boogie piano player who made a handful of recordings in the early 70s. He is a powerful performer, playing mostly original material. The Arhoolie album features him in the company of a discreet bass and drums. Alexander is now a Muslim and Imam Omar Sharriff is his Muslim name.

Arhoolie 1067 **The Rattler**
His best.
CASSETTE ONLY RELEASE
Arhoolie C-207 **Imam Omar Sharriff**
Double-length cassette combining Arhoolie 1067 and the out-of-print 1071.

TEXAS ALEXANDER

Wonderful singer from East Texas, Alexander recorded quite extensively between 1927 and 1934. His singing was strongly rooted in the older field-holler tradition, with long, rhythmically free-flowing vocal lines. He did not play an instrument himself but, on record, was accompanied by some of the finest musicians of the era. Some of his best records feature the guitar playing of Lonnie Johnson, who, though not a rural musician himself, fashioned a perfect accompaniment technique that echoed and enhanced Alexander's vocal lines. The three Matchbox albums are part of a continuing program to reissue all of his recordings, while the Agram set presents a broad-based survey of his recording career and inevitably duplicates material on the Matchbox albums.

Agram 2009 **Texas Troublesome Blues**
As a sampler, this album covers recordings from his entire recording career from 1927 to 1950. Sixteen fine performances with wonderful vocals and accompaniments by Lonnie Johnson, Eddie Haywood, and Eddie Lang. Includes extensive notes based on new research, with pictures of record labels, lyric transcripts, analysis of the songs, and even Alexander's family tree! Good sound quality.

Matchbox 206 **Texas Alexander, Vol. 1**
His first 18 recordings from 1927–28 in chronological order, with guitarist Lonnie Johnson and piano player Eddie Heywood. The accompaniments by Johnson are sensational, providing a perfect counterpoint to Alexander's singing.

Matchbox 214 **Texas Alexander, Vol. 2**
Seventeen sides recorded between March 1928 and June 1929. Some wonderful singing and somewhat more varied accompaniments than on Volume 1. Guitars by Lonnie Johnson and/or Eddie Lang or Little Hat Jones, and a couple of cuts feature accompaniments by King Oliver and Clarence Williams.

Matchbox 220 **Texas Alexander, Vol. 3**
Sixteen sides recorded between June 1929 and June 1930. Two tracks feature him in the company of eccentric guitarist Little Hat Jones, including the lovely "Johnny Behrens Blues." Six sides feature

guitar by Carl Davis, who was apparently influenced by Lonnie Johnson, though with more of a rural sound. There are some fine tracks here, although their similarity becomes a little dull after a while. Side two features eight tracks with the great Mississippi Sheiks, but the group is in a more restrained mood than usual on these accompaniments. Sound quality varies from very good to just bearable.

RED ALLEN
Famed jazz trumpeter. The following recordings from the 30s feature him accompanying blues singers such as Frankie Jaxon and Blue Lu Barker.

Jazz Archives 46 **Red Allen and the Blues Singers, Vol.1**
Jazz Archives 47 **Red Allen and the Blues Singers, Vol.2**

LUTHER ALLISON
Contemporary Chicago singer/electric guitarist with some rock influences. He can play straight-ahead, Chicago-style blues with great skill, though he often favors some of the excesses of blues-rock.

Black and Blue 33.524 (d) **Love Me Papa**
1977 French recordings. Most of the songs here are a bit long (two songs over 11 minutes) and over-played, leaning toward rock excess. While his guitar playing is at times impressive, in the late 50s "West Side" style, Luther's attempt at Little Walter-style harp playing is weak. More often than not it's his expressive and soulful vocals that are most impressive. The rather anonymous backing doesn't help a lot, either. CD features three additional, previously unissued tracks. Last Night/Key To The Highway/I Feel So Good.

Blind Pig 2287 **Serious**
CD issue: Encore ENC 131C **Life Is a Bitch**
US issue of album originally on French Encore label as "Life Is a Bitch." Although there is a strong white rock element on this album, Luther's singing and playing are more restrained than usual. The songs, mostly originals, are good and varied, and the band of French musicians provide a solid and hard-driving accompaniment. Michael Carras' keyboard work is particularly good. An excellent good-time record. CD features two extra tracks.

Charly CRB 1105 **Power Wire Blues**
Recent live recordings originally issued on the Rumble label.

Charly CRB 1227 **Rich Man**
CD issue: Charly CD 201
Recorded in Europe in 1987 with European backing

group. Chicago/Cold As Ice/Freedom/Fight/Get Down.

Delmark 625 **Love Me Mama**
With The Blue Nebulae, including "Big Mojo" Elem (b) and Jim Conley (ten sax). Why I Love The Blues/4:00 In the Morning/Dust My Broom.

Encore ENC 133 **Here I Come**
COMPACT DISC
Buda 82469-2 **Live in Paris**
Hot hour-plus live set from 1979. Fans of hard-rocking contemporary blues will dig this energetic 10-song set. Sweet Little Angel/My Babe/The Thrill Is Me Baby.

ALBERT AMMONS
One of the great boogie-woogie pianists.

ESSENTIAL SELECTION

Blues Classics 27 **The King of Boogie Woogie**
One side features his first solo recordings from 1939, and the other features excellent sides with a hot small band from 1946–49, including a couple of vocals by Jack Cooley. Monday Struggle/Boogie Woogie Blues/Chicago In Mind/Boogie Woogie At The Civic Opera.

Oldie Blues 2807 **King of Blues and Boogie Woogie**
A great collection of solo sides from 1939 and small group sides from 1941–49.The latter include a couple of vocals by Sippie Wallace or Mildred Anderson; accompanying musicians include Lonnie Johnson or Ike Perkins (gtr) and Gene Ammons (ten sax). Shout For Joy/Boogie Woogie Blues/Bass Going Crazy/Chicago In Mind/Buzz Me/Sweet Patootie Boogie.

Oldie Blues 2822 **Albert Ammons, Vol. 2**
Sixteen fine sides recorded between 1939–49, mostly with small bands. Includes quite a few of his wonderful mid-to-late 40s recordings where he took standards, such as "Roses of Picardie" and "Red Sails In The Sunset," and performed them as boogies. Woo Woo (with Harry James)/Mighty Blues/St. Louis Blues/Bass Gone Crazy/Mister Bell Boogie. Great!

PINK ANDERSON
A fine South Carolina singer and guitarist whose musical career began in 1915 and who recorded a handful of sides in 1928 and was later recorded in the early 60s.

O.B.C. 504 **Vol. 1–Carolina Blues Man**
This album is a reissue of Bluesville 1038, recorded in 1960. Warm and sensitive vocals and pleasing guitar. My Baby Left Me This Morning/Mama

Where Did You Stay Last Night/Meet Me in the Bottom.

FERNEST ARCENEAUX and HIS LOUISIANA FRENCH BAND
COMPACT DISC
JSP CD 220 Zydeco Stomp!
Fernest is no Clifton Chenier, but this is an enjoyable set of Zydeco, R&B, blues, and swamp pop. Victor Walker (b, pno) performs several vocals including a lovely Lightnin' Slim-flavored "I Can't Live Happy" and duets with Fernest on a couple of swamp pop items.

ARCHIBALD
Wonderful New Orleans singer and piano player who was a popular and influential figure, although he made few recordings.
Krazy Kat 7409 The New Orleans Sessions
Features his entire output of 14 sides recorded between 1950–52, accompanied by top New Orleans sidemen, including Dave Bartholomew, Ernest MacClean, and Herb Hardesty. Includes his one "hit," "Stack-A-Lee," plus "Great Big Eyes" and "Ballin' With Archie." Classic New Orleans blues.

ALPHONSE "BOISEC" ARDOIN
Arhoolie 1070 La Musique Creole
Excellent duet performances by Boisec, who is Amadé Ardoin's first cousin, and Caray Fontenot, blending Boisec's sturdy accordian style with Fontenot's lively and creative fiddle. Side one, from 1973, features duets in the older-style Creole music they have been playing together since the 1930s, as on the sadly out-of-print 1966 Melodeon LP, "Les Blues du Bayou." Side two, from 1971, brings in Boisec's sons, Gustave and Morris, on guitar and bass, for a more modern band setting, with both capturing the warmth, skill, and variety of these engaging performers. Home Sweet Home/Laccasine Breakdown/Les Barres de la Prison/Chere Ici, Chere La Bas/Opelousas Waltz/Canray's One Step/Petite et La Grosse/Ses Parents Ne Veulent Plus Le Voir/Joe Pitre A Deux Femmes/Le Boss/Jupe Courte/Jolie Catin.

AMADÉ ARDOIN
Pioneer Zydeco singer and accordion player.
Old Timey 124 His Original Recordings, 1928–38

LAWRENCE "BLACK" ARDOIN
Arhoolie 1091 (c) And His French Zydeco Band
Delightful album of Zydeco music by this excellent band fronted by singer/accordion player Ardoin, son of the great accordion player Alphonse "Boisec" Ardoin, and featuring the splendid fiddle of Edward

Poulard, brother of Bay Area Cajun musician Danny Poulard. Their music has more of a Cajun flavor than some of the Zydeco bands, though they can also turn in some fine bluesy stuff too. The material includes old songs from the 30s made famous by Amadé Ardoin, South Louisiana R&B, the J. B. Lenore song "Talk to Your Daughter," and a lovely Cajun waltz, "The Lonely Waltz."

BILLY BOY ARNOLD
Excellent Chicago singer/harmonica player.
Blue Phoenix 33 726 Ten Million Dollars
Recorded in France in 1984, Billy is accompanied by a splendid band including Jimmy Johnson and John Watkins (gtrs), Saint James Bryant (pno), Larry Exum (b), and Fred Grady (drm), who provide solid, swinging accompaniment. There are several originals, including a remake of his big Vee Jay hit "I Wish You Would," plus some other good songs like the slow and powerful title song and the fascinating "Yellow Rose From Texas Just Love Won't Do." Most of the rest of the songs are Billy's versions of traditional items like "Sugar Mama" and "I Done Got Over," or covers of old favorites like "My Babe," "Just A Little Bit," and "Last Night."
Charly CRB 1016 Crying and Pleading
Recorded for Vee Jay between 1955 and 1957. Great sides with Henry Gray (pno) and Jody Williams (gtr). Much of this is duplicated on Red Lightnin' 0012, but this LP is from master tapes. Includes his classic "I Wish You Would" plus Don't Stay Out All Night/I Ain't Got You/My Heart Is Crying/Prisoners Plea.
Prestige 7389 More Blues on the South Side
Enjoyable 60s stuff, with Mighty Joe Young and Lafayette Leake.
Red Lightnin' 0012 Blow the Back Off It
Fine 50s Vee Jay sides with Henry Gray (pno) and Jody Williams (gtr). Most of this is on Charly CRB 1016 with better sound.
Red Lightnin' 0014 Sinner's Prayer
1970 Chicago recordings with Louis Myers, Sammy Lawhorn, and "Big Moose" Walker.
Smokestack Lightnin' 0174 Checkin' It Out
Interesting set, originally issued on Red Lightnin' 0024 in the late 70s. Arnold takes control of this tight session, backed by Mighty Groundhogs guitarist Tony McPhee, bassist Alan Fish, and drummer Wilbur Campbell. While the sound is not quite rootsy, there are plenty of solid moments: Check out the cover of Little Walter's "Blue And Lonesome" for some pure blues atmosphere and distinctive chromatic harp. Billy Boy's own "Mary Bernice" is solid, as well as the remake of his one big hit "I Wish

You Would." Other favorites are a rocked-out "El Dorado Cadillac (I Ain't Got You)" and a "Dirty Mother Fuyer" that will get a few smutty chuckles out of you risque blues buffs!

KOKOMO ARNOLD

Fine 30s singer/slide guitarist originally from Georgia. Best selection of his recordings are the half-albums on Blues Classics and Yazoo.

ESSENTIAL SELECTION

Blues Classics 4 **Kokomo Arnold/Peetie Wheatstraw**

Eight songs by each. Arnold's tracks include his most famous songs, "Milk Cow Blues" and "Old Original Kokomo Blues," plus "Front Door Blues" and "Stop, Look and Listen."

Document 512 **Master of the Bottleneck Guitar, 1930–38**

A beautiful collection of 18 sides, 13 not previously on LP. It includes his first two recordings from 1930, issued under the name of "Gitfiddle Jim," including the incredible "Paddlin' Madeline Blues," featuring some of Arnold's most spectacular playing. Kokomo did not return to the recording studio until 1934, and the remaining 16 sides are from the period 1935–38. About half of the cuts are Kokomo on his own, while the rest feature a piano player, usually Peetie Wheatstraw. On one track, Arnold and Wheatstraw accompany Signifying Mary Johnson on "Delmar Avenue." Although there is a lot of similarity in the tunes Arnold used, there is great variety in the lyrics, and his singing and playing are always excellent. A few tracks are from noisy 78s, but the sound is generally satisfactory.

Yazoo 1049 **Bottleneck Trendsetters**
One side of album features Arnold, while the other features Casey Bill Weldon.

JOSEPH "MR. GOOGLE EYES" AUGUST

New Orleans' Mr. "G" was a shouter in the Roy Brown/Wynonie Harris tradition who experienced considerable recognition in the late 40s and early 50s. His later efforts, a mixture of jumping jive and crying blues on a slew of large and small labels, give us an indication of how well Mr. "G" could weep and whip up a storm.

Route 66 KIX 32 **Rock My Soul**
A fine selection of 40s and 50s recordings. With good sound, fine pics, and interesting notes by Almost Slim.

DEFORD BAILEY/D. H. "BERT" BILBRO

Matchbox 218 **Harmonica Showcase**
Presents the complete recordings of harmonica players DeFord Bailey and D. H. "Bert" Bilbro. As the first black artist to appear on Nashville's famed Grand Ole Opry, Bailey is a significant performer in the history of American music. His 11 performances are all solo harmonica instrumentals and demonstrate his skill, versatility, and powers of mimicry on such pieces as "Pan American Blues," "Old Hen Cackle," and "The Fox Chase," along with fine performances of blues numbers. Bilbro was for many years thought to be a black performer, but recent research shows that he was white. He recorded five tracks between 1928–31: three harmonica solos and two vocals with a small string band, and they are all enjoyable.

LAVERN BAKER

Atlantic 90980-1 (c) **Lavern Baker Sings Bessie Smith**
Reissue of Atlantic 1281 featuring Lavern doing individualistic interpretations of 12 Bessie Smith classics. She is accompanied by an all-star group of jazz musicians, including Buck Clayton (tpt), Paul Quinichette (ten sax), Nat Pierce (pno), and Danny Barker (gtr). Gimme A Pigfoot/ On Revival Day/I Ain't Gonna Play No Second Fiddle/Empty Bed Blues/Nobody Knows You When You're Down And Out/Young Woman's Blues.

CLASSIE BALLOU

Krazy Kat 800 **All Night Man**
Rather unexceptional album of Zydeco and South Louisiana blues by singer/guitarist Ballou, accompanied by a band including veteran accordion player Preston Frank. Although Ballou and Frank are accomplished musicians, the rest of the band doesn't seem to have a lot of spirit and the overall sound just doesn't quite jell. The most successful cuts are the R&B instrumental "Classie's Shuffle," the slow blues "Swamp Cabbage Blues," and the traditional "Church Point Special."

BARBECUE BOB
Superb 20s Georgia singer/12-string guitarist.

Collector's Classics CC 36 Barbecue Bob
Matchbox 1009 The Remaining Titles, 1927–30
A marvelous collection of 16 tracks, which together with Mamlish 3808 and Agram 2001 (currently unavailable), and Collector's Classics 36, comprises his entire recorded output. Although most of the tracks here have been reissued before, many are on out-of-print collections. This album includes his only two gospel recordings, "When The Saints Go Marching In" and "Jesus' Blood Can Make Me Whole." There are a couple of the fascinating spoken/sung dialogues he performed with his brother, Charley Hicks (aka Charley Lincoln), as well as more straight-ahead blues like "Goin' Up The Country," "She's Gone Blues," "Good Time Rounder," "Trouble Done Bore Me Down," "She Moves It Right," "Darktown Gamblin'," and, of course, the ever-popular Georgia standard "Yo Yo Blues," with stunning slide guitar. One not to be missed.

JOHN HENRY BARBEE
Storyville SLP 4037 John Henry Barbee
Also available as Storyville 171. Country bluesman recorded in Denmark in 1964. Some Big Bill Broonzy influences and some nice slide on a couple of cuts, with excellent notes by Paul Oliver.

Storyville SLP 4074 John Henry Barbee and Sleepy John Estes: Blues Live
Recorded live in Denmark in 1967, with seven tracks by Estes with Hammie Nixon and five by Barbee.

ROOSEVELT "BOOBA" BARNES and THE PLAYBOYS
Rooster Blues 2623 (c,d) The Heartbroken Man
Tough Mississippi Delta blues band.

LOTTIE BEAMAN/ LUELLA MILLER
Wolf 124 Complete Recordings in Chronological Order
The title of this album is a little misleading, as the Beaman sides complement those by her on Wolf 114 and the ones by Miller complement those on the yet-to-be released Wolf 125. Kansas City singer Lottie Beaman was a very fine singer who also recorded under the name of Lottie Kimbrough. Her 1928 recordings on Wolf 114 are particularly fine. The ones here from 1924 and '26 are less interesting due mainly to rather pedestrian accompaniments from either the rather out-of-tune Pruiett Twins, Jimmy Blythe, and Papa Charlie Jackson or Paul Banks' Kansas City Seven. Luella Miller was a fine and obscure singer who recorded some 22 sides between 1926–28. The eight tracks here are from 1928 and, although most of the accompanying musicians are uncertain, they are generally very good. Nothing really essential here but enjoyable material.

CAREY BELL/LURRIE BELL
Carey Bell is one of the finest living blues harmonica players; his son Lurrie is a fine blues guitarist and vocalist.

Blues Southwest BSW 0001 Carey and Lurrie Bell with The Junkyard Angels
Carey and Lurrie on their first headlining tour of Europe in 1986, backed by a spirited though mediocre British blues band; marred by only fair sound quality. Although father and son are in fine shape, most of the time they don't seem to mesh with the band. Magic Sam's "I Need Your Love So Bad" and the original "So Tired Of Being Alone" were recorded live, the rest in the studio. Mystery Train/I'm Ready/I Want You To Love Me/A Man and The Blues/Detroit Michigan.

Delmark 622 (c) Carey Bell's Blues Harp
On these 1969 recordings, Bell is heard in the company of such fine musicians as Eddie Taylor or Jimmy Dawkins (gtr) and Pinetop Perkins (pno). The songs are a mixture of originals and songs from Willie Dixon, Elmore James, and Little Walter.

L+R 42.051 Goin' on Main Street
Good album with his sons Lurrie (gtr) and Carey Jr. (b), plus guitar, organ, and drums. Mostly original songs; includes a solo performance by Lurrie and an unaccompanied harmonica duet with Billy Branch.

Rooster Blues 2617 Son of a Gun
On this outstanding album, featuring mostly original material, Carey shares the spotlight with his talented son Lurrie. Backed by a solid rhythm section, they work their way through nine vocals (four by Carey, five by Lurrie) and three instrumentals.

COMPACT DISC
JSP CD 211 Harpslinger
JSP CD 222 Dynasty!
Recorded in Chicago with Steve, Tyson, and James Bell.

JSP CD 227 Everybody Wants to Win
An album of good solid Chicago blues by Carey Bell's eldest son, Lurrie (vcl, gtr), with dad Carey or brother James on harp, Pete Allen (gtr), and brothers Steve and Tyson on bass and drums. Lurrie is a powerful singer and effective guitarist. The material is a mixture of originals and old favorites. Nothing outstanding but worth a listen.

ED BELL

Excellent Alabama country blues singer and guitarist who recorded in the 20s under the names of Sluefoot Joe, Barefoot Bill, and his real name.

Mamlish 3811 **Ed Bell's Mamlish Moan**

Fourteen beautiful sides. Considering the rarity of the originals, the sound here is excellent, and the notes, based on recent research, are detailed and informative. Mamlish Blues/From Now On/Mean Conductor Blues/One More Time/Big Rock Jail/Frisco Whistle Blues/House Top Blues.

Mamlish 3812 **Barefoot Bill's Hard Luck Blues**

A collection that extensively features Bell. See *Alabama Blues Collections* for full information.

LURRIE BELL and BILLY BRANCH

L+R 42.049 **Chicago's Young Blues Generation**

Good album by two excellent young blues musicians, guitarist Lurrie Bell and harmonica player Billy Branch, with solid backup from the band. The main drawback to the album is the overly familiar material.

BUSTER BENTON

Fine Chicago singer/guitarist.

Blue Phoenix 33.722 **First Time in Europe**

Recorded in France in 1983 with John Littlejohn or Joe Beard (gtr), Lafayette Leake (pno), Bob Stroger (b), and Odie Payne (drm). Some pleasant performances of mostly original songs. Benton is very good on the straight songs but is less effective when he tries his hand at soul.

Ichiban 1023 **Why Me?**

Decent, though unmemorable, album with accompaniment by a small band including guitar and keyboard player Gary B. B. Coleman, who also produced the album. All nine songs were written by Benton and are quite good. He is a good singer with some Bobby Bland inflections but is a very unimaginative guitar player.

Ichiban 1046 (c,d) **Money's the Name of the Game**

Recorded in Atlanta with Gary B. B. Coleman producing. Sweet 94/You Accuse Me/Sit Your Fine Self Down/Sweet Sixteen.

Red Lightnin' 0026 **Bluesbuster**

Reissue of sides recorded for Jewel. Fine 1974 recordings with Carey Bell, Jimmy Johnson, and Lafayette Leake.

COMPACT DISC

Blue Phoenix 59.001 2 **Blues at the Top**

Fifteen tracks recorded in France in 1983 and 1985, previously issued on Blue Phoenix 33.728 and 33.730. The 1983 session includes John Littlejohn (gtr) and Lafayette Leake (pno), and the '85 session includes Billy Branch on harp. Mostly original songs, though all are pretty derivative. Nothing really special here, but you do get value for money with almost 79 minutes playing time.

P-Vine PCD 2150 **Spider in My Stew**

Reissues recordings made for Jewel in the 50s. Benton is accompanied by top-notch Chicago musicians, including Carey Bell, Lafayette Leake, Mighty Joe Young, and Jimmy Johnston.

BIG BOY HENRY

Fine singer and guitarist from Beauford, North Carolina. Henry is a warm and affecting singer and an exceptionally fine, imaginative, and flowing guitarist. Many of his songs are original compositions.

Audio Arts 007 (45 rpm) **Mr. President/Cherry Red**

Some nice down-home blues. Topside is an excellent topical blues about the plight of the poor man in contemporary America. Henry's guitar is accompanied by piano, bass, and drums. Flip side lets us hear his East Coast guitar style on a more traditional risque blues.

Audio Arts 008 (EP) **Big Boy Henry**

Four track EP; three cuts are straight country with guitar accompaniment, and the fourth features a small band. "Warehouse" is based on Lightnin' Hopkins' "Mr. Charlie." Mr. Ball's Warehouse/Spank The Baby/Drunken Woman/New Bern.

Swingmaster 2114 **I'm Not Lyin' This Time**

These recordings were apparently made on tape for broadcast on a radio show out of New Bern, NC. Most of the tracks are from 1947, with two from 1952. The sound quality on the tape from 1947 seems almost too good to be true and most of the songs are four minutes long or more, which is atypical for the era. Maybe I'm cynical, but it sounds like these recordings were made much later. Still, whatever their real origin, they are very good. Henry is a distinctive, husky vocalist and a melodic player in the Northeast mold. Most of the songs are originals, and the performances—some on acoustic and a couple on electric guitar—are consistently good.

Swingmaster 2117 **Raised Up with the Blues**

Excellent collection of songs recorded between 1987–89. Most of the songs are originals including the personal "Arthritis Is Killing Me" and the fascinating "Miss Maybelle (The Root Woman)." This is one of the best new country blues recordings I've heard in quite a while. Highly recommended.

BIG MACEO

Magnificent and influential singer and piano player. Although based in Detroit, he is intimately associated with Chicago, having recorded with many of the important Chicago blues artists of the 30s and 40s. Maceo was a superb piano player with a rolling style that was equally effective on pounding boogies or slow blues. He had a lovely smoky voice, and the 32 sides recorded by him between 1941 and 1947 are among the finest group of recordings made by one artist. The recordings all feature brilliantly effective guitar by Tampa Red and, on the later sides, solid drumming by Melvin Draper, Tyrell Dixon, or Chick Saunders. The recordings reissued on Blue Classics are essential to any blues collection. Subsequent to 1947, ill health cut short his career and he recorded infrequently up to his death in 1953.

ESSENTIAL SELECTION

Blue Classics 28 **The King of Chicago Blues Piano, Vol. 1**
Sixteen sides from 1941–42. Worried Life Blues/County Jail Blues (absolutely exquisite!)/ So Long Baby/Tuff Luck Blues/It's All Up To You/Why Should I Hang Around/Some Sweet Day/My Last Go Round.
Blues Classics 29 **The King of Chicago Blues Piano, Vol. 2**
Seventeen sides from 1945-47, including a previously unissued acetate from around the same period. Kidman Blues/Things Have Changed/ Maceo's 32-20/Texas Stomp/Winter Time Blues/Big Road Blues/ Broke and Hungry Blues/It's All Over Now.
CASSETTE ONLY RELEASE
Arhoolie C-210 **Big Maceo**
Double-length cassette combining Blues Classics 28 and 29.

BIG MAYBELLE

Charly CDX 27 **The Okeh Sessions**
CD issue: Charly CD 108
Reissue of great two-LP set (originally available on Epic in the US) featuring 22 tracks recorded by this outstanding blues shouter for Okeh between 1952–55. Accompanied by great New York session musicians like Sam "The Man" Taylor, Lee Anderson, Mickey Baker, and Panama Francis, she wraps her gravel voice around the original recording of "Whole Lotta Shakin' Goin' On" plus Just Want Your Love/Gabbin' Blues/Rain Down Rain/Stay Away From My Sam/Maybelle's Blues/You'll Never Know.

Savoy 1143 (c) **Big Maybelle**
Twelve songs recorded for Savoy between 1957 and 1959. Most of her best sides have been reissued on Savoy 2221, 2233, and 2256 (all out-of-print), so this is pretty much from the bottom of the barrel. Although there are some great belting blues sides here, most of this album is composed of pop-style ballads, some with string accompaniments.
Savoy 1168 (c,d) **Blues, Candy and Big Maybelle**

THE BIG THREE TRIO

This Chicago-based blues harmony group consisted of Leonard Caston Sr. (lead vcl, pno), Bernardo Dennis (gtr), and the incomparable Willie Dixon (lead vcl, b). Between 1947–51, they produced some fine doo-wop harmony blues ballads and novelty jumpers. Their sound was unique and copied by no one (with the possible exception of The Four Blazes, who also recorded a little later in Chicago).

Columbia 46216 (c,d) **Willie Dixon: The Big Three Trio**
Varied material includes blues, boogie, jazz, novelty, and pop-flavored items. All the musicians were very fine and there is some wonderful boogie piano from Caston and imaginative soloing from the guitarists. The vocals are often sung in three-part harmony or with the rest of the group harmonizing behind the lead singer. Five of the tracks here are previously unissued. Booklet has notes by Mary Katherine Aldin and some fine vintage photos.
Dr Horse H 804 **I Feel Like Steppin' Out**
The group's strongest efforts were the ballads, a handful of which appear here for the first time in any shape or form for almost 40 years. Detailed sleeve notes and rare pics. Highly recommended.

BIG TIME SARAH

B.L.U.E.S. R&B 3601 **Undecided**
A mixture of soul and blues, though I find the soul a little too pop-oriented and the blues a little too

funk-oriented for my taste. Sarah is a good singer and the band is good, but I am just not too happy with the material or arrangements.

BIG TWIST and THE MELLOW FELLOWS
Alligator 4732 (c) **Playing for Keeps**
Flying Fish FF 229 **Big Twist and The Mellow Fellows**
Flying Fish FF 268 **One Track Mind**

BIG WALTER (PRICE)
Ace CHD 246 **Boogies from Coast to Coast**
Enjoyable if somewhat frustrating collection by fine Texas singer and piano player Big Walter Price (not to be confused with blues harmonica player Big Walter Horton). Price recorded for a number of small labels in the 50s and 60s with only a modicum of success. The 12 tracks here are from a previously unissued 1971 session recorded for Roy Ames, some with Walter on solo piano and others with a rhythm section. The material is varied, including some fine blues covers ("I Don't Know" and "Bloodstains On The Wall"), some originals ("Walking Across Texas"), swamp pop ("Louise") and even country ("Clock On The Motel Wall"). The only problem is that this was obviously a demo session and so some of the playing is sloppy and chaotic and not always good listening. Still there are some good moments here.

ELVIN BISHOP

Alligator 4767 (c,d) **Big Fun**
After taking about a decade off from recording, Elvin returned with an album packed with fine material, including many originals featuring suprisingly effective vocals, snappy Texas/Louisiana-influenced arrangements, and mature blues guitar delivered with intensity. Includes some sharp piano work by Dr. John.

BILLY BIZOR
Home Cooking 111 **Blowin' My Blues Away**
Mostly previously unissued recordings from 1969 by Texas singer/harmonica player Bizor plus two tracks from 1968 with vocals and guitar by his cousin Lightnin' Hopkins.

BLACK ACE
Fine Texas country blues singer with a deep rich voice and a melodic slide guitar style. He recorded for Decca in 1937 and was rediscovered in 1960 and recorded an excellent album for Arhoolie. He didn't record again and died in 1972. Some of Ace's prewar recordings are reissued on Yazoo 1026 and Mamlish 3801.
Arhoolie 1003 **Black Ace**
Thirteen lovely recordings. I Am the Black Ace/Santa Fe Blues/Evil Woman/Your Leg's Too Little/Santa Claus Blues.

BLACK BOY SHINE
Blues Documents 2039 **Complete Recordings in Chronological Order**
Harold Holiday ("Black Boy Shine") was one of the "Santa Fe" group of south Texas pianists recording in the late 30s; with the exception of three tracks available on Blues Classics and Magpie, none of these lovely performances is currently available on LP. While not the most versatile pianist to come out of Texas in this period, Shine's playing was characterized by a unique rolling left hand, which suited his understated vocals to a "tee," and each of these 18 performances contains original vocal lines, which make for moving and compelling performances. Highly recommended to all lovers of Texas (and other) piano blues.

OTIS BLACKWELL
Flyright 575 **Singin' the Blues**
Reissue of 1957 album featuring recordings cut in 1953 and 1954.

SCRAPPER BLACKWELL
One of the all-time great blues guitarists. Best known for his accompaniments of Leroy Carr, Blackwell was also a superb performer in his own right. Scrapper was one of the greatest of all blues guitarists, with a uniquely distinctive style. An intensely melodic guitarist, he makes effective use of string snapping and dazzling arpeggios. The Yazoo and Agram LPs reissue his early 20s and 30s sides, while the Ace album features more recent recordings.
Ace CH 255 **Mr. Scrapper's Blues**
This is a fabulous album, originally issued as Bluesville 1047 in 1961. Scrapper's playing isn't quite as

flowing as it was 30 years previously and his voice shows the sign of age and the tough life he led but, nonetheless, these are outstanding performances. The songs include songs made famous by Carr ("Blues Before Sunrise"/"George Street Blues"), remakes of some of his own early recordings ("Penal Farm Blues"), blues standards ("Nobody Knows You When You're Down And Down"), and songs not recorded elsewhere ("Little Girl Blues"). There are also two sublime instrumentals—"'A' Blues" and "'E' Blues"—which send shivers down my spine. On one track, Scrapper plays piano and shows that he is equally adept on that instrument. Beautifully recorded and remastered, bringing out all the wonderful resonances of Scrapper's guitar. If you love acoustic country blues, this album is not to be missed.

Agram 2008 **Blues That Make Me Cry**
Complements Yazoo 1019 by reissuing the rest of his solo recordings cut in the 20s and 30s along with a couple of accompaniments to Bumble Bee Slim.

Yazoo 1019 **The Virtuoso Guitar of Scrapper Blackwell**
A beautiful set, including accompaniments to Leroy Carr and Black Bottom McPhail.

BLIND BLAKE
Great 20s East Coast singer/guitarist whose recordings epitomize the best of raggy East Coast fingerpicking styles. The Yazoo album is a representative cross-section of his recordings and is noteworthy for the exceptional sound.

Matchbox 1003 **The Remaining Titles**
Eighteen fine sides. This album, taken together with the out-of-print Whoopee 101 and the Biograph LPs, presents the complete recorded works of Blake. This is a great collection including many sides that are not readily available elsewhere, including three great sides with legendary clarinetist Johnny Dodds. Generally good sound and fine notes by Paul Oliver.

Wolf 133 **The Accompanist, 1926–31**
Eighteen tracks featuring Blake mostly in an accompanying role. It includes his rare first recordings, "Early Morning Blues" and "West Coast Blues," his dialogue with Papa Charlie Jackson, plus accompaniments to Leola B. Wilson, Daniel Brown, Elzadie Robinson, Irene Scruggs, and Laura Rucker. About half of these tracks have been reissued before.

Yazoo 1068 (d) **Ragtime Guitar's Foremost Fingerpicker**
Two-LP set; a superb collection of 28 sides recorded between 1926 31, 19 by Blake himself, and nine

accompaniments to Leola B. Wilson, Irene Scruggs, and Bertha Henderson. Wonderful singing and playing throughout. Although there is much duplication with the out-of-print Biograph issues, the remastering here is so superior that it is almost like hearing them for the first time.

BOBBY "BLUE" BLAND
One of the great original soul/blues singers. His 50s and 60s recordings for Duke (now available on MCA) feature great vocals with outstanding bands. All the Duke albums reissued by MCA are worthwhile, with "Two Steps From The Blues" and "Here's The Man" being among the best. His later albums for ABC, MCA, and Malaco show poor influences, though there is some good stuff among the dross, and Bobby's lovely vocals are nearly always worth a listen.

Ace CH 132 **Blues in the Night**
An enjoyable collection of 14 sides recorded for Duke between 1960–69. Unlike the straight-ahead gospel-tinged blues Bobby recorded in the 50s, these 60s recordings show more diverse influences, including pop, jazz, and country. As always, Bobby's vocals are superb and Joe Scott's arrangements are just right. Most of the tracks here are available on MCA albums, but this is a good cross-section and does include some fine sides that are not readily available. Blue Moon/Ask Me 'Bout Nothing (But The Blues)/When You Put Me Down/Chains of Love/Blues In the Night/The Feeling Is Gone/Black Night.

MCA 883 **Here We Go Again**
Originally MCA 5297. A better than average 80s album from Bobby, in spite of the strings and vocal choruses.

MCA 884 **Tell Mr. Bland**
1984 album contains three fine blues, some contemporary soul ballads and funk, and one totally irrelevant instrumental.

MCA 2-4160 (c) **Together for the First Time**
With B. B. King.

MCA 27012 (c,d) **Together Again**
With B. B. King.

ESSENTIAL SELECTION

MCA 27013 (c,d) **The Best of Bobby Bland**
Reissue of Duke LP84. Poverty/Someday/I Pity The Fool/Turn On Your Love Light/Ain't Nothin' You Can Do/Further Up the Road/I Smell Trouble.

MCA 27036 (c,d) **Two Steps from the Blues**
Reissue of Duke LP69, a great collection. Cry, Cry, Cry/ Don't Cry No More/I Pity The Fool/Little Boy Blue/I'll Take Care Of You.

MCA 27037 (c) **The Barefoot Rock and You Got Me**
One side of this album is by Bland, the other by Junior Parker.

MCA 27038 (c) **Here's the Man**
Reissue of Duke LP75. You're The One/Who Will The Next Fool Be/Blues In The Night/Ain't That Lovin You/Stormy Monday Blues/ Turn On Your Love Light.

MCA 27040 (c) **Ain't Nothin' You Can Do**
Reissue of Duke LP78. If I Hadn't Called You Back Today/After It's Too Late/Loneliness Hurts/If You Can Read My Mind.

MCA 27041 (c) **The Soul of the Man**
Reissue of Duke LP79. I Can't Stop/Deep In My Soul/Ain't Nobody's Business/Too Late For Tears/ Soul Stretch/Play Girl.

MCA 27042 (c) **Call on Me/ That's the Way Love Is**
Reissue of Duke LP77. Honky Tonk/Wishing Well/That's The Way Love Is/No Sweeter Girl/Ain't It A Good Thing/The Feeling Is Gone.

MCA 27043 (c) **Reflections in Blue**
Reissue of ABC 1018.

MCA 27044 (c) **Come Fly with Me**
Reissue of ABC 1075.

MCA 27047 (c) **A Touch of the Blues**
Reissue of Duke LP88. Set Me Free/Road Of Broken Hearted Men/Driftin' Blues/Sad Feelin'/ One Horse Town.

MCA 27048 (c) **Spotlighting the Man**
Reissue of Duke LP89. Chains Of Love/Since I Fell For You.

Malaco 7429 **Members Only**
First album for his new label. It includes a higher proportion of straight soulful blues than most of his more recent MCA albums.

Malaco 7439 (c) **After All**

Malaco (c,d) 7450 **Midnight Run**
CASSETTE AND CD RELEASE ONLY

Malaco 7444 **Blues You Can Use**
Bobby still manages to sound contemporary and timeless at the same time. This album leans more on soul than blues, has nine tunes, eight written by the Malaco staff, including George Jackson and Earl Forrest. Backup group includes Fame drummer Roger Hawkins and the Muscle Shoals Horns with Jim Horn. Lots of songs about cheating and breaking up. Get Your Money Where You Spend Your Time/Let's Part As Friends /For The Last Time.
CASSETTE ONLY

MCA 2-4172 **Introspective of the Early Years**

MCA 27045 **The Best of Bobby Bland, Vol. 2**
Reissue of Duke LP86. 36-22-36/I Don't Believe/I Lost Sight Of The World/You've Got Bad Intentions/I Learned My Lesson.

MCA 27073 **I Feel Good, I Feel Free**
Reissue of MCA 3157 from 1969.

MICHAEL BLOOMFIELD
Popular white blues interpreter who died in 1980.

Demon FIEND 92 **I'm with You Always**
First time issue of this live set recorded at McCabe's Guitar Shop in 1977 with Mark Naftalin (pno), Buell Neidlinger (b), and Buddy Helm (drm). Mike plays acoustic and electric guitars on this very relaxed, low-key set of blues ("Eyesight To The Blind"), traditional tunes ("Frankie and Johnny"), rock ("Don't You Lie To Me"), even a few originals ("I'm Glad I'm Jewish").

Edsel 228 **Triumvirate**
Reissue of Columbia 32172 from 1973. Enjoyable jam band, with John Hammond on vocals, guitar, and harp, Bloomfield on lead, and Dr. John on keyboards and guitar, joined by producer Thomas

Jefferson Kaye on guitar, Burrito Bros. bassist Chris Etheridge, and Fred Staekle on drums, with a horn section that includes George Bohanon and Blue Mitchell. Some tunes are blues, which even back then were overdone, like "Rock Me Baby" and "It Hurts Me Too." The rest are fine New Orleans R&B, blues, and rock, including covers of Art Neville's "Cha-Dooky-Doo," Little Walter's "Last Night," and King Floyd's "Baby Let Me Kiss You."

THE BLUES BUSTERS
The Blues Busters are a quintet from Memphis (vocals, two guitars, piano, bass, and drums) who have been working together with varying personnel since 1982.

High Water 1006 **Busted!**
On this album, they perform a mixture of blues, R&B, rock 'n' roll, and a novelty song—the pointless and expendable "Campbell's Soup Song." They are at their best on the three very slow blues—a real Memphis forte—where the group produces a seething and chilling intensity. The singing is generally good, as is the instrumental work. An interesting, if not totally successful, album. With more rehearsals and a better choice of material they could probably have turned out a very good record.

THE BLUES CARAVAN
This group is a mixed band of black and white musicians (guitars, keyboards, sax, trumpet, drums, and occasional harmonica).

GNP Crescendo 2178 **The Blues Caravan**
Extended all-instrumental workouts on a selection of mostly originals, along with tunes by Bill Dogget and Freddie Hubbard. They play competently, although, occasionally, guitarist Neil Norman gets into some rock excesses. Interesting, if not terribly exciting.

LUCILLE BOGAN
Best Of Blues BOB 17 **1923–35**
Eighteen sides, most of which were issued some years ago on Roots 317, though the three early sides from 1923 have not been reissued before.

ZUZU BOLLIN
Dallas Blues Society 8900 **Texas Bluesman**
ZuZu Bollin certainly has a right to sing the blues. In the early 50s, he survived a run-in with Dallas club owner Jack Ruby (a stroke of luck, considering Ruby's treatment of Lee Harvey Oswald a few years later) as well as a car wreck that ended his nationwide tour with Jimmy Reed's band. Soon afterward, he quit music for a safer and cleaner life in the drycleaning business, and now, thanks to the Dallas Blues Society, he's back on wax again with Duke

Robillard, David "Fathead" Newman, and the Juke Jumpers. The sound is solidly 50s, with more than a nod to T-Bone Walker on the horn arrangements, loping shuffle grooves, and ZuZu's delicate guitar style. His laid-back vocals take command of the material—a nice mix of standards, obscure R&B covers, and ZuZu's truly original tunes ("Headlight Blues," "Zu's Blues," "Why Don't You Eat Where You Slept Last Night?").

SON BONDS
Wolf 129 **Complete Recordings in Chronological Order**
A lovely collection of 20 tracks featuring Tennessee singer/guitarist "Brownsville" Son Bonds, one of the many fine performers to come from west of the Tennessee River. Bonds was a fine singer with a warm vibrato and a basic but effective guitarist. Side one features 10 songs from 1934—six blues and four gospel songs. He is joined by brilliant harmonica player Hammie Nixon on these; on the gospel songs, Hammie provides vocals and/or jug backup. Side two includes six tracks from a wonderful session in September 1941, featuring Son on vocal and kazoo, Sleepy John Estes on vocal and guitar, and Raymond Thomas on bass. These tracks, issued under the name of The Delta Boys, are wonderfully exuberant and infectious performances that are utterly irresistible. The album is rounded out by four more performances by Son, with Estes on guitar. Includes brief informative notes by Paul Oliver.

JUKE BOY BONNER
Texas singer/guitarist/harmonica player who wrote amazingly observant songs about his life and surroundings. His Arhoolie albums are particularly fine.

Ace CHD 269 **They Call Me "Juke Boy"**
Fourteen fine sides recorded in Houston in 1967 and '69 by this brilliant and underrated bluesman. Like his first musical influence, Lightnin' Hopkins, Bonner was a creative bluesman who, in addition to the usual songs of lost love, also wrote perceptive songs about his experiences, the dangers of the big city, and the plight of the black man in America. Although occasionally a bit self-conscious, his songs are powerful and often moving. Four of the songs are from a 1967 session with Bonner accompanied by bass and drums, two are from a solo acoustic session, and the rest from 1969 are from an electric solo session and are, to my mind, the finest performances here.

Arhoolie 1036 **I'm Going Back to the Country**
Fine performances. She Turns Me On/Trying to Be

Contented/Life Is A Nightmare/Stay Off Lyons Avenue.

Arhoolie 1045 **The Struggle**
Has very effective drum accompaniment by Alvin J. Simon. Struggle Here In Houston/Watch Your Buddies/When the Deal Goes Down/I'm In the Big City.

Flyright 548 **The One Man Trio**
Previously on Flyright 3501; excellent 1967 club session, though sound quality is poor.

GNP Crescendo 10015 **Legacy of the Blues, Vol. 5**

BOOGIE WOOGIE RED
Detroit singer and piano player.

Blind Pig 003-77 **Red Hot!**

ROY BOOKBINDER
Acoustic blues/traditional jazz vocalist and guitarist whose deadpan vocal delivery brings to mind a cross between Leon Redbone and Ry Cooder. Roy plays good-time music, occasionally with a small ensemble, covering material from a variety of blues giants.

Flying Fish 098 **Going Back to Tampa**

Rounder 3107 (c,d) **Bookaroo**

JAMES BOOKER
Eccentric but outstanding New Orleans singer and piano player. Booker's music draws on elements as diverse as blues, jazz, pop, soul, and classical. Most of his currently available material features him in a solo setting, although he was also brilliant when working with a small band. His sudden death in 1983 at age 44 was a great loss to the blues world.

Rounder 2027 (c) **New Orleans Piano Wizard: Live!**
Reissue of fine live set recorded in Switzerland in 1977 and originally issued on the Swiss Gold label. Booker gives his unique treatment to a selection of blues, soul, pop, and jazz standards. Beautifully packaged with excellent notes by New Orleans music expert Almost Slim.

Rounder 2036 (c) **Classified**
Fine 1982 album is a mixture of blues and R&B along with bizarre oddities typical of Booker, like "Swedish Rhapsody" and "King Of The Road." Most cuts are solo but a few feature a small group with Alvin Red Tyler on tenor sax.

COMPACT DISC

Junco Partner JP 1 **King of the New Orleans Keyboard**
A great collection of 19 sides recorded live in Europe in the late 70s. These solo recordings (previously available on two JSP LPs) find this unique performer in top form on a selection of blues and R&B favorites given his original treatment, along with some originals. Although recorded live, the sound is excellent.

EARL BOSTIC
Though most famous for his smooth romantic mid-to-late 50s stylings like "Flamingo" and "Liebestraum," Bostic was, in his early days, the leader of a jumping combo.

Oldie Blues 8007 **Sax 'O' Boogie**
Sixteen tracks from his early recording days (1948–51), including hot, driving jump blues and R&B led by Bostic's hot alto sax, complemented by the tenor of Lowell Hastings, Roger Jones (tpt), and Gene Redd (vibes).

PRISCELLA BOWMAN
Kansas City blues shouter Bowman was a singer in Jay McShann's band when, in 1955, she recorded "Hands Off" for Vee Jay backed by the band, which spent an unprecedented 16 weeks at #1 on the R&B charts and has recently been covered by Aretha Franklin and June Carter.

Sounds Great 5008 **An Original Rock 'n' Roll Mama**
Fourteen fine Vee Jay recordings from 1955–59, with terrible discographical information. Liner notes state that dates and personnel are unknown. For the record, the first session is from August 13, 1957, with The Al Smith Orchestra, and yielded two Falcon singles. All four sides are here—"Sugar Daddy" plus three others. The second session is from July 30, 1958, with a quintet made up of Smith Orchestra members and Cliff Davis on tenor, and two sides with The Spaniels, released on Abner ("Rockin' Good Way" and "I Ain't Givin' Up Nothin'"), plus two unreleased tracks, both here. A third unreleased session from July 30, 1959, with most of the same musicians, produced "Like A Baby" and three others.

EDDIE BOYD
Chicago blues singer and piano player who started his recording career in 1947 and has continued performing up to the present day. Besides his singing and piano skills, he is also a fine and insightful songwriter. His best recordings date from the 40s, 50s, and 60s. His more recent recordings, mostly cut in Europe, where he now makes his home, are less inspiring. The Crown Prince album is a particularly fine cross-section of his recording career in the 40s and 50s. The many fine sides he recorded for small labels in

the late 50s and 60s are not at present represented on LP.

Crosscut 1002 Eddie Boyd and His Blues Band
Reissue of album cut in England in 1967 on which he is accompanied by some of Britain's leading blues interpreters—Peter Green, John McVie, Aynsley Dunbar, John Mayall, and Tony McPhee. On new songs and remakes of some old songs, Eddie plays and sings very well, and the backup is in good taste.

Crown Prince 400 Ratting and Running Around
Sixteen cuts recorded between 1947 and 1956 with sidemen like Willie Lacey, Ransom Knowling, Robert Lockwood, Lee Cooper, and Alfred Elkins. Rosa Lee Swing/Blue Monday Blues/You Got To Love That Gal/What Makes These Things Happen To Me/Eddie's Blues/Chicago Is Just That Way.

GNP Crescendo 10020 Legacy of the Blues, Vol. 10

L+R 42.005 Five Long Years
Excellent 1965 session recorded in Europe with a small band, including some splendid guitar by Buddy Guy plus Jimmie Lee Robinson (b) and Fred Below (drm). Mostly remakes of his most popular 50s recordings.

Stockholm RJ 204 Lovers Playground
A nice selection of 80s recordings. Accompanied by a Finnish rhythm section, including some surprisingly effective accordion by Pedro Heitanen. Eddie performs an excellent mixture of 10 original songs and instrumentals, many of them recent compositions.

CALVIN BOZE

Moonshine 113 Havin' a Ball
Excellent West Coast jump blues by fine and undeservedly obscure singer and trumpet player, recorded between 1949 and 1954 with mostly unknown musicians, though many of the tracks feature the tenor sax of the fine and ubiquitous Maxwell Davis. His recordings often are reminiscent of Louis Jordan with their easy-going swing and slyly witty lyrics. Most enjoyable.

Route 66 KIX 35 Choo, Choo's Brings My Baby Home
Boze's Aladdin output from 1949–52 proves him to be a fine singer and writer. It really helps that he had Maxwell Davis arranging, playing tenor, and providing the hottest session players. Drinkin', fish fries, house-rent parties, big-legged women, and BBQ—they're all here, presented with wit and style. Some duplication with Moonshine 113. Nineteen cuts in all: Good Time Sue/Stinkin' From

Drinkin'/Beale Street On A Saturday Night/Safronia B/Blow, Man, Blow.

ISHMAN BRACEY
Superb Mississippi singer/guitarist. He often worked with the great Tommy Johnson and Charlie McCoy. He recorded a number of sides for Paramount and Victor in 1928 and 1930 and the Wolf album below reissues all those recordings except for one Paramount that has not yet been found!

Wolf WSE 105 Ishman Bracey
Sixteen lovely sides, some solo, some with Charlie McCoy (gtr), and a few with the slightly bizarre New Orleans Nehi Boys, who accompany him on clarinet and piano. Saturday Blues/Leavin' Town Blues/My Brown Mama Blues/Trouble Hearted Blues/Jake Liquour Blues.

TOMMIE BRADLEY/JAMES COLE
Matchbox 211 Tommie Bradley–James Cole Groups
Fifteen recordings cut between 1930–32 by various groups that featured singer/violin player Cole and/or singer/guitar player Bradley. A mixture of blues, hokum, vaudeville-type songs, and jazzy items. Other instrumentation includes piano, mandolin, jug, and washboard. Only a few of these cuts have been reissued before.

JACKIE BRENSTON and HIS DELTA CATS
Chess (UK) GCH 8107 Rocket 88
Brenston's exciting "Rocket 88" was a big R&B hit in 1951 and has been reissued several times over the years, but this is the first time any more of his Chess material has been reissued. This album features 14 cuts recorded in the early 50s, of which about half are not listed in any discographies! A fine selection of rocking R&B and occasional slow blues with a rural flavor. The personnel fluctuated but, besides Brenston's vocals and tenor sax, included vocals by Billy Red Love and Edna McRaney, guitar by Willie Kizart and Calvin Newborn, piano by Ike Turner and Billy Red Love, and tenor sax by Raymond Hill. Excellent stuff. I Want To See My Baby/Jackie's Chewing Gum/Make My Love Come Down/In My Real Gone Rocket/Mule/My Baby Left Town.

JIM BREWER
Mississippi bluesman based in Chicago. Brewer is stylistically similar to Big Bill Broonzy.

Earwig 4904 Tough Luck
Enjoyable album. Most of his material here comprises blues standards, though he does have a couple of originals.

JOHN BRIM

Fine Kentucky-born Chicago blues singer who recorded some classics in the 50s. He had a lovely relaxed vocal style in the mold of Jimmy Rogers and played basic but effective guitar, and worked with some of Chicago's finest musicians.

Chess 9114 (c) Elmore James/John Brim: Whose Muddy Shoes
A classic reissued: Brim sides feature Little Walter and Jimmy Rogers. Ice Cream Man/You Got Me/Rattlesnake (an all-time classic with great harp from Little Walter)/Be Careful/Tough Times.

Flyright 568 John Brim/Little Hudson
Lovely album of low-key 50s Chicago blues, featuring 11 cuts by John or his wife Grace accompanied by Sunnyland Slim, and five by Little Hudson Showers with Lazy Bill Lucas (pno); great stuff!

Wolf 120.858 John Brim/Pinetop Perkins Chicago Blues Session, Vol. 12
Four songs by each: Brim with John Primer, Billy Branch, Willie Kent, and Timothy Taylor; Perkins with Taylor or Michael Strasser. Brim made some wonderful recordings for various labels in the 50s, but at the time of these tracks his voice was pretty shot and he sounded very different from the man who had recorded 30 years earlier. Perkins gives nice performances of mostly familiar songs like "High Heel Sneakers" and "Drivin' Wheel."

COMPACT DISC

Chess (France) 600119 Elmore James, John Brim, Floyd Jones
Features all the Chess recordings of these three artists. Fabulous music but, as usual for French Chess, the sound is not as good as it should be.

HADDA BROOKS

Jukebox Lil 1107 Romance in the Dark
A fine reissue of this torch singer and boogie-woogie piano player from Los Angeles, with 18 cuts from 1945–52 and one from c. 1972. The liner notes offer a detailed life history in a gatefold sleeve full of photos. There's also some tasty guitar work from Teddy Bunn on some cuts.

Oldie Blues 2826 Queen of the Boogie
A nice selection of piano blues and boogie numbers recorded between 1945–50. Although a technically accomplished player, she sometimes lacks the fire to really drive boogie along and, on some cuts, the accompaniments get in her way. Sound is pretty good and there is a wonderful color picture of Hadda on the cover.

LONNIE BROOKS (GUITAR JUNIOR)

Chicago-based singer/electric guitarist, originally from Louisiana. Powerful performer.

Alligator 4714 (d) Bayou Lightning
With Billy Branch (hca) on two cuts. Voodoo Daddy/Watchdog/In the Dark/Alimony.

Alligator 4721 (c,d) Turn on the Night
Unlike Alligator 4714, which featured rhythm section only, this one features horns on several cuts for a richer sound. Eyeballin'/Teenage Boogie Man/I'll Take Care Of You.

Alligator 4731 Hot Shot
Possibly his best Alligator album. Raw, emotion-charged vocals, and hard-driving guitar from Lonnie and solid support from his regular road band, with Abb Locke guesting on tenor sax. The songs are new originals or obscure older songs plus a powerful remake of his 50s "hit," "Family Rules."

Alligator 4751 (c,d) Wound Up Tight
Another winner from Lonnie, who also wrote most of the LP. Johnny Winter lends a hand on "Got Lucky Last Night" and the title tune, and Jim Liban guests on harp on "Musta Been Dreamin'" and "Belly Rubbin' Music."

Alligator 4759 (c,d) Live/Bayou Lightnin' Strikes

Black and Blue 33.554 Sweet Home Chicago
Originally issued as 33.512. Enjoyable album of electric Chicago blues, with Hubert Sumlin, Little Mac, Willie Mabon, Dave Myers, and Fred Below. Sweet Home Chicago/Crosscut Saw/ Things I Used To Do.

Crosscut 1006 Broke and Hungry
This album is a reissue of his 1969 Capitol album, produced by the son of Goldband's owner Eddie Shuler. It's a pleasing set of Louisiana-flavored performances of songs from Chuck Berry, Guitar Slim, Professor Longhair, and Lightnin' Slim. Good singing and playing from Lonnie and tasty backup by a small group with guitar, bass, harmonica, and drums.

BIG BILL BROONZY

Popular and prolific blues singer/guitarist, originally from Mississippi. His 20s/early 30s recordings feature great raggy guitar; these are reissued on Yazoo and Matchbox. His 30s and 40s recordings (reissued on Best Of Blues, Blues Documents, Columbia, and Document) are more urbane, with small groups. These were recorded in Chicago, which was his home from the 20s on. In addition to his own recordings, he performed on hundreds of sides cut in that city by other musicians. He became a father figure in the Chicago blues scene. His later 40s/early 50s recordings are mostly solo and show him catering to a folk audience. They are sometimes a little self-conscious, though his singing and guitar playing was always strong. He visited Europe several times in the 50s and recorded several times there. He died in 1958.

Best Of Blues BOB 2 **1935–41**
A fine collection of 18 sides, 17 previously unavailable on LP. Bill is heard in a variety of settings with a range of accompanying musicians. Includes three tracks with the State Street Boys, a delightful group featuring the alley fiddle of Zeb Wright. Washboard Sam shares the vocal with Bill on "Down In The Alley," and on the lively "Unemployment Stomp" he is joined by the jazzy trumpet of Punch Miller. Sound is satisfactory.

Blues Documents 2012 **1935–39**
Twenty tracks recorded between 1935–39, mostly not previously on album. There are two tracks by Bill with the State Street Boys—a fine string band with nice fiddle by Zeb Wright or Carl Martin. Other songs feature accompanying musicians like Black Bob, Charlie McCoy, Punch Miller, Blind John Davis, Buster Bennet, and Ranson Knowling. Sweet To Mama/You Need My Help Someday/Seven-Eleven (Dice Please Don't Fail Me)/Terrible Flood Blues/Barrel House When It Rains/Come Home Early/Hattie Blues/Fightin' Little Rooster/Ride, Alberta, Ride.

Chess 9251 (c) **Big Bill Broonzy and Washboard Sam**
Reissue of Chess 1468 (originally issued in 1962) features four songs by Broonzy and eight by Sam recorded in 1953. The lineup is basically the same on all cuts, with Broonzy and Lee Cooper (gtrs), Sam (washbd), Big Crawford (b), and, on a few cuts, Memphis Slim (pno). It seems that Lee Cooper is playing lead guitar on most cuts, although a lot of it does sound like Broonzy. Although these recordings do not capture either artist at his best, they are enjoyable enough. Little City Woman/Jacqueline/By Myself/Diggin' My Potatoes/Minding My Own Business/Horse Shoe Over My Door.

ESSENTIAL SELECTION
Columbia C 46219 (c,d) **Good Time Tonight**
1930–40 recordings originally made for Vocalion, including seven unissued takes and seven previously unreleased sides. Although there is no shortage of Broonzy reissues, this is a fine addition to what is already out there and, of course, boasts superior

sound and packaging over most others. There are four tracks from the early 30s with Bill on solo guitar or with second guitar by Frank Brasswell (displaying his awesome prowess on the instrument). The remaining tracks are from the late 30s and feature Bill with various small groups with piano, bass, and occasional trumpet, sax, clarinet, and drums. All of the performances are fine and the set comes with excellent notes by the series producer Larry Cohn.

Document 510 **Vol.1, 1934–37**
This album is noteworthy for the inclusion of Broonzy's brilliant 1934 version of "C. C. Rider," on which Bill plays violin for the only time on record, showing him to be very adept at that instrument. The rest of the album is a diverse and enjoyable selection including the fine "Sweetheart Land" from 1938, with some pioneering electric guitar by George Barnes, and other good tracks like "It's Your Time Now," "Please Be My So And So," "Lone Wolf Blues," and "Green Grass Blues." Most of these tracks have never been on LP before. Sound is satisfactory and the album comes with full discographical information.

Document 539 **Vol. 2, 1935–1949**
A typically fine selection of 30s Broonzy along with a few later items. There is so much Broonzy out there that's good it's not easy to recommend yet another one, but this does have a brilliant opening cut, "Something Good," with Bill's guitar joined by Louis Lasky. There is also the excellent, melodic "I'm a Southern Man," plus other good sides like "You Do Me Any Old Way," "Come Home Early," and "Why Do You Do That to Me?" Generally good sound and only a few tracks have been reissued elsewhere.

GNP Crescendo 10004 **Feeling Lowdown**
GNP Crescendo 10009 **Lonesome Road Blues**
Matchbox 1004 **Big Bill Broonzy, 1927–32**
A beautiful collection of 16 of Broonzy's earliest recordings, most of which have never been on LP before. This set complements Yazoo 1011 amd 1035, which cover material from the same era. Although the sound quality is not as good as that on the Yazoos, the music is and includes Bill's very first recording, "House Rent Stomp." Most of the other tracks feature Bill on his own and, besides his lovely rich vocals, they show his prowess as a ragtime-flavored blues guitarist. There are two raucous cuts from 1932 on which Bill is joined by a small group including trumpet, trombone, piano, and jug, an aggregation that goes under the name of Big Bill and His Jug Busters.

Smithsonian/Folkways SF 40023 (c,d) **Big Bill Broonzy Sings Folk Songs**

Reissue of Folkways FA 2328, put together from tapes that Moses Asch made of Broonzy at various times. This album represents Broonzy's more "folk-oriented" style of the 50s. This Train/Martha/Tell Me No/Bill Bailey/Alberta/John Henry/Glory Of Love.

Yazoo 1011 **The Young Big Bill Broonzy**

Great early recordings from 1928–36, with wonderful guitar. Includes some cuts with second guitar. Brownskin Shuffle/Starvation Blues/Good Liquour Gonna Carry Me Down.

Yazoo 1035 **Do That Guitar Rag**

More great early sides from 1928–35. Pigmeat Strut/Terrible Operation Blues/Leave My Man Alone/Grandma's Farm.

CASSETTE AND CD RELEASE ONLY

Portrait RJ 44089 **Big Bill's Blues**

It's great to have this classic album available again, and on CD too! Originally issued as Epic 22017 in the late 60s, this is probably the best collection of his late 30s/early 40s recordings. The 16 tracks include some of his most popular and most influential sides like the title song, "Bullcow Blues," "Baby I Done Got Wise," and "Just A Dream," along with other equally fine tracks like "Trucking Little Woman," "Southern Flood Blues," and "Night Time Is the Right Time." Accompanying Bill are such Chicago stalwarts as Black Bob, Joshua Altheimer, Washboard Sam, and Memphis Slim. Much is made of the digital remastering on the cover, but this sounds no better than the original Epic reissue, which is to say, excellent. But why replace the original, attractive cover photo with a hideous painting and why leave off the discographical details? Apart from these minor quibbles, this is an outstanding set.

COMPACT DISC

Sequel NEX CD 119 **The 1955 London Sessions**

Eleven tracks recorded in 1955 in England for the Nixa label. As usual for material from this period, Broonzy plays and sings wonderfully, but his choice of material is somewhat self-conscious. Two of the tracks feature him accompanied by a group of British jazz musicians who seem to have little idea of what Bill's music was all about.

Vogue 600041 **Big Bill Blues**

Fifteen songs recorded in Paris in 1951–52. Contains "Louise Louise," "Lonesome Road," "Baby Please Don't Go," "Down By The Riverside," "John Henry," "How Long," and a nine-and-a-half-minute version of "Hollerin' And Cryin' The Blues"!

Vogue 670401 **Feelin' Low Down**

A fine collection of 14 tracks recorded in 1951–52, mostly previously issued on various Vogue LPs and EPs. Although Broonzy's postwar recordings are sometimes written off as being self-consciously aimed at a white audience, there is a lot of wonderful blues here with intense, rhythmic, and unique guitar and powerful declamatory vocals. "House Rent Stomp," "The Moppin' Blues," "What I Used To Do," "Low Down Blues," and "Lonesome Road Blues" are very exciting and more than make up for the more self-conscious items like "Black, Brown and White," "When Did You Leave Heaven," and "Blues In 1890." With the exception of two rather poorly recorded live tracks from 1952, the sound here is excellent.

ANDREW BROWN

Excellent Chicago blues singer/guitarist who was active on the blues scene until his sudden death in 1985. He was a powerful, rich-voiced vocalist slightly reminiscent of Little Milton and an effective guitarist.

Black Magic 9001 **Big Brown's Chicago Blues**

His first album is good, solid, no-nonsense modern blues with fine vocals and guitar by Brown on mostly original songs and rock-steady accompaniment by the rhythm section. Produced by blues expert Dick Shurman, who also provides the extensive notes.

Double Trouble DT 3010 **On the Case**

Excellent second album. On this album, he performs a mixture of excellent original songs like "This Time You Gotta Pay," "The Blues Do Something To Me," and the splendid minor key "I Can Hear My Baby Talking," plus some excellent covers, including Bobby Bland"s "I'm So Tired." He is accompanied by a solid band, which includes Jimmy Johnson (gtr), Al Irono (sax), and Professor Eddie Lusk (kybds).

BUSTER BROWN
Charly CRB 1209 **Good News**
A fine collection of 14 sides recorded by this distinctive singer and harmonica player for the Fire and Gwenn labels between 1959–62. It includes his big hit "Fannie Mae" along with other songs. Good News/Gonna Love My Baby/Sugar Babe/Blueberry Hill/Slow Drag, Parts 1 and 2/Don't Dog Your Woman.
Collectables 5110 (d) **The New King of the Blues**
Reissue of Fire 102 from 1961 with extra tracks, 16 in all. This is the same as Fire (Japan) PLP 6004. Sharp harp, wild guitar from Jimmy Spruill and Riff Ruffin, and fine Bobby Robinson production. Dr. Brown/I Get The Blues When It Rains/Good News/Raise A Rukus Tonight/Gonna Love My Baby. Note: The previously unreleased "Corena" and "Going On A Picnic" are listed on the cover and are not on the LP!

CHARLES BROWN
Fine and important West Coast blues singer whose 40s recordings pioneered a whole new style of blues/ballad singing, with sensitive accompaniments by Johnny Moore's Three Blazers. His classic early recordings are reissued on the superb Route 66 albums. His more recent recordings are, for the most part, rather syrupy straight ballads.

Alligator 4771 (c,d) **One More for the Road**
Reissue of highly regarded album originally issued on the now defunct Blueside label. Eleven tunes, most cut with a trio of Brown (pno, vcl), Billy Butler (gtr), and Earl May (b), capturing the feel of The Three Blazers, with appearances by Harold Ousley (ten sax) and Kenny Washington (drm). A wide variety of material given the late-night Brown treatment, from pop ("One For My Baby," "Cottage For Sale"), country ("He's Got You," "Who Will The Next Fool Be?"), and R&B ("Route 66," "I Miss You So," "Travellin' Blues").
Gusto 5019 **Please Come Home for Christmas**
Twelve Christmas songs by Brown plus four by Bill Doggett.
Hollywood 329 (c,d) **Please Come Home for Christmas**
Jukebox Lil 1106 **Sail On**
This collection of three Modern sides and 15 late 40s Exclusive sides focuses on the upbeat numbers. In fact, they even find a way to jazz up "St. Louis Blues." Brown is joined by Johnny Moore (gtr) and Eddie Williams (b) on all the tunes, with Oscar Moore (gtr) added for three numbers. The leisurely night-club style blues still makes up the lion's share, with Brown's slurred vocals and deliberate piano style lulling the listener into a dream-like state. Moore's combination of alternately picking and strumming his guitar is pure genius and fits in perfectly, although I should also note that Brown, as the latecomer, fits in well. Wonderful stuff. Check out the great photo on the back showing the quartet with Satchel Paige. Sail On Blues/Johnny's Boogie/Bobby Sox Blues/Band B Blues/Cold In Here/Lost In The Night.
King 775 (c,d) **Sings Christmas Songs**
Please Come Home for Christmas/Christmas in Heaven/It's Christmas All Year/Merry Christmas Baby.
Route 66 KIX 5 **Sunny Road**
Sixteen fine sides recorded between 1945–60. New Orleans Blues/Soothe Me/Merry Christmas Baby/Traveling Blues.
Route 66 KIX 17 **Race Track Blues**
Sixteen songs recorded between 1945–56, with Johnny Moore's Three Blazers, Chuck Norris, Lee Allen, and other fine sidemen. Jukebox Lil/More Than You Know/Snuff Dippin' Mama/Peek-A-Boo/Homesick Blues.
Stockholm RJ 200 **I'm Gonna Push On**
Recorded live in Sweden with a Swedish band.
COMPACT DISC

Sequel NEX CD 133 **Hard Times and Cool Blues**
Twenty-five great Aladdin sides (two previously unissued). Driftin' Blues/Seven Long Days/Black Night/Fool's Paradise/My Baby's Gone/Still Water/Love Is A Gamble/How High the Moon/It's Nothing/Merry Christmas Baby/Evening Shadows/Seven Kisses Mambo/Goodnight My Love.

CLARENCE "GATEMOUTH" BROWN

Immensely talented Texas singer, guitar, fiddle, and harmonica player who has been an important force in Texas blues since the 40s and continues to make fine records in the 80s and 90s.

Alligator 4745 (c) Pressure Cooker

An enjoyable selection of tracks drawn from the five LPs "Gate" recorded in France for the Black and Blue label in the 70s. These jazzy blues usually find him in a trio or quartet format accompanied by organ player Milt Buckner or piano player Jay McShann with the occasional assistance of the great Texas tenor sax player Arnett Cobb. The material includes new recordings of some of his old Peacock classics, new songs, and a couple of tracks from his tribute album to Louis Jordan. Fine singing and lots of splendid Texas blues guitar by "Gate" plus solid accompaniment by the band.

Alligator 4779 (c,d) Standing My Ground

This one was recorded in New Orleans using some of the city's top musicians, and, as one might suspect, it sounds great. His guitar playing is as eloquent and inventive as ever, while still retaining that raw Texas blues sting, as he moves from style to style with a veteran's ease. Some tunes are self-explanatory, such as "Cool Jazz" and "Louisiana Zydeco" (featuring Terence Simien on accordion). Gate also plays fiddle, piano, and even drums on some cuts, while the nice punchy horn arrangements shine throughout.

Black and Blue 33.550 Okie Dokie Stomp

Reissue of Black and Blue 33.033 from 1971 with new packaging and remixed and remastered for better sound. A fine selection of songs with great vocals, guitar, violin, and harmonica by Gatemouth, accompanied by Mickey Baker and Jimmy Dawkins (gtr), Mac Thompson (b), and Michel Denis (drm). If I Get Lucky/Piney Brown Blues/Love Sick Soul.

Black and Blue 33.561 More Stuff

Some nice previously unissued sides recorded in France in 1973. Side one features Gate with a rhythm section only (Jay McShann [pno], Roland Lobligeois [b], and Paul Gunther [drm]), and offers some relaxed extended workouts on three songs. Side two features him with a larger band including Al Grey (trb), Hal Singer (ten sax), and Stan Hunter or Milt Buckner (org). Some nice performances.

Blues Boy 305 Atomic Energy

This fine release presents an excellent cross-section of vintage recordings. It includes his two earliest recordings from 1947 along with 14 others recorded between 1949 and 1959, ranging from the T-Bone Walker-flavored "Guitar in Hand," to the rockin' commercial "Pale Dry Boogie," to the sweet pop-jazz-flavored "September Song," on which Gate plays some fine violin. Excellent sound and fold-out jacket with extensive notes, photos, and full discographical information.

Chess (UK) LPM 7003 The Nashville Session—1965

After Gate's long and successful stint at Peacock, he hit the road for Nashville and cut this session for Hermitage Records. Chess eventually purchased the masters and they were released on Chess Japan a few years ago. He got the chance to break out of his blues mold a bit, utilizing his country and jazz influences, and also had a chance to play his fiddle on record. He's in a relaxed mood here, no "Atomic Energy" or "Okie Dokie Stomp" blues blasters. He must have had Sonny Boy Williamson on his mind, covering three of his tunes: "Cross My Heart," "Don't Start Me Talking," and "Ninety Nine." There are two takes of his version of Little Jimmy Dickens's very silly "May The Bird Of Paradise Fly Up Your Nose," but some great guitar and fiddle on the rest, including "Gate's Salty Blues" and "Goin' Down Slow."

Red Lightnin' 0010 San Antonio Ballbuster

Sixteen of his best vintage recordings from 1949 to 1959. Many of these tracks have been reissued elsewhere with better sound.

Rounder 2028 (c) Alright Again

Good 1981 album recorded in New Orleans with good band including Alvin "Red" Tyler on sax. Gate is in good form vocally and on guitar and throws in a little violin for good measure. A wide variety of material here. Frosty/Give Me Time To Explain/Sometimes/Slip/Alligator Boogaloo.

Rounder 2034 (c) One More Mile

This album is a more exciting set than Rounder 2028. Gate sings and plays with more enthusiasm and he is accompanied by a fine band, with some excellent horn arrangements by Bill Samuel and Homer Brown. The repertoire is a mixture of new originals and some older songs. Besides blues, the performances touch on jazz, country, Cajun, and pop music.

ESSENTIAL SELECTION

Rounder 2039 (c) The Original Peacock Recordings
Twelve vintage recordings cut for the Peacock label between 1952–59. Unlike the later recordings that featured him performing a variety of music, this album is all Texas blues at its best. It includes two previously unissued sides. With full discographical information and excellent notes by Dick Shurman.

Rounder 2054 (c,d) Real Life
Fine 1986 album that was recorded live in Fort Worth with Gate's regular working band. A powerful collection of Peacock remakes, blues standards, a couple of new songs, and a wild version of the jazz standard "Take The A Train." Most of the tracks feature tough guitar by Gate, but on "Catfish" (a new composition; no relation to the traditional blues), he takes out his violin for some lively jazz/blues improvisations.

COMPACT DISC

Black and Blue 59.096 2 Cold Storage
This 69-minute CD features 14 tracks recorded by Gate in France in 1973 and previously issued on various Black and Blue LPs. There are remakes of some of his 50s Peacock classics, a selection of Louis Jordan songs taken from the tribute album, and some others. Gate is in generally good form but the performances are generally rather restrained due, no doubt, to the rather effete accompaniments by mostly jazz musicians.

P-Vine PCD 2109 Hot Times Tonight
An interesting collection of 13 tracks recorded in the mid-60s. A few were issued on local Texas labels, but most have not been issued before. Accompanied by a couple of different bands, Gate turns in an eclectic mixture of blues, jazz, and country, featuring him on vocals, guitar, fiddle, and harmonica. About half the tracks are instrumental and include a Latin blues-flavored version of "When My Blue Moon Turns To Gold Again" on fiddle(!), hot R&B ("I Want You For My Girlfriend"), and a jazzy version of "Milkcow Blues." The vocal performances are equally eclectic. Nothing spectacular here, but an enjoyable selection from an extremely talented performer.

Rounder CD 11527 Texas Swing
Seventeen tracks taken from his Grammy-winning album "Alright Again" (Rounder 2028) and the Grammy-nominated "One More Mile" (Rounder 2034). Frosty/I Wonder/Baby Take It Easy/I Feel Alright Again/Dollar Got The Blues/Gate Walks To Board.

GABRIEL BROWN
Florida country bluesman who recorded for New York record producer Joe Davis between 1943–52. Brown was a fine artist with a rich and distinctive vocal style and a basic but effective guitar style though with an occasional tendency to play noticeably out of tune!

Flyright 591 Gabriel Brown
Some fine cuts. With detailed notes by Bruce Bastin and excellent and previously unpublished cover photos.

Krazy Kat 785 1944–52
Sixteen sides, 11 never issued before! This album complements Flyright 591, and is possibly better than that.

J. T. BROWN
Hot Chicago tenor player who appeared on many 40s and 50s recordings. The Pearl album reissues United recordings with his own band, while the Krazy Kat features tracks on which he was a sideman as well as recordings under his own name.

Krazy Kat 7420 Rockin' with J. T.
Reissue of album issued on Flyright some years ago but with several tracks changed to avoid conflict with the Pearl LP. Most of the cuts here feature him as sideman rather than leader, but all feature lots of his distinctive sax work. Artists whose cuts he is featured on include Roosevelt Sykes, Eddie Boyd, Booker T. Washington, and Washboard Sam. On most of the cuts under his own name, he is accompanied by Elmore James and Johnny Jones. Some exciting music.

Pearl 9 Windy City Boogie
Fine 1956 recordings cut for Chicago's United label; many previously unissued.

LEE BROWN
Blues Documents 2005 Piano Blues Rarities
Sixteen songs recorded between 1937–40 by singer/piano player Brown. The four earliest cuts—two with Sleepy John Estes—are the most downhome and include the first recording of his most popular song, "Little Girl, Little Girl." The later tracks find him with various small groups, some with a jazzy flavor. Brown is a decent singer and piano player, though his vocal inflections get a little tedious after a while.

NAPPY BROWN

Black Top 1039 (c,d) Something Gonna Jump Out of the Bushes
Recent recordings with Anson Funderburg and Ronnie Earl.

Ichiban 1056 (c,d) Apples and Lemons
This 1990 release is pretty much a straight blues album including songs like "Fishin' Blues," "Lemon Squeezin' Daddy," and "You Showed Me Love." He also does a remake of his hit "Don't Be Angry." Accompaniments are competent if not very interesting; the harmonica player on a few tracks is particularly overbearing.

Mr. R&B 100 That Man
Sixteen sides recorded between 1954–61. That Man/Is It True/ Open That Door/Little By Little/My Baby/A Long Time/Baby, I Got News For You

Savoy SJL 1149 Don't Be Angry
Sixteen cuts recorded between 1954–56 featuring a mixture of straight blues, blues ballads, and rocking R&B. Nappy's distinctive voice is accompanied by top New York session musicians: Sam Taylor (ten sax), Al Sears (ten sax), Mickey Baker (gtr), and Sam Price (pno). Although quite a few of these tracks were previously reissued on Mr. R&B, these cuts are taken from original master tapes. With informative notes by Colin Escott and full discographical information.

Stockholm RJ 205 I Done Got Over
On this 1984 album, Nappy proves that he can still belt it out, as witnessed by cuts like the remake of "Down In the Alley," ably backed by Knut Reiesrud (gtr) and Willie Cook (tpt). Recorded in Norway and Sweden in 1983 with Scandinavian musicians (except Cook), this album ably recreates the mood and tone of Nappy's glory days in the 50s. Notes by Jonas Bernholm.

CASSETTE AND CD RELEASE ONLY

Alligator 4792 With The Heartfixers
This 1985 set finds Nappy in fine vocal form, with a distinctive voice. He is accompanied by the Georgia white blues band The Heartfixers, along with several guest musicians who give the record a full sound. A varied selection of material on this enjoyable album. Originally issued as Landslide 008.

ROY BROWN

Popular and influential 40s/50s blues shouter who tragically passed away in 1981 just as he was on the verge of a comeback. At this point, many of his vintage recordings have been reissued on King, Mr. R&B, and Route 66 and they are all worthwhile.

Charly CRB 1199 The Bluesway Sessions
Eleven tracks recorded for Bluesway in 1967–68 and originally issued on Bluesway 6056.

King 5036X Hard Luck Blues
Two-LP set with 22 excellent 50s sides. Travelin' Man/Trouble At Midnight/Ain't It A Shame/Worried Life Blues/Hard Luck Blues/Train Time Blues/ Wrong Woman Blues/Big Town/Lonesome Love.

Mr. R&B 104 Saturday Night
This album focusses on his more rock 'n' roll oriented material recorded between 1952–59. Seventeen hot sides, many of them recorded in New Orleans with top sidemen like Lee Allen, Justin Adams, and Alvin Tyler; some cuts feature marvelous guitar by Jimmy Davis. Beautifully remastered, with a fold-out cover with fine photos and extensive notes.

Route 66 KIX 2 Laughing but Crying
Sixteen tracks recorded between 1947–59. Roy Brown Boogie/Rainy Weather Blues/New Rebecca/A Fool In Love/ Butcher Pete.

Route 66 KIX 6 Good Rockin' Tonight
Sixteen cuts, 1947–54. Whose Hat Is That?/Dreaming Blues/Old Age Boogie/Miss Fanny Brown Returns.

Route 66 KIX 26 I Feel That Young Man's Rhythm
This album focuses on the early years of Brown's career. Most of the tracks were recorded between 1947 and 1949. Includes his first recordings, cut in a club in 1947, and also an excellent four-song New Orleans session from 1949 that has never been issued before. The album is rounded out by three tracks from the early 50s. Consistently fine singing by Roy and some excellent bands. As usual for this label, the sound is superb, the record is attractively packaged, and it comes with a touching tribute to Roy by Art Fein.

RUTH BROWN

Fantasy 9662 (c,d) Blues on Broadway
This 1990 release has an after-hours blues feel about it, with Ruth sounding more like a supper-club singer than at any time since her re-emergence in the 80s. Some of the songs come from her Tony Award-winning performance in "Black and Blue," a Broadway show, including "St. Louis Blues," "If I Can't Sell It, I'll Keep Sittin' on It," and "Tain't Nobody's Business If I Do." Accompanists include Bobby Forrester on smooth Hammond organ and tasty piano, soulful tenor sax from Red Holloway, alto embellishments from Hank Crawford, and solid stickwork from Grady Tate. Ruth's voice is not as

youthful as it once was, but she can get smokey on the back-alley blues songs.

ROY BUCHANAN

Alligator 4741 (c,d) When a Guitar Plays the Blues

Roy's first all-blues album. Clean production, tight backup (Morris Jennings, former Chess session drummer, is on hand), and plenty of solos are sure to make this LP a special occasion for long-time fans.

Alligator 4747 (c,d) Dancing on the Edge

Alligator 4756 Hot Wires (c,d)

1987 session featuring Donald Kinsey on guitar. Roy declared this one to be "my best one yet."

Krazy Kat 7450 The Early Years

CD issue: Krazy Kat CD 02

Fourteen sides from the late 50s/early 60s. In addition to recordings under his own name, it includes accompaniments to Bobby and The Temps, Al Jones, and Cody Brennan. CD includes four additional tracks, two previously unissued.

BUCKWHEAT ZYDECO ILS SONT PARTIS BAND

Excellent Zydeco band led by singer, accordion, piano, and organ player Stanley "Buckwheat" Doral, formerly with Clifton Chenier. Although he is a fine artist, it does seem that he has been over-recorded in recent years. The best of his albums are Black Top 1024 and Blues Unlimited 5017.

Black Top 1024 (c,d) 100 Percent Fortified Zydeco

Excellent and delightful 1983 album. On this album, the band tackles a wide range of material: R&B, Zydeco, Cajun two-steps and waltzes, and pop songs; it all comes off well and ends up being stamped with that distinctive south Louisiana flavor.

Blues Unlimited 5006 (c) Ils Sont Partis

First solo album from 1979. Mostly original songs. I Bought A Raccoon/Zydeco Honky Tonk/Bim Bam, Thank You Mam/One For The Floor.

Blues Unlimited 5009 Take It Easy Baby

Their second album, a little slicker than the first and lacking a little of its punch but a fine selection nevertheless.

Blues Unlimited 5017 People's Choice

One of their best albums, from 1982. Buckwheat sings well and plays fine accordion, organ, and piano, and his band is very strong, with outstanding guitar by Paul Senegal and tenor sax by John Bell. The material is a nice mix of blues, R&B, Zydeco, and Cajun songs.

Blues Unlimited 5022 Ils Sont Partis

Their fourth Blues Unlimited album, a good selection of blues, R&B, and Cajun music but not as strong as "Peoples Choice" or "100 Percent Fortified."

Island 842 925-1 (c,d) Where There's Smoke There's Fire

Tough album by one of Zydeco's leading lights, accompanied by a driving band with various guest musicians, including David Hidalgo (who produced this set) on a couple of cuts. The best tracks here are the driving R&B and Zydeco originals like the title tune, "What You Gonna Do?," and "Pour Tout Quelqu'un." Buckwheat also does a good job on the jazz/blues/R&B standard "Route 66," though his versions of the Rolling Stones' "Beast of Burden" and Hank Williams's "Hey Good Lookin'" (with Dwight Yoakam!) are not quite as successful. All in all, an enjoyable set.

Island 90961 (c,d) Taking It Home

Stanley "Buckwheat" Doral's second LP for Island is, like the first, a mix of pop and Zydeco that seems tamed down for the pop market, but nonetheless is fun to listen to. "Why Does Love Got to Be So Sad," with Eric Clapton is pretty bad, but "Down Dallas Alley" and Roy Montrell's "Ooh Wow" cook along at a good clip, while "Drivin' Old Grey" and "Taking It Home" are hot Zydeco instrumentals. The two versions of the Rockin' Sidneyish "Creole Country" are expendable, but "These Things You Do" adds some badly needed passion to the proceedings. A mixed bag.

Rounder 2045 (c,d) Turning Point

Music is fine, though Buckwheat's voice is buried in the mix. I was a little taken aback to see him wearing a crown on the cover; he's got a long way to go before he can take the crown away from Clifton Chenier!

Rounder 2051 (c) Waitin' for My Ya Ya

On this varied 1986 album, Buckwheat and the band perform lively contemporary Zydeco renditions of the Dirty Dozen's Brass Band's "My Feet Can't Fail Me Now," the traditional Cajun song "Lache Pas La Patate," the Fats Domino classic "Walking To New Orleans," Lee Dorsey's "Ya Ya," which is given a bit of a reggae rhythm, and the popular soul ballad "Warm and Tender Love." Nothing special here but some enjoyable dance music.

COMPACT DISC

Rounder CD 11528 Buckwheat's Zydeco Party

Sixteen tracks drawn from Rounder 2045 and 2051 plus the previously unreleased "Hot Tamale Baby."

MOJO BUFORD

Good Chicago-style blues singer and harmonica player who, for a while, worked with the Muddy Waters band.

Rooster Blues 7603 Mojo Buford's Chicago Blues Summit

Reissue of a fine set originally issued on Mr. Blues label in 1980. Buford is joined by four top Chicago guitarists playing in various combinations—Sammy Lawhorn, Oliver "Sonny" Rogers, James "Pee Wee" Madison, and Abe "Little Smokey" Smothers. Rounding out the rhythm section are bass player Earnest Johnson and drummer Sam Lay. Half the songs are Buford originals, while others are from the repertoires of B. B. King, T-Bone Walker, and others. The music has a very tough, gutsy feel.

COMPACT DISC

JSP CD 233 State of the Harp

Solid collection of Chicago blues. Most tracks are originals and feature him with a good band of musicians; recorded in London in 1989. Detailed and informative notes by Norman Darwen.

BULL CITY RED

Blues Documents 2030 1935–1939 Complete Recordings in Chronological Order

Bull City Red accompanied Blind Boy Fuller on washboard on numerous ARC sides, but was also a good exponent of the Piedmont blues style in his own right, if not as skilled a guitarist as Fuller. Here we get the added bonus of the great Gary Davis' blues guitar accompanying Red on two cuts, along with six gospel sides recorded with Sonny Terry on vocals in 1939. An important gap filler for Carolina blues fans, since almost none of this is currently obtainable on LP.

BUMBLE BEE SLIM

Best Of Blues BOB 9 1934–1937

No surprises here (Slim's appeal to black record buyers of the day lay precisely in his familiarity; there were never any surprises), but a representative selection of this prolific performer's recorded output from these years. The usual Chicago studio regulars provide the backup, including wonderful piano from the obscure Eddie Miller and Myrtle Jenkins, and the reliable guitar of Big Bill Broonzy. Eighteen titles, only half of which are otherwise available on LP.

Blues Documents 2085 Vol. 1, 1932–34

Eighteen early tracks by this very popular and prolific performer. Although he is not an intense performer, his approach is a most engaging one, and he was usually accompanied by fine musicians.

M And O Blues, Parts 1 and 2/Runnin' Drunk Blues/Busy Devil (one of his more intense performances, with some nice mandolin, possibly by Howard Armstrong)/Step Child/Cruel Hearted Woman Blues, Parts 1 and 2/Blue Blues/Ain't It a Crying Shame/I Tried Everything I Could.

Document 506 1931–1937

An excellent collection of 18 sides by this popular and prolific 30s bluesman. The album opens with one of his earliest cuts from 1931, "No Woman No Nickel," a lovely country blues on which Slim accompanies himself with some fine guitar. He abandoned guitar after this session and the remaining tracks feature him with small groups including Jimmie Gordon, Myrtle Jenkins, Honey Hille, or Black Bob (pno), and Big Bill Broonzy or Willie Bee James (gtr). Slim was a lovely, relaxed vocalist and the material is varied, ranging from the mournful "Bye Bye Baby Blues" to the stomping "Deep Bass Boogie." Climbing on Top of the Hill/Can't You Trust Me No More/Steady Roll Mama Blues/You Don't Mean Me No Good.

JIM BUNKLEY/HENRY BUSSEY

Two fine Georgia country-blues singer/guitarists recorded in the 60s.

Rounder 2001 Jim Bunkley/George Henry Bussey

TEDDY BUNN

Blues Documents 2069 Complete Sessions in Chronological Order, 1930–39

Bunn was a renowned jazz/blues guitarist and this collection includes 16 tracks on which he is present. Side one is eight hokum duets with the insufferable Spencer Williams, while side two features accompaniments to Buck Franklin, Cow Cow Davenport, and Fat Hayden. With the exception of the Davenport sides, this is all pretty dull stuff. Bunn's guitar playing is not even very interesting. For completists only!

EDDIE BURNS

Excellent Detroit singer/guitarist/harmonica player.

CASSETTE AND CD RELEASE ONLY

Blue Suite 103-2 Eddie Burns

Eleven new recordings by the Motor City blues legend. Good vocals with fairly standard contemporary blues accompaniment.

R. L. "RULE" BURNSIDE

Excellent Mississippi country-blues singer and guitarist.

Arion ARN 33765 Mississippi Blues

Enjoyable set of performances, mostly recorded live

in France in 1983. Most of the songs are versions of traditional Mississippi pieces like "Poor Black Mattie" and "Rolling and Tumbling," along with some Lightnin' Hopkins songs. Burnside sings well and plays some good acoustic guitar, but the record suffers from overly familiar material.

Swingmaster 2101 Mississippi Delta Blues
European recordings, spirited renditions of mostly familiar Mississippi blues standards.

Swingmaster 2111 The Blues of R. L. Burnside
An excellent collection of 13 sides. This is one of the more interesting albums of Burnside because, not only is he in particularly good form vocally and instrumentally, but the selection of material is better than usual. Much of Burnside's repertoire comes from 50s bluesmen like Muddy Waters, Lightnin' Hopkins, and John Lee Hooker, but here he concentrates on traditional songs ("Skinny Woman," "Rolling and Tumbling," and "Mellow Peaches") or songs he learned locally ("Miss Maybelle," "Jumper On The Line," and "Long Haired Donkey"). The last four songs are all from one session recorded in Holland in 1984, and Burnside sings and plays with a passion and intensity not often heard on his recordings. Recommended!

HAROLD BURRAGE
Chicago singer and piano player. Not the greatest singer, but he recorded for Cobra with a very exciting band.

Flyright 579 She Knocks Me Out
Recorded between 1956–58, with Wayne Bennett, Henry Gray, Jody Williams, Harold Ashby, Willie Dixon, Odie Payne, Sonny Boy Williamson, and Otis Rush! Betty Jean/One More Dance/Satisfied/I Cry For You.

J. C. BURRIS
Sonny Terry's nephew, who at present lives in the Bay area and is a much-beloved figure due to his frequent performances at clubs, concerts, and festivals. Burris sings, plays fine harmonica, and also plays bones and does hand jive.

Arhoolie 1075 One of These Mornings

CHARLIE BURSE/JIMMY DE BERRY
Old Tramp 1214 1939—Complete Recordings in Chronological Order
Singer/guitarist/banjo and ukelele player Charlie Burse was a fixture on the Memphis scene from the 20s on and played and recorded quite extensively with the Memphis Jug Band. The 16 sides here feature him with his own group, The Memphis Mudcats, an unknown group featuring alto sax, piano,

bass, and drums. They perform blues and novelty songs with a jug-band flavor and, although there is not a lot of variety, the music is quite entertaining. The same can be said for Jimmy De Berry, who is, perhaps, better known for his postwar recordings. He's an engaging singer and is accompanied on his five songs here by trumpet, clarinet, piano, guitar, and bass. Sound is good.

W. E. "BUDDY" BURTON
Wolf WJS 1006 South Side Chicago Jazz and Blues Piano (1928–36)
Best known for his duets with Jimmy Blythe ("Blythe and Burton") and Bob Hudson (known as the "Black Diamond Twins," they produced the classic "Block And Tackle," reissued in several anthologies over the last two decades), Burton was a talented exponent of the South Side barrelhouse-style of hybrid piano, equally comfortable playing raggy instrumentals or accompanying a variety of singers. He is heard in both contexts here. This reissue restores a number of musically fine (and quite rare) performances to LP. Sound is poor-to-fair.

GEORGE "WILD CHILD" BUTLER
Charly CRB 1104 Open Up Baby
Some fine Chicago blues recorded for Jewel between 1966–68. Butler is an excellent singer and harmonica player and, on these sessions, produced by Willie Dixon, he is accompanied by top Chicago sidemen like Jimmy Dawkins, Big Mojo Elem, Lafayette Leake, and Phil Upchurch. Most of the songs are originals by Butler or Dixon. Open Up Baby/Axe and The Wind/ Hold Me Baby/She Walks Like Mary Ann/My Forty-Year-Old Woman.

Rooster Blues 7611 Lickin' Gravy
1976 recordings originally issued on the Roots label, with new 1986 overdubs. Butler is a deep, gruff, but not terribly expressive singer. He is a good harmonica player with a style that owes a debt to Sonny Boy Williamson #2 and Walter Horton. Most of the songs are Butler originals, with a couple of Willie Dixon oldies. The band is competent, if not terribly exciting, and the overdubs by Jimmy Rogers on guitar and Pinetop Perkins on piano and organ neither add nor detract from the music. Not really an essential purchase.

THE BUTLER TWINS
Blues Factory 1001 Live in Detroit
Nice set of down-home blues with a Chicago flavor featuring twins Clarence (vcl, hca) and Curtis Butler (gu) with a small combo (gtr, b, and drm), recorded live in Dearborn, Michigan, in May 1988. Clarence is a good, expressive vocalist and a decent, if not

terribly creative, harmonica player. Curtis and the rest of the band provide a solid backdrop to his singing and playing. Most of the songs are originals by Clarence, along with a couple of Little Walter songs. Nothing exceptional here, but some good, no-nonsense blues.

BUTTERBEANS AND SUSIE
Bluetime 2009 **Daddy's Got the Mojo**
A most welcome reissue featuring 16 tracks by this excellent vaudeville duo who recorded quite prolifically between 1924 and 1930. Susie (Edwards) was an excellent blues singer and gets to show her talents on numbers like "Kiss Me Sweet" and "My Daddy's Got The Mojo, But I Got The Say So," but the emphasis of their recordings was on the humorous musical dialogue between the two on items like the homicidal "A-Z Blues," the accusatory "Taint None Of Your Business," and the risque "Papa Ain't No Santa Claus." They are accompanied by some fine musicians like Joe "King" Oliver, Clarence Williams, and Eddie Heywood. Sound quality is generally good.

PAUL BUTTERFIELD
Edsel 212 **East-West**
CD issue: Elektra 7315-2 (J)
Reissue of Butter's second album, originally issued in the mid-60s by Elektra. If Butter's first LP was to be a classic in white and electric blues, he transcended that with his second LP, with the same lineup except drummer Billy Davenport, replacing Sam Lay. The Blues covers are down to a minimum, including "Walkin' Blues" and "Two Trains Running" (aka "Still A Fool"), along with covers of Lee Dorsey's "Get Out Of My Life Woman," and The Monkees' "Mary Mary." But what really set this apart are the two long tracks, a hard harp workout on Cannonball Adderly's "Work Song," and the 13-minute title track that experimented in modal playing and turned Mike Bloomfield into a superstar.

Edsel 301 **The Resurrection of Pigboy Crabshaw**
CD issue: Elektra 74015-2 (J)
A welcome reissue of Butterfield's third LP from the late 60s. In my humble opinion, this was his last consistently good album, made before he started stretching every song to the boredom limit. He fronts an eight-piece band including Elvin Bishop (gtr), Mark Naftalin (kybds), and David Sanborn (alto sax). They storm through some uptown-style blues reminiscent of Bobby Bland and Little Milton with thoughtful, powerful arrangements of "One More Heartache," "Driftin' And Driftin'," "Drivin'

Wheel," "Born Under a Bad Sign," and five others. A classic.

Red Lightnin' 008 **An Offer You Can't Refuse**
Rhino 70877 (c) **Paul Butterfield's Better Days**
Reissue of Bearsville 2119 from 1973. After breaking up the Blues Band, Butter headed to Woodstock and formed this all-star band, kind of a folkie version of the Blues Band, with Amos Garrett, Geoff Muldaur, Ronnie Barron, and Billy Rich and Chris Parker on bass and drums. Technically, the band is incredible, but the LP seems to snooze, aided by the inclusion of such war horses as "Baby Please Don't Go," "(New) Walkin' Blues," "Nobody's Fault But Mine," and "Please Send Me Someone To Love." Vocals by Butter, Geoff, and Ronnie.

Rhino 70878 (c) **It All Comes Back**
Reissue of Bearsville 2170 from 1974. After a promising start with a blazing version of Smokey Hogg's "Too Many Drivers," it goes downhill rather quickly. The overdone blues standards are replaced by new material written by Butter, Barron, and Bobby Charles, with lots of not really successful funk and New Orleans R&B experiments, the best being the Barron-Dr. John-penned "Louisiana Flood."

Rhino 70879 (c) **Put It in Your Ear**
Reissue of Bearsville 6960 from 1975. Why would anybody want to reissue this? Not only is Butter's voice shot but he plays more synthesizer than harp! Dozens of session men play backup to a whole LP of imitation funk produced by legendary King producer Henry Glover. Here I Go Again/(If I Never Sing) My Song/The Animal.

Rhino 70880 (c) **North South**
Reissue of Bearsville 6995 from 1981. Butter's only LP between "Put It In Your Ear" (1975) and his aborted comeback (shortly before his death) isn't much to talk about. Paul recorded this in Memphis with Willie Mitchell producing. Tons of synthesizers on this LP, finding Butter plodding through Boz Scaggs-ish white soul.
COMPACT DISC
Elektra 7294-2 (J) **The Paul Butterfield Blues Band**
CD issue of Elektra 7294 from 1965. Butterfield led the first major white Chicago blues band, a move that would spark the great late 60s blues revival. Butter originally had Elvin Bishop on guitar, with backup by the Howlin' Wolf rhythm section, Jerome Arnold (b), and Sam Lay (drm). He added Mark Naftalin (kybds) and, to round out the recording, future guitar legend Mike Bloomfield. These recordings still sound fresh and alive, and include the

classic Nick Gravinites tune "Born In Chicago," Elmore James' "Shake Your Moneymaker," Little Walter's "Mellow Down Easy" and "Blues with a Feeling," and originals like "Screamin'" and "Thank You Mr. Poobah"

JOHN BYRD and WALTER TAYLOR
Blues Documents 2008 Complete Recordings in Chronological Order
A fine collection of country blues and hokum. Side one includes eight sides featuring vocals by singer/washboard player Washboard Walter and singer/guitarist John Byrd. Byrd was a very fine guitarist who, on some tracks, plays some very effective 12-string. Includes two gospel recordings that probably also feature the vocals of Mae Glover, Byrd's magnificent "Old Timbrook Blues," and the facsinating tribute to Blind Lemon Jefferson, "Wasn't It Sad About Lemon?" All these tracks have been out before. Side two features singer/washboard player Walter Taylor with kazoo, guitar, and occasional banjo or mandolin. These are mostly hokum songs like "Thirty Eight and Plus," "Deal Rag," "You Rascal You," but also include the lovely blues "Coal Campuses." About half of these have been out before, but most are not currently available.

BUTCH CAGE
Fine Louisiana singer/fiddle player who usually worked with Willie Thomas to produce some raucous, down-home but exciting string-band music.
Arhoolie 2018 Country Negro Jam Session
Wonderfully exuberant 1959–60 recordings, includes five cuts by Cage and Thomas plus superb recordings by Robert Pete Williams, Clarence Edwards, and others. Great, spirited country blues.

EDDIE C. CAMPBELL
Fine Chicago singer/guitarist who has, in recent years, settled in Europe. Though not a great original, he is a strong singer and a tasteful guitar player in the West Side Chicago style.
Black Magic 9007 Let's Pick It
Half the songs here are good originals by Eddie and the remainder come from the repertoires of Albert King, Magic Sam, and Jimmy Reed, and all are given top-notch treatment.
Double Trouble-Rooster 7602 King of the Jungle
Reissue of 1977 album originally issued on Mr. Blues label. This reissue has been remixed for a tougher sound, has a new cover and notes, and two extra tracks not on the original album. The album represented 70s Chicago blues at its best. Eddie's singing and guitar playing are accompanied by an

excellent band, which includes some brilliant harp by Carey Bell and piano by Lafayette Leake. Material includes some originals ("Santa's Messin' With The Kid," "Weary Blues," and the title track), plus songs from Muddy Waters, Willie Dixon, and Magic Sam. An excellent set.
Double Trouble 3014/5 Mind Trouble
One-and-a-half LP set consisting of one full LP and a 12" 45 in a gatefold LP jacket.
COMPACT DISC
JSP CD 216 Baddest Cat on the Block
CD reissue of JSP 1087; songs from the repertoires of Albert King, Muddy Waters, and Johnny Taylor, along with a couple of good originals. He is accompanied by a band of British musicians who provide effective, if not terribly exciting, accompaniment.

GENE CAMPBELL
Wolf WSE 112 Texas Blues Pioneer
Twelve sides from this very obscure Texas bluesman who recorded some 24 titles between 1929–31 and has had practically nothing reissued up to now. Campbell is a good, if unexceptional, singer and guitar player very firmly in the Texas mold, with long vocal lines and single-string guitar work. Most of his songs are original, primarily based on traditional themes.

BLIND JAMES CAMPBELL (and HIS NASHVILLE STRING BAND)
Arhoolie 1015 Blind James Campbell and His Nashville String Band
Raucous Nashville string band with guitar, fiddle, banjo, trumpet, and tuba recorded in 1962.

JOHN CAMPBELL
Crosscut 1019 A Man and His Blues
Texas white blues interpreter strongly influenced by Lightnin' Hopkins. A couple of tracks have guest appearances by Ronnie Earl and Jerry Portnoy.

CANNED HEAT
Seminal 60s blues-guitar boogie band, noted for their collaboration with blues originals (such as John Lee Hooker). Bob "The Bear" Hite and Alan "Blind Owl" Wilson, both blues collectors and scholars, were the main force behind the band, sharing the vocal chores. The contrast between Hite's gruff singing and Wilson's mournful moaning (and great harp) kept things interesting, while Henry Vestine cranked up the excitement level with some very nasty distorted guitar.
EMI (UK) GO 2026 The Best of Canned Heat—Let's Work Together
Really good 16-tune selection of the best of Canned Heat's recorded output, leaving out most of the

hippy-dippy nonsense and self-indulgent jams that diluted a basically fine white-trash blues band. Boogie Children/On The Road Again/Amphetamine Annie/Rollin' And Tumblin'/Going Up The Country/Sugar Bee.

See For Miles SEE 62 Boogie with Canned Heat

Reissue of Liberty LST 7541 from 1968; their second LP found them masters of the electric John Lee Hooker-inspired boogie, enabling the group to take Floyd Jones' "Big Road Blues," redone as "On The Road Again," to the US and UK Top 10. Includes "Whiskey Headed Woman #2," the anti-drug "Amphetamine Annie," the guitar-and-horn Texas-blues instrumental, "Marie Laveau," "Turpentine Moan," with guest star Sunnyland Slim, and their 10-minute "Fried Hockey Boogie." New liner notes by Brian Hogg.

See For Miles SEE 268 Canned Heat

Reissue of Canned Heat's debut album originally released on Liberty in 1967. This was before their FM radio hits and live concert acclaim, but it's probably still the highlight of their long career. They played with power and vision, unsullied by the later blues bombast they used live and on record. The Bear and his crew work their mojo on city blues and country blues alike. Rollin' And Tumblin'/Bullfrog Blues/Catfish Blues/Dust My Broom/Big Road Blues.

Note: See under JOHN LEE HOOKER for their collaboration.

GUS CANNON'S JUG STOMPERS
Yazoo 1082/83 (c,d) The Complete Works, 1927–30

Two-LP/cassette or one-CD repackaging and reissue of long-out-of-print Herwin 208, featuring the complete recordings of one of the greatest of all Memphis jug bands, plus Cannon's solo recordings.

CAROLINA SLIM

The enigmatic Ed Harris (aka Carolina Slim, Country Paul, Lazy Slim Jim, and Jammin' Jim) recorded some 27 sides between 1950 and 1952 for several labels. Harris was a fine singer and guitar player who was strongly influenced by both Lightnin' Hopkins and Blind Boy Fuller.

Savoy SJL 1153 Blues Go Away from Me
Travelin' Man TM 805 Carolina Blues and Boogie

Fourteen fine tracks. There is a nice mixture of slow blues and lively boogies. Some cuts feature a second guitar and occasional unobtrusive drums or washboard. The exuberant "Carolina Boogie," with Slim exchanging remarks with an unknown second

guitarist and vocalist, is particularly fine. Fine country blues.

LEROY CARR

Between 1928 and 1935, Carr and his guitar-playing partner Scrapper Blackwell put out some of the finest and most influential blues recordings of the era. Leroy's smooth but intense vocals were complemented by his melodic piano and counterpointed by Blackwell's acerbic guitar. All his recordings are worthwhile and all the reissues merit a listen, with perhaps the Magpie album having the slight edge on choice of material and superior sound.

Best Of Blues BOB 13 1929–35

Eleven tracks, most of which have not been on LP before. Four tracks feature Carr and Blackwell in their famous duets; the remaining seven tracks feature Blackwell on his own or as accompanist to Black Bottom McPhail. Most of these have been on LP before, though some are not currently available.

Biograph BLP C-9 Singing the Blues

Great sides from 1934, including six previously unissued takes. Hard-Hearted Papa/Broken-Hearted Man/Good Woman Blues/You Got Me Grieving Mama/Tight Time Blues.

Blues Documents 2074 Remaining Titles and Alternate Takes

The 10 tracks here by Leroy and his long-time partner Scrapper Blackwell include hard-to-find rarities like "Hard Times Done Drove Me To Drink," "Nineteen Thirty One Blues," "The Depression Blues," plus alternate takes of "Hard-Hearted Papa," "Black Wagon Blues," and others. The four Blackwell cuts are from a 1958 session and were previously issued many years ago on a long-out-of-print EP, and show that Blackwell was still an outstanding performer.

Collectors Classics CC 38 Leroy Carr

Sixteen songs, 1928–34. How Long, How Long Blues No. 2/You Don't Mean Me No Good/Baby Come Back To Me/Cruel Woman Blues/Muddy Water.

Collectors Classics CC 50 Leroy Carr, Vol. 2

Sixteen songs, 1932–34. I Ain't Got No Money Now/Stormy Weather Blues/Hard Hearted Papa/Evil Hearted Woman/You've Got Me Grieving/Suicide Blues.

Document 543 1929–1934

Sixteen titles organized in chronological order. Side one emphasizes the popular side of the Blackwell/Carr repetoire, and includes the curious "I Know I'll Be Blue," which switches in mid-song from a blues piece to a sentimental Jolsonesque number. Side two is mostly blues and features some nice guitar by Scrapper as well as two previously unissued titles, "Rozetta Blues" and "Church House Blues." The material here seems to me to drone in places. Not one of the more essential reissues.

ESSENTIAL SELECTION

Magpie 4407 (d) **Leroy Carr, 1930–1935**
CD issue: Magpie CD 07

The best-sounding reissue and best selection of Carr's material; 16 beautiful songs beautifully remastered from excellent condition 78s. CD has four additional tracks, including the previously unissued and magnificent "Suicide Blues" and an unissued alternate take of "You Left Me Crying." Sloppy Drunk Blues/Alabama Woman Blues/How Long, How Long Blues, Part 2/Take A Walk Around The Corner/Barrel House Woman No. 2/Don't Start No Stuff/Good Woman Blues/Going Back Home.

Matchbox 210 **Leroy Carr, 1928**
This album reissues Carr's first 15 recordings, cut in 1928, including his first recording of his most famous song, "How Long, How Long Blues," a blues standard. Most of the songs here have not been reissued before. Some of them are very rare and have rather poor sound, but most of the album is very listenable and the music is great! My Own Lonesome Blues/Tennessee Blues/ Mean Old Train Blues/Low Down Dirty Blues/How Long, How Long Blues, Part 3/Tired Of Your Low Down Ways.

Old Tramp 1204 **Great Piano-Guitar Duets (1929–35)**
A beautiful collection of 18 sides recorded between 1929–35 by Carr and Scrapper Blackwell. The material is consistently fine and includes some great mournful blues like "Gambler's Blues," "That's All Right," "Rainy Day Blues" (with great guitar by Scrapper and interesting sound effects!), and "Prison Cell." There are some lively novelty songs like "There Ain't Nobody Got It Like She's Got It" and "Papa's On The House Top." The opening track, the rolling "The Truth About The Thing," is a rarity— a song with an effective kazoo solo that sounds almost like a violin. The main problem with this album is the high degree of surface noise on the original 78s used. With current technology, it is possible to remove much of this without harming the sound, and it's a shame these techniques weren't used here.

Yazoo 1036 **Naptown Blues**
Fourteen songs; great sound though perhaps an overemphasis on novelty and pop songs. Naptown

Blues/Papa Wants A Cookie/Four Day Rider/Carried Water For The Elephant/What More Can I Do?/I Keep the Blues.
CASSETTE AND CD RELEASE ONLY

Portrait RJ 44122 **Blues Before Sunrise**
One of the first and best reissues of Carr and Blackwell, originally issued in the mid-60s. Helped introduce their recordings to a broad audience. Sound quality is mediocre.

WYNONA CARR

Wynona Carr, like Ann Cole and Varetta Dillard, falls into the ex-gospel school of hard-singing female soloists. One of the much admired but rarely appreciated R&B talents of the 50s era.

Specialty 2157 **Jump Jack Jump**
A collection of Wynona's finest secular recordings in straight-ahead mono, beautifully remastered from original session tapes, backed by the incomparable "Bumps" Blackwell Orchestra. The album showcases six of the ten secular singles issued on Specialty between 1956–60. This includes an alternate nonvocal group version of "Hurt Me" recorded in 1956. Of the six remaining hitherto unissued cuts on this compilation, only "Bippity Bop" falls short of excellence.

BO CARTER

Excellent Mississippi singer/guitarist with a wonderful touch for double-entendre lyrics, who recorded prolifically between 1928–40 and was a sometime member of The Mississippi Sheiks. All three Yazoo albums are fine, with 1064 focusing exclusively on risque songs. Earl 610 fills in some useful gaps.

Document 524 **1928–38**
A few tracks have been on collections but most have not been on LP before. Includes a couple of lovely string-band sides with Bo on violin with Charlie

McCoy (mdln) and Walter Vincson (gtr), and one on which Bo's brother Lonnie plays fiddle. The rest is Bo and his guitar on a fine selection of blues and a few of his risque songs. Sound on a few tracks is a bit rough but is generally satisfactory.

Earl 610 Bo Carter, Vol. 1
Eighteen fine sides recorded between 1928–40. Only about one-third of these cuts have been issued, some on out-of-print collections. A few cuts have effective violin accompaniment. Corrine Corrina/Mean Feeling Blues/Loveless Love/Baby, How Can It Be/Please Warm My Weiner/Ride My Mule/Sue Cow.

Earl 618 The Rarest, Vol. 2
Seventeen rarities recorded between 1930–38, including Part 2 of his classic "All Around Man." Most tracks not on LP before.

BO CARTER 1931-1940

Old Tramp 1203 Bo Carter, 1931–40
Eighteen fine sides, mostly not issued elsewhere. A few tracks have dubious sound, but otherwise an enjoyable set. I Love That Thing/So Long, Baby, So Long/I Keep On Spending My Change/Old Shoe Blues/Spotted Cow Blues/You Better Know Your Business.

Yazoo 1014 Bo Carter's Greatest Hits
I Want You To Know/Dinner Blues/Bo Carter's Advice/Who's Been Here/Country Fool/Arrangement For Me Blues.

Yazoo 1034 Twist It Babe
Policy Blues/My Baby/Some Day/Doubled Up In A Knot/Rolling Blues/Let Me Roll Your Lemon/Howlin' Tom Cat Blues/The Law Gonna Step On You.

Yazoo 1064 Banana in Your Fruit Basket
All risque songs. My Pencil Don't Write No More/Pin In Your Cushion/Ram Rod Daddy/Howling Tom Cat Blues/Blue Runner Blues/Mashing That Thing.

Note: Other Bo Carter recordings, not on the above albums, are featured on Agram 2011. See also THE MISSISSIPPI SHEIKS.

THE CARTER BROTHERS
Intense California-based blues group. Vocals heavily influenced by B. B. King, but the band has a raw Southern feel to it.

Charly CRB 1023 Blues in Session
Sixteen sides recorded for Jewel in the mid-60s, including six previously unissued sides.

GOREE CARTER
Houston singer/guitarist influenced by T-Bone Walker but no slavish imitator.

Blues Boy 306 Rock Awhile
Seventeen sides recorded between 1949–51. Carter's band is unexceptional but appropriate, with some particulary good piano by Lonnie Lyons. As usual for this label, sound is exemplary, there are extensive notes by Dick Shurman, and rare photos are included. A most worthwhile issue.

BOWLING GREEN JOHN CEPHAS and PHIL WIGGINS
Excellent country blues duo from Washington, DC. Cephas is a fine singer and melodic guitarist in the East Coast style, while Wiggins complements him with some very effective harmonica. Sort of a latter-day Sonny Terry and Brownie McGee, with a different approach and material.

Flying Fish 394 Dog Days of August
Some lovely singing and playing by both and a couple of very effective interpretations of songs from the repertoire of the great Mississippi blues man Skip James.

Flying Fish 470 (d) Guitar Man
L+R 42.031 Bowling Green John and Harmonica Phil Wiggins
L+R 42.054 Sweet Bitter Blues
Nice mixture of familiar and original material including an engaging tribute to Skip James.

FANNIE BELL CHAPMAN
Gospel singer from Centreville, MS.

Southern Culture 1702 Gospel Singer
Album of gospel singing featuring Fannie Bell accompanied by members of her family; some cuts are sung a cappella.

SAM CHATMON
Sam Chatmon was the brother of Bo Carter and, although he recorded briefly with the Mississippi Sheiks in the 20s, he did not record at any length until the 60s and 70s, when he made a handful of fine recordings. He was a fine singer and guitarist and was stylistically not unlike his brother Bo, and, like Bo, had a penchant for some remarkable double entendre songs. He died in 1984.

Flying Fish 202 Sam Chatmon and His Barbecue Boys
Excellent album. Chatmon is singing and playing strongly, with sympathetic backup by Colin Linden (gtr) and Jim MacClean (hca, perc).

Rounder 2018 Sam Chatmon's Advice
Includes some of his delightful risque songs.

BOOZOO CHAVIS
Unlike many artists who seem to be jumping on the Zydeco bandwagon, Boozoo Chavis has been playing the music for over 30 years and in 1954 had one of the first Zydeco hits, "Paper In My Shoe." While not the world's best singer or accordionist, he has a rough, compelling style that is quite effective.

Maison De Soul 1017 Louisiana Zydeco Music
An enjoyable album of no-nonsense Zydeco on which Boozoo and his accordion are joined by his sons Rellis, J. W., and Anthony on drums and washboards, plus Carlton Thomas (gtr) and Shelton Jackson (b). Most of the tunes are uptempo dance tunes, though there are also a couple of effective slow blues and the obligatory version of "My Toot Toot."

Maison De Soul 1021 (c) Boozoo Zydeco!
Backed by a tight rhythm section with Charles Barry on rubboard, son Rellis Chavis on drums, and Carlton Thomas on guitar, Boozoo does nice versions of Charles Brown's "Driftin' Blues" and John De La Fosse's "Uncle Bud," and some interesting originals, including "Boozoo's Baby" and "Jealous Man Two-Step."

Maison De Soul 1028 (c) Zydeco Homebrew
Ten new, snappy and energetic tunes. The propulsive rhythms and persuasive vocals by Boozoo make this irresistible music, but Boozoo sure does get a lot of mileage out of one or two accordion riffs, speeding up or slowing down to fit in with his fine band. Make It With Me/Last Dance Waltz/Johnnie Billie Goat/Zydeco Hee Haw/Keep Your Dress Tail Down.

Rounder 2097 (c,d) The Lake Charles Atomic Bomb
Fourteen recordings originally issued on Goldband.

BOOZOO CHAVIS/NATHAN and THE CHA-CHAS
Rounder 2069 (c,d) Zydeco Live! From Richard's Club, Lawtell, LA
First of two LPs testifying to the continuing vitality and popularity of Zydeco in Louisiana. This features a veteran, Boozoo Chavis, and a rookie, Nathan Williams. Boozoo performs the infectious "Dog Hill," the risque "Deacon John," and "I'm Drifting," aided by son Wilson and the Magic Sounds. He's a little repetitive, but nice and funky. Nathan and his Zydeco Cha-Chas, with Paul Daigle on guitar, is a nice discovery, with a fine Clifton Chenier-like accordion style (indeed most songs are Clifton's) with plenty of "stomp down Zydeco." Only 26, he displays commendable versatility, a soulful voice with an engaging tremolo, and forceful and creative accordian. A comer. Good sound and genuine Zydeco ambience.

C. J. CHENIER
Arhoolie 1098 (c) Let Me in Your Heart
C. J. Chenier, Clifton's son, has his first LP out, and it is a hot one. Recorded with Clifton's preeminent Red Hot Louisiana Band, including brother Cleveland on rubboard, it places him firmly in line to inherit his father's mantle. While the French influences are lessened, C. J. is a very strong blues singer, as he shows on Clifton's lovely "I'm Coming Home" and seductive "Banana Man," as well as his own "Used and Abused" and "She's My Women." His formidable accordion and sax technique storms through the upbeat "I'm All Shook Up" and the frantic Zydeco "My Baby Don't Wear No Shoes," as well as the moody "Blue Flame Blues." Altogether, a tremendous debut from a man who has learned his lessons well and looks to perpetuate and renew the tradition.

CLIFTON CHENIER
King of that musical gumbo of Cajun music, blues, and R&B called Zydeco, Chenier was a tremendous singer and accordion player who led one of the hottest bands in the land. Many of his 70s recordings feature the tremendous driving tenor sax of John Hart and all feature the distinctive rubboard playing of his brother Cleveland. From the late 70s until his death, Clifton suffered from diabetes, which required extensive surgery and regular medical attention. As a result, he was not able to perform or record regularly. Of his records, Arhoolie 1076 and 1078 are probably the best, with Arhoolie 1024 and Maison De Soul 1003 close behind, though he rarely made a bad one.

Alligator 4729 (c,d) I'm Here
1983 album. Although his severe illness in the early
80s had taken its toll on his voice and playing, he
was still an immensely exciting artist. This album
has a tough big-band feel to it with its three-horn
lineup.

Arhoolie 1024 (c) Louisiana Blues and Zydeco
Wonderful 1965 recordings, some with a small
group with Elmore Nixon (pno), and some with
Cleveland's rubboard and drums only. On a couple
of tracks, Clifton plays some very effective Jimmy
Reed-flavored harmonica. Accordian Boogie/
Banana Man/It's Hard/Clifton Waltz/Louisiana Two
Step/I Can Look Down On Your Woman.

Arhoolie 1031 (c) Bon Ton Roulet
1966 recordings, some with his uncle, Big Chenier,
on violin. Includes his local hit from 1964, "Ai Ai
Ai," plus Oh Negresse/Baby Please Don't Go/Keep
On Scratchin'/If I Ever Get Lucky/Sweet Little
Doll/Can't Stop Loving You.

Arhoolie 1038 (c) Black Snake Blues
1967 recordings with musicians who were to be the
core of his regular band for the next 10 years:
Cleveland Chenier (rubd), Robert St. Judy (drm),
Felix Benoit (gtr), and Joe Morris (b). Black Snake
Blues/Walking To Louisiana/Wrap It Up/Johnny
Can't Dance/Can't Go Home No More.

Arhoolie 1052 (c) King of the Bayous
A nice mixture of blues, waltzes, pop songs, two
steps, and R&B recorded in 1969 and 1970 with
Antoine Victor or Raymond Monett replacing Felix
Benoit on guitar plus Elmore Nixon on piano on
some cuts. Tu Le Ton Son Ton/Who Can Your Good
Man Be/Gone a la Maison/Release Me/Ton Na
Na/Josephine Par Sa Ma Femme.

Arhoolie 1059 (c) Live at a French Dance
CD issue: Arhoolie CD 313
Recorded at Richmond, California, in 1971 with
Felix Benoit back on guitar. CD has four additional
tracks. A lively selection. Zydeco Cha Cha/Cher
Catin/Tu Le Ton Son Ton/ Tighten Up Zydeco.

Arhoolie 1072 (c) Out West
With the addition of the brilliant John Hart on tenor
sax and the replacement of Felix Benoit by Paul
Senegal on guitar, Clifton had his strongest band yet.
His music emphasized the blues and R&B elements,
at the expense of the old-time Cajun two steps and
waltzes. On these 1971 and 1973 recordings cut in
California, they are joined by Elvin Bishop on guitar
and Steve Miller on piano, who provide some effective accompaniments. This album features two of
Clifton's all-time classics: The wonderful minor-key
blues "I'm On A Wonder" and the rocking "I'm A
Hog For You."

Arhoolie 1076 (c) Bogalusa Boogie
CD issue: Arhoolie CD 347
This 1975 album is possibly Clifton's best, a tremen-
dously exciting collection of blues and R&B with
great playing by Clifton and all the band. CD has one
previously unissued track. One Step At A
Time/Quelque Chose Sur Mon Idee/Ma Mama Ma
Dit/Allons A Grand Coteau/Ti Na Na.

Arhoolie 1078 (c) Red Hot Louisiana Band
This 1977 album adds Stanley "Buckwheat" Doral
on piano and organ and has a spirit and excitement
similar to Arhoolie 1076. Grand Prix/Parti De
Paris/Party Down/Easy, Easy Baby/Do Right Sometime.

ESSENTIAL SELECTION

Arhoolie 1082 (c) Classic Clifton
CD issue: Arhoolie CD 301
Twelve of the best cuts selected from his first eight
Arhoolie albums. CD has three additional tracks.
Zydeco Sont Par Sale/Louisiana Blues/Zydeco Cha
Cha/Black Gal/I'm A Hog For You/Allons A Grand
Coteau.

Arhoolie 1086 (c) The King of Zydeco
CD issue: Arhoolie 355
Recorded live at the Montreux Jazz Festival in 1979,
distilled from the previously released Tomato two-
LP set. Features some great cover photos of Clifton
wearing his crown as the undisputed "King of
Zydeco." Jambalaya/Boogie Woogie/Cher Catin/
I'm On a Wonder/Hush Hush.

**Arhoolie 1093 (c) Live at the San Francisco
Blues Festival**
Clifton's performance at the 1982 San Francisco
Blues Festival was the highlight of that great festival
and one of Clifton's finest live gigs. Accompanied
by a great band, with his son C. J. on trumpet, brother
Cleveland on rubboard, Sherman Robertson on
guitar, and other fine musicians, Clifton rocked his
way through a great selection of Zydeco tunes, R&B

standards, waltzes, and tough blues, mostly old Chenier standards but given a new lease on life here.

Arhoolie 1097 Sings the Blues

Although the blues is a major part of Clifton Chenier's music, this is one of the few albums almost exclusively devoted to the blues. Features recordings made by Houston enterpreneur Roy Ames and previously issued on the Prophesy and Home Cooking labels. With his brother Cleveland on washboard and a solid, if somewhat thin, rhythm section, he does versions of blues classics like "Be My Chauffeur" and "Worried Life Blues," originals like "Ain't No Need Of Crying" and "Gone A La Maison" (the latter sung in French), and jumping R&B like Fats Domino's "Rose Mary" and a revitalised verison of Glenn Miller's "In the Mood."

GNP 2119 (c,d) Clifton Chenier in New Orleans

Jin 9014 Boogie in Black and White
With Rod Bernard.

Maison De Soul 1002 (c) Bayou Soul
Say Too Koreck/La Coeur De La Louisiana/Oh! Lucille/You Know That I Love You/A Worried Life Blues/Goin' To Big Mary's/Big Mamou/(High As A) Georgia Pine.

Maison De Soul 1003 (c) Boogie 'n' Zydeco
1975 album recorded shortly after his classic "Bogalusa Boogie" (Arhoolie 1076), this album finds Clifton and his band at their peak on a selection of mostly rocking R&B. Shake It, Don't Break It/Choo Choo Ch Boogie/You Can't Sit Down/You Used To Call Me/Je Me Fu-Pas Mal.

Maison de Soul 1012 (c) Country Boy Now Grammy Award Winner 1984!
Fine album, a mixture of blues, Zydeco, R&B, and a waltz. Although this is not one of his stronger efforts, Clifton manages to maintain a level of excitement in his music that is absent from most of his contemporaries.

Specialty 2139 (c,d) Bayou Blues
Wonderful mid-50s recordings, some previously unissued, with Phillip Walker or Lonesome Sundown (gtr) and James Jones (pno). Boppin' The Rock/Yestrday/I'm On My Way, Parts 1 and 2/All Night Long/Zodico Stomp.

Note: His early 60s recordings for Jay Miller are reissued on Flyright 539 and his 1956–57 recordings for Checker are available on Chess (Japan) PLP 6035.

CASSETTE AND CD RELEASE ONLY

Arhoolie C/CD 329 Louisiana Blues and Zydeco
All of Arhoolie 1024, half of 1038, and one unissued track.

Arhoolie C/CD 345 Bon Ton Roulet
All of Arhoolie 1031, plus the other half of 1038 and several unissued tracks.

COMPACT DISC

Arhoolie (Japan) PCD 2502 Louisiana Blues and Zydeco/ Bon Ton Roulet
Clifton's first two Arhoolie albums (1024 and 1031) on one CD.

Maison De Soul CD 105 Zydeco Legend
Eighteen great sides, 10 from his classic 1975 Maison De Soul album, "Boogie 'n' Zydeco," and eight from his 1984 album, "Country Boy Now Grammy Award Winner."

CLIFTON CHENIER/ROCKIN' DOPSIE

COMPACT DISC

Flyright CD 17 Clifton Chenier & Rockin' Dopsie
A fine collection featuring eight tracks by the King of Zydeco, Clifton Chenier, recorded between 1958–60, and 12 by the now very popular Rockin' Dopsie, recorded between 1970–74. The Chenier sides are all blues and R&B with great vocals and accordion by Clifton, hot tenor by Lionel Prevost, and tough guitar from Travis Phillips, including a shattering solo on "Worried Life Blues." The Dopsie sides are also strongly blues and R&B-oriented with some fine performances on "Blues," "Run Here to Me Baby," "Things I Used to do," and "You Told Me Baby."

CHESTER D. (WILSON)

CASSETTE ONLY RELEASE

Blue Jazz Heritage BZJ 153 Going Back Home
Eight songs from 74-year-old San Francisco street singer and guitarist Chester D. Wilson. He is an excellent and expressive singer and a limited but effective electric guitarist with a style strongly rooted in the Texas/Louisiana tradition with which he grew up. The songs are mostly originals though based on traditional themes. On several tracks, he is given discreet but effective backup by Gary Bergman (rhythm gtr) and/or Peter Chase (hca). In between the tracks, there are brief autobiographical reminiscences by Chester. With so few artists still performing in this style, this release is a most welcome one.

WILFRED CHEVIS and HIS TEXAS ZYDECO BAND

Zydeco group based in Houston, Texas. Accordion player and leader Chevis is a good player who gets a rich, full sound from his accordion; the rest of the band provides solid, powerful accompaniment, featuring a horn section, giving the band a different sound.

Maison De Soul 1013 **Foot Stompin' Zydeco**
Enjoyable album. The material is a nice mixture of straight-ahead, mostly original Zydeco, blues, soul, and R&B. Vocals are handled by Phillip Steward, an excellent and distinctive singer who, on the soul-flavored items, sounds like Otis Redding! A fine debut album.

CHICAGO BOB and THE SHADOWS
High Water 1010 **Just Your Fool**
Chicago Bob is actually from Louisiana, though he did spend a few years in Chicago. He is quite a good singer and harmonica player though rather one-dimensional in his approach. His accompanying band is competent though unexceptional. They perform a mixture of originals ("Call My Landlady," "Your Time To Choose," "Bogaloosa Boogie") and covers ("Just Your Fool," "Mama, Talk To Your Daughter," "Sloppy Drunk").

THE CHICAGO STRING BAND
Testament 2220 **The Chicago String Band**
A delightful album of black string-band music by a group that includes, in various configurations, John Lee Granderson (vcl, gtr), Carl Martin (vcl, vln), Johnny Young (vcl, mdln, gtr), and John Wrencher (vcl, hca). They perform a spirited mixture of blues songs, beautifully sung and played.

SAVANNAH CHURCHILL
Very fine torch-ballad singer of the decade directly following WWII. Savannah was the first female vocalist of any significance to head a black all-male R&B vocal quartet (the Four Tunes and Striders) after the war years, when female ballad singers usually fronted large bands and orchestras.

Jukebox Lil JB 1101 **Time Out for Tears**
Most of Savannah's finest songs with the Four Tunes and Striders are featured here. Includes the beautiful "Is It Too Late?"; "I Want to Cry," a ballad of beauty and sadness; the gospel-like arrangements of "Once There Lived a Fool"; and the ever-popular "Foolishly Yours." Informative sleeve notes and discographical details.

WILLIAM CLARKE
Alligator 4788 (c,d) **Blowin' Like Hell**
1990 set.
Double Trouble 3016 **Tip of the Top**
Fine LP of LA-based Chicago blues. There are no recording dates, but they appear to be from the mid-80s. Plenty of great-sounding help from a

myriad of guest stars including Hollywood Fats, Ronnie Earl, George "Harmonica" Smith, Charlie Musselwhite, and Mighty Flyers guitarist Junior Watson. Includes "Chromatic Blues," recorded live at a "Battle of the Harmonicas." Drinkin' Straight Whiskey/Tribute To George Smith/Drinkin' Beer/ Charlie's Blues.

Rivera 502 **Can't You Hear Me Callin'**
Reissue of his rare first LP, originally Watch Dog 1005 from 1983. Added to the eight tunes are the previously unreleased "West Coast Walk," a nice original instrumental, and John Brim's "Ice Cream Man," accompanied by Fred Kaplin (pno) and Joel Foy (gtr); the other eight tunes add Junior Watson (gtr). Includes B. B. King's "She's Trouble," Buddy Guy's "No Lie," Jimmy McCracklin's "The Pleaser," Tampa Red's "Give Me Mine Now," plus a few fine originals.

Rivera 503 **Rockin' the Beat**
Captures the band live at Redondo Beach in April '87. Unfortunately, the excitement of seeing the band live does not translate well to vinyl. There's nothing wrong with the LP and Clarke's one of the finest White harpists around. However, though fine for dancing, the grooves he gets into are a bit boring and, as all but one tune is a cover, nothing is added to the original versions. Good selection of tunes includes Muddy Waters' "Iodine In My Coffee," Johnny Young's "Deal The Cards," and Jimmy McGriff's "All About My Girl."

EDDIE CLEARWATER
Chicago singer/guitarist who also plays Chuck Berry-style rock 'n' roll.

Rooster Blues 2615 **The Chief**
Good, solid set of mostly original songs, with Lurrie and Carey Bell. Find You A Job/Blue, Blue, Blue Over You/I Wouldn't Lay My Guitar Down/Bad Dream.

Rooster Blues 2622 **Flimdoozie**
Enjoyable 1986 album. Eddie is accompanied by a talented group of musicians including Will Crosby (gtr), Leo Davis (kybds), and Herman Applewhite (b). There are several fine guest musicians including Otis Rush (gtr), who contributes some of his mighty string bending to five cuts. Sugar Blue plays fine harp on a couple of cuts, and Abbe Locke plays sax on a couple. The songs, mostly originals, are a mixture of upbeat blues, slow blues, Chuck Berry-flavored rock 'n' roll, and a dance tune ("Flimdoozie"). Nothing earthshaking here, but some fine contemporary blues sounds.

ANN COLE
Ann Cole was a wonderfully exciting blues and

R&B singer who recorded for various New York labels between 1956 and 1958.

Krazy Kat 782 **Got My Mojo Working**

These recordings are a mixture of driving uptempo numbers and bluesy ballads. Many cuts feature the excellent Dave McRae Orchestra. Includes Ann's recording of "Got My Mojo Working"; Muddy Waters learned the song from her!! Also includes "Easy Easy Baby" (later recorded by Magic Sam), "Are You Satisfied," and "My Tearful Heart." Based on the evidence here, Ann was an outstanding singer and deserves to have been a lot more successful.

GARY B. B. COLEMAN

Ichiban 1018 (c,d) **If You Can Beat Me Rockin'... You Can Have My Chair**

A good set of contemporary blues and R&B by this fine performer. Coleman is a good soulful vocalist and a decent guitarist, obviously influenced by that other B. B. The songs are a mixture of originals, including the title song and the raunchy "Watch Where You Stroke." There are a couple of nice minor key blues, some solid no-nonsense blues, an effective version of the standard "St. James Infirmary," and a driving version of "Hideaway."

Ichiban 1034 (c,d) **One Night Stand**

Ichiban 1049 (c,d) **Dancin' My Blues Away**

A Word Of Warning/I Gotta Play The Blues For You/Dancin' My Blues Away/Blues At Sunrise.

GEORGE COLEMAN

Unique and bizarre performer who sings surrealistic songs against his own backup on oil cans! Not exactly blues but not really anything else we can classify, either. Sort of a primitive precursor of rap music!!

Arhoolie 1040 **Bongo Joe**

Includes such gems as I Wish I Could Sing/Innocent Little Doggy/Listen At That Bull/Transistor Radio.

ALBERT COLLINS

Great Texas singer and guitarist with a driving and biting style. His classic early 60s recordings for TCF and Hall are reissued on Crosscut. The best of his late 60s/early 70s recordings are reissued on Charly. He seems to have found his niche with a series of excellent and powerful recordings for Alligator commencing in 1978.

Alligator 4713 (c,d) **Ice Pickin'**

Excellent album that brought him back to the attention of the blues-buying public. Honey Hush/Ice Pick/Too Tired/ Conversation With Collins.

ESSENTIAL SELECTION

Alligator 4719 (c) **Frostbite**

Another fine set with a powerful band recorded in 1980. If You Love Me Like You Say/Hangover/The Highway Is Like A Woman.

Alligator 4725 (c) **Frozen Alive**

Excellent live set recorded with his regular band at the Union Bar in Minneapolis in 1981. Frosty/I Got That Feeling/Things I Used To Do.

Alligator 4730 (c) **Don't Lose Your Cool**

This album by the "Master of the Telecaster" is more of the same high-energy electric blues that have made him so popular.

Alligator 4733 (c,d) **Live in Japan**

Tough set recorded live in Japan in 1982 with his regular band of A. C. Reed (ten sax), Larry Burton (gtr), Johnny B. Guyden (b), and Casey Jones (drm).

Alligator 4743 (c,d) **Albert Collins/Robert Cray/ Johnny Copeland: Showdown**

A marvelous combination of talents in which three masters of modern blues guitar join forces to have fun and make some exciting music. Albert Collins was an influence on Copeland in the 50s and on Cray in the 70s, so it is not too surprising that, in spite of the different directions these artists have gone in the intervening years, they sound perfectly comfortable performing together. Accompanied by a solid rhythm section of Alan Batts (org), Johnny B. Gayden (b), and Casey Jones (drm), they do a selection of new songs and old favorites, working together in duo or trio format, alternating vocals and guitar solos.

Alligator 4752 (c,d) **Cold Snap**

Albert chills another one, with help from the Uptown Horns. With a fabulous version of "Too Many Dirty Dishes" and eight more urban workouts.

Crosscut 1011 **The Cool Sound of**

Reissues some of Albert's recordings made early in his career in Houston in 1962 and 1963 for the TCF and Hall labels. Albert was an exciting, distinctive stylist even then with his staccato guitar picking, though his playing was somewhat more low key than it later became. This album features 11 great guitar instrumentals and one stunning vocal. The instrumentals are exciting, with Albert's distinctive choked-guitar style fronting a Texas band that includes impressive sax work by Big Tiny and Henry Hayes. All the tunes have a "cool" theme, including his much covered "Frosty." Albert sang very little in those days, but his one vocal, "Dyin' Flu," is a killer.

Munich 150 225 (d) **Albert Collins with The Barrelhouse Live**

Recorded in Holland in 1978 with a Dutch band. Not up to the standard of his Alligator LPs but quite good. Frosty/I've Got A Mind To Travel/Blue River Rising.

Red Lightnin' 004 **Live at Fillmore East**

Recorded in 1969; neither Albert nor the recording quality is outstanding, but there are some good moments. How Blue Can You Get/So Tired/Deep Freeze/Mustang Sally.

ALBERT COLLINS/ETTA JAMES/JOE WALSH

Verve 841 287-1 (c,d) **Jump the Blues Away**

CRYING SAM COLLINS

Fine Mississippi country bluesman who recorded quite extensively for Gennett and ARC between 1927 and 1932. Collins had a distinctive high voice reminiscent of Skip James. He plays simple but very effective guitar, usually with a slide. His repertoire was a mixture of blues and gospel and the occasional hokum song.

OJL 10 **And His Git-Fiddle**

Features a good proportion of his issued recordings. Besides the 13 tracks by Collins, this album also includes two tracks by King Solomon Hill, who was once thought to be Collins hiding behind a pseudonym. Devil In The Lions Den/Loving Lady Blues/Hesitation Blues/I Want to Be Like Jesus in My Heart/It Won't Be Long.

Note: Additional recordings by Collins can be found on OJL 2, Roots 302, Roots 303, and Yazoo 1038.

COOL PAPA and THE ALLSTAR BLUES BAND

TJ 1052 **Cool Papa and The Allstar Blues Band**

First solo album by West Coast blues singer and guitarist, accompanied by a small band. A rather ordinary set of performances with uninspired accompaniments.

DOLLY COOPER

Official 6019 **Ay La Bah**

Sixteen tracks recorded between 1952–57 by this obscure artist. Dolly is a decent singer with a Dinah Washington flavor to her approach. Her material, recorded in New York and Los Angeles with studio musicians, covers a broad spectrum, from driving blues ("My Man," "Ay La Bah") to pop ballads ("Is It True?", "Believe In Me") to syrupy teenage pop ("Teen Age Prayer," "Teen Age Wedding Bells"). Decent sound, full discographical information, and speculative liner notes by Dave Penny.

JOHNNY COPELAND

Gutsy Texas blues singer and guitar player with a gravel-voiced singing style and a gritty, tough guitar style. Johnny began his recordings career in the late 50s and recorded for a variety of mostly small labels until the early 70s. He moved to New York in the 70s and in the early 80s came to prominence in the blues world with a series of excellent albums for Rounder. Some of his 60s/early 70s recordings have been reissued by Mr. R&B, Ace, Home Cooking, and P-Vine.

Ace CHD 238 **Houston Roots**

A great collection of recordings from the early years of his career, about half previously unissued. Most of the tracks are from the 1959–62 period, along with his intense 1967 two-part rendition of "Night Time Is the Right." The material is varied and includes two lively versions of the blues standard "Rock Me Baby," a searing slow version of "Baby Please Don't Go," the first (previously unissued) recording of his powerful "I Wish I Was Single," the rocking instrumental "Late Hours," and a couple of pop blues ballads. Excellent sound and good notes by Ray Topping, though no discographical information.

Home Cooking 107 **The Copeland Collection, Vol.1**

Fifteen sides from the early 60s, including previously unissued tracks; some duplication with Ace CHD 238.

Mr. R&B 1001 **I'll Be Around**

Sixteen tracks from the 60s and 70s, a fine mixture of blues, R&B, soul, and rock 'n' roll, all given the distinctive Copeland treatment. Album features fold-out jacket with extensive autobiographical notes by Copeland himself and some great recent and vintage photos.

Mr R&B 1002 **Down on Bending Knees**

Sixteen songs recorded between 1962–73, a mixture

of blues and soul sides. The soul songs are, for the most part, not that exceptional except for "Sufferin' City" and "Love Prayer," but the blues are among his best from this era. "Down on Bending Knees," "It's My Own Tears Being Wasted," and "I Wish I Was Single" are tremendous.

Rounder 2025 (c) Copeland Special

Fine album; soulful and gritty vocals with a touch of Bobby Bland in his styling and solid guitar work with tight contemporary band stylings. Claim Jumper/I Wish I Was Single/It's My Own Tears.

Rounder 2030 (c) Make My Home Where I Hang My Hat

Superb album; powerful gruff vocals loaded with feeling, and intense, stinging guitar playing that is full of energy but without resorting to excesses. Excellent swinging band with tough rhythm section and fine four-piece horn section. Mostly original songs. Natural Born Believer/Devil's Hand/Cold Outside/Love Utopia.

Rounder 2040 (c,d) Texas Twister

Nine fine original songs and tunes. Tough singing and playing by Johnny and well-arranged backup by the band. I particularly like the hard-driving "Houston." Midnight Fantasy/Don't Stop By The Creek Son/Excuses.

Rounder 2050 (c) Bringing It All Back Home

Interesting 1986 album on which Johnny is featured on a selection of new songs recorded in the Ivory Coast, on which he is accompanied by his own band plus guest African horn and percussion players; one track is a solo by the great kora player Djeli Mousa. Most of the songs are based on Johnny's experiences during a long tour of Africa in 1982. This album is a fun mixture of different musical genres that works well though the sound is more African than bluesy. There are some nice tracks here and the playing is good, though there is not too much of Johnny's tough guitar playing.

Rounder 2055 (c,d) Ain't Nothin' but a Party

Six long songs recorded live at the Juneteenth Festival in Houston, Texas, in 1987.

Rounder 2060 (c,d) Boom Boom

COMPACT DISC

P-Vine PCD 2506 Soul Power

Twenty-one tracks from the 60s and early 70s. Soul Power/My Own Tears/ House Of So Many Tears/ Please Let Me Know/Year 'Round Baby.

P-Vine PCD 2509 Blues Power

Twenty blues songs, 15 are from the early-to-mid-60s and the rest from a live 1987 show. Some of the 60s recordings have been reissued by Ace and Home Cooking, but I think this is the first time they have appeared on CD. The live set is fine, though lacking a little of the energy of the earlier sides.

Rounder CD 11515 When the Rain Starts Falling

Over 60 minutes of powerful blues (16 tracks) drawn from Johnny's first four Rounder albums (2025, 2030, 2040, 2050). Midnight Fantasy/Down On Bended Knee/Bozalimalamu/Third Party/Old Man Blues/Same Thing/Rock 'n' Roll Lilly/Big Time.

MARTHA COPELAND

Fine, but obscure, singer who recorded 34 sides between 1923–28 that are reissued in their entirety on two Blues Docments LPs. She was a powerful and expressive singer, who, in addition to the familiar lightweight vaudeville songs, also sang some expressive blues.

Blues Documents 2071 Complete Recordings in Chronological Order, Vol. 1

Sixteen tracks recorded between 1923–27 with Eddie Heywood or Cliff Jackson (pno), Bubber Miley or Louis Metcalf (tpt or cnt), and Bert Howell (vln).

Blues Documents 2072 Complete Recordings in Chronological Order, Vol. 2

An even better selection than Volume 1. Eighteen tracks from 1927–28 with a range of accompanying musicians including Bob Fuller, Porter Grainger, Rube Bloom, Bubber Miley, J. C. Johnson, and Andrew Mead. Dyin' Crap-shooter's Blues/Police Blues/Hobo Bill/Shootin' Star Blues.

ELIZABETH COTTEN

Venerable singer/guitarist Elizabeth Cotten from North Carolina was not strictly a blues performer, but her music certainly had echoes of the blues in it. Most of her material was self-composed, and her raggy guitar style was an inspiration to folk and blues guitarists for many years. Although she was no great shakes as a singer, her vocals are charming and moving.

Arhoolie 1089 Live!

This set of performances was recorded live in the late 70s, when Elizabeth was in her 80s and reveals her as still an astonishingly good musician. Almost all the songs and tunes here have been previously recorded for Folkways (although two of Elizabeth's three fine Folkways albums are currently available only as special-order cassettes). It's delightful to hear how "Libba" relates to her audiences with some charming stories and jokes.

Smithsonian/Folkways SF 40009 (c,d) **Freight Train and Other North Carolina Folk Songs**
Reissue of Folkways FG 3526 from 1958. Cotten draws on a long and rich heritage on 14 folk-blues tunes. Wilson Rag/Freight Train/Vastopol/Spanish Flang Dang/Here Old Rattler Here.

SYLVESTER COTTEN
Krazy Kat 7422 **Detroit Blues, Vol. 1**
Splendid country blues singer recorded in Detroit in 1948 and 1949. Most of these cuts have never been issued before! Cotten was an excellent singer who composed some fine original songs, including the amazing "I Tried," expressing his feelings about being in a recording studio! Cotten was a basic but very effective guitarist who played a steel-bodied guitar.

JAMES COTTON
Well-known Chicago-based harp player and blues vocalist who first gained widespread success in the mid-60s. His more recent recordings still feature wonderful harp playing, but he has lost some of his original vocal capabilities.

Alligator 4737 (c,d) **High Compression**
Excellent mixture of straight-ahead Chicago blues and more contemporary stylings. On the former, he is accompanied by a Chicago rhythm section featuring Magic Slim (gtr) and Pinetop Perkins (pno), and on the latter by his regular touring band with an

excellent horn section. Cotton is in good voice and plays some great harp on a varied selection of material: a couple of originals, Washboard Sam's "Diggin' My Potatoes," Roscoe Gordon's "No More Doggin'," and Bobby Bland's "Ain't Doin' Too Bad."

Alligator 4746 (c,d) **Live from Chicago**
Fine set recorded live at Biddy Milligan's in February 1986. Jimmy is in fine form and is accompanied by an excellent band that, besides the usual guitars, bass, keyboards, and drums, also includes a horn section. Jimmy performs an excellent selection of blues and R&B songs, some familiar and some unfamiliar. Excellent sound.

Antones 0007 (c,d) **Live at Antones**
Recorded live at the famous Antones club in Austin, Texas, in 1987, accompanied by an all-star band with Matt Murphy, Luther Tucker, Calvin Jones, Willie Smith, and Pinetop Perkins. The material is mostly overdone old favorites like "Blow Wind," "It Ain't Right," "Oh Baby," "Midnight Creepers," and even "Hoochie Coochie Man"! There is nothing terribly exciting here.

Blind Pig 2587 (d) **Take Me Back**
Reissue of the recent Jackal LP. Excellent LP, first of a projected series of LPs with Cotton's version of the history of the blues. This set's got Sammy Lawhorn (gtr), John Primer (gtr), Pinetop Perkins (pno), Bob Anderson (b), and Sam Lay (drm). Front cover shows the original '66 Cotton band, with Anderson and Lay. Take Out Some Insurance/Killing Floor/My Babe/Dust My Broom.

COMPACT DISC

Sequel (UK) NEX CD 124 **Live and on the Move**
1975 double album reissued on one CD. High energy harmonica blues recorded live. Solid singing and playing from James and his band. Cotton Boogie/All Walks Of Life/Flip, Flop and Fly/Rocket 88/I Don't Know/Boogie Thing/You Don't Have To Go/Fannie Mae/Teeny Weenie Bit/How Long Can A Fool Go Wrong.

Vanguard VMD 79283 **Cut You Loose!**
Mid-60s recording of Cotton and his band in their heyday.

COUSIN JOE
Excellent singer and piano player from New Orleans who has been recording since the 40s. Joe has an engaging voice and writes some original and witty blues songs

Black and Blue 33.549 **Bad Luck Blues**
Originally issued as 33.035. Excellent set from 1971, with fine singing and playing by Joe on a selection of mostly original songs. Splendid guitar

by Clarence "Gatemouth" Brown, and accompaniment by Jimmy Dawkins, Mac Thompson, and Ted Harvey.

Great Southern GS 11011 **Relaxin' in New Orleans**

Charming 1986 solo album. Joe is featured on 12 songs which he has not recorded before. All of them are distinctive with astute lyrics. His song about the sinking of the Titanic has some very original elements. Well-recorded, with interesting notes by Jeff "Almost Slim" Hannusch.

Oldie Blues 8008 **Cousin Joe from New Orleans in His Prime**

A most welcome reissue featuring recordings made in 1946–47, some with Earl Bostic's Sextet or Orchestra, a couple with top-notch New Orleans sidemen (Lee Allen, Paul Gayen, Edgar Blanchard), and some with top New York session musicians (Sammy Price, Billy Butler, Pops Foster). A very entertaining selection. Some of these cuts were issued several years ago on the now defunct Riverboat label.

ROBERT COVINGTON

Red Beans 012 **The Golden Voice of Robert Covington**

IDA COX

Fine jazz/blues singer who started recording in the 20s.

Collectors Classics CC 56 **Ida Cox**

Eleven songs recorded between 1939–40; accompanied by Henry Allen, Hot Lips Page, J. C. Higginbotham, James P. Johnson, and Charlie Christian. Several songs are presented with two or more alternate takes, and there are four previously unissued songs.

Queen Disc 048 **Ida Cox/Bertha "Chippie" Hill**

1939–40 recordings by Cox with Her All Star Band, including Hot Lips Page, Edmond Hall, and James P. Johnson, along with 1947 recordings by Bertha "Chippie" Hill and The All Star Stompers, including Wild Bill Davison, Albert Nicholas, and Ralph Sutton.

Rosetta 1304 (c) **Wild Women Don't Have the Blues**

1961 Riverside session, with the Coleman Hawkins Quintet, including Roy Eldridge and Sammy Price. Excellent.

HARRY "FAT MAN" CRAFTON

Krazy Kat 818 **Harry Crafton 1949–1954**

Jump sides and easy blues tunes in the "Cleanhead" Vinson vein. Singer/guitarist "Fat Man" Crafton is no slouch on the axe and pitches a fine set of vocal

pipes to match. Many of these sides are ably supported by Joe Sewell (ten sax) and Doc Bagby (org), with whom Crafton cut many important early R&B sides.

JAMES "SUGAR BOY" CRAWFORD

Fine New Orleans blues and R&B singer and piano player.

Chess 2-92508 **Sugarboy Crawford**

Twenty-four cuts recorded in 1953–54 and previously issued on US Chess 2ACMB 209; many of the tracks here were not originally issued. A couple of the tracks feature vocals by Snooks Eaglin. Overboard/Jock-O-Mo/I Bowed My Knees/More Heartaches/Please Believe Me/Night Rider/Honey/Stop/Troubled In Mind/If I Loved You Darling.

ROBERT CRAY

One of the finest young blues artists in the country. Cray is a wonderful singer with a gospel-influenced approach, and a powerful and imaginative guitarist with touches of Magic Sam and Johnny "Guitar" Watson in his playing. He is also an excellent songwriter and, together with Bruce Bromberg and Dennis Walker, who have produced all his records, has produced some of the finest and most relevant contemporary blues

lyrics. Robert's band, though undergoing several changes throughout the years, is always strong and supportive, underpinned by the bass playing of Richard Cousins, who has been with Robert for many years. Most recently, Robert has attained the rare distinction of being the first black blues artist signed by a major label (Mercury) in many years and his albums for that label are winners all the way, with no concession to commerciality. He is also the first blues musician to appear regularly on MTV and VH-1 in videos to promote his songs, and has performed with rockers like Eric Clapton.

ESSENTIAL SELECTION

Hightone 8005 (c,d) **False Accusations**

A superb collection of nine songs from the pens of

Cray, Dennis Walker, and David Amy. A few cuts feature added instrumentation but most of the album is just the band. The album opens with the catchy "Porchlight" and continues with the excellent "Payin' For It Now," a mid-tempo item. The highlight for me is the beautiful slow and intense soul ballad "I've Slipped Her Mind," a brilliant Dennis Walker composition, which builds and builds with some of Robert's most emotional singing and stinging guitar. Throughout, Robert's guitar playing is assured, confident, and imaginative. CD has two bonus tracks. A must!

Mercury 830 568-1 (c,d) Strong Persuader

On this his first album for a major label, Robert does blues fans proud by bringing his own unique brand of blues to the record-listening public at large without compromising his music. The songs are all originals by band members and/or Dennis Walker and David Amy and, like other songs Cray has recorded, deal with contemporary urban themes rather than traditional blues elements. I'm sure several songs are destined to become contemporary blues classics: "Smoking Gun," "Right Next Door," and the brilliant "Foul Play." Like his previous albums on Tomato and Hightone, this was produced by Bruce Bromberg and Dennis Walker, who manage to get a thick, rich sound out of only a quartet of instruments (guitar, keyboards, bass, and drums). A few tracks feature additional horn work by The Memphis Horns that is most effective. This album was the first blues album in many years to get a gold record for sales of over 500,000 and was on its way to getting a platinum!

Mercury 834 923-1 (c,d) Don't Be Afraid of the Dark

Robert's first Mercury album, "Strong Persuader," was probably the biggest-selling blues album of all time, so you might think that his second one would be more pop-oriented. However, the contrary is true: On this album, Robert is singing with a more impassioned sound and playing more hard-edged guitar. Sure this is very polished music and the themes are aimed at middle-class life, but the feel and spirit of the blues is consistently present. All new songs mostly written by Robert, his band members, and Dennis Walker. The solid work of the band carries this album with occasional added impetus from The Memphis Horns. My favorite here is the intense minor key "I Can't Go Home," with intense, violent lyrics, marvelous singing, and stinging guitar from Robert. On "Across The Line," Robert plays one of his most powerful and driving guitar solos. Don't miss this album.

Mercury 846 652 (c,d) Midnight Stroll

The old debate continues: Is Robert Cray the saviour of the blues, or a mega-star who sold his soul to the corporate devils in exchange for the coveted "file under pop" tag? The truth no doubt lies in between these two extremes. For me, after seeing the potent performances of Cray's Northwest heyday, most of his recordings have seemed like carefully calculated fence-straddling. I am happy to report that his soulful voice, formerly so honey-sweet, has acquired an appealingly ragged upper edge over the years. If placed in a more convincing instrumental setting, this would be a legendary voice, right up there with the heart-wrenching wails of Otis Rush and Bobby Bland. But, restrained by these over-produced and unspontaneous arrangements where every plucked string, drum hit, and keyboard note sound like they've been rehearsed right into the ground, Cray's vocals and razor-sharp guitar just don't get a chance to break free and convey much real emotion. Songs like "The Forecast," "Consequences," with the funky Hi Records sound, "Move a Mountain," a deep minor-key blues, and the energetic "Walk Around Time" are exciting cuts nonetheless, packing enough of a punch to keep the fans coming back for more. The compact disc has one extra track.

CASSETTE AND CD RELEASE ONLY

Tomato 269653 Who's Been Talking

Reissue of Robert's excellent first album from 1980, originally on the now-defunct Tomato label, which was only available for a short while. This reissue has been digitally remastered, beautifully repackaged, with extensive notes by David Sinclair. Unlike Robert's more recent recordings which feature new material almost exclusively, this one is about half covers, including versions of Jessie Fortune's "Too Many Cooks," Freddy King's "The Welfare Turns Its Back On You," Howlin' Wolf's "Who's Been Talking," along with some excellent originals by Cray ("That's What I'll Do," "If You're Thinking What I'm Thinking") and David Amy ("The Score," "I'd Rather Be A Wino"). Apart from bassist Richard Cousins, the band lineup is different than on his more recent recordings; several cuts feature the harmonica of Curtis Salgado, who also contributes second vocal on one cut. This is a straight blues outing with imaginative guitar playing and excellent arrangements.

Hightone 8001 Bad Influence

The songs on this album are mostly good originals by band members and are a mixture of blues with a soul feel and soul with a blues feel. With excellent production and sound and good notes by Lee Hildebrand, this is an album to treasure.

PEE WEE CRAYTON

Fine West Coast singer/guitarist who died in 1985. Pee Wee recorded extensively over the years. His best recordings are those for Modern and Imperial.

Blues Boy 307 **After Hours Boogie**

A diverse collection of 20 tracks covering the period 1945–62. Usual high quality sound and production from this label.

Murray Brothers 1005 **Make Room for Pee Wee**

Excellent 1983 album; Pee Wee sings well and plays some fine stinging guitar. The backup band, featuring several horns, is pretty good, though I feel the harmonica on some cuts is rather superfluous. Smooth Groove/Brighter Day/Telephone Is Ringing/When I'm Wrong I'm Wrong/When Darkness Falls.

ARTHUR "BIG BOY" CRUDUP

Great Mississippi blues singer who was very active in the 40s. He was a limited guitarist but a brilliant singer who wrote some excellent and influential songs. Several of the songs he wrote and recorded became blues standards. His song "That's All Right" became the first hit for a young Elvis Presley. He recorded several times in the 60s, mostly recreating his 40s hits. Between the Crown Prince and Krazy Kat labels, a goodly proportion of his 40s recordings have been reissued, though some of the classic sides from his first two sessions in 1941 and '42 still await reissue.

Collectables 5130 (c,d) **Mean Ole Frisco**

Twelve songs recorded for Bobby Robinson's Fire label in 1962. Accompanied by an unknown bass player and drummer, Crudup turns in fine performances of his old favorites. Unfortunately, sound quality is mediocre; it sounds like this album was dubbed from a poor quality copy of the old Fire album. Mean Ole Frisco/That's Alright Mama/Standing At the Window/Rock Me Mama/Katie Mae/So Glad You're Mine.

ESSENTIAL SELECTION

Crown Prince IG 403 **Give Me a 32-20**

Sixteen songs recorded 1941–52. I Don't Know It/That's Your Red Wagon/Hoodoo Lady Blues/That's Why I'm Lonesome/Just Like A Spider/She's Just Like Caledonia/Tired Of Worry.

Delmark 614 **Look on Yonders Wall**

1967 recordings with rhythm section including veteran bass player Ransom Knowling and drummer "Judge" Riley. Mostly remakes of his earlier sides. Look On Yonder Wall/That's All Right/Dust My Broom/Coal Black Mare.

Delmark 621 **Crudup's Mood**

This long-unavailable album features some of the last recordings of this veteran country bluesmen made in 1967 and '69. Pleasant though restrained performances with Crudup accompanied by Willie Dixon or Ransom Knowling (b) and Edward El (gtr). Includes some remakes of his 30s and 40s recordings. Strictly A Woman/Rambling On My Mind/Crazy House Blues/I'm In the Mood For You/When I Lost My Baby.

Krazy Kat 7402 **Star Bootlegger**

Sixteen excellent 1945–52 sides that have mostly not been reissued before. I Want My Lovin'/Train Fare Blues/Love Me Mama/Dust My Broom/Cry Your Blues Away/Crudup's After Hours/Late In The Evening/Too Much Competition.

Krazy Kat 7416 **I'm in the Mood**

Sixteen sides recorded between 1942 and 1952. Second Man Blues/Come Back Baby/Crudup's Vicksburg Blues/Hey Mama, Everything's Alright/Mama Don't Allow/Pearly Lee.

ARTHUR "BIG BOY" CRUDUP and LIGHTNIN' HOPKINS

Krazy Kat 7410 **Previously Unissued 1960–62 Recordings**

One side of album by each artist.

JAMES CRUTCHFIELD

Swingmaster 2109 **Original Barrelhouse Blues**

Delightful album of old-style blues singing and piano playing by 73-year-old performer from St. Louis. Crutchfield is a powerful and expressive singer and a fine piano player with a loose flowing style. The material is, for the most part, based on traditional themes (but Crutchfield makes them his own) and also includes one topical item: "US–Russian Blues."

KING CURTIS

Red Lightnin' 0042 **That's Alright**

This album is full of surprises! Curtis is best known as one of the great blues and R&B tenor sax players; this album finds him featured as vocalist on all but one cut, he plays alto sax instead of tenor, and he even plays some tasteful blues guitar on one cut! Curtis is a good vocalist with a Ray Charles quality to his singing; the material comprises mostly blues standards, with Curtis accompanied by a good band with fine guitar by Al Casey.

DUSKY DAILEY
Document 537 Complete Recordings in Chronological Order
Fourteen tracks from 1937 and '39 by interesting and obscure singer and piano player Dailey. These, recordings find him in different settings; the first two from 1937 are as a member of The Jolly Three featuring vocals by Jim Whitehead and an unknown and very effective piano player. The other four tracks from 1937 are solo and include a lovely version of the familiar "Flying Crow." Two of the songs from this session almost fall into the pop music realm. The remaining eight sides are from 1939 and feature Dailey with a large and, at times, chaotic aggregation including trumpet, sax, harmonica, guitar, and drums. There are some good moments in these recordings, but in general they are rather dispensible.

JULIUS DANIELS/LIL McCLINTOCK
Matchbox MSE 219 Atlanta Blues, 1927–30
A beautiful album of old-time black rural music by two obscure singer/guitarists recorded in Atlanta, GA. Daniels recorded seven sides in 1927, and McClintock recorded four in 1930. All of their recordings are here along with alternate takes of four of Daniels's songs. Both artists were songsters who performed a variety of material in addition to blues, including older black song styles, songs of white origin, and religious songs. Daniels is a superb vocalist and an excellent guitarist in a variety of styles, including some very fine slide work. McClintock performs two humorous songs that get a little tedious after a while but his two religious songs are fine. All these tracks have been reissued before, but it is valuable to have them all together since the material is varied. Decent sound and excellent notes by Paul Oliver.

LARRY DARNELL
Route 66 KIX 19 I'll Get Along Somehow
Recordings from 1949–57 by popular artist whose material ranged from ballads to rockin' Roy Brown styled R&B.

"COW COW" DAVENPORT
Fine and influential piano player who popularized the "Cow Cow Blues." Davenport was a brilliant and fluid piano player from Alabama, whose playing has elements of blues, boogie woogie, and stride in it.
Best Of Blues BOB 7 1926–38
A fine selection of 20 sides, mostly not on LP before. In addition to songs under his own name, there are duets with Dora Carr, Ivy Smith, and Sam Theard, and accompaniments to Ivy Smith, the rather dull Hound Head Henry, and Sam Tarpley. The Davenport solo performances are excellent and include the brilliant instrumental "Struttin The Blues." Ivy Smith is also splendid, and one of her tracks, "My Own Man Blues," features some lovely violin by Leroy Pickett. Davenport's duet with Dora Carr, "Alabama Mis-treater," is an oustanding performance with a marvelous tempo change halfway through. A couple of tracks are from pretty worn 78s, but most of the LP is quite listenable.
Document 557 1927–29
Twenty tracks, 11 of which are accompaniments to the fine vocalist Ivy Smith, most of which have not been on LP before. There are two accompaniments to the dull Hound Head Henry, one to Memphis Sam and John (Sam Tarpley and Ivy Smith), and six solo piano sides. The solo tracks are all brilliant but all but one have been reissued before. Quite a few of the tracks are from rather worn 78s. A collection that is enjoyable in places but not really essential.
Magpie 1814 Alabama Strut
Limited-edition repressing of album originally issued nine years ago. There are three version of the ever-popular "Cow Cow Blues" here: a solo instrumental version from 1928, a version with cornet from 1927, and a vocal version with Dora Carr from 1925. Most of the album is solo instrumental (occasionally with spoken asides) including such wonderful performances as "Slow Drag," "Mootch Piddle," and "Alabama Mis-treater." There are three fine vocals by Ivy Smith and one track features scratchy fiddle from Leroy Pickett. Highly recommended.
Oldie Blues 2811 Cow Cow Davenport
Sides from 1925 to 1945, including vocals by Davenport himself, Hound Head Henry, Ivy Smith, and Memphis Joe.

EUNICE DAVIS
Rather unexciting performer.
L+R 42.016 Eunice Davis Sings the Classic Blues
Spivey 1022 What Is the Blues?

REVEREND GARY DAVIS
Great religious and blues singer and stunning six- and 12-string guitarist who was very influential. He recorded from the 30s through his death in the early 70s. He combined the intense vocal style of a gospel singer with wonderful ragtime-flavored guitar work, influenced by his mentor, Blind Boy Fuller. His best recordings are his first sides

reissued on Yazoo and the early 60s recordings reissued on Heritage, Prestige, and Fantasy.

Fantasy 24704 When I Die I'll Live Again
Great two-LP set reissuing early 60s albums ("Harlem Street Singer" and "A Little More Faith") originally recorded for Prestige. Moving and powerful performances. Twelve Gates to the City/Samson and Delilah/Motherless Children/I Belong to the Band/Sit Down on the Banks of the River/You Got To Move/I'll Be All Right Someday.

Heritage 307 I Am the True Vine
Lovely album of recordings from 1962–63 that were made at Davis's home in New York City in informal settings. Features gospel songs, infrequently recorded blues, and some of his astonishing instrumental pieces. Sound quality is very good, considering the circumstances of the recordings. Won't You Hush/Moon Is Going Down/Get Right Church/Slippin' 'Til My Gal Comes in Partner/Blues in E.

Heritage 308 Children of Zion
Reissue of Transatlantic 249 featuring Davis recorded live in concert. He is in top form on a selection of great religious songs, novelty items, and some mind-boggling instrumentals, including a seven-and-a-half-minute workout on "Soldier's March." I Heard the Angels Singing/When the Train Comes Along/Long Way to Tipperary/Come Down and See Me Sometime/Twelve Sticks.

Heritage 309 Ragtime Guitar
Reissue of Transatlantic 244, this is an all-instrumental set recorded 1962–70. The emphasis is on ragtime pieces, though there are also some fine blues. Gary plays some fine 6-string banjo on Blind Blake's "West Coast Blues."

O.B.C. 519 (c,d) Say No to the Devil
Davis' third Prestige/Bluesville album, recorded in 1961. Time is Drawing Near/No One Can Do Me Like Jesus/Trying to Get to Heaven in Due Time.

Prestige 7725 The Guitar and Banjo of Rev. Gary Davis
1964 recording of instrumentals. Maple Leaf

Rag/The Boy Was Kissing the Girl/US March/Please Baby.

Stinson 56 The Singing Reverend
50s recordings. Death Is Riding Every Day/Oh What A Beautiful City/Motherless Children/I Can't Make the Journey By Myself.

Yazoo 1023 Reverend Gary Davis
Beautiful recordings from 1935–40 with fabulous guitar. These are Davis's first recordings. The Angel's Message to Me/I'm Throwing Up My Hand/I Can't Bear My Burden By Myself/I Am the True Vine.

COMPACT DISC

Heritage CD 02 Reverend Gary Davis
Nineteen tracks drawn from Heritage 308 and 309.

JAMES "THUNDERBIRD" DAVIS
Black Top 1043 (c,d) Check Out Time
James Davis is best known for some outstanding 45s recorded for Duke in the early 60s. After a long absence from music, he was rediscovered living in Louisiana in 1988 and reunited with old friends Clarence Holliman (gtr), Grady Gaines (ten sax), and Lloyd Lambert (b). They recorded an excellent "comeback" album. Joining these veteran musicians are regular Black Top sidemen Anson Funderburgh, Ron Levy, and a small horn section. Although James' voice is a little rougher than on his 60s recordings, he is still a powerful and expressive vocalist. The album includes a couple of remakes of his Duke songs ("What Else Is There To Do," "Your Turn To Cry"), some blues and R&B oldies ("Bloodshot Eyes," "Dark End Of The Street"), and some good new items ("I'm Ready Now," "Come By Here," "A Case Of Love"). It's nice to have this fine performer back on the music scene.

BLIND JOHN DAVIS
Veteran Chicago blues and boogie piano player who played on hundreds of Chicago blues recordings in the 30s and 40s, but only recorded a handful of sides under his own name. In the 70s, he started performing regularly again and toured Europe often, where he recorded several albums. He died in 1985.

Alligator 4709 Stomping on a Saturday Night
Recorded in Germany in 1976.

Document DLP 505 In Memoriam
An excellent collection of 18 sides not previously on LP. There are six songs under his own name, eight accompaniments to Ruby Smith, and six to "St. Louis Red" (Mike Bailey), all from 1938. The tracks by Davis are a real treat, featuring husky vocals with rolling piano and some pioneering electric guitar

from George Barnes. These cuts have a real New Orleans flavor to them. Ruby Smith is the niece of the great Bessie Smith and, although a pleasant enough singer, she has none of the talent of her aunt. The obscure Bailey is a fine singer and, besides John's expressive piano, his recordings also feature lovely guitar by Lonnie Johnson. Packaging is minimal but sound is decent and there are full discographical details.

L+R 42.056 Blind John Davis
1982 album; a selection of mostly original songs, though many are based on standards. Davis is in good form vocally and instrumentally. I Had A Dream/Hey Hey Mama/I Heard An Echo/Harlem Blues.

Oldie Blues 2803 The Incomparable Blind John Davis
Recorded in Holland in 1974.

Red Beans 008 You Better Cut That Out
This album, recorded in 1985, features 14 mostly instrumental tracks, though with a few vocals thrown in for good measure. The material includes originals ("No Mail Today," "Bartender's Bounce"), a couple made famous by his former partner John Lee "Sonny Boy" Williamson, plus jazz and pop standards ("Born To Lose," "Mood Indigo," "She's Funny That Way"). The blues and boogie pieces are very fine, but the pop and jazz pieces are not quite as effective.

LARRY DAVIS
Fine Arkansas singer, bass player, and guitarist. Larry is an expressive vocalist, strongly influenced by B. B. King.

Pulsar 1001 I Ain't Beggin' Nobody
Unlike some over-recorded blues performers, new records by Davis are few and far between, but when they come, they are worth waiting for and treasuring. Like his last album, the critically acclaimed Rooster album "Funny Stuff," this album was produced by veteran St. Louis producer Oliver Sain, who also wrote most of the songs here and plays sax and keyboards. Larry is a splendid gospel-flavored singer and an excellent guitarist. The songs are fine and intelligent and, in addition to the Sain compositions, include one by Larry plus a couple of totally original covers, including B. B.'s "Sneaking Around," Chuck Willis's "Please Don't Go," and Little Walters' "Last Night." Larry's music is not of the high-energy, blast-you-into-submission school, but is beautifully crafted, subtle, soulful, and a joy to listen to. Let's hope we don't have to wait another seven years for his next one.

Rooster Blues 2616 Funny Stuff
Fine album, with excellent backup by various St. Louis musicians such as Oliver Sain, Phil Westmoreland, Johnnie Johnson, and Billy Gayles. With sensitive production by Sain and a good selection of songs, this album strikes the perfect balance between sounding contemporary and being nothing but the blues!

MAXWELL DAVIS
Ace CHAD 239 Father of West Coast R&B
Fourteen tracks featuring this fine tenor sax player and arranger who was an important figure in the development of West Coast blues and R&B. This beautiful package features Davis and his Orchestra, plus Davis performing with Gene Phillips and His Orchestra and Lloyd Glenn and His All Stars.

WALTER DAVIS
Incomparably fine singer/piano player from Alabama who recorded quite extensively in the 30s and 40s. He had a distinctive rolling piano style and a lovely warm and wistful vocal style.

Best Of Blues BOB 5 1937–41
A beautiful collection of 18 sides by this superb singer and piano player, most not on LP before. Although there is a degree of similarity in his performances, his songs are interesting enough and his performances engaging enough for him not to become boring. On many cuts, his vocals and piano are joined by the guitar of Henry Townsend, Robert Lee McCoy, or Yank Rachell. Sound is good, and there is discographical information.

Blues Documents 2084 Vol. 1
Another beautiful collection. In addition to the songs by Davis, it also includes eight accompaniments to the enigmatic Booker T. Washington, whose vocals are, if anything, even more mournful than those of Davis! He has some very interesting songs, including the superb and moving "Death of Bessie Smith" and the fascinating "Cotton Club Blues." Most of the Davis tracks have been reissued before, generally scattered over various collections, including one of his greatest performances, the magnificent two-part "Jacksonville Blues." Sound is very good. Recommended.

Krazy Kat 7441 The Bullet Sides
A wonderful collection of 16 postwar recordings, 12 songs recorded for Nashville's Bullet label in 1949 and 1950, plus four tracks recorded in 1952. Davis' style changed little from the 30s to the 50s. On most of the tracks, he is accompanied by the brilliant Henry Townsend on acoustic or electric guitar, his playing partner for 20 years. Townsend's playing perfectly complements Davis' singing and piano

playing. There are some beautiful songs here, including the magnificent "Tears Came Rollin' Down," a 1952 recording which is among the highlights of a very impressive recording career.

Old Tramp 1213 **1930–33**
A beautiful collection of 18 of the earliest recordings by this brilliant St. Louis-based performer. On most of his recordings from the mid-30s on, Davis accompanied his lugubrious vocals with his own sparsely effective piano playing. On these earlier recordings, he is usually accompanied by the magnificent Roosevelt Sykes or James "Stump" Johnson. One cut features the lovely percussive guitar of Henry Townsend, who was featured on many of Davis's recordings over the next 20 years. Only three of these tracks have been on LP before, and sound quality is generally excellent.

Yazoo 1025 **Walter Davis/Cripple Clarence Lofton**
One side of album by Davis.

Note: Other Davis recordings are reissued on Yazoo 1015, Mamlish 3801, Mamlish 3805, and Magpie 4412.

JIMMY DAWKINS
Fine Chicago blues singer/guitarist.
Delmark 623 **Jimmy "Fast Fingers" Dawkins**
Delmark 641 **Blisterstring**
COMPACT DISC
JSP CD 206 **Feel the Blues**

JIMMY DEBERRY/WALTER HORTON
Crosscut 1021 **Back**
First volume of previously unissued 1972–73 recordings reuniting Memphis singer/guitarist DeBerry and harmonica great Horton on a selection of remakes of their old records, blues standards, and originals. With guest musicians on a few tracks.
Crosscut 1022 **Back**

DAVID DEE
St. Louis singer/guitarist.
Edge 003 **Sheer Pleasure**
CD issue: P-Vine PCD 1253
This album of contemporary blues and soul is an improvement over his previous album on the Vanessa label. The album benefits from better production values and a strong band, with some nice horn work from The Memphis Horns. Side one is pretty much all straight blues with fine singing and playing from David. The opening, "On Your Way Fishing," is a follow-up to his minor hit on Vanessa "Going Fishing." I particularly like the hard-driving "Working Blues Man." To hedge his bets, Side two is all

contemporary soul; good enough but probably of little interest to most blues fans.
Vanessa 2001 **Going Fishing**
Enjoyable album of contemporary blues by Dee, produced by veteran St. Louis producer/arranger Oliver Sain. Most of the songs are originals by Dee or Sain. A few cuts have a funk or pop flavor with vocal groups and string sound (actually a synthesizer), but most of the LP is straight blues. Arrangements are good, though the album would have benefited from some good horns. The sound on the album is a little muffled, which is a bit distracting.

MERCY DEE
Great California singer/piano player and wonderfully creative songwriter. Mercy Dee was a lovely singer with a relaxed, drawled vocal style and an effective piano technique firmly rooted in the tradition of his native Texas.
Arhoolie 1007 **Mercy Dee**
Superb early 60s recordings.
Crown Prince IG 406 **G. I. Fever**
This album focuses on some of his lesser-known but very fine recordings cut for a variety of labels between 1949–55. What makes his songs so engaging are the wonderful original lyrics full of careful observations and brilliant witticisms. The mood is generally slow and mournful, but there are some delightful up-tempo items, including the title song (with some intriguing scat singing), an odd interpretation of Chuck Berry's "Maybelline," and the rocking "Romp and Stomp Blues." Excellent sound and perceptive notes by Hank Davis. Unreservedly recommended.

JOHN DELAFOSE
Excellent singer and accordian player from Eunice, LA, playing an older style of Zydeco with a lot of emphasis on dance rhythms; some good blues, too.
Arhoolie 1083 (c) **Zydeco Man**
Fine first album from Delafose and his band, including two of his original songs. Contains his big hit, "Joe Pitre A Deux Femmes." No Good Woman/One Hour Too Late/Madam Sosthane/Prudhomme Stomp/Co-Fe?/La Valse A Creole/You Took My Heartache.
Arhoolie 1088 (c) **Uncle Bud Zydeco**
One side of this album was recorded live at a festival in Louisiana and the other side offers studio recordings. Delafose and his group play a basic form of Zydeco, with the rhythm section supplying a solid backup for Delafose's elemental but propulsive accordion playing. Great for dancing!

Maison de Soul 1015 **Zydeco Excitement**
CASSETTE AND CD RELEASE ONLY
Arhoolie C/CD 335 **Got Two Women**
Most of Arhoolie 1083 and 1088, with two previously unissued tracks.

JOHN DELAFOSE/WILLIS PRUDHOMME
Rounder 2070 (c,d) **Zydeco Live! From Richard's Club, Lawtell, La.**
Fine LP of live Zydeco music, with John Delafose and the Eunice Playboys, and Willis Prudhomme and the Zydeco Express. Delafose's forte is an energetic, almost hypnotic groove created by his forceful, if limited, accordian and the powerful drumming of son Geno, son Tony's bass, Jermaine Jack's rubboard, and some tasty guitar from Gene Chambler. They are tight and irresistible on numbers like "Poor Man Two-Step," "Oh Yi Li'l Girl," and Guitar Slim's "I Done Got Over." Prudhomme, a late comer to the accordian at age 45, sounds a lot like Boozoo Chavis, and indeed does "Paper In My Shoe." While he and the Express put out a vigorous and bouncy sound, I find his style a little limited, though I liked his version of "Bernadette" and the waltz "Those Tears In Your Eyes Are Not For Me."

PAUL DELAY BAND
COMPACT DISC
Red Lightnin' RLCD 0081 **"You're Fired": The Best of the Paul Delay Band.**

SUGAR PIE DESANTO
Chess 9275 (c) **Down in the Basement: The Chess Years**
Twelve songs recorded between 1960 and 1967, including two previously unissued tracks.

VARETTA DILLARD
Popular R&B vocalist in the early and mid-50s whose repertoire included upbeat rockers, slow blues, and maudlin ballads.
Mr. R&B 106 **Double-Crossing Daddy**
Presents all the facets of her music with perhaps an overemphasis on the ballads. Varetta was usually accompanied by top-notch New York musicians.

FLOYD DIXON
Fine West Coast singer/pianist who mostly recorded in the 40s/50s. Floyd's singing has that delightful, plummy Charles Brown quality to it, although Floyd's style is somewhat more intense. Route 66 albums are fine retrospectives of his early recordings.
Route 66 KIX 1 **Opportunity Blues**

Route 66 KIX 11 **Houston**
Route 66 KIX 27 **Empty Stocking Blues**
Sixteen songs recorded between 1947–53. There are some excellent performances of mostly original songs with Floyd in the company of some excellent West Coast musicians, including brilliant guitarists like Tiny Webb, Chuck Norris, or Johnny Moore. The album also includes his two very rare and unexpected gospel performances, "Milky White Way" and "Precious Lord," which are very effective.

WILLIE DIXON
Renowned Chicago bass player and singer who has written many classic Chicago blues songs. He is a more interesting writer and bass player than singer.
Capitol C1 90595 (c,d) **Hidden Charms**
Features nine of his lesser-known songs sung by Willie with Lafayette Leake (pno), Cash McCall (gtr), and Sugar Blue (hca). As this album shows, Willie is a much better songwriter than singer and a few of the songs here are among his more pretentious. Accompaniments are good though a bit overblown in places.
Columbia PC 9987 (c) **I Am the Blues**
CD issue: Mobile Fidelity MFCD 872
Willie recorded in 1970, accompanied by a fine band including Johnny Shines, Shakey Jake, Sunnyland Slim, and Clifton James on a selection of some of Willie's most well-known songs. Back Door Man/Seventh Son/I Ain't Superstitious/I'm Your Hoochie Coochie Man/The Same Thing.
O.B.C. 501 **Willie's Blues**
A pleasing selection from 1959 (originally issued as Bluesville 1003) of mostly original songs with accompaniments by Memphis Slim (pno), Wally Richardson (gtr), Al Ashby (ten sax), and Gus Johnson (drm).
Spivey 1016 **Willie Dixon and His Chicago Blues Band**
COMPACT DISC
Varese Sarabande CD 5234-2 (SF) **Ginger Ale Afternoon Original Soundtrack**
Fifteen songs from a movie score.
Note: See also POSTWAR CHICAGO collections.

LEFTY DIZZ
COMPACT DISC
JSP CD 229 **Ain't It Nice to Be Loved**
Intense electric Chicago blues by singer and left-handed guitarist Dizz with Carey and Lurrie Bell and other members of the Bell Family. A mixture of originals and old favorites. Generally unexceptional.

JOHNNY DOLLAR

Johnny is a good mellow singer who occasionally brings to mind Fenton Robinson; a sturdy if not exceptional guitar player.

B.L.U.E.S. R&B 3603 **J. D.'s Blues**

Dollar's first US album is a nice mixture of contemporary blues and R&B. Most of the songs are good originals by Johnny. He is accompanied by a full band including horns and synthesizers, and the arrangements are full-bodied and well thought-out. Worth a listen.

GEORGIA TOM DORSEY

Twenties singer/pianist and master of risque songs who later became one of the great writers of gospel songs!

Yazoo 1041 **Come on Mama, Do That Dance**

Excellent.

K. C. DOUGLAS

Mississippi-born singer/guitarist with influences of Tommy Johnson in his music. Douglas moved from Mississippi to the San Francisco Bay Area in 1945 but, until the folk revival of the 60s, performed and recorded infrequently. K. C. had an engaging warm voice and his guitar playing was similarly warm and flowing.

Ace CH 254 **Big Road Blues**

Reissue of Bluesville 1050 from 1961. Mostly familiar material, including two songs he learned from the great Mississippi bluesman Tommy Johnson: "Big Road Blues" and "Canned Heat." Though K. C.'s music isn't terribly demanding, it is most enjoyable to listen to. Move To Kansas/Tore Your Playhouse Down/Whiskey Headed Woman/Key To The Highway.

Arhoolie 1073 **The Country Boy**

Country blues and some cuts with rockin' blues band.

O.B.C. 533 (c,d) **K. C.'s Blues**

Reissue of Bluesville 1023 from 1961.

Oldie Blues 2812 **Mercury Boogie**

Reissue of some of his rarest recordings. Includes his rare 1954 single with rhythm section and all cuts from his incredibly rare 1956 album, which were among the first recordings of a country bluesman for a white audience.

DR. JOHN (MAC REBENNACK)

Alligator 3901 **Gumbo**

Mac Rebennack's classic 1972 album is available again domestically. A blending of Dixieland jazz, R&B, and indigenous rock 'n' roll into a form best described by Mac as "basic good-time New Orleans blues and stomp music." The horn arrangements by Harold Battiste smoke, and the material chosen includes "Iko Iko," which epitomizes the spirit of Mardi Gras. "Blow Wind Blow" features Fats

Domino's premier saxman, Lee Allen; "Mess Around" is a spirited shuffle, and a tip-of-the-hat to Ray Charles. "Junko Partner," a brilliant rendition of a New Orleans anthem, and "Tipitina" a fine version of the '53 Professor Longhair gem, round out a superior selection. Dr. John contributes the liner notes on this reissue.

Alligator 3904 **Gris Gris**

Clean Cuts 705 (c) **Dr. John Plays Mac Rebennack**

Dr. John's first solo album finds him performing a mixture of blues, boogie, and pop, much of it with a New Orleans feel. All piano solos, letting us hear the "doctor" in all his glory, with just one vocal.

Clean Cuts 707 (c) **The Brightest Smile in Town**

This is Dr John's second solo album for Clean Cuts and has several more vocal cuts than his first. Fine singing and playing on a selection of New Orleans blues and R&B, a fine boogie, some standards, and some things that are just Dr. John.

Edsel 128 **Dr. John**

A generous collection of 14 tracks taken from two out-of-print Dr. John staples ("Right Place, Wrong Time" and "Desitively Bonnaroo").

Warner Brothers 25889-1 (c,d) **In a Sentimental Mood**

Popular songs of the 30s, including a duet with Rickie Lee Jones on "Ain't Misbehavin'" that was a minor hit for the pair.

DRIFTING SLIM (ELMON MICKLE)

Arkansas-born, West Coast-based singer/guitarist/harmonica player and sometimes one-man band Elmon Mickle also recorded under the pseudonym of Model T. Slim.

Flyright 559 Model T. Slim

Mostly previously unissued recordings from 1966 and 1967 with a small band.

Milestone 93004 Drifting Slim and His Blues Band

Features solo performances, one-man band cuts, and some songs with group.

DRINK SMALL

Rather dull East Coast country blues singer/guitarist.

Southland SLP1 I Know My Blues Are Different

HERVE DUERSON and TURNER PARRISH

Blues Documents 2025 The Piano Blues of Herve Duerson and Turner Parrish

Duerson and Parrish are best known for the eccentric instrumental blues "Trenches." They recorded for Paramount both solo and accompanying the undistinguished vocalist Teddy Moss; they are heard here also in the company of an absolutely dreadful clarinetist on several sides! Both were uniquely individual keyboard stylists whose solo performances invariably surprise. Only four of these sides are currently available, so this is recommended to piano blues freaks willing to cut through the pedestrian vocals.

ANDREW DUNHAM

Krazy Kat 7423 Andrew Dunham and Friends

Fifteen mostly previously unissued recordings of country blues recorded in Detroit in the late 40s. Ten of the songs feature singer/guitarist Andrew Dunham, a powerful and distinctive performer, though a rather limited one. The other four songs are by the excellent Sylvester Cotton, two of which are alternate takes of songs on Krazy Kat 7422.

CHAMPION JACK DUPREE

Excellent and prolific blues singer and piano player from New Orleans who has lived in Europe for several years. Most of his best recordings from the 40s and 50s are now available on Gusto/King, Krazy Kat, Red Pepper, and Travelin' Man. His later 60s, 70s, and 80s recordings—mostly for European labels—lack some of the bite of his earlier sides but are still very good.

Best Of Blues BOB 14 1940–50

Eighteen songs, including sides not previously on LP, along with tracks from the long-out-of-print and hard-to-find Continental LP. Includes several cuts with Sonny Terry and Brownie McGhee.

Blue Moon BMLP 058 Rockin' the Boogie

Recorded in Germany in 1982, accompanied by young German electric guitarist Kenn Lending. Lending is a good guitarist, but it seems that his ideas are in conflict with what Jack is singing and playing, and the two often don't jell. Jack is in fine form on a selection of remakes of some of his older recordings plus newer ones. My Baby's Coming Back/I Don't Know/I Had That Dream/Be A Man/Good Lord Born On Christmas.

Blue Moon BMLP 2074 The Jubilee Album—75 Years of Champion Jack Dupree

Double LP commemorating Dupree's 75th birthday, a celebration/performance that took place in Hamburg, Germany, on Sept. 8, 1984. It's very sad that he had to leave America (like so many other black blues and jazz artists) to garner the respect and admiration he deserves. Dupree won't be thought of as an all-time great, but he was always dedicated to spreading the blues experience, and he has a lot to offer with his blend of piano blues and boogie woogie, wit, humor, and homespun philosophy. He's helped out by blues stalwarts like Mickey Baker (gtr), Axel Zwingenberger (pno), Memphis Slim (vcl, pno), and Louisiana Red (vcl, gtr). There's a lot of carrying on and noodling about—it is a "concert" after all—but all in all there's plenty of enjoyable music throughout. Freedom/Ramblin' Boogie/Jump For Jack/New York City/I Hate To Be Alone.

Detour 33-007 Shake Baby Shake

Wow, this incredible album features all 17 songs recorded by Jack Dupree for Vik and Groove in 1956 and '57, including eight previously unissued songs plus five previously unissued takes of songs—most of which are every bit as good as the issued recordings. Dupree has had a long career; he's been performing for about 50 years and is still going strong. These are among his finest recordings, with fine guitar by Larry Dale and/or Sticks McGhee, Al Lucas (b), and Pete Brown (ten sax) on a few cuts. The songs are a mixture of slow, intense blues ("Down The Lane," "Story Of My Life," "My Baby's Like A Clock"), whimsical semi-novelty items ("Just Like A Woman," "Woman Trouble Again," "Rocky Mountain"), a lot of hard-driving rockers ("Old Time Rock 'n' Roll," "Shake Baby Shake," "You're Always Crying The Blues," "The Wrong Woman"), and even a country-and-western-flavored piece ("Lollipop Baby"). Superb sound, discographical information, and good notes by Bez Turner. Highly recommended.

GNP Crescendo GNP 10001 **Tricks**
With Mickey Baker.

GNP Crescendo GNP 10005 **Happy to Be Free**

GNP Crescendo 10013 **Legacy of the Blues, Vol. 3**

King 5037X **Blues for Everybody**
Two-LP set. Twenty-two great sides from the 50s, with small groups including Mickey Baker (gtr) and George Smith (hca).

Krazy Kat 801 **The Remaining Titles and Takes**
This somewhat frustrating album complements Red Pepper 701 by reissuing the remainder of Dupree's recordings for the Joe Davis label, cut in 1945 and 1946. The album features four fine songs not included on the Red Pepper album, including the very witty "Love Strike Blues" and the deliciously obscene "Wet Deck Mama." Most of the rest of the album consists of alternate takes and false starts of the songs on Red Pepper 701 and, although the alternates are interesting, they are generally not very different, and the many false starts, some as short as 10 seconds, are unnecessarily distracting. The album is rounded out by two tracks by jazz pianist Gene Rodgers: one a lovely swinging boogie and the other a jazz-flavored blues track.

Red Pepper 701 **The Joe Davis Sides**
Superb reissue of 16 sides recorded for the Joe Davis labels in 1944 and 1945. These recordings are among the finest of this prolific artist; the original 78s are very rare and were pressed on incredibly poor quality shellac, so these recordings taken from original master tapes are a double treat!

See For Miles 44 **Won't Be a Fool No More**
CD issue: London 820 568-2 (GM)
This album, recorded in England in 1966, features Jack accompanied by an all-star band of British musicians including Eric Clapton, John Mayall, Tony McPhee, and Keef Hartley. Jack is in good form, but the backup adds nothing and, much of the time, gets in the way. Mayall's harmonica playing is particularly obnoxious. There are a few decent solo cuts by Jack, but the rest of the album will only appeal to fans of Clapton and Mayall. Also available as "From New Orleans to Chicago" (Cross Cut 109).

Storyville 4040 **I'm Growing Older Everyday**
Nice sides recorded in Europe between 1960–62, originally issued as Storyville 161.

Travelin' Man 807 **Junker Blues**
Features 16 of the 24 sides recorded by Dupree in 1940 and '41, his first, and quite probably his best, recordings. Most cuts feature Dupree's singing and piano playing accompanied by Ransom Knowling or Wilson Swain (b) and occasional guitar by Bill Gaither or Jessie Ellery. Dupree sings beautifully and plays wonderfully swinging piano, with a strong New Orleans flavor. The classic title song was later to become a New Orleans standard; Fats Domino changed the lyrics and had his first hit, "The Fat Man," with it. There are some great songs here, with fine lyrics by Dupree; the moving "Warehouse Man Blues," about the economic situation of blacks at the time, "Chain Gang Blues" and "Angola Blues," about prison, and much more.

COMPACT DISC

EPM Musique FDC 5504 **Champion Jack Dupree**
This CD is drawn from later French sides, probably released on a small European label at the time. Definitely not his best stuff, but lots more enjoyable than I thought it would be. Probably was originally issued on two different LPs; the first session is from January 1977, with French sidemen, and includes a lot of references to Jimmy Carter on "Ham Hocks and Limer Beans," "Let Me In, I Am Drunk," and "Somebody's Done Changed The Lock." The final tunes are from an '83 session with a similar group with the addition of Louisiana Red on guitar on more topical tunes, including "President Reagan," along with "Feel Like Rockin'" and Big Joe Turner's "Ain't Gonna Be A Lowdown Dog No More."

Flyright CD 22 **The Joe Davis Sessions**
Reissue of all 20 sides recorded by this outstanding singer and piano player for the Joe Davis label in 1945 and '46. These are the only commercial recordings Jack made in his heyday that were completely solo. Jack is in great form on a superb selection of blues, boogies, some very raunchy risque songs ("Wet Deck Mama" and "Fisherman's Blues"), and a couple of touching tributes to the recently deceased Franklin D. Roosevelt. Sound from original acetates is excellent, there are informative notes by Ray Templeton, and discographical information.

JSP CD 231 **Live at the Burnley Blues Festival**
1989 recordings with the Big Town Playboys. Includes three solo tracks and eight band cuts. In the Evening/Junker's Blues/One Scotch One Bourbon One Beer/Now or Never.

King KCD 735 **Sings the Blues**
London (UK) 820 569-2 **And His Blues Band Featuring Mickey Baker**
Decca reissue from 1967, mostly new material graced by the gritty guitar of Mickey Baker. Sixteen tunes, 43 minutes.

Vogue 600096 **The Death of Louis**
Thirteen songs from a 1971 session in Paris, both solo and with small band including Mickey Baker on guitar and Hal Singer on tenor sax.

Vogue 670402 **I Had a Dream**
Thirteen tracks recorded for Vogue in 1968, 12 previously issued on Vogue 271 and one previously unissued. With Mickey Baker (gtr). Ugly Woman/Death Of Martin Luther King/In the Evening/Early In the Morning/My Next Door Neighbor.

BIG JOE DUSKIN
Cincinnati-based boogie and blues piano player.

Arhoolie 1080 **Cincinnati Stomp**
Solos and cuts with a small band.

Special Delivery 1017 **Don't Mess with the Boogie Man**
Recorded in England with a rather anemic group of English musicians led by guitarist/photographer Dave Peabody. Joe performs a selection of originals plus songs from the repertoires of Sonny Boy Williamson, Freddie Slack, Roosevelt Sykes, and Detroit Jr. Joe is a decent singer and piano player and the performances here are all satisfactory, but nothing really shines.

JOHNNIE DYER
Murray Brothers 1004 **Johny Dyer and The LA Dukes**
On this album, Dyer's band is OK, though their ideas outstrip their ability. The worst aspect of this album is the awful sound that turns everything into mush.

SNOOKS EAGLIN
Fine New Orleans singer/guitarist.

Arhoolie 2014 **Possum up a Simmon Tree**
Probably his best album. Spirited sides with Snooks singing and playing 12-string acoustic guitar. Accompaniments feature washboard, harmonica, and tom-tom. That's Alright/I Ain't Gonna Study War No More/Jack O' Diamond.

Black Top 1037 (c,d) **Baby, Get Your Gun**
With a sympathetic backing band of fellow New Orleanians David Lastie on sax, Smokey Johnson on drums, and Ewing Charles on bass, with help from Ron Levy on keyboards and Ronnie Earl on guitar, Snooks grabs hold of these tunes and doesn't let go! Whether an instrumental romp like "Providia" and

the meteorized "Drop the Bomb," the Earl King title tune, or his own "That Certain Door," he shows why the New Orleans brand of funk and blues is such a fountain of musical creativity.

Black Top 1046 (c) **Out of Nowhere**
With Anson Funderburgh and Sam Myers.

GNP Crescendo 10012 **Legacy of the Blues, Vol. 2**

GNP Crescendo 10023 **Down Yonder**
Fine sides with Snooks on electric guitar accompanied by a small New Orleans band.

Storyville 140 **Blues from New Orleans, Vol. 2**

Storyville 146 **Portraits in Blues, Vol. 1**

Sundown 709-04 **New Orleans, 1960–61**
A most welcome reissue, this album features 15 fine sides recorded in 1960–61, with Snooks accompanied by a small band. A nice mixture of R&B, blues, blues ballads, and some pop-type songs with fine soulful vocals and excellent guitar by Snooks.

ROBERT EALEY with THE JUKE JUMPERS
Amazing 1004 **Bluebird Open**
An enjoyable album of blues, R&B, and occasional soul from this Fort Worth-based singer accompanied by the popular Texas band, The Juke Jumpers. Mostly original songs by Ealey and members of the band. The sound quality is a little messy. Nothing memorable here but enjoyable listening.

RONNIE EARL and THE BROADCASTERS
Antones 002 **I Like It When It Rains**
CD issue: Line CD 9.00448
Extremely tasty set from the former Roomful of Blues guitarist, mostly instrumentals. First four tunes are electric, after which Earl switches to acoustic slide and National steel guitar for very low-keyed solos and guitar/piano duets (courtesy of Ron Levy), including beautiful versions of "Sitting On Top Of The World" (as an instrumental) and Tampa Red's "Anna Lee," closing with the mournful "Blues For Jimmie and Jesse," accompanied only by bass drum. Recorded live at Antones Club, Austin, Texas.

Black Top 1023 **Smoking**

Black Top 1033 (c) **They Call Me Mr. Earl**

Black Top 1042 (c,d) **Soul Searchin**
COMPACT DISC

Black Top CD 1033 **Deep Blues**
Seventeen tracks, with over 60 minutes of music. Ronnie Johnnie/She Winked Her Eye/Ridin' In the Moonlight/Sick and Tired/San Ho Zay/Follow Your

Heart/You've Got Me Wrong/Some Day, Some Way/ Waitin' For My Chance.

ARCHIE EDWARDS
L+R 42.036 The Road Is Rough and Rocky
Sixth album in the Living Country Blues series on L+R features country-blues singer/guitarist from Rocky Mount, NC, now based in Washington, DC. Pleasant performances of traditional and original songs.

CLARENCE EDWARDS
Sidetrack 001 Swamp's the Word
Clarence is a fine down-home singer and guitarist from Louisiana who first showed up on a collection of field recordings made by folklorist Harry Oster some 30 years ago. He has recorded sporadically since then, but this is the first full album under his own name. Edwards is an excellent, warm singer and a basic but effective guitarist. He plays both acoustic and electric guitar and is joined by various sidemen in various configurations, including Louisiana piano great Henry Gray, Harmonica Red, and Michael Ward, who contributes some effective fiddle on some tracks. The material is mostly fairly familiar blues standards, along with a couple of originals. Nice! I Done Got Over/Drivin' Wheel/ Stoop Down Baby.

DAVID "HONEYBOY" EDWARDS
Chicago-based Mississippi country bluesman. He recorded a handful of magnificent sides in the 40s and 50s, but his recent recordings are uninspired.
Blue Suit 102 White Windows
Recent recordings of this veteran bluesman. Edwards sings and plays acoustic and electric guitar on a fairly familiar selection of songs, along with a few originals. The performances are generally unmemorable; the years have taken a toll on Honeyboy's voice and guitar technique. 61 Highway/Shake 'Em on Down/Take a Little Walk with Me/Roll and Tumble Blues.

WILLIE EGANS
Krazy Kat 7404 Rock 'n' Roll Fever
Fine set of blues, R&B, and black rock 'n' roll recorded by this excellent singer/piano player between 1955–58 (his entire recorded output). With tough New Orleans-sounding band, including biting guitar by Lloyd Rowe.

TINSLEY ELLIS
Alligator 4765 (c,d) Georgia Blue
Debut work by acclaimed Heartfixers axeman, includes New Orleans classics "Double Eyed Whammy" and "Look-Ka-Py-Py."

Alligator 4778 (c,d) Fanning the Flames
SLEEPY JOHN ESTES
Fine Tennessee singer/guitarist who first recorded in the 20s and 30s and was rediscovered in the 60s and continued to record prolifically. Many recordings feature fine harmonica by Hammie Nixon. His early recordings are particularly fine; later recordings are stark but exciting.

Delmark 603 The Legend of Sleepy John Estes
1962 recordings with Hammie Nixon.

Delmark 608 Broke and Hungry
With Hammie Nixon and Yank Rachell.

Delmark 611 In Europe
Recorded live in London and in Copenhagen in 1964, accompanied on jug and harmonica by his old friend Hammie Nixon. They perform a mixture of old Estes favorites. Needmore Blues/Airplane Blues/Denmark Blues/I Stayed Away Too Long/The Woman I Love/Easin' Back To Tennessee.

Delmark 613 Brownsville Blues
With Hammie Nixon and Yank Rachell; a fascinating selection of songs about his hometown.

Delmark 619 Electric Sleep
With electric guitars and amplified harp, played by Earl Hooker, Carey Bell, and Sunnyland Slim.

Swaggie 1219 The Blues of Sleepy John Estes, Vol. 1
This and the next album contain all his Deccas.

Swaggie 1220 The Blues of Sleepy John Estes, Vol. 2

Wolf 120.913 Recorded Live
Eight songs recorded in Austria in 1966 with Yank Rachell, and six recorded in St. Louis in 1974 with Hammie Nixon.

SLEEPY JOHN ESTES/YANK RACHELL and SON BOND
Document 564 1929–30 and 1941

JOE EVANS and ARTHUR MCCLAIN
Earl 616 Two Poor Boys, 1927–31
A delightful collection of 16 songs by this fascinating and mysterious duo who both sing and between them play guitar, mandolin, kazoo, and piano. They perform a varied selection of music including minstrel-flavored items ("Little Son Of A Gun"), spirituals ("Two White Horses In A Line"), white country songs ("New Huntsville Jail," a variant of "Birmingham Jail"), hokum ("Take A Look At That Baby"), straight blues ("Mill Man Blues"), and even a sentimental ballad ("Georgia Rose"). All of it is

performed with great vitality and panache. This album features all of their discovered recordings (there are four songs that have never been found) and includes two versions of a couple of the songs. These are from very rare and often worn 78s, so sound is not that exceptional but the music is fine.

LUCKY LOPEZ EVANS
Borderline 001 **Chinaman's Door**
Chicago blues singer and guitarist recorded in England with a band of British musicians. Lucky is a decent singer with a voice a little reminiscent of Howlin' Wolf and plays good, solid guitar. The backup band provides solid accompaniments. There are only six songs here (less than 30 minutes all together), including the title song written by band guitarist Winston Weatherhill, a minor key blues version of James Brown's "If You Leave Me (I'll Go Crazy)," and B. B. King's "How Blue Can You Get?"
COMPACT DISC
JSP CD 234 **Southside Saturday Night**

MARGIE EVANS
L+R 42.050 **Mistreated Woman**
Debut solo album by this fine blues singer best known for her appearances with the Johnny Otis Show. Some decent original songs, some with a funk or jazz feel, accompanied by some young musicians from Los Angeles. A good album marred by overly long performances.

L+R 42.060 **Another Blues Day**
Interesting album on which Margie has written most of the songs in collaboration with guitarist Cash McCall, and performs accompanied by a small band that includes McCall on lead guitar, plus saxes, occasional flute, piano, rhythm guitar, bass, and drums. The arrangements tend to a funky jazz or soul flavor, and only one song is a straight blues.

BETTY EVERETT/LILLIAN OFFITT
Flyright 589 **Betty Everett/Lillian Offitt**
Some excellent Chicago blues and R&B by two outstanding female singers. Although Betty Everett is best known for her mid-60s recordings for Vee Jay, the nine tracks here are from her fine Cobra recordings cut in 1957 and '58, some with a Chicago band featuring Little Brother Montgomery and Wayne Bennett and some with Ike Turner's band. Lillian Offitt's six tracks here were recorded for Chief between 1959–61, and she reveals herself to be a very fine singer; it's unfortunate that she recorded very little else. Two of the cuts feature fine slide guitar by Earl Hooker, and all her tracks are very worthwhile.

WILL EZELL
Oldie Blues 2830 **Pitchin' Boogie**
A lovely collection of piano blues recorded by this fine but obscure performer between 1927–29. Half of the cuts are solo piano and show Ezell to be a brilliant musician who was equally at home with a slow blues, a rag, or a boogie. He was also a fine and powerful vocalist. The last session from 1929 features him with a small group that includes Baby Jay (cnt), Blind Roosevelt Graves (gtr), Uaroy Graves (tam), and occasionally an unknown banjo player. These are powerful stomping sides and probably the highlight of the album. Sound from the very rare 78 originals is satisfactory, and there are brief but informative notes by Martin Van Olderen.

THE FABULOUS THUNDERBIRDS
Powerful white blues and R&B band from Texas. Features plaintive lead vocals by chief songwriter Kim Wilson, who also plays harmonica. The heart of the band is lead guitarist Jimmie Vaughan (brother of Stevie Ray), who is a complete study in tasteful flowing leads.
CASSETTE AND CD RELEASE ONLY
CBS BFZ 40304 **Tuff Enuff**
Album produced by Dave Edmunds.
Chrysalis PV 41250 **The Fabulous Thunderbirds**
Originally issued as Takoma 7068.
Chrysalis PV 41287 **What's The Word?**
Chrysalis PV 41319 **Butt Rockin'**
Some excellent original songs.
Chrysalis FV 41395 **T-Bird Rhythm**

THE FAMOUS HOKUM BOYS
Matchbox 1014 **1930–31**

FERNEST AND THE THUNDERS
Excellent down-home Zydeco band from Louisiana.
Blues Unlimited 5005 **Fernest and the Thunders**

THE FIELDSTONES
High Water 1001 **Memphis Blues Today**
Splendid debut album by this exciting combo from Memphis. They have an individual touch with tough vocals from Willie Roy Sanders or Joe Hicks and effective twin electric guitar work from Sanders and Wordie Perkins, with solid backup by the rest of the band.

MARVIN and TURNER FODDRELL
Swingmaster 2106 **The Original Blues Brothers**
Despite the painful title, this is a very entertaining

album of country blues by two brothers from Virginia. They both play guitar and take turns in singing; both are fine and distinctive singers and good guitar players. Although the two guitars don't always mesh, the overall sound is very good. The material is mostly original though firmly based on traditional themes.

CHARLES FORD BAND
West Coast band.

Arhoolie 4005 **The Charles Ford Band**
Blue Rock'it 101 **A Reunion**
First recording together in many years by this famed band featuring Robben Ford (gtr, vcl), Patrick Ford (drm), Mark Ford (hca, vcl), with Stan Poplin (b) and Steve Czarnecki (pno), recorded live at Barney Steele's in 1982. High energy Chicago-style blues.

REDD FOXX and DUSTY FLETCHER

Savoy 1181 **Open the Door, Richard — Laughin' the Blues**
What a treat; reissue of a fine blues-melodrama recorded for National and Savoy during 1946 and 1947. Contained here are eight Fletcher comedy gems about booze, babes, and being broke, backed by The Jimmy Jones ('46) and The Hot Lips Page ('47) bands, including the title cut, which embraces Fletcher's original vaudeville routine, later set to music by Jack McVea, who scored with the hit version (one of many) in '47. The collection is rounded out with five fine blues songs (sung in the Wynonie Harris vein) by the teenage Redd Foxx of "Sanford and Son" fame; made during his glory days at The Apollo in Harlem, backed by Kenny Watts and His Jumpin Buddies. Recommended.

FRANK FROST
Fine Mississippi blues singer/guitarist and harmonica player. Jimmy Reed-influenced blues given the deep South sound.

Charly CRB 1103 **Ride with Your Daddy Tonight**
Fine 60s sides for Jewel.

P-Vine PLP 360 **Hey Boss Man!**
Exact repro of Phillips International 1975 from 1962 with an extra cut, reissuing all released tunes done for Sam Phillips (there's still a mess of unissued cuts). Frost on guitar, vocals, and harp, joined by Jack Johnson (gtr) and Sam Carr (drm). The 13th cut is "Crawlback," the instrumental flip side of the great "Jelly Roll King" single with the added guitar of Sun session vct Roland Janes. Big Boss Man/Now Twist/Jack's Jump/Just Come On Home.

COMPACT DISC
P-Vine PCD 2135 **Harp and Soul**
Thirteen fine Jewel recordings from 1966.

BLIND BOY FULLER
Great North Carolina country-blues singer/guitarist who recorded extensively in the 30s. An essential artist to listen to! There is very little duplication among the following albums. Yazoo has a slight edge because of the superior sound quality, but all are worthwhile.

Best Of Blues BOB 12 **The Remaining Titles**
A beautiful collection of 19 sides recorded between 1935–40. These complement the recordings on other reissues. Although half of these tracks have been out before, most are on long-out-of-print anthologies, and this does have several tracks not reissued before, including the fine "I'm Climbin' On Top Of the Hill" from his first recording session. There are four tracks from his superb 1937 Decca session including the lyrical "Working Man Blues." Several cuts feature the sensitive harmonica of Sonny Terry and a couple have Bull City Red on washboard. Sound varies from mediocre to excellent.

Blues Classics 11 **Blind Boy Fuller, 1935–40**
Fourteen great sides, mostly with Sonny Terry and Bull City Red. Shake It Baby/You've Got Something There/Step It Up And Go/Jitterbug Rag/Bus Rider Blues/Big House Bound/Three Ball Blues.

Old Tramp 1202 **Blind Boy Fuller, 1936–40**
Nineteen splendid recordings, mostly not on LP before. Babe You Got To Do Better/When Your Gal Packs Up and Leaves/Let Me Squeeze Your Lemon/Throw Your Yas Yas Back In Jail.

Oldie Blues 2809 **Death Valley Blues**
Eighteen fine tracks, recorded 1935–40, mostly by Fuller on his own. Evil-Hearted Woman/Keep Away From My Woman/Been Your Dog/You Never Can Tell/Hungry Calf Blues/Mama Let Me Lay It On You/ She's A Truckin' Little Baby.

Travelin' Man TM 801 **Blind Boy Fuller**
Fourteen sides recorded between 1935 and 1940. None of these cuts have been reissued before; most of them feature Sonny Terry on harmonica, some have him on vocal, and many cuts feature Oh Red on washboard and occasionally vocal. There are several of Fuller's rarely reissued gospel songs from 1940. Excellent sound.

ESSENTIAL SELECTION
Yazoo 1060 **Truckin' My Blues Away**
Fourteen tracks, recorded 1935–38. Some of his best songs, with exceptionally good sound. Weeping Willow/Truckin' My Blues Away/Homesick and

Lonesome Blues/Mamie/Funny Feeling Blues/
Meat Shakin' Woman.

Note: Other reissues on Blues Classics 6, Yazoo 1040, and Blues Classic 18.

COMPACT DISC

Travelin' Man CD 01 **Blind Boy Fuller 1935–40**
Twenty sides drawn from Magpie and Travelin' Man albums, ranging from his first recording ("Baby, I Don't Have to Worry") in July 1935 to his last ("Precious Lord") in June 1940. In fact, there are six tracks from this last session which, though good, did not feature his best performances. There are half-a-dozen solo sides by Fuller plus tracks with washboard player Bull City Red, guitarists Floyd Council, Blind Gary Davis, and Oh Red, and harmonica players Sonny Terry and Jordan Webb. Sound quality is generally pretty good, though some tracks are from rather worn 78s. An enjoyable, if not essential, collection.

JESSE FULLER
Fine West Coast-based country-blues singer, guitarist, harmonica player, and one-man band. Jesse was a fine vocalist who accompanied himself on 12-string guitar, harmonica, kazoo, cymbals, and his unique bass instrument—the fotdella. All his records are worthwhile.

Arhoolie 2009 **Frisco Bound**
Features some of his earliest recordings from the 50s; mostly 12-string guitar accompaniments with fine slide.

Good Time Jazz 10031 **Folk Blues and Sprituals**
Good Time Jazz 10051 **San Francisco Bay Blues**
Classic album from 1963. Includes the best version of his theme song, "San Francisco Bay Blues."

O.B.C. 526 (c,d) **The Lone Cat**
Reissue of 1958 Good Time Jazz LP, featuring 12 blues, spirituals, and good-time songs.

Topic 134 **Move on Down the Line**

JOHNNY FULLER
Mississippi-born bluesman Fuller was an eclectic performer whose 50s recordings included down-home blues, R&B, gospel, rock 'n' roll, Johnny Ace-type ballads, novelty songs, and more! He lived in the San Francisco Bay area.

Diving Duck 4303 **Fools Paradise**
All of the facets of his recording career are presented on this fine reissue that features 16 songs. His slow blues like "Roughest Place In Town" (a version of "Tin Pan Alley") and "Too Late To Change" are particularly fine, with wonderful "dirty" guitar by

Fuller and appropriate backing from the rest of the band.

Diving Duck 4311 **Fuller's Blues**
Reissue of Bluesmaker 4304 from 1974, coproduced by the author of this book! Fuller recorded plenty of classic Bay Area blues sides for such labels as Aladdin, Imperial, Hollywood, Flair, and Checker. These '74 recordings constituted his first-ever full LP, showing off a variety of styles, from acoustic country blues to jump to shuffle, all with wonderful success, featuring Walker on guitar and saxist David Li. Fool's Paradise/Tin Pan Alley/Mercy Mercy/Hard Luck Blues/Crying Won't Make Me Stay.

LOWELL FULSON
West Coast blues singer/guitarist who started as a country-blues performer (some of these recordings are reissued on Arhoolie 2003) and moved to small urban groups and then larger city bands. A consistently fine artist who has occasionally been saddled with poor production but is nearly always worth hearing.

Arhoolie 2003 **Lowell Fulson**
Country-blues-oriented recordings from the 40s. About two-thirds of the tracks feature Lowell accompanied by his own acoustic guitar and that of his brother Martin. The rest of the album features him with small urban groups, often with Lloyd Glenn (pno). A great collection.

Bear Family BFX 15279 **I Don't Know My Mind**
Relaxed 1972 sessions produced in Houston by Huey P. Meaux. Lowell fronts a four-piece, organ-dominated studio band on mostly slow tempo and shuffle pieces. Nonessential but pleasant. Includes eight of 10 cuts issued in 1978 as "Lowell Fulson" (Crazy Cajun 1090) and six from those same sessions never before released. Kansas City/I Want Affection, Not Protection/Getting Drunk/You Don't Know My Mind.

Blue Phoenix 33.724 **One More Blues**
Recordings cut in France in 1984 with Lowell accompanied by The Phillip Walker Blues Band. A mixture of old and new songs with fine singing and playing from Lowell and good backups by the band, with some very nice guitar by Phillip and sax by Mike Vannice. There is a certain degree of sameness to the performances, evidence of a rather hasty session, but worth a listen.

Blues Boy 302 **Lowell Fulson**
Sixteen fine sides recorded between 1946 and 1957 showing the remarkable versatility of this great blues artist. Excellent notes and packaging with a

brief analysis of Lowell's guitar style and lyrics to all songs on the album.

ESSENTIAL SELECTION

Chess 2-92504 Lowell Fulson
Two-LP set. Reissue of Chess ACMB 205 featuring 28 sides recorded for Checker between 1955 and 1962, most with Lloyd Glenn (pno) and fine horn work, including great alto sax by Earl Brown. I Want To Know/Lonely Hours/Lovin' You/It's A Long Time/Love Grows Cold/Hung Down Head.

Crown Prince IG 407/408 Baby Won't You Jump with Me
Two-LP set. A superb collection of 33 tracks recorded between 1946–51, ranging from country blues to small band blues. Album has superb sound, full discographical information, and extensive notes, plus some amazing never-before-seen photos including ones of Lowell's brother Martin and his grandparents in Oklahoma in the 30s!

Diving Duck DD 4306 The Blues Got Me Down
A nice collection of vintage recordings. The album covers tracks from 1946 to 1964, though most of the tracks are from 1946–53. Lovely small group sides with choice guitar by Lowell and usually Lloyd Glenn (pno) and Earl Brown (alto sax). Notes are not terribly informative and the lack of discographical information is regrettable. Street Walking Woman/The Blues Got Me Down/The Highway Is My Home/Be On Your Merry Way/You're Gonna Miss Me/Blue Shadows.

Rounder 2088 (c,d) It's a Good Day
Lowell's first new recordings in quite a while.

COMPACT DISC

Chess (France) 670403 So Many Tears
A great collection of 19 tracks from Checker, drawn from those originally issued on Chess ACMB 205 (now 2-92504). Although missing his most important Checker recordings, "Reconsider Baby" and "Tolling Bells," it does include such classics as "I Want To Know," "Hung Down Head," "So Many Tears," and "Blue Shadows." Most of the songs are originals by Lowell, featuring his warm, expressive vocals and effective guitar. The tracks were recorded in Los Angeles between 1955–62 and feature the great Lloyd Glenn on piano, along with other excellent West Coast musicians like Earl Brown, Jim Wynn, and Billy Hadnott. Sound is satisfactory.

Chess (UK) CD RED 15 Reconsider Baby
Twenty-four fine sides recorded for Checker between 1954–62, with various bands. Most of his best sides are here, including the classic title song, though, curiously, not his minor-key masterpiece "Tolling Bells." There are full discographical details

and informative notes by Tony Burke; however, this collection is marred by mediocre sound, muffled and lacking in presence. Trouble, Trouble/Took A Long Time/Blue Shadows/So Many Tears/Hung Down Head.

JSP CD 207 Think Twice Before You Speak
CD issue of JSP 1082, recorded in England with Eddie C. Campbell and some British musicians. An enjoyable, if not exceptional, set. Includes a couple of songs with Lowell accompanied by second guitar, trying unsuccessfully to recapture the feel of some of his 40s recordings. Parachute Woman/Think Twice Before You Speak/One-Room Country Shack/Come On.

ANSON FUNDERBURGH and THE ROCKETS
Tough white blues band from Dallas, Texas.

Black Top 1001 (c,d) Talk to You by Hand
Enjoyable versions of blues standards. Tore Up/Talk to You By Hand/How Long?/Nobody But You/Walking Dr. Bill/I Was Fooled.

Black Top 1022 (c,d) She Knocks Me Out

Black Top 1038 (c,d) Sins
With Sam Myers.

GRADY GAINES
Black Top 1041 (c,d) Full Gain

ROY GAINES
Fine Texas guitarist and singer based in Los Angeles.

Red Lightnin' 0035 Roy Gaines
1980 recordings featuring members of the Crusaders. A mixture of black music from down-home music to modern uptown funk. I would have preferred more of the former and less of the latter, though Roy handles it all very well.

BILL GAITHER
Although quite prolific in the 30s and early 40s, Bill Gaither has been under-represented on reissues. Although his music lacks the intensity of some of his contemporaries, Bill was an engaging vocalist and wrote some excellent songs, often with a whimsical quality. He was strongly influenced by the great Leroy Carr, and many of his recordings were issued under the sobriquet of "Leroy's Buddy." He was usually accompanied by his own guitar with the splendid piano of Honey Hill or sometimes Josh Altheimer or Jack Dupree.

Blues Documents 2090 Leroy's Buddy, 1936–41
Although there is not a lot of variety in Gaither's music, his voice is appealing, his lyrics are above average, his tunes catchy, and his accompaniments

usually feature the brilliant piano work of Honey Hill. Half a dozen of these tracks appeared recently on Bluetime 2019, but the rest have not been reissued before.

Bluetime 2019 **I'm Behind the Eight Ball Now**
Excellent selection of sides by this fine performer whose wry vocal style and cynical lyrics are most engaging. Most of the tracks here feature the brilliant piano of Honey Hill. More than half of them have been out before and some are currently available on Document and Old Tramp. But, all in all, this is a worthwhile collection.

Document DLP 508 **Vol. I: 1935–41**
Presents a fine cross-section of 18 sides that have not been on LP before. Well worth a listen.

Old Tramp 1212 **1936–1940**
Twenty sides, 18 featuring the lugubrious vocals of Gaither with the lovely rolling piano of Honey Hill, and two being instrumentals by Hill, including the archetypal "Boogie Woogie," which has been reissued several times before. Otherwise most of the tracks here have never been reissued before. The songs are varied and frequently witty; included is a tribute to his idol, Leroy Carr—"Life of Leroy Carr"—as well as an excellent version of Carr's "Mean Mistreater."

CECIL GANT
Oldie Blues 8004 **I'm Still Singing the Blues Today**
This reissue is somewhat disappointing since, besides the fine blues and boogie sides that are featured, there is also a fair proportion of rather unexceptional ballads, which Cecil recorded quite regularly but that have been avoided on most reissues. Sound quality isn't always the best.
COMPACT DISC
Krazy Kat CD 03 **Cecil Gant**
A splendid collection of 20 tracks recorded between 1944–46. There are several examples of his dynamic boogie playing on "Cecil's Boogie," "Rock The Boogie," "Syncopated Boogie," and the all-time classic "Hogan's Alley." There are also straight blues, jazzy jive numbers, and a couple of examples of his popular ballad stylings. Decent sound and brief informative notes from Bruce Bastin.

CLARENCE GARLOW
Flyright 586 **Clarence Garlow, 1951–1958**
Volume 28 in the series of reissues from the Jay Miller archives features 12 sides by this excellent Louisiana blues singer and guitarist who did the original version of "Bon Ton Roulet." This album has a remake of that song along with 11 other rare

and unissued titles. Most of this has an urban feel, with small band, but a few cuts are more down home with harmonica.

PAUL GAYTEN
New Orleans singer/piano player, producer, and bandleader whose band featured such fine sidemen as Edgar Blanchard and Lee Allen.
Route 66 KIX 8 **Creole Gal**
Features band vocalist Annie Laurie on many cuts.

GEORGIA TOM
Best Of Blues BOB 18 **1929–30**
Twenty rare sides not previously on album, including duets with Kansas City Kitty, Hannah May (Jane Lucas), and Laura Rucker.
Blues Documents 2061 **The Accompanist**
Twenty recordings from 1928–31, with Tom accompanying Aunt Mary Bradford, Stovepipe Johnson, Frank Brasswell, and The Famous Hokum Boys. Very little duplication with other reissues.
Document 563 **1928–32**
Twenty early sides with Tampa Red, The Hokum Boys, and Charlie McCoy.

CLIFFORD GIBSON
Superb 20s country-blues singer/guitarist from Alabama.
Yazoo 1027 **Beat You Doing It**
Note: Other cuts reissued on Yazoo 1006.

LACY GIBSON
Black Magic 9002 **Switchy Twitchy**
Good, solid album of modern Chicago blues by fine singer/guitarist accompanied by good band with Abb Locke (ten sax) and Sunnyland Slim or Allen Batts (pno). A good mixture of originals and familiar and unfamiliar songs. Good, dynamic sound.

JAZZ GILLUM
Popular 30s singer/harmonica player. Gillum was a fine and expressive singer and an effective, if limited, harmonica player. He was usually accompanied by top Chicago musicians like guitarists George Barnes, Big Bill Broonzy, and Willie Lacey, piano players Blind John Davis, Roosevelt Sykes, and Eddie Boyd, and washboard players Washboard Sam and the flamboyant Amanda Sortier.
Best Of Blues BOB 4 **1935–46**
Eighteen sides mostly never on LP before. This album features some of Gillum's earliest sides, including two 1935 recordings with the State Street Boys, a wonderfully exuberant band featuring guitarists Big Bill Broonzy and Carl Martin, pianist Black Bob, and bassist "Joe." Most of the other

tracks feature him with various groups, usually with Broonzy (gtr) and Josh Altheimer or Blind John Davis (pno). The music is consistently fine, though the sound is variable; some tracks are from worn 78s.

Bluetime 2013 Me and My Buddy

Sixteen tracks recorded between 1938–42, previously available on the long-out-of-print RCA (UK) INT 1177. All of the tracks feature the guitar of Big Bill Broonzy with Josh Altheimer, Horace Malcolm, or Blind John Davis on piano, and various other musicians. You're Laughing Now/Let Her Go/I'll Get Along Somehow/Keyhole Blues/I Got Somebody Else/Me and My Buddy/One Letter Home/I'm Gonna Leave You On the Outskirts Of Town.

Document 522 The Remaining Titles, 1935–47

Seventeen tracks. The album opens with the rural string band sound of The State Street Boys, with fine violin by Zeb Wright, and ends with the tough postwar Chicago blues sound of "Take A Little Walk With Me." Along the way we hear Gillum in various settings with fine accompaniments by Big Bill Broonzy, Blind John Davis, George Barnes (some pioneering electric guitar from 1938), Alfred Elkins, Big Maceo, and Willie Lacey. One track features tenor sax by John Cameron. An excellent collection by an underrated artist.

Travelin' Man 808 Jazz Gillum 1938–47

This LP is a repackaging of a long-out-of-print set originally issued in England almost 20 years ago. Some fine songs here, mostly by Gillum himself, along with several from Washboard Sam and Big Bill Broonzy. Excellent sound and informative notes by Neil Slaven. Sixteen tracks in all.

Wolf WBJ 002 Roll Dem Bones, 1938–49

Complements Document 522 above. The selection here is, if anything, even better, with such marvelous songs as "Reefer Head Woman" (with great electric guitar by George Barnes), "Down South Blues," the powerful "Afraid To Trust Them," and the ominous "Gonna Be Some Shooting." Highly recommended.

GENE GILMORE/THE FIVE BREEZES

Blues Documents 2065 Complete Recordings

Four tracks by Gilmore, two by Breezes member Baby Doo, and eight by The Five Breezes. A few on LP before.

LLOYD GLENN

Texas-born, West Coast-based pianist who was conversant with blues and jazz. He had a distinguished career going back to the 30s. He recorded extensively in the 40s and 50s, primarily as an arranger and sideman (most notably with Lowell Fulson) but also as a leader.

Jukebox Lil 608 Texas Man

Recordings from the 1946–59 period. Features some of his finest early recordings, including the title cut with vocals by Jerry Carter. The album dwells mainly on sides fronted by solo vocalists: Willis Threats, Red Miller, and Jesse Thomas. There also are tasty guitar licks by Tiny Webb and smooth alto parts by Henry Hayes.

Oldie Blues 8002 After Hours

This is an excellent selection of blues, boogie, and jazz instrumentals, mostly with bass and drums accompaniment, recorded between 1947–56.

LILLIAN GLINN/MAE GLOVER

Blues Documents 2009

Some wonderful music from two outstanding prewar women blues singers. Accompanied by a group with piano, banjo, and brass bass, Texas singer Lillian does some lovely vocalising on six fine and varied tracks from 1929. The 12 tracks by the mysterious Mae Glover feature all her discovered recordings. She was a gorgeous singer with a style slightly akin to that of the great Bessie Jackson. There are four incredible tracks with Mississippi 12-string guitarist John Byrd, including the amazing "Pig Meat Papa," on which Mae does some very effective yodelling! The other eight tracks have a slightly more urban feel with trumpet and piano accompaniment, but are also very fine, though some are from very worn 78s. About half of these tracks have been reissued before, but some are not currently available. A great collection.

THE GOLDEN EAGLES

Rounder 2073 (c,d) Lightning and Thunder

At last someone (Ron Levy) has made a live recording of a troupe of Mardi Gras Indians. The Golden Eagles, led by Monk Boudreaux, have long been one of New Orlean's best groups, both in terms of elaboration of their Indian-beaded costumes and their musical prowess, as well as their dedication to the Indian tradition. Here they chant and drum their songs—"Two-Way-Pak-E-Way," "Shoo Fly," "Indian Red," and "Hold 'Em Joe"—live in the Hand R Bar, capturing the essence of this unique celebration of black and Indian culture. With fine notes by Michael Smith.

CHARLIE GONZALES

Krazy Kat 810 Charlie Gonzales on Gotham

Charlie Gonzales, alias Bobby Prince, recorded jump songs and ballads in the Arthur Prysock vein for Ivin Ballen's Gotham label in 1950. This collection contains mainly laid-back blues ballads sung in a relaxed, polished style, backed by such notable outfits as Frank Motley and The Doc Bagby Orchestra. Includes eight previously unissued cuts and alternate takes.

GOOD ROCKIN' CHARLES
Double Trouble 7601 **Good Rockin' Charles**
Dutch reissue of a fine album originally on Rooster Blues.

IDA GOODSON
Florida Folklife 104 **Pensacola Piano**
A delightful album of blues, jazz, and gospel by this Florida performer. Ida is a fine piano player with a New Orleans flavor to her style and an engaging if not exceptional singer. Side one features a couple of originals along with some blues and jazz standards; on some cuts she is joined by a small band. Side two is all gospel and features some delightful instrumental versions of gospel songs along with some vocals on which she is joined by the Morning Star Missionary Baptist Church Choir. Comes with detailed four-page booklet.

JIMMIE GORDON
Pleasant, if unexceptional, bluesman.
Blues Documents 2075 **1934–41**
Twenty tracks with various groups, usually with trumpet and/or sax. Sidemen include Charlie McCoy, Odell Rand, Horace Malcolm, Sam Price, Teddy Bunn, Frankie Newton, and Buster Benett. Most tracks not previously on LP.
Document 515 **The Mississippi Mudder**
Eighteen sides recorded between 1934–41. Most of the tracks feature him with his Vip Vop Band, a small group featuring Sam Price or Horace Malcolm (pno) and various horn players, together with an unknown rhythm section. Like Gordon himself, the group is generally unexciting. Some good songs here, but generally a boring record.

ROSCOE GORDON
Slightly eccentric Memphis urban blues singer.
Mr. R&B 103 **Keep on Doggin'**
Sixteen sides recorded between 1951–69; fold-out jacket features extensive notes.
COMPACT DISC
Charly CD 213 **Let's Get High**
Great collection by one of the most distinctive of urban bluesmen, featuring 21 tracks recorded for Sam Phillips between 1952–57 and five recorded for Vee Jay in 1959. The Phillips' recordings feature several previously unissued songs and alternate takes, demonstrating Roscoe's flair for novel lyrics and rhythms; some consider him the father of

ska/bluebeat! His vocals are backed by some hot bands. Though not quite as raucous, his Vee Jay sides include some fine cuts, including his most famous song, "Just A Little Bit." Sound quality is much better than usual for Charly, and there are informative notes by Hank Davis. The lack of discographical information, however, is regrettable.

BLIND ROOSEVELT GRAVES
Wolf 110 **Blind Roosevelt Graves**
Some delightful music made by Mississippi singer/guitarist Roosevelt Graves along with his brother Uaroy (on vocal and tambourine). Twelve sides from 1929 with Baby Jay (clr) and Will Ezell (pno), and six sides from 1936, some with Cooney Vaughn (pno). The brothers liberally mixed secular and sacred material, and all of it has a lively good-time feel to it. The first track on Side one is almost unlistenable because of the poor quality of the original 78, but the rest of the album has perfectly adequate sound. About half of these cuts have been reissued before.

HENRY GRAY
Blind Pig 2788 **Lucky Man**
First US album by this brilliant Louisiana piano player who moved to Chicago in the 40s and whose piano playing illuminated so many great Chicago blues records of the 50s and early 60s. This album features him performing a mixture of original songs along with those from the repertoires of Fats Domino, Jimmy Rogers, Big Maceo, and J. B. Lenore. He is accompanied by a competent small group (bass, guitar, and drums). Although Henry is not a great singer, he is an effective one, and his piano playing skills are intact. His playing on slow or medium tempo items like the title song, "Mean Old World," or "Out On The Road" has a lovely rolling, cascading quality that one rarely hears anymore.

CAL GREEN
COMPACT DISC
Double Trouble DTCD 3020 **White Pearl**
Cal Green is a brilliant Texas blues guitarist who has recorded very little under his own name. In the 50s, he contributed to many blues and R&B recordings cut in Texas and for a while in the late 50s had a stint as guitarist with The Midnighters. Since the 60s, he has moved to more jazz/pop stylings in the vein of his idol George Benson, but he has continued to include blues in his repertoire. This album, recorded in Los Angeles with local musicians, is almost all blues and includes half a dozen originals by Cal along with a beautiful minor-key blues, "You Don't Know How It Feels," plus Hank Ballard's "24 Hours

A Day" and Muddy Waters' "Just Want To Make Love To You." Cal is not a great singer, though his distinctive high voice is effective, but throughout he plays some striking guitar and is given solid accompaniments by the rest of the band. There are informative notes by Dick Shurman in tiny print on Cal's career.

CLARENCE and CAL GREEN
COMPACT DISC
P-Vine PCD 1609 **Jumpin' Houston Guitarists, Entry 1**
A fine collection of 17 sides recorded for Houston's maverick record producer Roy Ames in the early 60s featuring brother-guitarists Clarence and Cal Green on a selection of mostly instrumental recordings. Most of these tracks have not been issued before. Who plays on what tracks is not clear, and since the two have stylistically similar approaches, identification is further confused. Still, this is an enjoyable set, if not an essential one.

LEOTHUS LEE GREEN
St. Louis-born Green was a warm singer with a rich vibrato in his singing, and he was a fluid piano player who is reputed to have originated the "44s" on the piano. He was also an interesting and imaginative songwriter.

Blues Documents 2050 **The Remaining Titles, 1929–37**
Eighteen songs, complementing the album on Earl 609 and the half album on Magpie 4418 (now out-of-print) in reissuing all of his recordings. Very few of the tracks here have been reissued before and, though the sound on some tracks is pretty noisy, the record is generally quite listenable. Most worthwhile.

Earl BD 609 **Leothus Lee Green**
Eighteen great sides recorded between 1929–37. About half of these cuts have been issued before, and six of them were available on Magpie with better sound, but there is enough unreissued material here to make it well worthwhile.

LIL GREEN
ESSENTIAL SELECTION
Rosetta 1310 **Chicago, 1940–1947**
Lil Green was a superb and expressive singer who died tragically at the age of 35. She is featured here in the company of guitar, piano, bass trios, or with small jazz-flavored bands with horns. The sound is, as usual for Rosetta, exemplary, although the liner notes spend too much time carping about the lack of available information on Green's career. In spite of

some reservations, the music on this album is fabulous and not to be missed.

BIG JOHN GREER
Official 6026 **R&B in New York City**
Fine collection of New York blues and R&B recorded between 1951–55 by singer and tenor sax player Greer.

GREY GHOST (ROOSEVELT THOMAS WILLIAMS)
Catfish 1001 **Grey Ghost**
Catfish Records is a label from Austin dedicated to preserving the Texas blues tradition; this first album features 1965 field recordings of veteran singer/piano player Roosevelt Thomas Williams, aka Grey Ghost. Ghost has been active since the 20s and is still performing at the age of 84. He is a musician in the Texas barrelhouse tradition. Unfortunately, on these sessions he was playing a very poor piano, and the recording quality is poor, resulting in some difficult listening at times. His material is varied, ranging from some fine original rolling blues and boogie like "Lonesome Traveler" and "Way Out In The Desert" to R&B songs like "Oke-She-Moke-She-Bop," pop songs like "A Good Man Is Hard To Find," to covers of Mercy Dee's "One Room Country Shack" and Dr. Clayton's "Hold That Train Conductor." Except for my reservations about the sound quality, this album is certainly worth a listen.

JOHNNY GRIFFIN with THE JOE MORRIS ORCHESTRA
Saxophonograph BP-504 **Fly Mister Fly**
Johnny Griffin was one of the many tenor players influenced by the great Charlie "Bird" Parker. Griffin straddled that transitionary fence in jazz when bebop and swing turned to R&B. Alas, Griffin rarely gets to show his colors on this album, featuring one of the pioneer big bands of R&B, The Joe Morris Orchestra. Highlights include the McNeely-like "The Spider" (1947), the bootin' "Weasel Walk" (1948), and "Beans and Cornbread" (1949), reminiscent of early Johnny Otis sides. Detailed sleeve notes by Jonas Bernholm. Good sound quality.

TINY GRIMES
Tiny was one of the most distinctive and accomplished R&B guitarists, with a forceful horn-like approach similar to T-Bone Walker's but even more inventive and fluid.

Krazy Kat 804 **Tiny Grimes and His Rocking Highlanders on Gotham, Vol. I**
Reissued here for the first time in album form is guitarist Grimes' best jump and ballad R&B

material, containing four cuts with Wynonie Harris-inspired vocalist J. B. Summers and two amazing sides by the weeping, wailing Screamin' Jay Hawkins at his first recording date. Other standouts include J. B. on "Hey Now" and "Hey Mr. J. B.," Doc Bagby on "My Baby Left Me," and George "Haji Baba" Grant on "I'm In Love With You Baby." No duplication with previous reissues. Great notes by Tony Burke.

Krazy Kat 817 **Tiny Grimes and His Rocking Highlanders, Vol. II**
Another collection of Tiny's frantic Gotham sides from the early 50s, all instrumentals except for a band vocal on "Ho Ho Ho," one of only four previously released tunes in this set (the others are "Call Of The Wild," "Pert Skirt," and "1626 Boogie"). There are four tunes never before issued in any form, including two takes of "Bananas" and hot, never-before-issued alternate takes of four tunes, including "Call Of The Wild" and "Frankie and Johnny Boogie." Lots of great John Hardee tenor sax.

Oldie Blues 8009 **Rockin' and Sockin'**
Whiskey, Women And . . . 706 **Loch Lomand**
COMPACT DISC
Krazy Kat KKCD 01 **Tiny Grimes and His Rockin' Highlanders**
Highlights from Tiny Grimes' Gotham recordings (issued on Krazy Kat LPs 804 and 817) are brought forth on this 20-track CD. Sadly the early Screamin' Jay Hawkins cuts are not included, but Gotham vocalists J. B. Summers, George Grant, and Claudine Clark all make appearances, backed up by Tiny, the Rockin' Highlanders, and tenor man Red Prysock (who became an ex-Highlander soon after kilts became the band's standard outfit). The sound on disc is greatly improved, due to the use of master tapes and re-equalization. So look no further if you're after jumpin' early R&B, with some of the finest solos and swingingest East Coast grooves ever heard.

HELEN GROSS
Document 542 **(1924–25)**
Seventeen sides by the obscure Ms. Gross, one of the early "classic" or vaudeville-type blues singers to record in New York. Although she is not the most compelling vocalist, these performances are nonetheless distinguished, apart from their extreme rarity, by some fine lyrics and the presence of some of New York's better jazz players, including Ellington greats Bubber Miley and Louis Metcalf and stride pianist Cliff Jackson. Taken in bulk, these quickly tire, but one-at-a-time there is some good

music to be heard here. Sound, for acoustical recordings, is better than I expected.

GUITAR GABLE
Flyright 599 **Cool Calm Collected**
From the archives of Louisiana record producer Jay Miller come 14 sides by an excellent band led by guitarist Gable. A mixture of blues, rocking R&B, and Louisiana-style ballads; most of the vocals are by King Karl, and the small band features one or two horns. Six of the cuts here are previously unissued. Goodbye Baby/Congo Mombo/String Bean/Please Operator.

GUITAR NUBBITT
Matchbox MB 1201 **Re-Living the Legend**
If you buy this seven track 12" 45 for no other reason, you owe it to yourself to hear Guitar Nubbitt's "Georgia Chain Gang," which is surely one of the greatest country blues recorded in the postwar era. Recorded for the small Boston label Bluestown in 1962, it is a truly remarkable performance. It is a story song full of weird, almost surrealistic images ("I whistled to my shotgun/It crawled down from the wall/I pulled its tongue and it bellowed and barked") sung with a passion and conviction in a distinctive and unique voice that is propelled along by his energetic and percussive guitar. Apparently an album was recorded of this outstanding performer, but the tapes have never surfaced; it is something to be hoped for! Absolutely recommended to anyone who loves country blues!

GUITAR SLIM (EDDIE JONES)
Eddie "Guitar Slim" Jones was a brilliant New Orleans singer and guitarist best known for the original version of the all-time blues classic "The Things I Used To Do." During his all-too-brief career (he died at age 33), he recorded some great sides and was a tremendous influence on many blues artists. His best recordings are those made for Specialty in 1954 and '55.

ESSENTIAL SELECTION
Ace CHD 110 **The Things That I Used to Do**
Sixteen cuts recorded for Specialty between 1953–56. Although this includes all the tracks previously reissued in the US on Specialty 2120, this album draws on the original master tapes; the Specialty LP draws on later versions that feature overdubbed organ and second guitar. This album has been digitally transferred for the best possible sound on Slim's voice and guitar.
Ace CHD 189 **Guitar Slim and Earl King: Battle of the Blues**
A full LP of hard-to-find Specialty material by Slim

and his number-one disciple. The nine Slim tunes on Side one are either new to LP or never before issued, including a jumpin' remake of "Certainly All," originally recorded for Bullet, plus "Goin' Down Slow," along with alternate takes of "Reap What You Sow" and "I Got Sumpin' For You." Earl's eight tunes are his impossible-to-find Specialty singles, including his first hit, "A Mother's Love," released as Earl Johnson, and "What Can I Do," released as by The Kings, who were Earl and Huey "Piano" Smith.

Atlantic 81760-1 (c) **The Atco Sessions**

Presents all the recordings he made for Atco between 1956 and '58, his last recordings. It includes both sides of his four Atco singles, one track that was only available on a long-deleted album, and six tracks that have never been issued before in any form. Six tracks were recorded in New Orleans with top New Orleans sidemen and the rest were recorded in New York with excellent bands. Although several of the songs fall into the novelty category, there are also some of Slim's distinctive blues ballads that give his gospel-flavored vocals and stinging guitar full reign. The unissued sides include a brilliant version of Gatemouth Brown's "My Time Is Expensive" and two takes of "Guitar Slim Boogie," his only recorded instrumental and one that also seems to owe a debt to Gatemouth. Excellent sound, informative notes by Jeff "Almost Slim" Hannusch, and full discographical information.

Specialty 2120 (c) **The Things I Used to Do**

Twelve classic Specialty recordings, although Ace CHD 110 (see above), with more songs, better sound, and undubbed masters, is a better choice.

Sundown 709-08 **Red Cadillacs and Crazy Chicks**

There are three great sides from his best period (1954–55), featuring Slim's wonderful gospel-tinged voice and distinctive guitar accompanied by a tough, hard-driving band. There are three sides from his first recording sessions in 1951; good, solid urban blues but lacking the unique sound that was to make Slim such a big influence. The remaining nine tracks were recorded between 1956–58 and are a mixed bag, as his record label was experimenting to get a more commercial sound, and so there are more pop R&B ballads and silly songs. But in spite of the occasional questionable material, there is some great singing and playing from Slim. Good sound, discographical information, and informative notes.

GUITAR SLIM and JELLY BELLY

Alec Seward and "Fat Boy" Hayes, recording under the names Guitar Slim and Jelly Belly, performed relaxed East Country blues from the 40s.

Arhoolie 2005 **Carolina Blues**

GUITAR SLIM

This is the third Guitar Slim to appear on record. This one is a fine country blues singer/guitarist and piano player from North Carolina recorded in the 70s.

Flyright 538 **Greensboro Rounder**

GUITAR SLIM, JR.

Orleans 4188 **Guitar Slim, Jr.**

Rodney Armstrong is, apparently, really the son of Eddie "Guitar Slim" Jones and, just to prove it, most of his first album features covers of his dad's songs performed very much in the style of his father. Nothing wrong with that except that his dad did it so much better. The only non-Guitar Slim songs are rather mediocre versions of a couple of soul songs. Forgettable.

ARTHUR GUNTER

Excello 8017 **Black and Blues**

BUDDY GUY

Fine Chicago singer and electric guitarist. His Chess recordings of the 50s and 60s and his 60s Vanguard LPs are particularly fine. His 70s recordings are often marred by an overabundance of vocal and guitar histrionics.

Alligator 4723 (c,d) **Stone Crazy**

Buddy accompanied by a rhythm section only on an album first released on the French Isabel label. Some good moments if a little excessive.

Chess 9115 (c) **Buddy Guy**

Twelve fine sides, previously issued in this form by English Chess; same mediocre cover, too! Broken Hearted Blues/First Time I Met The Blues/Hard But Fair/Stone Crazy/Stick Around/Leave My Girl Alone/I Got My Eyes On You.

Chess 9262 (c,d) **I Left My Blues in San Francisco**

Reissue of Chess 1527 from 1967. This is a bit of a mixed bag, featuring Buddy on a selection of songs recorded between 1962 and 1967, with most coming from the 1965–67 period when he was beginning to come to the attention of a rock audience; this is reflected in some exaggeration in his already intense vocal style. He is at his best on the intense slow numbers like "When My Left Eye Jumps" or "Leave My Girl Alone," but for my liking there are too many lightweight Willie Dixon compositions like "Goin' Home" or "Too Many Ways." Hopefully MCA will get around to reissuing the vastly superior Chess 409 one of these days.

ESSENTIAL SELECTION

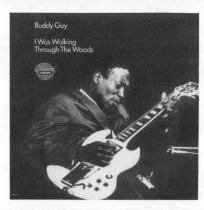

Chess 9315 (c,d) I Was Walkin' Through the Woods
Reissue of Buddy Guy's second Chess record, a collection of tracks culled from 1960–64 recordings. Ten fierce sides. Watch Yourself/Stone Crazy/First Time I Met The Blues/My Time After A While/10 Years Ago.

Red Lightnin' 001 In the Beginning
Great Chess and Artistic recordings, but all of them are available elsewhere with better sound.

Vanguard 79272 (d) A Man and the Blues
Vanguard 79290 This Is Buddy Guy
COMPACT DISC

Chess (France) 600176 Buddy Guy on Chess, Vol. I
This is the first volume in what promises to be an interesting series on French Chess reissuing all of Buddy Guy's US Chess recordings. It features his first 21 recordings cut for that label between March 1960 and February 1963 in chronological order, which are probably his best recordings. Intense heartfelt vocals and searing, imaginative guitar with accompaniments by great Chicago sidemen like Jarrett Gibson (ten sax), Donald Hankins (bar sax), Little Brother Montgomery (pno), Fred Below (drm), Otis Spann (pno), Junior Wells (hca), Bob Neely (ten sax), and Abb Locke (ten sax). Sound, like most French Chess CDs, is not outstanding though is satisfactory. Stereo mix on a couple of cuts is also a little dubious but otherwise this is a most worthwhile set. Broken Hearted Blues/First Time I Met the Blues/I Got A Strange Feeling/10 Years Ago/Stone Crazy (extended seven-minute version)/I Found A True Love/Hard But It's Fair/When My Left Eye Jumps/The Treasure Untold.

Chess (France) 600213 On Chess Vol. II
JSP CD 201 Live at the Checkerboard Lounge
1979 recordings; reedited version of JSP LP 1009 with extra tracks. Buddy's Blues/Tell Me What's Inside Of You/The Things I Used To Do/The Dollar Done Fell/Don't Answer The Door.

JSP CD 215 Breaking Out
This makes me want to break out in hives. Buddy recorded in 1980 with a small band, including his brother Phil on guitar. This is Buddy at his most excessive with overloud, distorted Hendrix-style guitar and aimless screaming. Not my cup of tea at all, I'm afraid.

BUDDY GUY and JUNIOR WELLS
Blind Pig 1182 (c,d) Drinkin' TNT 'n' Smokin' Dynamite
US issue of fine set previously available on Red Lightnin'. Some tasty performances recorded live in Montreux in 1974 with Bill Wyman, Pinetop Perkins, and Dallas Taylor.
COMPACT DISC

Black and Blue 59.530 2 Plus the Chicago Blues All Stars '78—Live in Montreux
CD reissue of Black & Blue 33.530 recorded live at Montreux in July 1977, with five previously unissued tracks. Buddy and Junior are accompanied by an all-star group including Jimmy Johnson, Eddie Clearwater, Hubert Sumlin, Dave Myers, and Odie Payne on 16 mostly familiar songs. One Room Country Shack/Everyday I Have the Blues/Help Me/Messin' with the Kid/Everything Gonna Be Alright/Hide Away/I Don't Know/Blue Shadow Is Falling.

PHIL GUY
Red Lightnin' 0062 Tough Guy
Eight tunes recorded live at Roma's in Chicago, Sept. 17, 1983. Performance is dull, plodding, boring, and poorly recorded. Features sax great A. C. Reed, who sounds here as if he's playing off-key more than on. Includes covers of Z. Z. Hill's "Down Home Blues," Amos Milburn's "Chicken Shack," and Albert Collins's "Frosty."
COMPACT DISC

JSP CD 214 All Star Chicago Blues Session
CD issue of 1982 tracks originally on JSP 1047 and 1061, with Buddy Guy (gtr), Professor Eddie Lusk (kybds), Maurice John Vaughn (sax), and Larry Cox (hca). Songs are a mix of originals and old favorites like "Texas Flood," "Blues With A Feeling," and "Born Under A Bad Sign" (here mistitled "Bad Luck Boy"). Guy is a decent, though unexceptional, singer and guitarist, and the band, though all Chicago stalwarts, are generally unexciting. This CD version has

been remixed and remastered and gives us 63 minutes of fairly dull music.

JSP CD 226 **Tina Nu**

JOHN HAMMOND

Urban blues revivalist (and son of noted record producer John Hammond Sr.), who has been active on the blues scene for more than 25 years.

Edsel 129 **Spoonful**

Sixteen tracks, 10 from his 1967 Atlantic album, "I Can Tell"—produced by Leiber and Stoller, with Robbie Robertson, Bill Wyman, and Rick Danko—and six tracks from his 1970 Atlantic album, "Southern Fried," with varied personnel, including horns on some tracks.

Rounder 3042 (c) **Mileage**

Rounder 3060 (c) **Frogs for Snakes**

Rounder 3074 (c) **Live**

Vanguard VSD 11/12 (c,d) **The Best of John Hammond**

Twenty-two tracks including My Babe/No Money Down/See That My Grave Is Kept Clean/32-20 Blues/Stones In My Passway/Statesboro Blues/Key To the Highway/Who Do You Love.

COMPACT DISC

Rounder CD 11532 **John Hammond**

Twenty-two tracks drawn from Hammond's three Rounder LPs; over 60 minutes of music.

MAJOR HANDY

GNP Crescendo GNPS 2177 **Wolf Couchon**

Zydeco with a soul flavor by singer/accordion player Handy and his group The Musical Wolf Couchons. Handy is a good soul-oriented singer whose voice is well-suited to most of the material here. Songs like "I've Reached The Turning Point" and "All About You" are pretty much straight soul with Zydeco instrumentation, while "Zydeco Cha Cha" and "Paper In My Shoe" are almost straight Zydeco. The album ends with a fine version of Clifton Chenier's wonderful minor-key blues "I'm On A Wonder." Nice singing and playing but not very good sound quality.

W. C. HANDY

Pioneer blues composer.

DRG 5192 **Father of the Blues**

Reissue of 1952 and 1953 recordings featuring Handy talking about his life and music. The spoken material is moderately interesting, but the musical excerpts by Handy and others are hideous!

THE HARLEM HAMFATS

The Hamfats were an unclassifiable septet whose repertoire ranged over blues, jazz, string band, pop, and hokum, all given a light, bawdy treatment. Featuring Joe McCoy (gtr, vcl), Charlie McCoy (mdln), and Herb Morand (tpt).

Blues Documents 2045 **Keep It Swinging Round and Round**

Enjoyable collection of 16 sides recorded between 1936–38 by this lively and popular 30s group. Nine of the vocals feature the distinctive gravel voice of Joe McCoy, while the rest have vocals by Alberta Smith or Lil Allen. Most of these tracks have not been on LP before and a few are from rather worn 78s.

Document 547 **Harlem Hamfats 1936–1939**

Twenty cuts featuring great swingin' trumpet and clarinet ("Take Me In Your Alley" and "Toodle Oo Blues"), raggy guitar and mandolin ("What's My Baby Doin'?" and "What's On Your Mind?"), fine piano ("Little Girl"), and exuberant vocals, blending elements of Louis Armstrong and Fats Waller. Marvelous good timey music!

Folklyric 9029 **Hot Chicago Jazz, Blues and Jive**

Wolf 1007 **The Remaining Titles**

Seventeen tracks recorded between 1936–39, including accompaniments to Rosetta Howard. Most tracks not previously on LP.

JAMES HARMAN BAND

Rivera RR 505 **Extra Napkins**

Pay no attention to the tasteless cover and obnoxious liner notes; it's what's in the grooves that counts, and this is a fine contemporary blues record. Harman and band jump, wail, and sweat their way through seven originals and five loving covers. James is a marvelous harp player (check out the title cut if you need convincing) whose blowing evokes Junior Wells, Big Walter, Snooky Pryor, and other Chicago greats. The guitar work by the late Hollywood Fats and Kid Ramos is blistering but seldom excessive. Find yourself a smoky room, break out the booze, call up your friends, and play this one LOUD!

Rivera RR 506 (d) **Strictly Live in '85**

A warts-and-all live set recorded at The Belly Up Tavern, Solano Beach, CA, in 1985. They warm up the crowd with a couple of slow blues tunes, then move to a boogie-paced "You're Gone" with Harman blowin' some mean harp and the remarkable Hollywood Fats ripping some mighty licks. Side two catches the show shifting into overdrive with a killer jump blues, "That's Not Your Baby," and a live version of "Goatman Holler."

COMPACT DISC

Rhino 70837-2 (21S) **Those Dangerous Gentlemens**

SLIM HARPO

Outstanding Louisiana blues singer and harp player. The Flyright albums are great, featuring issued and unissued recordings, and alternate takes of songs recorded by Jay Miller. The Rhino album is a great cross-section of his most popular sides.

Flyright 520 **Blues Hangover**
Flyright 558 **Got Love if You Want It**
Flyright 593 **Shake Your Hips**

Twelve great sides that were originally issued on Excello between 1959 and 1965, with Slim accompanied by fine musicians such as James Johnson and Rudolph Richard (gtr). Shake Your Hips/Harpo's Blues/My Little Queen Bee/Baby, Scratch My Back/Rainin' In My Heart.

ESSENTIAL SELECTION

Rhino R1 70169 (c,d) **The Best of Slim Harpo**

Repackaged and remastered version of album originally issued some years ago as Rhino 106. Fourteen great recordings cut for Excello between 1957 and 1967, plus one from 1970. It includes all his best-known songs and blues "hits," along with lesser-known songs. Harpo was a unique and distinctive stylist with his nasal vocal style and brittle but effective harmonica accompanied by Jay Miller's cadre of outstanding studio musicians. Sound is superb and, if you get the compact disc version, there are four extra songs, mostly lightweight but including the wonderful "Strange Love." If you want his most well-known songs get this collection; if you want rarities and unissued songs get the Flyrights; if you want a balanced collection of this fine artist get both. Baby Scratch My Back/I'm A King Bee/Blues Hangover/Shake Your Hips/Rainin' In My Heart/Don't Start Cryin' Now/Tip On In.

COMPACT DISC

Flyright FLYCD 05 **I'm a King Bee**

Twenty-one tracks by this distinctive Louisiana bluesman drawn from his two albums on Flyright (Flyright 520 and 558). Although some of the songs may appear to duplicate tracks on the Rhino collection, the versions here are alternate takes, along with unissued songs. Most of the tracks here are from the earlier years of his recording career (1957–61), including two of his very finest recordings, "This Ain't No Place For Me" and "That Ain't Your Business," which, remarkably, were never originally issued. Also included are alternate takes of some of his most famous songs ("I'm A King Bee," "I Got Love If You Want It," "Blues Hangover") and other gems, includ-

ing the very weird "Strange Love" that has long been one of my favorites. Sound is not up to the standard of the Rhino reissue but is certainly acceptable.

JIMMY LEE HARRIS

Southland SLP 11 **I Wanna Ramble**

Interesting new country-blues discovery from Alabama. Lee sings and plays regular and slide guitar and produces interesting harmonica-like sounds with his hands only. Several cuts also feature his brother Eddie on vocal and guitar. Mostly original songs

PEPPERMINT HARRIS

Urban blues singer from Houston, Texas.

Ace CHD 267 **Houston Can't Be Heaven**

This LP is a mixed bag. One side features really hot, recently unearthed Combo material (only one 45 rpm was ever issued) featuring the young Albert Collins on guitar. Eight tunes (plus an alternate take) cut at Goldstar for Jake Porter (Combo owner) are included here. Side two is made up of late 50s and early 60s material recorded at ACA studio in Houston, Texas. Harris's voice, never that strong to begin with, doesn't really cut it on these tunes; the strong backup band draws even more attention to the lack of good singing by Harris. I Got To Go/Let's Go To The Chicken Shack/Houston Can't Be Heaven/I Don't Care/ Foot Loose.

Home Cooking 116 **Being Black Twice**

Peppermint Harris was never a great singer, though he did make some good records; unfortunately, none of them are here. These 14 tracks come from four different sessions in 1958, 1960, 1974, and 1975. Most of the tracks are previously unissued and I'm not surprised; Harris's singing is dull and unemotional and the arrangements are unimaginative, some of it sounding like a lounge-club act. The tracks with only the piano of Honeymoon Davis are moderately listenable and his song about Watergate, "The President's Lawyer," is interesting, but most of this is expendable.

Route 66 KIX 23 **I Got Loaded**

A high-quality reissue, featuring 17 sides recorded between 1950 and 1953 in Houston and Los Angeles with small-band accompaniments.

PEPPERMINT HARRIS/ELMORE NIXON

Sundown 709-12 **Shout and Rock**

Side one features nine sides by plummy-voiced Texas blues shouter Peppermint Harris recorded in Los Angeles and Houston between 1950–55 with various small bands. The material is varied, as are the accompaniments. Some are a little ponderous for my liking, but the almost rockabilly-flavored "Angel Child" is a real treat. Side two features 10 sides by singer/piano player Elmore Nixon, who is best known for his accompaniments on many Houston blues recordings in the 40s, 50s, and 60s. Nixon was not a terribly exciting singer with a very light voice, and the instrumental work seems a little heavy handed to me.

PEPPERMINT HARRIS/PERCY MAYFIELD
COMPACT DISC
P-Vine PCD 2516 **Here Come the Blues**
Four songs by Percy and 15 by Peppermint.

WYNONIE HARRIS
Powerful 40s-50s blues shouter and R&B singer.

Gusto 5040X **Good Rockin' Blues**
Two-LP set; 22 excellent 50s sides.

Official 6024 **Here Comes the Blues**
Just about the last important Wynonie Harris sessions to appear for the first time in album reissue, including rare early sides circa 1945–46. Impressive shouters include "Wynonie's Blues," "Come Baby Baby," and "Good Morning Corinne." Good teasing version of "Somebody Changed The Lock On My Door," plus a handful of tasty straight-ahead blues ballads not found on other collections. Musical support is charted by such luminaries as Illinois Jacquet, Jack McVea, and Joe Morris. Some 78 rpm surface noise on a couple of cuts but good audio quality overall.

Route 66 KIX 3 **Mr. Blues Is Coming to Town**
Fine retrospective of his recordings.

Route 66 KIX 20 **Oh Babe!**
Sixteen sides from 1945–54. With notes by his longtime friend and associate Preston Love.

Route 66 KIX 30 **Playful Baby**
Reaches back to the early Apollo sides of 1945 with gems like "I Gotta Lyin' Woman," backed by the Oscar Pettiford All Stars, and forward to 1954 with stompers like "Git With The Grits," backed by the great Sonny Thompson Band. The album ends with "Good Mambo Tonight," a 1954 update of his big seller "Good Rockin' Tonight." Fine sleeve notes by Jonas Bernholm and a wealth of rare party pics of the shouter from Omaha himself.
COMPACT DISC

ESSENTIAL SELECTION
Charly CD 244 **Good Rockin' Tonight**
Twenty jumping sides recorded for King between 1947–53. Good Rocking Tonight/Blow Your Brains Out/All She Wants to Do Is Rock/Baby, Shame on You/Wynonie's Boogie/Good Morning Judge/

Lovin' Machine/Quiet Whiskey/Bloodshot Eyes/ Down Boy Down.

WYNONIE HARRIS/ROY BROWN
King 607 **Battle of the Blues, Vol. II**
COMPACT DISC
King KCD 627 **Battle of the Blues**

WILBERT HARRISON
Wilbert Harrison is a fine and distinctive singer who occasionally works as a one-man band. He has a recording career going back to 1953; since then, he has recorded for dozens of labels. He is a unique and eccentric artist whose music, though bearing a strong affinity to the blues, is often not straight blues.

Charly CRB 1102 **Lovin' Operator**
Brings together mostly sides recorded for Bobby Robinson's Fury label in the late 50s and early 60s along with assorted other sides, including the great driving title song recorded for Brunswick in 1974. Wilbert sings a wide variety of material—blues, R&B, ballads, even a great version of the old-time country tune "On Top of Old Smokey"—all given the distinctive Harrison touch with occasional reedy harp by him. It includes his big hit "Kansas City." Blueberry Hill/Why Did You Leave?/ Pretty Little Women/Let's Stick Together.

Grudge GR 0960 (d) **Greatest Hits**
This is a reissue of sides made by Wilbert in the late 60s for Sue. On these, Wilbert is a one-man band, singing and playing guitar, harmonica, and drums, which, together with his distinctive voice, makes for a unique sound. The album opens with Wilbert's version of the now popular "Stand By Me" and includes versions of other R&B favorites like "C.C. Rider," "Stagger Lee," and "What Am I Living For?," and a remake of his biggest hit, "Kansas City." The rest of the album includes Harrison specialties like "Tropical Shakedown," "Soul Rattler," "Cheatin' Baby," and his minor 1969 hit "Let's Work Together."

Krazy Kat 7439 **The Small Labels**
A delightful collection of songs recorded for various small labels between 1953 and the mid-60s. Includes variations on his most popular song, "Kansas City," including "This Woman Of Mine," which predates that hit by several years, and the lively "New York World's Fair." This album also features Caribbean-flavored songs like "Calypso Man" and a surprising version of "Cool Water." There are also teen ballads like "After Graduation" and "Off To School Again," and rocking R&B like "Off To Work Again" (an adult version of "Off To School Again") and Willie Mabon's "Poison Ivy." The accompaniments are as

varied as the material and some cuts include hot sax work—a few feature some bizarre harmonica playing—all held together by Wilbert's unusual slurred vocals.

Line 4.00434 **Let's Work Together**
Reissue of classic 1969 Sue album.

Savoy 1182 **Listen to My Song**
After leaving DeLuxe Records in 1953, Harrison signed with Savoy where he cut six singles (every one included here). Alas, they met with little success, which is sad because, after his DeLuxe efforts, these remain his finest sides, partly due to guitarist Mickey Baker, who played on almost all of the sessions, and support given by The Buddy Lucas Band. Great straight-forward uncomplicated 50s R&B. Includes four alternate takes and one cut with The Roamers. First-rate notes by Peter B. Lowry. Highly recommended.

COMPACT DISC

P-Vine PCD 1614 **Da-De-Ya-Da**
The material here ranges from hard blues ("I Will Never Trust Another Woman") to country (a truly anarchic version of "Cold, Cold Heart") to soul blues ("Near To You") to a version of "On Top Of Old Smokey," complete with tremolo guitar, traps, and fiddle!! I assume these tracks are from the late 50s and 60s. Jimmy Spruill's distinctive guitar playing is present on several tracks and presumably Wilbert is playing the tremolo guitar, harmonica, and traps. Not for the faint of heart!!

ROY HAWKINS
Fine West Coast singer and piano player active in the 40s and 50s.

Route 66 KIX 9 **Why Do Everything Happen to Me?**
Reissue of 40s and 50s recordings, some with great guitar by Ulysses James.

TED HAWKINS
Remarkable and original artist, singer, and songwriter who incorporates elements of blues and soul into his original and personal songs. Ted is a soulful blues singer who sounds at times like a blend of Sam Cooke, Taj Mahal, and Otis Redding. He uses basic open C guitar tuning and sings with overwhelming directness. The many trials and tribulations in his life have given his music that extra edge. Ted Hawkins' song-stories have that powerful, raw intensity that is lacking in most artists performing today!

American Activities BRAVE 2 **On the Boardwalk: The Venice Beach**
CD issue: Munich MRCD 123 **On the Boardwalk**
This was recorded in Nashville in '82. Hawkins performs mostly other people's material. He gives fresh interpretations to the C&W standards "Green Green Grass Of Home" and "Your Cheatin' Heart," and covers several soul/R&B gems—"Gypsy Woman," "Bring It On Home To Me," "I Got What I Wanted," "It Will Break Your Heart"—with remarkable conviction and simplicity. Ted strolls into the blues garden with his own "Ladder Of Success" and takes "Part Time Love" and the surreal "Quiet Place" to new heights.

Rounder 2024 **Watch Your Step**
Recorded by Bruce Bromberg in 1971 and 1972. Four cuts feature him with a tough, driving band led by Phillip Walker while the rest feature his own acoustic guitar accompaniment only. With excellent notes by Peter Guralnick.

Rounder 2033 **Happy Hour**
A superlative set of 12 tunes (10 originals) that embrace a multitude of genres. For the most part, Hawkins carries the album solely by his simplistic approach to acoustic guitar coupled with an honest, no-nonsense vocal delivery. On three tunes, "My Last Goodbye," "California Song," and the Hank Williams-flavored title track, Ted is joined by a backing quartet, the Angry Old Men. The other cover tune is the Curtis Mayfield classic "Gypsy Woman." Joining Ted on this and "You Pushed My Head Away" is guitarist "Night Train" Clemons, who sounds a lot like Robert Cray. Simple pleasures like Ted Hawkins are very rare these days.

WALTER "BUDDY BOY" HAWKINS
Excellent and mysterious blues singer. Hawkins is a unique stylist and a fine singer and a very fluid guitarist. Various suggestions place his home as Arkansas, Alabama, Mississippi, or Texas.

Matchbox 202 **Walter "Buddy Boy" Hawkins**
This album reissues all 12 songs recorded for Paramount between 1927–29; seven of these were previously issued on Yazoo 1010.

Yazoo 1010 **Buddy Boy Hawkins and His Buddies**
Half of the album is by Hawkins, the rest by Texas bluesmen like Will Day, Texas Alexander, and Willie Reed.

Note: Other reissues on Mamlish 3809 and Yazoo 1004.

CLIFFORD HAYES and HIS DIXIELAND JUG BLOWERS

Mostly jazz-oriented jug band with Hayes (vln) and Earl McDonald (jug).

Wolf WJS 1005 Vol. I: 1926–30

This album is all blues featuring 10 tracks by Sara Martin's Jug Band, including Hayes and McDonald. There are eight fine vocals and two spirited instrumental sides. Four tracks feature Hayes accompanying singer/piano player Kid Coley—a fairly undistinguished singer—and the remaining two feature singer John Harris, one of them featuring the jug band. Sound quality on some of the Sara Martin tracks is pretty rough but is generally satisfactory.

Yazoo 1054 Clifford Hayes and the Dixieland Jug Blowers

THE HEARTFIXERS

Good solid white blues band from Atlanta, GA, featuring black vocalist and harmonica player Chicago Bob Nelson.

Landslide 1007 Live

Live recordings cut at the Moonshadow Saloon in Atlanta, GA; mostly familiar songs. Night Train/A Losing Battle/Trick Bag/Talk To Me Baby.

Landslide 1010 Cool on It

1986 album, recorded without Nelson, is a lively mixture of blues, R&B, and rock 'n' roll. Most of the songs are originals. The vocals are generally undistinguished though the band is good and the use of several horns gives the music a thick sound.

Southland SLP 12 The Heartfixers

Some spirited performances of familiar and unfamiliar material.

JOHNNY HEARTSMAN

Crosscut 1018 (d) Sacramento

This is a real gem. Although singer/guitarist/keyboard and flute player Heartsman has been a significant contributor to the West Coast blues scene, this is only the third album under his own name and his first solid blues album. Johnny is a powerful, deep-voiced singer and one of the greatest of all contemporary blues guitarists, with a fleet-fingered but not fussy style accentuated by imaginative chording and effective tremolo effects using the volume control on his Stratocaster. All but one of the 10 songs here is a Heartsman original and show him to be a witty and sophisticated songwriter. In addition to vocals and guitar, Johnny also provides bass and organ accompaniment and is joined by fellow Sacramentan Rex Kline on drums. Two tracks also add the tenor sax of Gary Wiggins. This is the album those of us who've had a chance to see Heartsman

live have been waiting for him to record. Unreservedly recommended.

ERWIN HELFER

Chicago-based white piano player.

Flying Fish 210 Erwin Helfer and Friends

Blues, boogie, and jazz, with S. P. Leary and Odie Payne, Jr.

Red Beans 003 Live at the Piano Man

Red Beans 010 Erwin Helfer Plays Chicago Piano

Fine two-fisted solo piano, Chicago style. Recorded in 1986, Helfer does much to invoke the spirits of the great Chicago pianists—Meade Lux Lewis, Albert Ammons, and Jimmy Yancey—on four originals and seven standards. Pooch Piddle/After Work It's Just Me And A Empty Chair Blues/C.C. Rider/All Of Me/Since I Lost My Baby.

JESSIE MAE HEMPHILL

High Water 1012 Feelin' Good

Mississippi singer/guitarist Jessie Mae Hemphill is a unique and distinctive performer. She is a fine, moving singer, and her guitar playing draws on traditional Mississippi styles which she uses as a framework to generate hypnotic and haunting riffs. Her material is a mixture of originals and songs based on traditional elements. This is her first album on a US label. Side one has her accompanied by a second guitar and drums which gives it a slightly more contemporary feel. On Side two, she plays guitar and percussion at the same time. An excellent collection.

Vogue 513.501 She-Wolf

Fine Mississippi country-blues woman singing mostly original songs in traditional vein, accompanying herself on electric guitar and tambourine, with occasional second guitar and drums. Includes one track where she plays a home made "diddleybow" (mouthbow). Some fascinating and hypnotic music, produced by noted field researcher David Evans.

HEZEKIAH and THE HOUSE ROCKERS

High Water 421 (45 rpm) Do Your Thing/Low Down Dirty Shame

Fascinating Mississippi trio—vocal, guitar, harmonica, drums, and trombone! The trombone, believe it or not, fits in well with their arrangements.

High Water 1011 Hezekiah and the House Rockers

Hezekaiah Early's trio is a litle different than your usual blues group. In additional to the traditional lineup of guitar, harmonica, and drums (the latter two both played by Early), the group also features 80-plus-year-old Pee Wee Whittaker on trombone. The trombone is used as a lead instrument, rather than just riffing, and the effect, combined with the boogie guitar lines, is quite novel. Unfortunately, the playing is not exceptional and the choice of material is pretty dull, with Jimmy Reed covers, blues ballads, rock 'n' roll songs, and even "When the Saints Go Marching In." From a musical point of view, the most interesting tracks are those without the trombone, where Early gets to play some lively harmonica. A charming novelty item in small doses, but over an LP one's interest is likely to wane.

BLIND JOE HILL
L+R 42.059 **First Chance**
Joe Hill is one of the few surviving purveyors of the one-man band tradition, accompanying himself on guitar, bass, and drums. Hill's playing on all of these instruments is competent, though not exceptional, and after a while the sound becomes a little tiresome. He performs a mixture of original songs along with several from the repertoire of his hero Jimmy Reed. The album's title song is an interesting autobiographical piece, as is his "P. D. Blues."

Z. Z. HILL
Excellent artist who helped to bring back the blues to modern black consciousness by mixing blues and contemporary soul stylings. His vocal approach had touches of Bobby Bland and Johnny Taylor. He died in 1984.
Kent 018 **Dues Paid in Full**
Malaco 7402 **Z. Z. Hill**
Malaco 7406 **Down Home**
Includes his most celebrated song, "Down Home Blues," which has been one of the most popular blues song of the 80s.
Malaco 7411 **The Rhythm and the Blues**
Divided between contemporary blues stylings and modern soul and R&B. As a blues fan, I don't find the soul cuts too interesting but the blues are very good.
Malaco 7415 **I'm a Bluesman**
Like his previous albums, there are only a couple of straight blues; the rest of the album has a late-60s deep-soul flavor that is very gospel influenced. Cheatin' Love/It's Been So Long/Steal Away/Blind Love.
Malaco 7420 **Bluesmaster**
The last recordings made before his premature death in 1984. A fine mixture of soul-flavored blues and blues-flavored soul. You're Ruining My Bad Reputation/She Got The Goods On Me/Personally.

Malaco 7426 **In Memoriam, 1935–84**
A fine cross-section of sides drawn from his five Malaco albums recorded between 1980–84. It includes, of course, his most popular side "Down Home Blues," along with other fine sides like "When It Rains It Pours," "Someone Else Is Steppin' In," and "Get You Some Business." Unlike most of his albums that were a mixture of blues and soul, this one is just about all blues. With a touching tribute to Z. Z. by famous R&B deejay John R., who passed away himself in 1986.
Tuff City 4439 **Turn Back the Hands of Time**
An excellent collection of R&B, soul, and blues recorded in 1968 and 1972 and mostly issued on small Los Angeles labels, along with some previously unissued songs. Highlights of the album are the wonderful soul blues "Don't Make Me Pay For His Mistakes" and the beautiful soul ballad "Nine Pound Steel" that will send shivers down your spine. But it's all good, including covers of the Temptations' "Ain't Too Proud Too Beg" and Tyrone Davis' "Turn Back The Hands Of Time," and the topical song "Think People." The original recordings have been remixed and, in some cases, have horns overdubbed, but this is all done tastefully.

ALGIA MAE HINTON
Audio Arts AAEP 009 (EP) **Piedmont Folk Traditions**
Five tracks by this excellent country blues singer and 12-string guitarist from North Carolina. Algia Mae is an engaging singer and an effective guitarist. Material includes a bluesy and effective version of the soul hit "Steal Away" that she calls "I've Got To See You Somehow," a couple of lovely raggy traditional Piedmont blues, a combination guitar instrumental/buck-dance piece, and a version of the spiritual "You've Got To Move." Comes in a picture sleeve with brief notes.

SILAS HOGAN
Down-home Louisiana bluesman.
Blues South West 003 **The Godfather**
Recorded in 1988 with a group of mostly local musicians. He performs a mix of new originals, remakes of some of his classic recordings, plus songs from Lightnin' Slim and Clifton Chenier. Silas is in pretty good form, though at 78 it's not too surprising that his music doesn't have the energy of earlier sides. The band is competent but unexceptional.
Excello 8019 **Trouble**
When it comes to down-home Louisiana blues, they

don't come much more low down than the blues of Silas Hogan. Although they were recorded between 1962–65, the tracks on this album could have easily been recorded 10 years earlier. Hogan's rich vocals and basic guitar are complemented by guitar, harmonica (usually Sylvester Buckley or Whispering Smith), bass, and drums. Most of Silas's songs are originals, but have a strong traditional feel to them. Highly recommended. Out and Down Blues/I'm Going To The Valley/I'm Gonna Quit You Baby/Airport Blues/Trouble At Home Blues

Flyright 595 I'm a Free Hearted Man
Only eight of the 14 sides feature Hogan as vocalist; the remainder feature him as lead or rhythm guitarist in bands backing Jimmy Dotson, Blue Boy Dorsey, or an unknown and undistinguished singer on "I Wanna Join The Army" and "Sweet Little Things You Do." The best tracks are those featuring Hogan as vocalist ("I'm A Free Hearted Man," "Born In Texas," "My Baby Walked Out"), where his rich vocals are accompanied by his funky guitar and often the fine harp playing of Whispering Smith.

SMOKEY HOGG

Hogg was a very popular and prolific artist from Texas who recorded well over 100 cuts between the late 30s and late 50s. He was an engaging singer and an interesting, if somewhat limited, guitarist. He has been largely ignored on reissue albums due to the similarity in much of his material. Frequently, Smokey seems to be fighting with his backup bands, another reason that his work has not received the attention that it deserves.

Crown Prince 409 Too Late Old Man — Jivin' Little Woman
Seventeen tracks covering the period 1947–58.

Krazy Kat 7421 Goin' Back Home
This carefully compiled selection presents 14 of Hogg's best sides recorded between 1948–54, and shows just how interesting he could be. These cuts feature him with various small combos.

THE HOKUM BOYS

Novelty and risque blues by Georgia Tom, Big Bill Broonzy, and others.

Blues Documents 2022 The Remaining Titles, 1929
Complementing titles on Yazoo 1051, LE 300.003 (out of print), and the long-out-of-print Riverside 8803, this presents all the remaining recordings by this group whose members here include either Georgia Tom Dorsey, Alex Hill, or Jimmy Blythe (pno) and Ikey Robinson, Tampa Red, Bob Robinson,

Alec Robinson, or Dan Roberts (gtr), with most sharing the vocal honors, often in duets. The instrumental work is always fine, but I am not too wild about the generally nondescript and often risque lyrics and uninspired vocals.

Yazoo 1051 You Can't Get Enough of That Stuff

THE HOLLYWOOD BLUES BAND
High Water 1009 Hard Hitting Blues from Memphis
Excellent blues band from Memphis (Hollywood is a black suburb of that city) who have been working together for more than 10 years producing solid, no-nonsense blues with a down-home flavor. The leader of the group is singer/guitarist Ben Wilson, who also wrote two of the songs here. Wilson is a husky intense singer and an effective guitarist who patterns his playing after early B. B. King. The accompanying band features piano or organ, two saxophones, bass, and drums. The saxes mostly just riff along without adding too much, and although William Hubbard is good keyboard player, I would have liked more piano and less organ. Still this is a satisfying record, featuring a couple of originals by Wilson plus good versions of "I'm Tore Down," "Mannish Boy," "It's Too Bad," and "Let Me Play With Your Poodle." The album also includes one solo track by Wilson, a country blues he learned when he was growing up in Rosemark, Tennessee.

High Water 417 (45 rpm) Long Way from Home/ Mary Jo

ROOSEVELT HOLTS

Louisiana country bluesman influenced by Tommy Johnson.

Arhoolie 1057 Roosevelt Holts and Friends
With Blind Pete Burrell, Boogie Bill Webb, and others.

Note: Holts can also be heard on Rounder 2012.

HOMESICK JAMES

Chicago singer/slide guitarist. He can be very fine, though his recordings are sometimes marred by his erratic timing and tuning!

Krazy Kat 790 Shake Your Moneymaker
With singer/harmonica player Snooky Pryor recorded live in Germany in 1973, accompanied by a small band including Eddie Taylor (gtr). One side features vocals by James and the other by Pryor. An adequate, if uninspired, selection of performances.

Trix 3315 Goin' Back Home
Acoustic country blues set.

Wolf 0120409 Homesick James and Snooky Pryor
Recorded together in Austria in 1979. An uninspired offering.

EARL HOOKER

Great and highly respected Chicago guitarist. Particularly fine slide player. Most of his recordings are instrumental.

ESSENTIAL SELECTION

Arhoolie 1044 Two Bugs and a Roach
1968 recordings with Pinetop Perkins, Louis Myers, and Carey Bell.

Arhoolie 1051 Hooker and Steve Miller
With Louis Myers and Geno Skaggs.

Arhoolie 1066 His First and Last Recordings
Features 1955 unissued Sun sides, 1952 recordings, and 1968 and 1969 studio and live recordings.

Charly CRB 1134 Earl Hooker/Magic Sam: Calling All Blues
This album features eight tracks by Magic Sam recorded for Chief in 1960 and eight by Hooker recorded for Chief and Age between 1960–62. Most of the Sam sides are available on Flyright 590 and 605, including some tough vocal cuts like "My Love Is Your Love" and "Everynight About This Time," rocking instrumentals like "Blue Light Boogie," along with some novelty items. The Hooker sides are all instrumental, including two with Junior Wells on harp (also on Flyright) plus some other cuts not available elsewhere like the lovely slide instrumentals "Blues In D Natural" and "Blue Guitar." Full discographical information and detailed sleeve notes by Neil Slaven.

Red Lightnin' 009 There's a Fungus Among Us
Reissue of his Cuca album.

Red Lightnin' 0018 The Leading Brand
Reissue of early singles, plus cuts by Jody Williams.

CASSETTE AND CD RELEASE ONLY
Arhoolie C/CD 324 Two Bugs and a Roach
All of Arhoolie 1024 and over half of 1066.
COMPACT DISC
P-Vine PCD 2124 Blue Guitar
Twenty-one tracks recorded between 1959–63. In addition to some great blues instrumentals and vocals by Earl, there are some vocals by Junior Wells, Lillian Offitt, Harold Tidwell, and A. C. Reed.

JOHN LEE HOOKER

One of the most prolific and most original of postwar bluesmen. Originally from Mississippi. Hooker's early recordings, cut in Detroit, are among the most intense blues records ever made and achieve a rarely heard level of passion in the lyrics, singing, and playing, with a frequent streak of violence in the songs. Unfortunately his extensive late 40s/early 50s recordings for Modern are not, at present, available. His later recordings with a band tamed some of his ferocity. His 60s, 70s, and 80s recordings find him leaving most of the guitar work to the band and are noted for their rhythmic, hypnotic, and repetitive flavor that gave John Lee the reputation of being "King of Boogie."

Classic 40s and Early-to-mid-50s Recordings
Chess 2-92507 Mad Man Blues
Was Chess 9214, originally issued as Chess 60011. Twenty-three great sides from the early 50s. Down At the Landing/Leave My Wife Alone/In the Mood/It's My Own Fault/Stella Mae/Walkin' the Boogie/Hey Boogie.

ESSENTIAL SELECTION

Chess 9199 (c,d) Plays and Sings the Blues
Reissue of Chess LP 1454 originally issued in 1961. Twelve great sides recorded in his prime in 1951–52. Just him and his distinctive guitar. The Journey/Hey Baby/Bluebird/Apologize/Please Don't Go.

Chess 9258 (c,d) House of the Blues
Twelve more cuts from 1951–52 originally issued in the US in 1965 on Chess LP 1438. Walkin' the Boogie/Union Station Blues/Leave My Wife Alone/Sugar Mama/Louise.

Collectables (c,d) 5151 Gotham Golden Classics
Eleven sides recorded for the Gotham label in Philadelphia during 1950–51. According to the Ledbitter and Slaven blues discography, eight of these have appeared only on 78s, while the remaining three ("Feed Her All Night," "How Long Must I Be Your Slave," and "Ground Hog") are unissued! With

familiar titles like House Rent Boogie/Questionaire Blues/My Daddy Was A Jockey.

DCC Compact Classics DZS 042 (c,d) 40th Anniversary Album

A collection of mostly previously unissued recordings from the early days of Hooker's career. He was discovered in 1948 by record producer/distributor Bernie Bessman, who recorded over 200 sides by him between 1948–52. Some were issued on his own Sensation label and on Modern to great acclaim, but many remained unissued. In the blues boom of the late 60s/early 70s many of these unissued recordings were issued on United Artists or Specialty. This CD presents 15 more, mostly alternate, versions of songs issued elsewhere. John Lee was at his most intense in those early years with his dark vocals and free-flowing anarchic electric guitar style. Some of these tracks are solo and others feature added guitar, harmonica, or piano. Included on this set is the original recording of the classic "Boogie Chillun" from 1948 and, from 1961, "Blues From Abraham Lincoln." Notes by Hooker's producer Bessman and blues scholar Darryl Stolper and superb sound from original master tapes or acetates engineered by Steve Hoffman. A must have! House Rent Boogie/Baby How Can You Do It/Yes, Baby, Baby/Four Women In My Life/I'm Gonna Git Me A Women/Bluebird, Bluebird.

King 727 (d) 16 Selections Every One a Pearl

Reissue of famed 16-track collection that, in addition to 12 classic King sides by John Lee, features four sides (uncredited) by Earl Hooker!

Muse 5205 Sittin' Here Thinkin'

Excellent, previously unissued mid-50s recordings, some with Eddie Kirkland.

Red Lightnin' 003 No Friend Around

Fourteen great and rare sides from the 40s and early 50s. Stomp Boogie/Morning Blues/House Rent Boogie/Decoration Day Blues/Helpless Blues.

Specialty 2125 (c) John Lee Hooker Alone

Twelve previously unissued sides from 1949–51. Rollin' Blues/Do My Baby Think Of Me/Black Cat Blues.

Specialty 2127 (c) Goin' Down Highway 51

More great early sides, many previously unissued.

Mid–late 50s to Early 60s Recordings

Note: These mostly feature Hooker with sympathetic small groups. His Vee Jay material has been reissued often and many of his out-of-print Vee Jay albums are available again with original covers. The albums on Charly are carefully compiled cross-sections of the best of his Vee Jay recordings.

Charly CRB 1004 (c) This Is Hip

Sixteen Vee Jay sides, 1956–64, two previously unissued.

Charly CRB 1014 Everybody's Rockin'

Sixteen superb Vee Jay sides recorded between 1956–64.

Charly CRB 1029 Moanin' the Blues

Third album of Hooker reissues from Vee Jay features 16 sides recorded between 1955–64 in various settings and includes eight previously unissued cuts!

Charly CRB 1081 Solid Sender

Reissue of his "Travelin'" album (Vee Jay 1023) with four extra cuts.

Chess 9271 (c,d) The Real Folk Blues

This is a reissue of Chess 1508 from 1966 featuring recordings made that same year with Eddie Burns on guitar and a small band. These recordings have a similar feel to his Vee Jay recordings from the same era. They are powerful though lack the ferocity of his earlier sides. It includes the unusual introspective ballad "The Waterfront" that is very untypical of Hooker. It also includes an exciting remake of "I'm in the Mood," one of the few tracks on which he actually plays lead guitar. Let's Go Out Tonight/Stella Mae/You Know I Know/One Scotch, One Bourbon, One Beer.

Fantasy 24706 (d) Boogie Chillun

2-LP set of live solo performances from the 60s. One album previously issued on Galaxy, the other is previously unissued recordings.

Fantasy 24722 (d) Black Snake Blues

Vee Jay 1007 (c) I'm John Lee Hooker

His first and best Vee Jay album, recorded between 1955 and 1959.

Vee Jay 1049 (c) The Best of John Lee Hooker

Vee Jay 1058 (c) The Big Soul of

Vee Jay 1078 (c) Concert at Newport

Later Recordings

Ace CH 259 That's My Story

Reissue of Riverside 321 from 1960. In some ways this is a bit of a period piece. Back in the late 50s and early 60s, it was felt by certain jazz and folk entrepeneurs that the only true blues was a solo performer with an acoustic instrument and that electric blues was part of that somewhat disreputable musical genre "rhythm and blues." Hence Orrin Keepnews (who should have known better) produced two albums by John Lee Hooker playing acoustic guitar. On this, the second, he has added a straight laced jazz drummer and acoustic bass player "to free Hooker from the burden of carrying the full rhythm load." In spite of all the odds, John Lee turns in a fine set of performances (particularly on those tracks without the rhythm section!) including his unique modal reworking of the Barrett Strong hit

"Money" and the fascinating politically flavored blues "Democrat Man." Although it lacks the ferocity of his early recordings, this is well worth a listen though not essential.

Ace CH 282 The Folk-Blues of John Lee Hooker

This is a reissue of John Lee's first Riverside album recorded in 1959. Although he plays acoustic, rather than his more familiar electric guitar, he is not stifled by the bass player and drummer that were on the second Riverside album. He is in good form on a selection of songs that draws heavily from blues standards like "How Long Blues," "Pea Vine Special," "Bundle Up and Go," and "Good Mornin' Lil' School Girl," but all transformed into something uniquely John Lee Hooker. Superb sound due to digital transfer and direct metal mastering.

BGO BGOLP 39 (d) Live at Cafe Au Go-Go

Exact repro of Bluesway LP from 1967 complete with Stanley Dance's review of the live (August 1966) date. Despite the illustrious backup group—Muddy Waters, Otis Spann, and George Smith—this is a fairly lackluster set. Hooker is notoriously hard to backup anyway with his erratic electrified country blues approach, and, coupled with the fact that Muddy's band had already played a set to the young audience (". . . consuming enormous vases of ice cream and soda," according to Dance's review) the result isn't surprising. One for the completist. I'm Bad Like Jesse James/One Bourbon, One Scotch, One Beer/Seven Days/Heartaches and Misery.

BGO BGOLP 40 Simply the Truth

Exact repro of Bluesway LP from 1969. Hooker is backed here by an unknown (except for Pretty Purdie on drums) but talented ensemble on nine blues and boogies. He does some jumpin' tunes like "I Wanna Bugaloo" and "(Twist Ain't Nothin') But The Old Time Shimmy" but mostly sticks to his patently mournful style, especially effective on numbers like "I Don't Want To Go To Viet Nam," "Tantalizing With The Blues," and the haunting "One Room Country Shack."

Black and Blue 33.553 (d) Get Back Home

Originally 33.023 and 33.523. Solo performances from 1969; a little tepid.

Chameleon 74808 (c,d) The Healer

What a bunch of self-indulgent crap by producer Roy Rogers. He has partnered John Lee with such important blues artists as Santana, Bonnie Raitt, Los Lobos, and George Thorogood, and has him playing National steel guitar and 12-string. This record says nothing about John Lee Hooker's music but a whole lot about the producer's fantasies. With a cover that looks like something from "A Nightmare On Elm Street," this record is a real insult to a great artist.

Charly CDX 22 The Cream
CD issues: Charly CD 106; Tomato 269609-2
Reissue of Tomato 7009 from 1978. This two-LP set finds John in fine form, recorded live at the Keystone in Palo Alto in Sept. 1977, backed by a tight little band including Ron Thompson on second guitar and special guest harp by Charlie Musselwhite. This is a long set with most of the 15 tunes lasting over five minutes, including a 14-minute "Boogie On." Most tunes are either dark and brooding or mid-tempo. Includes some fine versions of Hook's classics, including "Tupelo," dedicated to the recently deceased Elvis, "When My First Wife Left Me," "Louise," even a chilling version of Van Morrison's "T. B. Sheets." Charly CD has only 11 tunes, leaving off "Little Girl" and all of Side four; Tomato CD has three less tunes than the two-record set, so is more complete.

Charly CDX 33 Original Bluesway Sessions
Two-LP set reissuing two albums originally issued on Bluesway: "Urban Blues" (6012), from 1967 with Wayne Bennett, Louis Myers, and Eddie Taylor, and "Simply The Truth" (6023), from 1968 with Wally Richrdson and Ernie Hayes

Rhino R2 75776 Hooker 'n' Heat
Blues great John Lee Hooker recorded live with Canned Heat and The Chambers Brothers at the Fox Venice Theatre in 1981. Hell Hound/Strut My Stuff/House of Blue Lights/It Hurts Me Too/Serves Me Right to Suffer.

See For Miles SEE 89 (d) Never Get out of These Blues Alive
Reissue of 1971 title album, plus four additional tracks taken from the 1970 album "Endless Boogie" and from the 1970 album "John Lee Hooker Featuring Earl Hooker."

Stax 4134 That's Where It's At
CASSETTE ONLY RELEASE

MCA 1365 Lonesome Mood
Seven lengthy performances recorded for Bluesway in 1969, with Earl Hooker, Johnny Big Moose Walker, and Jeff Carp.

Rhino RNDA 71105 John Lee Hooker and Canned Heat: Infinite Boogie
Reissue of the two-LP set "Hooker 'n Heat" from 1970. Side one and the first song on Side two are just Hook and guitar. Next come six tunes with sensitive backing by Canned Heat's second vocalist and harp wizard Al Wilson, on harp and piano on "Bottle Up and Go," "Burning Hell," and four others. Finally the whole group comes together for five pieces of end-

less boogie with Henry Vestine on guitar: "Boogie Chillun #2," "Pea Vine," "Whiskey and Wimmen," and two others. Insert has all the original photos and new liner notes by ex-Heat roadie Barrett "Dr. Demento" Hansen.

COMPACT DISC

Ace CD CHD 927 That's My Story/The Folk Blues of
Features most of Ace 259 and 282, with four tracks omitted so they could fit on one 72-minute CD.

Chameleon 74794-2 (21S) The Hook—20 Years of Hits and Hot Boogie

ESSENTIAL SELECTION

Charly CD 4 Boogie Chillun
Twenty-two Vee Jay sides recorded between 1956–64. Dimples/Little Wheel/I Love You Honey/I'm In The Mood/Hobo Blues/Drive Me Away/No Shoes/Will The Circle Be Unbroken/Boom Boom.

Charly CD 62 House Rent Boogie
Charly CD 4 had all the Vee Jay hits. This set has 22 lesser hits and LP cuts, the perfect complement to the hits package. John Lee rarely made bad records and this is your chance to hear songs other than "Dimples" and "Boom Boom." Over an hour of small group performances. Crawlin' Black Spider/I'm So Worried Baby/I'm Mad Again/Time Is Marchin'.

Charly CD 170 Let's Make It

Chess (France) 670404 Mad Man Blues
Seventeen tracks culled from Hooker's Chess recordings made between 1951–66. My First Wife Left Me/I'm In The Mood/Crawling King Snake/Mad Man Blues/Stella Mae.

MCA MCAD 31361 Never Get out of These Blues Alive
Reissue of 1972 ABC LP with Van Morrison on the title song. Accompanied by Charlie Musselwhite, Luther Tucker, Steve Miller, Mark Naftalin, Gino Skaggs, Mel Brown, and Elvin Bishop. Wow!

Suite Beat D 2012 The Best of. . .
Vee Jay sides.

JOHN LEE HOOKER/EDDIE BURNS

Krazy Kat 816 Detroit Blues, 1950–51
A great collection of down-home blues from Gotham featuring 11 cuts by Hooker (three previously unissued) and five by Eddie Burns (that were unknown until recently). This is Hooker in his prime: brooding intense vocals and fierce poignant guitar. Songs include the driving "Real Gone Gal" and "My Daddy Was A Jockey," the ferocious previously unissued "Feed Me All Night," and a unique treatment of the Mississippi blues standard "Catfish." Eddie Burns, who has frequently worked with Hooker, is a fine singer and harmonica player strongly influenced by John Lee "Sonny Boy" Williamson. He is accompanied here by Tennessee guitarist John T. Smith and, on one cut, by Hooker. Fine, if somewhat chaotic, cuts. Sound on this album is not as good as on some of the other Gotham reissues. Full discographical details and excellent notes by Mike Rowe.

JOHN LEE HOOKER/ALBERT KING

Tomato 269614-2 I'll Play the Blues for You
Recorded in 1977, with four tracks by Albert King, five by Hooker.

JOHN LEE HOOKER/STICKS MCGHEE

Audio Lab 1520 (c,d) Highway of Blues

LYNN HOPE
Bluesy/jazzy sax-led instrumentals by artist who was popular in the 50s and then disappeared from the scene.

Saxophonograph BP 508 Morocco

SAM "LIGHTNIN'" HOPKINS
Texas country bluesman Hopkins was one of the greatest bluesmen who ever lived, a performer whose singing and guitar playing seemed to evoke the spirit of the blues with every note. From his earliest recordings in 1946 for Gold Star to his last, he retained a remarkable consistency. His recordings for folk labels in the 60s are as fine as his 40s and 50s commercial recordings for a black audience. While his 40s-50s recordings were aimed at the black market and featured electric guitar with a small band backup, the 60s recordings, aimed at the "folk" market, usually were recorded with solo acoustic guitar (or acoustic guitar with muted bass and drums). He recorded extensively and, with few exceptions, almost every one of his records is worthwhile.

His Best Recordings

Arhoolie 1011 Lightnin' Sam Hopkins
Wonderful 1961–62 sides, some with electric and some with acoustic guitar. On a few cuts, Spider Kilpatrick joins him on drums.

ESSENTIAL SELECTION

Blues Classics 30 Houston's King of the Blues
Recorded when Hopkins was in his prime in 1952 and 1953, playing exciting intense guitar and singing with an unrivaled vitality. This album includes both sides of his rarest recording cut for TNT in 1953—"Moanin' Blues" and "Leavin' Blues"—with

moaning vocals and some of the funkiest electric guitar you've ever heard! Six tracks are from 1952 and early '53 with Lightnin' playing acoustic guitar with Donald Cooks on bass and, on some of the up-tempo tracks, tap dancing by L. C. Williams. Seven tracks are from 1953 with Lightnin' playing electric guitar with Cooks and drummer Connie Kroll. Great stuff!

Blues Documents 2066 **1946–60**
Twenty-one rare sides. Most of these tracks are from the mid-40s through early 50s and, although some have been available on LP at one time or another, very few are currently available. A few tracks are from very worn 78s, but most of this set is very listenable and most worthwhile. Mean Old Twister/Can't Get That Woman Off My Mind/You're Gonna Miss Me/Nightmare Blues/Come Back Baby/Howling Wolf Blues/(Mama's) Baby Child/Shining Moon/Papa Bones Boogie.

Candid 9010 (d) **Lightnin' in New York**
Some of the finest sides he recorded in the 60s, cut in Nov. 1960 for Candid. This album is an exact replica of the original Candid with the same cover and back liner. Lightnin' was in great form on this session, singing with great passion and playing both piano and guitar, and on one cut, the amazing "Take It Easy," he switches between both! It includes his brilliant song story "Mr. Charlie," along with such moving performances as "I've Had My Fun," "Trouble Blues," and "Wonder Why," as well as upbeat boogies like the amusing "Mighty Crazy" and "Lightnin's Piano Boogie." Recording quality is also excellent.

Collectables 5121 (c,d) **The Herald Records**
Lightnin's Herald sides are the rawest, rockinest records he ever produced. Previously released as two LPs on Diving Duck, this is a condensed single-LP version drawn from the same sessions. If you're not afraid of Lightnin's raunchy guitar grinding out the hard boogie in front of a stripped down and sweaty band, this is for you. Highly recommended.

Diving Duck 4307 **Flash Lightnin'**
This and Diving Duck 4308 reissue in their entirety some of Lightnin's last commercial recordings cut in 1954. These sides feature Lightnin' in top form accompanied by a bass and drums and include some of his fiercest recordings. Some tracks feature heavily amplified and distorted guitar, the latter particulary notable on the second set. This album features some wonderful introspective sides like "Sittin' Down Thinkin'," "Don't Think Cause You're Pretty," and the very moving "The Life I Used To Live," along with uptempo items like the

amusing "Lightnin's Boogie" and the storming "Grandma's Boogie." Dubbing from the original 45s is not exceptional but the music is.

Diving Duck 4308 **Lightnin' Hopkins**
Thirteen more great sides from 1954, including the powerful "Sick Feeling Blues," "Evil Hearted Woman," and "Nothing But The Blues," along with several romping boogies and a track where he backs the rather terrible vocalist Ruth Ames.

Document 577 **1948–61**
Twenty-two rare recordings. Mercy/No Mail Blues/Jackstropper Blues/Racetrack Blues/New York Boogie/New Worried Life Blues/Contrary Mary/Crazy About My Baby.

Other Recordings (Almost All Worthwhile!)

Ace CH 256 **Walkin' This Road by Myself**
Reissue of Bluesville 1057 from 1962, one of the best of the 10 albums he recorded for Bluesville and Prestige in the early 60s. Four tracks are from 1961 with Lightnin' accompanying himself on acoustic guitar. The remaining six tracks are from two sessions from early 1962, with Lightnin' on electric guitar, accompanied by fellow Houston musicians Spider Kilpatrick (drm), Billy Bizor (hca), and Buster Pickens (pno). The group is pretty ragged but gives the music the feel of the Houston juke joints Lightnin' played in at the time. In addition to Lightnin's unique reworkings of old blues favorites, the album also features one of his spontaneous topical creations, "Happy Blues For John Glenn." There are interesting notes by Mack McCormick on the creation of this song and the album has been beautifully remastered from original tapes.

Arhoolie 1022 **Lightnin' Hopkins**
With his brothers John Henry and Joel Hopkins.

Arhoolie 1034 **Texas Bluesman**

Arhoolie 1063 **In Berkeley**

Arhoolie 1087 **Po' Lightnin'**
Ten great sides recorded in 1961 and 1969. The eight 1969 cuts were previously issued on Tomato and are mostly versions of his most popular songs like "Mojo Hand" and "Rock Me Baby" where Lightnin' is accompanied by a small and tasteful rhythm section. The two 1961 cuts have not been issued before and feature rare examples of his piano and organ playing. The liner notes by Chris Strachwitz are a touching tribute to this great artist.

Bulldog BDL 1010 **Lightnin' Hopkins Live at the Bird Lounge**
Excellent live 1964 set recorded in Houston.

Charly CRB 1031 **Lightnin' Strikes Back**
Fourteen excellent cuts recorded in the early 60s,

partly recorded live in Los Angeles, and previously available on two long out-of-print Vee Jay albums.

Charly 1147 **Move on Out**

Fourteen Jewel sides recorded between 1965–69. These singles were recorded mainly for southern juke boxes, so Lightnin' really jumps here. These all feature a small group with harp (often by Wild Child Butler), piano, bass, and drums. Most of the tunes are reworkings of earlier material, including a fine version of "Mr. Charlie," plus the instrumental "Move On Out," and such gems (or Jewels) as Moaning Blues/Viet Nam Blues/Ride In Your Automobile/Wig Wearing Woman.

Charly CRB 1190 **Free Form Patterns**

Lightnin' recorded prolifically in the 60s and, although he rarely made a bad recording, there are several rather forgettable ones; this is one of them. On this set of recordings made for the International Artists label in 1968, he is accompanied on most tracks by harmonica player Billy Bizor and an unknown piano player, and on some by bass and drums. Although Lightnin' performs well, Bizor's contributions are unsympathetic and the recording quality is appalling. It sounds like the microphones had sheets draped over them!

Collectables 5111 (c,d) **Mojo Hand**

Most recently available as an expensive Japanese import, this album is a reissue of Fire FLP-104 from 1961. It features Lightnin' playing fine acoustic guitar, tastefully accompanied by bass and drums. It includes his minor hit "Mojo Hand" plus other fine songs like the moving and atypical "Awful Dream" and a fine "Have You Ever Loved A Woman" featuring some of Sam's unique piano playing. The album features a repro of the original cover and liner notes.

Collectables 5143 (c,d) **From the Vaults of Everest, Part One: Drinkin' in the Blues**

Collectables 5144 (c,d) **From the Vaults of Everest, Part Two: Prison Blues**

Collectables 5145 (c,d) **From the Vaults of Everest, Part Three: Mama and Papa Hopkins**

Collectables 5146 (c,d) **From the Vaults of Everest, Part Four: Nothin' But the Blues**

Four albums/CDs featuring recordings made between 1959–65, mostly previously issued on Tradition and Verve/Folkways. Mostly acoustic performances.

Collectables 5203 (c,d) **The Lost Texas Tapes, Vol. 1**

Collectables 5204 (c,d) **The Lost Texas Tapes, Vol. 2**

Collectables 5205 (c,d) **The Lost Texas Tapes, Vol. 3**

Collectables 5206 (c,d) **The Lost Texas Tapes, Vol. 4**

Collectables 5207 (c,d) **The Lost Texas Tapes, Vol. 5**

Fantasy 24702 (d) **Double Blues**

Two-LP set featuring 60s Prestige recordings.

Fantasy 24725 (c,d) **How Many More Years I Got**

Two-LP set featuring selections drawn from three out-of-print Prestige/Bluesville albums.

GNP Crescendo 10022 (d) **Legacy of the Blues, Vol. 12**

Krazy Kat 7410 **Lightnin' Hopkins and Big Boy Crudup**

An excellent set of previously unissued performances, six by Lightnin' from 1960 playing acoustic guitar and accompanied by bass and drums, and seven by Crudup from 1962 with bass and drums. Mostly familiar material.

O.B.C. 506 (c) **Blues in My Bottle**

Good acoustic set originally issued as Bluesville 1045 in 1961. Lightnin' is in good form on a mixture of blues standards and fine originals. Buddy Brown's Blues/Sail On, Little Girl, Sail On/Death Bells/Jailhouse Blues.

O.B.C. 522 (c) **Goin' Away**

Reissue of Bluesville 1073 from 1963. This album features Lightnin' on acoustic guitar on a collection of six songs and two instrumentals. He is accompanied by jazz bassist and drummer Leonard Gaskin and Herbie Lovell, who do a decent job of accompanying him, though I personally find Lovell's brush work irritating. This is one of Hopkins's lesser efforts, though his "Stranger Here" is a fascinating subjective view of the civil rights movement.

Prestige 7377 **Soul Blues**

Prestige 7592 **Greatest Hits**

Prestige 7714 **The Best of Lightnin'**

Prestige 7806 **Hootin' the Blues**

Prestige 7831 **Got to Move Your Baby**

Rhapsody 8 **At His Natural Best**

Good sides, probably from early 70s; their exact origin is uncertain.

Smithsonian/Folkways 40019 (c,d) **Lightnin' Hopkins**

Reissue of Folkways 3822 featuring 10 songs recorded in 1959 by Sam Charters.

CASSETTE ONLY RELEASE
Arhoolie C-201 **Lightnin' Hopkins**
Combines Arhoolie 1011 and 1087 on one cassette.
CASSETTE AND CD RELEASE ONLY
Arhoolie C/CD 330 **The Gold Star Sessions, Vol. 1**
Arhoolie C/CD 337 **The Gold Star Sessions, Vol. 2**
COMPACT DISC
Arhoolie (Japan) PCD 2501 **The Texas Bluesman**
A great collection featuring eight of the nine songs from Arhoolie 1011 recorded in California in 1961 and all of Arhoolie 1034, recorded in Texas in 1967. Wonderful recordings from the premiere Texas country bluesman at his best.

ESSENTIAL SELECTION
Arhoolie CD 302 **Texas Blues**
Sixteen tracks recorded between 1961–69, previously available on Arhoolie 1011, 1034, 1039, and 1063.

Charly CD 209 **Lightnin' Strikes Back**
Fifteen tracks recorded for Vee Jay between 1960–62, including cuts from his first live recording session.

P-Vine PCD 2523 **Blue Lightnin'/Talkin' Some Sense**
Nineteen tracks drawn from Lightnin's first two Jewel LPs recorded in the late 60s-early 70s. I Found My Baby Crying/Back Door Friends/Morning Blues/Wig Wearing Woman/Long Way From Home/Vietnam War, Parts 1 & 2/Walkin' Blues/Lonesome Lightnin'/Uncle Sam, The Hip Record Man/The Purple Poppy.

Vogue 600187 **Shake It Baby**
This CD features four songs from 1960 and nine from 1965. These were originally issued on the Verve/Folkways label and subsequently on several Everest labels. The 1960 recordings are live acoustic recordings, while the 1965 sides feature Lightnin' with a lightly amplified guitar accompanied by bass and drums and, on a couple of cuts, a totally incongruous trombone! Lightnin', as always, was fine, but these recordings are not among his most spirited and the bass and drums on the 1965 session add nothing. Sound is adequate, though there seems to be some distortion.

Vogue 670405 **Blues in the Bottle**
Thirteen sides recorded for Bluesville in the early 60s, drawn mostly from Bluesville 1045. The sound on this CD is not really satisfactory as it features an unreasonable amount of distortion.

LIGHTNIN' HOPKINS/SONNY TERRY and BROWNIE McGHEE
COMPACT DISC
Vee Jay (Japan) 30YD 1067 **Coffee House Blues**
Japanese CD of still-in-print Vee Jay album with two songs ("Blues For Gamblers," "Right On That Shore") by this mighty trio. Lightnin' does four tunes on his own, as do Sonny Terry and Brownie McGhee.

BIG WALTER "SHAKEY" HORTON
One of the best Chicago harmonica players. Horton has played on many Chicago recordings. His own recordings are all good though he is not as good a singer as harp blower. He died in 1981.

Ace CHD 252 **Mouth Harp Maestro**
A superb collection featuring all of his recordings made in Memphis at the Sun studios in 1951, including previously unissued songs and alternate takes. Includes accompaniments by Joe Hill Louis, Calvin Newbern, and Willie Nix. The album is rounded out with rare Memphis recordings of Jim Lockhart and Alfred Harris.

Alligator 4702 **Big Walter Horton**
One of his best solo albums with second harp by Carey Bell on some tracks plus accompaniments by Eddie Taylor, Joe Harper, and Frank Swan.

Black Magic 9010 **Harmonica Genius**
Black-and-white picture disc. The recordings come from sessions for Blind Pig records.

Blind Pig 006-78 (c,d) **Fine Cuts**
Excellent sides.

Blind Pig 1484 (c,d) **Can't Keep Lovin' You**
An outstanding set of recordings. All cuts feature John Nicholas on guitar; some feature a tough full band, one features added drummer only, and three feature duets with Walter and John. These recordings, along with his Alligator album, are probably his best 70s recordings.

Chess 9268 (c) **The Soul of the Blues Harmonica**
Originally issued on Argo (in England) in 1964 and only available for a short while. A nice set of performances with Walter accompanied by Bobby Buster (organ), Buddy Guy (gtr), Jack Myers (b), and Willie Smith (drm).

Pearl 12 **Harmonica Blues Kings**
Also features Alfred Harris. See POSTWAR CHICAGO Collections.

Red Lightnin' 008 **An Offer You Can't Refuse**
One side of the album is by Paul Butterfield. Some incredible playing by Horton.

COMPACT DISC
JSP CD 208 **Little Boy Blue**
1980 live recordings with Sugar Blue and Ronnie Horvath. Most tracks previously on an out-of-print JSP album.

SON HOUSE
Great Mississippi Delta blues singer who recorded classic sides for Paramount in 1930, the Library of Congress in 1941, and for various labels in the 1960s. Son was one of the most intense bluesmen of all times with a gruff and expressive voice and a driving slashing guitar style. He often played with a bottleneck slide. His 60s sides lack some of the technical prowess of his early recordings but make up for it in sheer intensity!

Biograph 12040 **Son House/Blind Lemon Jefferson**
One side of album features six of House's classic Paramount sides from 1930, the other side features six sides by Blind Lemon Jefferson.

Edsel ED 167 **Death Letter**
This album is a reissue of Columbia CS 9265 from 1965. This album features a couple of remakes of his 1930 Paramount classics (including "Death Letter" and "Preachin' Blues"), along with songs not previously recorded by him. It includes the chugging "Empire State Express," on which he is sensitively accompanied by the late Al Wilson of Canned Heat, the emotional a cappella performance of "Grinning In Your Face," and the beautiful "Sundown." Album features original cover and liner notes. An exciting and important album.

Folklyric 9002 **The Legendary 1941/2 Recordings**
Superb Library of Congress recordings.
COMPACT DISC

ESSENTIAL SELECTION

Travelin' Man CD 02 **The Complete Library of Congress Sessions**
Eddie "Son" House was at his prime when these recordings were collected by Alan Lomax in 1941–42. Most of them were previously issued on Folklyric 9002 and the rest on Flyright 541 (out-of-print), but this CD collects all of them in chronological order. The first seven tracks are with a wonderful string band featuring Willie Brown (gtr), Fiddlin' Joe Martin (mdln), and Leroy Williams (hca), who urges Son along with joyous shouts and additional vocalizing. The other 12 tracks are just Son alone with his steel-bodied National guitar. Although the CD reissue doesn't improve too much on the sound of the deteriorated acetates used, it is wonderful to have all this classic material in one place.

BEE HOUSTON
Dynamic Los Angeles singer/guitarist, performing mostly original songs.

Arhoolie 1050 **Bee Houston**
You Think I'm Your Good Thing/Be Proud To Be A Black Man.

JOE HOUSTON
Saxophonograph 1302 **Rockin' 'n' Boppin'**
Hot, unrelenting R&B saxophone from one of the legends, born in Texas but based in LA since the early 50s. Good remastering of 17 cuts from 1949–55 with one from 1963. Presented in a gatefold sleeve with lengthy liner notes and tons of photos. A must-buy if you like honking saxophones.

FRANK HOVINGTON
Very fine country blues singer/guitarist from Delaware.

Rounder 2017 **Lonesome Road Blues**

MAXINE HOWARD
COMPACT DISC
Line CD 9.00840 **Blue Shoes with No Strings**

ROSETTA HOWARD
Earl Archives 620 **With The Harlem Hamfats and The Harlem Blues Serenaders**
Sixteen tracks recorded 1937–39.

PEG LEG HOWELL
Wonderful 20s Georgia country blues singer/guitarist. The two Matchbox albums below feature all the recordings under his own name. The OJL LP duplicates some of these recordings and also includes tracks by some of the string bands Howell worked with.

Matchbox 221 **Peg Leg Howell, Vol. I**
Recordings from 1926–27 including seven solo performances and seven in the company of his "Gang" (Henry Williams [gtr] and Eddie Anthony [vln, vcl]). Howell's solo pieces are lovely and include the magnificent "Tishamingo Blues," the lovely "Fo' Day Blues," and the great "Skin Game Blues," a rare example of Howell's slide playing. The tracks with his Gang are absolutely delightful examples of black string-band music, with tremendous fiddle by Anthony. Although all of these tracks have been reissued before, it's a real pleasure to hear them all in a group.

Matchbox 205 **Peg Leg Howell, Vol. II**
All 16 sides recorded by Howell between April 1928 and April 1929. Lovely singing and guitar; some

cuts feature the violin of Eddie Anthony, giving the music an old-time string-band sound.

OJL 22 Peg Leg Howell and His Gang, 1927–30

HOWLIN' WOLF

One of the great Chicago blues singers with one of the most powerful and distinctive voices on record. His early sides were recorded in Memphis with a ragged but dynamic band. His Chicago recordings feature some of the finest blues players, usually including the brilliant guitar of Willie Johnson or Hubert Sumlin. Like other artists who recorded for Chess, his recordings have been repackaged again and again, which makes it very difficult to get a comprehensive cross-section of his recordings without extensive duplication. To help you decide we are listing as much detail as we can about the various albums. Now we need somebody to do a complete box set!

Ace CH 52 Ridin' in the Moonlight
Features all of his recordings cut for the RPM label in the Sam Phillips (Sun) studios around 1950. Although much of this material has been reissued before, this album includes three previously unissued alternate takes and is therefore the most complete selection of Wolf from this period. Sixteen titles of this great artist at his earliest and most savage, with shattering guitar by Willie Johnson, knocked-out piano by "Struction," and powerful drumming by Willie Steele. A must! (Bear Family has now issued all of the RPM material on two CDs; see below.)

Chess 9100 (c) Muddy and the Wolf

ESSENTIAL SELECTION

Chess 9107 (c) His Greatest Sides, Vol. I
Fourteen fine sides recorded between 1954–63, with great mono sound. Many of the cuts feature stunning guitar by Hubert Sumlin; other sidemen include Jimmy Rogers (gtr), Johnny Jones (pno), Otis Spann (pno), and Willie Dixon (b). Down In the Bottom/Sitting On Top Of The World/Red Rooster/Evil/Do the Do/No Place To Go/Smokestack Lightnin'/Spoonful/Killing Floor/I Ain't Superstitious/Who's Been Talking/300 Pounds Of Joy/Back Door Man/Wang-Dang-Doodle.

Chess 9183 (c) Rocking Chair
"Electronically re-inhanced" for stereo sound, but, thankfully, the electronic stereo is not too offensive.

Chess 9195 (c) Moanin' in the Moonlight
Reissue of Wolf's classic first album (Chess 1434) from 1959. Here are some of Wolf's greatest songs accompanied by the magnificent guitars of Willie

Johnson, Hubert Sumlin, and/or Jody Williams; and piano by Ike Turner, Otis Spann, or Hosea Lee Kennard. Moanin' At Midnight/Smokestack Lightnin'/No Place To Go/Evil/Moanin' For My Baby/Forty Four.

Chess 9273 (c,d) The Real Folk Blues
Reissue of Chess 1502 from 1966. A superb collection of tracks featuring four from the 50s including his updates of the traditional "Poor Boy" and "Sittin' On Top Of The World," and the chilling true story "The Natchez Burning." The remaining tracks were recorded between 1962–65. Although a few of these songs are a bit silly, they all have great singing from Wolf, fine arrangements, and stunning guitar from Hubert Sumlin. Excellent sound. Killing Floor/My Country Sugar Mama/300 Pounds Of Joy/ Built For Comfort/Tell Me What I've Done.

Chess 9279 (c,d) More Real Folk Blues

Chess 9297 (c,d) The London Howlin' Wolf Sessions
Wolf and Hubert Sumlin accompanied by British blues revivalists in the early 70s. Rockin' Daddy/I Ain't Superstitious/Sittin' On Top Of The World/The Red Rooster.

Chess 93001 (c,d) Change My Way
Reissue of a compilation that surfaced very briefly in the mid-70s. Not particularly unusual Wolf material, but a great collection of some of his most rip-roarin' sides, with Hubert Sumlin on all 15 cuts. Do The Do/I Ain't Superstitious/Hidden Charms/I Didn't Know/I Better Go Now/Just Like I Treat You.

Sundown 709-07 Live in Europe, 1964
Recorded live in Bremen, Germany, in November 1964 with Hubert Sumlin, Sunnyland Slim, Willie Dixon, and Clifton James. Enjoyable performances, though not among Wolf's most exciting, and the sound is not exceptional. A rare chance to hear this great artist live, including a couple of songs Wolf had not recorded elsewhere.

Rounder SS 28 (c,d) **Cadillac Daddy**
Wolf 120.000 **Live, 1975!**
This is a pretty despicable album. Recorded at the 1815 Club in Chicago just six months before his death, and after several years of ill health, it finds this great artist just a shadow of his former self. His singing and playing lack strength and conviction and, although the musicianship from the band is good, particularly from Hubert Sumlin, the sound quality is so poor that most of the music is reduced to mush. The producer's note tries to justify this recording by saying that its "documentary value cannot be overestimated," while stating that the recordings were produced by agreement with Wolf's widow. To my mind, these are cynical excuses to justify crass exploitation of Wolf's many fans and discredit the memory of a truly great performer.

COMPACT DISC

Bear Family BCD 15460 **Memphis Days: The Definitive Edition, Vol. I**
Fantastic collection of 21 tracks recorded in Sam Phillips' studios in Memphis in 1951 and 1952. It's amazing when listening to these performances to realize that not a single one was originally issued! Most of them resurfaced some years ago on various Charly albums but this CD issue also features previously unissued versions of six songs including "Oh Red," "Come Back Home," and "How Many More Years." These early recordings feature Wolf at his most ferocious, accompanied by a hard-driving band with the shattering guitar of Willie Johnson and the knocked-out piano of Albert Williams or William Johnson, plus drums and occasional horn. With the exception of two tracks drawn from a rather worn acetate, the sound on this collection is stunning, with a great presence that brings out all the force of Wolf's vocals and Johnson's over-amplified guitar. The set has full discographical information, informative notes by Colin Escott, and a startling early photo of Wolf in a grocery store dwarfing the electric guitar he is holding! Absolutely essential! Roll on Volume two!

Bear Family BCD 15500 **Memphis Days, Vol. II**
Nineteen songs, with six previously unissued tracks, and an eight-page booklet.

Chess CHD 5908 **Moanin' in the Moonlight/ Howlin' Wolf**
Two classic albums combined into one killer CD.

Chess (France) 670412 **I'm the Wolf**
Fifteen tracks, 10 of them from his 1973 album "Back Door Wolf." Although not among his better recordings, there are some good performances here, including "Trying To Forget You," "Moving," and the witty topical "Coon On The Moon" and "Watergate Blues." The remaining tracks are 50s classics like "No Place To Go," "Smokestack Lightnin'," and "I Asked for Water" that have been reissued many times before.

Chess (UK) CD RED 3 **Moanin' and Howlin'**
Twenty-four sides recorded between 1951–64 with unexceptional sound. Moanin' At Midnight/Forty Four/The Natchez Burnin'/I Walked From Dallas/Wang Dang Doodle/ Down In the Bottom/You'll Be Mine/Three Hundred Pounds Of Joy/Killing Floor.

JOE HUGHES
Black Top 1050 (d) **If You Want to See the Blues**
Double Trouble TX 3012 **Texas Guitar Master**
Enjoyable album issued in conjunction with a filmed tribute to T-Bone Walker; as a result, the album is mostly covers of Walker songs and tunes. Hughes is a fine singer and guitarist from Houston, recorded here in two different settings, one live and one in the studio, accompanied by two different small bands. On the live set, he shares guitar honors with another fine Houston-based guitarist, Pete Mayes. Hughes's singing and playing are fine though he is in the shadow of T-Bone and comes off second best. On the two original songs, Hughes shows that he can come up with good original material that is not obviously derivative of T-Bone.

Double Trouble (d) 3019 **Craftsman**
Ten songs (CD has three extra tracks) recorded in 1986 and 1987 with a couple of different bands. Hughes is a good, solid singer and an impressive guitarist, if not a memorable one. Songs are a mixture of originals plus items from the repertoire of his idol T-Bone Walker, Johnny Otis, and Gatemouth Brown. Joe is indeed a craftsman but not a master craftsman.

HELEN HUMES
Veteran blues and jazz singer whose career stretches back to the 20s. She is best known for her stint as vocalist with the prewar Count Basie orchestra.

O.J.C. 171 (c,d) **Songs I Like to Sing**
Muse 5217 (c) **Helen Humes and The Muse All Stars with Eddie Vinson, Arnett Cobb**
Muse 5233 **Helen Humes**
Savoy SJL 1159 (c) **Be-Baba-Leba: The Rhythm and Blues Years**
Four sessions from 1944–50 with bands led by Leonard Feather, Marshall Royal, Roy Milton, and

Dexter Gordon. Some duplication with Whiskey, Women, and. . . 701.

Whiskey, Women, and. . . 701 **Be-Baba-Leba**
Sixteen postwar recordings of blues, jazz, and boogie from 1944–52 with Leonard Feather's Hip-tette, The Bill Doggett Octet, Roy Milton's Band, and other top-notch musicians.

Whiskey, Women and. . . 707 **New Million Dollar Secret**
Postwar R&B sides cut in LA, with a notable exception, the opening "Garlic Blues," a classic blues the 14-year-old Helen cut for Okeh in 1927 with backing by guitarists Sylvester Weaver and Walter Beasley. The rest are big-band R&B extravaganzas: '45 Philo/Aladdin sides, a '46 Black and White session with Buck Clayton, and lots of early 50s live recordings released on Modern, Decca, and Gene Norman Presents, including "Hard Drivin' Mama" and the title tune, performed live with Roy Milton.

MARK HUMMEL and THE BLUES SURVIVORS

Double Trouble 3018 **High Steppin'**
Berkeley-based blues band had to go to Holland to get their LP released! This is a good LP by Little Walter-influenced harpist Hummel; 10 tunes including six originals (I like "Harp Shuffle") plus covers of "Keep A Knockin'" (pretty bad!), Howlin' Wolf's "Just Like I Treat You," Harold Burrage's "One More Time," and Little Charlie's "Livin' Hand To Mouth." Notes by Lee Hildebrand.

Rockinitus 101 **Playin' in Your Town**
Many originals; the varied material includes straight-ahead Chicago-style blues ("I'm Gone," "Let Me Go," and Otis Rush's "It Takes Time"), vintage R&B and soul ("Hey Doctor," "Last Thing," and a nice version of Arthur Alexander's "Sally Sue Brown"), rock 'n' roll ("Be My Girl"), and some Sonny and Brownie-styled country blues ("Changed My Ways").

Rockinitis 103 **Up and Jumpin'**
COMPACT DISC
Double Trouble DTCD 3021 **Harmonica Party**
Mid-80s recordings featuring Mark accompanied by Ron Thompson, Paris Slim, and Kevin Zuffi (from Joe Louis Walker's band) on a program of Chicago blues-inspired originals and covers. The band is pretty tough, with some fine guitar work by Pat Chase and Hummel's harp playing throughout in a solid Little Walter-ish vein.

ALBERTA HUNTER
Fine blues and jazz singer who started performing in the 20s and was still going strong at the time of her death in 1985 when she was in her 90s!

DRG 5195 (d) **The Legendary Alberta Hunter**
Sessions recorded in London, England, in 1934. Includes her version of "Miss Otis Regrets."

O.B.C. 510 **With Lovie Austin and Her Blues Serenaders**
Nice set recorded in 1961 and originally issued on Riverside 9418. It reunited Hunter with veteran piano player and bandleader Austin.

Stash 115 (c) **Alberta Hunter**
Reissue of 30s recordings with Buster Bailey, Lil Armstrong, and Al Casey.

Stash 123 **Young Alberta Hunter**
Fourteen fine songs from the early years of her career, 1921–29. Most of these songs are blues, some with a vaudeville flavor. She is accompanied by musicians such as Fletcher Henderson, Eubie Blake, Don Redman, Louis Armstrong, Sidney Bechet, Perry Bradford, and Fats Waller (playing pipe organ).
COMPACT DISC

ESSENTIAL SELECTION

Jass CD 6 **Young Alberta Hunter**
Gorgeous collection of 23 tracks recorded between 1921–40 and previously reissued on Stash 115 and 123. A nice mixture of blues and popular songs with Alberta accompanied by various groups ranging from the solo piano of Eddie Heywood to larger groups like The Fletcher Henderson Novelty Orchestra, and the Red Onion Jazz Babies (with Louis Armstrong, Sidney Bechet, and Lil Armstrong). Excellent sound courtesy of Jerry Valburn and Jack Towers and informative notes by Chris Alberston.
CASSETTE RELEASE ONLY
Columbia FC 37691 **The Glory of Alberta Hunter**
Columbia FC 38970 **Look for the Silver Lining**

CASSETTE AND CD RELEASE ONLY
Columbia PC 36430 **Amtrak Blues**
Excellent 70s recordings with Billy Butler (gtr) and Gerald Cook (pno).

IVORY JOE HUNTER
Excellent pop-blues singer, songwriter, and pianist who started out in 1942 with Johnny Moore's Three Blazers, later having a string of classic hits with MGM and Atlantic. The records below focus on his career as an urban blues singer.

Bulldog 1016 **The Artistry of Ivory Joe Hunter**
Not all of this album is by Hunter.

Home Cooking HCS 112 **I'm Coming Down with the Blues**
A couple of sessions in 1968 at Roy Ames' ACA studios in Houston produced these tunes. Hunter begins with a very country-and-western-sounding "I'll Give You All Night to Stop," then reprises his hit "I Almost Lost My Mind." The title tune has some heavy blues-rock guitar but Joe picks up the slack with the infectious rhythm of "Working On Me," featuring some great call and response. After a couple of smooth ballads, Joe dons his Stetson again for the honky tonkin' "The Cold Gray Light of Dawn." Side two showcases more of Hunter's barrier-breaking talents, with some fine blues, R&B, country, and even a bit of Tex-Mex on "Adios Senorita."

Route 66 KIX 4 **Seventh Street Boogie**
Sixteen fine sides from 1945–50 with various small bands.

Route 66 KIX 15 **Jumping at the Dew Drop Inn**
Sixteen cuts, 1947–51, some with Pee Wee Crayton (gtr).

Route 66 KIX 25 **I Had A Girl**
Sixteen sides from 1946–52.

COMPACT DISC
King KCD 605 **Sixteen of His Greatest Hits**

IVORY JOE HUNTER/BIG SAMBO
COMPACT DISC
P-Vine PCD 2507 **Gray Light of Port Arthur**
Fifteen previously unissued sides from 1968 by veteran blues/R&B/pop vocalist and piano player Hunter and six from 1963–64 by singer/sax player Big Sambo. The Hunter sides are presumably mostly demos and several feature Joe and his piano only, while others feature small groups with guitar, bass, drums, and occasional organ and sax. The material is extremely varied, including country songs, blues, R&B, and a rather high proportion of lounge-club pop. Big Sambo performs a mixture of pretty pedestrian Louisiana-flavored upbeat items and doo-wop-flavored ballads.

LONG JOHN HUNTER
Double Trouble TX 3011 **Texas Border Town Blues**
Excellent set of tough Texas blues recorded, for the most part, between 1961–63 by this fine singer/guitarist. Some of the tracks were issued in the 60s on the Yucca label but the majority have not been issued before, which is a surprise since most of them are very good. Hunter is a powerful singer and an imaginative and expressive guitarist. Half the tracks here are instrumentals that allow John to stretch out. The medium slow "Midnight Stroll" is particularly fine but all the tracks are worth a listen. Most of the songs and tunes are originals by Hunter.

MISSISSIPPI JOHN HURT
Magnificent country blues singer/guitarist with a distinctive and influential guitar style. One of the few blues artists whose 60s recordings were on a par with his 20s recordings. An interesting sidelight is that Hurt was rediscovered by blues collector Tom Hoskins, who listened to his 20s recording "Avalon Blues"; clues in this song led him to the guitarist, who was still living in the same town of Avalon, Mississippi.

Flyright 553 **Monday Morning Blues**
Shortly after the rediscovery of country blues legend John Hurt in 1963, Dick Spottswood took him to the Library of Congress to explore his repertoire. Over a period of a week he recorded dozens of songs, including remakes of his classic recordings and many others he learned as a young man. John was in fine form and in addition to the music we have some brief comments from John interspersed with the songs.

Heritage 301 **Mississippi John Hurt, Vol. II**
More Library of Congress recordings made in 1963. Mostly familiar Hurt pieces but beautifully performed.

Heritage 320 **Library of Congress Recordings, Vol. 3**
Complementing Flyright 553 and Heritage 301, this completes the reissue of recordings by this great songster made at the Library of Congress in July 1963. These are essentially relaxed, informal sessions, so John occasionally stumbles over words or guitar strings. He has recorded most of the songs elsewhere, sometimes in better versions. Side one is all secular, including "Pallet on the Floor," "I'm Satisfied," "C.C. Rider," and "Funky Butt." Side two is spirituals, including "Mary Don't You Weep," "Do

Lord Remember Me," "Glory Glory Hallelujah," and "Where Shall I Be."

OJL 8053 **The Piedmont Sessions, Vol. I— Folksongs and Blues**

Reissue of Piedmont 13157, issued in 1963. This was the first album recorded by John after he was "rediscovered." Features 12 fine songs, including remakes of his 1928 Okeh recordings ("Avalon Blues," "Spike Driver Blues," and "Louis Collins") and songs remembered from his early playing years ("Richland Woman Blues," "Cow Hooking Blues," and "Joe Turner Blues"). Singing and playing are fine though not quite as lucid as his later Vanguard recordings and the recordings are not as good.

OJL 8054 **The Piedmont Sessions, Vol. II— Worried Blues**

Reissue of Piedmont 13161, recorded in 1964. Recorded live in Falls Church, VA, it mostly features songs he had not recorded before. Like the first album, the sound and performances are not outstanding but these are important historical documents. Enclosed booklet features discussion of John's guitar style with some tablatures. Lazy Blues/Sliding Delta/Cow Hooking Blues #2/Weeping And Wailing/Oh Mary, Don't You Weep.

Rebel 1068 **Volume One of a Legacy**

Some of his last recordings. Although most of the songs had been recorded by Hurt several times before, these are particularly fine versions, especially the extended version of "Stack-O-Lee" and "Frankie and Albert." C.C. Rider/Coffee Blues/Do Lord Remember Me/Let the Mermaids Flirt With Me/Casey Jones.

Vanguard VSD 19/20 (d) **The Best of Mississippi John Hurt**

Two-LP set recorded live at Oberlin College in 1965. Here Am I, Oh Lord Send Me/Nearer My God To Thee/It Ain't Nobody's Business/Coffee Blues/Make Me A Pallet On the Floor.

Vanguard 79220 (d) **Today**

Recorded in 1964; superb performances. Pay Day/Candy Man/Talking Casey Blues/Coffee Blues/Hot Time In The Old Town Tonight/Spike Drivers Blues.

ESSENTIAL SELECTION

Yazoo 1065 (d) **1928 Sessions**

Beautiful reissue of his 1928 Vocalians with superb sound. Got The Blues, Can't Be Satisfied/Blue Har-

vest Blues/Blessed Be The Name/Frankie/Big Leg Blues/Praying On the Old Camp Ground.

COMPACT DISC

Flyright CD 06 **Avalon Blues**

The best of Hurt's 1963 Library of Congress recordings. Some of these were previously issued on Flyright and Heritage LPs. Avalon Blues/Frankie And Albert/Stackolee/Slidin' Delta/Nobody's Dirty Business/Hey Baby Right Away/Pay Day/Let The Mermaids Flirt With Me/Stocktime/Pera-Lee.

Vanguard VMD 79327 **Last Sessions**

J. B. HUTTO

Chicago singer and slide guitarist. Dynamic performer with powerful vocal style who died in 1983. Some of his classic early 50s recordings were reissued on the out-of-print Blues Classics 8. He recorded quite often in the 60s, 70s, and 80s with variable results.

Delmark 617 **Hawk Squat**

Probably the best of his 60s/70s recordings with Sunnyland Slim, Lee Jackson, and Frank Kirkland. Speak My Mind/Too Much Pride/20% Alcohol.

Testament 2213 **J. B. Hutto and The Hawks**

Recorded in 1966. These are some of the earliest recordings made by Hutto after his return to performing in the 60s and are some of his best, with exciting declamatory vocals and biting slide guitar by Hutto and solid accompaniment by Johnny Young, Big Walter Horton, Lee Jackson, and Fred Below.

Varrick 003 (c) **Slideslinger**

Some of Hutto's last recordings, accompanied by a tough small band. Most of this album was previously issued on the French Black and Blue label but this album has one different track.

Varrick 006 (c) **Slippin' and Slidin'**
This album features Hutto's last recordings recorded in March 1983, three months before his untimely death. Hutto is accompanied by his band, the New Hawks, and, on some cuts, there is added support from Ron Levy (pno) and The Roomful of Blues reed section. High-spirited, hard-driving blues; mostly original songs by J. B. Pretty Baby/New Hawk Walk/Black's Ball/Soul Lover/Jealous Hearted Woman/I'm Leaving You.

BESSIE JACKSON (LUCILLE BOGAN)

Blues singers often recorded under different names as a way to get around "exclusive" contracts with record labels. Bessie Jackson/Lucille Bogan is no exception to this rule, and it is unclear which (if either) name was her own. Whatever her real name, she was one of the greatest women singers ever to record. All her recordings are fine, but her 30s recordings are particularly distinguished by the wonderful piano of Walter Roland. All of the following albums are outstanding.

Agram 2005 **Women Won't Need No Men**
Sixteen sides not duplicated elsewhere. Beautiful vocals with accompaniments by Will Ezell, Charles Avery, and Walter Roland.

Blues Documents 2046 **1923–1935**
Twenty gorgeous tracks. Many have been reissued before on various collections but it's good to have these all in one place. The opening track from 1923 sounds very unlike Lucille but from then on it's that wonderful voice we know and love. There are 10 tracks featuring Walter Roland including one by Walter without Lucille and one on which she is accompanied by the dual guitars of Roland and Bob Campbell. There are some great songs here including the bizzarre "New Way Blues." What is she singing about?! Great stuff!!

Magpie 4406 **Piano Blues, Vol. 6**
The emphasis here is on the piano and vocals of Walter Roland, featuring tracks recorded between 1933–35, but there are several superb vocals by Bessie Jackson.

Yazoo 1017 **Bessie Jackson and Walter Roland, 1927–35**
Superb collection.

BO WEAVIL JACKSON (SAM BUTLER)

Matchbox 203 **Weavil Jackson**
Reissues all 12 recordings made in 1926 by this fine Alabama bluesman who also recorded under the

name of Sam Butler. He has a wonderful high declamatory vocal style and plays a mixture of blues and gospel songs—some with splendid slide guitar.

BULL MOOSE JACKSON
Urban blues singer and sax player.

Bogus 0214851 **Moosemania**
Moose is in good voice and is accompanied by The Flashcats, a seven-piece band that is joined at times by several other musicians, producing a big-band feel. Most of the material is new and written by members of the band, some with Moose's help. The album is rounded out by two tracks from a live performance.

Route 66 KIX 14 **Big Fat Mamas Are Back in Style Again**
Reissue of sides from 1945–1956.

Saxophonograph BP 506 **Moose on the Loose**
Moose's early sides (1945–47) with The Lucky Millender Orchestra, plus later grooves (1949–52) backed by Harold "Money" Johnson and Tiny Bradshaw's big bands. Joyful jiving and root-tooting abound on such houseshakers as "Hold Him Joe," "Jammin' and Jumpin'," and "Moose On The Loose." The set also includes soulful ballad singing on "Sometimes I Wonder" and "End This Misery," plus raunchy double entendre on "Oh John" and the legendary "Big Ten Inch Record." Star musicians include Bill Doggett, Sam "The Man" Taylor, Red Prysock, and Bernie Peacock.

GEORGE JACKSON
Amblin 14935 **Sweet Down Home Delta Blues**
Jackson is a very undistinguished singer and guitarist from Mississippi. Accompanied by a heavy-handed bass and drums, he performs a mixture of standards along with a few undistinguished originals.

JIM JACKSON
Distinctive Hernando, MS, country bluesman/songster who lived in Memphis and first popularized "Kansas City Blues." Jackson also sang novelty songs and country dance tunes from his many years on the medicine and minstrel-show circuits, providing a fascinating glimpse into the earlier traditions of black music. Many of the blues Jim sang had the same tune!

Agram 2004 **Kansas City Blues**
Sixteen sides recorded between 1927–29 by this Mississippi bluesman, whose music has strong links to the minstrel tradition. The LP includes several versions of his most famous song, "Kansas City Blues." Good sound, detailed notes, and lyric transcripts. He's in the Jailhouse Now/I'm a Bad

Bad Man/What a Time/Hey Mama It's Nice Like That/Foot Achin' Blues/I Ain't Gonna Turn Her Down.

Blues Documents 2037 **Remaining Titles and Alternate Takes**

Been looking for that elusive alternate take of "Kansas City Blues, Pt. 2"? Take 3 of "My Monday Woman Blues"? Take 2 of "I Heard The Voice Of A Pork Chop"? Look no further, it's all right here, in reasonably clear sound (with a few important exceptions!). Jackson's repertoire was actually much larger than his endless "Kansas City" variants suggest (including his classic "Old Dog Blue," included here), but his most interesting work has been reissued on the Agram and Earl collections. Still, if you have to have it all, here it is!

Earl BD 613 **Jim Jackson**

Sixteen sides recorded between 1928–30. Ten have been reissued before on LP and over half are still available. My Monday Woman Blues/Mobile Central Blues/Bootlegging Blues.

Note: Other reissues on Blues Classics 5, Mamlish 3803, Historical 32, Yazoo 1021, and Herwin 205.

JOHN JACKSON

Excellent Virginia country blues singer/guitarist with a distinctive vocal style and a fluid melodic guitar technique. There is quite a bit of white country material in his repertoire.

Arhoolie 1025 **Blues and Country Blues Songs from Virginia**

His first and possibly best recordings.

Arhoolie 1035 **More Blues and Country Dance Tunes**

Arhoolie 1047 **John Jackson in Europe**

Rounder 2019 **Step it Up and Go**

Rounder 2032 **Deep in the Bottom**

1983 album. John is in good form on a mixture of blues and country songs but this record is marred by a very obtrusive and unnecessary string bass on most cuts.

CASSETTE ONLY RELEASE

Arhoolie C-221 **John Jackson**

Double-length cassette combining Arhoolie 1025 and 1035.

LIL SON JACKSON

Excellent Texas country blues singer/guitarist who recorded commercially in the late 40s and early 50s and resurfaced briefly in the 60s.

Arhoolie 1004 **Lil Son Jackson**

Excellent early 60s recordings.

Note: Some of his superb 40s Gold Star sides are reissued on Arhoolie 2006.

PAPA CHARLIE JACKSON

One of the first country blues artists to record (in 1925). Charlie's material was a mixture of straight blues, hokum, old folk songs, and even a couple of topical pieces. He usually accompanied himself on 4- or 6-string banjo, although some recordings featured guitar.

Blues Documents 2036 **The Remaining Titles, 1924–34**

Matchbox 1007 **Mostly New to LP, 1924–29**

Eighteen songs. The sound from poorly recorded Paramounts is generally satisfactory and there are informative notes by Paul Oliver.

Yazoo 1029 **Fat Mouth**

Fourteen sides, recorded 1924–27. Airy Man Blues/I'm Alabama Bound/Texas Blues/Your Baby Ain't Sweet Like Me/Salty Dog Blues/Coffee Pot Blues/Shake That Thing.

NEW ORLEANS WILLIE JACKSON

Old Tramp 1215 **Complete Recordings in Chronological Order, 1926–28**

One of the more obscure bluesmen to have a whole album devoted to his music. Jackson is a pleasant enough singer with a style and repertoire indicating he probably came out of the vaudeville tradition. The accompaniments are very sparse: a basic piano with occasional banjo, sax, or guitar. A couple of tracks feature the guitar of Eddie Lang. Enjoyable in small doses, but the lack of variety in sound or material gets rather numbing after half a dozen tracks in a row.

WILLIS "GATOR" JACKSON

Whiskey, Women and. . . KM 705 **On My Own**

Sixteen fine cuts by the "Madman of The Saxophone" recorded between 1950–55.

ELMORE JAMES

The best and most influential postwar performer on slide guitar. James popularized "Dust My Broom" and was an incredibly powerful singer and guitar player. He recorded with some fine bands, often featuring the wonderful piano of Johnny Jones and the booting tenor sax of J. T. Brown. At his death in 1963, he was still at his peak. All his records are worth getting and he rarely, if ever, made a bad one! At this point, just about all his recordings have been made available and, although there is often duplication among albums, the real fan will want almost all of them in order to get the occasional track not available elsewhere or alternate takes.

Ace CH 31 The Best of Elmore James and His Broom Dusters

Reissue of United 7743, but with superior sound and different cover and notes. Twelve great sides, including "Dust My Blues," "Blues before Sunrise," "Standing at the Crossroads," and "Wild about You Baby."

Ace CH 112 The Original Meteor and Flair Sides

Fourteen classic sides featuring some of his greatest recordings. They have been lovingly remastered by Bob Jones and have never sounded better.

ESSENTIAL SELECTION

Ace CH 192 (c,d) Let's Cut It: The Very Best Of Elmore James

Eighteen tracks from the Flair and Modern labels. The sound on this release is excellent with lots of presence and an almost total absence of tape hiss, which is remarkable considering the condition of the original tapes. No real surprises here but there are a few previously unissued alternate takes. Plenty of great intense singing and playing from Elmore and top-flight backup from his band. Dust My Broom/No Love In My Heart/Standing At the Crossroads/Sunnyland/Happy Home/Long Tall Woman/Hawaiian Boogie/Dark and Dreary/I Believe.

Charly CRB 1008 (c) One Way Out

Sixteen classic sides from Trumpet, Vee Jay, Fire, and Enjoy. Talk To Me Baby/Can't Stop Lovin' My Baby/The Sky Is Crying/Something Inside Of Me/Coming Home/Take Me Where You Go/Person To Person/12-Year-Old Boy.

Charly CRB 1017 Got To Move

Sixteen more recordings cut between 1957–63 for Vee Jay, Chief, Fire, Enjoy, and Spheresound. Tremendous vocals and guitar and top-notch bands. Dust My Broom (60s version)/Knocking At Your Door/Pickin' The Blues/My Bleeding Heart/Early One Morning/Got To Move/It Hurts Me Too (60s version)/Held My Baby Last Night.

Charly CRB 1212 Come Go with Me

Sixteen tracks recorded by Bobby Robinson between 1959–63.

Chess 9114 (c) Elmore James/John Brim: Whose Muddy Shoes

Originally issued as Chess 1537 in 1969, this album features eight classic sides by James and six by Brim. Elmore plays some of his finest slide guitar ever on classics like "I Can't Hold Out," "Sun Is Shining," and "Stormy Monday," and there is great harmonica by Little Walter on Brim's "Rattlesnake." The packaging on this reissue is not the greatest but the music is!

Collectables 5112 (c) Golden Classics

Twelve great Fire sides (all of these are on the Japanese Fire 3-LP set). Hand In Hand/Every Day I Have The Blues/It Hurts Me Too/12-Year-Old Boy/I Gotta Go Now/Mean Mistreatin' Mama.

Collectables 5184 (c,d) The Complete Fire and Enjoy Sessions, Part 1

Collectables 5185 (c,d) The Complete Fire and Enjoy Sessions, Part 2

Collectables 5186 (c,d) The Complete Fire and Enjoy Sessions, Part 3

Collectables 5187 (c,d) The Complete Fire and Enjoy Sessions, Part 4

In the four years prior to his death, James was recorded quite extensively by New York producer Bobby Robinson for his Fire and Enjoy labels and these four LPs/CDs present these recordings pretty much in their entirety. Although most of these have been reissued before—most notably on the Japanese Fire 3-LP box—this set does have a couple of surprises and it's great to have these all available in compact disc form. The first volume from his 1959 and '60 sessions includes such gems as the lyrical "The Sky Is Crying," a stinging remake of his most famous song, "Dust My Broom," a supercharged citified version of the Mississippi blues standard "Rollin' and Tumblin'," and my personal favorite, "Done Somebody Wrong," with its distinctive rhythm and searing slide guitar. The second volume features recordings from 1960 and '61, including his long, moving, and intense "Something Inside Of Me," two takes of the Latin-flavored "Stranger Blues," a tough version of his mentor Robert Johnson's "Standing At The Crossroads," and a wonderful version of Big Boy Crudup's "Look On Yonder Wall" recorded in New Orleans in 1961 with lovely harmonica by Sammy Myers. Volume 3 starts off with more tracks from the '61 New Orleans session, including one of his best-known songs, the frequently covered "Shake Your Money Maker," three takes of the standard "Mean Mistreatin' Mama," and a remake of his own "Sunnyland." There are several other remakes of songs he had recorded earlier, including "Hand In Hand" and "It Hurts Me Too" from 1962–63 sessions. By this time, Elmore's health was failing and his singing and playing were not quite as strong, though still powerful and effective. Volume 4 features more tracks from his last sessions, again including quite a few remakes and somewhat tentative performances from Elmore and what sounds like mostly a pickup band. It includes several bits of studio chat among Elmore, Robinson, and piano player Johnny Walker. However, this album ends with a few surprises: three tracks which, to the best of my knowledge, have not been issued before, including a version of "Look On Yonder Wall" from a different session with different lyrics, the powerful "You Know You Done Me Wrong," with some fine piano, and the rocking instrumental "Black Snake Slide." As usual for Collectables, the packaging is minimal and there is no discographical information, though there are notes (somewhat generic) from George Moonoogian. Sound is better than usual for this label. Until someone does the definitive version of these recordings, these will keep me happy for a long time!

Fire (Japan) PLP 6005/6/7 Something Inside of Me
This beautiful 3-LP box set features all 47 tracks recorded for Bobby Robinson's Fire and Enjoy labels between 1959–63. Many of these tracks are available on Charly and Collectables, but the attractive packaging and high-quality mastering and pressing make this a worthwhile investment. This set does not include all of the alternate tracks from the last Fire sessions available on the Collectables reissue. Wonderful singing and slide guitar from Elmore and great work from the band. Includes booklet with photos, notes in Japanese, and lyric transcriptions in English.

Relic 1021 The Last Session (2/21/63)
Hot on the heels of the Collectables Fire/Enjoy reissues, Relic has made their bid for a share of the Elmore James market with this upcoming release. No track listing yet, but I'll bet that this one, mastered from original stereo tapes and pressed on audiophile vinyl, will have the competitve edge in terms of sound quality.

COMPACT DISC

Charly CD 34 Shake Your Moneymaker
Twenty-two tracks recorded for Chief, Vee Jay, Fire, and Enjoy. All these tracks have been available before on Charly LP but now you can listen to a solid

60 minutes of Elmore with better-than-usual sound for a Charly CD. Includes one of my all-time favorite Elmore tracks, the incredible "Done Somebody Wrong." Good notes by Alan Balfour but no discographical notes. Dust My Broom/Coming Home/Elmore's Contribution To Jazz/Take Me Where You Go/Held My Baby Last Night/Rollin' and Tumblin'/Fine Little Mama/I Need You/Something Inside Of Me/Baby Please Set A Date/Got To Move.

Charly CD 180 Come Go with Me
Twenty-four tracks recorded for Bobby Robinson's Fire, Fury, and Enjoy labels between 1959–63. All these tracks are available on a series of LPs/CDs issued on Collectables, along with all of Elmore's other recordings for Robinson. Stranger Blues/So Unkind/Sunnyland Train/12-Year-Old Boy/My Kind Of Woman/Hand In Hand/My Baby's Gone/Make My Dreams Come True/My Bleeding Heart/ Early One Morning/It Hurts Me Too/I Have A Right To Love My Baby.

Chess (France) 600119 Elmore James, John Brim, Floyd Jones
Features all the Chess recordings of these three great artists. Fabulous music but, as usual for French Chess, the sound is not as good as it should be.

ELMORE JAMES/JIMMY REED
COMPACT DISC
Muse MCD 5087 Street Talkin'

FRANK "SPRINGBACK" JAMES
Document 538 Complete Recordings in Chronological Order
Eighteen tracks recorded between 1934–37 by the brilliant singer/piano player, about half previously on LP but only a few still available.

SKIP JAMES
Great Mississippi country bluesman. His 1931 recordings are some of the most unique and moving performances on record. James's music was uncompromisingly bleak—a welling up of intense emotions that is sometimes almost painful to listen to. He had an expressive high voice that he accompanied on either guitar or piano; he was equally accomplished on both. His guitar playing was miraculous. Played, for the most part, in "cross-note" tuning, it produced a modal quality that was perfectly suited to the somber nature of his music. His playing is fluid and supple and at times his picking technique is awe-inspiring! His piano playing is also unique and effective. His 60s rediscovery recordings on Biograph and Melodeon (now out of print) and

Vanguard don't have quite the grandeur of his early recordings but are superb in their own right. His classic Paramount recordings from 1931 have been reissued several times but the definitive collection of these is Yazoo 1072, which has superior sound and packaging.

Document 523 Live at "The 2nd Fret"

Recorded live in Philadelphia in 1966. Skip is in fine form but the recording quality is mediocre and Skip sounds like he's singing in the bottom of a barrel. Since he has recorded all the songs elsewhere with better sound, this set is pretty expendable.

ESSENTIAL SELECTION

Yazoo 1072 Skip James : The Complete 1931 Session

All 18 tracks recorded by James for Paramount in 1931. All of these tracks were available on Matchbox 207 though the sound here is considerably better but still rather rough at times. You will probably want to get this, as the recordings here are some of the greatest blues ever recorded. Notes by Stephen Calt are, as usual for him, pompous but informative.

COMPACT DISC

Vanguard VMD 79219 Today!

Mid-60s recordings after James's "rediscovery"; powerful, although less moving than his 78s from 1931.

Vanguard VMD 79273 Devil Got My Woman

CD reissue of his second Vanguard album recorded in 1967, two years before his death at the age of 67. It includes remakes of a few of his 1931 Paramount recordings including the spine-chilling title song and the wonderful "Little Cow, Little Calf Blues," the latter featuring some of his amazing piano playing. There are his unique interpretations of familiar themes in "Worried Blues" and "Catfish Blues" and some songs recently composed by Skip including "Sickbed Blues" and a song for his wife, "Lorenzo

Blues." Exquisite and timeless music reproduced with crystal clarity.

FRANKIE "HALF PINT" JAXON

Distinctive, high-pitched vocalist who recorded in the late 20s and early 30s; noted for his outrageous performances of primarily "hokum" (novelty) songs.

Blues Documents 2049 The Remaining Titles

Nineteen tracks from a number of different sessions with varied personnel ranging from solo piano to large jazz-flavored band. Five songs that were not originally issued are included, a riotous version of Georgia Tom's risque "Operation Blues," a distinctive treatment of "Mama Don't Allow," and the weird "Mortgage Blues."

Collector's Item 013 Saturday Night Scrontch

Absolutely delightful album. Sixteen sides recorded between 1928–30 featuring accompaniments by Tampa Red—playing some lovely slide guitar—and various other musicians on piano, kazoo, washboard, and jug. Exuberant and bawdy songs that Jaxon sings with great enthusiasm. Very few of these tracks have been reissued before and the sound, mastered by the legendary John R. T. Davies, is superb. Excellent notes and fascinating cover art. Includes a truly amazing version of "How Long"!

Collector's Items 014 Can't You Wait Till You Get Home

Sixteen more sides recorded between 1926–33. These mostly feature Frankie accompanied by various piano players. Two feature him with Bill Johnson's Louisiana Jug Band, and four with a jazz group. Although it's not quite as strong as the previous album, there are some great performances here featuring Frankie's witty delivery. Fine sound and excellent notes. Hannah Fell in Love With My Piano/Can't You Wait Till You Get Home/How Can I Get It/Willie the Weeper.

Document 560 1937–1938

Eighteen tracks recorded between 1937–38, 14 with the Harlem Hamfats and the remainder with the Barney Bigard Quartet. Jaxon attacks all the songs with vigor, interjecting spoken comments between the verses, and the instrumental accompaniment is appropriately lively. Sound is excellent. Recommended.

BLIND LEMON JEFFERSON

Texas country bluesman active in the 1920s, who was probably the most popular country bluesman of all time among black audiences. The Yazoo 2-LP set is the best general compilation of his music, featuring some of his best recordings reproduced with exceptional fidelity.

Matchbox 1001 **The Remaining Titles**
Eighteen titles recorded between 1926–29. Most of
the tracks on this album have been available in the
US on Biograph and Melodeon. Got the
Blues/Matchbox Blues/He Arose From the Dead.
Milestone 2004 **Blind Lemon, Vol. I**
Milestone 2007 **Blind Lemon, Vol. II**
Milestone 2013 **Black Snake Moan**
Milestone 47022 **Blind Lemon Jefferson**
Two-LP set with 32 of the 36 songs on the previous
3 Milestone albums!

ESSENTIAL SELECTION

Yazoo 1069 (c,d) **King of the Country Blues**
Definitive 2-LP collection, with extensive notes on
Lemon's life and music. Against almost insurmount-
able odds—the incredibly bad sound quality of early
Paramount recordings—Yazoo has produced an
album on which one can hear Lemon's vocals and
guitar with a clarity never heard before! The enhanced quality means one can truly understand why
Lemon is considered to be one of the greatest
country bluesmen of all times and was held in such
great esteem by his contemporaries. The CD has
fewer tracks than the double LP.

GUS JENKINS
Diving Duck 4309 **Cold Love**
The long-awaited indispensible set of 50s sides by
this superb pianist who recorded fine down-home
blues and wild housewreckers under various pseu-
donyms, including Little Temple in '54 and The
Young Wolf for Combo in '53. All cuts recorded
between 1953–62. Rarities like "Weird," with Albert
and Charles Bedeaux and harp player Neal Johnson,
on Pioneer from '53, make this set a "must."

ELLA JOHNSON
Jukebox Lil 604 **Say Ella**
Sixteen sides recorded between 1942–57 by this fine
jazz/blues vocalist accompanied by her brother Bud-
dy Johnson and His Orchestra, one of the early
R&B-influenced big bands.

BIG JACK JOHNSON
Earwig 4910 **The Oil Man**
Debut album of no-nonsense, down-home blues by
singer/guitarist Johnson, who has worked with
Frank Frost for almost 25 years. Frost plays piano
on this album and they are joined by Clarksdale
musicians Ernest Roy on bass and Walter Roy on
drums. In spite of the small size of the group, they
generate a full sound thanks to Johnson's powerful
vocals and basic but energetic guitar style. The
material is a mixture of originals like the title song

and "I'm Gonna Give Up Disco And Go Back To the
Blues," which is based on Junior Parker's "Mystery
Train." Jack's guitar playing evokes the feel of early
Willie Johnson or Pat Hare. The rest of the album
includes songs from Howlin' Wolf, Tommy Johnson
(a pile-driving "Catfish"), and Johnny Taylor, all
given an original touch. It even includes an instrumental version of "Tom Dooley" and a nice
version of "Steel Guitar Rag." If you like Magic
Slim, you're sure to like Jack Johnson too. Recommended!

HERMAN JOHNSON
Excellent Louisiana country bluesman recorded
by Harry Oster in the 60s.
Arhoolie 1060 **Louisiana Country Blues**
I Just Keeps On Wanting You/Motherless
Children/She's A Looking For Me/I'm Growing
Older/Leaving Blues.

JAMES "STUMP" JOHNSON
Excellent St. Louis-based singer/piano player.
Agram 2007 **The Duck's Yas-Yas-Yas**
Fifteen sides recorded between 1928–32 and four
from a 1964 session for Euphonic.

JIMMY JOHNSON
Exciting Chicago blues singer/guitarist with a
gospel-flavored vocal style and a hard-driving
guitar technique. His band is excellent and between them they have written some excellent
blues songs. One of the best contemporary artists!
Alligator 4744 (c) **Bar Room Preacher**
Originally issued in France on Blue Phoenix in
1983. Although only accompanied by keyboards,
bass, and drums, the sound is full and rich. The
material is mostly covers but Jimmy brings his own
unique approach to songs like Fenton Robinson's
"You Don't Know What Love Is," John Lee
Hooker's "When My First Wife Quit Me," and a
spine-tingling version of T-Bone Walker's "Cold
Cold Feeling." There are also a few fine originals,
including the hard-driving "Happy Home," the
powerful and insightful "Heap See," and the rollicking instrumental shuffle "Missing Link."
Delmark 644 **Johnson's Whacks**
Mostly original songs.
Delmark 647 **North/South**
Splendid 1982 album; all original songs with fine
singing and playing by Johnson and solid backup by
the band. Although obviously a blues band, Johnson
and the group are aware of contemporary trends in
music and incorporate them into their sound in an
exciting and tasteful manner.

JOHNNIE JOHNSON
Pulsar 1002 Blue Hand Johnnie

Johnnie Johnson is the near-legendary piano player who backed Chuck Berry on many of his classic hits. However, his first solo album is disappointing. There's nothing wrong with his playing but the production stinks. Johnny is playing a horrible rinky-tink piano and the backing group is pretty mediocre; Steve Waldman's guitar playing is particularly obnoxious. Several tracks have vocals by the mediocre Barbara Carr or adequate Stacy Johnson. It's hard to believe that the excellent producer Oliver Sain had a hand in this mess. Johnnie may not have a solo album in him.

LARRY JOHNSON

Young New York-based country blues singer/guitarist. Fine picker.

L+R 42.046 Johnson! Where Did You Get That Sound?

Pleasant album of East Coast raggy blues performed by Johnson and harmonica player Nat Riddles. Two of the vocals are by Riddles and the rest are by Johnson.

Spivey 1034 Larry Johnson and Nat Riddles

Recorded at Larry's home in the early 80s, they perform songs from the repertoires of Robert Johnson, Gary Davis, Chuck Bradford, and Roosevelt Sykes. Some good performances but the recording quality, as is so often the case with Spivey, is mediocre.

COMPACT DISC
JSP 237 Railroad Man

1990 recordings with a small band.

LIL JOHNSON
Blues Documents 2083 1935–37

Complementing Document 516, this collection features 22 fine sides by this excellent Chicago singer. Lil was a powerful and expressive vocalist with a penchant for risque songs, and this collection features such delicacies as "If You Can Dish It (I Can Take It)," "Press My Button (Ring My Bell)," "Get 'Em From the Peanut Man," "Meat Balls," "You Stole My Cherry," and others served up with relish. There are also some fine slow blues like "Shake Man Blues" and "Scuffling Woman Blues." The first two tracks feature the brilliant piano of Frank "Springback" James, and many of the others feature the equally brilliant Black Bob. Other accompanying musicians include Big Bill Broonzy, Mr. Sheiks, and Arnett Nelson. Several tracks are from unissued test pressings. Most worthwhile.

Document 516 1936–37

Eighteen sides not previously on LP by this undeservedly obscure singer. Lil is a vibrant and powerful singer who is equally at home on slow, intense blues like "Black and Evil Blues" or "River Hip Papa," risque songs like "Get 'Em From the Peanut Man" and "Sam, The Hot Dog Man," and good-time stompers like "Rug Cutter's Function" and "Goofer Dust Swing." She is at her very best on the superb topical song "That Bonus Done Gone Through." She is joined by many fine musicians and about half the tracks feature the brilliant piano of Black Bob. Other musicians include Big Bill Broonzy (gtr), Blind John Davis (pno), and "Mr Sheiks" (tpt). Recommended.

LONNIE JOHNSON

One of the great and important blues singers and guitarists. His 20s and 30s recordings on his own or as a sideman are real classics. Johnson was a rare musician who was equally at home playing country blues and the more modern jazz stylings. He is famous for his guitar duets with white picker Eddie Lang and his wonderful sessions with Louis Armstrong's Hot Five. Most surprisingly, Johnson could switch from sophisticated guitar picking to eerie back-country blues fiddling! Certainly none of his contemporaries had this range. His later recordings from the 40s, 50s, and 60s are somewhat slicker, and some of his later blues ballads have a real "pop" flavour, but almost all of his recordings are worth a listen.

Blues Boy 300 (d) The Originator of Modern Guitar Blues

Fine selection of sides from 1941–52, including some pop ballads. Sound and packaging are superb with complete song lyrics.

Blues Documents 2064 1926–40

A varied collection of Johnson's music. "Very Lonesome Blues" features Lonnie and James Johnson both on violin providing a very eerie backdrop for Lonnie's vocals! On two tracks, Lonnie plays harmonium with James also on violin for a very unique, if not completely successful, sound. Other tracks feature Lonnie on fiddle or piano and, of course, there are several tracks with his distinctive and beautiful guitar accompaniments. He also accompanies the excellent Helen Humes on "Black Cat Blues" and "A Worried Woman's Blues." As far as I can tell, none of these tracks have been reissued before. Sound quality ranges from very good to poor.

Columbia C 46221 (c,d) Steppin' on the Blues

A magnificent survey of 19 recordings made between 1925–32. Johnson's supple guitar style was both lyrical and rhythmic, thoroughly innovative, and the envy of many of his contemporaries. He had a distinctive sly vocal style and wrote songs that were well out of the ordinary, as one can hear on "Got the Blues for Murder Only" and "She's Making Whoopee in Hell Tonight." He is equally comfortable duetting with white guitarist Eddie Lang or accompanying rural Texas singer Texas Alexander. This set also features four previously unissued solo guitar instrumentals and a couple of vocal duets with Victoria Spivey. The notes by Pete Welding include an informative survey of Johnson's career.

Document 546 1926–42

Eighteen tracks.

Mamlish 3807 Mr. Johnson's Blues

Superb selection of 14 sides from 1926–32. Vocals by Lonnie, Mooch Richardson, Katherine Baker, and Victoria Spivey. Excellent sound and detailed notes.

Matchbox 1006 Vol. 1, 1926–28

Eighteen mostly previously unavailable tracks recorded between January 1926 and March 1928, featuring Lonnie as vocalist or as accompanist to vocalists James "Steady Roll" Johnson, Raymond Boyd, or Joe Brown. Besides witnessing his renowned prowess as a guitarist, we also hear Lonnie on banjo, violin, and kazoo! The 1926 recordings are all from the acoustic era of recording and so the sound on these has a hollow, distant quality. The later electrically recorded sides from 1927–28 sound fine.

Matchbox 1013 Vol. 2, 1927–32

A gorgeous collection of 18 tracks, most of which have never been on LP before. These are all well-recorded sides made when Lonnie was in his prime. Side one features Lonnie in various settings: with the rolling piano of De Loise Searcy on his version of the then-popular hit "Kansas City Blues," duetting with Jimmy Foster on the hokum "I Want Some O' That What You Got," and trading lines with Victoria Spivey on the outstanding "You Done Lost Your Good Thing Now." The rest of the album is mostly Lonnie and his guitar, revealing why he is considered one of the all-time greatest blues guitarists and showing his abilities as a blues writer of great wit and originality. Sound is generally good; there are detailed notes by Paul Oliver, and full discographical details.

O.B.C. 502 Blues by Lonnie Johnson

Originally issued as Bluesville 1007 in 1960, this is a fine R&B-flavored session. Some powerful singing and electric guitar from Lonnie with Hal Singer (ten sax), Claude Hopkins (pno), Wendell Marshall (b), and Bobby Donaldson (drm).

OJL 23 Woke Up This Morning with Blues in My Fingers

Sixteen cuts from 1927–32, most never before reissued and four previously unissued in any form.

Oldie Blues 2819 Blues for Everybody

Eighteen sides recorded between 1942–46 with ubiquitous piano player Blind John Davis. Many of the songs here are updates of earlier Johnson compositions and his guitar playing is somewhat restrained. Davis provides impeccable backup, though his playing tends to become tedious after awhile. These drawbacks, coupled with inferior sound and the fact that nearly all the songs have identical tunes, makes this one of the less desirable reissues of Johnson.

Storyville 4042 Swingin' with Lonnie

Nice set recorded in Denmark in 1963 drawn from three old Storyville albums. With Otis Spann on piano on most cuts.

Swaggie 1225 The Blues of Lonnie Johnson

Sixteen sides recorded for Decca in 1937–38. Half of the tracks are solo and half are with a small group including Roosevelt Sykes on piano. Beautiful sound.

Swaggie 1229 Eddie Lang and Lonnie Johnson

Superb album of blues and jazz guitar instrumentals recorded in the 1920s, including solos and some stupendous duets. Lang took the pseudonym of "Blind Willie Dunn" for the duet sessions, to avoid the controversy of a white artist recording with a black musician.

Swaggie 1276 Eddie Lang and Lonnie Johnson, Vol. 2

Mostly focuses on jazz stylings of Lang but does include some great duets and a couple of accompaniments for Texas Alexander.

LONNIE JOHNSON/VICTORIA SPIVEY

O.B.C. 518 Idle Hours

Reissue of Bluesville 1044 from 1961. This album features nine solo performances by Lonnie and his guitar with Cliff Jackson (pno), two vocal duets with Victoria, and one solo performance by Victoria with her own piano. The duets are charming if not terribly exciting and Lonnie's solo performances are about par for the period—pleasant sentimental blues. The solo Spivey cut, "I Got The Blues So Bad," is a nice funky performance.

LUTHER "HOUSEROCKER" JOHNSON

Iciban 1060 (c,d) Takin' a Bite Outta the Blues

Fine set of 60s-style Chicago blues by this veteran singer/guitarist. Luther is a good singer and a melodic guitarist with the clipped phrasing popular on the West Side of Chicago. The songs are mostly familiar standards, but Luther and his group give them respectful treatment. There are a couple of good originals, too: "Trouble Blues" and "Big Money." Nothing flashy or high energy here; just down-to-earth, no-nonsense blues. Little Car Blues/Pretty Thing/Rock Me Baby/What'd I Say.

Rooster Blues 7607 Doin' the Sugar Too

Johnson performs a wide range of material—from the acoustic down-home blues of "Early in the Morning Blues" to the funk flavor of "Get on the Floor"—and it all works very well. On six cuts he is accompanied by a rhythm section (piano, organ, bass, and drums) and on four tracks he is joined by the Roomful of Blues Horns (tenor, alto, and baritone sax, trumpet, and trombone) for a richer sound.

COMPACT DISC

Black & Blue 59.519 2 Luther's Blues

Reissue of Black & Blue 33.519 with three extra previously unissued titles. Johnson is accompanied by Bob Margolin, Jerry Portnoy, "Pinetop" Perkins, Calvin Jones, and Willie Smith on a selection of old favorites recorded in 1976. Back at the Chicken Shack/Too Many Drivers/Luther's Blues/Nobody Wants to Lose/Better Watch Yourself/Boogie in the Dark.

MARY JOHNSON

Agram 2014 I Just Can't Take It

Eighteen sides by fine St. Louis-based singer recorded between 1929–36 with accompaniments by Ike Rodgers, Henry Brown, Tampa Red, and Peetie Wheatstraw.

MERLINE JOHNSON

Merline Johnson, aka "The Yas Yas Girl," was a good, mainstream Chicago blues singer who recorded extensively in the middle and late 30s, though very few of her recordings have been reissued.

Best Of Blues BOB 8 The Yas Yas Girl

Twenty tracks recorded between 1937–41, none previously on LP. With accompaniments by Black Bob, Big Bill Broonzy, and Blind John Davis.

Document 562 The Yas Yas Girl

Twenty tracks recorded between 1937–40, most not previously on LP.

Earl BD 601 The Yas Yas Girl

Fourteen songs recorded between 1938–41. Accompanists include George Barnes, Blind John Davis, and Big Bill Broonzy.

PETE JOHNSON

Great blues/boogie/jazz piano player.

ESSENTIAL SELECTION

Document 535 1938–47

Sixteen tracks featuring one of the greatest blues and boogie piano players of all time. Although many of these tracks have been reissued, most are not readily available at this time. Included are six songs featuring the vocals of his long-time partner Big Joe Turner, and a couple feature him fronting the Benny Goodman Orchestra. There are a couple of incredible duets with Albert Ammons, some numbers with a small group, and some solo performances. Johnson is in top form throughout, playing with a light, swinging touch that most piano players would kill for. Essential!

Oldie Blues 2801 Master of Blues and Boogie Woogie

Nine solos from 1944 and '46, four sides with a small band and two with a rhythm section from 1947.

Oldie Blues 2806 Master of Blues and Boogie Woogie, Vol. 2

Ten solos from 1939 and six by the Pete Johnson Quartet from 1947.

Oldie Blues 2823 Master of Blues and Boogie Woogie, Vol. 3

Four cuts from 1939 with excellent rhythm section, two solo cuts from 1939, three from 1946 with small group including excellent guitar by Jimmy Shirley and incongruous organ by Bill Gooden, and three from 1949 with a small band. Very nice!

Savoy SJC 414 Pete's Blues

Reissue of Savoy MG 12199 at a budget price. A

beautiful blues/jazz jam session with Johnson accompanied by two separate groups, including such great musicians as Albert Nicholas, Hot Lips Page, Jimmy Shirley, Ben Webster, Clyde Bernhardt, and Budd Johnson. The second side includes a couple of fine vocals by Etta Jones.

CASSETTE ONLY RELEASE

MCA 1333 **Boogie Woogie Mood**
Originally on French MCA, these are superb sides from 1940, '41, and '44. Eight tracks are solos, there are four with a rhythm section, and one with a band.

Note: See also Storyville 184 in PREWAR PIANO BLUES AND BOOGIE Collections. Johnson also recorded extensively behind Joe Turner.

ROBERT JOHNSON

Mississippi Delta singer/guitarist who recorded only a handful of songs in 1936 and 1937. Possibly the greatest country bluesman who ever lived and undeniably one of the most influential! He had an impassioned vocal style and a unique lyric approach that seemed to speak of an inner torment. This was complemented by an equally fervent guitar style with frequent use of bottleneck. The intensity of songs like "Hellhound On My Trail" or "Me And The Devil" is almost numbing in its dark ferocity. There is no other blues artist, to my knowledge, who uses imagery of this intensity so consistently. It's hard to believe that in live performance he actually did versions of "Yes Sir, That's My Baby" and "Tumbling Tumbleweeds"! Perhaps it is this dark intensity that strikes home so strongly for his listeners and crosses racial, cultural, and language barriers. Unlike some of the great Mississippi blues performers who preceded and influenced him, his music is much more accessible. His voice is high and clear and, while not all completely intelligible, most of the lyrics are easy to understand. His sound is transitional between the rough early Mississippi Delta feel and the shortly-to-come Chicago blues bands with his insistent and compulsive rhythms and memorable melody lines. Quite a few of his songs feature slide guitar and there have been few, if any, performers whose playing was so accomplished and moving, ranging from the lyrical beauty of "Come On In My Kitchen" to the mind-boggling pyrotechnics of "Preachin' Blues." His songs have been recorded hundreds of times by other musicians and his guitar techniques have provided the springboard for many postwar stylings. An essential artist for any blues lover to listen to.

Columbia C3 46222 (c,d) **The Complete Recordings**
Three-LP/cassette/two-CD compilation of all of Johnson's recordings. This magnificent collection features all 29 songs that he recorded in Dallas and San Antonio in 1936 and 1937, plus 12 alternate takes. The alternate takes are sometimes musically quite different (as in "Come On In My Kitchen"), but often the differences are more subtle but still significant: different verses, different guitar riffs, or different shadings in vocal emphasis. This makes it all the more frustrating to find out that there may have, at one time, existed other alternate takes that have not survived. The sound is generally excellent, although some of the rarer selections are a bit noisy. The set comes with a 48-page booklet that includes an essay by Steve LaVere that features much previously unpublished material based on his extensive research, along with many rare photographs of Robert, his family, and his musical associates, including an amazing early photo of Elmore James. Transcriptions of lyrics for all songs are included.

TOMMY JOHNSON

Another of the truly great Mississippi country bluesmen who, regrettably, only recorded a handful of sides.

Wolf WSE 104 **Tommy Johnson**
Twelve sides of exquisite beauty. These cuts have been reissued several times before, but it's great to have them in their entirety. Superb vocals, lovely guitar, and accompaniments by Charlie McCoy and Ishman Bracey.

COMPACT DISC

Document DOCD 5001 **Complete Recorded Works in Chronological Order**
All of Johnson's recordings from 1928–29, including some recently discovered acetates. Includes accompaniments by Charlie McCoy and the bizarre New Orleans piano and clarinet duo, The Nehi Boys.

BLIND WILLIE JOHNSON
ESSENTIAL SELECTION
Yazoo 1058 (d) **Praise God I'm Satisfied**
The greatest-ever rural religious singer/guitarist. Some of the most powerful and moving music ever committed to record; stunning singing form Willie (and sometimes his wife Angeline) and utterly magnificent guitar, including some gorgeous bottleneck stylings. Every track is a gem. His instrumental and humming version of the old spiritual "Dark Was the Night, Cold Was the Ground" never fails to raise the hairs on the back of my neck!

CASSETTE AND CD RELEASE ONLY
Yazoo 1078 **Sweeter as the Years Go By**
Sixteen tracks that, with Yazoo 1058, give the complete recorded output of this great gospel singer. Excellent sound with extensive notes by David Evans.

BESSIE JONES
Famed Georgia Sea Islands singer, folklorist, and group leader.
Rounder 2015 (c) **So Glad I'm Here**
Rounder 8004 **Step It Down**
Children's game songs.

CASEY JONES
Rooster Blues 7612 **Solid Blue**
Drummer Casey Jones's solid drum work has enlivened hundreds of blues sessions. Though not an outstanding singer, Casey is a very good one and is accompanied by an outstanding group of Chicago musicians spearheaded by the brilliant and lyrical guitarist Maurice Vaughn, who is rapidly becoming one of my favorite blues guitarists. Also included are keyboards player Allen Batts, bassist Johnny B. Gayden, and other musicians. Songs are all originals by Casey and include his dedication to great blues artists of the past ("Tribute to the Boogie Men"), the rocking "Big Cities Shuffle," and the wonderful minor key blues "News Is Bad."

COLEY JONES and THE DALLAS STRING BAND
Matchbox 208 **Coley Jones and The Dallas String Band, 1927–1929**
The complete recordings of the fine Texas singer and guitar player Coley Jones, as a solo artist and as leader of one of the very few black string bands on record, the exciting Dallas String Band. The four solo performances by Jones are fascinating examples of preblues and minstrel traditions; the eight tracks by the Dallas String Band are lively and exciting, highlighted by the oft-reissued "Dallas Rag." There are also four blues duets with Texas singer Bobbie Cadillac. Very little here has been reissued before. Brief but excellent notes by Paul Oliver.

CURTIS JONES
Enjoyable singer/piano player who first recorded in the 30s and is best known for his "Lonesome Bedroom Blues" and "Tin Pan Alley." Jones was a fine distinctive singer with a wistful vocal quality and he was a good piano player.
Delmark 605 **Lonesome Bedroom Blues**
Nice early 60s sides.
Document 592 **1937–40**
This album is a fine collection of his original songs. Curtis is, as usual, accompanied by Willie Bee James on guitar, with drums, bass, or washboard. Very few of these tracks have been reissued before. Decoration Day Blues/Drinking and Thinking Blues/Bad Avenue Blues/Let Me Be Your Playmate/Yours All Alone/Down in the Slums/Black Gypsy Blues.
O.B.C. 515 **Trouble Blues**
Reissue of Bluesville 1022 originally recorded in 1960. Jones is accompanied by a rhythm section and most incongruously by an organ player who sounds totally out of place here and almost ruins what is an excellent album. The songs are all Jones's originals and include a remake of one of his most popular 30s recordings, "Lonesome Bedroom Blues." Some nice stuff but oh that awful organ! Suicide Blues/Weekend Blues/Trouble Blues/Low Down Worried Blues.
Oldie Blues 2824 **Blues and Trouble**
Early recordings featuring 16 cuts recorded between 1937–53 with various small groups. A few cuts are from rough sounding 78s, but otherwise good sound.
See For Miles SEE 53 **Curtis Jones in London**
Reissue of 1964 Decca album plus two extra cuts recorded in London with, on some cuts, a small group with Alexis Korner (gtr), Jack Fallon (b), and Eddie Taylor (drm). Jones does a mixture of lively boogies, some remakes of his 30s recordings, new original songs, plus songs from the repertoires of Joe Liggins, Elmore James, and Percy Mayfield. The group featured on several cuts provides firm support for Curtis's singing and piano

DENNIS "LITTLE HAT" JONES/ J. T. "FUNNY PAPA" SMITH
Blues Documents 2010 **Texas Blues Guitar, 1929–35**
A fine collection of Texas country blues. Side one features all 10 sides recorded in 1929–30 by Dennis "Little Hat" Jones. Although all of these tracks have

been issued before on various albums, it is nice to have them all collected together here. Jones was a very fine singer with a loose, flowing vocal style, at times reminiscent of Texas Alexander. His guitar style counterpoints his vocals, being powerful and rhythmic. The 10 sides featuring J. T. "Funny Papa" Smith are all the remaining tracks by him that are not on Yazoo 1031; most of these have never been on LP before. Smith was a superb singer and guitarist with an intense vocal style and varied guitar technique. Two of the tracks feature him accompanying vocalist Bernice Edwards. Some splendid stuff!

FLOYD JONES
Floyd, who died in 1990, was a wonderful Chicago-based singer. Originally from Arkansas, he had a wonderful mournful voice and has written some powerful and significant songs.

Testament 2214 Masters of Modern Blues, Vol. 3 —Floyd Jones/Eddie Taylor
Two wonderful down-home performers recorded in 1966 with an all-star band, including Taylor (gtr), Jones (b), Big Walter Horton (hca), Otis Spann (pno), and Fred Below (drm). Most of the songs here are remakes of songs they had recorded earlier in the late 40s and 50s but these performances stand on their own. The recording quality is not exceptional.

COMPACT DISC
Chess (France) 600119 Elmore James, John Brim, Floyd Jones
Features all the Chess recordings of these three great artists. Fabulous music but, as usual for French Chess, the sound is not as good as it should be.

JOHNNY JONES
One of the finest Chicago piano players and a moving singer who recorded very little on his own before his tragic death in 1964. Best known for his accompaniments for Elmore James and Tampa Red.

Alligator 4717 Johnny Jones with Billy Boy Arnold
1963 club date. A lovely set of after-hours blues, some with vocals and/or harmonica by Billy Boy Arnold.

NYLES JONES
Jambalaya CW 204 The Welfare Blues
Reissue of rare LP originally issued on the obscure Gemini label in 1970. Nyles Jones is a singer and acoustic guitarist from South Carolina, although these recordings were made in Pittsburgh in 1970. Jones is an effective and warm singer and a decent guitar player who combines elements of East Coast blues with ideas drawn from Lightnin' Hopkins. Most of the tracks feature him accompanied by a

competent though unexceptional rhythm section (harmonica, piano, bass, and drums). His material is diverse, including old favorites like "Sweet Little Angel," "Betty and Dupree," and "Your Poodle Dog," which he gives a unique treatment, along with semi-talking blues like "Down On the Farm" and "Expressing The Blues." Jones seems to be having a good time, since he frequently lets out with a lively chuckle. A most interesting collection. Since Nyles was probably in his 40s when he made these recordings, does anyone know if he's still around or performing?

CHARLEY JORDAN
Excellent St. Louis-based singer/guitarist. Popular in the 30s, he not only recorded under his own name but accompanied several artists and also acted as a talent scout. He was a fine singer and guitar player in the St. Louis vein, combining lovely melodic lines with percussive sounds.

Agram 2002 It Ain't Clean
Sixteen sides from 1930–36 not reissued elsewhere.
Document 518 1932–37
Eighteen fine sides. In addition to nine tracks recorded under his own name or his pseudonym Uncle Skipper, there are also five accompaniments to the magnificent "Hi" Henry Brown, two to Mary and two to Verdi Lee. Many of these tracks have been reissued before, but some are on long out-of-print albums and several have never been reissued before.
Earl BD 604 Charley Jordan
Eighteen sides recorded between 1930–36. Keep it Clean/Stack O'Dollars Blues/Hunkie Tunkie Blues.

LOUIS JORDAN
Popular and influential urban blues singer and sax player. Particularly noted for his humorous witty songs, many of which have become blues standards. His 30s, 40s, and early 50s Decca recordings are reissued on MCA, Jukebox Lil, and Swing House. His later recordings for Mercury and RCA have more of a contemporary R&B flavor and are reissued on Bear Family. He recorded infrequently in the 60s and 70s—mostly recreating his earlier hits.

A Touch Of Magic ATOM 4 (d) Live Jive—Louis Jordan and the Tympany Five
Bear Family BFX 15201 Rockin' and Jivin', Vol. 1
The first of two albums to reissue all of Jordan's sides cut for Mercury between 1956–58. Twenty-one sides, including 14 from his first session from 1956, where he was accompanied by an all-star band

of New York sidemen. These are mostly remakes of some of his old Decca hits given a faster, contemporary, and more urgent sound than the originals and have great merit in their own right. The rest of the album is from two 1957 sessions with an unknown band, though it sounds like Mickey Baker is playing guitar on some cuts. It includes three previously unissued cuts: the rockin' "Fire," the poppish "I Want To Know," and the bluesy ballad "I Found My Peace Of Mind."

Bear Family BFX 15207 Rockin' and Jivin', Vol. 2

Features the rest of Jordan's 1957–58 Mercury sides; a bit of a mixed bag. One side is devoted to a session featuring the less-than-wonderful sound of the Hammond organ, although these cuts also feature some nice tenor sax by Austin Powell and guitar by Irving Ashby. There are four tracks from a 1958 session that has a more commercial R&B sound, including the rocking "Sweet Hunk Of Junk," a couple of previously unissued R&B ballads, and the calypso-like "Wish I Could Make Some Money." The rest of the album is mostly expendable previously unissued ballads.

Bear Family BFX 15257 Rock and Roll Call

Features all the recordings cut for RCA's X subsidiary in 1955–56, including four previously unissued tracks. The music is quite a change from his earlier Decca and Aladdin recordings featuring Jordan fronting one of the largest bands of his career on a selection of hard-driving, big-band R&B like the raucous title song, the powerful "Hard Head," "Baby Let's Do It Up," and "Baby You're Just Too Much," novelty songs like "Chicken Back" and "It's Been Said," and the occasional pop ballad like "Where Can I Go." Fold-out cover with notes by Colin Escott, full discographical information, and some great photos from the sessions. Most enjoyable.

Circle LP 53 Louis Jordan and His Tympany Five

Excellent selection of performances recorded as transcriptions for the World Broadcasting Company in Los Angeles or New York. Some of the songs here were also recorded commercially for Decca, but these treatments are different. Pinetop's Boogie Woogie/Papa Boy/Somebody Done Changed the Lock/G. I. Jive.

Jukebox Lil 602 G. I. Jive

Sixteen recordings of blues, jazz, jump, and humor recorded between 1940–47; not previously reissued on LP.

Jukebox Lil 605 Cole Slaw

Complementing Jukebox Lil 602, this album fea-

tures 16 sides recorded between 1947–52. Pettin' and Pokin'/Don't Burn The Candle At Both Ends/Push Ka Pee Shee Pie/Heed My Warning.

Jukebox Lil 619 Somebody Done Hoodooed the Hoodoo Man

Another exciting collection of early Jordan from the period 1938–41. Bjorn Almsledt's remastering from the original 78s is a joy to the ear on standouts like "Bounce The Ball," "Do You Call That A Buddy?" and "It's A Low Down Dirty Shame." More fine bluesy numbers here than on previous reissues. Great pics and fold-out sleeve notes by Tony Burke.

Krazy Kat 7414 Reet Petite and Gone

Eleven fine performances by Jordan and his band as featured in the soundtracks of his movies "Reet Petite and Gone" (1947) and "Caledonia" (1945).

Krazy Kat 7415 Look Out Sister

Sixteen fine sides by Jordan from film soundtracks. Twelve are from the 1948 movie "Look Out Sister" and the rest are from various short features made between 1942–52. Excellent sound.

Official 6061 The V-Discs

The V-Discs (V for Victory) were pressed by the War Department between 1942–48 for exclusive use by the Armed Forces Radio Service. These 12" 78s have become collector's rarities. The quality of these jump and jive recordings is excellent and constitute some of Louis Jordan's best work. Five of the cuts on this 14-track collection are from his first wartime jubilee session that took place in Hollywood in August 1943. Others are from two later 1943 Southern California sessions. Deacon Jones/Five Guys Named Moe/Knock Me A Kiss/Jumpin' At Jubilee.

Swing House SWH 14 Good Times

Radio broadcasts recorded in Hollywood in 1943 and 1948.

CASSETTE ONLY

MCA 1337 Greatest Hits, Vol. 2

Fourteen tracks from 1941–47, some previously issued on MCA 2-4079. Reet Petite and Gone/Is You Is Or Is You Ain't (My Baby)/Boogie Woogie Blue Plate/Open The Door Richard/What's The Use Of Gettin' Sober/Somebody Done Changed My Lock/Five Guys Named Moe.

COMPACT DISC

Black and Blue 59.059 2 I Believe in Music

Fifteen selections from Jordan's rarely documented later period, recorded in 1973. Nine previously available on Black and Blue, and six previously unreleased tracks (including four numbers with Louis and Dave Myers and Fred Below: "Caledonia," "Saturday Night Fish Fry," "Is You Is Or Is You Ain't (My Baby)," "'A' Train").

ESSENTIAL SELECTION
MCA MCAD 4079 (SF) The Best Of Louis Jordan

This is it, man! The great Decca recordings, previously collected as a 2-LP set, are on CD at last. Jordan's best would have to include "Choo Choo Ch' Boogie," "Ain't Nobody Here But Us Chickens," "Saturday Night Fish Fry," "Caledonia," "Knock Me A Kiss," "Five Guys Named Moe," "What's The Use Of Getting Sober," "Buzz Me," and "Barnyard Boogie," and they're all here plus more. Twenty of the jumpin'est wartime R&B sides ever put on wax.

TAFT JORDAN
Krazy Kat 793 Blues Women with Taft Jordan

Continuing Flyright's and Krazy Kat's documentation of the activities of veteran record producer and publisher Joe Davis, this album presents sides recorded in 1952 by three fine women singers—Irene Redfield, Millie Bosman, and Beulah Bryant—accompanied by a small jazz-flavored group led by veteran trumpeter Taft Jordan. Other members of the group include Sam Taylor (ten sax), Panama Francis (drm), and, for the Bryant sides, Will Bradley (trb). Rounding out the album are two instrumental tracks by the band and two boogie cuts by a small combo led by pianist Viola Watkins with Jimmy Shirley (gtr), Walter Washington (b), and Conrad Kirnon (drm). A nice set of jazz-oriented R&B.

THE JUBIRT SISTERS
Interesting trio from Memphis who do blues, R&B, and rock 'n' roll in harmony and also occasional solo efforts.

High Water 1008 Ladies Sing the Blues

A poor choice of material mars this otherwise interesting album, featuring the sisters accompanied by Memphis musicians on guitars, keyboards, bass, drums, and occasional harmonica and horns. Good vocal and instrumental arrangements. With a better choice of material, the girls could probably do a very good album, but this isn't it!

THE JUKE JUMPERS
Fort Worth-based blues bar band led by Jim Colegrove.

Amazing 1001 Border Radio
Amazing 1005 The Joint's Jumpin'
Varrick 016 Jumper Cables

KANSAS JOE (WILBUR MCCOY)
Country bluesman noted for his marriage to famed female blues singer, Memphis Minnie.

Earl BD 603 Kansas Joe, Vol. 1

Eighteen sides recorded between 1929–35. About half the sides have been reissued before on collections. Some great country blues—some with Minnie—plus two excellent and rare gospel recordings originally issued under the name of "Hallelujah Joe."

JO ANN KELLY
British blues interpreter noted for her husky vocals.

Document CSAP 101 (d) Retrospect, 1964–72

Although I am not a big fan of white blues performers, I have a lot of fondness for the music of Enlgish blues interpreter Jo Ann Kelly. Part of it is nostalgia, as she is one of the first people I saw performing in English clubs in the 60s, but I also think that she has a natural blues quality to her singing. This collection of recordings made between 1964–72 presents a wide range of country blues performances including Robert Johnson's "Walking Blues," Bessie Jackson's "Shave 'Em Dry," Memphis Minnie's "Boyfriend Blues," the traditional "When I Lay My Burden Down" (with Fred McDowell on slide guitar), and Howlin' Wolf's "Just Like I Treat You." In addition to her own guitar accompaniments, other featured musicians are Steve Rye (hca), John Fahey (gtr), and Bob Hall (pno). The music is consistently good but the sound quality is unexceptional: thin and, at times, distorted.

Open 001 Jo Ann Kelly
CD issue: Line CD 9.00712
With Steve Donnelly, Geraint Watkins, and Pete Emery.

CHRIS KENNER
COMPACT DISC

Charly CD 230 I Like It like That

Excellent collection of 24 Instant and Uptown recordings from 1961–67 with Allen Toussaint producing most of the tracks. This is essentially a reissue of Charly CRB 1163 with eight extra tracks, including the previously unissued "My Wife." Chris was an excellent writer and fine singer, though some of his best songs are known from cover versions by other artists, including "Land of 1000 Dances," "Something You Got," "Shoo-Rah," and the title tune. "Land" is heard here with a great gospel-like call-and-response intro that was chopped off the final release. Gonna Getcha Baby/Something You Got/She Can Dance/How Far/All Night Rambler, Parts 1 and 2/I'm Lonely, Take Me.

TROYCE KEY, J. J. MALONE, and THE RHYTHM ROCKERS

Excellent Oakland-based blues performers.

Red Lightnin' 0028 I've Got a New Car

Solo vocals by Key and Malone along with a couple of duets. Imaginative arrangements of older songs and some good new originals; nice horn work from the band and strong guitar work from Key.

Red Lightnin' 0043 Younger Than Yesterday

Excellent second album features their own brand of good-time blues and R&B, including some stand-ards along with a few originals. Good vocals and playing by Key and Malone and solid backup by the band, though I would have preferred more horns and less harmonica. Flip, Flop and Fly/It Should Have Been Me/Crazy Little Chicken/Sail On.

JUNIOR KIMBROUGH

High Water 418 (45 rpm) Keep Your Hands Off Her/I Feel Good, Little Girl

Powerful vocals over a hypnotically compelling backup of guitar, bass, and drums.

LOTTIE KIMBROUGH and WINSTON HOLMES

Wolf WSE 114 Lottie Kimbrough and Winston Holmes

Half of this album features seven sides by superb Kansas City singer Lottie Kimbrough recorded in 1928–29, six featuring splendid guitar by Milas Pruitt. Several tracks feature vocal effects by Kansas City promoter Winston Holmes. The other side features Holmes with singer/guitarist Charlie Turner on six tracks. Most of this is medicine-show and hokum-type material and is quite enjoyable. One track ("Kansas City Dog Walk") is a wonderful 12-string guitar instrumental by Turner.

AL KING

Diving Duck 4302 On My Way

A most welcome reissue from this excellent but obscure Northern California blues singer. King recorded a dozen or so singles in the 60s and this album features 15 of the best plus one cut from 1953. He is a fine singer and writes some witty lyrics. He is accompanied by top-notch bands and many cuts feature the superb guitar of the grossly underrated Johnny Heartsman.

ALBERT KING

One of the three great Kings of the blues. He is a powerful singer and distinctive electric guitarist with a much-copied string-bending style. He started recording in the 50s and reached his peak in the mid-60s with some great recordings for Stax, many of which are finally being reissued. In the last few years, he has been recording for Fantasy; these recordings recapture some of the spirit and fire of his mid-60s recordings.

Atlantic AD 2-4002 (c) Masterworks

Two-LP set featuring seven cuts from his legendary 1968 Stax album, "Born Under a Bad Sign," along with 11 titles issued on Utopia and Tomato between 1976–78, some produced by Allen Toussaint. It would have been better to have had the entire "Born Under a Bad Sign" album reissued but the rest of the material here is very good. With excellent liner notes by Robert Palmer.

ESSENTIAL SELECTION

Atlantic (Canada) 7723 (c) Born Under a Bad Sign

Reissue of Stax 723 from 1968. Though Albert's been recording since '53, this LP, his first for Stax, is still the zenith of his career. With backing by Booker T and the MGs, this LP has the tunes that King is still best remembered for and still are featured in his live show, including Booker T's "The Hunter" and the title classic. Crosscut Saw/The Very Thought Of You/As The Years Go Passing By/Oh, Pretty Wo-man/Laundromat Blues.

Edsel 130 Laundromat Blues

A great collection featuring 16 of Albert's best-ever recordings cut for Stax between 1966–68. Ten of the cuts were originally on his classic "Born Under a Bad Sign" album and the rest were originally on singles. Great songs, great singing and guitar by Albert, and solid accompaniments by Booker T and the MGs and The Memphis Horns. Born Under a Bad Sign/I Love Lucy/You Sure Drive a Hard Bargain/I Almost Lost My Mind/Oh Pretty Woman/The Hunter.

Fantasy 9627 (c) San Francisco '83

Possibly King's best since his classic 60s Stax recordings. He is in great voice and obviously enjoying the session and plays lots of his distinctive guitar. He is backed only by a four-piece rhythm section who drive the music along with great energy. The material is a mixture of familiar blues songs and some originals, including a couple of interesting topical numbers. The sound on this album is superb with great presence.

Fantasy 9633 (c) I'm in a Phone Booth Baby

Excellent 1984 album that, like Fantasy 9627, is a straight-ahead blues set with tough singing by Albert and lots of stinging guitar from his "Flying V." This album adds some tasty horns by Steve Douglas and Cal Lewiston to the solid, if unexceptional, rhythm section. Songs are a mixture of new and old, including songs by Robert Cray and Doug Macleod that sit nicely alongside some Elmore James standards.

King 852 (c,d) The Big Blues
Modern Blues Recordings 723 (c,d) Let's Have a Natural Ball

A brilliant collection of material licensed from the King label, featuring seminal recordings made by Albert for Bobbin and King between 1959–63. Eleven of the tracks were previously issued on the King LPs "Travellin' To California" and "The Big Blues," while the remaining three were only previously available as singles. Wherever possible, the tracks have been digitally remastered from the original master tapes, giving the recordings an immediacy and clarity not heard before. Albert's powerful vocals are well to the fore, along with his searing and distinctive string-bending guitar playing. He is accompanied by top-notch St. Louis musicians who perfectly complement Albert's singing and playing. With complete discographical information (some of it based on recent research) and informative notes by Daniel Jacoubovitch; an essential release for lovers of contemporary blues.

Stax 4101 (c) The Pinch
Previously unissued Stax sides.

Stax 4123 (c) Albert King/Little Milton
One side of album by each; good 60s sides.

Stax 4128 (c,d) Live Wire/Blues Power

Stax 8504 (c) Blues for Elvis
Albert does his unique versions of nine Elvis Presley hits. Hound Dog/All Shook Up/Heartbreak Hotel/One Night/ Love Me Tender.

Stax 8513 (c,d) I'll Play the Blues for You
Reissue of Stax 3009. Breaking Up Somebody's Home/I'll Be Doggone/Don't Burn Down Your Bridge.

Stax 8517 (c) Lovejoy
Reissue of 1970 album, somewhat more commercially oriented than his previous Stax albums with most songs written by blues/rock singer Don Nix.

Stax 8522 (c,d) Years Gone By
Stax 8534 (c,d) The Lost Session
An excellent, previously unissued, set of recordings that were only recently discovered in the Fantasy vaults. This album features 10 songs recorded in 1971 produced by British blues interpreter John Mayall, who also plays on the album. The rest of the band features a mixture of jazz and blues musicians, including sax players Clifford Solomon and Ernie Watts and trumpeter Blue Mitchell (who appear on a few cuts) and jazz drummer Ron Selico. The drumming, in particular, with its syncopated rhythms, gives the recordings a jazz flavor that is rarely heard in Albert's work. His singing and playing, though fine, are a little more restrained than usual, which might explain why it wasn't originally issued.

Stax 8536 (c) I Wanna Get Funky
Reissue of Stax 5505 from 1974. Albert was in fine form on a selection of blues and soul-flavored items with fairly lush arrangements featuring the Barkays, The Memphis Horns, the vocal group Hot Buttered Soul, and, on a couple of tracks, The Memphis Symphony Orchestra(!). However, this is, for the most part, integrated effectively with Albert's solid blues vocals and mighty string bending. It includes a remake of one of his first hits, "Crosscut Saw," and a superb version of the minor-key soul ballad "Walking The Back Street and Crying." Playing On Me/Flat Tire/ Travelin' Man/That's What the Blues Is All About.

Stax 8546 (c,d) Blues at Sunrise
Those relentless vault-probers at Fantasy Records have provided us with a newly discovered live tape from the 1973 Montreux Jazz Festival, and it is amazing. Aside from the previously issued "For The Love Of A Woman," this disc is an all-killer, no-filler, King-sized thriller. Potent vocals throughout, and, when he makes that guitar talk, you better hold on to your beret and listen up good. Nobody wrings as much emotion out of an amplified wire, and on this day he was ON, boy; we're talkin' about slash and burn playing with a level of inventive genius that other recordings only hint at. The recording (by Swiss radio engineers) is less than perfect, but who cares—this music is the real deal and the ticket is a steal

Stax MPS 8556 (c,d) Wednesday Night In San Francisco
Stax MPS 8557 (c,d) Thursday Night In San Francisco
COMPACT DISC

ESSENTIAL SELECTION
Atlantic 8213-2 (P) King of the Blues Guitar
The cream of the crop from Albert's first Stax LP, with six bonus tracks for a total of 17 high-voltage cuts. Many of these mid-60s numbers, like "Laundromat Blues," "Oh Pretty Woman," "Crosscut Saw," and "Born Under A Bad Sign," are electric blues classics. The rest, especially "Personal Manager," "I Almost Lost My Mind," "As the Years Go Passing By," "Cold Feet," and "You're Gonna Need Me," are just super, and certainly to be counted among King's most memorable sides.

Charly CD 136 Albert Live
Reissue of Tomato LP, recorded at the Montreux festival in Switzerland with special guests Rory Gallagher and Louisiana Red. I believe this was done a few years later than the excellent "Blues at Sunrise" album on Stax, but it does have versions of many of the same tunes, which were standards in King's repertoire during the mid-70s. Watermelon Man/Stormy Monday/Kansas City/I'll Play The Blues For You/Don't Burn Down The Bridge.

Stax CD 60-005 The Best of Albert King
Sixty-three minutes of Albert's Stax recordings, 1968–73. The 13 tunes here are all excellent (except perhaps a horrible "Honky Tonk Woman"), including such classics as "I'll Play The Blues For You," "Blues Power," and "Angel Of Mercy," plus hits "Breaking Up Somebody's Home," "I Wanna Get Funky," "Everybody Wants To Go To Heaven," and "Can't You See What You're Doing To Me," previously only available as a single. Good liner notes by Lee Hildebrand.

Tomato 269625-2 King Albert
Reissue of Tomato 6002 from 1978, deservedly long-out-of-print. Disco Albert, complete with background chorus, funky bass, wah-wah guitar, and flute! Sure, there's a few good blues here, notably "Ain't Nothing You Can Do" and a charged shuffle version of "I'm Ready," but the opener, "Guitar Man," is as bad as the crap Freddie King was being forced to record at RSO and some is even worse.

Tomato 269631-2 Truckload of Lovin'
Reissue of Utopia 1387 from 1975. Like a good number of Albert's 70s recordings, this one's more pop and funk than blues (but at least not disco), complete with strings and girl chorus. What does set this one apart is strong material written by soulster and former Falcon, Sir Mack Rice, including the hit "Cadillac Assembly Line," "Cold Women with Warm Hearts," and "Sensation, Communication Together." Usual group of 70s funk sessioners including Wah Wah Watson, Joe Sample, and Chuck Rainey.

Tomato 269633-2 New Orleans Heat
Reissue of album originally issued on the Tomato label in 1977. It features Albert recorded in New Orleans at the famed Cosimo studios under the guiding hand of Allen Toussaint. Includes remakes of a couple of his old hits, along with some new material.

ALBERT KING/OTIS RUSH
Chess 9322 (c,d) Door to Door
Reissue of Chess 1538, a great album featuring two

of the premiere exponents of modern blues guitar. There are six superb sides by Rush from 1960 including the magnificent "So Many Roads, So Many Trains," one of his greatest performances. The eight Albert King cuts were recorded for Parrot in 1953 and Bobbin in 1961. Newly remastered from original tapes with session credits and new notes.

B. B. KING
Probably the most influential blues guitarist of all time. B. B.'s single-string electric guitar playing has been copied by thousands of guitarists, but few can match the finesse and control of the master. He is also an outstanding singer whose style shows his debt to the gospel music he sang as a youngster. During most of the 50s, he recorded for RPM and Kent, making dozens of classics. Much of this is reissued on Ace. In the 60s and 70s, he recorded for ABC and Bluesway with varying results; the great albums are mixed with commercial dross. He currently records for MCA.

Ace CH 30 The Best of B. B. King
This is a straight reissue of B. B.'s first album, though the sound is far superior to the various Crown and United issues of the same material.

Ace CH 50 The Memphis Masters
Great collection of 12 songs recorded in Memphis between 1950–52. Most of these have been reissued before on various Kent albums, plus the album does feature one previously unissued track. No notes or discographical information.

Ace CH 119 Rock Me Baby
Essentially a reissue of Crown 5021 with additions and deletions to make a great 14-track album. Drawing on B. B.'s Kent recordings cut in the early 60s and beautifully remastered by Bob Jones, this set makes for great listening, though most of the tracks have already been reissued several times. Rock Me Baby/Worst Thing In My Life/Five Long Years/I Can't Lose/Eyesight to the Blind.

ESSENTIAL SELECTION

Ace CHA 198 (c,d) The Best of, Volume One

An excellent sampler, featuring 19 of his best RPM/Kent recordings. Digitally mastered to provide the best possible sound. You Upset Me Baby/ Five Long Years/ Beautician Blues/Three O'Clock Blues/Sweet Sixteen/Mean Ole Frisco/Going Down Slow/You Don't Know.

Ace CH 199 (c,d) The Best Of, Volume Two

Twenty-one sides recorded for RPM and Kent and digitally remastered for superb sound. Although the emphasis is on his more popular songs, this set does include a previously unissued instrumental, "Low Rider," and a couple of alternate takes. Many of the tracks are in real stereo. Bad Luck Soul/The Jungle/Ten Long Years/House Rocker/Shut Your Mouth/I've Got A Right To Love My Baby/You Done Lost Your Good Thing Now/B. B. Rock/It's My Own Fault/You're Gonna Miss Me.

Ace CHD 201 One Nighter Blues

Early recordings cut between 1951–54. These are digitally mastered from recently discovered master tapes and the sound is astounding. Includes three previously unissued songs and alternate takes of three other songs, plus 10 other superb tracks. Informative notes by Ray Topping and some amazing previously unpublished photos from the 50s.

Ace CHD 230 Across the Tracks

More early recordings, from 1951–57, with the majority being from sessions held in Los Angeles between 1954–57. Sixteen tracks, most not available on LP for many years, with five previously unissued alternate takes and four previously unissued songs, including "Bad Luck" and a fine version of the blues standard "Confessin' The Blues." Superb sound from digitally remastered master tapes, fine packaging, with another great early photo of B. B. and his band, and informative notes by Ray Topping.

Ace CHD 271 Lucille Had A Baby

Sixteen great sides from the mid-50s digitally remastered for exquisite sound.

BGO BGOLP 36 Lucille

Exact repro of what is probably B. B.'s most popular LP, at least for the general public. Released in 1968 during the height of the blues revival, this LP provided many a blues novice with their first exposure to the blues via the mesmerising autobiographical title tune. God knows how many bar bands were inspired by B. B.'s single-note soloing, to the long-lasting detriment of such slash-and-burn blues guitarists as Johnny "Guitar" Watson and Ike Turner. King is backed by Maxwell Davis and a rather large band on nine tunes, so if you need a new copy of this one, here 'tis. Country Girl/You Move Me So/I Need Your Love/Rainin' All The Time.

BGO BGOLP 37 His Best —The Electric B. B. King

Reissue of Bluesway LP from 1969, complete with lenghty Ritchie York liner notes, where he wonders if B. B. will ever make any big money with his music. Well, he didn't make Michael Jackson-type bucks but he did all right for himself. I don't think many blues aficionados will agree with the title "The Best," but this is a nice selection of his urbane mid-period blues. Tired Of Your Jive/Don't Answer The Door/Sweet Sixteen/Think It Over.

BGO BGOLP 42 (d) In London

Reissue of 1971 album recorded in London with Ringo Starr, Alexis Korner, Bobby Keys, Klaus Voorman, Duster Bennet, and other English "stars."

BGO BGOLP 69 (d) Blues on Top of Blues

Reissue of Bluesway 6011 from 1968, which includes his top-ten R&B hit "Paying The Cost To Be The Boss." Most of these recordings were "arranged and conducted by Johnny Pate" and are a bit overblown and poppish but there is some great singing and playing from B. B.

BGO BOGLP 71 (c,d) Guess Who

Blues Boy 301 The Rarest King

Sixteen cuts that have never been issued on LP before, including two from his first session in 1949. Great packaging with excellent photos, detailed notes, including a brief discussion of B. B.'s guitar style, and lyrics for all songs

MCA 5616 (c,d) Six Silver Strings

This 1985 album is, apparently, his 50th and includes three songs from the film "Into The Night." Although the album is well-produced with some good arrangements, the fact of the matter is that B. B. just doesn't have the vocal quality he had a few years back and his guitar lacks a lot of the bite and expressiveness. Highlight is the highly charged version of "In The Midnight Hour."

MCA 6455 (c,d) Live at San Quentin

Includes new versions of "Sweet Sixteen," "Sweet Little Angel," "The Thrill is Gone," and other favorites, plus one recent studio recording, "Peace to the World."

MCA 2-8016 (c) Now Appearing at Ole Miss

Two-LP set.

MCA 27005 (c,d) Live in Cook County Jail

Recorded in 1975.

MCA 27006 (c,d) Live at the Regal

Fabulous live set recorded at the Regal Theatre in Chicago in 1964. B. B. and his band are in great form and the enthusiasm of the audience eggs him on to great heights. Everyday I Have The Blues/It's My Own Fault/Please Love Me/Worry, Worry.

MCA 27007 (c,d) The Electric B. B. King

MCA 27008 (c,d) Live and Well

MCA 27009 (c,d) Completely Well

MCA 27010 (c,d) Back in the Alley
Reissue of Bluesway 6050 featuring 1964–67 recordings.

MCA 27011 (c,d) Midnight Believer
1978 album.

MCA 27012 (c) B. B. King and Bobby Bland: Together Again

MCA 27034 (c,d) There Must Be a Better World Somewhere
1981 album. In spite of sidemen like Dr. John, David Newman, and Hank Crawford, this album is little more than middle-of-the-road pop based on 12 bars.

MCA 27074 (c,d) The Best of B. B. King
Nine of his most popular ABC and Bluesway sides. Hummingbird/How Blue Can You Get/Sweet Sixteen/Why I Sing The Blues/The Thrill Is Gone.

MCA 27119 (c,d) Blues 'n' Jazz
Good 1983 set. Unlike some of his 80s albums, this is pretty much a straight blues set. B. B. plays some fine guitar though his voice is a little strained on some cuts. He is acompanied by top blues and jazz musicians like Harold Austin (ten sax), Billy Butler (gtr), Lloyd Glenn (pno), and Oliver Jackson (drm). A nice mixture of new and old songs.

MCA 42183 (c,d) King of the Blues, 1989
B. B. buried under a sea of drum machines, synthesizers, schlock rock guitar, vocal choruses, along with such exciting "guests" as Steve Cropper, Mick Fleetwood, and Stevie Nicks. The result? Music that could be anybody but B. B. King: musical anonymity. B. B. has made a lot of albums, some better than others; but this is certainly high on the list as one of his worst.

See For Miles SEE 216 Blues Is King
CD issue: MCA MCAD 31368 (CP)
Reissue of Bluesway 6001 from 1967. Extremely powerful live LP, probably unfairly overshadowed by the classic "Live At The Regal" from '64. B. B., hot on the charts with the million seller "Don't Answer The Door," recorded this set at Chicago's International Club on Nov. 5, 1966, with his working band, including Bobby Forte on tenor and organist Duke Jethro. The 10 tunes from the original LP are joined by the live non-LP single "Sweet 16, Pts. 1 and 2," thought to be recorded at the same show. B. B.'s singing and playing are both at their peak here

on such gems as "Gambler's Blues," "Blind Love," and Louis Jordan's "Buzz Me."
CASSETTE ONLY RELEASE

Ace CHC 801 The Best of B. B. King: The Memphis Masters
Double-cassette release combining Ace CH 30 and CH 50.

MCA 886 Love Me Tender
1985 album featuring a selection of 10 country songs, with vocal backup and 18-piece string section!
CASSETTE AND CD RELEASE ONLY

MCA 2-4124 Great Moments with B. B. King
Drawn from 1966–68 ABC/Bluesway cuts, some recorded live. Waitin' On You/Tired of Your Jive/Buzz Me/Baby Get Lost/I Know What You're Pullin' Down.
COMPACT DISC

Ace CDCH 187 Spotlight on Lucille
A great collection of 12 instrumentals recorded 1960–61, some of which were only discovered in 1985. Accompanied by various small groups and occasionally a full band, B. B.'s great playing shines through. Sound is superb; the crystal clear remastering allows us to hear every nuance of B. B.'s playing. Slidin' And Glidin'/King Of Guitar/38th Street Blues/Goin' South.

Ace CDCH 916 Do the Boogie!
Twenty selections from the LPs Ace CHD 201 and Ace CHD 230.

ESSENTIAL SELECTION

MCA MCAD 5877 Two on One
Great music and great value for the money with over 73 minutes of music. It combines two fine ABC LPs, "Live At The Regal" and "Live In Cook County Jail" (see listings under LPs above). There are only a couple of songs duplicated on both sets. Sound on the CD is very good, although since these are live recordings they don't have the punch or presence of a studio set.

MCA MCAD 31343 (CP) Indianola Mississippi Seeds
Nine selections. King's Special/Ain't Gonna Worry My Life Anymore/Hummingbird.

EARL KING
Excellent New Orleans singer/guitarist and songwriter.

Ace 2029 Let the Good Times Roll
US issue of Ace (UK) CH 15 (now out of print) featuring 14 great sides recorded for Ace and Rex in the 50s. An excellent collection of Louisiana-style blues and ballads with a healthy dose of upbeat

R&B. Fine mellifluous vocals and Guitar Slim-influenced guitar from King with top-notch accompaniments from Huey Smith, Lee Allen, and Robert Parker.

Black Top 1035 (c,d) Glazed
King, with support from the top-flight Providence, RI, band Roomful Of Blues, has fronted a smokin' R&B party. Includes Texas-flavored blues shuffles and some of Earl's older compositions reworked and given new life. The communication lines between King and fellow guitarist Ronnie Earl are exceptional and Earl shines on "Three Can Play The Game" and "One Step Beyond Love." Stellar production by Hammond Scott, and scintillating organ and piano courtesy of Ron Levy.

COMPACT DISC

Charly CD 232 Street Parade
1972 recordings originally issued on Charly LP 2021. Fine vocals but no guitar by Earl. Do the Grind/Love Look Out for Me/Up on Her Hill/The Real McCoy.

EDDIE KING BLUES BAND

Double Trouble 3017 The Blues Has Got Me
A good debut album by Chicago West Side singer/guitarist King along with his sister Mae Bee May and a solid hard-driving band. King is a powerful and gospel-flavored vocalist and versatile guitarist. Sister Mae is also a soulful vocalist and the arrangements are well thought out. Material is a mixture of familiar and less familiar blues and soul numbers, along with a couple of originals. Highlights include Mae's reworking of an Elmore James song as "12-Year-Old Girl," Eddie's lovely minor key original "The Blues Has Got Me," and Mae's rip-roaring version of Ann Peebles' "99 Pounds." Excellent!

FREDDY KING

Exceptional singer and electric guitarist. His 50s Federal recordings reissued on King, Charly, and Crosscut feature some very melodic playing based on the influence on Freddie of Jimmie Rogers and Eddie Taylor. A significant percentage of his early sides are instrumentals. His later recordings find him playing in a more intense and, at times, rock-influenced style.

Crosscut 1005 Rockin' the Blues—Live
Seven cuts recorded live in Germany in 1974–75. Freddy is in good form vocally and instrumentally and is accompanied by a solid, if unexceptional, band. Excellent sound. Hideaway/Key To The Highway/Wee Baby Blues/Blues Band Shuffle.

Crosscut 1010 Gives You a Bonanza of Instrumentals
Reissue of King 928 with four extra tracks, one previously unissued. A collection of mostly blues guitar and country-flavored instrumentals recorded for Federal between 1961–64. Freddy was a brilliant musician who can hold your interest over an LP of instrumentals. Surf Monkey/Remington Ride/Manhole/Funnybone/The Sad Night Owl/ Freddie's Midnite Dream/Side Tracked.

Double Dutch MMG 99003 "Texas Cannonball" Live
CD issue: P-Vine PCD 909 Live at the Texas Opry House, April 20, 1976
Mostly standard 70s concert fare ("It's Your Move," "Hideaway," "Sweet Home Chicago"), an uninspired backup band, and omnipresent "heavy rock" organ make this a nonessential item for all but hardcore Freddy King collectors.

Gusto 5033X Hideaway
Two-LP set featuring 22 great performances from Federal including a couple of duets with Lula Reed. Hideaway/Washout/Low Tide/See See Baby/I Love The Woman/Sen-Sa-Shun/Swooshy/Now I've Got A Woman/Man Hole/Sad Nite Owl.

King 773 (d) Let's Hide Away and Dance Away with Freddy King
Reissue of a great all-instrumental album. Eleven tracks. Hideaway/The Stumble/Heads Up.

King 5012 17 Original Greatest Hits
CD issue: Federal CD 1036
Superb collection of Federal sides; five duplicates with Gusto 5033X. You've Got To Love Her With A Feeling/Hideaway/San-Ho-Zay/I'm Tore Down/ Christmas Tears/What About Love/The Welfare Turns Its Back On You/Hi-Rise.

King Biscuit KBR 001 Live In Germany
Eight tunes recorded live in 1975 in Hamburg and Bremen. Sweet Home Chicago/Have You Ever Loved a Woman/Big Legged Woman/Let the Good Times Roll.

Modern Blues Recordings MB2LP-721 (d) Just Pickin'
A fabulous all-instrumental collection. This two-LP set, digitally remastered from the original session tapes, features Freddy's two all-instrumental King LPs (King 773, "Let's Hide Away And Dance Away" and King 928, "Freddy King Gives You A Bonanza Of Instrumentals") in one jacket. The first album (recorded in 1960–61) features Freddy with just a rhythm section on most cuts. The second album (recorded between 1962–64) features larger groups

with one or more saxes, but underpinning it all is Freddy's wonderfully melodic guitar work. Nice early photo of Freddy on the cover, full discographical details, and detailed liner notes.

ESSENTIAL SELECTION

Modern Blues Recordings MBLP 722 (c,d)
Freddy King Sings
Reissue of Freddy's first album for King featuring Freddy's intense vocals and plangent guitar on 12 great songs. He is accompanied by a solid rhythm section with producer Sonny Thompson on piano, plus, on some cuts, some effective horns. For this release, Modern Blues Recordings has digitally remastered the original two-track mono tapes and produced a true stereo master. The album features original cover and back liner plus an insert with extensive notes and discographical information. Have You Ever Loved A Woman/You've Got To Love Her With A Feeling/I'm Tore Down/I Love The Woman

CASSETTE AND CD RELEASE ONLY

Polydor 831 816-1 **Larger Than Life**
Reissue of Freddie's last LP, originally RSO 4811, from 1975. Six of the nine tunes were recorded live in Texas with Mike McNeil on slide guitar, Jim Gordon on organ, and a five-piece horn section led by Fathead Newman. Most of the live tunes are good blues covers including "Have You Ever Loved A Woman," "Woke Up This Morning," and "The Things I Used To Do." The studio tunes, produced by Mike Vernon, are pretty bad.

Polydor 831 817-1 **1934–76**
Reissue of RSO 3025 from 1977. Not a bad LP for a posthumous release. In fact, Side two is quite good, including three tunes from sessions with Eric Clapton's group, including an alternate take of "Sugar Sweet" plus "T. V. Mama" and "Gambling Woman Blues," and a live version of "Further On Up The Road" with Clapton on vocals. Side one's got three tunes from the "Burglar" session including a decent "Sweet Home Chicago" with just a quartet. The album ends with Freddie and his own group doing a couple of live tunes including "Ain't Nobody's Business If I Do."

COMPACT DISC

French Concerts FCD 111 **Live in Antibes, 1974**
Freddy recorded live in Antibes on July 24, 1974. He is accompanied by the same band featured on Crosscut 1005 who are tight if not exceptional. Over 50 minutes of high-energy electric blues. Good sound. Going Down The Highway/Woman Across The River/Ain't Nobody's Business If I Do/Let The Good Times Roll.

French Concerts FCD 126 **Live In Nancy 1975, Vol. 1**
French Concerts FCD 129 **Live In Nancy 1975, Vol. 2**
Polydor 831 815-1 **Burglar**
Reissue of RSO 4803 from 1974. Freddie's final studio LP isn't very good, full of an overblown group of studio musicians including Brian Auger, Bobby Tench, Pete Wingfield, and Steve Ferrone, plus a five-piece horn section, and produced by Mike Vernon. The best thing on this LP is the only cut not from these sessions, a fine "Sugar Sweet" done with Eric Clapton's group. Of the rest, "Pulp Paper" is a pretty good instrumental.

Shelter CD 8003 **Getting Ready. . .**
Reissue of 1970 session (recorded at the Chess studio in Chicago!) with 12 selections, including two unreleased cuts: "Gimme Some Lovin'" and "Send Me Someone To Love." Same Old Blues/Dust My Broom/Going Down/Tore Down.

FREDDY KING/LULU REED/SONNY THOMPSON

King 777 (d) **Boy-Girl-Boy**
Fine collection featuring four sides of King/Reed duets from 1962; the remaining eight tracks are by Lulu from 1955, '56, and '61. All the tracks feature excellent accompaniments by a band led by King house bandleader Sonny Thompson.

SAUNDERS KING

Blues Boy 303 **What's Your Story, Morning Glory**
Sixteen sides of blues with a jazz flavor recorded between 1942–54 by this fine West Coast singer and guitar player who is little known today, having retired from music. Although his guitar playing is not prominent on many of these sides, when he does play he is a fine and original guitarist and is accompanied by good small bands.

KING BISCUIT BOY

Red Lightnin' 0049 **Mouth of Steel**
First album in 10 years by popular Canadian singer and harmonica player. A selection of rockin' blues and R&B. Georgia Slop/Mama Luchie/Down The Line/Route 90/It's My Soul/Get It Right.

BIG DADDY KINSEY and THE KINSEY REPORT

Rooster Blues 2620 **Bad Situation**
Excellent debut album by family group from Gary, IN, that very neatly mixes traditional Muddy Waters-styled Chicago blues and very contemporary sounds with disco or reggae rhythms and female

choruses. Leader of the group is singer, guitarist, and harmonica player Lester Kinsey, an energetic Albert King-styled singer who also plays some fine slide guitar. He is joined by his sons Donald, Ralph, and Kenneth on guitar, bass, drums and percussion, and various other musicians including Nate Armstrong or Billy Branch (hca), Pinetop Perkins or Frankie Hill (pno), and occasional horn sections and female choruses. All the material is original and includes a couple of excellent topical songs. The mixing of traditional blues and contemporary sounds doesn't often work but here it is very effective.

Blind Pig 3489 (d) **Can't Let Go**

THE KINSEY REPORT
Alligator 4758 (c,d) **Edge of the City**
High-energy electric blues band from Gary, IN, featuring brothers Donald (vcl, gtr), Kenneth (b), and Ralph Kinsey (drm) together with guitarist Ron Prince. The songs are mostly written by the band members and touch on contemporary themes ("Poor Man's Relief," "Answering Machine") as well as

more traditional blues elements ("Got To Pay Some-day," "Give Me What I Want"). Tough vocals and guitar and energetic rhythms. On a few tracks, the band seems to make more than a passing nod to the songs and style of current blues superstar Robert Cray. CD has two bonus tracks.

Alligator 4775 (c,d) **Midnight Drive**

EDDIE KIRKLAND
Alabama-born, Detroit-based singer/guitarist who used to perform with John Lee Hooker. Eddie sings with a powerful raspy voice and plays some excellent guitar and occasional harmonica.

O.B.C. 513 (c) **It's the Blues Man!**
Reissue of Tru-Sound 15010 from 1962, which was also reissued a few years ago by Red Lightnin'. These are probably his best recordings. Kirkland is accompanied by a group of studio musicians—led by the great sax player King Curtis and featuring guitarist Billy Butler—who supply sympathetic accompaniments. I particularly like the intense "Have Mercy On Me," where Curtis's sax echoes Eddie's vocal lines. A good 'un.

Pulsar 1003 **Have Mercy**
Kirkland's customary high energy fails to surmount lackluster production and sidemen and a superfluous female backup group. Some good guitar and harp from the leader, but nothing ever really catches fire here. This release is all the more disappointing since Kirkland is still singing and playing very well and could produce a real blockbuster album one of these days.

CHRISTINE KITTRELL
Krazy Kat 7432 **Nashville R&B, Vol. 2**
Fifteen sides by this outstanding Nashville singer whose comparative lack of success was no reflection of her talents. She was a lovely singer with a powerful and expressive vocal style and this collection, mostly dating from the early 50s, finds her in the company of some outstanding bands. The album features her three minor hits from 1952–53: the lovely "Sittin' and Drinking," which includes "Buddy" Hagens and Wendell Duconge from Fats Domino's band, the hard-driving "Every Night In the Week," and the intense "I'll Help You Baby," which includes a nice piece of double timing from Christine and the band. "Lord Have Mercy" from 1953 almost certainly features Little Richard on piano. It's all urban blues at its best with excellent sound and informative notes by Bruce Bastin. Highly recommended.

ALEXIS KORNER
British blues revivalist most active in the late 50s and early 60s, famous for founding bands such as Blues Incorporated and inspiring the fledgling Rolling Stones, whose recordings inspired many of the blues rockers of the 60s.

Collector Series CCSLP 150 (d) **The Alexis Korner Collection, 1961–72**

Krazy Kat 789 **Alexis Korner and Cyril Davis**
Sixteen sides recorded in 1957–61. Korner sings on six cuts and plays guitar and mandolin, Davis sings on nine cuts and plays 12-string guitar and harmonica, and one cut features Lisa Turner on vocal. They are accompanied by Terry Plant (b) and Mike Collins (washbd). Twelve of these cuts were previously available but four cuts have never been issued before. Leaving Blues/Rotten Break/Skip to My Lou/County Jail/Alberta/Ella Speed.

Thunderbolt THBL 2.026 (d) Testament
1980 duo recordings, with Korner on vocal and
guitar and Colin Hodgkinson on bass and vocal.

Thunderbolt THBL 037 Hammer and Nails
Reissue of Jeton 1003305 from 1979. Ten solo blues,
recorded direct-to-disc in W. Germany in July 1979.
After a poor start with "Honky Tonk Woman,"
Korner sets down to a fine set of traditional blues
and bluesy originals. "Louise" and his own "And
Again" are guitar solos and Alex sits down at the 88's
for Leroy Carr's "How Long Blues" and Jimmy
Yancey's "East St. Louis Blues."

COMPACT DISC

Line CD 9.00634 Blues Incorporated
Ten tracks reissued from Transatlantic Records.
Woke Up This Mornin'/Stormy Monday/Chicken
Shack/Haitian Fight Song.

DENISE LASALLE
Malaco 7422 Love Talkin'
Memphis singer who mixes blues and soul with
some occasional funk and pop. Highlights are the
soulful "Talkin' In Your Sleep," the bluesy "Someone Else Is Steppin' In," the cynical "Love Is A Five
Letter Word," and the rocking "Get What You Can."
Arrangements have that Malaco assembly line
sound to them—very competent but lacking in expressiveness. But the album is worth a listen for
Denise's vocals and some of the songs.

BOOKER T. LAURY
**Wolf 120 912 One of the Last Memphis Blues
Piano Jewels**
This veteran pianist started playing on Beale Street
in 1932. This LP finds the 72-year-old Laury
recorded live in Austria during January 1987 as part
of the "Stars Of Boogie Woogie" tour. Nine fine
romps with Junior Parker's "Next Time You See
Me" and Roosevelt Sykes' "I Done You Wrong,"
plus seven originals, all solo piano with vocals.
Booker's Boogie/My Own Memphis Blues.

LAZY LESTER
Brilliant Louisiana harmonica player and singer
with a languid style (hence the nickname) who
recorded for Jay Miller in the late 50s/early 60s.

Alligator 4768 (c,d) Harp and Soul

Flyright 526 They Call Me Lazy
Twelve sides recorded for Jay Miller. These are
either unissued songs or alternates of those pre-

viously issued on Excello. Lester's Stomp/I'm So
Tired/Late Late in the Evening/They Call Me Lazy.

Flyright 544 Poor Boy Blues
Twelve more unissued songs or alternate takes. Poor
Boy Blues/The Same Thing Could Happen to
You/Sugar-Coated Love.

COMPACT DISC

Flyright FLYCD 07 Lazy Lester
A terrific collection of 20 sides recorded for producer Jay Miller between 1957–67. Lester was accompanied by the cream of Miller's session
musicians including guitarists Al Foreman, Bobby
McBride, and Guitar Gable; pianists Katie Webster
and Murton Thibodeaux; and, on a couple of cuts,
the searing sax of Lionel Torrence. Although many
of Lester's recordings were issued on Excello, all the
tracks here are unissued songs or alternate takes that
were previously issued on several Flyright albums.
Good sound and brief, but informative, notes by
Bruce Bastin. Tell Me Pretty Baby/They Call Me
Lazy/Quit Foolin' Myself/Lester's Stomp/I'm So
Tired/Late Late In The Evening.

LEADBELLY (HUDDIE
LEDBETTER)
12-string guitarist/vocalist/songwriter who became the darling of the late 40s/early 50s folk
revival. Leadbelly began his career as a "lead
boy" for noted bluesman Blind Lemon Jefferson,
and served several terms in prison, where he was
"discovered" by folklorists John and Alan
Lomax, who arranged for his release and hired
him as their chauffeur. Leadbelly performed a
wide variety of songs, from blues to playparties,
children's songs, hymns, worksongs, and his own
compositions.

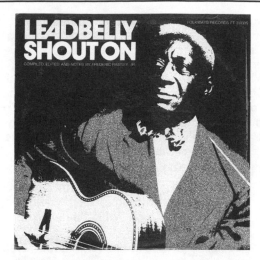

Document 544 (1934–46)

An interesting hodge-podge of blues and non-blues material, including a number of quite rare items alongside material that has already been reissued. Includes two tracks pairing Leadbelly with the Golden Gate Quartet, recorded for Bluebird in 1940. Live tracks from 1946 include "Good Morning Blues," with jazz band accompaniment (including Bunk Johnson and Omer Simeon!), and a fine piano "Eagle Rock Rag." All of this is fairly good Leadbelly, but given the abundance of Leadbelly on LP, the listener looking for an introduction to this magnificent artist should start elsewhere; for dedicated collectors there is enough scarce material to warrant checking it out.

Smithsonian/Folkways 40010 (c,d) Leadbelly Sings Folk Songs

The long-awaited reissue of Leadbelly's Folkways recordings has begun! Fifteen tracks with Woody Guthrie, Cisco Houston, and Sonny Terry. Formerly Folkways FTS 31006. There's A Man Going Around Taking Names/Stewball/Keep Your Hands Off Her/ Outskirts Of Town/The Blood Done Sign My Name (Ain't You Glad)/Jean Harlow/Little Children's Blues/Meeting At The Building.

Stinson 17 A Leadbelly Memorial, Vol. 1

Eight 1943 recordings made by Moses Asch.

Stinson 19 A Leadbelly Memorial, Vol. 2

Sixteen songs.

Stinson 39 Leadbelly Sings Play Party Songs

Stinson 48 A Leadbelly Memorial, Vol. 3

Eleven songs.

Stinson 51 A Leadbelly Memorial, Vol. 4

Sessions originally issued on the Musicraft label.

Stinson 91 Leadbelly Sings and Plays

With Woody Guthrie and Josh White

COMPACT DISC
ESSENTIAL SELECTION

Capitol 92075-2 (21K) Huddie Ledbetter's Best

CD issue of Capitol T-1821 originally issued in 1963. Recorded in October 1944, these were his last studio recordings and feature fine renditions of some of his most popular songs, including a particularly rousing version of his most famous song, "Goodnight Irene." There are also two wonderful tracks featuring Leadbelly playing some lovely ragtime-flavored blues piano. Many of the tracks feature Paul Howard on zither—an instrument not normally associated with the blues but which is remarkably effective here. Rock Island Line/Ella Speed/Western Plain/Sweet Mary Blues.

Columbia CK 30035 (998) Leadbelly

Superb recordings from 1935 made for the ARC label, some of his best.

RCA 9600-2 (CD-A) Alabama Bound

Another excellent entry in RCA's "Heritage" series, this CD features most of his recordings made for RCA in June of 1940. Sixteen songs, including the previously unissued "Can't You Line Em." Eight of the songs feature Leadbelly accompanied by the superb Golden Gate Quartet. They provide almost doo-wop type harmonies on some of the more popular numbers, while on the work songs like "Stewball" and "Can't You Line 'Em," they recapture the feel of the prison work gang that Leadbelly was quite familiar with. The remaining tracks are Leadbelly alone with his guitar and, although his guitar is a bit under-recorded, his powerful voice comes through clearly. Overall sound on this collection is a bit muffled but generally good. Informative notes by series producer Billy Altman in 16-page booklet that also includes discographical information and some excellent photos. Good Morning Blues/Alberta/Easy Rider/Roberta.

CALVIN LEAVY

COMPACT DISC

P-Vine PCD 2118 Cummins Prison Farm

Issued some 12 years ago on LP, this CD is a powerful collection of 16 tracks recorded for Calvin Brown's Soul Beat label in the late 60s-early 70s. Intense and basic blues and deep soul, including vocals by Hosea Leavy, Marie Price, and Jesse "Guitar" Box. It includes the hit title song about Arkansas's infamous penitentiary, along with follow-ups "I Met the Man from Cummins Prison" and "Free From Cummins Prison." Big Four/What Kind of Love/Heart Trouble/You Can't Lose What You Ain't Never Had/Give Me a Love (That I Can Feel)/I Won't Be the Last to Cry.

FRANKIE LEE
Hightone 8004 **The Ladies and the Babies**
Splendid debut album by this fine Bay Area singer. This album effectively mixes blues and soul to create music that is contemporary yet has an earthy bluesy quality to it. Frankie is a fine and expressive singer and has some good songs here, several written by Dennis Walker. Excellent arrangements, with effective use of horns arranged by Miles Grayson and good guitar by Frankie's regular guitarist, Bobby "Mr. Goodfingers" Murray.

JOHN LEE
Alabama country bluesman who made some incredible recordings in 1952. His rediscovery performances from the early 70s on Rounder are a little disappointing.
Rounder 2010 **Down at the Depot**
Note: One of his classic early cuts is reissued on the out-of-print Blues Classics 5 and the rest are on Mamlish 3812 (see PREWAR ALABAMA BLUES collections).

JULIA LEE
Fine urban blues singer and piano player from Kansas City who recorded for Capitol between 1944–52. She had a knack for risque songs.
Jukebox Lil 603 **Ugly Papa**
Sixteen sides recorded between 1945–57. Unlike other reissues that concentrate on her risque double-entendre material, this album presents a more balanced survey of her career, including blues, blues ballads, and jazzy pieces with some nice soloing by Julia and various band members.
Jukebox Lil 614 **A Porter's Love Song**
An excellent collection featuring Julia backed by some of the best jazz musicians of the day, including Billy Hadnott, Benny Carter, Baby Lovett, and Red Callender, on such pearls as "Breeze" and "On The Way Out." Other pleasing performances include the bluesy "Christmas Spirits," with tasty trombone licks from Vic Dickenson, and "When A Woman Loves A Man," with trumpet fills by Vernon "Geechie" Smith. A well-rounded album with good clean sound.

BOBBIE LEECAN and ROBERT COOKSEY
Matchbox 1010 **The Remaining Titles**
Sixteen sides recorded in 1926–27, many not previously on LP. A charming collection of old-time black music featuring the music of guitarist, vocalist, and kazoo player Bobby Leecan and harmonica player and vocalist Robert Cooksey. This album complements the currently unavailable Collector's Classics 53 that features the rest of their recordings. Six of the tracks feature the duo, four are by Cooksey with Alfred Martin, who produces a very similar sound, two are solo tracks by Leecan, including a nice version of "Nobody Knows You When You're Down and Out," and four are by the Dixie Jazzers—a jazz group featuring Leecan and Cooksey with Tom Morris (cnt), Mike Jackson (pno), and Eddie Edinburgh (washbd, drm). Only a few tracks on this album are strictly blues but, nevertheless, this is an entertaining set.

THE LEGENDARY BLUES BAND
Chicago-based group featuring former members of the Muddy Waters band: Pinetop Perkins, Jerry Portnoy, Calvin Jones, Willie Smith, and Peter Ward.
Rounder 2029 (c) **Life of Ease with Louis Myers**
Good, solid performances if not actually earthshaking.
Rounder 2035 (c) **Red Hot and Blue**
A mixture of originals and older songs. Vocals are by Portnoy, Jones, and Perkins—none of whom are exceptional vocalists. The accompaniments, featuring fine guest guitarist Duke Robillard, are competent without being very striking.
COMPACT DISC
Ichiban CD 1039 **Woke Up with the Blues**

J. B. LENOIR
Chicago singer/guitarist with a distinctive high-pitched voice. Recorded some fine rocking material in the 50s, and in the 60s recorded in an acoustic format, performing original social-protest songs.
Chess 9323 (c,d) **Natural Man**
Reissue of 1970 LP featuring fine sides recorded for Chess, Checker, and Parrot in 1955 and '56.
Flyright 564 **Mojo Boogie**
Reissue of superb early 50s J.O.B. recordings, including some unissued alternate takes. With Sunnyland Slim and J. T. Brown. Let's Roll/I Have Married/The Mountain/The Mojo/I Want My Baby.
L+R 42.001 **Alabama Blues**
Long unavailable 1965 acoustic session of original songs. Alabama Blues/God's Word/Move This Rope/Alabama March/ Mississippi Road/Vietnam.
L+R 42.012 **Down in Mississippi**
More fine acoustic sides, some with Fred Below (drm). Part of this was issued some years ago on Polydor with interview material with J. B.'s widow. Down In Mississippi/If I Get Lucky/Round and Round.
Relic 8017 **The Parrot Sessions, 1954–55**
Thirteen tracks recorded for Parrot in 1954–55, in-

cluding both sides of his four Parrot singles and five originally unissued takes, including two ("I'm Gonna Die Someday" and the first take of "Eisenhower Blues") that have never been issued before.

CASSETTE ONLY RELEASE

Chess 2-92506 **J. B. Lenoir**

Originally issued as Chess ACMB-208. Twenty-eight great sides recorded for Chess, Parrot, and Checker between 1951–58. Natural Man/Let Me Die With The One I Love/Mama What About Your Daughter/Five Years/I've Been Down So Long/Carrie Lee/Sitting Down Thinking/J. B.'s Rock.

COMPACT DISC

Flyright FLYCD 04 **His J.O.B. Recordings, 1951–54**

All of his recordings for the J.O.B. label including three tracks on which he accompanies Sunnyland Slim and two accompanying Johnny Shines. Lenore was equally at home with a rocking item like "Let's Roll" or an intense slow blues like the beautiful "Louise." All of the tracks feature the magnificent Sunnyland Slim on piano and some feature the acerbic sax of J. T. Brown. Two takes are featured of several of the songs. A wonderful collection

RON LEVY and THE WILD KINGDOM

Black Top 1034 (c,d) **Wild Kingdom**

With Ronnie Earl, Kim Wilson, Wayne Bennett, and Jimmie Vaughan.

Black Top 1040 (c,d) **Safari to New Orleans**

FURRY LEWIS

Excellent Memphis singer/guitarist and master of the slide. His classic 1927–28 recordings are available on Yazoo and Wolf 101. His 60s-70s rediscovery material is generally very good although he recorded many of the same songs again and again.

Ace CH 260 **Done Changed My Mind**

Reissue of a Bluesville LP from the early 60s. The songs are a mixture of remakes of songs he had recorded in the 20s ("Casey Jones," "I Will Turn Your Money Green"), other blues hits ("Goin' To Kansas City," "Frankie and Johnnny") and other songs drawing on familiar Memphis themes ("Done Changed My Mind," "This Time Tomorrow"). Furry's singing and playing are fine, but I am not too happy with the recordings; his voice and guitar are heavily echoed, which, for me, makes listening uncomfortable.

Fantasy 24703 **Shake 'Em on Down**
Southland SLP 3 **The Fabulous Furry Lewis**
Wolf 101 **The Remaining Titles**

Eleven cuts from 1927–29, complementing Yazoo's LP. Together, they give us his entire recorded output from this period. Mr. Furry's Blues/Billy Lyons and Stack O'Lee/I Will Turn Your Money Green.

ESSENTIAL SELECTION

Yazoo 1050 **In His Prime, 1927–28**

Superb sides. Rock Island Blues/Jellyroll/Good Looking Girl Blues/Mean Old Bedbug Blues/Furry's Blues/Mistreatin' Mama/Cannon Ball Blues.

JOHNNY LEWIS

Good country blues singer/guitarist recorded in Chicago, 1971.

Arhoolie 1055 **Alabama Slide Guitar**

MEADE LUX LEWIS

One of the giants of piano blues and boogie. The Oldie Blues albums are a good survey of his career.

Blues Documents 2031 **1939–1954**

A gap filler that would be of interest only to dedicated collectors were it not for the inclusion of the four classic Art sides of 1939. Also includes five solo cuts from 1944, two of which appear to have been recorded live, and some fairly uninteresting air checks from San Francisco's Club Hangover recorded 1953–54.

Document 534 **1927–1939**

A diverse collection of 14 performances. Starting with his frequently reissued 1927 recording of "Honky Tonk Train Blues," it continues with accompaniments to George Hannah and the dreadful Bob Robinson. There are two great recordings of Meade joined on piano by Albert Ammons and Pete Johnson, a couple of duets with Albert Ammons accompanied by The Benny Goodman Orchestra, and some fine solo performances. Many of these tracks have been reissued before, but this is an enjoyable set.

Euphonic 1209 **Meade Lux Lewis/Cripple Clarence Lofton**

One side of album by each, featuring 1939 recordings. The Lewis sides are from a CBS radio broadcast and the Lofton sides are alternate Solo Art masters.

Oldie Blues 2805 **Tell Your Story**

Fifteen sides, recorded 1930–44, including accompaniments to vocalists George Hannah and Bob Robinson. Also includes a duet from 1939 with

Albert Ammons and one on which Lewis plays celesta.

Oldie Blues 2820 Meade Lux Lewis, Vol. 1

Fourteen solo sides recorded between 1938–41, including four harpsichord solos from 1941.

Oldie Blues 2827 Chicago Piano Blues and Boogie Woogie, 1936–51

Lewis' Chicago recordings. Side one features 1936 solo recordings; Lewis is featured on celesta on two cuts. On the second side, recorded in 1951, he is joined by Israel Crosby (b) and Frank Williams (drm). A couple of tunes are repeated on the second side and it is interesting to compare the different approaches. Sound is excellent and music is, of course, superb.

SMILEY LEWIS

Superb New Orleans singer who recorded quite extensively in the 50s but with only moderate success. He was a powerful, rich-voiced vocalist and a limited, but effective, guitar player. His recordings feature the cream of New Orleans musicians, usually under the leadership of Dave Bartholomew.

K.C. 102 Hook, Line and Sinker

Superb collection of 16 sides recorded between 1950–56. Sidemen include Dave Bartholomew, Lee Allen, Red Tyler, Salvador Doucette, Justin Adams, and Earl Palmer. A must for lovers of New Orleans blues and R&B.

K.C. 103 Caledonia's Party

Sixteen sides recorded between 1950–53, with many of the same sidemen featured on K.C. 102. Baby Was Right/Lowdown/Dirty People/Bee's Boogie/Gumbo Blues.

K.C. 104 Down Yonder

This set, featuring sides from 1953–60, is one of his best, as it features some all-time Lewis classics. Down the Road/I Hear You Knocking/One Night (the original version of this song)/Shame, Shame, Shame/Real Gone Love/Queen of Hearts/Rootin' and Tootin'.

COMPACT DISC

K.C. CD 01 Volume 1

This CD (along with K.C. CD 02) features 48 songs from the best period of his career, 1950–60, and includes all of the material on the three K.C. LPs. Sound is very good and, although there are no notes or a detailed discography, there is a collective personnel listing. Noteworthy on Volume 1 is the original version of "Blue Monday," later made a hit by fellow New Orleanian Fats Domino. Lillie Mae/That Certain Door/Nobody Knows/No

No/Standing On The Corner/Gumbo Blues/Big Mamou/Playgirl.

K.C. CD 02 Volume 2

Some of his best and most well-known songs. I Hear You Knockin' (also recorded by Fats)/Shame, Shame, Shame/One Night (recorded by a certain Mr. Presley)/Down The Road/Lost Weekend/Come On/Please Listen To Me/The Bells Are Ringing.

ESSENTIAL SELECTION

Sequel NEXCD 130 New Orleans Bounce

Thirty classic Imperial recordings. All are also on the K.C. reissues but many tracks here are from master tapes.

JIMMY LIGGINS

Singer, songwriter, and guitar player Jimmy Liggins (Joe's younger brother) was one of a handful of musicians who shaped the emergence of R&B in the late 40s. Jimmy's sound was hard and unpolished, more akin to bebop. He led a fine West Coast urban blues band in the 40s and 50s.

Route 66 KIX 18 I Can't Stop It

Sixteen fine sides recorded between 1947–52 featuring Jimmy and his band. Excellent examples of jump, boogie, and blues, with a few cuts with nice stinging guitar by Jimmy.

Specialty SP 7005 (c,d) The Legends of Specialty—Jimmy Liggins and His Drops O

Contains many of his best recordings, plus a couple of shuffle boogie pieces not previously reissued, the novel, previously unissued "Hep Cat Boogie," and the easy-blues classic "Going Away." There is some duplication with Route 66 KIX 18 and an old, out-of-print English Specialty LP. The CD contains nine bonus tracks including the hit "Don't Put Me Down," and three jumping, previously unissued songs. Great "insider" sleeve notes by Billy Vera.

JOE LIGGINS

The brother of Jimmy Liggins, Joe is a fine and important bandleader and an excellent piano player. His 40s and 50s recordings with his band The Honeydrippers featured a mixture of blues, jazz, and popular music that helped lay the foundation for R&B. Liggins is still active and his present band continues in the spirit of his earlier music.

Jukebox Lil JB 601 Darktown Strutters Ball

Sixteen sides recorded in the 40s and 50s.

Jukebox Lil 622 The Honeydripper

One of the best reissues of Liggins' music, including 16 good sides recorded from 1945–49, including his original, "The Honeydripper," a million seller. As always, great packaging, although there are not as many photos as you've come to expect from this label.

Specialty 2160 Joe Liggins and His Honeydrippers

Classic sides from the late 40s–early 50s. Excellent sound on such all-time greats as "The Honeydripper" and "Pink Champagne."

Specialty SP 7006 (c,d) Legends of Specialty—Joe Liggins and The Honeydrippers.

Features many of his best-known jumping sides like "Pink Champagne," the 1950 remake of "The Honeydripper," "Frankie Lee," and the unstoppable "Rag Mop." Contains three unissued sides including the frantic "Flying Dutchman," on which tenor saxman Maxwell Davis blows the roof off. The CD includes nine bonus tracks, two previously unissued. No duplicaiton with Jukebox Lil 622. Fascinating notes by Billy Vera.

PAPA GEORGE LIGHTFOOT

Crosscut 1001 Natchez Trace

Reissue of album originally issued on Vault in 1970. Fine Mississippi blues singer and harmonica player recorded informally in Jackson, MS, with a small group. Some primitive playing and production but quite effective.

LIGHTNIN' SLIM

Fine Louisiana country/down-home bluesman who recorded for Excello. With his deep, rich vocals, basic but very effective guitar, and the harmonica of Wild Bill Phillips or Lazy Lester, his music epitomized blues at its funkiest. His early recordings are superb examples of low-down swamp blues.

Excello 8000 Rooster Blues

Twelve great down-home blues recordings cut for Jay Miller in the late 50s by this superb artist. Alternate takes of some of the songs here have appeared on Lightnin' Slim albums in Flyright's superb reissue program, but these are the versions that were popular in Louisiana. Includes the tremendous witty talking blues "G.I. Slim," the soulful "My Starter Won't Work," and the hard-driving "Rooster Blues." Long Leanie Mama/Bed Bug Blues/It's Might Crazy/Tom Cat Blues.

Excello 8004 Bell Ringer

Another great collection of mostly early sides. Some songs have appeared in alternate versions on various Flyright albums, but these are the versions originally issued as singles. Includes one of his finest, the doomy "Wintertime Blues," and his unique version of Sonny Boy Williamson's "Don't Start Me To Talkin'." Love Me Mama/ Have Mercy On Me/If You Ever Need Me/Baby Please Come Back/Somebody Knockin'/You Move Me Baby.

Excello 8023 London Gumbo

Some of Slim's last recordings, cut in London in 1972 with a whole slew of blues-rock musicians. Slim is in pretty good voice but the arrangements tend to somewhat overpower him. Just A Little Bit/Too Much Monkey Business/I Won't Give Up/Mean Ole Frisco.

Flyright 524 The Early Years
Flyright 583 The Feature Sides, 1954

Superb sides from the Jay Miller vaults, featuring the six earliest recordings Slim made, two cuts by Slim's harmonica player, Schoolboy Cleve, and four cuts recorded later by Slim in the style of his earliest recordings. Sparse, down-home blues at its most earthy. Includes fine notes by Bruce Bastin.

Flyright 612 We Gotta Rock Tonight

Unissued songs and alternate takes from the Jay Miller archives. Lightnin's dark mournful voice and rudimentary but effective guitar are featured on 14 songs in the company of such brilliant musicians as Lazy Lester and Katie Webster. The songs include such wonderful, slow, intense items as "It's Been A Long Long Time," "I Hate To Leave You Baby," and the magnificent "Wintertime Done Rolled By," alongside propulsive upbeat titles like "Long Leanie Mama" and "We Gonna Rock Tonight." Excellent.

COMPACT DISC

Flyright CD 08 Rollin' Stone

This CD features 18 tracks recorded between 1954 and the mid-60s, drawn from the Flyright LPs, including both sides of his first three singles on Feature, alternate takes of some of his best Excello recordings, plus a couple of unissued sides. Many of the sides feature the brilliant harmonica playing of Lazy Lester and other top-notch sidemen like Al Foreman, Bobby McBride, and Warren Storm, and a variety of very effective percussion effects. Excellent!

LIL' ED and THE BLUES IMPERIALS

An exciting West-Side Chicago blues band that has been tearing up the clubs for 10 years but has only recently made it to record. Fronting the combo is singer/guitarist Lil' Ed Williams. Ed is not a great singer, but he gets the song across effectively and his guitar playing is in the mold of Hound Dog Taylor and his uncle, J. B. Hutto, with a lovely dirty tone and lots of stinging slide playing. The Imperials are a rock-solid accompanying group (second guitar, bass, and drums) who provide a propulsive rhythm.

Alligator 4749 (d) Roughhousin'
The songs here are mostly originals by Ed, along with a few old favorites: Percy Mayfield's "You Don't Exist Any More," a driving boogie version of "Mean Old Frisco," and a wild version of "Walking The Dog."

Alligator 4772 (c,d) Chicken, Gravy and Biscuits

CHARLEY LINCOLN

Matchbox 212 Charley Lincoln
Fourteen wonderful sides recorded between 1927–30 by excellent Atlanta, GA, singer/12-string guitarist Lincoln. Lincoln was the elder brother of the more famous Barbecue Bob and had a similar style. All these sides have been reissued before, spread over various collections, but it is nice to have them all together.

HIP LINKCHAIN

Black Magic 9011 Airbusters
Enjoyable album of Chicago blues from singer/guitarist Linkchain. Most of the recordings are from two sessions held in 1985 and 1987 with different musicians, plus a spirited version of "Diggin' My Potatoes" recorded live in 1984. Most of the songs are originals from Hip, along with a couple of covers. Nothing really exceptional here but good playing and singing throughout.

MANCE LIPSCOMB

One of the great country blues discoveries of the 60s. Superb Texas singer and guitarist whose

repertoire also included non-blues material. His best albums are the first three Arhoolies but all are worthwhile.

ESSENTIAL SELECTION

Arhoolie 1001 Texas Songster and Sharecropper
1960 recordings; beautiful singing and guitar. Fred-

dy/Going Down Slow/Rock Me All Night Long/ Jack O' Diamonds/ Shake Shake Mama.

Arhoolie 1023 Texas Songster, Vol. 2
Recorded 1964. Joe Turner Killed A Man/Silver City/Alabama Jubilee/Come Back Baby/Boogie In A/Cocaine Done Killed My Baby.

Arhoolie 1026 Texas Songster, Vol. 3
Recorded live.

Arhoolie 1033 Texas Songster, Vol. 4

Arhoolie 1049 Texas Blues
1968 and 1969 recordings, some with second guitar or rhythm section. Black Gal/Oh Baby/Angel Child/Whiskey Blues/Haunted House Blues.

Arhoolie 1069 Texas Songster, Vol. 6

Arhoolie 1077 You'll Never Find Another Man Like Mance
1964 live concert in Berkeley; fine music and a valuable glimpse of Mance's rapport with his audience.

COMPACT DISC

ESSENTIAL SELECTION

Arhoolie CD 306 Texas Songster
Twenty-two great tracks recorded in 1960 and '64, previously issued on Arhoolie 1001 and 1026. Booklet includes extensive notes that were originally included with 1001.

LITTLE CAESAR

Fine West Coast urban blues singer who was quite popular in the 50s but in the 60s turned to acting and now regularly appears on TV shows. In addition to the usual songs, Caesar also specialised in dramatic vignettes, in the form of dialogues between him and his lady friend, sometimes amusing and sometimes tragic.

Route 66 KIX 24 Lying Woman...Goodbye Baby
Nice accompaniments by bands that included Que Martin (ten sax), King Soloman (pno), Maxwell Davis (ten sax), Chico Hamilton (drm), Gene Phillips (gtr), and J. D. Nicholson (pno). Excellent notes, packaging, and full lyrics.

LITTLE CHARLIE and THE NIGHTCATS

Alligator 4753 (c,d) All the Way Crazy
First LP by California jump-blues band, led by Little Charlie Baty on guitar, Rick Estrin on vocals, and Little Walter on harp and shiny suit. This LP has the one thing the band lacks in person: restraint. Live, Charlie tries to play the entire history of blues, jazz, and rockabilly guitar on every solo; here he just plays what the song needs. Songs are on the humorous side. Some good originals like "T. V.

Crazy," "Short Skirts," and "Poor Tarzan," and a great choice of covers including the Five Royales' "Right Around The Corner" and the Boo-ga-loo's "Clothes Line."

Alligator 4761 (c,d) Disturbing the Peace

Alligator 4776 (c,d) The Big Break
The Big Break/Don't Do That/Dump That Chump/ Jump Start/Some Nerve/Lottery.

LITTLE JOE BLUE

Joe was born in Louisiana, lived in the San Francisco Bay Area, and recorded in Los Angeles. He has a vocal style strongly influenced by B. B. King and a guitar style influenced by Freddie King! Despite being on the scene for over 20 years and turning out consistently worthwhile records, he has never achieved true commercial success.

Evejim 1991 Dirty Work Going On
This album benefits from better-than-usual production from veteran producer Leon Haywood. Joe's singing and playing is accompanied by an excellent band with some fine horn work. The LP includes remakes of the title song originally recorded for Checker in 1966 and "Encourage Me Baby," recorded for Jewel in the 70s. Most of the rest of the album is well thought-out covers, including Israel Tolbert's "Big Leg Woman" and Sonny Boy Williamson's "Don't Start Me To Talkin'." My only complaint is that there are only eight songs and barely 30 minutes of music.

Evejim 4009 I'm Doing All Right Again
Decent singing and guitar playing by Joe and good small-band arrangements by John Stephens and the album's producer Leon Haywood.

LITTLE MILTON

Excellent Memphis blues/R&B/soul singer. His early Sun/Meteor recordings (reissued on Red Lightnin') are mostly straight blues with good guitar. His Checker recordings from the early 60s are a nice mixture of blues and R&B, while the Stax sessions throw in a bit of soul for good measure plus some hot arrangements. His most recent recordings for Malaco find him returning to a more blues-oriented style.

ESSENTIAL SELECTION

Chess 9252 (c) We're Gonna Make It
Reissue of Milton's first Checker LP 2995 from 1965. Twelve songs that neatly straddle the line between soul and blues. He is accompanied by a solid band of Chicago musicians and we get to hear a few flashes of his excellent guitar playing. Songs include the big hit title song, a great version of the

Bobby Bland hit "Blind Man," the old blues standard "I'm Gonna Move To the Outskirts Of Town," the

pop blues "Blues In the Night," and the straight blues "Life Is Like That."

Chess 9265 (c) Little Milton Sings Big Blues
Reissue of Checker 3002 from 1966. Milton does great versions of blues standards. Tough vocals and guitar from Milton and solid accompaniment by the band. Feel So Long/Stormy Monday/Hard Luck Blues/Sweet Sixteen/Sneakin' Around.

Malaco 7419 Little Milton Playing for Keeps

Malaco 7427 I Will Survive
Enjoyable, if somewhat predictable album. A mixture of blues and soul, some new and some old with Milton singing well. There is some decent guitar but it's hard to tell if it's Milton playing or not. Arrangements are slick in the typical Malaco style.

Malaco 7435 (c) Annie Mae's Cafe
Malaco records are becoming so predictable that they are beginning to sound about as exciting as computer music. Nothing very wrong about it; some decent songs, well sung, with tasteful playing from all the musicians. The songs are a mixture of blues and soul with strings and vocal choruses on some selections. The problem is that the heart and individuality of the main performer is missing.

Malaco 7445 Movin' To The Country
Excellent LP, a very strong selection of mostly blues with some soul and even a tiny bit of funk. Most of the 10 are from the Malaco stable of writers, with covers of Billy Vera's yuppie hit "At This Moment" (soon forgotten) and Billy Myles's classic "Have You Ever Loved A Woman?" Lots of great Milton guitar. Lovin' On Borrowed Time/You're So Cold/You Just Can't Take My Blues.

Red Lightnin' 0011 Raise a Little Sand
Sixteen fine sides from Milton's early days, 1953–59. Homesick For My Baby/Lonesome For My Baby/Begging My Baby/ Love At First Sight.

Rounder SS 35 (c,d) The Sun Masters
Great collection of 13 sides recorded by Milton for Sun in 1953–54, featuring some of his most intense

singing and sensational stinging electric guitar. All these tracks have been out before, most notably on Zu Zazz 2007.

Stax 8514 (c,d) Walking the Back Streets

Excellent collection of mostly previously unissued sides. Somebody's Tears/ Married Woman/Open the Door To Your Heart.

Stax 8518 (c,d) Blues 'n Soul

Reissue of 1974 album. Some good material along with some pop-oriented songs and arrangements.

Stax 8529 (c) Grits Ain't Groceries

Excellent set recorded live at the Summit Club in Los Angeles in 1972 and unissued until now. Accompanied by a good band, Milton works his way through extended versions of six of his best-known songs. Grits Ain't Groceries/Blind Man/I Can't Quit You Baby.

Stax 8550 (d) What It Is—Live at Montreux
Zu Zazz 2007 Hittin' the Boogie

Marvelous collection of sides recorded for Sun in 1953–54; much duplication with Rounder SS 35. Features several songs that have never been issued before, alternate takes, and completely different versions and tracks that have not been available on LP for many years. This is Milton at his rawest and most energetic, accompanied by a solid riffing small band with Ike Turner (pno) and a couple of horns. Milton sings in a powerful, heartfelt style and plays some wonderful searing electric guitar in that over-amplified distorted style we have come to associate with Memphis guitarists like Willie Johnson and Pat Hare. Excellent sound from digitally remastered tapes, informative notes by Colin Escott, and some rare early photos.

CASSETTE ONLY RELEASE

Chess 9112 His Greatest Sides

Fourteen fine blues and R&B sides recorded between 1962–71. Grits Ain't Groceries/Just A Little Bit/Losing Hand/More And More/We're Gonna Make It/Man Loves Two/Feel So Bad.

MCA 902 Age Ain't Nothin' But A Number

1983 album features one quite good blues; the rest is more or less contemporary soul music.

COMPACT DISC

Chess CHD 5906 We're Gonna Make It/
Little Milton Sings Big Blues

Two fine LPs combined into one excellent CD.

Chess (France) 670407 If Walls Could Talk

Seventeen Checker sides. Losing Hand/We're Gonna Make It/What Kind of Love Is This/So Mean to Me/Woke Up This Morning/Just A Little Bit/All Around the World (Grits Ain't Groceries)/Baby I Love You/Many Rivers to Cross.

LITTLE SONNY (AARON WILLIS)

Stax 8533 (c) New King of the Blues Harmonica

Reissue of Enterprise album originally issued in the early 70s. Aaron "Little Sonny" Willis is a fine Detroit singer and harmonica player. Most of this album is instrumental with only two vocals by Sonny, the old standby "Baby What You Want Me To Do" and his own fine "Don't Ask Me No Questions." A solid, hard-driving rhythm section provides the accompaniment, with the sound filled out by an electric organ that, for the most part, is quite effective.

LITTLE WALTER (JACOBS)

Little Walter was possibly the finest blues harmonica player to record in the postwar era and undeniably the most influential. A pioneer in the use of electrification for the harp, his playing reveals an awe-inspiring level of creative imagination. His control of tone, coupled with his immense energy, made for some truly stirring music. Add to this the fact that he was a truly fine singer and was usually accompanied by some of Chicago's foremost sidemen and you can understand why his records are prized as among the finest records to come out of Chicago. Except for his last few sessions, all of his recordings are worth getting. Although many of his best recordings are available, they are scattered over several albums with duplications, and there are several fine unissued titles and alternate takes that are not available at present.

Chess 2-92503 (c) Boss Blues Harmonica

Two-LP set. Twenty-four Chicago blues classics, with sidemen like Muddy Waters, Louis Myers, Robert Jr. Lockwood, Willie Dixon, and Fred Below. Includes all the tracks on Chess 9192 plus Off the Wall/You Better Watch Yourself/Blue Lights/Tell Me Mama/Back Track/It's Too Late Brother/Just A Feeling/Teenage Beat/Just Your Fool/Flying Saucer/I Got To Go/Shake Dancer/Too Late/Thunderbird/Ah'w Baby/Boom Boom, Out Go the Lights.

ESSENTIAL SELECTION

Chess 9192 (c,d) The Best of Little Walter

Reissue of Chess 1428 from 1958 featuring 12 classic performances recorded between 1952–55, accompanied by Louis Myers, Robert Jr. Lockwood, Willie Dixon, Jimmy Rogers, and Fred Below. My Babe/You're So Fine/Blues With A Feeling/

Juke/Off The Wall/Blue Light/Sad Hours/Last Night/Can't Hold Out Much Longer/Tell Me Mama/You'd Better Watch Yourself/Mean Old World.

Chess CH 9292 (c,d) **The Best of Little Walter, Vol. 2**
A great selection of 10 sides recorded for Chess between 1950–60 (including the terrific instrumental "Boogie") that have not been available before on American LP. It includes two of his hits, "Mellow Down Easy" and the utterly magnificent "Key to the Highway"—my favorite version of this oft-recorded song. Accompanists include Robert Jr. Lockwood, Willie Dixon, Louis Myers, Fred Below, Muddy Waters, and Luther Tucker. Digitally remastered from the original master tapes, the sound is outstanding. The CD has two extra tracks, the incredible Muddy Waters' instrumental "Evans Shuffle" and "Just A Feeling." Too Late/Crazy Mixed Up World/Oh Baby/It Ain't Right.

Chess 9321 (c,d) **Hate to See You Go**
A great collection of tracks originally recorded between 1952–60, including such classics as his hit "Oh Baby," his lyrical rendering of "Key to the Highway," and the intense minor-key masterpiece "Blue and Lonesome." Sidemen include Muddy Waters, Jimmy Rogers, Robert Jr. Lockwood, Otis Span, Willie Dixon, and Fred Below. 'Nuff said!

Delmark 648 (c) **The Blues World of Little Walter**
Note: Walter's earliest recordings are available on the following collections: Nighthawk 102 and Blues Classics 8. See also CHICAGO BLUES COLLECTIONS.

LITTLE WILLIE LITTLEFIELD
Fine West Coast singer and piano player with a distinctive vocal style who performed boogie, blues, and ballads. He was at his best on his 40s and 50s recordings.
Oldie Blues 8003 **House Party**
Enjoyable set recorded in Holland in 1978. Primari-

ly a set of skillfully performed boogies, but also includes some blues and ballads.
Oldie Blues 8006 **I'm in the Mood**
Recorded in Holland in 1983. Willie is in excellent form on a selection of blues and boogies. Unfortunately, the Dutch drummer and sax player who join him on several cuts are unexceptional and, on a few cuts, really get in the way.
Route 66 KIX 10 **It's Midnight**
1949–57 recordings.

JOHNNY LITTLEJOHN
Excellent Chicago blues singer and slide guitarist.
Arhoolie 1043 **John Littlejohn and The Chicago Blues Stars**
His best record, recorded in 1968 with an excellent small band. Produced by Willie Dixon and Chris Strachwitz. The material is varied and includes the intense "What In The World You Goin' To Do," the lyrical slide-guitar outing on "Dream," and a bluesy version of the Brook Benton pop/R&B hit "Kiddeo."
Rooster Blues 2621 **So Called Friends**
This is Littlejohn's best album since his 1968 Arhoolie set. Johnny is in good form both vocally and instrumentally and plays some of his fine and distinctive slide guitar, along with some powerful single-string work. The album was recorded at several sessions with different bands but most tracks feature a very effective horn section which, on occasion, has as many as eight members! Material here is mostly new songs from Littlejohn and bassist Aaron Burton along with a couple of old favorites and a tasteful version of B.B.'s "Just A Little Love."
COMPACT DISC
Arhoolie (Japan) PCD 2107 **Chicago Blues Stars**
CD issue of Arhoolie 1043 with two previously unissued tracks, including the traditional-sounding "Nowhere To Lay My Head."

JOHNNY LITTLEJOHN/WILLIE KENT/TAILDRAGGER
Wolf 120.859 **Chicago Blues Sessions, Vol. 13: John Littlejohn's Blues**
Nine tracks recorded in 1989, including six songs by Littlejohn, one by Taildragger, a rather mediocre Howlin' Wolf imitator, and two by Kent, a powerful and effective singer. Fine accompaniments by Luther Adams and John Primer (gtr), Billy Branch (hca), Willie Kent (b), and Timothy Taylor (drm).

ROBERT JR. LOCKWOOD
Great Chicago blues singer/guitarist from Mississippi (and stepson of Robert Johnson). Fine

singer and superb and original guitarist with a jazz-influenced style.

Black and Blue 33.740 **Plays Robert and Robert**
Recorded in France in 1982, featuring Lockwood accompanied only by his electric 12-string guitar. Side one is devoted to the songs of Robert Johnson ("Ramblin' On My Mind," "Walkin' Blues," "Sweet Home Chicago"). Few artists perform these songs with as much command and conviction as Lockwood. Side two is mostly original songs or traditional pieces like "Western Horizon," "Little Boy Blue," or "Take A Little Walk With Me" that Robert performs with skill and authority. The only problems are that Lockwood has recorded all these songs before and I personally find the sound of the electric 12-string guitar irritating.

COMPACT DISC

P-Vine PCD 2134 **The Baddest New Guitar**
A great collection of 18 tracks recorded in the early 60s. Most of them were recorded for the J.O.B. label. There are several vocals including his great (and incredibly rare) version of "Sweet Home Chicago" (called "Aw Aw Baby"), "Sweet Woman from Maine," and two powerful versions of "Dust My Broom." There are also eight great vocals by Sunnyland Slim, who plays piano on all of the tracks, and two by drummer Alfred Wallace. Sound is good, if not state of the art.

Note: Lockwood's few 40s and 50s recordings can be found on Blues Classics 7 and Nighthawk 101.

ROBERT JR. LOCKWOOD and JOHNNY SHINES

Flyright 563 **Dust My Broom**
CD issue: Flyright CD 10
Includes their entire sessions from J.O.B. in the early 50s. They do not perform together on this album.
Note: For more information, see under JOHNNY SHINES.

Rounder 2023 **Robert Jr. Lockwood and Johnny Shines**
Includes acoustic guitar duets and electric blues with Robert's band.

Rounder 2026 **Mister Blues Is Back to Stay**
Nice mixture of blues, ballads, and jazz with good work from Robert's band, though Johnny's voice is showing the effect of his stroke in 1980.

CRIPPLE CLARENCE LOFTON
Superb 30s/40s piano player with a distinctive and innovative style. Highly recommended.

Euphonic 1208 **Cripple Clarence Lofton/Meade Lux Lewis**
Great album. Lofton sides are Solo Art alternates and the Lux sides are from radio broadcasts.

Oldie Blues 2817 **Clarence's Blues**
Some duplication with the out-of-print Magpie 4409 but mostly reissues from a long-unavailable 1939 Chicago session.

Yazoo 1025 **Cripple Clarence Lofton/Walter Davis**
Great! Most of Lofton cuts are from a previously unissued private session recorded in the late 30s.

LONESOME SUNDOWN (CORNELIUS GREEN)
Fine Louisiana singer/guitarist. Sundown was a wonderful singer with a rich expressive voice and a fine and fluid guitar player. He recorded classics for Excello in the 50s and was in equally good form in the 70s when he recorded his new album for Joliet (now available on Alligator).

Alligator 4716 **Been Gone Too Long**
Great set recorded in Los Angeles in 1977 with Phillip Walker and his band.

Excello 8012 **Lonesome Sundown**
Twelve great sides from the late 50s/early 60s. He is accompanied by top Excello sidemen like Lazy Lester (hca), Lionel Torrence (ten sax), and Katie Webster (pno). Some of these tracks have also been reissued on Flyright 587. The main drawback of this album is that it is has been reprocessed into some rather heavily echoed electronic stereo.

Flyright 529 **Bought Me a Ticket**
Twelve excellent Jay Miller recordings, unissued and alternate takes of Excello material.

Flyright 587 **Lonesome Whistler**
Twelve superb cuts recorded for Jay Miller between 1956–58. Unlike many other albums in the Jay Miller series, this one features nine original recordings that were issued on Excello, along with two unissued titles and one alternate take. Lovely relaxed vocal and guitar by Sundown and expressive harp by Lazy Lester. Leave My Money Alone/Mojo Man/Don't Say a Word.

Flyright 617 **If Anybody Asks You**
Previously unissued songs and alternate takes from the Jay Miller archives. There are six previously unissued songs, two fairly forgettable ballads, one interesting instrumental, and three fine blues including the intense "You Give Me All Kinds Of Misery," with some unusual but effective reverb/delay effects on Sundown's guitar. The rest of the tracks are alternate takes of songs issued on Excello, including the title song (a variation on the song issued as "My Home Ain't Here"), the moving "My Home Is Prison," and the rocking "Learn To Treat Me Better." Accompaniments are by stalwarts of the Miller

recording studios such as Lazy Lester, Katie Webster, and Warren Storm. Excellent!

COMPACT DISC

Flyright CD 16 **Lonesome Sundown**

Twenty-one sides recorded for Jay Miller between 1956–64. These are drawn from the three Flyright albums of mostly unissued songs and alternate takes from his Excello sessions. Every track is a gem featuring Sundown's warm smokey vocals and rolling guitar in the company of such stellar accompanists as Lazy Lester, Lionel Torrence, Katie Webster, Warren Storm, and Guitar Gable.

LONESOME SUNDOWN and PHILLIP WALKER

Rounder 2037 (c) **From La. to L.A.**

Excellent album featuring 11 recordings made between 1969–81 by two excellent Louisiana bluesmen who worked together originally in the 50s. There are six solo performances by Phillip accompanied by various groups that show him to be one of the finest contemporary blues singers and guitarists. There are four solo performances by Sundown (accompanied by Phillip) in his down-home style, and one vocal duet. Great stuff.

LOUISIANA RED

Excellent down-home singer/guitarist who plays excellent slide, though he has been over-recorded in recent years.

L+R 42.011 **Reality Blues**

Electric set with Hubert Sumlin and Odie Payne.

L+R 42.045 **Anti-Nuclear Blues**

All topical and political songs. Red accompanies himself on acoustic and electric guitar with occasional second guitar by Gerhard Engbarth. One can't argue with the sentiments of such songs as "Anti-Nuclear Blues," "Reagan Is For The Rich Man," "Starving In Detroit," and "Tribute To Tampa Red," but the songs and performances are a little self-conscious.

L+R 42.055 **Boy from Black Bayou**

This album, subtitled "A Tribute To Muddy Waters," finds Red accompanied by a Chicago band including Jimmy Rogers (gtr), Carey Bell (hca), and Lovey Lee (pno). Mostly original songs.

L+R 42.061 **My Life (with Carey Bell)**

Vogue 522 004 **Lowdown Backporch Blues**

Reissue of Red's first and best album, originally issued on Roulette in 1962. Red sings and plays some powerful guitar (plus harmonica on two cuts) and is tastefully accompanied by bass and drums. Mostly traditionally flavored blues plus two politi-

cally aware songs: the amusing "Red's Dream" and the powerful "Ride On Red, Ride On." Working Man Blues/Sweet Alesse/I'm a Roaming Stranger/Sad News.

COMPACT DISC

Tomato 26934-2 **Midnight Rambler**

Nineteen tracks recorded in 1975, including eight previously unissued sides. Red plays acoustic guitar, with some nice slide playing from time to time.

CLAYTON LOVE

Mississippi blues singer and piano player based in St. Louis.

Red Lightnin' 0029 **Come on Home Blues**

Recorded live with a good small band.

PRESTON LOVE

Fine alto and tenor sax player who started his career with Count Basie in the 40s and is best known for his association with Johnny Otis in the 50s.

Saxophonograph BP 501 **Preston Love and His Orchestra**

Excellent selection of urban blues, R&B, and R&B-flavored jazz. A couple of the cuts were recorded live in Sweden in 1980 and show Love to be still in fine form. About half the cuts are instrumental and the rest feature vocals by Love, Charles Maxwell, and others.

WILLIE LOVE

Oldie Blues 2825 **Shout Brother Shout**

Reissues all 14 cuts recorded by this fine Mississippi piano player between 1951–53. Love is accompanied by a small group; they have a rough juke-joint quality, with declamatory vocals and barrelhouse piano by Willie and loose but exciting backup by the band. Several cuts feature fine Mississippi guitarist Joe Willie Wilkins.

PROFESSOR EDDIE LUSK

Delmark 650 (c) **Professor's Blues Revue**

Eddie Lusk is best known for his session work on keyboards, and this is his first solo album. The vocals are spread among Lusk, Karen Carroll, and guitarist Joey Woodfalk. The performances are decent, though unexceptional, and the band sounds unfocussed and uncertain what direction they should be taking.

NELLIE LUTCHER

A fine piano player and singer who was very popular in the late 40s and early 50s. She is more of a jazz than a blues artist, though quite a bit of her material is blues-based.

Jukebox Lil 1100 **My New Papa's Got to Have Everything**
Sixteen sides recorded between 1947–55. She performs a mixture of blues, boogie, jazz, and pop numbers, sometimes livening things up with some scat singing. Her singing and piano playing are usually accompanied by a rhythm section, though her later recordings feature a bigger band. Beautifully packaged with some wonderful photos.

Jukebox Lil JB 1103 **Ditto from Me to You**
Sixteen tracks, 1947–55.

WILLIE MABON
Fine and distinctive Chicago singer and piano player with a sly and effective vocal style and a witty way with a lyric.

Chess 9189 (c) **Willie Mabon**
Reissue of Mabon's Chess recordings, originally reissued on the German Teldec label. It's a pretty good selection though some of the unissued sides used are not all that good and the version of his big hit "I Don't Know" is from a rather awful-sounding phony stereo master.

Crown Prince IG 402 **The Seventh Son**
Sixteen recordings cut between 1952–56 (his entire issued output during this period), recorded in Chicago with excellent small bands.

Flyright 580 **I'm the Fixer**
Reissues his 1963–64 U.S.A. recordings. Enjoyable selection of original urban blues songs, including two previously unissued tracks and his fine harmonica instrumental "Harmonica Special."

L+R 42.003 **Chicago Blues Session**
1979 recordings with Hubert Sumlin and Eddie Taylor.

DOUG MACLEOD
Hightone 8002 **No Road Back Home**
An impressive debut album by young blues singer/guitarist from Southern California. MacLeod is a rich-voiced singer and a striking guitar player with a relaxed Louisiana quality to his playing. On most cuts he is accompanied by a top-notch rhythm section (keyboards, bass, and drums). A couple of songs feature some very tasty horn parts and one cut features some pleasing harp by George Smith. All songs are written by MacLeod and are very good.

ALBERT MACON and ROBERT THOMAS
Swingmaster 2105 **Blues and Boogie from Alabama**
Country blues duo. Some spirited, if occasionally chaotic, performances.

MAGIC SAM
Superb Chicago singer/guitarist whose tragic death at an early age robbed the blues world of a great talent. A wonderfully expressive singer and an imaginative and powerful guitarist. His brilliant 1956 recordings for Cobra are available on Flyright and Charly and his superb 60s recordings are available on Delmark, L+R, and Black Magic.

Black Magic 9003 **Live at Sylvio's**
Recorded live by Belgian blues collector George Adins in 1968 at Sylvio's Lounge in Chicago. Sam is in stunning form both vocally and instrumentally and is accompanied by a solid rhythm section (Mack Thompson [b], Odie Payne [drm]). Shakey Jake sings or plays harmonica on about half the cuts and is better than usual. Considering the circumstances, the recording quality is quite good.

ESSENTIAL SELECTION
Charly CRB 1108 **Easy Baby**
CD issue: Charly CD 218
All of his classic Cobra recordings are here along with two sides not originally issued, plus cuts from the Crash and Chief labels and two excellent tracks from Artistic on which Sam backs his uncle, Shakey Jake, with some stunning guitar. All these sides are available on Flyright, so if you have those reissues, this is expendable; if you don't, here is your chance to pick up on some great blues singing and guitar playing.

Charly CRB 1134 **Magic Sam/Earl Hooker: Calling All Blues**
This album features eight tracks by Magic Sam, recorded for Chief in 1960, and eight by Hooker, recorded for Chief and Age between 1960–62. Most of the Sam sides have been reissued on Flyright 590 (out-of-print) and 605, including some tough vocal cuts like "My Love Is Your Love" and "Everynight About This Time," and rocking instrumentals like "Blue Light Boogie," along with some dispensable

novelty items. The Hooker sides are all instrumental, including two with Junior Wells on harp. Full discographical information and detailed sleeve notes by Neil Slaven.

Delmark 615 (d) West Side Soul
His first and best Delmark album. Recorded in 1966 with great backup by Mighty Joe Young, Stockholm Slim, and Odie Payne, this is a fabulous collection of songs and instrumentals.

Delmark 620 Black Magic

Delmark 651 (c) The Magic Sam Legacy
Features unissued songs and alternate takes from his 1967–68 Delmark sessions, plus two songs from a 1966 session that he later redid for Delmark. The unissued songs are mostly Chicago blues standards like "Walkin' By Myself" and "That Ain't It," so most of the material here will be pretty familiar territory, but Sam's outstanding performances do a lot to lift them out of the rut. If you've not heard Sam before, you'd be better off with Delmark 615 or 620, plus of course the Charly or Flyright reissues of his classic Cobra recordings from the late 50s.

Flyright 561 Magic Rocker with Shakey Jake
Reissue of 12 great Cobra recordings from 1956.

Flyright 562 The Other Takes, 1956–58
Includes all the takes of Cobra songs not on Flyright 561. Also features Otis Rush.

Flyright 605 Chiefly Wells
Most of this album is by Junior Wells, but it does include four fine Chief sides by Sam.
See under JUNIOR WELLS.

L+R 42.014 The Late, Great Magic Sam
Recordings from 1963, 1964, and 1969. Some fine performances, although with fairly uninspired accompaniment.

COMPACT DISC

P-Vine PCD 2123 Out of Bad Luck
Twenty-six tracks, including his complete Cobra, Chief, and Crash recordings, with a couple of alternate takes.

MAGIC SLIM AND THE TEARDROPS
Excellent Chicago singer and electric guitarist with an original guitar style and a powerful voice. Usually performs with a trio that produces some incredibly raw and exciting music.

Alligator 4728 (c,d) Raw Magic
Eight superb cuts drawn from his two albums on the French Isabel label (900.505 and 900.511). Slim has

solid and effective backup from the rhythm section of guitar, bass, and drums.

Blind Pig 3690 (c,d) Gravel Road
1990 LP from the always excellent Magic Slim, performing gritty versions of Albert King's "Cold Women With Warm Hearts," Otis Reddings's "Hard to Handle," Eugene Church's "Pretty Girls Everywhere," and Percy Mayfield's "Prisoner of Love."

Wolf 120.849 Chicago Blues Sessions, Vol. 3
Excellent no-nonsense Chicago blues. The songs are all familiar or based on familiar themes, but Slim gives them his touch with his rich expressive vocals and dynamic vibrato-laden guitar. Nothing fancy here; nothing else but the blues. You can't go wrong with Slim.

Wolf 120.856 Chicago Blues Sessions, Vol. 10
1989 recordings. Although they have little original material, the Teardrops feature the soulful singing and intense guitar of Slim and the rock-solid backup of John Primer, Nick Holt, and Michael Scott, making for a unique and instantly identifiable sound. Vocals are shared by Slim and bassist Holt on fine versions of Eddie Taylor's "Bad Boy," Bo Diddley's "Before You Accuse Me," "Everybody in Town," and "That Will Never Do" (a variation of "Tin Pan Alley"). I'm a real sucker for minor-key blues and the group's versions of "That Will Never Do" and the Charles Brown classic "Driftin' Blues" are simply spine-tingling with truly marvelous guitar by Slim. Among their better recordings.

COMPACT DISC

Black & Blue 59.525 2 Highway Is My Home
Reissue of Black & Blue 33.525 with one previously unissued extra track. Recorded in France in 1978 with Alabama Junior, Nick Holt, and Fred Below; this is not one of his most inspired releases, but

anything by Slim is worth a listen. Includes intense versions of Wolf's "Highway Is My Home," Jimmy Reed's "I Love You Baby," Junior Parker's "Man or Mouse," Elmore James' "The Sky Is Crying," and others, including a couple of good originals.

J. J. MALONE
Cherrie 2401 **The Enemy Called Hate**
Quite different from his work with his partner Troyce Key. Much of the album is with a large band and the arrangements have more than a hint of funk to them. Some good original songs though sometimes Malone is overpowered by the arrangements.

SARA MARTIN
Best Of Blues BOB 19 **1922-1928**
Twenty sides by this popular and prolific vaudeville blues singer. In general, her accompaniments are more interesting than her somewhat inexpressive vocals. The early sides feature the solo piano accompaniments of Clarence Williams or Fats Waller, while the later ones feature her with small jazz groups, including musicians like Bubber Miley, Shirley Clay, Barney Bigard, Richard M. Jones, and King Oliver. About half of these tracks have been reissued before, but most are not currently available.

MARTIN, BOGAN, and ARMSTRONG
Fine black string band who play a wide range of material including blues, pop, jazz, and country. Entertaining.

Fine Catch 27003 **Martin, Bogan and Armstrong**
Fine Catch 27056 **That Old Gang of Mine**
Rounder 2003 **Barnyard Dance**

TONY MATTHEWS
West Coast singer and guitar player who was a member of the Ray Charles band for eight years.
Alligator 4722 **Condition Blue**
Interesting mixture of blues, soul, jazz, and funk with an emphasis on the blues. Good singing and guitar by Matthews and very varied arrangements.

PETE MAYES
Houston-based bluesman who is strongly influenced by the great T-Bone Walker. Mayes' guitar playing owes a little to T-Bone but his vocals are uncannily like those of his mentor.
Double Trouble TX 3013 **I'm Ready**
Mayes is accompanied by a small band with horns and keyboards who do a good, if not memorable, job. There are only eight songs on the album—six originals plus covers of Jay McNeely's "Something On Your Mind" and Chuck Willis's "My Life," but Pete doesn't sound too comfortable on these blues ballads. Poor sound quality.

PERCY MAYFIELD
Excellent California singer and brilliant and renowned blues writer. Percy had a distinctive vocal style. His Specialty recordings were very influential, though he rarely recorded anything that wasn't worth a listen. Many of his fine 60s recordings are, unfortunately, at present unavailable.
Route 66 KIX 22 **The Voice Within**
A most welcome reissue featuring 16 sides recorded between 1949–56, including one previously unissued. Urban blues at its best with smooth vocals by Percy, wonderful lyrics (mostly by Percy), and fine bands.

ESSENTIAL SELECTION
Specialty 2126 (c) **The Best of Percy Mayfield**
Twelve classics from the 50s. Please Send Me Someone To Love/Lost Mind/Memory Pain/ Louisiana/Strange Things Happening/River's Invitation.
Specialty 7000 (c) **The Legends of Specialty— For Collectors Only**
This incredible compilation of Percy, revealing pain and poetry, is indeed "for collectors only." It contains seven masterful alternates, five previously unissued gems, a revealing false start, and an amazing a cappella demo of "Hit the Road Jack" that Percy's friend Ray Charles later laid to wax.
Timeless SJP 170 **Hit the Road Again**
1982 album of recordings cut in Holland with Percy accompanied by the Phillip Walker Blues Band. Most of the songs are remakes of Percy's old hits. The performances are good though the mood is, perhaps, a little too laid back and Percy's vocals are a little too slurred for comfort. The band is fine with splendid guitar from Phillip and fine tenor sax from Hollis Gimore.

ESSENTIAL SELECTION

Specialty CD 7001 The Legends of Specialty—Percy Mayfield: Poet of the Blues
Twenty-five cuts, 20 of which have been available before on various LPs. Tracks includes his most well-known songs like "Please Send Me Someone to Love," "Strange Things Happening," "What a Fool I Was," and "Lost Love," along with the prophetic, previously unissued sizzler "Advice (For Men Only)," the beautiful "Life Is Suicide," and "Memory Pain." Twenty-four-page booklet with notes, discographical information, photos, and memorabilia. Essential to the beginning blues collector.

JERRY MCCAIN
Excellent Alabama singer and harmonica player. Capable of being an outstanding performer, his records are often bogged down by an over-reliance on novelty songs and inferior production.

Ichiban 1047 (c,d) Blues 'n Stuff
Excellent 1989 recordings. All new songs with Jerry accompanied by a solid band (mercifully, not the usual Ichiban houseband).

White Label 9966 Choo Choo Rock
Fine, previously unissued 50s recordings.

CASH MCCALL
Fine singer and electric guitar player who was a writer and producer for Chess in the 60s and 70s.

L+R 42.058 No More Doggin'
Excellent first album. Most of the songs were written by McCall in collaboration with Margie Evans and he is backed by a good band including nice horn by Andre Avila and piano by Arthur Woods. Some of the songs have a modern funky flavor.

Stone 1945 Cash Up Front
A nice mixture of contemporary blues and soul, much of it written by McCall himself. He is a good singer and a solid, if not terribly original, guitarist. Accompaniment is provided by a tight band including Richard Tee, Phil Upchurch, and Les McCann, and a powerful horn section.

TOMMY MCCLENNAN
Exciting Mississippi blues singer and guitarist. McClennan was a wonderful singer with a gruff voice and a basic but effective guitarist, accompanying himself on a steel-bodied guitar. He sang mostly traditional material and enlivened his recordings with spoken asides. Great stuff!

Travelin' Man 804 Cotton Patch Blues
Sixteen sides recorded between 1939–42, including six tracks from his first and best session in 1939. You Can Mistreat Me Here/Bottle It Up and Go/Cotton Patch Blues/ My Baby's Gone.

Travelin' Man CD 06 Travelin' Highway Man
Twenty-track collection is as fine a cross-section of his recordings made between 1939–42 as you are likely to find and marks their first appearance on CD. Music is consistently fine, sound is generally excellent, and there are informative notes and discographical information. Wonderful stuff!

CHARLIE MCCOY
Mississippi blues guitarist/mandolin player/singer who recorded in the late 20s and 30s, noted for his varied repertoire of blues, country, and novelty songs.

Earl BD 602 Charlie McCoy
Eighteen songs and tunes recorded between 1929–36; about one-third have been reissued before on various collections. Enjoyable mixture of country, hokum, and string-band music, with Bo Chatmon, Walter Vincson, Joe McCoy, and Black Bob.

CHARLIE MCCOY and WALTER VINCSON
Earl BD 612 Charlie McCoy and Walter Vincson
A delightful collection of 18 sides recorded between 1928–36 featuring one or both of these excellent Mississippi musicians (singer/guitarist/mandolin player McCoy and singer/guitarist Vincson). The material is varied, including two lovely Ishman Bracey cuts with McCoy on guitar, the hokum sound of the Jackson Blue Boys with McCoy, Vincson, and Bo Carter, two great duets by McCoy and Carter with Bo playing great fiddle, and the intense sound of Sam Hill (from Louisville) with Vincson on guitar. About half of these cuts have been on LP before, but many of the previous reissues are no longer available.

GEORGE and ETHEL MCCOY
Swingmaster 2106 At Home with the Blues
Some nice country blues by this brother and sister from St. Louis (Memphis Minnie was their aunt). Although they are somewhat limited in technique, they make up for it with the wonderful, dark, brooding quality of their vocals that epitomizes the blues.

ROBERT MCCOY
Alabama singer and piano player.

Oldie Blues 2814 Blues and Boogie Classics

JIMMY MCCRACKLIN
Important and prolific West Coast blues and R&B singer, piano player, and songwriter. McCracklin is equally at home with a down-home

solo piano blues or with big-band R&B, and his recordings reflect this. The albums below feature recordings from all phases of his career (he is still active) and are all worthwhile.

Crown Prince IG 405 **You Deceived Me**
Sixteen sides recorded between 1945–54, including some of his earliest sides, "Mean Mistreated Lover" and "Highway 101." These feature him singing in the 30s Walter Davis style, with piano accompanied by a group including the brilliant guitarist Robert Kelton. On the rocking "Special For You" and "Rock and Rye," he is accompanied by a jump band with horns. Great sound and informative notes.

Route 66 KIX 12 **Rockin' Man**
Sixteen sides from 1945–56, from his Walter Davis-influenced sides to his rockin' mid-50s R&B.

Route 66 KIX 29 **I'm Gonna Have My Fun**
A superb collection of 16 early McCracklin sides covering the period 1949–57, with an emphasis on his more upbeat, R&B sounds. Many of the cuts here feature the brilliant guitarist Lafayette Thomas. The music throughout is exciting and solid.

Stax 8506 **High on the Blues**
Reissue of 1971 album produced by Willie Mitchell and Al Jackson. Some good performances, but a few cuts are a little overarranged.

FRED MCDOWELL
Absolutely magnificent Mississippi country blues singer and guitarist. Incredibly powerful player and master of the slide. Most of his records

have merit, with Arhoolie 1021, 1027, and 1046, Testament 2208, and Heritage 302 being particularly fine. An essential artist.

ESSENTIAL SELECTION
Arhoolie 1021 **Delta Blues**
Absolutely superb. Write Me A Few Lines/Louise/I Heard Somebody Call/'61 Highway/Mama Don't Allow Me.

Arhoolie 1027 **Fred McDowell, Vol. 2**
Another fabulous selection; two tracks feature Fred with veteran Mississippi bluesman Eli Green. I Ain't Gonna Be Bad No More/I Looked At the Sun/Brooks Run Into The Ocean/ I Walked All The Way From St. Louis.

Arhoolie 1046 **Fred McDowell and His Blues Boys**
The first album on which Fred played electric guitar, with second guitar, bass, and drums. The result is very effective. My Baby/When The Saints Go Marching In/Dankins Farm/You Ain't Treating Me Right.

Arhoolie 1068 **Keep Your Lamp Trimmed and Burning**
An excellent selection of mostly spirituals. I Heard Somebody Calling/Where Could I Go But To the Lord.

Heritage 302 **Mississippi Fred McDowell**
CD issue: Flyright CD 14
1962 recordings, his first following his discovery by Alan Lomax in 1959. McDowell is in tremendous form and, although the technical quality is not quite up to the standard of some of his later recordings, these are some of his most spirited performances and feature several songs not recorded by him elsewhere. His version of "Red Cross Store" is absolutely spellbinding. CD has six additional, previously unreleased songs. Unreservedly recommended!

O.B.C. 535 (c,d) **Long Way from Home**
This is a reissue of Milestone 93003 originally issued in 1968. To my mind, there can never be too much Fred McDowell; he was a truly magnificent performer and possibly the greatest blues discovery of the 60s. A rich, powerful, and expressive singer, he was also a unique and brilliant guitarist whose playing embodied some of the most hypnotic rhythms to be heard anywhere. He was also a brilliant slide guitarist. What makes this collection somewhat unique is that it includes several songs that Fred had not recorded elsewhere. In addition to his unique interpretations of traditional songs like "Poor Boy, Long Way from Home," "Milk Cow Blues," and "Sail on Little Girl," it also includes less familiar items like "The Train I Ride," "Millionaire's Daughter Blues," and "You Drove Me from Your Door." Superb.

OJL 8051 **Levee Camp Blues**
Previously unissued 60s recordings featuring some of the earliest songs Fred learned.

Red Lightnin' 0053 **Standing on the Burying Ground**
Recorded live in England in 1969 with Jo Ann Kelly on some cuts. OK recordings.

Rounder 2007 **Fred McDowell and Johnny Woods**
Fred with fine Mississippi harmonica player.

Testament 2208 **Fred McDowell**
Some of the earliest and best recordings by Fred from 1963–64. One side is all blues and the other side is all spirituals with Fred's wife, Annie Mae. Wonderful impassioned vocals and stunning slide guitar. A classic.

COMPACT DISC

Tomato 269637-2 **Shake 'Em on Down**
Reissue of 1971 recording. Nine tunes. You Got To Move/Someday/Baby Please Don't Go.

FRED MCDOWELL and PHIL GUY
Red Lightnin' 0063 **A Dose of Double Dynamite**
A rather odd coupling of performers. Side one by McDowell was recorded in London in 1969 and features him in good form on a selection of some of his best-known songs. The Phil Guy set was recorded live in Chicago in 1983 with a band including tenor sax player A. C. Reed. A rather unexceptional set of performances that is made even more unexceptional by mediocre sound.

TOM MCFARLAND
Talented blues singer/guitarist from the Northwest. He is a decent vocalist and better-than-average guitarist and writes good songs.

Flying Heart 332 (c) **Just Got in from Portland**
Tom fronts a crack eight-piece band, he sings from the heart, and plays with a lot of soul. The production is high-calibre and McFarland's lead guitar is perfectly mixed up-front. The three-piece horn section is used tastefully and does not intrude upon the proceedings. The Tickler/Rainy Day Blues/Goin' Back to Oakland.

BROWNIE MCGHEE AND SONNY TERRY
One of the giants of East Coast country blues. McGhee's career dates back to the late 30s when he was groomed to be the successor to the great Blind Boy Fuller. Over the years, he has recorded in a range of different styles with varied accompaniments and is best known for his acoustic duets with harmonica player Sonny Terry. Brownie and Sonny worked together regularly from the early 40s up to a few years before Sonny's death in 1985, and most of the recordings below feature them together.

BGO BGOLP 75 (d) **Home Town Blues**
Reissue of Mainstream 56049 (it has also had several other catalog numbers) featuring recordings made for Bob Shad's Jax and Sittin' In With labels in 1952–53. These are among the duo's finer recordings. Half of the tracks feature a small band with Brownie on electric guitar and the great Bob Gaddy on piano, including his amusing "challenge" to Lightnin' Hopkins, "Lightnin's Blues." The rest are acoustic duo performances. Excellent.

Blue Rock'it 104 **Facts of Life**
1985 album by Brownie recorded on the West Coast, where he now lives. He is accompanied by various Bay Area musicians, including the famed Robben Ford on guitar, Mark Hummel on harp, and Clay Cotton on piano. It's nice to hear Brownie again in an electric-band context, though the album lacks the spark to make it a really exciting production

Collectables 5198 (c,d) **Sonny Terry and Brownie McGhee**

Muse 5131 **You Hear Me Talking**
1961 Choice recordings.

Muse 5177 **Hootin'**
Reissue of recordings cut for the Choice label in 1959 and 1961.

O.B.C. 505 **Brownie's Blues**
Originally issued as Bluesville 1042 in 1961. Typical set with Sonny Terry and nice second guitar by Benny Foster. Jump, Little Children/One Thing For Sure/Little Black Engine.

ESSENTIAL SELECTION

Savoy SJL 1137 **Climbin' Up**
Reissue of long-out-of-print Savoy 14019 with new cover and notes. This enjoyable set features four sides from January 1952 on which Brownie is accompanied by Sticks McGhee on second guitar. Four sides are from March 1952 on which Sonny and Brownie are accompanied by a discreet bass player and drummer, performing typical Sonny and

Brownie fare. The most interesting cuts are the four from 1955 on which Brownie and Sonny are accompanied by a small R&B combo with fine guitar by Mickey Baker.

Smithsonian/Folkways SF 40011 (c,d) Brownie McGee & Sonny Terry Sing
Remastered, repackaged version of Folkways 2327 originally issued in 1958 with Gene Moore (drm).

Storyville 4007 Brownie and Sonny

COMPACT DISC

A&M 0829 (CD-Q1) Sonny and Brownie
Early 70's pop-oriented reissue, with "People Get Ready," "Bring it on Home to Me," "On the Road Again," and nine more.

Fantasy FCD 24708-2 Back To New Orleans
Two-LP set on one CD.

See For Miles SEECD 92 I Couldn't Believe My Eyes
Sixteen of Sonny and Brownie's bluesiest recordings of the 60s, thanks to the tough-playing group of Earl Hooker (gtr), Ray Johnson (pno), Jimmy Bond (b), and either Panama Francis or Earl Palmer (drm). The six tunes with Palmer first appeared as part of "A Long Way from Home" (Bluesway 6028 from 1969), while the 10 with Francis came out 4 years later as "I Couldn't Believe My Eyes" (Bluesway 6059 from 1973). Lots of great guitar throughout by both Brownie and Hooker. Black Cat Bone/When I Was Drinkin'/You Just Using Me for a Convenience.

Sequel NEX CD 120 The 1958 London Sessions
A better-than-average collection from Sonny and Brownie recorded in England in 1958 and originally released on a Nixa LP and EP. This CD includes all those sides plus two previously unissued titles. The duo is in fine form on a selection of mostly familiar items. A few tracks feature sympathetic piano support by Dave Lee, and there are a couple of solo cuts by Brownie. Sound quality here is excellent. Just a Dream/Woman's Lover Blues/Southern Train/Gone but Not Forgotten/Cornbread, Peas and Black Molasses/Brownie's Blues/Auto Mechanic Blues/Wholesale and Retail/The Way I Feel.

Tomato 269610-2 Rainy Day
Twelve tunes. The Blues Had a Baby/Walk On/Mean and Evil/Wine Sporty Orty/Key to the Highway.

Travelin' Man CD 04 1944–55
Excellent cross-section of Brownie's recordings from the 40s and early 50s. Most of the tracks feature him with small groups with sidemen like Sonny Terry, Big Chief Ellis, Jack Dupree, and Bob Gaddy.

Also includes accompaniments to Sticks McGhee and Bobby Harris.

Note: Only one of the many albums McGee and Terry recorded for Folkways have yet to be reissued by Smithsonian/Folkways, but are available on special order cassette directly from the Smithsonian. See also SONNY TERRY for the albums featuring Terry as vocalist and also those without McGhee.

STICKS MCGHEE
Crown Prince IG 401 Drinkin' Wine Spo-Dee-O-Dee
Sixteen sides recorded between 1949–53 by this fine singer who was the brother of Brownie McGhee and is best remembered for the original version of the title song on this album. Features various small groups, some including Brownie on guitar or second vocal.

BIG JAY MCNEELY
One of the great honking tenor players, Jay has had a long career dating back to the 40s culminating in his big hit "There Is Something On Your Mind" in 1959. He was in retirement through the 60s and 70s but returned to performing in 1983, when he also formed his own record label, Big J.

Big J 101 Loose on Sunset
Live at Club Lingerie in LA on Halloween night, 1983.

Big J 103 The Swingin' Cuts
Sixteen tracks recorded for the Los Angeles Swingin' label between 1957–61. Lots of hard-driving music, including the unedited version of the hit "There Is Something On Your Mind," with Little Sonny Warner on vocals, lots of honkin' instrumentals, and even a rockabilly track.

Saxophonograph BP 505 Roadhouse Boogie
Features a variety of swing styles, sometimes bop, sometimes Latin, sometimes just wildly frantic. Side one features eight sides recorded in 1949, including the title tune, with screaming vocals by Ted Shirley, and the mellow "Midnight Dreams," featuring the voice of Clifford Blivens. Side two gives us a glimpse of six of Jay's excellent Aladdin cuts plus two from Federal. Junie Flip/Real Crazy Cool/Deac's Blowout.

Saxophonograph BP 1300 The Best Of Big Jay McNeely, Vol. 2
Previously unreissued cuts, focussing on Big Jay's best booting from the much-coveted Federal period, including the jet-speed "3D," the bouncy "Let's Work" with fine Ed Moody piano, and the positively frantic "Nervous Man Nervous." Some duplication with other albums.

Note: Eight of Jay's Savoy sides can be found on Savoy 2234, The Roots Of Rock 'n Roll, Vol. 6.

JAY MCSHANN

Jazz band leader who featured many of the finest blues vocalists.

Black Lion 30144 **The Band That Jumps The Blues**

Splendid set of 1947–49 recordings reissued from Swingtime. Instrumentals and vocals featuring Jimmy Witherspoon, Lois Booker, Crown Prince Waterford, Art Farmer, Tiny Webb, and Maxwell Davis. West Coast urban blues at its best.

MCA 1338 **The Early Bird Charlie Parker**

Features seven fine blues vocals by Walter Brown including the first recording of the blues standard "Confessin' The Blues." Recordings from 1941–43 with McShann (pno), Charlie Parker (alto sax), and band.

BLIND WILLIE MCTELL

One of the giants of country blues whose recording career spanned the period from 1928–56. A marvelous singer, he was also probably the finest of all 12-string guitarists. His recordings are consistently fine, with his early sides (reissued on Yazoo 1005 and 1037) being among the greatest country blues ever recorded.

Document 531 **1929–31**

Seventeen tracks, including accompaniments to Alfoncy and Bethenea Harris, Ruth Willis, and Ruby Glaze (probably Kate McTell). One of the Willis cuts and the Ruby Glaze cut are vocal duets with Willie and are truly superb: "Rollin' Mama Blues" by Willie and Ruby has some incredibly raunchy lyrics. The Harris tracks are dull hokum with minimal contributions from Willie. In addition to the fine blues, there are some excellent gospel performances. Although most of these tracks are not currently available, almost all have been reissued before 1970, mostly on Roots 324 and Magnolia 502—so you might want to check your collections.

Melodeon 7323 **The Library of Congress Session**

Beautiful 1940 recordings.

Wolf 102 **The Remaining Titles**

Fifteen sides recorded between 1927–49, complementing other reissues (some now out of print). Mr. McTell Got the Blues/Loving Talking Blues/ Lonesome Day Blues/Searching the Desert for the Blues/Death Cell Blues.

ESSENTIAL SELECTION

Yazoo 1005 (d) **The Early Years**

Tremendous! Probably the best reissue of his early recordings made in 1927–33. Fabulous singing and 12-string guitar by Willie. Mama 'Taint Long Fore

Day/Love Changin' Blues/Three Women Blues/ Broke Down Engine Blues/ Travelin' Blues.

Yazoo 1037 **Blind Willie McTell, 1927–1935**

Another superb selection. Stole Rider Blues/Kind Mama/Scarey Day Blues/My Baby's Gone.
CASSETTE ONLY RELEASE

MCA 1368 **Blind Willie McTell**

Twelve great sides recorded for Decca in 1935, five with Kate McTell on second vocal. Although all of these have been reissued before, these are taken from original Decca metal parts and have superb sound. Let Me Play With Your Yo Yo/ Cold Winter Day/Cooling Board Blues/Hillbilly Willie's Blues.
Note: See also JEMF 106 in PREWAR GEORGIA COUNTRY BLUES collections.

JACK MCVEA and HIS ALL STARS

Alto blower McVea was one of the creators of the R&B idiom, who, after leaving the Lionel Hampton Band at the close of WW II, formed his own unit and recorded some of the finest boogie, blues, and R&B sides of the time. His "Open The Door Richard" (included on Jukebox Lil 607), recorded in 1946, became a best-selling disc and has since become McVea's trademark. McVea had a strong "tight" driving sound rarely matched during the early days of R&B.

Jukebox Lil 607 **Open the Door Richard**

Includes some able lead vocals by trumpet player Cappy Oliver and drummer Rabon Tarrant. Titles from 1945–47. Scrupulous sleeve notes by Greg Drust. Bartender Boogie/O-Kay for Baby/Ooh Mop/Frisco Blues/Don't Let the Sun Catch You Crying.

Jukebox Lil 612 **Two Timin' Baby**

Features drummer Rabon Tarrant's best vocal blues ballads cut between 1945–47, including the "New Worried Life Blues" and the fine "Lonesome Blues." The set is also peppered with solid blues and R&B instrumentals, notably "Silver Symphony" and "Frantic Boogie."

MEMPHIS JUG BAND

Great 20s/early 30s jug band with varying personnel but always including Will Shade on vocals, guitar, and harmonica. Other members included Ben Ramey, Will Weldon, Walter Horton, Charlie Polk, and Hattie Hart.

Matchbox 1008 The Remaining Titles
Rounds up all the titles by this great group that are not on other reissues. The music is a delightful collection of blues, breakdowns, and even a jug band waltz! Wonderful stuff!

Yazoo 1067 The Memphis Jug Band
Two-LP set featuring 28 great performances.
Note: Also on collections: Historical 36, OJL 4, OJL 19, and Blues Classics 2.

EDDIE MILLER/JOHN OSCAR

Blues Documents 2060 The Piano Blues of Eddie Miller and John Oscar
Fourteen tracks featuring eight Miller numbers, including accompaniments to Charles "Speck" Pertrum, Lizzie Washington, and Eddie Morgan, plus six never-before-reissued Oscar tracks.

MEMPHIS MINNIE

Wonderful country blues singer and guitarist. Her 20s/early 30s recordings featuring duo guitar with her husband Kansas Joe (McCoy) are especially fine (reissued on Blues Classics 13, Document 559, Earl 608 and 617, and Travelin' Man 803). All of her recordings are fine; she was an outstanding guitarist and immensely powerful singer to the end of her career.

Blues Classics 1 Memphis Minnie, Vol. 1
Fourteen tracks from 1928–42, including some of her most popular recordings. In My Girlish Days/Black Rat Swing/Nothing In Rambling/Me and My Chauffeur Blues/Joe Louis Strut/Boy Friends Blues/When The Levee Breaks.

Blues Classics 13 Memphis Minnie, Vol. 2
Superb 1930–31 sides with Kansas Joe on second guitar and occasional vocals. New Dirty Dozens/She Put Me Outdoors/What's The Matter With The Mill/Pickin' The Blues/After While Blues.

Document 559 Keep You Goin'
In case you were wondering if you need yet another Memphis Minnie album, just listen to the first few bars of the opening cut "Don't Bother It," with the lyrical twin guitars of Minnie and husband Kansas Joe, and you'll know the answer is a resounding yes! Minnie was one of the greatest of all blueswomen: a superb, powerful singer, magnificent guitarist, and an imaginative songwriter. She was equally at home with the country blues she performed with Joe, and

the urban small-group sounds she performed after she settled in Chicago. This collection covers the whole spectrum, featuring recordings made between 1931–41. Most of the tracks have not been on LP before, including a couple of her very rare 1935 recordings issued as "Texas Tessie," where she is accompanied by an unknown second guitarist with a two-guitar sound that is very different from early sides with Kansas Joe. Sound is generally good and the music is exceptional!

Earl BD 608 Memphis Minnie, Vol. 1
Eighteen sides, about half of which have been reissued before but some are on long out-of-print albums. Eleven of the songs are solo with guitar accompaniment only, two songs have a jug-band accompaniment, and the rest are with small groups. Classic stuff!

ESSENTIAL SELECTION

Earl BD 617 Memphis Minnie, Vol. 2
A beautiful collection of 19 sides from 1929–41. Eleven of them were previously on the out-of-print Paltram 101, while the rest were previously on collections or never reissued before. Ten of the tracks feature the twin guitars of Minnie and her husband Kansas Joe McCoy, an ecstatically beautiful sound, as they weave around the vocals. On "Stinging Snake Blues," Minnie is accompanied by her own guitar, and her playing is spine-tingling with some wonderful string snapping. The remaining tracks feature her with small groups that include piano, second guitar, mandolin, bass, and drums in various combinations, including her tribute to Joe Louis ("He's in the Ring") and the very liberated "You Can't Rule Me."

OJL 24 Gonna Take the Dirt Road Home
Recordings from 1944–49, featuring mostly unissued or alternate takes with Little Son Joe and Blind John Davis.

Travelin' Man 803 In My Girlish Days
Sixteen early and incredibly rare sides recorded between 1930–35, when Minnie was at her peak. Most of the tracks find her in combination with husband Joe McCoy (on second guitar), a truly lovely sound. On a few tracks, Joe joins her on vocal. The sound on a few cuts is quite bad, but they are so rare that we are lucky to have them at all. A superb album!

CASSETTE ONLY RELEASE

Arhoolie C-215 Memphis Minnie
Double-length cassette combining Blues Classics BC 1 and BC 13.

MCA 1370 Moanin' the Blues
One Vocalion side from 1930 and nine Decca sides

4s

from 1934 and 1935. Most of these have been reissued before, but they are taken from original metal masters so they have superb sound. Great country blues.

Note: Other prewar sides are reissued on OJL 6,OJL 21, Yazoo 1008, Yazoo 1021, Mamlish 3801, Mamlish 3803, Magpie 4413, and JEMF 106. Postwar sides available on Flyright 585.

MEMPHIS SLIM

Prolific blues singer and piano player who lived in Europe in the 70s and 80s up to his death in 1989. His recordings range from mostly solos to large bands. Slim is a deep-voiced singer and a very good piano player, though he has recorded so often that many of his albums are rather pedestrian. Favorites are the the King recordings with an excellent band and the Charly, Pearl, and Vee Jay sides recorded with a band featuring superb guitar by Matt Murphy.

Antones ANT 0003 Together Again One More Time

The reunion of Memphis Slim with his former partner, guitarist Matt Murphy, after not playing together for 20 years. Although the magic and excitement of their earlier recordings is gone, there are some enjoyable moments here.

Candid 9023 (d) Tribute to Big Bill Broonzy, Leroy Carr, and Others

Slim pays homage to some of the great artists who influenced him or were his contemporaries with a selection of songs and tunes from the repertoire of Big Bill Broonzy, Leroy Carr, Cow Cow Davenport, Curtis Jones, and Jazz Gillum. He is joined on guitar and harmonica by Arbee Stidham and Jazz Gillum, respectively, who each contribute a couple of vocals.

Candid 9024 Memphis Slim, USA

Charly CRB 1030 (d) Rockin' the Blues

CD issue: Charly CD 210

Sixteen excellent cuts recorded for Vee Jay in the late 50s and early 60s with a hard-driving band including superb guitar by Matt Murphy. Most of this album has appeared before on Slim's "Gate Of Horn" album but a few cuts have only been previously available on singles.

Chess 9250 (c) Memphis Slim

Reissue of Chess 1455 from 1961, featuring sides originally recorded for the Premium label between 1950–52. Most tracks feature Slim with a small band (bass, drums, and saxes) and are a mixture of driving boogies, relaxed after-hours-type blues, and doo-wop flavored ballads.

GNP-Crescendo 10002 The Blues Is Everywhere

GNP-Crescendo 10017 Legacy of the Blues, Vol. 7

1973 recordings with band including Billy Butler (gtr) and Eddie Chamblee (ten sax).

Muse 5219 I'll Just Keep on Singing the Blues

A much better-than-average Slim album, recorded in 1961 and originally issued on the Strand label, with a fine small band including Matt Murphy (gtr).

O.B.C. 507 All Kinds of Blues

1960 recordings originally issued on Bluesville 1053. A typical set from Slim. Blues Is Troubles/ Three-in-One Boogie/Churnin' Man Blues/The Blacks.

ESSENTIAL SELECTION

Pearl 10 Memphis Slim, USA

Some of his best recordings cut for United in 1954, with an excellent band and stunning guitar by Matt Murphy.

COMPACT DISC

Charly CD 249 Life Is Like That

Seventeen sides recorded for Miracle and King between 1946–49 in Chicago with sidemen such as Ernest Cotton, Willie Dixon, Big Crawford, and Alex Atkins.

Esperance ESPCD 1909 Memphis Slim Story

A fine collection of 20 tracks from the 70s and 80s by this ubiquitous performer. Four of the tracks feature Slim narrating the story of his life to his piano accompaniments. Some of his claims seem a little unbelievable, but it certainly makes for interesting listening! The rest is a mix of solo tracks, tracks with drummer Michel Denis, and some with a small band with horns. The most effective ones are those by Slim on his own or with Denis. Slim is in excellent form, singing and playing with great spirit. Recording is excellent, with a lot of presence.

AMOS MILBURN

One of the finest urban blues artists of the 40s and 50s with his smokey vocals and brilliant piano in the company of some hot combos.

Route 66 KIX 7 Amos Milburn and His Chicken Shackers

Sixteen great cuts, 1946–64. Amos Blues/I Love Her/Pool Playing Blues/Real Pretty Mama Blues/ Let's Make Christmas Merry Baby.

Route 66 KIX 21 Rock, Rock, Rock

Sixteen fine ballads, blues, and boogie numbers recorded between 1947–57. No duplication with any other reissues. The usual superb sound and packaging we have come to expect from this label.

Route 66 KIX 28 **Let's Rock a While**

Seventeen blues, ballads, and boogies. Includes the slow blues ballad "After Midnite," with Amos' smoky voice used to great effect, the wonderful boogie "Blues at Sundown," with some great sprightly piano from Amos, "Walking Blues," with nice guitar by Johnny Brown, his distinctive version of the country song "Birmingham Bounce," and many more great sides.

COMPACT DISC

ESSENTIAL SELECTION

Sequel NEX CD 132 **Blues & Boogie—His Greatest Hits**

This marvelous 23-track collection gathers together some of his finest and most popular recordings from the 40s and early 50s.One of Amos' favorite hobbies was drinking, and he had a string of successes with such songs (included here) as "Good, Good Whiskey," "Bad, Bad Whiskey," "Thinkin' and Drinkin'," and "Let Me Go Home, Whiskey." Most of the recordings here were cut in Los Angeles with top West Coast sidemen like Maxwell Davis, Don Wilkerson, Chuck Norris, and Wayne Bennett. It also includes his second version of "Chicken Shack Boogie," recorded in 1956 in New Orleans with an all-star New Orleans band, which is one of the greatest rock 'n' roll records ever made! Sound is generally excellent, there are informative notes by Dave Penny, and full discographical information. Essential! It Took a Long Long Time/Chicken Shack Boogie/Bewildered/Hold Me Baby/Roomin' House Boogie/Real Pretty Mama Blues/Tears, Tears, Tears/Let's Rock Awhile.

EDDIE MILLER/JOHN OSCAR

Blues Documents 2060 **The Piano Blues of Eddie Miller and John Oscar**

Fourteen tracks featuring Miller, including accompaniments to Charles "Speck" Pertum, Lizzie Washington, and Eddie Morgan, plus six by Oscar. A half dozen of these tracks have been reissued before.

LUCKY MILLINDER

One of the foremost pioneer exponents of big-band R&B.

Jukebox Lil 609 **Shorty's Got to Go**
Jukebox Lil 613 **Let It Roll Again**

A mixture of material cut between 1941–51, including war-propaganda novelties sung with bravado by all the band members. Although much of the vocal work by Trevor Bacon and Judy Carol sounds dated, Arbee Stidham does a fine job on the bluesy "Your Heart Belongs To Me," Big John Greer wails on "Let It Roll Again," Annisteen Allen hollers "The Blues Done Got Me," and Wynonie Harris belts out the Ruth Brown hit "Teardrops From My Eyes" with much virtuosity.

CASSETTE ONLY RELEASE

MCA 1319 **Lucky Days, 1941–45**
With Rosetta Tharpe, Dizzy Gillespie, and Wynonie Harris.

MCA 1357 **Let It Roll**
With Rosetta Tharpe.

ROY MILTON

West Coast blues/R&B bandleader and singer popular in the 40s and 50s. Milton was one of the key artists in the development of R&B from the merging of blues and jazz.

Dooto 223 **Rock 'n' Roll Versus Rhythm and Blues**
Half of the album is by Chuck Higgins; 50s recordings.

Jukebox Lil 600 **Grandfather of R&B**
Seventeen sides recorded between 1945–51 with excellent vocals and band work. Album cover and inner liner feature some amazing rare early photos.

Jukebox Lil 616 **Big Fat Mamas**
More fine postwar blues and rhythm ballads and swinging instrumentals including sides from his own Roy Milton picture label, most of which have remained unreissued up to this point. Standouts include the rollicking "Big Fat Mama," with fine piano triplets from Camille Howard, the ballad hit "So Tired" from 1952, great scat and vocal harmony on "Blue Turning Grey," good solid rock 'n' roll on "T-Town Twist," and "Let Me Give You All My Love." Boss R&B.

Specialty 2159 (c) **R. M. Blues**
Milton's Boogie/Information Blues/Night and Day.

ESSENTIAL SELECTION

Specialty SP 7004 (c,d) **The Legends of Specialty—Roy Milton & His Soul Senders**
Sixteen nuggets from the 1945–50 period. Includes hits like "Milton's Boogie," "R. M. Blues," "Keep A Dollar in Your Pocket," and "The Hucklebuck." The Solid Senders were modeled on the Lucky Millinder Band. They included the great alto sax player Jackie Kelson and legendary boogie pianist Camille Howard, who also recorded for Federal and Specialty. Camille and Jackie "spiced" the Milton band with tireless excitement. The CD features nine additional hits from the same period, including "Best Wishes," "T-Town Twist," and "I Have News for You." There is only minimal duplication with Jukebox Lil 600 and 616.

MISSISSIPPI DELTA BLUES BAND

Down-home blues group of obscure musicians.

T.J. 1002 Mississippi Delta Blues Band in Europe

T.J. 1050 Mississippi Delta Blues Band

With vocals and harp by Sammy Myers and good slide guitar by Robert Deance.

T.J. 1054 Chromatic Style

Features the lead vocals and chromatic harmonica of Sam Myers. Some decent singing and playing from Myers but rather unexceptional backup from the band.

THE MISSISSIPPI SHEIKS

Popular 20s Mississippi black string band featuring the first family of Mississippi blues, the Chatmon brothers—Bo (aka Bo Carter), Sam, and Lonnie—with additional musicians like Walter Vincson or Charlie McCoy. Their combination of guitars, fiddles, and mandolin made for exhilarating music.

Document 595 1930–35

A superb collection from the greatest of the black string bands, featuring, in various combinations, Bo Chatmon (Carter; vcl, gtr, vln), Sam Chatmon (vcl, gtr), Lonnie Chatmon (vln), and Walter Vincson (vcl, gtr). The music is consistently fine and exhilarating. Unfortunately, quite a number of the tracks are from very worn 78s, making for tough listening.

Mamlish 3804 Stop and Listen

Superb selection including their most famous song, "Sitting On Top Of The World." Yodeling Fiddling Blues/Your Good Man Caught The Train and Gone/ Honey Babe, Let the Deal Go Down/Ramrod Blues.

Matchbox 1005 Mostly New to LP—Vol. 1

Delightful compilation of 18 recordings from 1930. Dubbed from rare 78s, the sound is mostly good and the music is wonderful. These recordings showcase the simple yet infectious guitar-violin interplay that makes the Sheik's sound so distinctive. There's plenty of hard-edged yet lilting fiddle by Lonnie and Bo (who also plays guitar) and Walter Vincson's gritty voice and string-popping guitar lend fierceness and authority to his sides. The Sheik Waltz/The Jazz Fiddler/River Bottom Blues/Church Bell Blues.

Note: Other sides reissued on Yazoo 1007, Yazoo 1014, and Roots 316.

MONKEY JOE

Old Tramp 1208 1938–39

Mississippi singer/piano player Jesse Coleman, aka Monkey Joe, recorded some 34 sides between 1935–39 but, up to now, very few of his recordings have

been reissued. This enjoyable collection features 18 sides recorded in 1938 and 1939 and show him to be a fine vocalist and a fluid piano player, though some of the tracks feature Blind John Davis on piano. Accompaniments are typical for the period, featuring in various combinations Charlie McCoy (mdln), Fred Williams (drm), Buster Bennet (alto and tenor sax), and Willie B. James (gtr). Sound on a few cuts is pretty rough, though it is generally satisfactory.

LITTLE BROTHER MONTGOMERY

Fine blues singer and piano player who started his recording career in 1935 and was active up to his death in 1985! Some nice ragtime influences in his playing.

Ace CH 263 Chicago—the Living Legends

Reissue of the 1961 Riverside album that was recorded live at The Birdhouse in Chicago. Montgomery works his way through a fine selection of blues tunes, both solo and with a varying group of traditional jazz instrumentalists. Home Again Blues/Up the Country Blues/Trouble in Mind/ Riverside Boogie.

Magpie 4452 "Those I Liked, I Learned"— Unissued Recordings, Vol. 2

The second album from Magpie, featuring previously unissued recordings (made by Francis Smith) of blues pianists who visited England in the early 60s. This album features 16 sides made in 1960 by Little Brother Montgomery. Although the recordings were made under informal living room conditions, the sound is very good with a lot of presence on Brother's singing and playing. Brother was in good form at the time of these sessions, which feature a number of songs he had not performed for a long while and indicate that his abilities included other kinds of music in addition to blues. Wang Wang Blues/Caledonia Numbers 1 and 2/Careless Love/A Married Man's a Fool/Do Right Mama/Gulf Coast Blues/The Cooter Crawl/Lonesome Road Blues.

LITTLE BROTHER MONTGOMERY/SUNNYLAND SLIM

Redita 133 Chicago Blues Session

Limited edition reissue of long-out-of-print 1960 album; originally issued on the 77 label, featuring these two splendid piano players recorded at an informal session, with occasional bass by Corky Robertson and drums by legendary Chicago drummer Jump Jackson. Although the recording quality of these home tapes is unexceptional, there are some fine performances of some of their most popular songs. Sunnyland does seven songs, including "One Room Country Shack," "Brownskin Woman," "Devil Is a Busy Man," and "Everytime I Get to Drinkin'." Little Brother does 12 songs, including "Trembling Blues," "I Keep on Drinkin'," "Farrish Street Jive," "Cow Cow Blues," and "Pinetop's Boogie Woogie."

ALEX MOORE

Texas blues singer/pianist who has been active since the 20s.

Arhoolie 1008 **Alex Moore**
Arhoolie 1048 **Alex Moore in Europe**

Note: Some of his prewar recordings are reissued on Magpie 4415 and Historical 32.

JOHNNY B. MOORE

Excellent contemporary blues singer/guitarist who emerged from Koko Taylor's backing band.

B.L.U.E.S. R&B 3604 **Hard Times**

Fine debut album featuring some good originals along with some impressive updatings of a couple of songs from the 30s.

JOE MORRIS and HIS ORCHESTRA
Jukebox Lil 610 **Lowdown Baby**

Spans the years 1949–57, highlighting the vocal talents of Fay Adams (Scruggs): "That's What Makes My Baby Fat" (a duet with Morris) and "Crazy Mixed Up World." Little Laurie Tate, hired to emulate the Little Esther sound, sings an amazing high-pitched soprano on four cuts including "You're My Darling" and "I Hope You're Satisfied." Teen idol Al Savage is here with his hit "I Had a Notion," issued in 1953. A fascinating musical document of the emergence of New York R&B.

BUDDY MOSS

Superb Georgia country blues singer and guitarist who recorded some brilliant sides in the early 30s. He had a rich, relaxed, warm vocal sound and a flowing guitar style, often complemented by the second guitar of Curley Weaver and others. He was rediscovered in the 60s but has performed only infrequently.

Travelin' Man 800 **Georgia Blues**

Sixteen recordings cut between 1930–33. Four cuts feature him playing harmonica in the group the Georgia Cotten Pickers that featured Curley Weaver and Barbecue Bob (gtrs), and two cuts feature him as a member of the Georgia Browns with Curley Weaver and Fred McMullen (gtrs). The remaining sides feature Moss accompanied by his own guitar with second guitar by Fred McMullen, Curley Weaver, or Josh White. Great!

Travelin' Man 802 **Red River Blues**

Sixteen great sides, duplicating the out-of-print Kokomo 1003, which was issued about 20 years ago, but this album has better sound and the records have been transferred at the correct speed. On a few cuts there is second guitar by Curley Weaver, Josh White, or Brownie McGhee, and a few have a small group. Highly recommended.

COMPACT DISC
Travelin' Man CD 05 **1930–41**

Twenty tracks, 14 with Moss's singing and guitar playing up front (usually with the second guitar of Curley Weaver, Fred McMullen, or Josh White), and six with Moss playing harmonica as a member of the Georgia Browns or Georgia Cotton Pickers (featuring Curly Weaver and/or Barbecue Bob on vocals and guitar). Although the group tracks are superb in their own right, I would have preferred to have heard more Moss vocals. Sound is quite good and there are informative notes by Bruce Bastin and full discographical details. Despite my caveats, this is a worthwhile collection.

Note: See also under TALLAHASSEE TIGHT/BUDDY MOSS.

FRANK MOTLEY
Krazy Kat 805 **Frank Motley on Gotham**

Motley's "Crew" is one of the most important early innovative blues-based swing outfits and the originator of the classic "Honkin' At Midnight." This collection contains three of Motley's Gotham 78s plus six unissued and three alternate cuts. The set rocks, driven by the solid drums and vocal chops of the great T.N.T. Tribble. Contains the classic "Hurricane Lover."

MUDDY WATERS

The father of Chicago blues. In the 40s, he moved from Mississippi to Chicago and there he, along with other emigres from the South, electrified the traditional Mississippi blues of their youth and produced a style that was to take Chicago by storm and, much later, the whole world. His bands have nurtured such sidemen as Little Walter, Jimmy Rogers, Otis Spann, James Cotton, and many others who have gone off to have impressive blues careers of their own. A great singer, he was first recorded by the Library of Congress in 1941 and 1942 while still in Mississippi and these magnificent recordings are now available on Testament. His 40s and 50s recordings for Aristocrat and Chess are among the greatest blues records of the postwar era and are consistently fine. In the 60s he and his producers experimented with different sounds with varying results. In the late 70s he returned to his old style with a series of albums for Columbia, produced by Johnny Winter, but these recordings don't have the conviction of his early sides. He died in 1983, leaving behind an unforgettable legacy.

CFPC 401 Live, 1965–68
Ten sides recorded by Muddy and his band at various unspecified locations between 1965–68. Muddy is in fine form on a selection of old favorites, and the band is top-notch, featuring the guitars of Sammy Lawhorn and Pee Wee Madison and some excellent harp by Carey Bell. The piano player is listed as Pinetop Perkins but, on some recordings, sounds more like Otis Spann. Sound is rather muffled but acceptable. Blow Wind Blow/Honey Bee/Walking through the Park/Going Down Slow/All Night Long.

Chess 9100 (c) Muddy and the Wolf
Selections from the Muddy Waters album "Fathers and Sons" with Michael Bloomfield and Paul Butterfield, and from the "The London Howlin' Wolf Sessions" with Eric Clapton, Steve Winwood, and Bill Wyman. With good notes by Peter Guralnick.

Chess 9101 (c) Rolling Stone
Wonderful collection of 14 sides. Six cuts were previously on the "Best of Muddy Waters" set. The sound on this album is superb and the album includes a wonderful previously unissued take of "Rollin' Stone." Walking Through the Park/She Moves Me/Tiger in Your Tank/Got My Mojo Working "Live"/Baby Please Don't Go.

Chess 9197 (c) Muddy Waters Sings Big Bill Broonzy
Reissue of Chess LP 1444 issued in 1960 featuring Muddy doing a tasteful musical tribute to his musical mentor. Accompanied by his great band (James Cotton, Pat Hare, Otis Spann, Andrew Stephenson, and Francey Clay). Tell Me Baby/When I Get To Thinking/Double Trouble/I Done Got Wise/Lonesome Road Blues.

Chess 9198 (c) Muddy Waters at Newport
CD issue: Chess 31269
Reissue of Chess LP 1449 from 1960 featuring excerpts of Muddy and his band's performances at the Newport Jazz Festival in July of that year. Some great performances from Muddy and the band, which included James Cotton, Pat Hare, Otis Spann, Andrew Stephenson, and Francis Clay. I Got My Brand On You/Baby, Please Don't Go/Tiger In Your Tank/I've Got My Mojo Working.

Chess 9180 (c) Rare and Unissued
Fourteen recordings ranging from "Little Anna Mae"—recorded at his first session in 1947 with Sunnyland Slim (pno) and Ernest "Big" Crawford

(b), echoing the prewar sound of Leroy Carr and Scrapper Blackwell—to the full electric band sound of "Deep Down in My Heart," recorded in 1960. Although most of the tracks here have been reissued at one time or another, some of them have only been available on poor quality bootlegs or on the long-unavailable Genesis series. Superb performances; fine singing and great guitar by Muddy with Leroy Foster, Jimmy Rogers, Little Walter, Junior Wells, and Willie Dixon. Full discographical information. Superb album!

ESSENTIAL SELECTION

Chess 9255 (c) The Best Of Muddy Waters
CD issue: Chess 31268
Reissue of Muddy's first classic LP (Chess 1427) from 1958. Twelve archetypal Chicago blues performances. With original cover and liner notes by Studs Terkel. I Just Want To Make Love To You/Louisiana Blues/Rollin' Stone..

Chess 9261 (c) Folksinger
Reissue of Chess 1483. An all-acoustic set of blues standards recorded in 1963 with Buddy Guy (acst gtr) and Willie Dixon (b). An interesting experiment that doesn't quite come off. My Home Is In the Delta/My Captain/You Gonna Need My Help/Big Leg Woman/Feel Like Going Home.

Chess 9274 (c,d) The Real Folk Blues
Reissue of Chess 1501, a great album originally issued in the 60s and featuring 12 fine Muddy cuts from the 40s through the early 60s. Mostly material not reissued on other LPs. Mannish Boy/ Screamin' and Cryin'/Just To be With You/Walking In The Park/Walking Blues/Canary Bird/Same Thing/ Gypsy Woman/ Rollin' and Tumblin'/40 Days and 40 Nights/Little Geneva/ You Can't Lose What You Ain't Never Had.

Chess 9278 (c,d) More Real Folk Blues
Reissue of Chess 1511. Twelve sides mostly from the late 40s and early 50s and mostly unavailable elsewhere. Great! Sad Letter Blues/You're Gonna

Need My Help/Sittin' Here Drinkin'/Down South Blues/Train Fare Blues/Kind Hearted Woman/Appealing Blues/Early Morning Blues/Too Young To Know/She's All Right/My Life Is Ruined/Honey Bee.

Chess 9286 (c,d) Muddy, Brass and the Blues

Reissue of Chess 1507 from 1966. Hardly one of the essentials of the Muddy canon, and perhaps the most maligned besides "Electric Mud," this set has Muddy and the mid-60s band including James Cotton, Otis Spann, and Sammy Lawhorn, but they try to turn Muddy into Big Joe Turner. The 10 tunes are mainly from the 30s and 40s (and even includes Big Joe's "Piney Brown Blues"); throw Pinetop Perkins in on organ (!), and then have a group of horns, led by soulster Gene Barge, overdubbed. Black Night/Trouble in Mind/Sweet Little Angel/Corinne Corinna.

Chess CH 9291 (c,d) Trouble No More

A great collection of 10 sides that were issued on Chess between 1955–59 and, surprisingly, have not been issued on a US album before now. It is particularly surprising when you consider that three of the songs—"Sugar Sweet," "Don't Go No Further," and "Close to You"—were R&B hits, and one of the songs, the original recording of "Got My Mojo Working," is one of his most famous. After having been ponderously done to death by Muddy and others so many times, it is a relief to hear the gently swinging arrangement of the original recording with lovely lyrical harp by Little Walter. Other highlights include the beautiful arrangement of "Rock Me," with some of James Cotton's finest playing, the terrific "All Aboard," with Walter and Cotton sharing the harmonica work, and the powerful title song, which is a rearrangement of "Worried Life Blues." Sound is excellent, there are informative notes by Don Snowden, and full discographical details. The CD version has two extra songs—"Take the Bitter with the Sweet" and "She's into Something."

Chess 9298 (c,d) The London Muddy Waters Sessions

This one's not as effective as the Wolf London session, partially due to the cluttered arrangements (with backing vocals and brass) and the uninspired backing musicians (Rory Gallagher [gtr] and Mitch Mitchell [drm]). Recorded in 1971, Muddy and his unwieldy conglomeration run through the Morganfield and Dixon songbook: Key to the Highway/Young Fashioned Ways/Walkin' Blues/I'm Ready/Sad Sad Day.

Chess 9299 (c,d) They Call Me Muddy Waters

Twelve cuts recorded between 1951–67 with Little Walter, Jimmy Rogers, James Cotton, Otis Spann, and Pinetop Perkins; originally issued on LP in 1971. There is no particular focus to this collection, and Chess didn't concern themselves too much with rarities and collector's editions back then, but once the needle hits the groove, none of that really matters. Previously reissued by Chess (France) 515 036. Crawlin' Kingsnake/When the Eagle Flies/Howlin' Wolf/Two Steps Forward

Chess 9319 (c,d) Can't Get No Grindin'

Reissue of 1972 LP featuring Muddy with James Cotton, Pinetop Perkins, Pee Wee Madison, and Sammy Lawhorn.

Chess 2-92522 (c,d) Fathers and Sons

Reissue of Chess 50023, a two-LP set featuring recordings cut in 1969, half live and half in the studio. Features sidemen Otis Spann, Michael Bloomfield, Paul Butterfield, Donald "Duck" Dunn, Sam Lay, and Buddy Miles. Mostly remakes of his 50s classics. Walking Through The Park/Twenty Four Hours/40 Days and 40 Nights/You Can't Lose What You Ain't Never Had/Blow Wind Blow/Long Distance Call/The Same Thing.

Chess CH6-80002 (c,d) The Chess Box

This is one of the most impressive blues packages ever put out by a major US label. Although not as comprehensive as the now-out-of-print Japanese box set of a few years ago, this set is an extensive survey of the recordings of the greatest Chicago bluesmen, covering recordings from 1947 through the early 70s. It features a couple of surpises for owners of the Japanese set, including the previously unissued Aristocrat track "Good Lookin Woman," an alternate take of "Take the Bitter with the Sweet" (complete with studio dialogue between Muddy and Len Chess), and a version of "Black Night" (from the much-berated "Muddy, Brass and The Blues," with the brass mixed out). The 72 tracks have all been newly remastered from original masters or, in some cases, from clean 78s. Included is a 32-page booklet with discographical information, notes by Robert Palmer and Mary Katherine Aldin, plus photos and memorabilia. Available as six LPs or three cassettes or CDs.

Chess (France) 427 005 Muddy Waters

Two-LP set, reissue of US Chess 2ACMB-203. Twenty-four classic performances with Little Walter, Jimmy Rogers, Willie Dixon, Otis Spann, and Elgin Evans. Great music in a stupid cover! Walking Through the Park/Still A Fool/ You Can't Lose What You Ain't Never Had/I Can't Be Satisfied/I Want You To Love Me/ Rolling and Tumbling/Just To Be With You/You're Gonna Need My Help/Same

Thing/My Life Is Ruined/Baby Please Don't Go/Got My Mojo Working, Part 1.

Chess (France) 515 037 Live at Mister Kelley's

Originally issued as Chess 50012 in 1977, this features Muddy recorded live in Chicago in 1971 with Paul Oscher (hca), Pinetop Perkins (pno), Pee Wee Madison and Sammy Lawhorn (gtrs), Calvin Jones (b), and Willie Smith (drm). James Cotton guests on harmonica on three cuts. Pleasant though not exceptional performances. What Is That She Got/Strange Woman/Country Boy/Stormy Monday Blues.

Columbia PZ 35712 (c,d) Muddy "Mississippi" Waters

Live with Winter, James Cotton, and "Pinetop" Perkins.

French Concerts FC 116 (d) Live in Antibes, 1974

Thirteen sides recorded in July 1974 with Bob Margolin, Luther "Guitar Jr." Johnson, Pinetop Perkins, Jerry Portnoy, Calvin Jones, and Willie Smith.

French Concerts FC 121 (d) Live in Paris, 1968

This excellent, albeit rather brief, concert from November 1968 features Muddy along with Otis Spann on piano, Luther Johnson and Pee Wee Madison on guitars, and Paul Oscher on harmonica romping through a set of fairly familiar material. Otis Spann, in particular, is in fine form throughout and sings two of the disc's eight tunes: Muddy's "Long Distance Call" and his own "Ring Up." The record's only shortcoming is its length. The eight tunes clock in at just over 35 minutes and, no, there aren't any extra tracks on the CD. Hoochie Coochie Man/Worried Life Blues/Got My Mojo Working.

Krazy Kat 7405 Muddy Waters, 1958

Fine set recorded in Manchester, England, in 1958 during his infamous tour. The critics were not prepared for Muddy's brand of electric blues and blasted him for not sounding like Big Bill Broonzy! Accompanied by Otis Spann and a drummer, Muddy turns in a fine set of versions of his early Aristocrat and Chess sides along with some he had not yet recorded for Chess. In this trio format, Spann truly shines.

Moon 007 Unreleased in the West

Eight tracks recorded live in 1976. Very little detail is given about these recordings, but I would assume they were made in Warsaw, Poland and were originally issued on the Polish Polijazz label. Muddy's band included Bob Margolin and Luther Johnson (gtrs), Jerry Portnoy (hca), Pinetop Perkins (pno), Calvin Jones (b), and Willie Smith (drm). There are three instrumentals by the band and five vocals by Muddy. The performances are adequate

but certainly don't present Muddy at his best and I feel that Jerry Portnoy's harmonica playing is lacking in subtlety. Junior Shuffle/G. P.'s Boogie/Soon Forgotten/Hoochie Coochie Man.

Syndicate Chapter 001/2 Back in the Early Days

Two-LP set, featuring 28 great sides, recorded 1947–55. Sound is not very good. I Feel Like Going Home/You're Gonna Miss Me/Streamline Woman/Evans Shuffle/All Night Long/My Fault/Please Have Mercy/Who's Gonna Be Your Sweet Man/Lovin' Man/Blow Wind Blow/She's So Pretty/Oo Wee/ Clouds In My Heart/My Eyes Keep Me In Trouble/Sugar Sweet.

Syndicate Chapter 002 Good News

Fourteen fine sides, recorded 1955–58. Trouble No More/ Don't Go No Further/Evil/I Love The Life I Live/Rock Me/Recipe For Love/Come Home Baby/Close To You.

Testament 2210 Down on Stovall's Plantation

These are Muddy's first recordings, made in 1941 and 1942 by Alan Lomax for the Library of Congress while Muddy was still a fieldhand in Mississippi. Several of the songs here are ones that Muddy would later record for Aristocrat or Chess, so this is one of those pivotal links between the music of the Mississippi Delta and the Chicago blues. Several cuts feature second guitar by Henry "Son" Sims or Charles Berry and four cuts are with a string band featuring Muddy (vcl, gtr), Percy Thomas (gtr), Louis Ford (mdln), and Sims (vln).

CASSETTE ONLY RELEASE

Chess 91513 "Unk" in Funk

Reissue of Chess 60031 from 1974. A selection of old Muddy favorites along with some later compositions. Muddy is accompanied by Paul Oscher, Pinetop Perkins, and Luther Johnson Jr. Muddy and the band sound bored and I suspect you will be too!

CASSETTE AND CD RELEASE ONLY

Columbia PZ 34449 Hard Again

Produced by Johnny Winter, as are all the Columbia sets. Recorded in 1977 with Winter, James Cotton, and "Pinetop" Perkins. Mannish Boy/Jealous Hearted Man/The Blues Had A Baby/Crosseyed Cat.

Columbia PZ 34928 I'm Ready

1978 album with Winter, Walter Horton, and Jimmy Rogers.

Columbia PZ 37064 King Bee

COMPACT DISC

Chess CHD 5907 Sings Big Bill Broonzy/Folk Singer

Two LPs combined onto one CD. Not exactly an

obvious choice for the first Muddy Waters CD on US Chess.

Chess (France) 600052 **Muddy Waters on Chess, Vol. 1**

Twenty classic early sides from Aristocrat and Chess. The sound on this CD is a little harsh and not of the same quality as some of the available records of the same material. Gypsy Woman/Down South Blues/Little Geneva/Rolling and Tumbling/You're Gonna Need My Help/Appealing Blues/Too Young To Know.

Chess (France) 60059 **Muddy Waters on Chess, Vol. 2**

Twenty songs from the period 1951–59. Some great music though, like the above CD, the sound quality is not all it could be.

Chess (UK) CD RED 1 **Rollin' Stone**

23 tracks recorded between 1948–59. I Can't Be Satisfied/Screamin' and Cryin'/Walkin' Blues/Louisiana Blues/Honey Bee/Still a Fool/Standing Around Crying/I Want You to Love Me/I'm Your Hoochie Coochie Man/I'm Ready/Forty Days and Forty Nights/ Just a Dream.

Muse MCD 6004 **Mud in Your Ear**

Twenty tunes originally issued on the Douglas label, then issued on Muse on the "Mud in Your Ear" and "Chicken Shack" LPs. These are often overlooked, but worthwhile, efforts recorded in 1967 with Otis Spann, Francis Clay, Sam Lawhorn, and Mojo Buford and Luther Johnson adding guest vocals.

THE MUDDY WATERS BLUES BAND

The 60s band without the boss!

Muse 5008 (c) **Mud in Your Ear**

Spivey 1008 **The Muddy Waters Blues Band**

Spivey 1010 **The Muddy Waters Blues Band, Vol. 2**

MATT "GUITAR" MURPHY

Antones ANT 0013 (c,d) **Way Down South**

This one is a real gem. Matt Murphy is most certainly one of the giants of postwar guitar, whose deft playing has enlivened the recordings of many blues artists like Bobby Bland, Memphis Slim, James Cotton, and many others. This is his first solo album, and shows that, besides his dazzling guitar playing, he is also a most pleasing singer and songwriter. He is accompanied by an excellent band, including his brother Floyd on guitar, Mel Brown on piano, Chester King on harmonica, and "Kaz" Kazenoff on sax, who provide a perfect backdrop for Matt's brilliant excursions. The focus, of course, is on Matt's guitar playing, and he shows that one doesn't have to indulge in pyrotechnics to get the point across—why play three notes when one says it all? He never ceases to surprise with his imagination, technique, and good taste, and, most importantly, feeling. The material is varied, ranging from the Mississippi feel of "Thump's Time" to the contemporary urgency of "Blue Walls." Too many backup musicians do not come across well when they take the lead, but this album is a most welcome exception.

CHARLIE MUSSELWHITE

Excellent Chicago-style blues revivalist singer and harmonica player.

Alligator 4781 (c,d) **Ace of Harps**

Arhoolie 1056 **Takin' My Time**

Arhoolie 1074 **Goin' Back Down South**

With Lafayette Leake, Tim Kaihatsu, and Robben Ford.

Blue Horizon 005 **Cambridge Blues**

A rollicking set of accoustic blues with British blues vets Dave Peabody (gtr) and Bob Hall (gtr), recorded live at the Cambridge (UK) Blues Festival on Aug. 1, 1986. Seven tunes, including the original "Up and Down the Avenue," plus versions of Jazz Gillium's "Key to the Highway," Robert Jr. Lockwood's "Take a Little Walk with Me," and Jimmy Rushing's "Miss Bessie."

Blue Rock'it 103 **Tell Me Where Have All the Good Times Gone?**

Good album accompanied by the Charles Ford Band with excellent guitar by Robben Ford. A mixture of Musselwhite originals and old favorites, including one surprise: a country blues track on which Charlie plays some surprisingly effective lightly amplified guitar.

Crosscut 1008 **Memphis, Tennessee**

Crosscut 1013 (d) **Mellow Dee**

Twelve sides recorded in Germany in 1985. Eight tracks feature him with German bands, some featuring the strong guitar work of Jim Kahr. The remaining four tracks feature Charlie accompanying himself with some relaxed acoustic guitar. Charlie is in good form on a selection of songs from the repertoires of Jimmy Rushing, Walter Horton, Big Joe Williams, and Mose Allison.

Kicking Mule 305 The Harmonica According to Charlie Musselwhite
All-instrumental instruction-oriented album.
CASSETTE AND CD RELEASE ONLY
Arhoolie C-203/CD 303 Memphis Charlie
Comprises two albums from 1971 and 1974: Arhoolie 1056, "Takin' My Time," and 1074, "Goin' Back Down South;" aided by Robben Ford and Tim Kaihatsu on guitar, Lafayette Leake and Skip Rose on piano, and Pat Ford on drums. The CD sports a catchy likeness of Charlie by Lynda Barry.

LOUIS MYERS
Fine Chicago singer/guitarist and harmonica player who has worked with almost every major Chicago blues artist. Best known for his recordings with the Aces, his first solo album shows him to be a performer of consummate ability.

Advent 2809 I'm a Southern Man
Louis sings and plays regular guitar, slide guitar, and harmonica. He is accompanied by an excellent group of West Coast musicians, including some superb guitar by Freddy Robinson.

SAM MYERS
Excellent Mississippi blues singer/harmonica player who recorded in the 50s for Ace and Fury. His Black Top and T.J. recordings are recent and decent though not outstanding.

Black Top 1032 (c) My Love Is Here to Stay
Decent 1985 album featuring Myers in the company of popular white Texas blues band Anson Funderburgh and The Rockets. Sam performs a mixture of good originals along with songs from the repertoires of Elmore James and Little Walter. Sam is a strong singer though perhaps a little one-dimensional. He plays some good harp, though we hear too little of it. Funderburgh and his band provide some good solid accompaniments though nothing exceptional.

T.J. 1030 Down Home in Mississippi
T.J. 1040 Mississippi Delta Blues

NATHAN and THE ZYDECO CHA-CHAS
Rounder 2092 (c) Steady Rock
Catchy new album from Lafayette's young accordionist, Nathan Williams, selecting R&B and Zydeco numbers in the style of his inspirations, Clifton Chenier and Buckwheat Zydeco. He can slip through frothy numbers like "If You Got a Problem"

or "Zydeco Joe," get bluesy on Ron Levy's "I'm Back" or "Steady Rock," and save enough to burn through down-home Zydecos like "Hey Bebe." While not of the depth or subtlety of a Clifton, he has an amiable, but supple, sound that marks him as someone to watch. With a fine backup band.

KENNY NEAL
Kenny Neal is the son of famed Louisiana singer/harmonica player Raful Neal. He is a good, solid singer and guitar player, though not particularly distinctive.

Alligator 4764 (c,d) Big News from Baton Rouge
Enjoyable album. This was originally issued in 1989 on the King Snake label as "Bio on the Bayou." For this release, the album has been remixed to give it a richer sound, and three previously unissued tracks have been added. Neal is a decent, if unexceptional, singer and a good solid guitarist. He is accompanied by a serviceable band on a selection of mostly original songs. No real surprises here, but some decent singing and playing throughout.

Alligator 4774 (c,d) Devil Child

RAFUL NEAL
Blue Horizon 003 Louisiana Legend
The fine Louisiana singer and harmonica player Raful Neal has been performing for more than 30 years, but this is his first album, and a most worthwhile one it is, too. Raful is a powerful singer and distinctive harmonica player and, on this recent session, he is accompanied by a fine band, which includes his son Kenny on lead guitar and an excellent horn section including Noble Watts on sax. Includes some fine remakes of songs he had previously recorded as 45s ("Blues on the Moon" and "Late in the Evening"), a couple of covers (Jimmy Reeds's "Honest I Do" and Wilburt Harrisons's "Let's Work Together"), and some fine new songs, including the excellent "Luberta," a song which is lyrically a murder ballad and musically jumping Louisiana R&B.

ARNETT NELSON
Magpie 1803 When the Music Sounds Good 1935–1938
Sixteen tunes by New Orleans clarinetist Arnett Nelson, concentrtating on his backups to blues singers Bumble Bee Slim, Tampa Red, Victoria Spivey, and Washboard Sam. Brown Skin Mama/ Street Walkin' Blues/Oh! Red/Christmas Time Blues/Waiting Blues.

JIMMY NELSON
Texas blues shouter.

Ace CHD 228 Watch that Action
Sixteen fine sides recorded for RPM, some with his regular band, The Peter Rabbit Trio. It includes his one minor hit—the classic "T-99"—as well as a few previously unissued titles. Excellent sound and good notes by Ray Topping, though some discographical information on the sessions would have been useful. Cry Hard Luck/Meet Me with Your Black Dress On/Raindrop Blues/Bad Habit Blues/Sweetest Little Girl.

COMPACT DISC
P-Vine PCD 1620 Sweet Sugar Daddy
1965 and 1970 recordings, with Texas tenor titan Arnett Cobb and guitarist Pete Mayes. Eighteen songs, not all of them brilliant, but there are plenty of hot tracks here.

RED NELSON
Document 545 1935–38
Red Nelson (real name Nelson Wilborn) was an excellent singer with a distinctive sly vocal style who wrote some imaginative songs. The 19 songs here are from six sessions held between 1935–38 and feature him with a variety of accompanying musicians, including Charles Avery, Horace Malcomb, Big Bill Broonzy, Blind John Davis, and Tampa Red. In small doses, this is most enjoyable, but when heard in depth the melodic similarities and rather ponderous accompaniments get a little tiring.

SONNY BOY NELSON
Wolf 128 Complete Recordings in Chronological Order, 1936
Eugene Powell, aka Sonny Boy Nelson, was a brilliant singer and guitarist from the Murphy-Hollandale area in Mississippi. This superb collection presents 19 tracks recorded in New Orleans on October 15, 1936. All tracks feature Nelson with second guitarist Willie Harris, Jr., and together they produce that lovely flowing guitar interplay that has rarely been heard since the 30s. There are six vocals by Nelson, three by his wife Mississippi Matilda, and ten by obscure singer/harmonica player Robert Hill. The tracks by Nelson and Matilda are fine, intense blues that are all outstanding. Hill is a less interesting performer, a fairly nondescript singer and harmonica player who performs mostly hokum material, though his tracks are enlivened by Nelson's and Harris' guitar work.

NEW MISSISSIPPI SHEIKS
Blues string band with Sam Chatmon, Walter Vincson, Carl Martin, and Ted Bogan.
Rounder 2004 The New Mississippi Sheiks

JACK NEWMAN
Document 550 Complete Recordings, 1938
Seventeen sides featuring the talents of singer/guitarist Jack Newman, six under his own name and the rest accompanying vocalists Frankie Jones (a female singer) and Black Bottom McPhail. In addition to Newman's guitar, most of the tracks feature the piano playing of Jesse Coleman, so the songs tend to have a similar feel. Newman and Coleman are not exceptional instrumentalists, but these tracks are noted for the fine singing (particularly by McPhail) and the interesting songs. Very few of these tracks have been reissued before and some are unissued recordings from test pressings. Sound is satisfactory, and these tracks are worth a listen.

ROBERT NIGHTHAWK
Absolutely superb Chicago blues singer and guitar player particularly noted for his melodic single-string slide guitar playing that was very influential. Recorded prewar under the name Robert Lee McCoy. These sides are all reissued on Wolf 120 and 121. His 60s recordings on Rounder and Testament are also fabulous.

Pearl 11 Bricks in My Pillow
After many years, this classic album featuring his 1951–52 United recordings is back in print. Essential.

Rounder 2022 Live on Maxwell Street, 1964
Superb and dynamic recordings, with Carey Bell and Johnny Young.

ESSENTIAL SELECTION
Testament 2215 Robert Nighthawk/Houston Stackhouse
This is a beautiful album. The eight cuts by Nighthawk are among his best, with moving vocals and exquisite slide guitar. On most of these, he is accompanied by John Wrencher (hca) and Johnny Young (gtr), and the overall sound is stunning. The four Stackhouse cuts have Nighthawk playing backup guitar and James "Peck" Curtis on drums, and feature pleasing versions of Tommy Johnson songs.

Wolf 120 Robert Lee McCoy (Robert Nighthawk)—Complete Recordings in Chronological Order, Vol. 1
The first of two albums to reissue all of the prewar recordings of McCoy, who was later to change his name to Robert Nighthawk. Features his 13 recordings from 1937 with second guitar by Joe Williams, harmonica by Sonny Boy Williamson, and occasional piano (possibly by Walter Davis). There is little opportunity to hear much of his trademark

single-string slide, though it is present on the very fine "G-Man Blues." The music here is fine, though there is a certain lack of variety.

Wolf 121 Robert Lee McCoy (Robert Nighthawk)—Complete Recordings in Chronological Order, Vol. 2

Features eight recordings from 1938 and four from 1940. The 1938 tracks have not been reissued before and feature him with Sonny Boy Williamson (hca) and probably Speckled Red (pno). Two of the four sides from 1940 feature rather terrible vocals by Robert's then-wife Ann Sortier, who also plays washboard. The final two sides are the best, featuring Robert alone with his guitar, and include the superb "Friar's Point Blues," though this has been reissued several times before. It was the finest thing that Robert recorded until his magnificent 40s recordings for Aristocrat.

THE NIGHTHAWKS

Energetic rock 'n' blues bar band from the Washington, DC, area. This quartet is fronted by Mark Wenner, who sings and plays harp, and lead guitarist Jim Thackery, who also shares the vocal chores. These guys play simple straight ahead blues with a frenzy.

Adelphi 4105 Open All Night
With Pinetop Perkins.

Adelphi 4110 (c) Live 1976
Recorded at the Psyche-Delly.

Adelphi 4115 Side Pocket Shot

Adelphi 4120 Jacks and Kings
With guest appearances by Pinetop Perkins, Guitar Jr., and Calvin Jones.

Adelphi 4125 Jacks and Kings "Full House"

Adelphi 4130/35 Times Four
Two-LP set, recorded 1976–78, with live and studio cuts.

Adelphi 4140 Best of the Blues
Nine tunes, the best from their Adelphi (pre-Varrick) LPs. High-powered covers, mostly taken from the Elmore James's songbook, including "Madison Blues," "Red Hot Mama," and "You Got to Move"; along with Sonny Boy's "Nine Below Zero" and "Bring It on Home"; even Motown, with a long live version of Junior Walker's "Shake and Finger Pop," and a cover of a cover when they do Savoy Brown's version of The Temptation's "Can't Get Next to You."

Varrick 001 (c) Ten Years Live

Varrick 007 (c) Rock 'n' Roll
Cover versions of tunes made famous by Johnny Otis, The Temptations, and the Rolling Stones.

Varrick 009 (c) Hot Spot

Varrick 022 (c,d) Hard Living

Varrick 033 Live In Europe
CD issue: Crosscut CCD 11014
Mixed bag, recorded live in Bremen, West Germany on July 10, 1986. Seems to me that the best things here are the nonblues covers—nice versions of Elvis's "Hard Headed Woman," Bo Diddley's "I Can Tell," and Steve Earle's "Nothin' but You" stand out, but their version of Sonny Boy's "Mighty Long Time" almost sounds like a parody and the 11-minute "Black Night" is as bloated as the worst of Canned Heat. Probably worked OK live, but doesn't transfer to vinyl. CD has one extra track.

Varrick 036 (c,d) Backtrack
Live recordings with guests Toru Oki, John Hammond, and Pinetop Perkins. CD has extra tracks.
COMPACT DISC

Genes CD 4120/25 Jacks and Kings, Vols. 1 and 2
Combines Adelphia 4120 and 4125.

Genes CD 4140/45 Best of the Nighthawks

OLLIE NIGHTINGALE

Retta 0001 Troubled in Mind
A nice mixture of blues, R&B, and soul from this fine Southern singer. The title song is the old blues standard "Trouble in Mind," and there are other blues like "I'm Changing My Ways" and the rocking "I Can't Set You Free." Other tracks like "Six Nights and a Day" and "Too Busy" fall into more of an R&B/soul vein. The instrumental arrangements are unexciting; Chick Willis' guitar playing is very limited, and the rest of the band is unexceptional.

HAMMIE NIXON

Fine Tennessee singer and harmonica player.

High Water 1003 Tappin' That Thing
Eleven mostly traditional blues songs, accompanied by a group of young blues interpreters, giving the album somewhat of an old-time jug-band feel. Hammie sings and plays harmonica, kazoo, and jug. A pleasant though not terribly exciting album, and I don't care too much for the overuse of echo.

ST. LOUIS JIMMY ODEN

Blues Documents 2058 1932–48
Sixteen tracks, most not on LP before.

ODETTA

O.B.C. 509 Odetta and the Blues
1962 album, originally Riverside 9417. Popular folk singer Odetta tries her hand at the classic blues and does an OK if somewhat histrionic job. Accompaniments by Buck Clayton (tpt), Vic Dickenson (trb),

and Herb Hall (clr). Hard, Oh Lord/Oh, Papa/ Hogan's Alley/Oh, My Babe.

JOHNNY OTIS

One of the pioneer figures in blues and R&B in the 40s and 50s and still a significant contributor. Besides making many fine records under his name featuring many important singers and musicians in his bands, he also discovered and recorded with many important performers. His 40s and 50s recordings for Savoy and other labels are reissued on Savoy double sets and Jukebox Lil. All the other albums listed are 60s, 70s, and 80s recordings.

Ace CH 299 (c,d) **Good Lovin' Blues**

What an amazing man Johnny Otis is: He has been playing, leading bands, producing, and discovering new talent for about 45 years now and is still going strong, as this 1990 release convincingly shows. On this album Johnny fronts a solid band, which includes son Shuggie on guitar, bass, and organ, son Nicky on drums, and veteran horn men Clifford Solomon and John Ewing; the sound they produce is beefy and unpretentious. Besides his own vocals, there are three new vocalists, including the brilliant Ramona, a truly outstanding singer who brings to mind Ann Peebles or Candi Staton in their prime. Also includes the fine La Dee Streeter and the excellent Jackie Payne. The material is mostly blues and hard-driving R&B with an occasional soul ballad. Most of the material is Otis originals along with a few old favorites, like "Open House at My House" and "Rock Me Baby." The compact disc has two extra tracks: a driving instrumental "Pop and Sons Boogie" and the fine "Hey Bartender." Solid and exciting music from one of the true rhythm and blues greats.

Alligator 4726 **The New Johnny Otis**

1982 album by Otis was his first in almost 10 years and is an excellent one. A fine mixture of blues and R&B with excellent vocal work by Otis himself, Delmar Evans, and other vocalists. Outstanding guitar work by son Shuggie Otis, plus backup by Plas Johnson, Zaven Jambazian, and Earl Palmer.

Jukebox Lil 611 **Barrelhouse Stomp**

Fine early sides.

Jukebox Lil 617 **Gee Baby**

Fiteen incredible pieces of LA R&B recorded between 1947–52 featuring Otis's superfine orchestra, with Pete Lewis, Don Johnson, James Von Streeter, Lady Devonia, Paul Quinichette, and K. C. Bell, and vocals by Mel Walker, Ada Wilson, and Joe Swift. Also includes two tunes by Otis associates—Von Streeter's "Square Dance Hop" and Preston Love's 1951 version of "Voodoo." The usual beautiful Jonas Bernholm package, with an 18-year-old (pre-mustache!) Johnny playing drums with Count Otis Matthews' West Oakland House Rockers on the cover!

Savoy 2230 **The Original Johnny Otis Show**

Two-LP set featuring 32 sides from 1945–51. Vocals by Jimmy Rushing, The Robins, Mel Walker, Otis, and Little Esther Phillips.

Savoy 2252 **The Original Johnny Otis Show, Vol. 2**

Two-LP set featuring 32 more sides from 1945–51. Vocals by Dee Williams, Mel Walker, Little Esther Phillips, and Linda Hopkins.

Snatch 101 **Snatch and The Poontangs**

Otis and friends performing unexpurgated "blue" blues, based on the dozens and toasts. For adults only! The Signifying Monkey, Parts 1 and 2/That's Life/The Great Stack-A-Lee/The Pissed Off Cowboy/Hey Shines.

COMPACT DISC

Capitol 92858-2 (21Z) **The Capitol Years**

CD equivalent of 2-LP retrospective set.

JACK OWENS

Testament 2222 **It Must Have Been the Devil**

A beautiful album of Mississippi country blues recorded by David Evans in 1970. Owens is from Bentonia, MS, which was also the home of the great Skip James. Although his playing is not as complex as James', it is powerful and imaginative and his singing is marvelous. There are only six songs on this album, including an almost 10-minute version of the magnificent "It Must Have Been the Devil," which James also sang. There are traditional favorites like "Good Morning Little Schoolgirl" and "Catfish Blues," along with songs unique to Owens, like "Can't See, Baby" and "Jack Ain't Had No Water." On some tracks, Jack is joined by harmonica player Benjamin "Bud" Spires (the son of "Big Boy" Spires) who provides some effective accompaniments. Owens's music is not for casual listening, but your attention will be rewarded by a beautiful and moving musical experience. Highly recommended.

PARIS SLIM

Blue Sting 014 **Blues for Esther**

Debut LP by longtime Bay Area blues guitarist Paris Slim, originally from France. With Tim Kaihatsu, Bobby Murray, and Dave Wellhausen.

(LITTLE) JUNIOR PARKER

Excellent blues singer and harmonica player. Much of his repertoire is not now available on record.

CASSETTE ONLY RELEASE
MCA 27037 Blues Consolidated
One side of the album is by Bobby Bland. Parker cuts include Next Time You See Me/Mother-In-Law Blues/Barefoot Rock/That's Alright/Wondering/ Sitting and Thinking.

MCA 27039 Driving Wheel
Twelve sides originally issued as Duke 76. Sweet Talkin' Woman/The Tables Have Turned/Someone Somewhere/Annie Get Your Yo Yo/Driving Wheel/ Foxy Devil.

MCA 27046 The Best of Little Junior Parker

CHARLEY PATTON
One of the very greatest Mississippi Delta blues singers. His 20s and 30s recordings are masterpieces, with his deep rough voice accompanied by his powerful and rhythmic guitar. He sometimes uses slide to great effect. He is occasionally accompanied by the second guitar of Willie Brown or the wild fiddle of Henry Sims. Perhaps difficult listening for the beginning blues listener, his music is ultimately rewarding on every level. Between them, Herwin 213 (currently unavailable), Wolf 103, and Yazoo 1020 reissue all of his recordings.

OJL 1 The Immortal Charley Patton
The first reissue of this great artist, though all these tracks are available elsewhere, often with better sound.

OJL 7 Charley Patton, Vol. 2
More great sides but again all are available elsewhere.

Wolf 103 The Remaining Titles
Twelve magnificent sides complementing Yazoo 1020 and Herwin 213. Pea Vine Blues/Prayer of Death/I'm Goin' Home/Devil Sent the Rain/Mean Black Moan/Love My Stuff.

ESSENTIAL SELECTION
Yazoo 1020 (d) The Founder of the Delta Blues
A classic two-LP set featuring a broad cross-section of his recordings. Extensive notes and song transcripts. Some of the tracks feature the fiery fiddling of Henry Sims or the guitar of Willie Brown. The bond between Patton and Brown's playing is positively psychic. Considering the age, rarity, and pressing quality of the original Paramounts used, the sound quality is good. Essential. LPs have 28 tracks, CD has 24 (to fit on a single 74-minute disc). Screamin' and Hollerin' the Blues/Mississippi Bo Weavil Blues/A Spoonful Blues/Moon Going Down/When Your Way Gets Dark/High Water Everywhere, Parts 1 and 2.

PEG LEG SAM (ARTHUR JACKSON)
COMPACT DISC
Tomato 26966502 Joshua
Reissue of LP issued on Blue Labor label in 1975. Sam was discovered in 1972 working one of the last of the travelling medicine shows and subsequently played regularly at festivals up to his death in 1977. He was an outstanding singer and harmonica player whose music was strongly rooted in the traditions of his North Carolina heritage. On many of the tracks, he is accompanied on guitar by Louisiana Red, whose urban stylings don't always jell with Sam's playing, but at least he keeps discreetly in the background. Joshua Fit the Battle of Jericho/John Henry/Mr. Ditty Wah Ditty/I Got a Home/Early in the Morning/Along the Navaho Trail.

PINETOP PERKINS
Pianist who formerly played with Muddy Waters's band.

Black and Blue 33.520 Pinetop Is Just Top
Recorded in France in 1976 with Luther Johnson, Jr. (gtr), Calvin Jones (b), and Willie Smith (drm).

Blind Pig 73088 After Hours
COMPACT DISC
Black and Blue 233520 Pinetop Perkins/ Luther Johnson Jr.: Boogie Woogie King
Twelve tracks drawn from two Black and Blue albums (33.520 and 33.519), the former by Perkins and the latter by Johnson; all recorded at a 1976 session. The Johnson tracks have the same personnel as the Perkins' sessions (see LP listing above), but add Bob Margolin (b) and Jerry Portney (hca).

KING PERRY
Krazy Kat 7438 King Perry

JAMES "LUCKY" PETERSON
Alligator 4770 (c,d) Lucky Strikes!
King Snake 4031 (c,d) Rough and Ready

ROBERT PETWAY
An exciting Mississippi bluesman with a style very much like Tommy McClennan.

Wolf 108 Robert Petway
Presents all 14 sides he recorded in 1941–42. His version of "Catfish Blues" is an all-time classic!

BREWER PHILLIPS
Wolf 82 007 Ingleside Blues
Solo album by guitarist who was a member of Hound Dog Taylor's House Rockers in the Hound Dog tradition of raw high-energy down-home blues. The material is a mixture of originals and unbearably familiar pieces like "Sweet Home Chicago."

LITTLE ESTHER PHILLIPS

Wonderful and expressive singer who died in 1984.

Savoy SJL 2258 (c,d) **The Complete Savoy Recordings**

Superb two-LP set presents all the recordings she made for Savoy. The first LP is devoted to her classic sides recorded with the fabulous Johnny Otis Orchestra in 1950 and includes several sides that have not previously been on LP. The first side on the second LP features tracks from 1956 with an excellent studio band and includes three previously unissued alternate takes. The last side is from her 1959 Savoy session, again with a New York studio band, and also featuring some alternate takes. All the music is of the highest calibre, the packaging is very appealing, and there are excellent notes by Dan Nooger.

PIANO RED (DR. FEELGOOD; WILLIE PERRYMAN)

Georgia singer and piano player who also recorded as Dr. Feelgood. A fairly limited performer, he tends to record the same songs again and again! His best albums are the Arhoolie that features 60s recordings along with some reissued from the 40s, and the Oldie Blues that is all 50s recordings.

Arhoolie 1064 **Dr. Feelgood Alone**

Euphonic 1212 **Percussive Piano**

L+R 42.019 **Music Is Medicine**

Oldie Blues 2821 **Dr. Feelgood**

Matchbox MB 902 **Wildfire**

Most of these 12 wild rockin' blues and boogie tunes have been out recently on various budget LPs but they really benefit from the complete Matchbox attentiveness here: nice sound quality and sessionography is included. Red really hammers it out. Rockin' With Red/Red's Boogie/Wild Fire/Diggin' the Boogie.

PIANO SLIM (ROBERT T. SMITH)

Texas blues singer/piano player who now lives in St. Louis, where the following albums were recorded.

Swingmaster 2103 **Mean Woman Blues**

Enjoyable album of mostly original piano blues and boogie. Good solid singing and playing.

Swingmaster 2110 **Gateway to the Blues**

Slim is joined by a band that includes guitar, sax, trumpet, harmonica, bass, and drums. A pleasing selection of mostly original songs with good vocals and piano by Slim. The band provides solid, workmanlike accompaniments. Nothing outstanding here but some good down-home blues.

BUSTER PICKENS

Excellent Texas blues singer and pianist recorded in 1960.

Flyright 536 **Buster Pickens**

DAN PICKETT

Krazy Kat 811 **1949 Country Blues**

What a masterpiece! Back in the 60s, some of the most highly prized 78s among blues collectors were the rare Gotham records of Dan Pickett. These were valued not only for their rarity, but because they were among the finest commercial recordings of country blues in the postwar era. At that time, no one could have imagined that there would be an album available of Pickett's recordings, but here it is! Not only do we get all of Pickett's sides issued on 78 rpm but four previously unissued titles, mostly from original master tapes, thanks to Gotham's foresight in recording on tape as early as 1948. Pickett, whose real name was apparently James Founty, was a stunning performer. A distinctive vocalist, he had a remarkable vocal technique in which he sometimes compressed an amazing amount of syllables into one line. He was also a stunning guitar player, performing in either a rhythmic percussive picking style or a lovely melodic slide style, accentuating his playing with rapping on the guitar. The songs are mostly versions of songs originally recorded in the 30s, including Leroy Carr's "How Long," Buddy Moss' "Ride to a Funeral in a V-8," Blind Boy Fuller's "Let Me Squeeze Your Lemons" (which Pickett calls "Lemon Man"), and others, including a spellbinding version of "99½ Won't Do," Pickett's only gospel performance. Pickett transforms the songs into totally unique ones. The unissued songs are every bit as good as the issued ones. The album has excellent sound and informative notes by Chris Smith. A special thanks to Bruce Bastin, whose foragings in the Gotham vaults have turned up this gem. One of the best blues reissues of the last five years.

BILLIE and DEDE PIERCE

O.B.C. 534 (c,d) **Vocal Blues And Cornet In The Classic Tradition**

Reissue of Riverside 370 from 1961. Nine sides with Billie on piano and vocals, Dede on cornet, and Albert Jiles on drums. St. Louis Blues/Careless Love/Algiers Hoodoo Blues/Gulf Coast Blues/Love Song of the Nile.

"DOC" POMUS

Whiskey, Women, and... KM 700 **Send for the Doctor**

Sixteen recordings made between 1944–55. Pomus

is best known as one of the greatest R&B and rock 'n' roll songwriters of the 50s and 60s but here he is revealed as a fine urban blues vocalist in the Joe Turner/Wynonie Harris mold. He is accompanied by top musicians such as Tab Smith, Leonard Feather, Bill Moore, Rex Stewart, Pete Brown, King Curtis, and Mickey Baker.

JIMMY PRESTON
Krazy Kat 806 Jimmy Preston on Gotham Vol. 1
Philadelphia alto saxman/singer Jimmy Preston recorded jump tunes and occasional slow blues items for Gotham between 1948–50. Most of the Prestonians upbeat material is of little importance as far as the development of the R&B genre is concerned, but this collection does contain two worthwhile blues items: the soulful "Early Morning Blues" and the striking "Credit Blues."

BOBBY PRICE
Blues Unlimited 5025 Two Trains a Runnin'
Primarily a blues and soul album featuring vocalist Price accompanied by the excellent accordion player Fernest Arceneaux and his Zydeco band, The Thunders. Some nice singing and playing though nothing outstanding.

SAMMY PRICE
Veteran jazz/blues piano player with a recording career stretching back to the 30s.
Black and Blue 33.560 Rockin' Boogie
Twelve sides recorded in France in 1975 and previously unissued, featuring Price with an all-star band including Doc Cheatham (tpt), Ted Buckner (alto sax), and Gene Connors (trb). The result is a mixture of jazz, blues, and boogie. Includes a couple of vocals by Cheatham and two Bessie Smith songs performed by Mary Buggs.

ESSENTIAL SELECTION
Blue Time 2002 Singing with Sammy
Enjoyable collection recorded between 1938–44. Sammy takes the vocals on the excellent and risque "Queen Street Blues," accompanied by Lem Johnson and His Washboard Band. The rest of the album finds him performing with small groups accompanying various singers, featuring vocals by Johnson (including a very tasty version of "Going Down Slow"), Perline Ellison, Ollie Shephard (a fascinating "Numbers Blues"), Bea Booze, Jimmie Gordon, the powerful Yack Taylor, and the unexceptional Christine Chatman. Good sound, brief notes, and full discographical details.

Circle LP 73 Sammy Price and His Blusicians
A nice album of instrumental jazz-flavored piano

blues and boogie recorded as radio transcriptions in 1944. Accompanying Price are such fine musicians as Ike Quebec (ten sax), Bill Coleman (tpt), and Oscar Pettiford (b). The album includes all the alternate takes, incomplete takes, and false starts, which gets a little tiresome.

Sackville 3029 Black Beauty
With Doc Cheatham.
Savoy 2240 Rib Joint
CD issue: Savoy 4417
Two-LP set of excellent 1956–59 sessions with small R&B band including Mickey Baker and King Curtis.

Swingtime 1029 Sweepin' the Blues Away, Vol. 2
Eighteen tracks recorded between 1940–45 by pianist Price and his group, The Texas Blusicians. In addition to instrumentals and vocals by Price himself, there are also vocals by Yack Taylor, Ruby Smith, Jack Meredith, Mabel Robinson, and Warren Evans.

Whiskey, Women and. . . KM 702 Play It Again, Sam
Features nine sides recorded in 1983 along with four from the early 60s. The 1983 sides are a mixture of blues and boogies with some wistful vocals by Sam. The 60s recordings feature pleasant but unexceptional vocals by Marie Briggs on four Bessie Smith songs.

Whiskey, Women and. . . KM 704 Do You Dig My Jive
Sam's excellent 40s sides on which he is, at times, backed by such notables as "Moon" Mullins (tpt), Duke Jones (b), and "Doc" West (drm). Good solid "jive blues." Rare pictures from the Frank Driggs collection plus extensive sleeve notes by Dan Kochakian.

BIG WALTER PRICE with ALBERT COLLINS
COMPACT DISC
P-Vine PCD 1615 Texas Thunderbird
I'm not sure that this Big Walter (the piano-pounding Price, not the better known Horton) has a reputation of sufficient size to justify a 20-song Japanese CD, but the inclusion of six vintage cuts with fellow Texan Albert Collins is sure to sway a few of you. Two of the Collins pairings are live recordings from 1964, which are powerful in spite of the low-fi sound, and the other four are effective and well-produced 1963 studio duets where the ice man plays an unusually restrained, yet solid role. The remaining 14 tracks from 1971 are really hit-and-miss;

Price is an able singer whose piano playing is just OK, playing material that is not consistently exciting. Standout tracks are two takes of "I Wanta Be Your Chauffeur," a couple of mellow Slim Harpoish talking blues, and the aforementioned cuts with Collins.

JOHN PRIMER

Wolf 120.852 Chicago Blues Session, Vol. 6

Excellent debut album by vocalist/guitarist Primer, who worked for several years with Muddy Waters and more recently with Magic Slim, who joins him on guitar on several cuts. John is a powerful singer and a gritty guitarist in the tough Magic Slim vein. Accompanied by a solid rhythm section, he performs some originals plus Muddy's "My Eyes Keep Me in Trouble" and Magic Slim's "I'm a Blues Man," the latter with some nice slide guitar.

PROFESSOR LONGHAIR

Father of New Orleans blues piano who passed away in 1980, just as his brilliant Alligator album was about to be released. Great and original performer.

Alligator 4718 (c,d) Crawfish Fiesta

Superb album recorded in 1979, just a few months before his death. Longhair's singing and playing are at their peak, the band is top-notch, and guest pianist Dr. John adds some tasty licks.

Atlantic SD 2-4001 (c) The Last Mardi Gras

Two-LP set featuring live recordings cut at Tipitina's in New Orleans in 1978 with his band at the time. Some good performances, but most of the songs Fess has recorded elsewhere better.

Atlantic SD 7225 (c,d) New Orleans Piano

Thirteen great sides recorded for Atlantic in 1949 and 1953, including six previously unissued or alternate takes. CD has three extra tracks. In the Night/Hey Now Baby/Hey Little Girl/Professor Longhair Blues/Ball The Wall/Boogie Woogie.

Dancing Cat 3006 (c,d) Rock 'n' Roll Gumbo

A classic revisited and improved! This album was recorded in 1974; it has been remixed by the album's original producer, Philippe Rault, and two previously unissued songs from the session have been added. The remix gives added emphasis to Fess' superb piano and the sound is brighter and crisper. On this session, Fess was joined by a superb rhythm section and splendid guitarist Clarence "Gatemouth" Brown. Fess is in top form on a selection of New Orleans classics ("Junco Partner," "Rockin' Pneumonia," "Tipitina"), R&B favorites ("Mean Ol' World," "Dr. Professor Longhair"), a calypso ("Rum and Coke"), and a country favorite "Jambalaya" (with bluesy fiddle by Gate).

Krazy Kat 7408 Mardi Gras in New Orleans

This live set was recorded in Hamburg, Germany, in 1975. Longhair is in good form on a familiar selection of his tunes and the band is pretty good, though the inclusion of a harmonica player is a little incongruous in this setting.

Nighthawk 108 (d) Mardi Gras in New Orleans

Sixteen classic recordings cut between 1949–57. Many familiar songs but these are the original recordings. Beautifully packaged with excellent notes by Leroy Pierson.

Rounder 2057 (c,d) House Party New Orleans Style

The legendary lost sessions made in 1971, soon after he was rediscovered. Two quartet sessions here, both featuring Snooks Eaglin on guitar. Includes 10 of the 34 Baton Rouge "demos" with Will Horvey (b) and Shiba (drm), and "Tipitina," "Dr. Professor Longhair," and "G Jam" from the June '72 Memphis sessions featuring Ziggy Modeleste of the Meters (drm) and George Davis (b). Fess' voice is a bit shaky, but the piano is superb, as is Snooks.

COMPACT DISC

JSP CD 202 The Complete London Concert

This is essentially the same as the out-of-print JSP 1025 with one extra track, a recording of a concert by Fess in London in March 1978. Fess was in great form at the concert, accompanied only by his conga player, Alfred Roberts, giving his great piano playing a lot of opportunity to shine. The material is mostly Longhair favorites; sound quality is quite good. Mess Around/Whole Lot of Loving/Baldhead/Big Chief/Everyday I Have the Blues/Rockin' Pneumonia/P. L. Boogie.

SNOOKY PRYOR

Very fine Chicago harmonica player and singer.

Blind Pig 2387 Snooky

Fine new album by this veteran Chicago singer and harmonica player teams him with a tough small band, featuring Steve Freund (gtr), Bob Stroger (b), and Willie Smith (drm). Snooky is in good form on a selection of new songs, revamped versions of traditional items, and remakes of some of his old recordings. The band does an excellent job complementing Snooky, and Freund's Eddie Taylor-flavored guitar is impressive. Broke and Hungry/Judgement Day/It Hurts Me Too/Cheatin' and Lyin'/Key to the Highway.

Flyright 565 Real Fine Boogie

Early-to-mid-50s J.O.B. sides, about half previously unissued. Vocals by Snooky and Moody Jones, with Sunnyland Slim on guitar.

COMPACT DISC

Flyright CD 20 **Snooky Pryor**

A wonderful collection of Chicago blues. Snooky's playing is transitional, between the 40s style of John Lee "Sonny Boy" Williamson and the more urgent, intense style of Little Walter. The first six tracks are from rare recordings made in 1947 and '48 for the Planet and Marvel labels, featuring Snooky accompanying Floyd Jones (the brilliant "Stockyard Blues"), Moody Jones, and Johnny Young, as well as two sides under his own name, including the wonderful instrumental "Boogie" which was, in some respects, a precursor of Little Walter's later instrumental efforts. The remaining tracks were recorded for J.O.B., mostly from the early-to-mid-50s, along with a couple from the 60s. Accompanying Snooky are outstanding musicians like Moody Jones (who does a couple of lovely mournful vocals), Alfred Elkins, Sunnyland Slim, and Alfred Wallace. These are consistently fine performances. Like many Flyright CDs, the sound is a little muffled, but not distressingly so, and there are discographical details and informative liner notes from Klaus Kilian.

P-Vine PCD 2158 **Real Fine Boogie**

Eighteen tracks recorded for J.O.B. and Cobra between 1960–62, including several not originally issued songs. Sidemen include Leroy Foster, Moody Jones, Sunnyland Slim, and Eddie Taylor.

Note: See also HOMESICK JAMES.

RED PRYSOCK
Saxophonograph 502 **Cryin' My Heart Out**

JOE PULLUM
Agram 2012 **Black Gal**

Eighteen sides by this excellent Texas singer, 17 from the 30s and one from 1948. Pullum was a fine singer with a high voice and a range that was unusual among his contemporaries. He was accompanied by the brilliant Texas piano players Robert Cooper or Andy Boy. The album opens with the first version of his most famous song, "Black Gal What Makes Your Head So Hard," a song he recorded with slight variations five more times and which many other artists have recorded. Joe's songs have a lot of variety and many do not fall into a straight 12-bar structure. There are extensive notes and a booklet that includes lyrics to all of Joe's songs, not just those on this album. Sound is quite good.

QUEEN IDA and THE BON TEMPS ZYDECO BAND

Talented and vivacious accordion player and singer from Daly City, CA. Originally from Lake Charles, LA, she learned some accordion at an early age from both her parents, only to give it up for over 20 years. After raising three kids, she picked it up again, and the West Coast hasn't been the same since.

GNP 2101 (c) **Zydeco**

First LP from 1976. Here, aided by brothers Al and Wibert, she gives the world a sumptious taste of her talent. Rosa Majeur/Oh' Teres/Je Vas Revenir/Creole de Lake Charles.

GNP 2112 (c) **Zydeco à la Mode**

Second fine album from 1978. Al sings, Wilbert rubs, and Ida squeezes out 11 fine numbers. Frisco Zydeco/La Veuve/Moi Mademoiselle/Colinda/Moi Tete Feye O' Paradise/Uptown Zydeco.

GNP 2131 (c) **New Orleans**

Recorded in 1980 after her first appearance at the New Orleans Jazz and Heritage Festival, this album reflects her increasing confidence and zest for Zydeco. Capitaine Gumbo/Mon Paradis/Vieux Paris/La Vierge/La Louisianne.

GNP 2147 **On Tour**

Live recordings cut in Europe in 1982, her last recording with brother Al Rapone. It nicely captures the blend of traditional Zydeco and pop flavoring that defines their style together, as exemplified by the tune "Frisco Zydeco." Capitaine Gumbo/Grand Basile/Mazuka/La Louisianne/P'tit Fille O' Paradis/Madame Ben/Bayou Polka.

GNP 2158 (c) **In San Francisco**

Ida's singing and accordion is complemented by fine guitar by Douglas Dayson and fiddle by Pierre Allen. The material is a mixture of Zydeco, old-time Cajun, pop, R&B, and country.

GNP 2172 (c) **On a Saturday Night**

Ida's brand of Zydeco mixes in some Cajun elements on this album courtesy of the excellent fiddler Tom Rigney. The band romps its way through a selection of mostly original songs and tunes. Great party or dance music; one of her best.

GNP 2181 (c,d) **Caught in the Act**

1986 album was recorded live at the Great American Music Hall and features Ida with her current band performing a selection of original songs plus the obligatory "My Toot Toot."

GNP 2197 (c,d) **Cookin' with Queen Ida**

Queen Ida's latest features a punchier sound than previous efforts, with horns, background vocals, slide guitar from Gary Myrick, and second accordion from son, Myrick Guillory. He writes and sings half of the tunes, with mixed results. "Gator Man" and "I-10 Express" cook along nicely, but "Love Is the Answer" and "Lady Be Mine" are pretty insipid. Lonnie Brooks' "Zydeco" is fine and "The Ranger's

Waltz" is given a light, almost Parisian air that is quite lovely.

QUEEN SYLVIA

Chicago's Sylvia Embry is an excellent singer, a little reminiscent of Big Mama Thornton. She also plays solid bass.

L+R 42.057 Midnight Baby

On this, the first album under her own name, she is backed by a solid Chicago group including Jimmy Dawkins, Richie Kirch and Phillip Meeks (gtrs), and Tyrone Centuray (drm). Mostly original songs. Some good performances, though I think the band could have used a bit more rehearsal.

RUFUS and BEN QUILLIAN

Matchbox 217 Complete Recordings, 1929–31

A rather dull album of hokum by these two brothers from Georgia. The two sing in harmony, adding an occasional third singer on a selection of novelty risque songs, almost all of which have the same tune and similar corny lyrics! Instrumental work is good but doesn't do much to bring the tedious vocals to life.

JAMES "YANK" RACHEL

Fine Tennessee singer/guitarist and mandolin player best known for his accompaniments of Sleepy John Estes, though his own recordings are very good too.

Blind Pig BP 1986 Blues Mandolin Man

Delmark 606 Mandolin Blues

With Hammie Nixon, Sleepy John Estes, and Big Joe Williams.

Delmark 649 Chicago Style

Old-style electric Chicago blues featuring singer/mandolin player Rachell accompanied by Pete Crawford (gtr), Floyd Jones (b), and Odie Payne (drm). Most songs are old favorites, like "Roll Me Over Baby," "Check Up on My Baby," and "Early in the Morning," along with a couple of originals, including the semi-topical "Depression Blues." Nice, if not earthshaking, music.

Wolf 106 Complete Recordings, Vol. 1

First of two albums to reissue all of his recordings, except for those with Sleepy John Estes that are available elsewhere. Comparatively little of his early recordings have been reissued before, so it's a pleasure to hear these 18 sides that include six of Rachel as accompanist to singer/guitarist Elijah Jones.

Wolf 107 Complete Recordings, Vol. 2

Complementing Wolf 106. The rest of Rachel's prewar recordings, featuring 18 songs recorded be-

tween 1938–41. Enjoyable small group performances with Sonny Boy Williamson playing harp on all cuts. Unfortunately, many of the songs sound similar, making for dull listening.

MA RAINEY

One of the all-time great female blues singers who recorded extensively for Paramount in the 20s. Unlike many of the other singers of the period, Rainey was a very powerful down-home singer with strong roots in traditional rural music, even though she often recorded with small jazz bands and she wrote many of her own songs.

Biograph 12001 Blues the World Forgot

Biograph 12011 Oh My Babe Blues

Biograph 12032 Queen of the Blues

Black Swan WCH 12001 The Paramounts Chronologically, Vol. 1

Black Swan is a new label from the indefatigable George Buck, devoted to reissuing material from the famed Paramount label. This album is identical to VJM VLP81 and features the first 17 songs recorded by Rainey between December 1923 and May 1924, plus three alternate takes, for a total of 20 songs. Most tracks feature her accompanied by the excllent Lovie Austin and Her Blues Serenaders with Austin (pno), Tommy Ladnier (cnt), and Jimmy O'Bryant (clr). There are two tracks with the bizzarre Pruitt twins on banjo and guitar. Sound on these ancient acoustic recordings is very good and the album comes with good notes by Frank Driggs.

Milestone 2001 The Immortal Ma Rainey

Milestone 2008 Blame It on the Blues

Milestone 47021 Ma Rainey

VJM VLP 81 The Complete Recordings, Vol. 1

First in a series issuing all of her recordings including all known alternate takes. Dubbing from 78s is better than any other issues except for the Yazoo.

VJM VLP 82 Complete Recordings in Chronological Order, Vol. 2: August 1924– July 1925

ESSENTIAL SELECTION

Yazoo 1071 Ma Rainey's Black Bottom

A superb collection of 14 sides recorded between 1924–28. All of these tracks have been reissued before but the superb packaging, with hand-colored cover photo and Yazoo's state-of-the-art mastering, makes this the best-looking and best-sounding reissue. She is accompanied by a wide variety of musicians, from the solo piano of "Don't Fish In My Sea," the twin guitars of "Farewell Daddy Blues," to the full jazz band on "Stack O' Lee Blues" (including

Buster Bailey, Coleman Hawkins, and Fletcher Henderson).

WILLIE GUY RAINEY
Excellent Georgia country blues singer and slide guitarist.

Southland SLP 7 **Willie Guy Rainey**

AL RAPONE and THE ZYDECO EXPRESS
L+R 44.012 **C'est La Vie—Cajun Creole Music**

MOSES RASCOE
Flying Fish 454 (c) **Blues**

A. C. REED and HIS SPARK PLUGS
Chicago singer and saxophone player.

Alligator 4757 (c,d) **I'm in the Wrong Business**
A. C. sings more than he blows on this 1990 LP, with less-than-satisfactory results. All 10 tunes were written by A. C.; the lyrics are witty and insightful (especially the title tune), but "Don't Drive Drunk" is anti-drug and drinking doggerel, and something

about the tunes make them forgettable. Reed really appears to be reaching for the Yuppie white audience with prominent inclusion of "bluesmen" Bonnie Raitt and Stevie Ray Vaughan. Includes his recent Ice Cube single "Fast Food Annie" and "This Little Voice."

Rooster 7606 **Take These Blues and Shove 'Em**
A collection of mostly original songs, including his minor hit "I Am Fed Up With This Music" about the trials and tribulations of trying to make a living as a blues musician. Accompanying musicians include Casey Jones, Larry Burton, Lurie Bell, Phil Guy, Allen Batts, and Billy Branch.

A. C. REED/MAURICE VAUGHN
Blue Phoenix 33.727 **I Got Money**
A bit of a frustrating album featuring veteran singer and sax player Reed and up-and-coming singer/guitarist Vaughn accompanied by bass and drums. Reed takes the vocals on one side of the album and Vaughn the other. The latter is a very good singer and an outstanding guitarist, but the choice of material is mediocre except for a remake of "Computer Took My Job" that was on Vaughn's excellent Reecy album. Reed's side features even more expendable songs done Jimmy Reed style, but, again, Vaughn gets to take some nice guitar licks and Reed plays some decent sax.

JIMMY REED
One of the most popular blues performers of all time, and one of the most influential. His lazy voice, limited but effective harmonica playing, and hypnotic guitar beat have entranced generations of fans and fellow musicians. His early Vee Jay recordings are fine, but his later recordings find his distinctive features reduced to a rather stylized parody. His Vee Jay recordings have been licensed to so many companies and been repackaged so many times that it is almost impossible to avoid duplication. The original Vee Jay LPs themselves are now being reissued. Probably the best cross-section of his Vee Jay recordings are on the four Charly albums.

ESSENTIAL SELECTION
Charly CRB 1003 (c) **Upside Your Head**
Excellent collection of 16 Vee Jay sides from 1955–64, with good notes. Shame, Shame, Shame/I Ain't Got You/Down the Road/Too Much/I'm Going Upside Your Head/Honest I Do/Aw Shucks, Hush Your Mouth/Baby, What You Want Me To Do.

Charly CRB 1013 **High and Lonesome**
Sixteen sides including his first recording and three previously unissued sides. She Don't Want Me No More/I'm Gonna Ruin You/You Upset My Mind/Baby, Don't Say That No More/I Love You Baby/It's You Baby/You Know I Love You/You Gonna Need My Help/High and Lonesome/Pretty Thing.

Charly CRB 1028 **Got Me Dizzy**
Sixteen more Vee Jay sides, including some hits and some B-sides. I'm A Love You/Take Out Some Insurance/Caress Me Baby/I'll Change My Style/You Got Me Dizzy/Meet Me.

Charly CRB 1082 **I'm the Man Down There**
This set covers his entire recording career for Vee Jay from his first session in 1953 to his last in 1965. From his early sessions, we have such great sides as "I Found My Baby" and the rarely reissued "Shoot My Baby." From the mid-50s there are fine rare and unissued tracks like "Come On Baby," "When You Left Me," and the fascinating previously unissued instrumental "State Street Boogie," featuring some amazing fiddle work by Remo Biondi. The second side of the album is all 60s recordings and, although Reed wasn't always at his best then, the album's compilers have carefully chosen the best titles from this era.

Krazy Kat 786 **Cold Chills**
Compiled from recordings made by Reed for Al Smith between 1966–71. Although these later recordings aren't a match for his 50s Vee Jay classics, there are some nice moments here from Reed and from his top-class sidemen: Wayne Bennett, Eddie Taylor, Louis Myers, and Phil Upchurch.

Vee Jay 1004 (c) **I'm Jimmy Reed**
Reissue of his classic first album featuring 12 great sides. Honest I Do/My First Plea/You Got Me Crying/You Got Me Dizzy/Can't Stand To See You Go/You're Somthing Else.

Vee Jay 1008 (c) **Rockin' with Reed**
Vee Jay 1022 (c) **Found Love**
A classic Reed album available again in its original format. This one features 12 sides recorded for Vee Jay between 1955–61, including such blues hits as "Baby What You Want Me to Do," "Found Love," "Hush Hush," and "Big Bossman," along with other fine tracks like "Meet Me," "Going to the River," "Where Can You Be," and the atypical "I Ain't Got You," with piano by the great Henry Gray. Before Jimmy's lazy drawled vocals became an affectation, these tracks show just what an appealing vocalist he was. He accompanies himself on guitar and rack-mounted harmonica with Eddie Taylor (gtr) and Earl

Phillips (drm) on most cuts.

Vee Jay 1025 (c) **Now Appearing**
Excellent selection. Close Together/I Want To Be With You/Tell the World I Do/I've Got The Blues/Down the Road/ You're My Baby.

Vee Jay 1035 (c) **At Carnegie Hall**
CD issue: Suite Beat D3001
Two-LP set. A classic collection. In spite of the title, these are all studio recordings.

Vee Jay 1039 (c) **The Best of Jimmy Reed**
Twelve songs. Baby What You Want Me To Do/Hush Hush/Honest I Do/Big Bossman/Boogie In The Dark.

Vee Jay 7303 **Blues Is My Business**
An excellent collection of 12 sides from the 50s. Several of these were not originally issued as 45s by Vee Jay, including such fine performances as "When You Left Me" and "Shoot My Baby." However, many of the best sides here are also available on the four Charly albums. You in that Sack/Please Don't/My Baby/Go Get My Baby/I'm Gonna Love You.

COMPACT DISC

Charly CD 3 **Big Boss Blues**
Twenty-two great Vee Jay sides, 1953–63. The sound on these early recordings is not particularly better on this CD issue and, in fact, the earlier sides sound a little more muffled and echoey than on LP reissues. You Don't Have To Go/Ain't That Loving You Baby/You Got Me Dizzy/Down In Virginia/I Wanna Be Loved/Take Out Some Insurance/Hush Hush/Big Boss Man/Bright Lights, Big City/Good Lover/I'll Change My Style.

Charly CD 61 **Rockin' with Reed**
An hour's worth of Vee Jay sides, 1955–64. This one doesn't have the hits (those are on Charly CD 3); it has 22 more fine sides including the instrumentals "Roll and Rhumba," Reed's first Vee Jay recording, and the title tune. I'm Going Upside Your Head/Baby What's Wrong/Shoot My Baby/The Sun Is Shining.

Flyright CD 15 **Jimmy Reed**
Twenty-one tracks recorded between 1966–71 and available on two Krazy Kat LPs (781 [out of print] and 786). By the time of these recordings, Reed's career was in decline and his distinctive sound had become pretty much a formula. Nevertheless, there is some good music here from Reed and his stellar accompanists, including Eddie Taylor, Lefty Bates, Phil Upchurch, Louis Myers, and Fred Below.

GNP Crescendo GNPD 20006-2 **The Best of Jimmy Reed**
Twenty Vee Jay sides. Ain't that Lovin' You

Baby/Honest I Do/Baby What You Want Me to Do/I Ain't Got You/Big Boss Man/Bright Lights Big City/Shame Shame Shame.
Note: See also under EDDIE TAYLOR/JIMMY REED.

SONNY RHODES

Excellent contemporary West Coast singer/guitarist who often performs on steel guitar. He is, however, much more interesting on regular electric guitar as on his Rhodesway album. He is also a good songwriter though some of his songs tend to be a bit self-conscious.

Rhodesway 4501 **Just Blues**
This 1985 album is easily the best by him since his (currently unavailable) Amigo/Advent album. He is accompanied by his working band, which features some pleasing horn work by Bernard Anderson and Jonathan Paul. He sings well on a selection of blues favorites like "I Can't Lose," "Please Love Me," "Think," and "Strange Things Happening," along with a couple of good originals, "House Without Love" and "Cigarette Blues." Album has a tough, ballsy sound.

TODD RHODES
Jukebox Lil 615 **Your Daddy's Doggin' Around**

WALTER "LIGHTNIN' BUG" RHODES

North Carolina singer/guitarist who has been active since the early 50s, performing in a variety of blues, gospel, and R&B groups.

Swingmaster 2116 **Giving You the Blues**
An acoustic country blues set, with 10 songs featuring his warm vocals and fluid Carolina-flavored guitar. Tasteful second guitar by Dutch player Fred Reining is featured on three tracks, including a remake of "Picking Cotton" that he recorded in 1965 as Little Red Walter. The songs are all originals and include the provocatively titled "Sex," and the interesting story-song "Shot At Dobbin Height." An enjoyable collection. Bull in the Pasture/Your Whole Life Through/Mean Little Woman.

TOMMY RIDGELY
Flyright 519 **The NEW King of the Stroll**
Great blues and R&B from New Orleans. Fourteen sides, mostly recorded for the Ric label in the early 60s. A mixture of rockin' R&B, hard blues, and blues ballads, all with that distinctive New Orleans feel, with great vocals by Ridgely and all-star accompanists: Lee Allen, Eddie Bo, Roy Montrell, and Charles "Hungry" Williams. Great!

BOB RIEDY BLUES BAND
Chicago blues band led by piano player Riedy; more notable for guest appearances by people like Jimmy Rogers and John Littlejohn than for Riedy himself.

Fine Catch 27006 **The Bob Riedy Blues Band**
Guest appearances by Carey Bell and Eddie Clearwater.

Rounder 2005 **Lake Michigan Ain't No River**
THE JAMES RIVERS QUARTET
Spindletop 101 **The Dallas Sessions**
New Orleans R&B, blues and jazz featuring groups led by saxophonist and flute player Rivers.

Rounder 3103 (c,d) **Swing**

DUKE ROBBILARD and THE PLEASURE KINGS
Rounder 3079 (c) **Duke Robbilard and The Pleasure Kings**
Solo album by the former guitarist with Roomful of Blues, accompanied by rhythm section only on a selection of mostly original songs. Decent vocals and some excellent guitar.

Rounder 3082 (c) **Too Hot to Handle**
Rounder 3100 (c,d) **You Got Me**
Guests like Dr. John (with some very nice piano), Jimmy Vaughan of the Fabulous Thunderbirds, and Ron Levy put together a pleasant sound in a gentle blues-rock vein.
COMPACT DISC
Rounder CD 11548 **Rockin' Blues**
Seventeen-track compilation from Robillard's first two Rounder albums, "And The Pleasure Kings" and "Too Hot to Handle."

WILLIAM ROBERTSON
Georgia country blues singer and guitarist. Nice, though a little primitive.

Southland 5 **South Georgia Blues**

ELZADIE ROBINSON
Document 588 **1926-29**
I know very little about Elzadie Robinson other than the fact that she was from Shreveport, LA, and worked the barrelhouses in Texas and Louisiana with pianist Will Ezell, who accompanies her on many of the 16 tracks here. What is clear, though, is that she was an outstanding singer with an intense moaning style that puts her up among the best. Her songs are often topical, with subjects like "Sawmill Blues," "Galveston Blues," and "Arkansas Mill Blues." Ezell's accompaniments are excellent, though sometimes the recording balance has his playing dominate her vocals. A few tracks also feature a small group with cornet. The tracks here are from rare, worn, and poorly recorded Paramounts so sound is not too great, but these outstanding perfor-

mances are well worth a listen. Practically none of these has been reissued before.

FENTON ROBINSON

Marvelous Chicago singer and guitarist with a fine and powerful voice and a highly melodic and fluid guitar style. The Alligator and P-Vine albums are all very fine.

Alligator 4705 (c,d) Somebody Loan Me a Dime
Excellent set with fine singing and guitar by Fenton, and splendid accompaniment by a small solid band. Mostly remakes of songs he had recorded before. Directly From My Heart To You/You Say You're Leaving/You Don't Know What Love Is/Country Girl/Texas Flood.

ESSENTIAL SELECTION

Alligator 4710 I Hear Some Blues Downstairs
An even better album than 4705 with some great new songs, brilliant singing and playing by Fenton, and outstanding instrumental arrangements. West Side Baby/I Wish For You/Going West/As the Years Go Passing By.

Alligator 4736 (c) Night Flight
1984 album originally recorded for the Dutch Black Magic label. Fenton is in fine form on a selection of mostly original songs and is accompanied by an excellent band of Chicago musicians, with Junior Wells guesting on one track.

P-Vine PLP 9001 The Mellow Blues Genius
CD issue: P-Vine PCD 1256
It's great to have this marvelous album back in print. The LP features 11 tracks recorded for Chicago's Giant and Palos labels between 1965–74. Some were issued on 45s, but several were unissued until the original appearance of this LP. It includes the original recording of his all-time classic "Somebody Loan Me a Dime," the beautiful minor key "Nothing but a Fool," with some of the most lyrical guitar playing I've ever heard, and a brilliant hard-driving version of "One Room Country Shack." The CD adds another version of "I Put My Baby in High Society" and the fine "You're Cracking Me Up." These are my favorite recordings by Fenton and I unequivocally recommend them to any lover of electric blues.
COMPACT DISC

Black Magic CD 9012 Special Road
Although marred by less-than-spectacular production values and accompaniments that don't always do him justice, this 1990 collection proves, once again, that Fenton is one of the greatest contemporary blues performers. He is a wonderfully soulful singer with a gospel tinge to his vocals. His guitar playing is unique—dazzlingly imaginative with a hint of jazz in his approach but 100 percent blues in his execution. The material here includes a few new songs (the title track and "Money Problem"), some remakes of songs he had previously recorded, including a spellbinding version of "Blue Monday," and some blues standards including a version of "Baby Please Don't Go" that breathes new and unique life into this hoary old chestnut. In spite of my minor reservations, it's quite likely the best contemporary blues album of 1990.

BANJO IKEY ROBINSON
Document 509 1929–35
Ikey Robinson was a moderately prolific artist on both blues and jazz records in the late 20s and 30s. This album features 12 of his blues and hokum sides along with six jazz items. Most of these tracks have not been on album before. The general mood here is upbeat hokum, which is not my favorite music, though there are a couple of nice blues opening the album with some effective finger-picked banjo by Ikey. The two tracks by Ikey with his Bull Fiddle band feature some hot fiddle by R. Waugh and the outrageous vocals of Frankie Jaxon, which elevate them above most of the material here.

L. C. "GOOD ROCKING" ROBINSON

Excellent California singer who plays regular and steel guitars and fiddle.

Arhoolie 1062 Ups and Downs
One side of album features the Muddy Waters Blues Band.

"SUGAR CHILE" ROBINSON

Remarkable blues and boogie piano player who recorded between the ages of 9 and 11.

Oldie Blues 2828 Go Boy Go
Sides recorded between 1949–52 by this amazing prodigy who specialized in piano blues and boogie. Accompanied by a nondescript rhythm section, Sugar Chile plays some good piano and shouts the blues in his squeaky preteen voice. Although Sugar Chile was a decent musician, it must be admitted that the music wears thin after the novelty wears off.

ROCKIN' DOPSIE and THE CAJUN TWISTERS

Enjoyable Louisiana Zydeco group who have become particularly successful in Europe in recent years.

Flyright 592 Rockin' Dupsee
Blues and Zydeco recorded for Jay Miller between 1970–74. Most of these recordings have not been issued before.

GNP 2154 (c) **Big Bad Zydeco**
Fine album. A familiar selection of blues, Cajun, and Zydeco tunes.

GNP 2156 **Hold On**
Features some great tenor sax by former Clifton Chenier sideman John Hart.

GNP 2167 **Good Rockin'**
Enjoyable album with a nice mixture of R&B, Zydeco, blues, and New Orleans R&B. Besides Dopsie's own vocals, guest guitarist Russell Gordon contributes three songs (two in French) and blues singer Joshua Jackson sings two numbers. Clifton Chenier's former guitar player, Paul Senegal, is also featured on the album.

Maison De Soul 1020 **Crowned Prince of Zydeco**
Excellent set of R&B, Cajun, and Zydeco numbers backed by long-time stalwarts from Clifton Chenier's band: Paul Senegal and Sherman Robertson on guitars and John Hart on sax. The result is hard-driving Zydeco on Dopsie's "Crazy 'Bout That Married Woman" and "Zyde-Cool," also Chuck Martin's hit "Make It Hot," and the classic "Back Door."

Maison De Soul 1025 (c) **Saturday Night Zydeco!**
CD issue: Maison De Soul CD 104
OK, maybe Dopsie doesn't possess the greatest voice, play the hottest accordian, or write the best songs. But he does have John Hart on sax and Paul Senegal on guitar from Clifton Chenier's old band, and an easy, good-timing swing to his music that is hard to resist. Aided by sons David and Alton Jr. on scrubboard and drums, he romps through old R&B favorites like "Mardi Gras in New Orleans," "Please Don't Leave Me," "Calinda," and "High-Heeled Sneakers," complete with son David's "Zydeco Rap," not to mention the familiar sounding "Dopsie's Boogie," "Dopsie's Cajun Stomp," and "Footstompin' Zydeco." Nothing earthshaking, but a lot of fun and downright hot when Hart or Senegal lets loose with some tasty solos.

Rounder 6012 **Rockin' Dopsie and The Twisters**
Sampler from his three Sonet albums.

Sonet 761 **Zy-De Blue**

Sonet 872 **French Style**
Cajun musicians Dewey Balfa (fdl), Tony Balfa (acoustic gtr), and Jay Pelsia (steel gtr) join Dopsie to create a mix of Cajun and Zydeco sounds. The combining of black and white French Louisiana traditions is most effective on this selection of Zydeco songs, R&B numbers, blues, and Cajun songs.

COMPACT DISC
Gazell GCCD 3003 **Zy-De-Co-In'**
CD combines Dopsie's first two Sonet LPs, "Doin' the Zydeco" and "Zy-De Blue."

ROCKIN' SIDNEY

Fine Louisiana singer and accordion player who over the years has recorded a mixture of blues and Zydeco. In 1986 he had a hit with his song "My Toot Toot" that led to national stardom and a whole slew of cover versions of this catchy novelty song.

Bally Hoo 2001 **Joy to the South**
A pleasant mixture of mostly original blues and Zydeco. The blues are generally more interesting than the Zydeco songs. The sound on the album is rather thin.

Flyright 515 **They Call Me Rockin'**
Reissue of his 60s recordings for Floyd Soileau's Jin and Fame labels. These are mostly blues.

Maison De Soul 1007 **Give Me a Good Time Woman**
Good solid album of Zydeco music.

Maison de Soul 1008 **Boogie, Blues and Zydeco**

Maison De Soul 1009 **My Zydeco Shoes Got the Zydeco Blues**
Pleasant album of Zydeco by Sidney who wrote, sang, and arranged all of the songs on the package and played all of the instruments as well—harmonica, accordion, rhythm and lead guitars, bass, and drums. Some enjoyable performances but the total sound is a little thin and Sidney could have used some extra musicians!

ZBC 100 **A Holiday Celebration**
Sidney's Zydeco Christmas album.

ZBC 101 **Hot Steppin'**
Snappy, fun-filled Zydeco. There are a couple of songs that recall his hit "My Toot Toot" ("Don't Mesh With My Tush" and "Dance A Little Bit"); some songs of almost innocent braggadocio ("I Need A Man To Ring My Bell" and "I'm Your Man" [with Katie Webster on piano]); plus the irrepressible humor of "Lonely Lost Frog" and "Every Dog Has His Day." Sidney plays almost everything: accordion, guitar, harmonica, and even banjo on "Cajun Cowboy 2-Step."

ZBC 102 (c) **Creola: The Talk of the Town**
Original songs by the "Toot Toot" man is a mixed bag of Zydeco, R&B, and pop. Nothing really stands out here, though it is a pleasant collection.

ZBC 103 (c) **Squeeze that Thang!**
This album continues Sidney's catchy, poppish style, forever in search of that next hit. "Kicking, Asking, and Taking Names" and "Squeeze that Thing" have clever, suggestive lyrics coupled with frothy rhythms that are enjoyable, and his two versions of "Harlem Shuffle (and Zydeco Shuffle)" rock out nicely. Some of the other selections seem a bit mechanical, but it's all good fun. Dat's Dat Zydeco/ May I Have the Pleasure/Throw on Me/King Zydeco.

COMPACT DISC
JSP CD 213 **Live with the Blues**

JIMMY ROGERS

Superb Chicago singer with a lovely relaxed vocal style and a melodic guitar style. He was a member of the Muddy Waters blues band from the late 40s to mid-50s, and many of the recordings from that period under his own name feature fellow band members. These have now all been reissued on various Chess albums. He retired from music for a while but returned to recording in the 70s.

Antones 0012 (c,d) **Ludella**
1990 recording. The Chicago blues legend has assembled a 10-song studio and live set that puts most contemporary blues records to shame. Enlisting some heavy hitters from his Muddy Waters days—his recent touring partner Pinetop Perkins, bassist Calvin Jones, and drummer Willie "Big Eyes" Smith, along with producer/harpman Kim Wilson (of Fabulous Thunderbirds fame)—Rogers and company have recaptured the swaggering urban intensity that powered his original 50s Chess recordings. He dusts off "Chicago Bound," "Ludella," "Sloppy Drunk," and the old chestnut "Got My Mojo Working," with additional help from Hubert Sumlin, drummer Ted Harvey, and Antone's regular Derek O'Brien. Jimmy's voice still has its bittersweet clarity, and you can count on hearing some excellent playing by Kim Wilson and "Big Eyes" Smith, who really tear it up live.

Black and Blue 33.544 **Sloppy Drunk Nice**
1973 sides with Louis Myers, Willie Mabon, Dave Myers, and Fred Below. Half of the cuts were previously on Black and Blue 33.504 and the rest are new to record. Mostly familiar Rogers songs.

ESSENTIAL SELECTION

Chess 93000 (c,d) **Chicago Bound**
Long-awaited reissue of 14 early-to-mid-50s

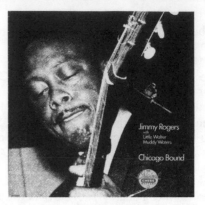

recordings. Only one tune, "You're the One," is duplicated on Chess 2-92505, making this a valuable addition to any Chicago blues collection. A real treat! Last Time/Sloppy Drunk/That's All Right/ Chicago Bound/Walkin' By Myself.

Shelter SRZ 8016 **Sings the Blues**
CASSETTE ONLY RELEASE
Chess 2-92505 **Jimmy Rogers**
Includes the "Chicago Bound" album plus half of the cuts on the Japanese/French twofers. Great music, of course, but minimal packaging and no notes.

COMPACT DISC
Chess (UK) CD RED 16 **That's All Right**
If it wasn't for the fact that the sound on this set is unexceptional, this would be the definitive collection of Rogers' Chess recordings. Jimmy's warm melodic voice and flowing guitar are always a joy to hear, the material is varied, and his accompanists include Little Walter, Eddie Ware (a unique and very effective piano player), Big Crawford, J. T. Brown, Johnny Jones, Willie Dixon, Muddy Waters, Otis Spann, Fred Below, Walter Horton, and Robert Jr. Lockwood. The ensemble playing is unbelievably tight, and this seamless integration pays tribute not only to the brilliantly talented musicians but also to the production talents of Leonard Chess. Ludella/Today Today Blues/Money, Marbles and Chalk/Back Door Friend/Out On the Road/Chicago Bound/Walking By Myself.

WALTER ROLAND

Superb Alabama piano player and singer who, besides many fine recordings on his own, also provided some outstanding accompaniments to the great Bessie Jackson, who is featured on the following albums.

Magpie 4406 **Piano Blues, Vol. 6**
Recordings made between 1933–35, including

several tracks with vocals by Sonny Scott or the magnificent Lucille Bogan (aka Bessie Jackson).

Yazoo 1017 Bessie Jackson and Walter Roland, 1927–1935
Note: Other recordings are reissued on Blues Classics 7. See also BESSIE JACKSON.

ROOMFUL OF BLUES
Nine-piece band from Rhode Island that is hard to categorize because they dabble in everything: swing jazz, R&B, and a strong backbeat. They have a hard-driving, five-piece horn section and tackle everything from Duke Ellington to Big Joe Turner to the Nighhawks. Rockin' good time music.

Varrick 018 (c,d) Dressed Up to Get Messed Up
This is their fourth album. Greg Piccolo's "What Happened to the Sugar (In My Lemonade)" is a knockout. Also praiseworthy is guitarist Ronnie Earl's work on "Whiplash" and guest vocalist Kim Wilson (from the Fabulous Thunderbirds), who lets it rip on "The Last Time."

Varrick 021 (c,d) Hot Little Mama
Varrick 024 (c,d) Live at Lupo's

DOCTOR ROSS
Fine singer/guitarist/harmonica player and sometimes one-man band. His best recordings are the driving performances he cut for Sun in the early 50s that are reissued on Arhoolie 1065, which are the only ones currently available.

Arhoolie 1065 His First Recordings

JAMES "SPARKY" RUCKER
Young black blues interpreter from Tennessee.

Green Linnet 1032 Heroes and Hard Times
June Appal 017 Cold and Lonesome on a Train
L+R 42.062 Drive Back the Night
Pleasant album of folk-flavored blues, mixing originals with songs from Mississippi John Hurt, Robert Johnson, Peg Leg Sam, and a couple of traditional ones. With occasional electric guitar by Louisiana Red and harp by Carey Bell.

OTIS RUSH
One of the greatest contemporary blues singers and guitarists alive. An intense and moving blues singer, he is also a guitarist of considerable skill and unparalleled imagination. Between 1956–58, Rush recorded some incredible impassioned recordings for the Cobra label out of Chicago. Accompanied by such brilliant sidemen as Walter Horton, Lafayette Leake, Harold Ashby, Willie Dixon, Little Walter, Jody Williams, Odie Payne, Little Brother Montgomery, and Jackie Brenston,

he turned in some amazing vocal and instrumental performances that should be in every blues fan's collection. These have been reissued several times. The complete recordings, including many alternate takes, are available on a couple of Flyright albums. His later recordings are somewhat more erratic, ranging from mediocre to sensational. Of these, his best is the superb 1971 session for Capitol that was issued by Bullfrog in 1976 and subsequently reissued by Hightone in 1986. He is now back on the road after a period of retirement and it is to be hoped that he will record another album that does his great talents their full justice.

Blind Pig 73188 Tops
Live recordings from the 1985 San Francisco Blues Festival. This set finds Otis doing a mixture of originals ("Right Place Wrong Time," "Tops," and a painfully short "Keep on Loving Me Baby") and standards like "Crosscut Saw," "Gambler's Blues," and "Feel So Bad." While it's really not a bad album, it's not very exciting either. Because of his reluctance to put together his own band and do it right, Otis continues to short-change his own talent and legendary status. The backup band is solid, but they simply aren't familiar enough with Otis and his choice of material. Vocally he is in fine form; his guitar playing is imaginative and sometimes fiery. The thing is, if this were the debut of a new artist it might be looked at differently, but this is Otis Rush, and the name alone deserves more.

Chess 9322 (c,d) Albert King/Otis Rush: Door to Door
Originally Chess 1538. A great album featuring two of the premier exponents of modern blues guitar. There are six superb sides by Rush from 1960 including the magnificent "So Many Roads, So Many Trains" that is one of his greatest ever performances.

Delmark 643 So Many Roads
Live in Japan, 1975.

Flyright 560 Groaning the Blues
Cobra sides previously issued on an out-of-print
Blue Horizon album. Includes some alternate takes
and all-time classics.

**Flyright 562 Otis Rush and Magic Sam:The
Other Takes 1956–58**
Alternate takes not previously reissued plus a few
issued takes not on 560. Ten tracks by Otis and ten
by Sam.

ESSENTIAL SELECTION

Hightone 8007 (c,d) Right Place, Wrong Time
Arguably the best recordings of this great Chicago
singer/guitarist with the possible exception of his
recordings for Cobra in the 50s. Originally recorded
for Capitol in 1971, it was not released by them and
was subsequently bought by Bullfrog in 1976; in
1986 the rights were acquired by Hightone. Accompanied by a superb band of San Francisco-based
musicians, Otis turns in superb versions of original
songs like the title song, "Take a Look Behind," and
the superb instrumental "Easy Go." He also turns in
outstanding versions of Ike Turner's "Tore Up,"
Albert King's "Natural Ball," Little Milton's "Lonely Man," and a remarkably sensitive version of
"Rainy Night in Georgia." Otis' singing throughout
is outstanding—passionate and intense but not out
of control, as is sometimes the case on his 70s and
80s recordings. He is also one of the world's greatest
blues guitarists, and there is a lot of opportunity for
his playing to shine here. Highly recommended!
COMPACT DISC
**Flyright FLYCD 01 1956–1958: His Cobra
Recordings**
What can possibly be said about these incredible
recordings that hasn't been said before? Here for the
first time on CD are 20 of the finest sides ever cut in
Chicago, the issued takes along with four alternates.
While the originals weren't recorded all that well,
the sound here is uniformly excellent. Despite some
distortion and hiss, the vocals have a lot of presence
and the guitar stings. If you don't already have these
in your collection, it's an absolutely essential purchase. Double Trouble/Checking on My Baby/My
Baby's a Good'un/All Your Love/Three Times a
Fool.

JIMMY RUSHING
Great jazz/blues singer who started his career
with the Basie band in the 30s.
Fresh Sound FSR 642 Five Feet of Soul
Exact reissue of Colpix CP 446 from 1963 on the
Spanish Fresh Sounds label. "Mr. Five by Five" belts

out ten standards, backed by an incredible big-band
lineup put together for the two-day session. Person-
nel include Phil Woods (alto sax), Zoot Sims (ten
sax), Joe Newman (tpt), Urbie Green (trb), Freddie
Green (gtr), and Milt Hinton (b)! Just Because/
'Tain't Nobody's Biz-ness if I Do/Trouble in Mind/
You Always Hurt the One You Love.
Official 3020 I Want a Little Girl
Definitely some of the big man's finest cleffings
from the 1945–57 period, backed by The Johnny
Otis, Dick Vance, and Buddy Tate Orchestras.
Standouts include Jimmy's original version of
"Round the Clock Blues," one of the most recorded
double entendre blues classics of the 40s; "Good
Morning Blues," suppported by great trumpet fills
from Harry Edison; "Go Get Some More You Fool,"
with fine "watery" piano triplets from Al Williams;
and "In the Moonlight," with tasty guitar licks from
Jimmy Shirley. Sixteen titles in all. Excellent easy-
blues singing with first-rate support.
COMPACT DISC
**Bluebird 6460-2 RB You and Me That Used to
Be**
With Al Cohn, Budd Johnson, Earl Hines, and Dave
Frishberg.

SAFFIRE
Alligator 4780 (c,d) The Uppity Blues Women

ST. LOUIS BESSIE
Matchbox 223 1927–30
Eighteen sides by excellent but obscure St. Louis
singer Bessie Mae Smith from six sessions between
1927–30, with Lonnie Johnson, Wesley Wallace,
and Henry Brown. Most tracks have not been reissued before.

BON TON ST. MARY
Goldband 7793 Highway Zydeco
Promising, but uneven, first LP from Sacramento,
CA-based Zydeco artist St. Mary. He can get a good
steam up on songs like "Hey Hey Josephine" and
"No Need to Cry," but is sometimes betrayed by an
uncertain voice and backup and some weak
material. Still an enjoyable first outing.

SAM BROTHERS FIVE
Five brothers from Lafayette, LA, who play hot
Zydeco music.
Arhoolie 1081 The Sam Brothers Five
Enjoyable first album recorded when the band mem-
bers were aged between 11 and 18.
Blues Unlimited 5014 Cruisin' On
Second album is a rather dull effort.

Maison De Soul 10929 **Zydeco Brotherhood**

SAMPY AND THE BAD HABITS

Zydeco band from Carenco, LA. Decent though primitive sounding.

Caillier 1001 **Zydeco Gumbo**

DERYCK SAMPSON

Enjoyable boogie-woogie piano player who recorded for Joe Davis's Beacon label in 1943–44. Only 17 at the time of the first recordings, Sampson was a powerful and imaginative performer. Although his playing doesn't have the drive or fire of an Ammons or Lewis, he is most pleasing and his "Boogie Express" is particularly impressive.

Harlequin HQ 2006 **Boogie Express**

THE SAN FRANCISCO BLUES BAND

T.J. 1056 **The San Francisco Blues Band**
Some decent if unexceptional singing and playing on a selection of mostly original songs. Lead vocals are taken by band member Craig Horton.

CHARLIE SAYLES

Dusty Road 701 **The Raw Harmonica Blues of Charlie Sayles**
Originally issued in 1976. When he was 28, Sayles was discovered as a street musician in New York, singing and playing with a maturity that belied his age. An excellent singer and a brilliant harmonica player, Sayles writes original songs based on his experiences travelling the country and a sojourn in Vietnam. He is given basic but effective accompaniment by guitar and sometimes bass and drums. On a few cuts, he plays his own hi-hat. Sayles was a formidable discovery.

ISAAC SCOTT

Fine contemporary-styled singer/guitarist from Seattle.

Red Lightnin' 0023 **Isaac Scott Blues Band**
Mostly recorded live at various Seattle clubs.

MABEL SCOTT

Jukebox Lil 606 **Fine Fine Baby**

MARILYN SCOTT/MARY DELOATCH

Whiskey, Women and . . . 710 **I Got What My Daddy Likes**
Marilyn Scott is Mary Deloatch, who recorded some excellent blues and gospel for the Lance, Free, Savoy, and Regent labels between 1946–51. As Marilyn Scott, she cut outstanding blues, accompanying herself on guitar, and as Mary Deloatch, she

cut gospel tunes with and without The Evan's Gospel Quartet, a female outfit. On many of her blues sides, she is accompanied by The Johnny Otis Orchestra and is billed as The Carolina Blues Girl. No artist switched from God to the Devil with such apparent ease, even to the extent of playing both roles on consecutive Savoy recording sessions. A full page is needed to describe the merits of this collection, which is easily one of the best reissues to surface in 1990. Highly recommended.

SONNY SCOTT

Blues Documents 2020 **The Complete Recordings in Chronological Order**
A beautiful collection of 17 country blues recorded in 1933 by obscure Alabama blues singer/guitarist Sonny Scott. Not much is known about Scott; he seems to have worked regularly with the great Walter Roland, who appears on several tracks here on guitar, piano, or vocal. Scott was an excellent and distinctive vocalist and a varied guitarist whose style at times brings to mind Mississippi guitarists with its churning rhythm and at other times has a more melodic cast. The songs are mostly unique to Sonny, though many are based on traditional themes. Only a few of these tracks have been reissued before and very few are currently available. Sound quality is rough on a few tracks but is mostly very good. This collection is eminently worthwhile.

IRENE SCRUGGS

Blues Documents 2095 **1924–30**
Irene Scruggs was a fine St. Louis singer who was recorded in some very fine company, as can be heard on this collection of 17 tracks. There are two tracks with Irene accompanied by Clarence Williams, two with a superb small band including King Oliver, Kid Ory, Albert Nicholas, and Luis Russell (!), two with DeLoise Searcy and Lonnie Johnson, two duets with Johnny Hodges (a different one), five with piano player J. Norman Ebron and an unknown guitar player who plays some fine slide on a few tracks, and finally four tracks with Little Brother Montgomery. Curiously enough, she sounds like more of a rural artist on the later sides than on the earlier recordings. All in all, a most worthwhile reissue with good sound on most tracks and little duplication with other reissues.

SON SEALS

Good, strong contemporary singer/guitarist from Chicago. Style somewhat influenced by Albert King.

Alligator 4703 **The Son Seals Blues Band**
Tough set with rhythm section accompaniment only.

Mother-in-Law Blues/Look Now Baby/All Your Love/Hot Sauce.

Alligator 4708 (d) Midnight Son
Son's first album with horns. I Believe/Four Full Seasons Of Love/Don't Bother Me/Don't Fool With My Baby/Going Back Home.

Alligator 4712 (c) Live and Burning
Recorded live in 1978 at Wise Fools Pub in Chicago, with A. C. Reed (ten sax) and Lacy Gibson (gtr). I Can't Hold Out/Funky Bitch/Help Me Somebody/Call My Job.

Alligator 4720 Chicago Fire
1980 album. Buzzard Lope/Leaving Home/Gentleman From The Windy City.

Alligator 4738 (c,d) Bad Axe
Another dose of high-energy guitar blues from Seals.

WILL SHADE/GUS CANNON
Document 561 With Friends
1961 recordings.

RAY SHARPE
Former R&B rocker, good singer/guitar player.

Flying High 6502 Texas Boogie Blues
Excellent album. Nice mixture of straight blues, R&B, and bluesy rock 'n' roll, with Delbert McClinton (hca).

Flying High 6507 Live at the Bluebird, Vol. 1
Live set with Ray accompanied by a tough band performing mostly blues standards. Dust My Blues/Every Day I Have the Blues/Chili Con Como/Gotta See My Baby.

EDDIE SHAW
Rooster Blues 7608 King of the Road
A nice cross-section of recordings made by singer, songwriter, and blues saxophonist Shaw between 1966–84. A wide variety of musicians is featured on these recordings including guitarists Magic Sam, Hubert Sumlin, Milton Houston, and Shaw's son Eddie Shaw Jr. I generally prefer the 60s and 70s sides to those from '84 that are a little heavy-handed.

OLLIE SHEPARD
Old Tramp 1210 1937–41
Twenty tracks by this rather urbane blues vocalist with his Kentucky Boys. Most of these tracks have not been on LP before.

JOHNNY SHINES
Excellent singer and guitarist. Originally from Tennessee, Johnny spent many years in the South performing with artists like Robert Johnson. He is the finest interpreter of Johnson's songs. Shines was equally fluent as a solo country bluesman or in the company of small blues bands. He is an immensely powerful vocalist and a fine guitar player, playing some especially exciting slide guitar.

Black and Blue 33.541 Nobody's Fault But Mine
Previously issued as Black and Blue 33.520, this set primarily features Johnny accompanying himself on the electric guitar (Luther Johnson plays second guitar on three tracks). Some powerful declamatory vocals and fine playing by Johnny.

ESSENTIAL SELECTION

Flyright 563 Johnny Shines and Robert Lockwood: Dust My Broom
CD issue: Flyright CD 10
Simply tremendous! The complete early 50s sessions for J.O.B. by these two great bluesmen (they do not perform together here). Some of these sides have been issued before, but three of the Shines cuts were only on a long-out-of-print P-Vine album. Four sides have never been issued before in any form, including Shines's tremendous reworking of Robert Johnson's "Terraplane Blues" that he calls "Fishtail" and that is a true postwar classic. CD has five additional tracks, with Lockwood accompanying Shines; sound is no better than LP.

Rounder 2020 Hey Ba-Ba-Re-Bop
Recorded live in 1974. An all-acoustic set focusing on old favorites. Sweet Home Chicago/Kind Hearted Woman/When Your Troubles Get Like Mine/Hey Ba-Ba-Re-Bop.

Rounder 2023 Robert Jr. Lockwood and Johnny Shines
Includes acoustic guitar duets and electric blues with Robert's band.

Rounder 2026 Mister Blues Is Back to Stay
With Robert Jr. Lockwood.

Testament 2212 The Johnny Shines Band
Fine 1966 album of Johnny with a Chicago band including Big Walter Horton (hca), Otis Spann (pno), Lee Jackson (b), and Fred Below (drm). A fine group of performances with Johnny in top form: powerful declamatory vocals and hard-edged electric guitar with some fine slide work. Rollin' and Tumblin'/Mr. Tom Green's Farm/What Kind of Little Girl Are You?/Sweet Home Chicago/Black Panther.

Testament 2217 Johnny Shines with Big Walter Horton
A fine selection of recordings drawn from two sessions: one in Chicago in 1966 with Otis Spann (pno), Lee Jackson (b), and Fred Below (drm), and one in LA in 1969 with Luther Allison (gtr), Prince Candy

(b), and Bill Brown (drm). All but one of the vocals are by Shines and most of the songs are Shines' originals. As always, Shines' vocals are outstanding and Horton plays some brilliant and innovative harp. The presence of a young Luther Allison on the LA sessions gives the music a slightly more contemporary feel but it is all down-home blues.

Testament 2221 Standing at the Crossroads
Reissue of excellent all-acoustic set originally issued in early 70s.

Tomato 269636-2 Too Wet to Plow
1975 recording with Louisiana Red and harpist Sugar Blue. Hot Tamale/Moanin' the Blues/30 Days in Jail.

Wolf 120.914 Recorded Live
This set was recorded live in St. Louis in 1974 and finds him in a rather restrained mood, playing acoustic guitar and singing a variety of mostly traditional blues songs. Most of the performances are rather lengthy and somewhat aimless. Johnny is rarely bad but this one is unexceptional.

COMPACT DISC

P-Vine PCD 2013 Johnny Shines
CD issue of the out-of-print LP Advent 2803 with one extra radio recording. Includes solo acoustic and electric tracks, and cuts with the Phillip Walker Blues Band.

J. D. SHORT
Excellent Mississippi bluesman who was based in St. Louis.

GNP Crescendo 10018-2 Legacy of the Blues, Vol. 8

Wolf 118 J. D. Short: 1930–33
Five superb country blues known to be by Short (recorded under a pseudonym) and four guitar accompaniments to other artists. Most of these recordings have been reissued before.

SILENT PARTNERS
Antones 0010 If It's All Night
High energy and totally forgettable blues-rock by a trio of musicians who have mostly worked as sidemen in various blues bands: Mel Brown (vcl, gtr, kybds), Russell Jackson (vcl, b), and Tony Coleman (vcl, drm), with various guest musicians and vocalists.

CLARENCE "GUITAR" SIMS
Eli Mile High 1001 Born to Sing the Blues

FRANKIE LEE SIMS
Excellent Texas country bluesman who recorded some fine rockin' blues in the 50s, many of which are reissued on Specialty. Some recently dis-

covered demos of Frankie recorded in New York in 1960 have been issued on Krazy Kat.

Krazy Kat 7428 Walkin' with Frankie
These recently rediscovered cuts are Sims' last recordings. He is accompanied by a small group—piano, bass, and drums—performing several remakes of his Ace and Specialty sides along with songs he had not recorded before. Frankie's singing is, as always, superb. His guitar is powerful and distinctive though his playing is, at times, rather sloppy.

Specialty 2124 (c) Lucy Mae Blues

BUDDY SKIPPER and THE CODE BLUES BAND
Buddy and his band, The Jetty Jumpers, were big in the Carolinas in the late 50s–early 60s. He is a white blues singer in the style of Big Joe Turner and Jimmy Rushing.

Gutter 001 Boogie the Joint
This comeback LP jumps just right, with Buddy backed by the two-man studio group Code Blues. Of the 10 tunes, three are different mixes of Sonny Burgess' "Red Headed Woman," plus Billy Emerson's "Shim Sham Shimmey," and Tabby Thomas' "Goin' To New Orleans."

FREDDIE SLACK
Oldie Blues OL 2829 Boogie Woogie
An excellent selection of boogie recorded between 1941–49. Slack is featured in a wide variety of band formats from quartets to 16-piece bands. Though there are some good instrumentalists featured, the spotlight is always on Slack's excellent piano playing. Most of the tunes are Slack originals and are instrumentals, though a few feature some expendable vocals by Don Raye.

"SLOPPY" HENRY
A fine and obscure singer from Georgia who recorded a diverse mixture of material, including straight blues, old ballads, and hokum songs.

Blues Documents 2063 Complete Recordings In Chronological Order, 1924–29
The eight songs on Side one feature him accompanied by the fine piano of Eddie Heywood. Some fine performances, but sound on most of these tracks is very noisy. Four of the remaining tracks feature the guitar of Peg Leg Howell with Eddie Anthony on violin on two tracks. The remaining four feature Henry with cornet and piano. Some good material, if a bit similar; Side one is for diehards only!

AL SMITH
O.B.C. 514 Hear My Blues
This is a reissue of the first Bluesville album (1001)

from 1959. Smith was originally a gospel singer and this is evident in his melismatic approach to the eight songs here, which include a version of "Night Time Is the Right Time," a couple of blues ballads originally made famous by Johnny Ace, and several originals. Al's singing is good, but the arrangements leave a lot to be desired; in spite of the presence of the fine tenor sax of Eddie "Lockjaw" Davis, most of the backing instrumentation focuses on the Hammond organ of Shirley Scott, producing a sound which, to my ears, is totally inappropriate to the blues.

BESSIE SMITH

One of the greatest female blues singers, Bessie was not called the "Empress of the Blues" for nothing! The best single album sampler of her recordings is the incredible BBC set that has a great selection of music and truly remarkable sound.

ESSENTIAL SELECTION

BBC REB 602 (c,d) **Great Original Performances, 1925–33**
A remarkable effort from the studio of Australian engineer Robert Parker, who has been doing an amazing job of restoring the sound of classic jazz and blues recordings and putting them into synthetic stereo. This album is a wonderful cross-section of sides by Bessie, including the two-part "Empty Bed Blues," the grim "Send Me To The 'Lectric Chair," the exuberant "Alexander's Ragtime Band," and the risque "You've Got To Give Me Some" (with lovely guitar by Eddie Lang). The sound is incredible, with a clarity and definition to the vocals and instruments that is not heard on any other reissue of Bessie's recordings. Preachin' The Blues/Trombone Cholly/Kitchen Man/He's Got Me Goin'/Devil's Gonna Git You/Baby Doll/Young Woman's Blues.

Biograph M-3 **Bessie Smith, Louis Armstrong, and Cab Calloway**
Featuring the soundtrack of her only movie, "St. Louis Blues."

Columbia CJ 44441 (c,d) **The Collection**
Selected recordings from 1923–33.
COMPACT DISC

Hermes 6003 **1925-33**
A wonderful collection of 20 tracks beautifully remastered for CD release; 63 minutes of classic blues. Foldout sheet with extensive notes and full discographical information. No duplications with BBC 602. Yellow Dog Blues/Careless Love Blues/I Ain't Gonna Play No Second Fiddle/Muddy Water/Lock and Key Blues/Nobody Knows You When You're Down and Out/Do Your Duty/Give Me A Pigfoot.

BYTHER "SMITTY" SMITH

Smitty is an expressive and emotional singer and plays tough, dirty guitar with elements of Otis Rush and Magic Slim, though Smitty is very much his own man.

Razor 5105 **Housefire**
What a welcome and pleasant surprise. This album was originally issued a few years ago as a limited edition on the Japanese Mina label and has been unavailable for far too long. Razor is to be commended for acquiring the tapes and finally issuing it in this country. Byther is accompanied by a solid band, including a couple of fine horn players. The songs are mostly originals and include the slow, intense opener "Live On and Sing the Blues," the hypnotically rhythmic "Wait and See" (a song about suicide), and the unusual "Here I Am" with its coupling of sacred and secular images. But it is all good and most definitely recommended.

Red Lightnin' 0061 **Tell Me How You Like It**
Reissue of excellent Chicago blues LP originally issued on the Grits label. Accompanied by a solid, if not particularly imaginative, rhythm section, he performs some original songs plus a couple of Willie Dixon compositions, a Junior Wells tune, a B. B. King song, and a couple of others. I particulary like his minor key "I Don't Like To Travel." If you didn't

get this album the first time around, you should check it out this time. You won't be disappointed.

COMPACT DISC

JSP CD 232 Addressing the Nation with the Blues

A better-than-average contemporary blues offering from JSP. Blyther is accompanied on these 11 songs (mostly originals) by his regular band. The sound is a little low-key, but otherwise this is an enjoyable set.

CLARA SMITH

Document 566 Complete Recorded Works in Chronological Order, Vol. 1

The first of several LPs reissuing the entire recorded output of this popular 20s and early 30s singer. This volume features 18 sides recorded between June 1923 and January 1924 and they are among her least interesting takes. Although she was a powerful and expressive singer and some of the songs are good, most of the recordings feature the ponderous and lifeless piano playing of Fletcher Henderson. A couple of the tracks are of interest because they are duets with the great Bessie Smith, but these are also rather draggy. Things pick up with her January 1924 session when she is accompanied by a small jazz group. Good sound quality.

Document 567 Vol. 2
Eighteen tracks from 1924.

Document 568 Vol. 3
Eighteen tracks from 1924–25.

Document 569 Vol. 4
Eighteen tracks from 1925–26.

Document 570 Vol. 5
Eighteen tracks from 1926–28.

Document 571 Vol. 6
Eighteen tracks from 1928–30.

Document 572 Vol. 7
Seventeen tracks from 1930–32, including four duets with Lonnie Johnson.

CLARENCE "PINE TOP" SMITH

Oldie Blues 2831 Clarence "Pine Top" Smith/Romeo Nelson—Their Complete Recordings

Features all known recordings by these two superb piano players: eleven tracks by the brilliant and influential Smith, including several alternate takes, and four by Nelson. There are two takes of Smith's classic "Pinetop's Boogie Woogie," two very different takes of "Pinetop's Blues," and two takes of "Jump Steady Blues." Smith was a brilliant singer and piano player and, although his tracks have been reissued many times before, it is good to have them all together. Nelson was another outstanding per-

former whose handful of recordings have been reissued before, but, again, it's good to have all these tracks together, though his version of "Midnight Special" is probably the weakest cut on the album. Good sound and informative notes by Martin Van Olderen.

GEORGE SMITH

Excellent West Coast singer/harmonica player who recorded on and off from the 50s until his death in 1983. He was particularly adept at playing the chromatic harmonica, an instrument not often favored by blues harmonica players.

Ace CH 60 Oopin' Doopin' Doopin'

This album reissues all the sides he recorded for the R.P.M. label in 1955–56, including two previously unissued sides. Some excellent material; accompaniment ranges from just small rhythm sections to West Coast-style small bands with horns.

Crosscut 1015 ...of the Blues

Reissue of Bluesway 6029 from 1973. This album finds this fine singer and brilliant harmonica player in good form on a selection of five vocals and four instrumentals. Most tracks feature George with a small band, with Marshall Hooks or Arthur Wright playing some nice guitar. On a few tracks, he is joined on harmonica by his student Rod Piazza, who also takes an expendable vocal on "Help Me." George's vocals include a version of "Got My Mojo Working" and the soulful "If You Were a Rabbit," while the instrumentals include the splendid "Juicy Harmonica" and bluesy versions of "Hawaiian Eye" and "Ode to Billy Joe."

J. T. "FUNNY PAPA" SMITH

Popular and influential Texas country bluesman who was the first to use the sobriquet Howling Wolf.

Yazoo 1031 The Original Howling Wolf

MAMIE SMITH

Document 551 Complete Recorded Works in Chronological Order, Vol. 1

The first of five volumes featuring all of the recordings by this popular prewar artist. She is generally credited with having made the first commercial blues recording, "Crazy Blues," which is one of 20 songs on this album recorded between February 1920 and February 1921. The album starts with her very first recording "That Thing Called Love" which is quite bluesy in its own right. She is featured with various jazz-flavored groups, most featuring the cornet of Johnny Dunn and many with the soaring trombone of the delightfully named Dope Andrews. Included are several instrumental cuts. Although not as interesting as some of the singers to follow her lead, Mamie was certainly quite engaging; however, these recordings are not for the casual listener, as they were recorded in the acoustic era. The Document label does not have access to techniques that compensate for this, so it often sounds like you are listening to the music through the telephone! Still, there is some most worthwhile music here.

Document 552 Complete Recordings in Chronological Order, Vol. 2
Features 20 songs recorded at nine different sessions in 1921. The recordings feature her with a small jazz band, mostly of unknown and unmemorable musicians. A lot of the songs would be considered "vaudeville" rather than blues. The last three tracks feature her with a band including Bubber Miley, Coleman Hawkins, and Leroy Parker.

Document 553 Vol. 3
Document 554 Vol. 4
Document 555 Vol. 5

TAB SMITH and HIS ORCHESTRA
Talmadge Smith, unlike most swing sax players, could play alto and tenor with much proficiency. He could sing well and blow (usually buried in echo-chamber effects) the most mellow alto ever on wax.

Saxophonograph BP 503 I Don't Want to Play in the Kitchen
These sides were made after he left the Lucky Millinder band, when he was strongly influenced by Coleman Hawkins. The excellent "All Night Long"—with Tab's first featured vocalist, Trevor Bacon—is included. Bacon was replaced by Robbie Kirk, who sings on two numbers. Much of this jump material predates his echo-ballad work that culminated in the haunting "Echo Blues" from a 1949 session. Other featured vocalists are Frank Galbreath, Ray King, and Betty Mays.

TRIXIE SMITH
Blues Documents 2068 1922–29

SMOKEY BABE
Excellent Louisiana country blues singer and guitarist. Originally from Itta Bena, MS, Smokey Babe (Robert Brown) settled in Scottlandville, LA. At times his style is a little reminiscent of his neighbor, Robert Pete Williams, but without Williams' anarchic approach. Babe is a wonderful vocalist with a deep, expressive voice and is an intensely rhythmic guitarist. His material includes traditional items like "Now Your Man Done Gone" and "Something Went Wrong With My Machine," as well as more personal items.

Ace CH 261 Hottest Brand Goin'
This is a reissue of Bluesville 1063 originally issued in 1963 from recordings made in 1961 by folklorist Harry Oster. "Hottest Brand Goin'" is a marvelous performance in which he expresses his feelings about the gas station where he works. "I'm Goin' Back To Mississippi" voices his nostalgia about his birthplace. On a couple of tracks, he is joined by Clyde Causey or Henry Thomas on harmonica. Excellent all round.

Arhoolie 2019 Hot Blues
Originally issued as Folklyric 118, these fine sides feature Smokey with occasional accompaniment by Henry Thomas or Clyde Causey (hca) and occasional vocals by William Dotson or Sally Dotson. Splendid stuff.

OTIS "SMOKEY" SMOTHERS
Red Beans 009 Got My Eyes on You
Unexceptional 1986 recordings by Chicago singer/ guitarist.

KING SOLOMON
Diving Duck DD 4303 Non Support Blues
Sixteen sides recorded in the 60s and early 70s by this West Coast singer. Mostly original songs recorded with various groups. Solomon is a good singer with a strong gospel flavor. Includes his hit "Non Support Blues." Little Dab Will Do It/Please Mr. President/Big Things/Separation.

SONS OF BLUES
One of the younger generation of Chicago blues bands that attempts to fuse down-home blues with more contemporary R&B and soul sounds. The group has undergone several changes over the years but has included guitarist Lurrie Bell, harmonica player Billy Branch, and guitarist Elisha Murray.

L+R 42.053 Live Recorded
1982 German live recordings. OK vocals but the rhythm section is very stodgy.

Red Beans 004 Where's My Money?
Includes two excellent cuts with veteran singer/ piano player Jimmy Walker that are firmly in the 50s vein and sound more coherent. There is some fine harmonica playing on the album by Billy Branch, but the songs and arrangements lack excitement.

SONS OF BLUES/CHI-TOWN HUSTLERS
Blue Phoenix 33.728 Romancing The Blue Stone
Contemporary Chicago blues featuring Billy Branch (hca), J. W. Williams (b), Carlton Weathersby (gtr), and Mose Rutues (drm), with Francois

Rilhac (pno) and Buster Benton guesting on vocals and guitar on the unexceptional "In the Ghetto." The songs are mixture of old favorites and originals. Most of the band members take vocals; I particularly like the singing of Williams, who turns in a fine version of the much-recorded "As The Years Go Passing By." Branch plays some fine harp, though it could have used some added amplification.

CHARLIE SPAND
Superb and influential Detroit-based piano player.

Blues Documents 2035 (1929-40) The Remaining Titles
Well-served on an out-of-print Magpie reissue, Spand's remaining output is reissued with no loss of musical quality, even if Blues Document's sound quality doesn't measure up to the standard set by Magpie. Side one, which includes a particularly rare Paramount test, was recorded in 1929-30, while Side two jumps to 1940, with guitar accompaniment by Little Son Joe and Bill Broonzy, and is up to the same fine musical standard, if lacking some of the loose, ragtimey feel so important to Spand's earlier efforts.

OTIS SPANN
Simply magnificent singer and piano player who was a member of the Muddy Waters band for many years.

Black Cat 001 Half Ain't Been Told
Superb album recorded in 1964 in England with Muddy Waters (gtr), Ransom Knowling (b), and Willie Smith (drm). Twelve of the cuts were originally issued on a long out-of-print Decca album, one track was only available on a 45, and one on an Ace Of Clubs album. Spann and the band are in fine form.

London (UK) 810 177-2 Cracked Spanner Head
Ten tracks from 1964 and four from 1967 recorded in England. Although most of the tracks were recorded with the Muddy Waters band, including the master himself on guitar, London has decided to use versions which had been overdubbed with such blues "giants" as Eric Clapton, Jimmy Page, and other utterly boring English musicians. I'm sure this will help sell this disc, and I'm sure the added musicians had the best intentions, but the result does no credit to Spann or to them. On the few places where the accompaniments don't overwhelm, one can hear some beautiful singing and playing by Spann but, alas, those moments are too infrequent.

Prestige 7719 The Blues Never Die
Excellent sides with James Cotton and the Muddy Waters Blues Band.

Storyville 4041 Good Morning Mr. Blues
Beautiful solo recordings made in Denmark in 1963. Lonnie Johnson adds some tasteful guitar licks on one cut. Riverside Blues/Jelly Roll Bake/Worried Life Blues/Spann's Boogie/Goin' Down Slow.

ESSENTIAL SELECTION :

Testament 2211 Otis Spann's Chicago Blues
One of his best, featuring 14 superb recordings cut in 1965. Eight of the cuts feature Otis and piano only, one cut adds a drummer, and five cuts feature an excellent small group with Johnny Young (gtr) and James Cotton (hca). All aspects of Spann's great talent are presented on this album.

COMPACT DISC

Candid CD 9001 Otis Spann is The Blues
Classic 1960 recordings with Robert Jr. Lockwood.

Candid CD 9025 Walking the Blues

THE SPARKS BROTHERS
Blues Documents 2054 Complete Recordings in Chronological Order, 1932–35
A beautiful collection of piano blues featuring the St. Louis duo Milton "Lindberg" Sparks (vcl) and Aaron "Pinetop" Sparks (pno). In addition to recordings under their own name, it also includes accompaniments to Tecumsah McDowell and Charlie McFadden, plus two by Milton with an unknown small group and four vocal sides by Aaron, with Henry Townsend on guitar, including possibly the earliest version of "Every Day I Have the Blues." The performances are consistently fine. Milton was a fine and expressive singer and Aaron's playing is fluid and imaginative. Many of these tracks have been out before, but this LP brings them all together in one place. Highly recommended.

SPECKLED RED
Raucous blues singer and barrelhouse piano player from Georgia. He was the brother of Piano Red (q.v.).

Wolf 113 Speckled Red
Features all 18 sides recorded by him between 1929–38. His early sides from 1929–30 are solo recordings, while his 1938 cuts feature accompaniments by Robert Lee McCoy (Robert Nighthawk, gtr) and Willie Hatcher (mdln). Unfortunately these accompaniments tend to make Red's rather loose style somewhat rigid. About one-third of these cuts have been reissued before.

VICTORIA SPIVEY
Document 590 1926-31
This is a truly marvelous collection. Victoria Spivey's prolific activities in the 60s and 70s somewhat overshadowed her earlier recording career in

the 20s and 30s but, as this album makes clear, she was one of the greatest of all female singers to record in this period. Her powerful and clear voice had a spine-tingling intensity that can't fail to move you. Most of the tracks feature piano accompaniment (usually John Erby, Porter Grainger, or Clarence Williams), and many feature the guitar of her long-time partner, Lonnie Johnson. On a couple of tracks, she is accompanied by The Clarence Williams Blue Five with King Oliver and Eddie Lang. The songs, quite a few of them risque, are also exceptional. Very few of these tracks have been reissued before and sound is generally excellent. Highly recommended. Black Snake Blues/Steady Grind/No. 12 Let Me Roam/Garter Snake Blues/Blood Thirsty Blues/Your Worries Ain't Like Mine/My Handy Man.

WILD JIMMY SPRUILL

Brilliant New York guitarist best known for his accompaniments on Wilbert Harrison's "Kansas City" and Buster Brown's "Fannie Mae." He had a distinctive style, often concentrating on treble notes with use of much tremolo.

Krazy Kat 7429 **The Hard Grind Bluesman**
An excellent tribute to one of the great unknowns of New York blues. Features seven instrumentals issued under his own name, including the magnificent "Hard Grind," along with accompaniments to Buster Brown and His Rockin' McVouts, Charles Walker, Wilbert Harrison, and Noble "Thin Man" Watts (on his classic "Hard Times").

HOUSTON STACKHOUSE

Wolf 120 779 **Houston Stackhouse, 1910–1980**
Although he was an important figure in the postwar Mississippi blues scene, most of Stackhouse's recordings do not live up to his reputation. This album is no exception. Eleven of the 14 sides were recorded in 1967 with Carey Mason helping on vocals and/or guitar, and three were recorded in Austria in 1976, with accompaniments by an Austrian bass player and drummer. Most of the songs are overly familiar Mississippi/Chicago songs given turgid treatments. The high point is the track "Travelling Blues," on which he is joined by Tommy Johnson's brother, Mager.

THE STATE STREET SWINGERS

Blues Documents 2047 **And The Chicago Black Swans**
The State Street Swingers (who recorded two tracks as The Chicago Black Swans) were a fine, jazzy, bluesy, hokum group featuring the vocals of Washboard Sam, Bob Robinson, Mary Mack, or Big Bill Broonzy, with trumpet by Herb Morand, clarinet by Arnett Nelson, and piano by the superb Black Bob

or Myrtle Jenkins, and various other musicians on bass and guitar. Their music covers the same territory as The Harlem Hamfats, but I think this group had more interesting vocals and more imaginative musicianship. Very little of this has been reissued before and sound quality is generally good. Some exhilarating material here.

ARBEE STIDHAM

Rather unexciting urban blues singer who was quite popular in the late 40s and early 50s. He has a very unusual voice, very deep, with a lot of vibrato, that tends to be rather monotonous in large doses.

Crown Prince IG 404 **My Heart Belongs to You**
Features 16 recordings cut between 1947–57. There are some good songs and some good band accompaniments, but many will find Arbee's voice an acquired taste.

FRANK STOKES

Superb Memphis country blues singer and guitarist with a nod toward minstrels. His twin guitar work with Dan Sane (performing as The Beale Street Sheiks) is simply stunning, and sometimes the fine fiddle of Will Batts was added to their recordings for good measure. The Yazoo LP is essential for the choice of material and sound quality.

Matchbox 1002 **The Remaining Titles**
Twenty songs recorded between 1927–29, representing all the sides (except for two that have never been found) that are not on Yazoo 1056 or the out-of-print Biograph 12041. However, almost all of these performances were available on Roots a while back, so, if you have all the Roots albums, this album is not essential. Sound quality is variable, due to the age of the original 78s.

Yazoo 1056 **Creator of the Memphis Blues**
Classic sides.

STOVEPIPE NO. 1 and DAVID CROCKETT

Blues Documents 2019 **Complete Recordings in Chronological Order**

So tell me: How many stovepipe players have you heard? None? Well, have I got a record for you. Stovepipe No. 1 (real name: Sam Jones) sang, played guitar, harmonica and, yes, stovepipe. The stovepipe sounds a little bit like a tuba, a little bit like a jug and, er, a little bit like a stovepipe. This set features 16 tracks recorded between 1924–30 by Jones and singer/guitarist David Crockett (honest!), including six tracks by King David's Jug Band, which is actually a stovepipe band with mandolin. The 1924 tracks are mostly preblues traditional pieces like "Lonesome John" and "Fisher's Hornpipe," and, being taken from rare and worn acoustically recorded 78s, are a bit tough to listen to. The 1927 and 1930 recordings are mixture of blues and hokum material. Fascinating if not essential listening.

NOLAN STRUCK

Ichiban 1045 **Hard Working Man**

Another from the Ichiban assembly line, produced by Gary B. B. Coleman. Struck is a decent singer doing a mixture of originals and covers with nice but predictable arrangements.

HUBERT SUMLIN

Superb blues guitarist best known for his magnificent accompaniments to Howlin' Wolf. His own recordings are unexceptional.

Black and Blue 33.548 **My Guitar and Me**

1975 session (previously available as 33.511) with Lonnie Brooks, Willie Mabon, Dave Myers, and Fred Below.

Black Top 1036 (c,d) **Hubert Sumlin's Blues Party**

His best LP to date, though the magic he showed on his accompaniments to Howlin' Wolf seems to be gone for good. This LP has good arrangements, with some nice horn work and fine vocals by Mighty Sam McCain. Hubert's own vocals are pleasant, if unexceptional, and Ronnie Earl's vocals are expendable.

Black Top 1053 **Healing Feeling**

Blind Pig 3389 **Heart and Soul**

CD issue: Blind Pig 73389

With James Cotton and Little Mike and The Tornadoes.

L+R 42.008 **Hubert Sumlin and Carey Bell**

Hubert plays acoustic guitar on most tracks.

Vogue 512 503 **Funky Roots**

Originally issued as Vogue 30.285.

SUNNYLAND SLIM

Fine Mississippi-born, Chicago-based blues singer/piano player who has recorded quite prolifically under his own name as well as a sideman on hundreds of recordings. Most of his recordings are worth a listen, particularly the ones from the 50s.

Black and Blue 33.743 **Travelin'**

Recorded in France in 1974 with Slim in fine form. It includes original pieces like "Miss Bessie Mae," "I Make Love," and "Travelin'," and old favorites like "Throw This Old Dog A Bone," "Goin' Down Slow," and "One Room Country Shack."

Earwig 4915 **Be Careful How You Vote**

Collection of sides originally recorded in the late 70s and early 80s for Slim's own Airway label. In addition to Slim's fine singing and piano playing, he is joined by musicians like Hubert Sumlin, Robert Stroger, Eddie Taylor, Sam Buchardt, and Magic Slim. Unfortunately, Slim plays organ on many cuts, and he is much less effective on this instrument.

Flyright 566 **Sunnyland Slim**

Fifteen great sides recorded between 1951–55 for J.O.B., featuring sidemen J. B. Lenoir, Johnny Shines, and Robert Jr. Lockwood. Includes one previously unissued instrumental by Snooky Pryor.

GNP 10021 **Legacy of the Blues, Vol. 11**

Solo performances.

L|R 42.015 **Decoration Day**

1980 recordings with Hubert Sumlin, Jeff Swan, and Carey Bell.

Prestige 7723 **Slim's Shout**

With King Curtis.

Red Beans 002 **Sunnyland Train**

January 1983 recording of Sunnyland accompanied by his piano only. Sometimes I Worry/All My Life/ Unlucky One/Worried About My Baby.

Red Beans 007 **Chicago Jump**

Storyville 4043 **Sad and Lonesome Blues**

1973 recordings with Swedish band.

SUNNYLAND SLIM/DR. CLAYTON

Blues Documents 2062 **Dr. Clayton and His Buddy**

Eleven tracks by the distinctive Dr. Clayton and eight by his protege Sunnyland Slim. A few previously on LP.

SUNNYLAND SLIM/J. B. LENOIR

COMPACT DISC

P-Vine PCD 2164 **Original J.O.B./Cobra Recordings**

SUNNYLAND SLIM/LITTLE BROTHER

COMPACT DISC

Southland SCD 10 **Chicago Blues Session**

Originally issued on the English 77 label and more recently available as a limited-edition reissue on the Redita label, this is an enjoyable informal session featuring two blues piano giants produced by Paul Oliver. Also featured on many of the tracks are Corky Robertson (b) and legendary Chicago drummer Jump Jackson. This CD reissue adds four previously unissued sides from the session. Although the quality of these home recordings is unexceptional, there are some fine performances of their most popular songs. Sunnyland does 10 numbers, Little Brother does six. One Room Country Shack/Brownskin Woman/Devil Is A Busy Man/Everytime I Get to Drinkin'/Trembling Blues/I Keep On Drinkin'/Farrish Street Jive/Cow Cow Blues/Pinetop's Boogie Woogie.

ROOSEVELT SYKES

Great blues singer and piano player (nicknamed "The Honeydripper") who was in fine form right up to his death in 1983 after 50 years of recordings! Most of his albums are worthwhile, though there is some repetition of songs among them. His Yazoo and Matchbox albums feature his earliest recordings, while the Oldie Blues, Blues Documents, Bluetime, and Best Of Blues feature 30s and 40s recordings, often with small bands; all are particularly fine. Some of his outstanding 50s recordings are available on Delmark 642. His later 60s and 70s recordings are generally worthwhile, with Delmark 607 being particularly good.

Best Of Blues BOB 3 **1929–1942**

An excellent collection. Here we have a whistle-stop tour through his prewar career from his answer to "Pinetop's Boogie Woogie" called "Boot That Thing," on through some fine 30s sides in the company of Kokomo Arnold and others, to his slicker, jumpy 40s output—a sound that in part paved the way for postwar R&B. Sound quality varies a little but is generally acceptable, full discographical information is provided, and the packaging is sturdy.

Blind Pig 005 **The Original Honeydripper**

ESSENTIAL SELECTION

Blues Documents 2013 **The Honeydripper, 1929–41**

An excellent cross-section of recordings. Many of these tracks have been reissued before and some are still available, though this does have some tracks that

have never been reissued or are on long-out-of-print LPs. Includes a wonderful jazzy duet with violinist Artie Mosby on "Mosby Stomp," the powerful "Soft and Mellow," and his theme song, "The Honeydripper," with great slide guitar by Kokomo Arnold. A bit of a frustrating issue for the long-time collector but consistently fine music.

Blues Documents 2088 **Vol. 2, 1936–51**

Most of the recordings are from the 1936–41 period, plus two rare tracks from 1951, where Sykes accompanies Grace Brim.

Bluetime 2008 **Dirty Mother for You**

Fourteen great sides recorded between 1936–42. About half of these have been on LP before, though only a few are currently available. Some great music, but sound quality on several tracks is poor.

Bluetime 2018 **Get Your Row Out**

An excellent collection of tracks recorded between 1936–41. Includes a couple of songs that have become blues standards ("Night Time Is the Right Time" and "Driving Wheel"), plus several of his witty risque titles ("My Baby's Playground," "Bread Pan," and "Jet Black Snake," the latter with lovely slide guitar by Kokomo Arnold). The great Sid Catlett urges Sykes along on a couple of lively jive pieces ("Doin' the Sally Long" and "47th Street Jive"), which have a Fats Waller feel to them. Some of the tracks have been on LP before but most are new to microgroove.

Delmark 607 **Hard Driving Blues**

Mostly solo sides though a couple feature Homesick James on bass or guitar.

Delmark 616 **In Europe**

Delmark 632 **Feel Like Blowing My Horn**

1973 sides with small band including "Sax" Mallard (ten sax, clr) and Robert Jr. Lockwood (gtr).

Delmark 642 **Raining in My Heart**

A great collection of urban blues recorded by Sykes with various sidemen for Chicago's United label between 1951–53. These tracks were issued a few years ago on the Japanese P-Vine label. Accompanying Sykes' piano and expressive vocals are sidemen like Robert "Sax" Crowder (ten sax), "Sax" Mallard (alto sax), John "Schoolboy" Porter (gtr), J. T. Brown (ten sax), and "Big" Crawford (b). Seven of the tracks feature some very effective blues violin by Remo Biondi. Five tracks were not originally issued on singles. Good sound, full discographical information, good notes by Tad Jones, but ridiculous cover art.

Document 526 **At Webster College**

This album features this great piano bluesman recorded live at Webster College in St. Louis in

1974. Roosevelt was in fine form on a selection of his old favorites. In addition to the fine singing and playing, there are charming and interesting introductions to the songs by Roosevelt. Sound is generally good. 44 Blues/Night Time Is the Right Time/Driving Wheel/Goin' Down Slow/St. James Infirmary Blues/On the Sunny Side of the Street.

Fantasy 24717 Urban Blues
Double album, one by Little Brother Montgomery.

Matchbox 1011 Mostly New to LP
This excellent collection features 18 tracks recorded between 1929–34. There are five superb vocals by Sykes himself, and the rest of the album features him accompanying other artists. In many cases, his playing is much more interesting than the vocalists, particularly on the cuts with Isabel Sykes, Clarence Harris, and Johnnie Strauss. Charlie McFadden is a splendid singer and Roosevelt trots out some of his best playing on the four tracks by him. Carl Rafferty is also excellent, and his track, "Mr. Carl's Blues," is one of the first to feature the line "I believe I'll dust my broom." Generally good sound and informative notes by Paul Oliver.

Oldie Blues 2818 Boogie Honky Tonk
Great sides with small groups, 1944–47.

Prestige 7722 The Honeydripper

Southland SLP 2 Dirty Mother for You

Yazoo 1033 The Country Blues Piano Ace
Classic early sides, 1929–32, some with great guitar accompaniments by Clifford Gibson.

COMPACT DISC

EPM Musique FDC 5514 Music Is My Business
Sixteen sides recorded in New York in 1977. The nine tracks of Sykes alone find him in top form. There are also six tracks with an "unknown" guitarist, and one with an "unknown" singer. In both cases, I am sure the performer in question is Louisiana Red, whose contribution to the proceedings seems inappropriate. There is also one track without Sykes at all (!) which features vocals and

guitar by Johnny Shines with Red and an unknown harmonica player; an excellent performance. Sound quality is excellent.

T-LOU and HIS LOS ANGELES ZYDECO BAND
Maison De Soul 1014 T-Lou and His Los Angeles Zydeco Band
West Coast Zydeco from a Los Angeles band led by T-Lou from Grand Coteau, Louisiana. T-Lou is a decent singer and accordion player and the band provides competent backup, though occasionally guitarist Craig Printup gets into some inappropriate blues-rock excesses. Mostly original songs. Nothing special here but some OK singing and playing.

T. V. SLIM
Slim was a fascinating artist who recorded a wide variety of styles of blues: acoustic boogies, down-home small-band stylings, and novelty songs, mostly for his own label, Speed.

Moonshine 101 Flat Foot Sam
Thirteen sides recorded mostly in the early 60s, including the classic and hilarious "Don't Reach Cross My Plate."

BLIND JOE TAGGART
Wolf WSE 122 The Remaining Titles

TALLAHASEE TIGHT/BUDDY MOSS
Blues Documents 2092 Country Blues from the Eastern States
An excellent collection of blues from the Southeast. Side One features all of the blues recordings of Tallahassee Tight, aka Louis Washington (his four gospel recordings have not shown up). Apart from the fact that he was probably the only active Florida bluesman to record, little is know about him. He is a solid if not exceptional singer and guitarist in the East Coast tradition, with a number of interesting songs about his home state ("Quincy Wimmens" and "Tallahasee Women"). By contrast, Buddy Moss, who is represented by ten songs, is much more familiar and is truly one of the greats of East Coast blues. His warm vocal style and lyrical guitar technique are used to great effect on these recordings, most of which have not been reissued before. A most worthwhile release.

TAMPA RED
Fine and influential singer and guitarist particularly noted for his single-string slide playing. He recorded both as a solo artist and as an accompanist to many other blues singers. His records were consistently good, though some of his late

30s Bluebirds lack variety, and some feature too much of his kazoo playing.

Best of Blues BOB 15 **1928–46**
Twenty sides including tracks under his own name and accompaniments to Foster and Harris, Madilyn Davis, Jenny Pope, and the Gospel Camp Meeting Singers. About one-third of these tracks have been reissued before, mostly on out-of-print collections.

ESSENTIAL SELECTION

Blues Classics 25 **The Guitar Wizard**
Good cross-section of his recordings covering the period 1935–53. With Blind John Davis, Big Maceo, Ransom Knowling, and Sonny Boy Williamson.

Blues Documents 2001 **It's Tight Like That**
Eighteen tracks recorded between 1928–42, mostly from 1928–31. Most of these tracks have not been issued before. In addition to tracks under his own name, accompaniments to Papa Too Sweet, Mary Johnson, and Sweet Papa Tadpole (!) are included, along with a bizarre trio with Georgia Tom and Frankie Jaxon.

Blues Documents 2086 **Vol. 2, 1929–30**
Excellent collection of early Tampa Red sides, mostly with Georgia Tom Dorsey on piano. There are vocal duets on some of the hokum numbers, which include the third version of their big hit "It's Tight Like That." There's a lot of Red's fine slide guitar and a welcome absence of the kazoo that intruded on many of his later recordings. Unfortunately, many of these tracks are from rare and worn 78s, so sound on quite a few tracks is pretty noisy. Very few of these have been reissued before.

Old Tramp OT 1201 **The Guitar Wizard**
Eighteen tracks recorded between 1935–42. Tampa is heard here in various settings. Some tracks feature him with piano and bass accompaniment only, others feature him with a small hokum-flavored group, and on two tracks Tampa plays piano with guitar by Willie B. James. The selection of material is good though there are no particularly outstanding tracks. Sound is satisfactory.

Oldie Blues 2816 **You Can't Get That Stuff No More**
Late 30s/early 40s recrdings.

Oldie Blues 8001 **Crazy with the Blues**
Sixteen sides recorded between 1929–49—from his early duets with Georgia Tom Dorsey to cuts with a full Chicago band, including Johnnie Jones and Ransom Knowling. No duplications with other reissues.

O.B.C. 516 (c) **Don't Tampa with the Blues**
Reissue of Bluesville 1030 from 1960. Tampa has an impresssive recorded legacy, but this is not part of it. Tampa sounds past his prime, singing with little fervor and playing some rather sloppy electric guitar. Most of the songs are remakes of old recordings he had previously done many times in better versions. To make matters worse, we now get to hear his wretched kazoo in hi-fi! If you really want to sample just how good Tampa could be, try one of the many reissues of 20s, 30s, and 40s material around.

Wolf WBJ 001 **Keep Jumping**
There's no shortage of Tampa Red reissues around, and here's another one covering a diversity of sides recorded between 1934–52. Side one features tracks mostly from 1934–47, featuring Tampa in various settings with musicians like Blind John Davis, Ransom Knowling, "Sax" Mallard, "Big" Crawford, "Judge" Riley, and Bob Call, and is fairly typical stuff. Side two, featuring tracks recorded between 1950–52, is generally more interesting, featuring the wonderful piano and occasional second vocal of the magnificent Johnny Jones, plus the solid rhythm of Ransom Knowling and Odie Payne.

Yazoo 1039 **Bottleneck Guitar**
Mostly early sides from 1928–37, including recordings with Frankie Jaxon, Georgia Tom, Ma Rainey, and Madilyn Davis. Great stuff!

TAMPA RED/BIG MACEO
Swingtime BT 2014 **Get It Cats!**
Sixteen blues numbers recorded in Chicago, 1941–46. Tampa Red was already a well-established star in the windy city when he teamed up with Big Maceo and his cathouse piano. Unfortunately, acclaim came too late for Maceo, who was crippled by a stroke shortly after the last of these sessions. Although most of Big Maceo's life was spent in obscurity, we should be thankful for these inspired duets. Let Me Play with Your Poodle/She's Love Crazy/Don't Jive Me Mama/She Want to Sell My Monkey.

FRANK TANNEHILL
Blues Documents 2027 Complete Recordings in Chronological Order
Fourteen tracks recorded between 1932–41 by this excellent singer/piano player, most not on LP before.

TARHEEL SLIM (ALLEN BUNN)
Krazy Kat 7430 Wildcat Tamer, 1951–62
Sixteen rare gems from four facets of Slim's long and varied musical career. Two cuts with the vocal group The Larks are featured here: "My Kinda Woman" and "Little Side Car." Side one also includes four very fine earthy blues numbers, "Guy With the 45"—recorded in 1952 with fine harp by Sonny Terry—"My Flight," "I'm Gonna Throw You Out," and the superb "Too Much Competition," recorded for Red Robin in 1953. Side two starts out with his classic 1959 recordings of the rockin', stompin' "Wildcat Tamer" and the all-time classic "Number 9 Train." In 1957 Bunn met his future wife, and they started recording as Tarheel Slim and Little Ann. Eight sides by the duo are here, including their 1957 recording of "Don't Ever Leave Me," the flip of their big hit "It's Too Late," along with seven other tracks recorded between 1957–62.

EDDIE TAYLOR
Brilliant Chicago singer/guitarist whose distinctive vocal and instrumental style contained elements of the music he learned as a young man growing up in Mississippi. His 50s recordings for Vee Jay are true Chicago blues classics. He also accompanied Jimmy Reed on most of his Vee Jay recordings and added his distinctive and effective guitar licks to many other artists' recordings. His later recordings do not always do justice to his talents. His death on Christmas day, 1985, closed another significant chapter in the history of the blues.

Antones 005 Still Not Ready for Eddie
CD issue: Line CD 9.00452
Eddie Taylor, who died on Christmas Day, 1985, was a great performer who never quite had the fame he deserved. He was a splendid singer and guitar player who was able to reach back to the music he heard when he was growing up in the 20s and 30s and give it a contemporary sensibility. This fine set was recorded at Antones in Austin, TX, with an all-star band including Luther Tucker (gtr), Sunnyland Slim (pno), and Snooky Pryor (hca), plus guest appearances on guitar by Hubert Sumlin and Jimmy Rogers. The material is mostly songs that Eddie had recorded before—"Bad Boy," "Clouds in My Heart," "Sittin' Here Thinkin'," "Look on Yonders Wall," and "Boogaloo Farm"—all performed in fine style. Includes an insert sheet with some photos of Eddie and touching liner notes by Paul Ray, plus a poem dedicated to Eddie by Clifford Antone.

L+R 42.009 My Heart Is Bleeding
1979 recordings with Carey Bell (hca) and Sunnyland Slim (pno).

Wolf 120.711 I Found Out
1983 album. Eddie is in fine form vocally and instrumently on a mixture of familiar and new material. However, his backing group is stodgy and overpowering and the recorded sound is thin and lacks punch. On a few cuts, Eddie plays some nice acoustic guitar but his playing is almost drowned out by the mediocre drumming of his son Larry.

COMPACT DISC
P-Vine PCD 2102 I Feel So Bad
CD issue of the out-of-print LP Advent 2802 with extra tracks.

P-Vine PCD 2159 Live in Japan, 1977
Available some years ago with fewer tracks, this December 1977 recording features accompanists Louis Myers, Bob Myers, and Odie Payne, Jr. There are 10 vocals by Eddie, two by Louis Myers, and one by Payne. Hoy Hoy/Bad Boy/There'll Be A Day/Blow Wind Blow/Kind Hearted Woman/Tin Pan Alley/Baby Please Don't Go/I Don't Know.

EDDIE TAYLOR/JIMMY REED
COMPACT DISC
ESSENTIAL SELECTION
Charly CD 171 Ride 'em on Down
A terrific collection of 24 tracks, 12 by Eddie Taylor and 12 by his long-time associate Jimmy Reed. Many of the tracks here feature them playing on each other's recordings. Reed's tracks, recorded between 1953–64, include his magnificent first recording "High and Lonesome," plus "I'm Gonna Ruin You," "Honey Don't Let Me Go," "My Bitter Seed," and "A String to Your Heart." Taylor's contributions include such classics as "Bad Boy," "Ride 'em on Down," and "Big Town Playboy." In addition to these are such fine performances as "You'll Always Have Home," "I'm Gonna Love You," "Stroll Out West," and "I'm Sitting Here." All the tracks here have been available on Charly LPs, but it is great to have them on CD, even if Charly's remastering is not exactly state of the art. Essential!

EVA TAYLOR
Retrieval FJ 121 Eva Taylor and Clarence Williams
Seventeen sides recorded in 1925 and 1926, most featuring the vocals of Eva Taylor with accompani-

ments by various groups led by her then-husband Clarence Williams, along with a few instrumentals. The varying personnel includes Buster Bailey, Bubber Miley, Don Redman, Charlie Ives, Arnett Nelson, Tommy Ladnier, Coleman Hawkins, and Leroy Harris. The songs are a mixture of blues, hokum, pop songs, and jazz vocals. A couple feature some nice fiddle, probably by Eddie South. Sound, considering the age of the recordings, is outstanding thanks to the genius of John R. T. Davies. There are informative notes by Dave Gladen and full discographical data.

GREG "FINGERS" TAYLOR
Red Lightnin' 0058 **Harpoon Man**
Good set of white blues by this decent singer and excellent harmonica player from Mississippi. On this album, he is accompanied by Anson Funderburgh and The Rockets and various additional musicians, resulting in a solid, driving sound. Most of the material is familiar from the repertoires of Chuck Berry, Junior Wells, Muddy Waters, Little Walter, and Eddie Taylor.

HOUND DOG TAYLOR
High-energy Chicago blues singer and electric slide guitarist whose style is based on that of Elmore James. His recordings are basic jumping music, with Hound Dog's singing and guitar accompanied by the rock-solid instrumental support of Brewer Phillips (gtr) and Ted Harvey (drm).
Alligator 4701 (d) **Hound Dog Taylor and The Houserockers**
His first album from 1973. She's Gone/Held My Baby Last Night/It's Alright.
Alligator 4704 (c,d) **Natural Boogie**
Second album from 1974. Take Five/See Me In The Evening/ Sitting Home Alone.
Alligator 4707 **Beware of the Dog**
Possibly Hound Dog's most exciting album. Recorded live in 1974, this atmospheric recording captures those rare moments that can only be experienced in a live setting. Give Me Back My Wig/Kitchen Sink Boogie/Comin' Around The Mountain.
Alligator 4727 (c) **Genuine Houserocking Music**
Ten previously unissued cuts from 1971–73 Alligator sessions find "Dog" in typical form with his unique brand of hard-driving blues and boogie often featuring his slashing slide guitar. Includes one vocal by guitarist Brewer Phillips.

LITTLE JOHNNY TAYLOR
Fine singer who, like Bobby Bland, falls midway between blues and soul in his approach. His early sides for Galaxy (reissued on Fantasy and Red Lightnin') are more on the blues side, while his later Jewel sides (previously available on Charly) are more on the soul side.

ESSENTIAL SELECTION
Fantasy 4510 **Greatest Hits**
Twelve great sides of gospel-influenced blues recorded between 1963–68. Includes his classic "Part Time Love." About half of the songs here are also on the Red Lightnin' album. Most cuts feature the tough guitar work of Arthur Wright. Compiled and with excellent notes by Lee Hildebrand.
Ichiban 1022 **Stuck in the Mud**
Some of Johnny's more recent albums found him in a contemporary funk-flavored bag. This album returns to the bluesy soul (or is it soul-flavored blues?) that he sang in the 60s and early 70s. Johnny is a wonderful singer with a melismatic gospel style and here he sings new versions of some of his old songs, like "Full Time Love" and "Everybody Knows about My Good Thing," new songs like "Stuck in the Mud," and covers of Big Jay McNeely's "There Is Something on Your Mind" and Jimmy Reed's "You Can Help Yourself." Good small-band accompaniments, with fine honking tenor by Morris Atchison. Maybe, in the light of contemporary music trends, this is a little dated but it certainly sounds good to me and it's gratifying to see a commercial company like Ichiban putting out this kind of music.
Ichiban 1042 **Ugly Man**
Little Johnny is accompanied here by "The Blue Guys," including Steve McRay (pno), Jody Worrell (slide gtr), and Ted Dortch (alto and tenor sax). The set kicks off in nightclub style with "Have You Ever Been to Kansas City," and soon slides into deep soul with "Never Be Lonely and Blue," handled with soulful delicacy. Other enjoyable readings include the popular disco jam "L. J. T.," the soulful "How Can A Broke Man Survive," and a fair rendition of "It's My Own Fault." Little Johnny's vocal intensity seems to have fizzled, if this collection is any indication.
Red Lightnin' 0030 **I Shoulda Been a Preacher**
Great collection of Galaxy sides.

JOHNNY TAYLOR
Fine soul/blues singer. Often confused with Little Johnny Taylor, this Taylor is more of a soul than blues singer.
Malaco 7421 **This Is Your Night**
With most of the songs written by Malaco staff

writer George Jackson and the Malaco house band, the album has a rather predictable feel. Most of the songs are soul rather than blues, though there are a couple of the latter. Good professional stuff.

Malaco 7431 **Wall To Wall**
Another predictable mixture of blues, soul, pop, and rock from Malaco. Some great singing from Johnny but the songs and arrangements are unmemorable.

Malaco 7440 **Lover Boy**
Johnny's third for Malaco is a winner. Ten tunes, eight written by the Malaco crew (only two by George Jackson!). The set is worth it for "Something Is Going On" alone, a classic soul blues in the Bobby Bland mold, complete with Hammond organ and blaring horns. Some tunes stray close to Lionel Ritchie-dom ("Universal Lady," "Nothing Like A Lady") without being mawkish. The rest are a combination of late night music and classic soul. Liner notes by Almost Slim.

Stax 8508 (d) **Raw Blues**
Reissue of his first Stax album, with Stax's usual fine production.

KOKO TAYLOR
Powerful Chicago blues singer. She is very popular, though I find her raucous shrieking style a little uncomfortable to listen to. Most of her recordings find her in the company of first-class Chicago musicians.

Alligator 4706 **I Got What It Takes**
1975 album with Mighty Joe Young and Sammy Lawhorn. Trying To Make A Living/Mama He Treats Your Daughter Mean/ Be What You Want To Be/Big Bossman.

Alligator 4711 (c) **The Earthshaker**

Alligator 4724 (c) **From the Heart of a Woman**
Mixture of blues and soul.

Alligator 4740 (c,d) **Queen of the Blues**

Alligator 4784 (c,d) **Jump for Joy**
1990 release (her first in three years) includes four original songs, a duet with Lonnie Brooks, a version

of Ted Nugent's "Hey Baby," and horn arrangements by veteran Chess and Stax arranger Gene Barge.

Black and Blue 59.542 2 **South Side Lady**
Reissue compilation of live and studio Black and Blue recordings from 1973, with two unreleased selections. Fifteen tracks in all, with an all-star band of Jimmy Rogers, Louis Myers, Dave Myers, Willie Mabon, and Fred Below. Previously issued as Black and Blue 33.542, with five songs from 33.505.

Chess 9263 (c) **Koko Taylor**
CD issue: Chess CHD 31271 (CP)
Reissue of Checker 1532 from 1969. Though Koko recorded over 50 sides for Checker, this is the only LP that was released, a dozen tunes recorded between 1965–69. Most of the personnel isn't known, but includes Buddy Guy, Johnny Shines, Lafayette Leake, Shakey Horton, Matt Murphy, and Sunnyland Slim, as well as Willie Dixon, who played bass, produced, wrote eight of the tunes (including the classic "Wang Dang Doodle"), and even sang on his "St. James Infirmary" rewrite, called "Insane Asylum." Love You Like a Woman/Don't Mess with the Messer/Nitty Gritty.

Chess (France) 600179 **I Got What it Takes**
Twenty-one Chess sides. Don't Mess with the Messer/I'm a Little Mixed Up/Blues Heaven/Tell Me the Truth/Egg or the Hen.

MELVIN TAYLOR
Taylor is a fine young Chicago blues singer and guitarist with a hard-edged Buddy Guy-style guitar sound. He suffers from the occasional tendency to go overboard with displays of expertise at the expense of feeling.

Isabel 900.512 **Blues on the Run**
A good debut album, with solid accompaniment by Johnny Dollar and Big Moose Walker.

Isabel 900.520 **Plays the Blues for You**
A disappointing, self-indulgent album, with Taylor trying to impress with his blazing speed at the expense of feeling. He is a fine singer and, when not going overboard, an excellent guitarist. There are some fine tracks here: "T. V. Mama," "Born To Lose," and "Cadillac Assembly Line." There are a couple of attempts at jazz that don't work and the two-part "Talking To Anna Mae" finds him at his most excessive. He is accompanied by an unexciting rhythm section.

MONTANA TAYLOR
One of the all-time great blues piano players and also an excellent singer.

Oldie Blues 2815 **Montana's Blues**
All of his known recordings, from the 20s–40s.

JOHNNIE TEMPLE

An excellent performer who was born and raised in Mississippi and moved to Chicago in the mid-30s, where he became a popular performer. He is best known for his recording (possibly the first) of "Louise Louise Blues." Although recording in Chicago with small urban groups, Temple's singing had a loose, free-flowing, rural quality, no doubt from his Mississippi upbringing.

Blues Documents 2067 **1936–40**

Nineteen tracks accompanied by the Harlem Hamfats, Joshua Altheimer, Sam Price, Teddy Bunn, Lonnie Johnson, Buster Bailey, and Henry "Red" Allen. Includes two versions of "Louise Louise Blues," including his original 1936 recording. A few of the tracks have been reissued before but none is currently available. Nice!

Document 511 **1935–39**

Fine collection of 18 sides. The first four recordings from 1935 are straight Mississippi country blues, with Johnnie accompanying himself on guitar, usually with Charlie McCoy on second guitar. These include the risque "Lead Pencil Blues" and a lovely version of Skip James' "Devil Got My Woman." The remaining tracks feature Johnny accompanied by various small groups (guitar, piano, saxophone, and sometimes clarinet) in the popular style of the period. Although the feel of these recordings is more urban, Johnny's singing and some of the songs have strong roots in the Mississippi country blues. Sound is generally quite good. Most of the tracks here have not been on LP before.

SONNY TERRY

Fine North Carolina singer and harmonica player best known for his partnership with Brownie McGhee. Sonny died in 1986.

Alligator 4734 (c,d) **Whoopin'**

This album is a bit different than most of Sonny's albums, because, instead of the usual folky feel, Sonny is accompanied by a tough, Chicago-style band, including Johnny Winter (elec and acst gtr, pno), Willie Dixon (b), and Steve Homnick (drm). Sonny is in good form vocally and instrumentally and the accompaniments are tasteful and appropriate. One could have only wished that Sonny would have played amplified harp for an even tougher sound!

Document 536 **1938–1955**

A fine collection of 17 early sides. The first four tracks are Sonny alone with his harmonica and feature brilliant effects on "Fox Chase" and "Train Whistle Blues," the latter originally issued in a classical music series! The remaining tracks find him with various accompaniments, including washboard player Oh Red, guitarists Blind Boy Fuller, Woody Guthrie, and, of course, Brownie McGhee. There is also a raucous session with McGhee, a piano player, and a drummer that sounds like it was recorded in a tunnel, and two tracks on which Sonny, Brownie, and piano player Bob Gaddy accompany the fine singer Alonzo Scales. Some of the tracks have been reissued before but very little is currently available elsewhere.

Krazy Kat KK 807 **Sonny Terry**

Nice sides recorded for Gotham in 1952. Includes many alternate takes and some unreleased songs.

O.B.C. 503 **Sonny's Story**

Originally issued as Bluesville 1025 in 1960. Enjoyable acoustic set with J. C. Burris (2nd hca) on some cuts, Sticks McGhee (gtr), and Belton Evans (drm).

O.B.C. 521 (c) **Sonny Is King**

Reissue of Bluesville 1059 from 1960. Side one features Sonny with the unexpected backing of Lightnin' Hopkins on guitar, plus Leonard Gaskin (b) and Belton Evans (drm). Gaskin and Evans provide spot on but insufferably dull accompaniments and Lightnin' is more restrained than usual, playing under-recorded acoustic guitar. Side two is back to familiar territory, with Sonny backed by his long-time partner Brownie McGhee. Sonny is fine throughout, though not terribly inspired. Not an essential album unless you are trying to complete a Sonny Terry collection.

Stinson 55 **Sonny Terry and His Mouth Harp (With Woody Guthrie)**

COMPACT DISC

Fantasy 24723 **California Blues**

Reissue of Fantasy albums originally issued in 1957 and 1960. Enjoyable sides.

Note: See also under BROWNIE MCGHEE and SONNY TERRY.

SONNY TERRY and BUSTER BROWN

Sundown 709-11 **Toughest Terry and Maddest Brown**

A nice collection of nine songs each by these two harmonica players from Georgia. The nine Terry sides are from the period 1950–59; they were all issued as singles for a black audience and are less folky than some of his other recordings. Most of the tracks feature guitar by his long-time partner Brownie McGhee and additional instrumental work by fine musicians like Mickey Baker, Bob Gaddy, and Big Chief Ellis. Buster Brown is not in the same league as Terry as a harmonica player, but he's an enjoyable and powerful performer. Most of his tracks are from the 1961–64 period, plus one rather unexceptional side from his last session in 1976. Most of the musicians are unknown, but three tracks feature the brilliant guitarist Jimmy Spruill.

LOVIN' SAM THEARD

Wolf WJS 1008 **Complete 1934–1940 Recordings in Chronological Order**

Sam Theard was a popular singer and songwriter in the 30s, though few of his recordings have been reissued. He had a relaxed, engaging vocal style and his material was a mixture of blues, hokum, and jazz on which he was accompanied by small jazz-flavored groups. A couple of tracks feature fine piano by John Oscar and a couple feature some of Kokomo Arnold's distinctive slide guitar. Enjoyable.

CHRIS THOMAS

Chris Thomas is a young (25-year-old) Louisiana black blues stylist, the son of Tabby Thomas. Like many younger blues performers, Chris draws on a variety of influences including Lightnin' Hopkins, B. B. King, Chuck Berry, and Jimi Hendrix!

Arhoolie 1096 (c) **The Beginning**

Chris produced, wrote all of the songs, arranged them, and performed them on this album. His songs are original, though mostly based on familiar themes, and his harsh vocal style seems to be derived from white blues and blues-rock bands. He is a good guitar player with a powerful funky sound, though the occasional rock-flavored excesses are a little painful. He is accompanied by a satisfactory but rather pedestrian rhythm section. A promising, if not totally satisfying, debut.

HENRY THOMAS

Yazoo 1080/81 (c,d) **Texas Worried Blues**

Reissue and repackaging of long-out-of-print album Herwin 215 featuring all of the recordings of this brilliant Texas songster of the 1920s. Thomas is noted for playing panpipes along with his backwoods blues guitar on a number of songs.

JAMES "SON" THOMAS

Mississippi country bluesman. "Son" is a good singer and guitarist, though most of his repertoire tends to be familiar, traditional, or popular blues songs. Since he was discovered in the 60s, he has been recorded rather often.

Black and Blue 33.744 **Good Morning School Girl**

Recorded in France in 1986. Pleasant selection of 11 country blues standards. Rollin' and Tumblin'/Good Morning School Girl/Standing at the Crossroads/Big Fat Mama/Whiskey Head Woman.

Flying High 6506 **Son Down on the Delta**

Enjoyable set of live performances of mostly blues standards, recorded in Fort Worth, TX, in 1981.

L+R 42.048 **The James "Son" Thomas Album**

Southern Culture 1701 **Highway 61 Blues**

Twelve sides recorded between 1969–82. Mostly interpretations of familiar songs. Fast Boogie/Bottle Up and Go/Catfish Blues/Highway 61 Blues/Good Morning Little Schoolgirl.

Swingmaster 2102 **Delta Blues Classics**

Recorded in Holland in 1981. Nice performances of mostly well-known songs.

RAMBLIN' THOMAS

Excellent Texas country bluesman who recorded for Paramount and Victor in the late 20s and early 30s. Thomas played some very fine guitar, sometimes with a slide, and sang some excellent songs.

Matchbox 215 **Ramblin' Thomas**

This album features all of his Paramounts plus one of his Victor recordings.

TABBY THOMAS

Down-home Louisiana singer, guitarist, and piano player.

Blues Unlimited 5007 **25 Years with the Blues**

With Whispering Smith on harmonica.

Flyright 621 **Hoodoo Party**

Fourteen tracks from the Jay Miller archives. Drawing from a variety of sessions recorded between 1954 and the early 60s, this features him in a variety of settings from hard-rocking blues to swamp-pop ballads and even some gospel! The earliest sides from 1954 have a strong New Orleans flavor with hot guitar from "Big Charlie" Morris. There are several unissued tracks, including an alternate take of his most famous song, "Hoodoo Party," with fine harmonica from Lazy Lester. Other highlights include a fine reworking of "C. C. Rider," "Playgirl," with tough guitar from Rudolph Richard, and the Guitar Slim-flavored "Keep On Trying."

Maison De Soul 1010 **Rockin' with the Blues**
Unpretentious album with Tabby accompanied by a tight band of musicians including legendary piano player Henry Gray. The band, while not exceptional, maintains a good solid groove behind Tabby and the whole record has a down-to-earth quality to it. Most of the songs are originals by Thomas.

Maison De Soul 1016 (c) **Blues Train**

Maison De Soul 1026 **King of Swamp Blues**
One might quibble with the album title, but this is certainly an enjoyable selection of solid no-nonsense blues. Backed by a good band, Tabby sings 10 originals. There are touches of soul, swamp pop, and rock 'n' roll, but it all ends up being blues. Never Get Rich in Bed/Louisiana Woman/Honey Dripper (a Thomas original, not the old favorite)/Fortune Teller Blues/Lord Please Have Mercy.

BIG MAMA THORNTON

Marvelous West Coast singer and occasional harmonica player. Her 50s recordings for Peacock, including the original version of "Hound Dog," are classics; some of these are available on Ace. In the 60s and 70s, she recorded for Arhoolie and Vanguard; the Arhoolies are particularly fine.

Ace CHAD 277 **You Ole Houn' Dawg, Vol. 2**
This deluxe gatefold LP collects 10 Peacock recordings from 1953–57 as well as a Duke release from '54 and two each from Backbeat ('69) and Kent ('65). There's no drop off in quality from label to label, with everything being uniformly excellent due to Thornton's mighty pipes and the lowdown and dirty baritone sax honking on almost every tune. She does duets with Johnny Ace ("I Just Can't Help Myself"), and a funny bit with Elroy Peace called "Tarzan and the Signified Monkey." Hound Dog/I Smell a Rat/Me and My Chauffeur/Walking Blues/They Call Me Big Mama.

Arhoolie 1028 **In Europe**
With Walter Horton, Eddie Boyd, and Buddy Guy. Also includes two wonderful cuts on which Mama is accompanied by Fred McDowell on slide guitar. Swing It On Home/The Place/Unlucky Girl/My Heavy Load/School Boy.

Arhoolie 1032 **Big Mama with the Chicago Blues Band**
Big Mama accompanied by James Cotton, Otis Spann, Muddy Waters, and Frances Clay.

Arhoolie 1039 **Ball and Chain**
Features Lightnin' Hopkins and Larry Williams.

Vanguard VSD 79351 (d) **Jail**
Live recordings from prison shows in Washington and Oregon. With George Smith on harmonica. Little Red Rooster/Ball 'n' Chain/Hound Dog/Rock Me Baby.

CASSETTE ONLY RELEASE

Arhoolie C-204 **Big Mama Thornton**
Double-length cassette combining Arhoolie 1028 and 1032.

COMPACT DISC

ESSENTIAL SELECTION

Ace CD CHD 940 **The Original Hound Dog**
Twenty-two tracks featuring Big Mama's best Peacock sides, leading off with the classic "Hound Dog." My Man Called Me/Willie Mae's Trouble/I Smell a Rat/They Call Me Big Mama/I Ain't No Fool Either/Let Your Tears Fall Baby/Rock-A-Bye Baby/Nightmare/Laugh, Laugh, Laugh/The Fish.

Arhoolie CD 305 **Big Mama Thornton**
Tracks from her three Arhoolie albums.

Arhoolie (Japan) PCD 2518 **In Europe/With the Chicago All Stars.**
Ten tracks from her first Arhoolie album (1028) and nine from her second (1032). Some great performances backed by Muddy Waters, Otis Spann, Buddy Guy, and Fred McDowell. Quite a bit of overlap with Arhoolie CD 305.

GEORGE THOROGOOD and THE DESTROYERS

Powerful white blues/rock band. Three-piece group featuring hot vocals and dynamic slide by Thorogood.

Rounder 3013 (c,d) **George Thorogood and The Destroyers**

Rounder 3024 (c,d) **Move It on Over**

Rounder 3045 (c,d) **More George Thorogood and The Destroyers**

JOHN TINSLEY

Good country blues discovery from Virginia.

Swingmaster 2104 **Sunrise Blues**
Recorded in Holland. Nice peformances but a little restrained.

HENRY TOWNSEND

Brilliant St. Louis country bluesman who performs equally well on guitar and piano. His superb 20s and 30s recordings, mostly featuring Henry on guitar, are available on Wolf. Since his rediscovery in the 60s, he has concentrated more on piano. His recordings in the 60s, 70s, and 80s have generally been excellent, with Nighthawk 201 being particulary fine.

Nighthawk 201 **Mule**
Excellent 1979 recordings, mostly featuring Henry on piano.

Swingmaster 2107 **Hard Luck Stories**
1981 recordings. Townsend sings and plays guitar and piano on a selection of 11 original songs. Some nice performances.

Wolf 117 **Henry Townsend and Henry Spaulding**
Some beautiful country blues by two St. Louis musicians recorded between 1929–37. Singer/guitarist Spaulding only recorded two cuts (in 1929) and both of these are here along with 13 of the 17 recorded by Townsend (four have never been found). Both are wonderful wistful singers and play lovely, flowing guitar in a style that seems to have several exponents in St. Louis. Seven of Townsend's cuts feature him with his guitar only and are quintessential country blues, two feature fine piano accompaniments by Roosevelt Sykes, and four feature a small combo with piano, second guitar, and harmonica by Sonny Boy Williamson. Although not as striking as his solo performances, they are brilliant in their own right.

Wolf 120 495 **St. Louis Blues**
Recorded in Austria in 1980, featuring Thomas mostly on guitar. Side one was recorded in a studio and is very good; Side two was recorded live and the poor recording quality detracts from some good performances. Includes one cut by his wife Vernell.

T.N.T. TRIBBLE
Krazy Kat 809 **The Gotham Sides**
A set of exciting blues and R&B sides by singer/drummer Tribble backed by The Frank Motley and Albert Pritchett Combos. Includes five of the six singles cut for Gotham (two cuts are alternates) between 1951–54, plus seven hitherto unissued takes, the foremost being two righteous versions of Sonny Thompson's 1947 hit, "Long Gone." Solid stuff.

BESSIE TUCKER/IDA MAE MACK
Magpipe 1815 **The Texas Moaners Accompanied by Mr. '49**
Limited edition reprint of this album featuring 14 tracks by two superb Texas singers accompanied by K. D. Johnson (pno), recorded in Memphis in August 1928. Both singers are outstanding with soulful voices that, at times, bring to mind field hollers. Sound on this reissue is excellent and it comes with informative, if slightly dated, notes by Paul Oliver.

TOMMY TUCKER
Blues/R&B/Soul singer famous for his hit "Hi-Heel Sneakers." He died in 1982.

Red Lightnin' 0022 **Mother Trucker**
Red Lightnin' 0037 **The Rocks Is My Pillow**
Nice set of 1979 recordings cut in New York. A mixture of blues and R&B, some with a funk feel to them. Some nice guitar by Bo Diddley Junior.

IKE TURNER
Blues/R&B singer, guitarist, piano player, and talent scout best known for his R&B recordings with Tina Turner. Ike was more interesting as a musician and arranger than as a singer and most of the recordings under his name feature various band members as vocalists.

Flyright 578 **Kings of Rhythm**
Mostly previously unissued recordings cut for Cobra in 1958. Vocals by Ike, Jackie Brenston, and Tommy Hodge. Fine down-home-influenced urban blues with tough guitar by Ike.

Red Lightnin' 0016 **The Kings of Rhythm**
Various Southern blues artists accompanied by the Ike Turner Band, including Billy Gayles, Jackie Brenston, and Clayton Love.

Red Lightnin' 0047 **The Legendary Ike Turner and The Kings of Rhythm**
Two-LP set. The title is a little misleading, because only about half the cuts feature Turner. Features 22 sides recorded for the small St. Louis label Stevens in 1959, featuring local blues and R&B artists. Features Turner and his band (under the pseudonym of Icky Renrut!) with vocals by Jimmy Thomas and Tommy Hodge; Bobby Foster with Turner and his band; Johnny Wright; and the much-sought-after Little Cooper. Several of these recordings have not been issued before. Most of the performances are rather average, though there are some good moments, particularly when Ike plays some of his shattering guitar. It's also nice to hear the rare Little Cooper tracks. Full discographic information, rare photos, and extensive notes.

COMPACT DISC
P-Vine PCD 2161 **Cobra Sessions 1958**
Cobra and Artistic label material, including unreleased songs and alternates. Ten cuts by Ike's Kings of Rhythm and seven with The Kings and The Willie Dixon Band backing Betty Everett. This is certainly vintage material, recorded in Chicago in the late 50s; check out the personnel here: Jackie Brenston, Willie Dixon, Odie Payne, Little Brother Montgomery, and Wayne Bennett.

BIG JOE TURNER

One of the all-time great blues shouters. Joe was originally based in Kansas City and first recorded in the 30s and continued recording regularly up to his death in 1985. His earliest recordings, featuring his long-time playing partner, Pete Johnson, on piano, are available on MCA C 42351 and are superb. Other great recordings from the 40s and early 50s are available on Savoy 2223, Arhoolie 2004, and Jukebox Lil 618. His 50s recordings, showing the influence of rock 'n' roll and R&B, are available on Atlantic 81663. His later recordings are often of lesser interest because, while Joe is usually in good form as a singer, his accompaniments are not always up to the task, and there is frequent repetition of his 40s and 50s material.

Ace CHD 243 **Steppin' Out**

Another great collection of vintage Big Joe. Side one features eight sides recorded for the Freedom label in Houston with mostly local musicians like Lonnie Lyons, Goree Carter, and Joe Hourton. Joe was in peak form on uptempo jumpers like "Adam Bit the Apple" and "Feeling Happy" or soulful slow blues like "Still in the Dark" and "Life Is like a Card Game." Several of these tracks have also been reissued on Jukebox Lil. Side two features live recordings from a 1947 "Just Jazz" concert organized by Gene Norman. There are four great tracks by Joe accompanied by Pete Johnson and an unknown rhythm section. The rest of the side features three great boogie instrumentals by Johnson and a vocal by pop/jazz vocalist Kay Starr. Superb sound and excellent notes by Tony Collins.

Arhoolie 2004 **Jumpin' the Blues**

Great 40s sides from Swingtime with Pete Johnson's Orchestra.

Atlantic 81663 (d) **The Rhythm and Blues Years**

A fine double LP of some of Joe's best R&B efforts with an emphasis on titles that were not hits. The album includes "T. V. Mama," featuring the slide guitar of Elmore James and piano of Johnny Jones, some stomping early sides fuelled by the legendary Van "Piano Man" Walls, "Teenage Letter," charged by Sam "The Man" Taylor on alto, and "Honey Hush," driven by a legion of first-rate session men including King Curtis, Al Sears, and Mickey Baker. There is some duplication with Charly CRB 1070 (out-of-print) but this album includes several cuts never on LP before. Sleeve notes contain fond memories of Joe from the likes of Jerry Wexler and Doc Pomus plus a scatter of pics.

Atlantic 81752 (c,d) **Greatest Hits**

It don't get much better! This single LP has Joe's 14 biggest Atlantic sides, 1951–56, the birth of rock 'n' roll! Shake Rattle and Roll/Flip Flop and Fly/Honey Hush/Corrine Corrina/Oke-She-Moke-She-Mop/Chains Of Love. CD has seven bonus tracks: The Chill Is On/After My Laughter Came Tears/Bump Miss Suzie/I'll Never Stop Loving You/Baby I Still Want You/Red Sails in the Sunset/Blues in the Night.

Atlantic Jazzlore 90668 (c,d) **Big Joe Rides Again**

Reissue of Atlantic 1332 from 1960. Joe shouts blues originals and sings standards in front of a great eight-piece Basie-esque big band, including such luminaries as Coleman Hawkins, Ernie Royal, Vic Dickenson, and Jimmy Jones on piano, with arrangements by Ernie Wilkins, recorded in September 1959. Also includes a real Basie-esque "Pennies from Heaven" from '56 with a rhythm section including Walter Page, Freddie Green, and Pete Johnson, along with Lawrence Brown, Pete Brown, and Seldon Powell! I Get the Blues When it Rains/Time After Time/Don't You Make Me High (aka "Don't You Feel My Leg").

Black and Blue 33.547 **Texas Style**
CD issue: Black and Blue 59.547

Enjoyable 1971 set with Joe accompanied by Milt Buckner (pno), Slam Stewart (b), and Jo Jones (drm), originally issued as 33.028.

Jukebox Lil 618 **I Don't Dig It**

This beautiful set features 16 sides recorded between 1940–49 with Joe in his prime accompanied by a variety of bands ranging from trios to large bands. All of these are rare tracks that have never been on LP before and show Joe's remarkable versatility as a singer. He sounds equally at home on a romping boogie like "Boogie Woogie Baby" (accompanied by a fine West Coast band with the great Pete Johnson on piano), a blues standard like Jimmy Rushing's "Goin' to Chicago Blues," a pop standard like "I Can't Give You Anything but Love" (given a very bluesy treatment), or the original "Mardi Gras Boogie." Album has superb sound and comes in a fold-out jacket with extensive notes and lots of rare early photos.

Muse 5293 (c,d) **Big Joe Turner and Roomful of Blues**

Enjoyable album recorded early in '83 by Joe accompanied by this top-notch R&B band. Joe is undoubtedly past his prime but the result is quite enjoyable. Dr. John guests on piano on one cut.

Pablo 2310 709 (c) **The Bosses with Count Basie.**

Pablo 2310 800 (c) **The Things I Used to Do**

Pablo 2310 818 (c) **Everyday I Have the Blues**
1975 recordings with Sonny Stitt, Pee Wee Crayton, and J. D. Nicholson.

Pablo 2310 844 (c,d) **The Midnight Special**

Pablo 2310 859 (c) **Kansas City Shout**
With Count Basie.

Pablo 2310 863 (c) **Have No Fear, Big Joe Turner Is Here**

Pablo 2310 883 (c) **Life Ain't Easy**

Pablo 2310 904 (c) **Kansas City, Here I Come**
Enjoyable set of familiar songs with Joe in good form. Down Home Blues/Since I Fell for You/Big Leg Woman.

Pablo 2310 913 (c) **Joe Turner Meets Jimmy Witherspoon—Patcha, Patcha, All Night Long**
Joe's last recordings. Four of the six tracks here are performed solo and two of them feature 'Spoon and Joe alternating verses. They are accompanied by an excellent band that includes veteran New Orleans' musician Lee Allen on tenor, Red Holloway on alto, Bobby Blevins on keyboards, and fine guitar by Gary Bell. Although both artists are past their prime and the material is the same old stuff, there are some enjoyable moments here and the instrumental work is first rate.

Savoy 2223 Have No Fear, Big Joe Turner Is Here
Two-LP set featuring wonderful sides recorded for National, 1945–47, with Frankie Newton, Pete Johnson, Wild Bill Moore, Teddy Bunn, Albert Ammons, Ike Perkins, Don Byas, and Camille Howard.

Southland SLP 13 With Knocky Parker and His Houserockers
Joe is accompanied by veteran piano player Parker and a varied selection of instrumentalists including the fine Eddie Chamblee on alto or tenor and the embarrassing David Ostwald on tuba or bass saxophone. Big Joe sounds tired and works his way mechanically through his same old repertoire.

Spivey 1020 **Big Joe Turner**
CASSETTE/COMPACT DISC RELEASE

MCA C 42351 **Volume 1: I've Been to Kansas City**
The first in a series that is intended to reissue all of Joe's classic Decca recordings. This one covers 16 sides from 1940–41. Joe is featured in the company of such jazz and boogie greats as Willie "The Lion"

Smith, Art Tatum, Hot Lips Page, Don Byas, and Sammy Price. Includes two takes of a couple of songs.
COMPACT DISC

Atlantic CD 8812 **The Boss of the Blues**
Reissue of excellent 1956 album. Ten blues standards with Joe in top form acompanied by Pete Johnson, Freddie Green, Joe Newman, and Pete Brown, with the original liner notes by Whitney Balliet.

P-Vine PCD 908 **Live!**
Eight Big Joe standards ("Flip Flop and Fly," "Corrine Corrina," "T. V. Mama," and "Honey Hush") recorded live in the late 70s, with Mike Bloomfield on guitar!

Pablo PACD 2310-937-2 **Flip, Flop, and Fly**
1972 recordings with the Count Basie Orchestra, typical of Big Joe's material. Nine cuts in all. Corrine Corrina/Shake Rattle and Roll/T. V. Mama.

Pablo PACD 2405-404-2 **The Best of Joe Turner**
Eight selections. Backup by the likes of Roy Eldridge, Milt Jackson, Cleanhead Vinson, Lloyd Glenn, Pee Wee Crayton, and Sonny Stitt. The Things I Used to Do/Corrine Corrina/Everyday I Have the Blues.

BIG JOE TURNER/T-BONE WALKER
RCA Bluebird 8311 (d) **Bosses of the Blues, Vol. 1**
Not a whole lot of music, timewise, on this LP (even considering the budget price), but oh what music! The two blues giants get a side apiece, with selections taken from the Bob Thiele sessions, both made in 1969 in LA. While both performers were well past their best and most influential recording years, neither were they ready for the old-age home. Turner belts out his big numbers like "Shake Rattle And Roll" and "Corinne Corinna." Walker obliges with the standard "Everyday I Have the Blues" and the topical "Viet Nam."

JOHNNY TURNER/ZAVEN JAMBAZIAN
Testament 227 **Blues with a Feeling**
This is a live set recorded in California in the late 70s of singer/guitarist Johnny Turner and his small band. Turner, who grew up in Arkansas, moved to California in 1965 and has been playing the blues steadily ever since, touring all over with Joe Houston's band as well. Jambazian is an Armenian blues harp player! Checkin' On My Baby/Hard Luck Blues/Tomorrow Night/Last Night.

TWO ACES AND A JACK
Blue Suit BS 101 **Hot as You Get**
Fine set of tough blues by some Detroit bluesmen transplanted to Toledo, OH. Side one features six tracks by brothers Art and Roman Griswold; both are good singers and Art plays some intense B. B. King-flavored guitar. This duo brings to mind the Carter Brothers' sound. I could have done without such overdone songs as "Got My Mojo Working" and "The Thrill Is Gone." Side two features singer/guitarist/harmonica player Big Jack Reynolds, who sings and plays in a somewhat older style. Both the Griswolds and Reynolds are accompanied by the Toledo band, The Haircuts, who generally do a creditable job, though some of guitarist Larry Gold's solos go a bit overboard.

UNCLE BEN AND HIS NEPHEWS
High Water 423 (45 rpm) **Mean Woman Blues/ Mama, Look at Sis**
Some tough primitive blues recorded live on Beale Street by Memphis-based singer/guitarist. On one cut, he is accompanied by Roosevelt Briggs (hca) and on the other by Ken Welch (gtr).

STEVIE RAY VAUGHAN and DOUBLE TROUBLE
Tough white blues band from Texas. Intense vocals and guitar by Vaughan accompanied by bass,

guitar, and drums. Vaughan tragically died in a helicopter crash after performing on a triple bill with Eric Clapton and Robert Cray in the summer of 1990.
CASSETTE AND CD RELEASE ONLY
Epic BFC 38734 **Texas Flood**
About two-thirds original songs along with songs by Buddy Guy and Larry Davis.
Epic FE 39304 **Can't Stand the Weather**
1984 album. Some hard-driving performances including versions of Guitar Slim's "The Things I Used To Do," Ray Agee's "Cold Shot," and an impressive version of the West Coast blues standard "Tin Pan Alley." Also includes an homage to Jimi Hendrix with a very Hendrix-influenced version of "Voodoo Chile." Brother Jimmy Vaughan (of the Fabulous Thunderbirds) guests on a couple of cuts.
Epic FE 40036 **Soul to Soul**
Mostly original material.
Epic E2 40511 **Live Alive**

STEVIE RAY VAUGHAN/JIMMY VAUGHAN
Epic 46225 (c,d) **Family Style**
As the finishing touches were being put on this long-awaited brotherly collaboration, a tragic accident ended Stevie Ray Vaughan's stellar career. And so, what should have been a joyous musical celebration is now a bittersweet memorial to his talent. Stevie Ray and brother Jimmie (of the Fabulous Thunderbirds) obviously had a ball in the studio, swapping vocals and guitar leads on a set that unfolds like a top-flight bar band kicking up their heels on a Friday night. Needless to say, the guitar-slinging is hot as a bowl of Texas chili, perhaps due to a little sibling rivalry that coaxes the best out of both men. I love the four tough instrumentals, each with its own memorable mood and series of masterful solos. Stevie deftly handles the lead vocal on four numbers, being especially effective on the understated soul of "Tick Tock," and the blues rockers "Long Way from Home" and "Telephone Song." He completely overshadows his brother's capable but under-confident singing, which takes center stage on the least exciting two songs here. But Jimmie's licks, always my favorite part of any T-Birds album, are terse and tasteful as ever, an effective foil to Stevie Ray's expansive style. When the grieving is over, I think we'll all be glad to have a recording like this that's so full of life.

MAURICE JOHN VAUGHN
Alligator 4763 (c,d) **Generic Blues**
This is a fine debut album by a young Chicago blues singer/guitarist and tenor sax player. Some fine singing and playing by Vaughn on a selection of mostly original songs and solid accompaniments by the small group with some particularly nice keyboard work by Leo Davis. Maurice is a fine and distinctive vocalist with a tough, crisp electric guitar style. Six of the eight songs are originals and are good, intelligent compositions.

EDDIE "CLEANHEAD" VINSON
Blues shouter and alto player with a distinctive vocal style.

Black and Blue 33.543 **Kidney Stew**
Excellent 1969 LP, previously issued as Black and Blue 33.021. Mostly Vinson standards on which he is accompanied by Hal Singer, T-Bone Walker, and Jay McShann.

Circle CLP 57 **Kidney Stew**
Recorded in Holland in 1976 with Vinson accompanied by Ted Easton's Jazzband, a Dutch group. Both Vinson and the band are in very good form, though this album suffers from an overabundance of familiar material. Cleanhead Blues/Kidney Stew/Juice Head.

Delmark 631 **Eddie "Cleanhead" Vinson**
Excellent late 60s set recorded in France, with T-Bone Walker (gtr), Hal Singer (ten sax), and Jay McShann (pno).

Gusto 5035x **Cherry Red Blues**
Twenty-two splendid late 40s and early 50s King sides with "Cleanhead" accompanied by some marvelous bands, including sidemen like Eddie "Lockjaw" Davis, Wynton Kelly, Slide Hampton, Milt Larkins, and Milt Buckner. Ashes On My Pillow/I'm Weak But Willing/Bald Headed Blues/Peas and Rice/My Big Brass Bed Is Gone/If You Don't Think I'm Sinking/Rainy Mornin' Blues/Lonesome Train/I Need You Tonight.

Muse 5116 **The Clean Machine**
1979 session with Lloyd Glenn and Larry Gales.

Muse 5208 **Live at Sandy's**
Excellent blues and jazz jam recorded in 1978 at Sandy's Club in Beverly, MA, with Vinson supported by Ray Bryant, Arnett Cobb, and Alan Dawson.

Muse 5282 (c) **And A Roomful of Blues**
Excellent selection of blues, jazz, and R&B. Vinson is accompanied by a leading white R&B band.

Muse 5310 **Sings the Blues**

Pablo 2310 866 (c) **I Want a Little Girl**
A relaxed, jazz-flavored set, featuring a couple of jazz instrumentals and some familiar and unfamiliar blues songs given Vinson's distinctive treatment. He is accompanied by first-rate musicians like Art Hillery (pno, org), Cal Green (gtr), and Roy McCurdy (drm).

ESSENTIAL SELECTION

Saxophonograph 507 **Mr. Cleanhead Steps Out**
Vinson's early alto and vocal recordings (1945–51) with the Cootie Williams Orchestra, plus sides with a host of star talent including Sam Taylor, Eddie "Lockjaw" Davis, Wynton Kelly, Billy Taylor, Milt Larkins, and Clarke Terry. Five swinging instrumentals and 11 "squeaky" blues vocals by the man himself. There is something here to please everyone. Detailed sleeve notes by Dave Perry.

COMPACT DISC

Black and Blue 233021 **Kidney Stew**
Excellent CD taken from three star-laden French sessions for Black and Blue. The first 10 songs are from a '69 Paris session with Hal "Cornbread" Singer, T-Bone Walker, and Jay McShann, available on Black and Blue LP 33.543. The second session is from '72 with Al Grey, Floyd Smith, and Wild Bill Davis, and includes "Person to Person" and "Alimony Blues." The final two songs are from a '78 Nice session with Lockjaw Davis, Bill Doggett, Milt Hinton, and J. C. Heard, including a never-before-issued "Totsy," plus Doggett's "Hey Little Doggey." Excellent sound, an hour long.

Charly CD 50 **Back in Town**
Jazz blues recorded in 1957 and originally issued on Bethlehem. Twelve songs with "Cleanhead" accompanied by Joe Newman (tpt), Henry Coker (trb), Ed Thigpen (drm), and Paul Quinichette (ten sax).

JSP CD 204 **Fun in London**
CD issue of JSP 1012, recorded in May 1980. Eddie's joined by a British rhythm section with John Burch on piano. Except for Dizzy Gillespie's "The Theme," everything's original; the only real R&B are fine remakes of Cleanhead's "Racetrack Blues" and "High Class Baby," the rest is straight-ahead jazz. Cleanhead's Thing/Roxanne/Straight Away.

JSP CD 223 **Meat's too High**
Cleanhead's second JSP LP is now out on CD with fine sound. Recorded in London on March 19, 1982, this nine-song set has a very jazzy feel, mainly due to too much solo space given to guitarist Les Davidson, a rock-session guitarist, part of this competent but not very exciting British rhythm section. Somebody's Got to Go/Home Boy/Old Maid Boogie/Investigation Blues.

EDDIE "CLEANHEAD" VINSON/ OTIS SPANN

RCA Bluebird 8312-2 **Bosses of the Blues, Vol. 2**

EDDIE "CLEANHEAD" VINSON/JIMMY WITHERSPOON

King 634 (d) **Battle of the Blues, Vol. 3**

WALTER VINSON

Mississippi singer/guitarist who was often a member of The Mississippi Sheiks.

Agram 2003 **Rats Been on My Cheese**
Sixteen songs recorded between 1929–41, including one previously unissued track.

Note: See also under CHARLIE McCOY and THE MISSIS-SIPPI SHEIKS.

JIMMY WALKER
Wolf 120.712 **Original South Side Blues Piano**
First solo album by this veteran Chicago singer and piano player, featuring 12 sides recorded in 1983. Some quite good performances, though Walker doesn't have the ability or imagination to sustain interest throughout a whole album. On some cuts, he is accompanied by drummer Pete Crushing, who is competent at best.

JOE LOUIS WALKER
Hightone 8006 (c,d) **Cold Is the Night**
Hightone does it again with the first album by a talented young blues artist. Joe, a Bay Area-based performer, is a striking and powerful singer and an imaginative guitarist who can play both fast or with restrained feeling. He is backed by a basic but effective rhythm section (bass, keyboards, and drums), which is occasionally augmented by sax or added keyboards. As is usually the case, producers Bruce Bromberg and Dennis Walker get a thick sound out of only a handful of instruments. The songs include seven fine originals by Joe Louis and three from the brilliant pen of Dennis Walker, including the moving and soulful title song and the fine "Ten More Shows To Play," written in collaboration with Lowell Fulson. Highly recommended.
Hightone 8012 (c,d) **The Gift**
Hightone 8019 (c,d) **Blue Soul**
Hot new LP by Bay Area favorite may be his best yet. Mostly original songs.

JOHNNY "BIG MOOSE" WALKER
Fine Chicago singer and piano player.
Isabel 900.502 **Going Home Tomorrow**
Excellent session recorded in France in 1980. "Moose" sings and plays well and is given good accompaniment by Willie James Lyons (gtr), Big Mojo (b), and Odie Payne (drm).
Red Beans 005 **Blue Love**
"Big Moose" is a fine singer and piano player but you wouldn't know it from this solo album. The performances are so low key that you're likely to find yourself nodding off by the end of the first side. Uninteresting material and performances.

PHILLIP WALKER
Outstanding singer and guitar player. Originally from Louisiana, Phillip worked with Clifton Chenier and Etta James before settling in California.

Alligator 4715 **Someday You'll Have These Blues**
Excellent set originally on Joliet.
Hightone 8013 (c,d) **Blues**
Phillip Walker is a fine artist who consistently delivers high-quality soulful vocals and expressive guitar. This album offers just what the title promises—10 blues with Phillips accompanied by a solid rhythm section, occasional horns from The Memphis Horns, and crisp production from Bruce Bromberg and Dennis Walker, who have produced most of Phillips's recordings over the past 15 years. The album is mostly new songs written by Dennis Walker, David Amy, and others. Phillip also turns in fine versions of Howlin' Wolf's "How Many More Years" and Lonesome Sundown's "I Had A Dream." Nothing really spectacular here, just good solid blues by one of the most consistent artists around.
Hightone 8020 (c,d) **The Bottom of the Top**
Reissue of his first album from 1973. In many ways, this is his best album, with his strongest and most assured singing and expressive guitar playing, including some dazzling fleet-fingered work that in spite of speed is always in good taste. The songs were recorded over a three-year period and are tremendously varied, with several fine originals including the wonderful loping Louisiana rocker "Hello My Darling" and the fine soulful ballad "It's All In Your Mind." His covers include the familiar "Tin Pan Alley," which sounds fresh in his hands, a gorgeous version of Lightnin' Hopkins' "Hello Central" with solo guitar accompaniment only, and fine versions of Long John Hunter's "Crazy Girl" (with some of his most fiery guitar) and Jimmy Johnson's "The Bottom of the Top." There is even a remarkably effective blues-drenched version of Buck Owens' classic "Crying Time." Excellent production from the indefatigable Bruce Bromberg, newly remastered by Bernie Grundman, with informative notes by Pete Welding. Now's your chance to replace your old worn-out Playboy album or to pick up for the first time this outstanding release.
Rounder 2038 (c) **Tough As I Want to Be**
Splendid 1984 album. Backed by a tough small band, Phillip works his way through a grand selection of nine songs: a couple of originals, three new songs written by Lowell Fulson, a Dennis Walker composition, and top-notch updatings of Jimmy McCracklin's "Think," and Percy Mayfield's "A Lyin' Woman." Highlights of this album are two first-class slow blues, his own semi-autobiographical "Port Arthur Blues," and Fulson's "The Blues and My Guitar."

Note: See also LONESOME SUNDOWN and PHILLIP WALKER.

T-BONE WALKER

Great Texas-born singer/guitarist who was one of the most influential blues guitarists of the postwar era.

ESSENTIAL SELECTION

Atlantic (Canada) 8258 (c) **T-Bone Blues**
At last this classic album has been reissued in its entirety. Here we have T-Bone at his peak, recorded at three different sessions. There are three tracks from a 1955 Chicago session with a small band of Chicago musicians, including Eddie Chamblee, Mc-Kinley Easton, and Ransom Knowling. On one of these tracks, the horns drop out and T-Bone is joined by Junior Wells on harp for a down-home "Play on Little Girl." The five tracks from a 1955 Los Angeles session are the best, with T-Bone accompanied by Lloyd Glenn, Billy Hadnott, and Oscar Lee Bradley. He does stunning remakes of "Mean Old World," "Stormy Monday," and "T-Bone Blues." The 1959 session, also from LA, features an interesting lineup with two more guitars (R. S. Rankin and Barney Kessel), ace sax player Plas Johnson, plus Earl Palmer on drums. There is an emphasis on instrumental work on this album, with some truly outstanding playing. Essential!

Bear Family BFX 15277 **I Don't Be Jivin'**
Mostly late 60s T-Bone produced by Huey P. Meaux, with session men Jimmy Jones on bass and Piano Slim Burton on keyboards. T-Bone hadn't cut anything since his classic late 50s Atlantic sides and doesn't even play lead guitar on these sessions (he plays rhythm guitar and organ), though his voice is excellent. Most of the LP is taken from a two-hour session from Sept. 8, 1966, with local guitar hero Joey Long on histrionic lead. Of the dozen tunes cut, three were leased to Brunswick in '68, three came out on Meaux's Jet Stream label in '67, and two were released in '78 on Meaux's Home Cooking label, with the rest unissued. Many tunes have a horn section, including Arnett Cobb on tenor. The final three cuts are from a 1970 session with Johnny Copeland on guitar, the only good cuts from the horrible "Stormy Monday Blues" LP (Wet Soul 1002). Reconsider Baby/Further on up the Road/T-Bone's Back on the Scene.

Black and Blue 33.552 **Feeling the Blues**
1968 recordings.

Blues Boy 304 **The Inventor of the Electric Guitar Blues**
Complementing the three albums on Charly and the four out-of-print albums on Pathe, this LP reissues most of the rest of T-Bone's 40s and early 50s recordings. There are 16 sides from 1945–53, and one side of a 1929 recording in a country-blues vein. These are classic and influential recordings of urban blues featuring his outstanding guitar playing and emotive vocals accompanied by various fine groups.

Charly CRB 1019 (c) **T-Bone Jumps Again**
Sixteen superb sides recorded for Black and White and Capitol between 1942–49. T-Bone is backed by jazz-styled groups. Includes the first and best recording of his classic "Call it Stormy Monday." A treat for blues lovers.

Charly CRB 1037 **Plain Ole Blues**
Second album of 16 marvelous sides with small jazz groups recorded for Capitol in the 40s. A must.

Charly CRB 1057 **The Natural Blues**
The third reissue of T-Bone's classic recordings made for Capitol in 1942 and for Black and White and Capitol between December 1946 and April 1949, featuring six songs never issued before (some that were only recently discovered). Mellow vocals and great guitar by T-Bone accompanied by various small bands.

Delmark 633 (c) **I Want a Little Girl**
CASSETTE ONLY RELEASE

MCA 1366 **Dirty Mistreater**
Ten fine sides recorded for Bluesway in 1968 with good bands. Stormy Monday/Jealous Woman/Long Skirt Baby Blues/Treat Me So Low Down.
COMPACT DISC

ESSENTIAL SELECTION

Atlantic 8020-2 (M) **T-Bone Blues**
Now this is what compact discs are all about! This CD features all of T-Bone's recordings made for Atlantic in 1955 (Chicago), 1956, and 1957 (both Los Angeles). This includes tracks not previously on LP, along with what appears to be several previously unissued titles. T-Bone was in great form on these sessions and was accompanied by top session musicians like Plas Johnson, Earl Palmer, Lloyd Glenn, Eddie Chamblee, and Barney Kessel. A couple of the tracks have a more down-home feel, with Jimmy Rogers (gtr) and Junior Wells (hca); the latter does a fine solo on the previously unissued "T-Bone Blues Special." All of these sessions were beautifully recorded, and this comes over on this well-remastered compact disc. This one is a must!

Charly CD 7 **Low Down Blues**
Twenty-two of T-Bone's classic 40s recordings for Black and White and Capitol. Sound is OK, though, like most Charly CDs, it does not do justice to the medium; it sounds like the high end has been filtered to reduce noise. Don't Leave Me Baby/It's A Low

Down Dirty Deal/T-Bone Jumps Again/Call It Stormy Monday/Midnight Blues/Too Much Trouble Blues/The Natural Blues.

Sequel NEX CD 124 The Hustle Is On

The first CD in a series to reissue all of T-Bone's classic Imperial recordings. This one feautres 28 tracks recorded between April 1950 and October 1953. Walker was at his peak in these sessions, and he was accompanied by top-notch West Coast sidemen, including Jim Wynn, Robert "Snake" Sims, Maxwell Davis, and Willard McDaniels. I Got the Blues/Strollin' with Bones/Street Walkn' Woman/Cold Cold Feelin'/I Get So Weary/The Sun Went Down/Party Girl/Tell Me What's the Reason.

T-BONE WALKER/ROY GAINES
COMPACT DISC

Black and Blue 59.552 2 Feeling the Blues

69-minute CD featuring nine tracks recorded by T-Bone in France in 1968 and originally issued on Black and Blue 33.019 (now 33.552), and four tracks by Roy Gaines recorded in France in 1975 and originally issued on Black and Blue 33.088. The T-Bone tracks feature a good small group, including Hal Singer on tenor and George Avanitas on piano. Good, standard T-Bone fare with good singing and playing all around. Gaines was one of the many people influenced by T-Bone, though his music has taken a more jazz-flavored approach. Accompanied by Milt Buckner on organ and Panama Francis on drums, he performs good versions of a couple of originals, plus a reworking of Lightnin' Hopkins' "Once I Was a Gambler" and a ponderous version of T-Bone's "Stormy Monday."

FRANCES WALLACE and CLARA BURSTON

Document 584 Complete Recordings in Chronological Order, 1929–30

I don't know anything about the two artists featured here other than the fact that they are both excellent singers and that Wallace is a very fine piano player. There are four solo performances by Wallace with her own piano or that of John Oscar, and two solos by Burtson with an unknown piano player plus banjo or mandolin. There are four songs by Burston with Wallace on piano (two from unissued test pressings), two vocal duets, and three terrific tracks with vocals by Burston with a small group featuring Wallace on piano, James Cole on violin, and Walter Cole or Tommy Bradley on guitar. Consistently fine performances, sound ranges from adequate to excellent and, as far as I can tell, none of these tracks has been reissued before.

SIPPIE WALLACE

Another classic female blues singer who recorded in the 20s and 30s, continuing to record until her death in the 1970s. She authored many popular blues, several of which have been covered by Bonnie Raitt.

Document 593 1923–1929

Eighteen of her early recordings, where she is accompanied by solo piano or small jazz-flavored groups. It includes two versions of one of her most famous songs, "I'm a Mighty Tight Woman." Sound is generally quite good and very few of these tracks have been reissued before. Up the Country Blues/Caledonia Blues/Strangers Blues/Section Hand Blues.

Storyville 4017 Sippie Wallace Sings the Blues

SIPPIE WALLACE/OTIS SPANN

Mountain Railroad 52672 With Jim Kweskin and the Jug Band: Jug Band

Now here's a pleasant surprise. I don't know the origin of these recordings, but they include some superb moments. Eight of the 12 tracks feature Sippie accompanied by Kweskin and his group (Kweskin [gtr/comb], Geoff Muldaur [gtr, mdln, clr, washbd, kazoo], Bill Keith [5-string banjo], Richard Greene [vln]), and are nice performances re-creating some of her old favorites, like "Lovin' Sam," "Mighty Tight Woman," and "Up the Country." However, what makes this album essential for blues lovers are the four cuts on which Sippie is accompanied only by Otis Spann—"Black Snake Blues," "Jelly Roll Blues," "Muhammed Ali," and the utterly exquisite "Gambler's Dream." Sippie really lets the vocals rip on these and Spann's accompaniments are incredible, accentuating the vocals and weaving around them, proving once again that he was one of the greatest blues pianists who ever lived.

VAN WALLS

Whiskey, Women, and. . . 711 They Call Me Piano Man

Pianist extraordinaire Van Walls started his recording career in 1949, playing on Frank Culley's great stompers "Cole Slaw" and "Floorshow." He went on to be the preferred session piano player on Atlantic, backing Sticks McGhee, Ruth Brown, Big Joe Turner, The Drifters, and The Clovers, as well as moonlighting with other bands and record companys too numerous to mention (it's all in the liner notes). Side one is comprised of a recent ('87) solo set recorded in Boston, where the 70-year-old Walls lays down some inventive boogie-woogie. Side two collects nine tunes from 1949–52 that feature his virtuoso piano playing. These tunes show how well his talent lent itself to various styles, like blues (Brownie McGhee), hard-driving R&B (The Freddie Mitchell Orchestra), jazzy R&B (Nelson Clark's Orchestra with Hot Lips Page), and vocal groups (The Rockets). Open the Door/Air Mail Boogie/Idaho Boogie/Chocolate Candy Blues/Big Leg Mama.

J. W. WARREN
Swingmaster 2113 **Blues by J. W. Warren**
1981–82 recordings by Alabama country bluesman Warren. He is a good singer and a decent guitarist and performs a mixture of traditional songs, original pieces, and songs learned from the records of Blind Boy Fuller. He doesn't quite have the ability to pull off the raggy Piedmont style of Fuller, but his playing is quite good and he also plays some nice slide. Highlight of these recordings is the six-minute story/song, "The Escape of Corinna," with some particularly nice slide. Not an outstanding album, but it's so rare to hear any new country blues recordings with a degree of originality; this one is most welcome.

WASHBOARD DOC
L+R 42.010 **Early Morning Blues**
Spivey 1021 **Washboard Doc and His Hep 3**

WASHBOARD SAM
Popular singer, washboard player, and blues writer who was very active in the 30s and 40s. Although the washboard is a rather limited instrument, Sam's playing is subdued and the emphasis on his recordings is on his rich vocals and the playing of his sidemen, usually including Big Bill Broonzy on guitar. Other sidemen include piano players Black Bob, Joshua Altheimer, Horace Malcolm, and Roosevelt Sykes, and various string bass players.

Best Of Blues BOB 1 **1936–42**
Eighteen sides recorded between 1936–42, 16 not previously on LP. Several cuts feature some nice alto sax by Buster Bennett. Some of the material is a little similar but most of it is gently swinging. Good sound and full discographical details, though no notes.

Blues Classics 10 **Washboard Sam**
Fourteen sides recorded between 1935–41. Probably the best cross-section of his recordings. Mama Don't Allow/Big Woman/Back Door/Out with the Wrong Woman/I'm on My Way/Low Down Woman/Lovers Lane Blues/Digging My Potatoes.

Blues Documents 2091 **Vol. 1: 1937–47**
Twenty tracks, about one-third previously reissued on LP.

Chess 9251 (c) **Big Bill Broonzy and Washboard Sam**
See under Big Bill Broonzy.

Document DLP 507 **Volume 1**
Eighteen sides recorded between 1935–47, most never on LP before. This is an enjoyable collection of good-timey blues with Sam's rich vocals and washboard accompanied by the likes of Black Bob, Big Bill Broonzy, Arnett Nelson, and Blind John Davis, including pioneer electric guitarist George Barnes, who takes a lovely solo on "It's Too Late Now." Who Pumped the Wind In My Doughnut/Ladie's Man/Barbecue/Hand Reader Blues/Somebody Changed That Lock On My Door/She's A Bad Luck Woman/He's A Creepin' Man.

DINAH WASHINGTON
Although well-known as a jazz singer and, to a lesser extent, as a pop singer, Dinah's recordings of blues are not as well-documented. The following albums reveal what an excellent blues singer Dinah was, with elements of Billie Holiday in her approach.

Emarcy 814 184 (c) **A Slick Chick on the Mellow Side**
A wonderful two-LP set featuring 27 songs recorded between 1943–54 by this outstanding artist. She is accompanied by top musicians: The Lionel Hampton Septet, The Tab Smith Orchestra, and The Cootie Williams Orchestra. Some of the later recordings from the 50s have a pop flavor, but the 40s recordings are consistently fine.

Jukebox Lil 1102 **If You Don't Believe I'm Leaving**
"The Queen of the Jukeboxes" delivers the goods in her own inimitable style on choice sides like "Mean and Evil Blues" (1947), "Pillow Blues" ('52), an ode to the sopping wet pillow slip, and the saucy, seductive "Big Long Slidin' Thing" (the trombone, of course) on which Dinah is backed by some tasty licks from members of the Leroy Kirkland Orchestra. Fine informative notes by Dave Penny plus a treasury of rare photos grace the fold-out sleeve.

Rosetta 1313 **Wise Woman Blues**

LEROY WASHINGTON
Obscure but fine Louisiana singer and guitarist who recorded for Jay Miller in the late 50s. Washington is a good singer with a relaxed vocal style popular with Louisiana singers. His guitar playing is right in the Louisiana tradition, but with elements of more contemporary styling.

Flyright 574 **Leroy Washington**
Excellent backup by Guitar Gable and Katie Webster.

TUTS WASHINGTON

Influential piano player from New Orleans who died in 1984.

Rounder 2041 (c,d) **New Orleans Piano Professor**
Wonderful album by then 76-year-old New Orleans piano player who was an inspiration to such artists as Professor Longhair, Allen Toussaint, and James Booker. This is, surprisingly, his first and only solo recording and shows him to be a wonderful performer who showed no sign of his advancing years in his playing, and was equally at home with blues, boogie, jazz, or pop tunes. At times his playing brings to mind Jimmy Yancey, but Tuts is very much an individual performer. CD includes bonus tracks. Delightful!

WALTER "WOLFMAN" WASHINGTON

Charley LIM 100 **Good and Juicy**
Fine New Orleans guitarist who has worked with many of the great Crescent City legends like Lee Dorsey, Irma Thomas, and Johnny Adams. These tunes are taken from his work for Hep'me Records in the early 80s. Get On Up (The Wolfman's Song)/Good and Juicy/Honky Tonk/It's Rainin' In My Life.

Rounder 2048 (c,d) **Wolf Tracks**
Rounder 2068 (c,d) **Out of the Dark**
Mainly uninspired funk/R&B cuts by legendary Federal sideman, issued as part of Rounder's "Modern New Orleans Masters" series. Unfortunately, this one sounds like a misdirected bid for Top 40 airplay, conveying little of the spirit and soul of the Crescent City. Exceptions are Washington's skillful arrangement of Jimmy Hughes' "Steal Away," a laid-back Louisiana groove propelled by a bubbling bass line, and a swampity-boot-a-shake version of Otis Redding's "Nobody's Fault but Mine." His reworking of Buddy Johnson's "Save Your Love for Me" features his most noteworthy and expressive vocal, as well as giving him a chance to stretch the strings a little—a welcome change from the constricted feel that dominates the rest of the soloing here. Walter has a chunky rough-hewn guitar sound that stands out in sharp contrast to the otherwise slick production, a tough, distinctive tone sharpened by years of work with Lee Dorsey, Irma Thomas, and Johnny Adams. His playing is the one memorable element in what is otherwise just another piece of low-cal pop fodder.

CROWN PRINCE WATERFORD

Oldie Blues 8011 **Shoutin' the Blues**
Excellent collection of 14 sides by this fine under-recorded blues shouter. Seven tracks are from a 1947 session featuring Waterford with an excellent small band, including the brilliant piano of Pete Johnson and the fine tenor sax of Maxwell Davis. The other tracks were recorded between 1945–49 with various bands, including Jay McShann on piano. Waterford was a fine and expressive singer who was equally at home on a jumping boogie ("Merry Go Round Blues," "Leaping Boogie," "Coal Black Baby") or a soulful slow blues ("Weeping Willow Blues," "C. P. Blues"). Recommended.

ETHEL WATERS

Blues/jazz/vaudeville singer who recorded quite extensively in the 20s, 30s, and 40s. Her 20s recordings are pretty much blues, while her later ones are more pop and jazz flavored.

Rosetta 1314 **1938–40**
Ethel's complete Bluebird recordings, 16 sides recorded at four sessions between November 1938 and September 1939. Backing band is The Eddie Mallory Orchestra, with the trumpeter joined by such greats as Benny Carter, Shirley Clay, Tyree Glenn, Garvin Bushell, and Milt Hinton. Fold-out cover has Ethel's full biography and lots of rare photos.

Wolf WJS 1009 **1924-28**
Twenty tracks not previously on album.

JOHN "MAD DOG" WATKINS

Blue Phoenix 33.725 **Here I Am**
Young singer/guitarist recorded in France with rhythm section including the brilliant Jimmy Johnson on guitar. Watkins is a pleasing though not very striking performer. He mostly performs old favorites. As the Years Go Passing By/Call the Plumber/Gangster of Love.

JOHNNY "GUITAR" WATSON

Fine West Coast blues singer/guitarist with a powerful percussive style who has adapted well to the times; a few years ago he enjoyed some success as a disco performer! His early recordings issued on Ace and Red Lightnin' are all excellent and highly recommended.

Red Lightnin' 0013 **The Gangster Is Back**
Sixteen great sides, 1955–61. Too Tired/Hot Little Mama/I Love To Love You/Oh Baby/She Moves Me/Gangster Of Love.
COMPACT DISC
Ace CDCH 909 3 **Three Hours Past Midnight**
Recordings made from 1955–56 for RPM, plus two

1959 tracks recorded for Class and his early Combo recording of "Motor Head Baby" with The Chuck Higgins Orchestra.

JAMES "WEE WILLIE" WAYNE
Sundown 709-02 Travellin' from Texas to New Orleans
A most welcome reissue of 18 fine sides of urban blues and R&B by this excellent Texas singer who recorded quite extensively in New Orleans. Wayne is best known for the original versions of the classic songs "Junco Partner" and "Travellin' Mood" (both here). Recordings from 1951–61; the New Orleans sides feature such great names as Lee Allen and Justin Adams.

CURLEY WEAVER
Blues Documents 2004 Georgia Guitar Wizard
A retrospective of this brilliant Georgia singer and guitarist has been long overdue and, although the packaging and sound on this album are not exceptional, the music certainly is. Weaver was a splendid performer—a warm singer and an exceptional guitarist who played equally well in regular or bottleneck style. Weaver worked closely with fellow Georgians Buddy Moss, Blind Willie McTell, and Fred McMullen, who all appear here in accompanying roles, and, on the superb "Some Cold Rainy Day," Ruth Willis adds some lovely vocal harmonies. Many of these tracks have been issued before, but mostly on currently unavailable albums. Highly recommended. Sweet Petunia/Baby Boogie Woogie/No No Blues/Tippin' Tom/Decatur Street 81/City Cell Blues.

Document 594 1933-1950
Documents many aspects of Weaver's recording career. Most of Side one features Weaver as an accompanying guitarist to Buddy Moss; Moss was a magnificent singer and guitarist, and the seven sides with them together are terrific. From 1935 there are two excellent and rare sides by Weaver, with Blind Willie McTell on second guitar! The remaining seven titles are from Weaver's postwar recordings (1949 and '50) that show that his talents were undiminished; his versions of "Ticket Agent" and "Some Rainy Day" are as good as anything he recorded. Some of the cuts on this album have been reissued before, but most are not currently available elsewhere. Sound on a few tracks is rough but is generally good.

SYLVESTER WEAVER
Wonderful and pioneering blues guitarist who was the first black blues guitarist to accompany a singer.

Agram 2010 Smoketown Strut
Sixteen superb sides recorded between 1923–27. Features four instrumentals by Weaver, including his original version of "Guitar Rag," which later became famous as "Steel Guitar Rag." There are four vocals by Weaver, and he accompanies E. L. Coleman, Sara Martin, Helen Humes, and Walter Beasley. Includes extensive notes based on recent research, two photos of Weaver, label photos, and more. Many of these recordings are very rare and the sound on some of the cuts is very poor, but the music is so great that it is worth suffering through some of the almost unlistenable tracks.

Blues Documents 2026 The Accompanist 1923–1927
This LP contains both sides of Weaver's historic first recording, accompanying Sara Martin, plus 16 other titles with Sylvester backing either Sara Martin (13 cuts) or Helen Humes (later a vocalist with Count Basie). The tracks with Martin are slow blues and, save for "Strange Lovin' Blues," on which Weaver plays bottleneck, all feature jazzy, ragtime guitar stylings. The three titles backing Helen Humes are wonderful, with Walter Beasley on second guitar, Weaver playing slide throughout, and some bizarre lyrics to boot. Complements Agram 2010, with only four titles previously available.

Earl 615 The Remaining Titles, 1924–27
A lovely collection of 18 sides, complementing Agram 2010 by reissuing all of the remaining solo performances by Weaver, with the exception of two undiscovered tracks. It also includes one accompaniment to Sara Martin on the fine gospel song "Where Shall I Be." Weaver was a master musician whose material included straight blues, ragtime guitar, and bottleneck-style, all performed with equal skill and imagination. There are solo guitar instrumentals, vocal and guitar pieces, and guitar duets with fellow Kentuckian Walter Beasley. The album includes one of his two versions of "Guitar Rag." Many of these tracks have been reissued before, scattered over various albums, many now out-of-print. Some of the tracks are from worn 78s, but the sound is generally quite satisfactory and the music is fabulous.

BOOGIE BILL WEBB
Flying Fish 700506 (c) Drinkin' and Stinkin'
Thirteen tracks by a Mississippi bluesman based in New Orleans. Webb was an associate of the great Tommy Johnson and many of his previous recordings focused on Johnson's influence on him. This release draws on a more diverse repertoire. There is the obligatory Johnson song, "Canned Heat," but

this collection also features Bill doing Leadbelly's "Red Cross Store," Lowell Fulson's "Black Nights," and an unexpected "Cuttin Out Baby," which Bill learned from Professor Longhair (whom he played with in the 50s). Plus there are several originals, including the humorous title song, and the instrumental "Bill's Boogie Woogie." Bill sings and plays electric guitar and is given sympathetic backup by Ben Sandmel on drums and Reggie Scanlan on bass. Album comes with a detailed eight-page booklet by Nick Spitzer.

KATIE WEBSTER

Fine Louisiana singer and piano player who was house pianist for Excello Records for many years. Katie now lives in California. Her Flyright

albums are mostly previously unissued recordings from the late 50s. Her 70s recordings for Goldband are unexceptional. Her recent recordings for Ornament, Arhoolie, and Alligator are all very good but Katie has to be seen live to be appreciated.

Alligator 4766 (c,d) The Swamp Boogie Queen
Excellent new album by Louisiana's Queen of blues, boogie, and soul. Accompanied by her band—the fine three-piece Silent Partners—she performs a selection of blues, soul, swamp pop, and boogie. The emphasis is on a 60s soul sound, with driving versions of Johnny Taylor's "Who's Making Love," her former boss Otis Redding's "Fa-Fa-Fa-Fa-Fa," "Try a Little Tenderness" (the latter with a nice up-tempo ending), and Joe Tex's "Hold on to What You've Got," with a new and witty spoken section by Katie. She also does a fine version of the old swamp-pop hit, "Sea of Love," and gets in a splendid boogie workout on her own "Black Satin," with a whimsical intro from "Clare de Lune." Several guest musicians appear, including Robert Cray (adding some trademark licks on "Who's Making Love"), and the splendid Memphis Horns round out the sound on a couple of tracks. Other guests include Bonnie Raitt and Kim Wilson, whose contributions are fairly

expendable. Still, a most worthwhile album from a major talent.

Alligator 4777 (c,d) Two-Fisted Mama!
1990 album with her new road band and guest appearance by The Memphis Horns on three cuts.

Arhoolie 1095 (c) You Know That's Right
1985 LP, possibly her best. It's great to hear her driving, inventive piano clearly. Here she is backed by Hot Licks, led by guitarist John Lumsdaine. The songs, mostly originals, have that catchy Louisiana feel, from the rollicking title song, "Voodoo Blues," and the soulful "Jimmy, Jimmy," to the torchy "Don't Accuse Me," and the lively piano solo on "Katie's Boogie Woogie." Katie has rarely sung better and, coupled with the fine production and backup, we finally get to hear her at her best.

Flyright 530 Whooee Sweet Daddy
Superb late 50s recordings cut for Jay Miller, mostly previously unissued.

Flyright 613 Katie Webster
Volume 48 of the Legendary Jay Miller Sessions presents 14 sides recorded in the late 50s and early 60s by this marvelous singer and piano player, accompanied by various musicians. This complements Flyright 530 and includes versions of songs that were previously issued in alternate-take form only, along with alternate takes of songs issued then and some newly discovered songs. The album opens with the tremendous "Baby Baby," a classic talking blues with great singing and playing by Katie. There are two versions of the blues ballad "Sunny Side of Love," a beautiful previously unissued version of the swamp-pop hit "Sea of Love," and a fine version of "Your Cheating Heart." Some of the tracks seem to be rough demos, but Katie is such a fine talent that they are well worth a listen.

Goldband 7780 Katie Webster has The Blues
Uninspired 70s recordings.

Goldband 7785 You Can Dig It
Uninspired 70s recordings.

Ornament 7.123 Live + Well
Recorded live in Germany. A solo selection of blues, boogies, and R&B songs, plus Katie's version of "Satisfaction"! She is in fine form with great vocals and her piano playing is top-notch whether on a low-down blues or romping boogie. The only complaints are that the sound of the piano is a little thin and the audience noise is a bit distracting, but otherwise a very fine album.

Ornament 7.529 200% Joy
Unlike her first Ornament release, which was recorded live, this is a studio set, making for generally better listening, although her playing is slightly

lacking in spontaneity. She performs a diverse selection of songs and tunes, some originals, along with songs by Stevie Wonder, Otis Redding, Helen Humes, and Percy Mayfield.

Swamp Boogie 8701 (12" 45 rpm) **Whoo Wee Sweet Daddy**

COMPACT DISC

Flyright CD 12 **Katie Webster**

Fine collection of 20 sides recorded by this brilliant Louisiana singer, piano player, and entertainer for Jay Miller in the early 60s. Drawn from Flyright 530 and 613, it includes songs originally issued on 45s by Miller, along with many previously unissued songs. The material is varied and includes the marvelous duet with her husband Ashton Conroy on "No Bread, No Meat," jumpin' numbers like "Baby Come On," "The Katie Lee," and "Don't You Know," and soulful swamp ballads like "Glory of Love," "Sunny Side of Love," and "Sea of Love." Fine singing and playing from Katie and solid band accompaniments.

WILL WELDON

Excellent prewar singer and slide guitarist.

Document 565 **Remaining Titles and Alternate Takes**

Eighteen tracks recorded between 1935–37.

Earl BD 605 **Will Weldon**

Eighteen fine sides, recorded between 1927–37, complementing reissues on RCA (France) PM 42050 (now out of print) and Yazoo 1049. These recordings range from the Memphis country-blues guitar duet, "Turpentine Blues," to the more urban small-group stylings of "Christmas Time Blues." Accompanying musicians include Vol Stevens, Peetie Wheatstraw, Black Bob, and Big Bill Broonzy.

Old Tramp 1206 **Master of the Steel Guitar**

This album features 18 tracks recorded between 1936–37. Most of these tracks have not been on LP before, though some are alternate takes of songs available elsewhere. There are also two takes each of "Keyhole Blues" and "Streamline Woman," which are not terribly different from each other. The album includes his topical songs "Flood Water Blues" and "Casey Bill's New W.P.A.," plus his version of "We Gonna Move (to the Outskirts of Town)," which, I believe, is one of the first recordings of this song. Bill is accompanied by such sidemen as Black Bob, Tampa Red, Charlie McCoy, Horace Malcomb, and Big Bill Broonzy. "Pokino Blues" features a vocal by Blind Teddy Darby. There is not a whole lot of variety in the performances here, but most of the performances are individually enjoyable.

Yazoo 1049 **Bottleneck Guitar Trendsetters**

One side of album by Kokomo Arnold.

VALERIE WELLINGTON

Rooster Blues R 2619 (c,d) **Million Dollar Secret**

Fine young blues singer from Chicago. Her debut album features an interesting selection of songs, including updates of several blues from the 20s and 30s such as the title song, "Down In The Dumps," and Bessie Smith's "Dirty No Gooders Blues." There are several originals by Valerie along with songs by Howlin' Wolf and Roy Brown. Valerie has a vocal style akin to that of Koko Taylor, though she is a more subtle performer. She is given solid support by some top Chicago blues musicians, including some great guitar by Magic Slim.

JUNIOR WELLS

Brilliant Chicago blues singer and harmonica player. His classic recordings for States in 1953 are reissued on Delmark 640. His later 50s recordings for States and Profile (which do not always feature his harp) are available on Flyright and Red Lightnin'. His 60s and early 70s recordings, often with Buddy Guy, are consistently good. His later recordings are more variable; Junior attempts to perform James Brown-type soul, not the ideal selection of material to showcase his talents.

Delmark 612 (c,d) **Hoodoo Man Blues**

The first, and one of the best, Delmark albums, from 1965. Junior is accompanied by Buddy Guy (gtr), Jack Myers (b), and Billy Warren (drm). This album presents Chicago blues at its best, with great singing and playing by Wells.

Delmark 628 (c) **Southside Blues Jam**

Another splendid 60s album, with Buddy Guy, Louis Myers, Otis Spann, and Fred Below.

Delmark 635 **On Tap**

1974 set with A. C. Reed, Charles Miles, and Sammy Lawhorn.

ESSENTIAL SELECTION

Delmark 640 Blues Hit Big Town
Essential sides recorded for States in 1953–54 with Junior accompanied by incredible musicians like Elmore James, Muddy Waters, Louis Myers, Johnnie Jones, and Otis Spann. Includes several great tracks not originally issued. Classic performances. Hoodoo Man/Junior's Wail/Ways Like An Angel/Blues Hit Big Town (two versions)/'Bout The Break Of Day/So All Alone.

Flyright 588 Universal Rock
Twelve excellent sides from 1957–63 recorded for Profile, Chief, and U.S.A. Not a lot of Junior's harp here, but fine tough vocals and superb bands, including Syl Johnson, Willie Dixon, Earl Hooker, Lafayette Leake, and Fred Below. About half these tracks are on Red Lightnin' 007, but this one, from original master tapes, has much better sound.

Flyright 605 Chiefly Wells
Eleven tracks recorded for Chief and U.S.A. between 1957–63. Although he only plays harp on a few tracks, there are some great vocals and superb accompaniments by such artists as Syl Johnson, Willie Dixon, and Earl Hooker. A couple of the Wells cuts are expendable pop items but most are very good. There are also four Magic Sam cuts, three recorded for Chief in 1960 and the other recorded for Crash in 1966. The album is rounded out by two cuts by Shakey Jake, who is no great shakes (!) as a singer, but he turns in a creditable job, and the accompaniments by Louis Myers (hca), Otis Spann (pno), and Magic Sam and Mighty Joe Young (gtrs) make these cuts well worth a listen.

Red Lightnin' 007 In My Younger Days
Classic States, Chief, and Profile sides. All these area available with better sound on Delmark and Flyright.

Vanguard 79262 (d) Coming At You
COMPACT DISC

Flyright FLYCD 03 Messin' with the Kid
23-track collection of recordings by Junior made for the Profile, Chief, and USA labels between 1957–63. Although only a few tracks feature Junior's great harp playing, there are some fine songs here and great accompaniments, including some beautiful slide guitar by Earl Hooker, along with other fine musicians like Syl Johnson, Willie Dixon, Lafayette Leake, Dave Myers, Jarrett Gibson, Moose John Walker, Johnny Jones, and Billy Emerson. Come on in this House/So Tired/It Hurts Me Too/Messin' with the Kid/You Couldn't Care/Two-Headed Woman/Lovey Dovey Lovey One.

Vanguard 73120 It's My Life Baby
Note: See also under BUDDY GUY and JUNIOR WELLS.

JUNIOR WELLS/EARL HOOKER
COMPACT DISC

Charly CD 219 Messin' with the Kid
24-track collection of recordings cut for Chief, Profile, and Age by Junior with Hooker and Hooker with Junior. Most of these tracks are also available on Flyright. Little By Little/Come on in this House/Prison Bars All Around Me/Love Me/It Hurts Me Too/The Things I'd Do for You/Universal Rock/So Tired/I Need Me a Car/Calling All Blues/These Cotton Pickin' Blues.

PEETIE WHEATSTRAW
An incredibly popular and influential bluesman in the 30s and early 40s. He was a lovely singer with a rich, expressive voice. His "ooh well, well" was a trademark he used on many of his recordings and was copied by many other performers. He was a basic but effective piano player. Peetie tended to use the same tune on many of his songs, but his songs are usually interesting enough that this is not a problem.

Best Of Blues BOB 10 The Devil's Son-in-Law, 1937–1941
This collection of 18 tracks focuses on Peetie's talents as a vocalist. There are two titles with accompaniments by Teddy Bunn and Sammy Price and two with Lonnie Johnson and Lee Brown. Half of the LP consists of two 1941 sessions with Jonah Jones, Lil Armstrong, and Big Sid Cattlett, which have a decidedly jazzy feel. I especially like Jones' growl trumpet on "Jaybird Blues," and his blowing on "Pocketknife Blues." Four tracks with Robert Lee McCoy and Jack DuPree round out the LP. Peetie's songs are often similar, but the diffent accompanists help to diversify things. This record reissues the long-out-of-print White Label 8 LP, with the addition of one track.

Blues Classics 4 Peetie Wheatstraw and Kokomo Arnold
One side of album by each.

Blues Documents 2011 The Devil's Son-in-Law
Twenty tracks recorded between 1930–41 by this distinctive and popular performer. Although many of these tracks have been reissued before, most have been unavailable for many years. Here we have Peetie's fine vocals, trademark "Ooh Well, Well," and distinctive piano style with varied accompanying musicians, including Charlie Jordan, Kokomo Arnold, Lonnie Johnson, and Lee Brown. Songs include the odd "Fairasee Woman," the risque "I Want Some Sea Food," and other fine numbers.

Don't Feel Welcome Blues/These Times/Santa Claus Blues/Meat Cutter Blues/Beggar Man Blues/Third Street's Going Down.

Old Tramp OT 1200 **The Devil's Son-in-Law, 1931–34**

Eighteen fine tracks, mostly not reissued before. Most of the tracks feature him in the company of a guitar player, including such fine performers as Charlie McCoy, Charlie Jordan, and Lonnie Johnson, and a few feature the lovely slide guitar of Kokomo Arnold. The last few tracks on the album feature small combos including one with the fine harmonica of Robert Lee McCoy. Sound is generally good and there are full discographical details.

Note: Other Wheatstraw recordings are available on Yazoo 1030, Mamlish 3805, and OJL 20.

ARTIE "BLUES BOY" WHITE

Chicago-based singer.

Ichiban 1008 (c) **Nothing Takes the Place of You**

A nice mixture of contemporary blues and deep soul. The blues include the lively "Wondering How You Keep Your Man," Little Milton's "How Could You Do It to Me," and "Ever Loving Man," while the soul tracks include a version of the classic Toussaint McCall title song, Willie Nelson's "Funny How Time Slips Away," and the very fine "I Need Someone." Good singing and nice no-nonsense arrangements.

Ichiban 1026 **Where It's At**

Excellent album is two-thirds blues and one-third 60s-style soul. Artie is a fine vocalist, at times reminiscent of Albert King. He is accompanied by a fine band, with strong horn section and nice, if sometimes fussy, guitar by Chris Johnson.

Ichiban 1044 **Thangs Got to Change**

A nice mixture of old favorites like "You Upset Me Baby" and "Reconsider Baby" alongside good new ones like the title song, "Rainy Day," and "I Wonder Why." Several of the songs were written by Artie and Little Milton, and Milton plays tasty lead guitar on many of the tracks. Artie is a good singer in the Milton/Albert King mold, and the arrangements with a big band are very effective.

Iciban 1061 (c,d) **Tired of Sneaking Around**

Fine 1990 album of blues, R&B, and soul. Along with some good new songs by Travis Haddock, there are also some excellent covers, including B. B. King's "Sneaking Around" and even Merle Haggard's "Today I Started Lovin' You Again," which comes across very well as a bluesy shuffle! Good singing from Artie and solid backup by a small band with a couple of horns and some very tasty guitar from Larry Williams.

Ronn 8000 **Blues Boy**

Some good contemporary blues with a touch of funk/soul. Accompanied by a solid band with effective horns, he works his way through eight songs including a couple of originals and versions of the country-soul standard "Funny How Time Slips Away" and Don Covay's "Chain of Fools." The weakest point of this album is the very rock-flavored guitar, but otherwise this is an enjoyable set.

BOOKER (BUKKA) WHITE

Great Mississippi country-blues singer and guitarist. He was a powerful slide player and a creative composer of blues songs. His incredible 1930 recordings are available on the following anthologies: Yazoo 1009, 1026, OJL 12, and OJL 13. His superb 1937–40 tracks are available on Travelin' Man. His 60s recordings are all very fine, with the two Arhoolie's being of particular interest with the lengthy performances giving a remarkable insight into a bluesman's creative process.

Arhoolie 1019 **Sky Songs, Vol. 1**

Bukka sings and plays guitar on a series of lengthy and highly creative songs. Jesus Died On The Cross To Save The World/Sugar Hill/My Baby/Alabama Blues.

Arhoolie 1020 **Sky Songs, Vol. 2**

More remarkable performances. Bald Eagle Blues/Single Man Blues/Georgia Skin Game/Mixed Water.

Biograph 12049 **Big Daddy**

GNP Crescendo 10011 (d) **Legacy of the Blues, Vol. 1**

His first recordings after being rediscovered in the early 60s. Originally issued as Takoma 7001.

ESSENTIAL SELECTION

Travelin' Man 806 **Aberdeen Mississippi Blues, 1937–40**

These recordings are among the greatest country blues ever made so it is a pleasure to have them available again. Bukka, in addition to being a great singer and guitar player, was also a brilliant songwriter whose lyrics were more inventive and original than those of many of his contemporaries. Many of his songs are based on personal experiences. Several songs deal with the subject of sickness and death, and there are several songs about his stay at the dreadful Parchman prison farm and other events in his life. All this is sung in Bukka's beautiful rich voice with its powerful vibrato and effective use of slurs and slides. He accompanies himself with rhythmic, complex guitar parts, with occasional use of slide. Excellent sound and informative notes by Simon Napier. If you don't already have these classic sides on a previous reissue, these are a must.

CASSETTE AND CD RELEASE ONLY

Arhoolie C/CD 323 **Sky Songs**
All of Arhoolie 1019 and half of 1020.

COMPACT DISC

ESSENTIAL SELECTION

Travelin' Man CD 03 **The Complete Sessions, 1930–40**
Twenty flawless masterpieces. Incorporates material from the Travelin' Man LP. Sound is OK.

GEORGIA WHITE

Excellent Chicago-based singer and piano player who recorded quite extensively between 1936–41.

Rosetta 1307 **Sings and Plays**
Sixteen fine sides, including her 1936 recordings of "Trouble In Mind"— the first version of this classic. Most of the performances feature piano and guitar and a few cuts have larger jazzy accompaniments.

JOSH WHITE

Although best known for his slick folky renditions from the 40s and 50s, White was, in his early days, an excellent East Coast country-blues singer and fluid guitarist.

Document 597 **1929–41**
A diverse selection by this popular and prolific performer. It starts with a 1929 harmonica instrumental by The Carver Boys with Josh on guitar. There are half-a-dozen tracks from the mid-30s with fine vocals and guitar by Josh and occasional second guitar or piano. Two tracks from 1940 feature him with Sidney Bechet (clr) and Wilson Myers (b). There are also five tracks with Myers only; these are fine performances, but with an odd hollow sound, as though they were recorded at a concert. There is a track by Joshua White and The Carolinians, a gospel group in the vein of the immensely popular Golden Gate Quartet, and the set is rounded out by Josh with a small group, including Edmond Hall on clarinet, which doesn't really work. I don't think any of these have been on LP before.

Earl BD 606 **Joshua White, Vol. 1**
Eighteen sides recorded in 1932–33, about two-thirds blues and one-third gospel songs. Some fine music, though some of the tracks are taken from rather worn 78s.

Earl BD 619 **Joshua White, Vol. 2**
Twenty beautiful blues and gospel sides recorded between 1929–35 during Josh's prefolk era.

M.C.A. 2-4170 **The Legendary Josh White**
Two-LP set featuring recordings from the late 50s. Josh at his folkiest.

Stinson 14 **Josh White Sings the Blues**
Stinson 15 **Josh White Sings the Blues, Vol. 2**
Storyville 123 **Blues Singer and Balladeer**
Note: Other early tracks are available on Historical 22 and Rounder 4007.

JOHNNY WICK'S SWINGING OZARKS

Pearl PL 13 **Jockey Jack Boogie**
An interesting album featuring recordings from a session held in Chicago in March 1952 by a jazz-flavored group from Louisville, KY, led by bass player John Wicks and including fine tenor sax playing by Scott Johnson and nice piano by Gerald Blue. It features vocals by "Preacher" John Stephans, who also plays the tuba on several cuts, giving them a unique sound. Many of the tracks were never issued originally, and the album includes quite a lot of studio chat. A couple of the cuts feature guest violinist Remo Biondi, who mostly just noodles away.

ROBERT WILKINS

Absolutely marvelous Mississippi country-blues singer and guitarist with a wonderful complex picking style. The Wolf LP reissues his magnificent 20s and 30s recordings. Wilkins turned to the ministry in the late 30s, and his 60s and 70s recordings are all gospel, though all feature his magnificent guitar playing.

OJL 8052 **Memphis Gospel Singer**
Reissue of one of my favorite albums, originally issued in 1964 on the Piedmont label. Features some of the few recordings made in the postwar era by this wonderful singer and guitar player. Mostly original compositions, including his 11-minute retelling of the story of the prodigal son using the tune of one of his early blues songs, the highlight of an outstanding album.

Wolf 111 **Robert Wilkins**
All 17 cuts that have so far been discovered of Wilkins' recordings from 1928–35. Fourteen of these cuts have already been reissued by Herwin on a now out-of-print LP. Absolutely superb country blues.

JIMMY LEE WILLIAMS
Swingmaster 2115 Blues by Jimmy Lee Williams

Excellent country-blues guitarist and singer from Porlan, GA, recorded by folklorist George Mitchell in 1977 and 1982. Williams is a powerful singer and a rhythmic and effective electric guitarist. Much of his material is original, though he also draws on traditional songs and blues hits. Well worth a listen.

BIG JOE WILLIAMS
Great Mississippi country-blues singer and guitarist noted for playing a nine-string guitar and for his powerful vocal style. Joe had an almost unbroken recording career from the mid-30s up to his death in 1983, and there was little change in the style or the quality of his music over the years. Some of his 30s recordings can be found on the superb Mamlish 3810, while his 40s recordings (with Sonny Boy Williamson on harmonica) are featured on Blues Classics 21. Oldie Blues 2804 features some fine early 50s demos. Many of his 60s and 70s recordings are very fine, with standouts being Arhoolie 1002 and Delmark 627.

Arhoolie 1002 Tough Times
Superb recordings from 1959–60. Sloppy Drunk Blues/ President Roosevelt/Graystone Blues/Mean Stepfather.

Arhoolie 1053 Thinking of What They Did to Mc
Fine 1969 set, with Charlie Musselwhite (hca) on some cuts.

Blues Classics 21 Big Joe Williams and Sonny Boy Williamson
Fourteen great sides, 1941–47.

Delmark 627 (d) Nine-String Guitar Blues
Fine 1971 set, with Ransom Knowling (b) on some cuts.

GNP Crescendo 10016 Legacy of the Blues, Vol. 6

L+R 42.047 Big Joe Williams
CD issue: L+R CD 2047
Excellent selection of recordings made between 1973–80. Most were recorded at Joe's home in Crawford, MS, and have a relaxed, informal quality. Some of these songs will be familiar to Joe's fans but some are not as well-known. Tailor Made Baby/Dark Road Blues/Delta Blues/Don't Your House Look Lonesome.

Mamlish 3810 Big Joe Williams, 1935/1941
Fourteen superb sides, some with incredible fiddle by Chasey Collins.

Milestone 3001 Classic Delta Blues
Oldie Blues 2804 Malvina, My Sweet Woman
Ornament CH 7.713 Back to the Roots
Informal recordings mostly cut at Big Joe's home between 1973–78. Joe is in good form singing and playing six-, nine-, and 12-string guitars. The record comes with a detailed booklet.

Storyville 224 Big Joe Williams
Recorded in Denmark in 1972. Big Joe hardly ever made a bad record and this one is no exception. A mixture of old favorites and less familiar titles. Pretty Willie Done Me Wrong/Tell Me, Who's Been Telling You/My Baby/Turnroad Blues.

Wolf 120.918 Live, 1974
Recorded live in November 1974 in Jackson, MS. Although Joe is in fine form on a selection of his old favorites, like "Shake Your Boogie," "Don't Your Peaches Look Mellow," and "Baby Please Don't Go," the sound is appallingly bad. It sounds very much like a poor-quality cassette recording and, with so much first-rate Big Joe material available, including versions of most of these songs, I really cannot see any point to this release.
CASSETTE AND CD RELEASE ONLY

Arhoolie C/CD 315 Shake Your Boogie
All of Arhoolie 1002 and most of 1053.

LESTER WILLIAMS
Excellent Houston-based urban blues singer and guitarist. Williams is a mellow singer who plays some T-Bone Walker-influenced guitar.

Krazy Kat 7412 Dowling Street Hop
Twelve sides including his 1950 blues hit "Wintertime Blues."

PAUL WILLIAMS AND HIS ORCHESTRA
Rockin' East Coast blues and R&B band featuring the alto or baritone sax of leader Williams and the driving tenor of Noble Watts.

Saxophonograph BP 500 The Hucklebuck

ROBERT PETE WILLIAMS
Discovered in the Louisiana State Penitentiary in 1959, Robert Pete was one of the great country blues discoveries of the period. A moving singer and original guitar player; his style is intense and uncompromising and can be hard going for the casual listener but is incredibly rewarding. His finest recordings are probably the reissues of his Folklyric records on Arhoolie and his Prestige recordings that are available on a Fantasy double set. Williams died in 1980.

Arhoolie 2011 Angola's Prisoner's Blues
Superb album recorded at the Louisiana State

Penitentiary at Angola. Five cuts by Williams including his tremendous "Prisoner's Talking Blues," one of the most moving blues ever recorded! Other artists featured on this collection are Hogman Maxey and Robert Welch.

Arhoolie 2015 Those Prison Blues

Fabulous performances recorded by Harry Oster between 1959–61, while Robert was in jail at Angola. Pardon Denied Again/This Wild Old Life/Texas Blues/Up and Down Blues/ Louise.

Fantasy 24716 Robert Pete Williams and Snooks Eaglin

Double set; one album by each.

GNP Crescendo GNP 10019 The Legacy of the Blues, Vol. 9

Southland 4 When I Lay My Burden Down

Storyville 225 Robert Pete Williams

Recorded in Denmark in 1972. This album does not feature Robert Pete at his best. Some cuts feature 12-string guitar and some slide, neither of which is terribly effective.

SONNY BOY WILLIAMS

Wolf 135 Complete Recordings in Chronological Order, 1940–42

Under no circumstances should this artist be confused with either of the artists who recorded as Sonny Boy Williamson. Sonny Boy Williams (real name: Enoch Williams) was a dull New York-based singer and pianist who is more of a pop and jazz singer than a blues singer. Many of the songs here are of only marginal blues interest.

WILLIE WILLIAMS

P-Vine PLP 9055 Raw Unpolluted Soul

Reissue of album originally issued some 10 to 15 years ago on the Supreme Blues label, featuring drummer/vocalist Williams with "Pinetop" Perkins (pno), Eddie Taylor and Hubert Sumlin (gtrs), and Carey Bell (hca). Indifferent vocals and poor recordings mar what might have been a very interesting album.

SONNY BOY WILLIAMSON, #1 (JOHN LEE WILLIAMSON)

John Lee Williamson, called Sonny Boy Williamson, was a fine, distinctive singer and an excellent and very influential harmonica player. He recorded extensively in the 30s and 40s, often in the company of sidemen like Big Bill Broonzy, Walter Davis, Blind John Davis, Big Maceo, and Eddie Boyd. All his recordings are excellent.

Blues Classics 3 Sonny Boy Williamson, Vol. 1

Sixteen great sides, 1937–44, with Walter Davis, Yank Rachell, Big Bill Broonzy, and Blind John Davis. Collector Man Blues/You Give An Account/Joe Louis and John Henry Blues/Welfare Store Blues/Jivin' The Blues/Shotgun Blues/ Black Panther Blues.

Blues Classics 20 Sonny Boy Williamson, Vol. 2

Skinny Woman/Train Fare Blues/Big Apple Blues/Shady Grove Blues/Broken Heart Blues/G, M, and O Blues/Hoodoo Hoodoo.

Blues Classics 24 Sonny Boy Williamson, Vol. 3

My Little Baby/Something Going on Wrong/I Have Got to Go/Love Me Baby/Miss Stella Brown/ Sonny Boy's Jump/Alcohol Blues/Wonderful Time.

Old Tramp 1205 1937–45

Eighteen great sides from Sonny Boy with accompaniments by Joe Williams, Robert Lee McCoy, Yank Rachell, Walter Davis, Big Bill Broonzy, Blind John Davis, and Eddie Boyd. Most of the tracks are available elsewhere, though this is a great collection covering most of his recording career, including his classic 1945 recording of "Elevator Woman." Sugar Mama Blues/Black Gal Blues/Suzanna Blues/ Decoration Blues/Sunnyland/Doggin' My Love Around/Sugar Mama Blues #2/Tell Me Baby/I'm Gonna Catch You Soon.

CASSETTE ONLY RELEASE

Arhoolie C-216 Sonny Boy Williamson

Double-length cassette combining Blues Classics BC 3 and BC 20.

SONNY BOY WILLIAMSON #1/BIG JOE WILLIAMS

RCA Heritage 9599-2 Throw a Boogie Woogie

A tremendous selection of eight songs each by two brilliant but very different bluesmen who frequently accompanied each other on record. Sonny Boy's songs are drawn from his first four Bluebird sessions in 1937 and '38, several including Big Joe on guitar. Other musicians include guitarists Robert Lee McCoy (aka Robert Nighthawk) and Henry Townsend and mandolin player Yank Rachell. Here are some of his best-known and influential songs: "Good Morning Little School Girl," "Sugar Mama Blues," and "Early in the Morning." Big Joe's tracks feature Sonny Boy's lovely harmonica punctuating Big Joe's vocals and guitar, including versions of some of Big Joe's best-known songs: "Brother James," "Peach Orchard Mama," "Crawlin' Kingsnake," and "Please Don't Go." Also included are two songs—"North Wind Blues" and "Throw a Boogie"—which, as far as I can tell, are not only previously unissued but also are not listed in the prewar blues discography! Apart from these two, all of the tracks have been reissued before. However, most are not currently available elsewhere, and the digital remastering from original metal parts brings a crystal clarity to these 50-year-old recordings. Kudos to Bill Altman for another outstanding production!

SONNY BOY WILLIAMSON, #2 (RICE MILLER)

Rice Miller, who also recorded under the name of Sonny Boy Williamson, was a superb blues singer and harmonica player whose style was completely different from that of John Lee Williamson. A unique artist, he was not only a superb singer and distinctive harmonica player, he also wrote some fine original songs, often displaying great wit and sometimes a bizarre, almost surrealistic quality. A truly great performer, he hardly ever made a bad record. His classic first recordings for the Trumpet label in Mississippi are reissued on Arhoolie 2020, while his Checker recordings are available on various Chess albums, including a complete boxed set. His later recordings are almost all worthwhile, though the pairings with various British rock bands are not that exciting.

Alligator 4787 (c,d) Keep It to Ourselves
Twelve tracks drawn from recordings made in Europe for Storyville in 1963. Most cuts feature Matt Murphy on acoustic guitar, Memphis Slim joins in on piano on a couple of cuts, and Billy Stepney is on drums on one cut.

Arhoolie 2020 King Biscuit Time
CD issue: Arhoolie CD 310
Sixteen classic recordings made for Trumpet in 1951 with fine local musicians including the great guitar of Joe Willie Wilkins. CD includes an additional 15-minute radio broadcast, plus the original recording of Elmore James' "Dust My Broom." Do It If

You Wanna/Come on Back Home/Eyesight to the Blind/I Cross My Heart/Nine Below Zero/She Brought Life Back/Mr. Downchild/Pontiac Blues.

Chess 9116 (c,d) One Way Out
Originally issued as Chess 417 in 1970. A classic collection of performances recorded between 1955–61, several never issued as singles, with Muddy Waters, Otis Spann, Robert Jr. Lockwood, Willie Dixon, Luther Tucker, and Fred Below. Born Blind/You're Killing Me/Don't Lose Your Eye/Too Close Together/Good Evening Everybody/Like Wolf (Sonny Boy's witty impersonation of Howlin' Wolf!)/Work with Me/Keep It to Yourself.

ESSENTIAL SELECTION

Chess 9257 (c,d) Down and Out Blues
Sonny Boy's classic first album (Checker 1437) from 1959, reissued with the original front cover (though reproduction of the original picture is not the greatest) and new back cover; features the original notes by Studs Terkel plus new notes by Don Kamerer and full discographical details. Here is this magnificent singer, songwriter, and harmonica player at his peak in the company of musicians of the calibre of Muddy Waters, Robert Jr. Lockwood, Willie Dixon, Otis Spann, and Fred Below. Essential! Don't Start Me to Talkin'/All My Love in Vain/Keep It to Yourself/Fattening Frogs for Snakes/Your Funeral and My Trial/Cross My Heart.

Chess 9272 (c,d) The Real Folk Blues
Reissue of Chess 1503 from 1965 with original cover, original notes by Willie Dixon, new notes by Chris Morris, and full discographical details. It features 12 sides recorded between 1957–63, mostly from the early 60s. Sidemen include Robert Jr. Lockwood, Lafayette Leake, Otis Spann, Luther Tucker, Willie Dixon, and Fred Below. Another must if you don't already have these songs. One Way Out/Trust My Baby (a truly beautiful performance)/Sad to Be Alone/Bring It on Home/Peach Tree/That's All I Want/Checkin' Up on My Baby (among his greatest).

Chess 9277 (c,d) More Real Folk Blues
Reissue of Chess LP 1509 from 1967. Another brilliant collection of 12 songs recorded between 1960–64, some of his last Checker recordings. Sonny Boy's magnificent vocals and harmonica playing are accompnied by musicians like Lafayette Leake, Matt Murphy, Robert Jr. Lockwood, Luther Tucker, and Fred Below. Original front cover is reproduced, but there are new notes with full discographical information, and the sound is superb. If you don't already have these cuts elsewhere, this is an essential

set. Help Me/Nine Below Zero/The Goat/Decoration Day.

Chess (France) 427 004 Sonny Boy Williamson
Reissue of Chess 2ACMB 206. Twenty-eight superb Checker sides on a two-LP set. One Way Out/Keep It to Yourself/Let Your Conscience Be Your Guide/I Never Do Wrong/Don't Start Me to Talking/Key to Your Door/Let Me Explain/All My Love in Vain/Nine Below Zero/She Got Next to Me/I Can't Be Alone.

GNP 10003 In Paris

L+R 42.020 (c) Sonny Boy Williamson and the Yardbirds: Live In London
Recorded at the Crawdaddy Club in England in 1963, including seven previously unissued alternate takes and titles.

Storyville 4016 A Portrait in Blues
1962 sides cut in Europe with Memphis Slim and Matt Murphy.

Storyville 4062 (d) The Blues of Sonny Boy Williamson
Superb album originally issued on European Storyville in 1965 but unavailable for several years. Features solo performances and accompaniments by Memphis Slim, Matt Murphy, and Bill Stepney in various combinations.

COMPACT DISC

Charly Chess Box CD 1 The Chess Years
The complete Checker recordings of this great artist. Four CDs in a sturdy box, 89 Checker songs including alternate takes. Includes all the tracks on the Japanese Chess box and single albums except a couple of unimportant alternate takes, false starts, and studio chat. It does include some fine and different alternate takes of "The Key," "Checking Up On My Baby," and "One Way Out" that are not available anywhere else. Tracks are roughly in chronological order, but there are many tracks out of sequence, and most of the alternate takes are confined to the fourth disc rather than within the body of the recordings, which, unfortunately, disturbs the flow of the recordings. Set comes with attractive illustrated booklet with good notes by Neil Slaven and accurate and detailed discography.

Charly CD 215 With the Animals
Eighteen cuts from the early 60s, when Sonny Boy spent a lot of time touring England in the company of young local R&B bands like the Animals and the Yardbirds.

Chess (UK) CD RED 14 Work with Me
Twenty-four great tracks with unexceptional sound.

Chess (France) 670411 Stop Crying
Seventeen great Checker recordings. All My Love in Vain/Key to Your Door/"99"/Sad to Be Alone/Nine Below Zero/I Can't Be Alone.

Chess (Italy) CD 35 The Best of Sonny Boy Williamson
Twenty-two classic Checker recordings from the 50s and early 60s, with accompaniments by some of Chicago's finest musicians. No surprises here, but 60 minutes of great songs. Sound is generally very good. Don't Start Me to Talkin'/Let Me Explain/The Key/Cross My Heart/Ninety Nine/Let Your Conscience Be Your Guide/It's Sad to Be Alone/Lonesome Cabin/Too Close Together/Help Me/Decoration Day.

SONNY BOY WILLIAMSON, #2/BIG WALTER HORTON

Document 575 Solo Harp
Six tracks by Williamson from 1963 and five by Big Walter from 1965.

SONNY BOY WILLIAMSON, #2/ WILLIE LOVE

Trumpet AA 700 (c,d) Clownin' with the World
This fine collection includes eight previously unissued Williamson recordings drawn from three sessions in 1953 and '54 with different groups. These include a song about Trumpet's owner, Lillian McMurray ("309 Blues"), one about the train that took him and his good friend Willie Love to Houston for a session ("City Of New Orleans"), and the upbeat instrumental "Clownin' with the World." Willie Love is less well-known but was a wonderful and engaging singer and a rolling barrelhouse piano player. His material is strongly rooted in traditional elements. This collection features six of his issued tracks dubbed from 78s, along with two beautiful previously unissued tracks from 1953. The sound on the tracks from tape is very good, though a bit echoey, but the ones dubbed from 78s sound hollow and have quite a few clicks and pops. However, this is a small price to pay for some excellent music.

CHICK WILLIS

Collectables 5193 (c,d) Stoop Down Baby

Ichiban 1012 Chick Sings Chuck

Ichiban 1054 (d) Footprints in My Bed
New album from the man who made "stoop down" a household phrase. Mercifully, there is not another version of his theme song here, but there are plenty of raunchy songs, like the title track, "Use What You Got," "Big Red Caboose," that hoary old chestnut (sorry!) "Hot Nuts," and even a version of the old Max Romeo bluebeat classic, "Wet Dream," which

is rendered here as "Jack You Up." Chick moves his mind to higher things on the socially conscious ballad, "What's to Become of this World," and does a nice down-home version of Lightnin' Hopkins's "Hello Central." Usual Ichiban backing musicians on most of the cuts.

RALPH WILLIS

Excellent Carolina country blues singer/guitarist who recorded in New York in the 40s and early 50s, sometimes with Sonny Terry and Brownie McGhee.

Blues Classics 22 **Carolina Blues**

EDITH WILSON

Fine vaudeville blues singer whose recording career dates back to 1921. She later achieved fame on T.V. commercials as "Aunt Jemima." She died in 1981.

Delmark 637 **He May Be Your Man**
Nice 60s recordings.

HOP WILSON

Fine singer and steel guitar player from Houston, Texas.

Ace CHD 240 **Steel Guitar Flash**
A fine collection of 17 sides recorded by Houston steel guitarist Hop Wilson, his band, and various vocalists. This was recorded for drummer Lee Semiens' Ivory label between 1958–61, and includes nine previously unissued tracks. Wilson was a fine singer and an excellent, if somewhat chaotic, guitarist. Accompanying Hop are Semiens on drums, Elmore Nixon on piano, and various other musicians. In addition to Hop's own vocals, there are also some by Lee and the recent surprise discovery of vocals by Larry Davis and Fenton Robinson. On "My Woman Done Quit Me," Fenton also contributes a dynamic guitar solo. There are also two instrumental tracks which really give Hop a chance to work out on the steel.

Goldband 7781 **Blues with Friends**
60s recordings. Six songs by Wilson plus tracks by Guitar Junior, Big Chenier, and Ashton Savoy. As with most Goldband productions, the recording quality leaves a lot to be desired, but there is some exciting music here.

COMPACT DISC

P-Vine PCD 1607 **Houston Ghetto Blues**
Twenty-three tracks featuring all of his Ivory recordings (also on Ace) and his Goldband recordings.

JIMMY WILSON

A wonderful 50s West Coast singer with a soulful brooding quality who sang some fine "doomy"

songs with excellent bands, often featuring the great guitar of Lafayette Thomas.

Diving Duck 4305 **Trouble in My House**
Excellent collection of 50s recordings. Several songs here echo his big hit, "Tin Pan Alley" (featured on Arhoolie 2008), including the superb "Tell Me," with stunning guitar by Thomas. Every Dog Has His Day/Ethel Lee/Call Me Hound Dog (an "answer song" to "Hound Dog")/Oh Red.

LEOLA B. and "KID" WESLEY WILSON

Document 549 **1928–33**
Husband-and-wife team Leola B. and "Kid" Wesley Wilson recorded quite prolifically in the 20s and early 30s and also wrote a number of popular blues songs. Their duets, often with a humorous or risque slant, are delightful, their solo performances are less interesting, and the tracks with Wesley and Harry McDaniels issued as Pigmeat Pete and Catjuice Charlie are downright dull. Only a couple of tracks here have been reissued before and sound quality is generally pretty good.

SMOKEY WILSON

Excellent California blues singer/guitarist originally from Mississippi. Powerful style at times reminiscent of Howlin' Wolf.

Murray Brother 1003 **88th Street Blues**
Wilson is a good performer but on this album shows very little evidence of an original style because he copies the styles of Elmore James, Jimmy Reed, and Howlin' Wolf. Well done but irrelevant. The backup by Rod Piazza and Hollywood Fats is competent but unexciting.

COMPACT DISC

Black Magic CD 9013 **And the William Clarke Band**
Dull recent recordings with the oppressive harmonica of William Clarke. Covers of songs from the repertoires of Jimmy Reed, Johnny Copeland, Roy Brown, and John Lee Hooker.

U.P. WILSON

Double Trouble DTCD 3023 **Wild Texas Guitar**
Ten tracks, mostly recorded live in 1988 and 1989, featuring this high-energy Fort Worth singer and guitarist accompanied by a rather nondescript band.

Red Lightnin' 0078 **On My Way**
Although performing in the Dallas-Fort Worth area since the late 50s, these were the first recordings of singer/guitarist Wilson. Accompanied by a solid rhythm section and occasional horns or harmonica, he performs a selection of originals plus tunes from the repertoires of Lowell Fulson, Little Walter, and

Albert King. He is a decent singer, though not terribly distinctive, and a tough, energetic, and imaginative guitarist with a gritty sound. Good contemporary blues.

JOHNNY WINTER

Alligator 4735 (c,d) **Guitar Slinger**
1984 album by this popular artist is a straight blues effort on which Johnny brings his histrionic vocal and guitar style to bear on songs originally recorded by Bobby Bland, Muddy Waters, Sly Williams, and Junior Parker. This album, recorded in Chicago, features well-known Chicago sidemen Johnny B. Gayden (b) and Casey Jones (drm), and there are guest appearances by Gene Barge (ten sax) and Billy Branch (hca).
Alligator 4742 (c,d) **Serious Business**
Alligator 4748 (c,d) **3rd Degree**
1986 recordings, some tracks with Dr. John on piano.
Collector Series CCSLP 167 **The Collection**
Two-LP set with 20 tunes from his six Columbia LPs (1969–74), mostly with Johnny Winter And... (with the ex-McCoys including Rick Derringer) as back-up band. Twelve of the 20 tunes are covers of rock tunes—"Jumpin' Jack Flash," "Highway 61 Revisited," and "Slippin' and Slidin'"—and the two blues tunes that he does probably also qualify as rock 'n' roll: "Good Morning Little Schoolgirl" and "Rock Me Baby," plus his big hit "Rock 'n' Roll Hoochie Koo."
President PRCV 116 (d) **Early Winter**
Fine early sides (late 50s/early 60s) from singles originally on KR and Frolic. Ease My Pain/Gangster of Love/Creepy.
Relix 2034 **Birds Can't Row Boats**
When Johnny first hit the majors in '68, it seemed like every budget label was putting out his early sides going back to '59 ["First Winter," "Early Winter," etc.]. Here's another 15 tunes, half never before issued, with the rest probably out of print. Includes "Icecube" from '59, the long unedited ver-

sion of his '67 Cascade single "Coming up Fast," a '67 single release of "Tramp" by The Traits on Universal (no, not the Jars label), a very rare '65 MGM single "Gone for Bad," and Johnny playing blues behind Calvin "Loudmouth" Johnson and straight country behind Isaac Payton Sweat.
Showcase SHLP 132 **Livin' in the Blues**
Interesting and, at times, bizarre collection of early Winter recordings from the 60s. The highlights are the straight country-blues interpretations with Winter accompanied by his own acoustic or electric guitar and restrained rhythm section: "Going Down Slow," "Leavin' Blues," "32-20," and "Kind Hearted Woman." Less effective is the jazz blues "Parchman Farm" and his interpretation of James Brown's "Out of Sight." The bizarre tracks are a weird parody of Bob Dylan in his "Highway 61" period called "Avocado Green" and an impersonation of Jimi Hendrix on the title song!
CASSETTE AND CD RELEASE ONLY
Columbia PC 9826 **Johnny Winter**
Columbia PC 9947 **Second Winter**
COMPACT DISC
P-Vine PCD 1611 **The Johnny Winter Story**
Hey, there are some suprisingly good tracks among these early, early recordings, regardless of what you think about Winter's later blues-rock efforts. Twenty-one cuts in all, many of them creditable straight-ahead versions of classics like "Parchman Farm," "Going Down Slow," "Road Runner," and "Gangster Of Love." Johnny's hard-core fans will love this one, and the quality of the material is bound to win over those of you with interest in 60s blues, and even garage rock/Texas punk enthusiasts.

JOHNNY WINTER and UNCLE JOHN TURNER
Thunderbolt THBL 077 **Back in Beaumont**
1981 recordings done by Winter, who was reunited with his old drummer from the early days, John Turner. Winter plays some excellent guitar and some surprisingly good harp, while Turner handles the drums and vocals, the former much more adequately than the latter. They ramble through a timeless set that could've been heard in any of the last 30 years or so. Redbeans Stewardon, on accordion, joins the band for a couple of nice Zydeco efforts, "Allons Dancez" and "Struggle in Houston." Nice LP for Winter fans. They Call Me Lazy/Family Rules/Ooh Pooh Pah Do/Drivin' Wheel.

JIMMY WITHERSPOON
Fine urban blues shouter who has been active since the 40s and has recorded with various bands

including some rock-oriented groups but is at his best with bluesy jazz-flavored groups.

Black Lion 30147 **Ain't Nobody's Business**
Twelve cuts recorded in 1947–48 for Swingtime. These are among Spoon's best, with accompaniment by Jay McShann, Tiny Webb, Forrest Powell, and Louis Speigner.

Chess 93003 (c,d) **Spoon So Easy**
Twelve tracks (14 on the CD) recorded in 1954, '56, and '59, including several previously unissued cuts.

Fantasy F 9660 (c,d) **Rockin' LA**
One is immediately impressed by the fine musicians on this collection: the gospel-tinged piano of Gerald Wiggins, the flawless mellow tenor sounds of Teddy Edwards, and the "just right" bass and drum support of John Clayton and Paul Humphrey. Some great blues-inspired songs here, including the R&B finger-snapping "You Got Me Running" and the evergreen "Once There Lived a Fool," "Stormy Monday Blues," and "Careless Love." Spoon's rich baritone voice manages to emote and stay on top of the melody (a miracle, since he has recently suffered a bout of throat cancer) and the unit swings when swing is required. Two extra tracks on the CD: "Don't Gotta" and a medley of "Ain't Nobody's Business/Please Send Me Someone to Love."

Fantasy 24701 (d) **The Spoon Concerts**
Two-LP set, with Roy Eldridge and Coleman Hawkins.

Muse 5288 **Sings the Blues**
Reissue of excellent set, originally on the French Black and Blue label, featuring Spoon in fine form, accompanied by a nine-piece band put together by Panama Francis, in honor of the famous Harlem band of the 30s, Al Cooper's Savoy Sultans. The material is mostly jazz/blues standards, with five songs originally made famous by Jimmy Rushing. A very enjoyable set. Also available as Black and Blue 59.1772.

Muse 5327 (d) **Midnight Lady Called the Blues**
1986 set with Dr. John, David "Fathead' Newman, Doc Pomus, and Hank Crawford.

ESSENTIAL SELECTION

O.B.C. 511 (c,d) **Evenin' Blues**
Reissue of Prestige 7300 from 1963. This album found Spoon in particularly good form, shoutin' the blues on a collection of mostly old favorites like "Money's Getting Cheaper," "Baby, How Long," "Good Rockin' Tonight," "Kansas City," the superb title blues ballad "Evenin'," and a rousing version of the Roy Hamilton hit, "Don't Let Go." He is accompanied by a fine band, which includes the great T-Bone Walker on guitar, contributing some lovely

riffs, and Clifford Scott on tenor, alto sax, and flute. Recommended.

O.B.C. 527 (c,d) **Baby, Baby, Baby**
Reissue of Prestige 7290 from 1963.

Prestige 7327 **Blue Spoon**
Prestige 7475 **Blues for Easy Livers**
1967 set with Pepper Adams (bar sax) and Bill Watrous. Lotus Blossom/Travelin' Light/I'll Always Be in Love with You/Easy Living.

Prestige 7713 **The Best of Jimmy Witherspoon**
Selections from his Prestige albums. Good Rocking Tonight/Drinkin' Beer/Bad Bad Whiskey/Cane River/Mean Old Frisco/Kansas City.

Route 66 KIX 31 **Hey Mr. Landlord**
The first half of this collection highlights Spoon's Jay McShann-supported sessions dating from 1945–47. Included is a version of Walter Brown's very fine "Confessing the Blues." The flip side skims through a mix of labels and session dates, the most notable being "Oh Boy" (1953), "Big Daddy" (1954), and "Daddy Pinnochio" (1953).

Vogue 600161 **Jimmy Witherspoon and Jimmy Rushing**
The two Jimmies in seperate Paris concerts from the 60s. Spoon is heard with an outstanding all-star band from the Basie Orchestra: Buck Clayton (tpt), Emmett Berry (tpt), Dicky Wells (trb), Earl Warren (alto sax), Buddy Tate (ten sax), Sir Charles Thompson (pno), Gene Ramey (b), and Oliver Jackson (drm). The April 22, 1961 set starts with two never-before-issued instrumentals, the rhythm section doing "I Get a Kick Out of You" and the band doing Buck's "Swingin' at the Copper Rail," before Spoon comes out for eight songs, including "C.C. Rider" and "Gee Baby, Ain't I Good to You." Rushing is heard from July 19, 1967, backed by the Earl Hines Quartet with Budd Johnson (ten sax), performing five tunes including "Exactly Like You" and "Am I Blue?"
CASSETTE ONLY RELEASE

MCA 1367 **Jimmy's Blues**
Seven sides recorded for Bluesway in 1969, with Earl Hooker and Mel Brown (gtrs) and Charles Brown (pno). Parcel Post Blues/Bags Under My Eyes.
COMPACT DISC

Charly CD 169 **Meets the Jazz Giants**
Reissue of Hi-Fi-Jazz label recordings done live in '59. Spoon's usual repertoire ("Everyday I Have The Blues," "C.C. Rider," "Corrine Corrina," and "St. Louis Blues") is given the deluxe treatment by sidemen such as Ben Webster, Gerry Mulligan, Roy Eldridge, Coleman Hawkins, and Earl Hines. Fifteen tunes.

JSP CD 205 Big Blues

CD issue of JSP 1032. June '81 London session with Spoon and veteran tenor saxman Hal "Cornbread" Singer in a two-sax band with a solid group of British sessionmen, including saxist Pete King and Oblivion Express guitarist Jim Mullen. Includes Jimmy Reed's "You Got Me Runnin'" and "Big Boss Man" plus "Nobody Knows You When You're Down and Out" and "Whiskey Drinkin' Woman."

JOHNNY WOODS

Swingmaster 2112 The Blues of Johnny Woods

1981 and '84 recordings of Mississippi harmonica player.

OSCAR "BUDDY" WOODS

Document 517 1930–1938

A great collection of 16 tracks featuring brilliant Louisiana singer and slide guitarist Oscar Woods. Many of these cuts have been reissued before, but this does include a few that have never been reissued, and it's great to have all these gems together. Woods was a fine singer with a sly vocal style and a wonderfully melodic slide guitarist. Highlights are the tracks featuring Oscar on his own or with a second guitarist, including the magnificent and often reissued "Evil Hearted Woman" and "Lone Wolf Blues." There are several tracks with a small group with piano, drums, and occasional trumpet. Although the accompaniments are a little heavy handed, they are enlivened by Oscar's fabulous singing and guitar. The album also includes the four tracks on which Oscar accompanied white country singer Jimmie Davis. These are superb, though they were reissued a year ago on the Jimmie Davis album on Bear Family.

BILLY WRIGHT

Fine urban singer from Atlanta who was very popular in the late 40s–mid 50s and was also a big influence on singers like Little Richard.

Ace CHA 193 Don't You Want a Man Like Me

Four Peacock tracks from 1955 by Wright. The rest of the album features the rare 1953 Peacock sides by Little Richard with Ray Taylor's Tempo Toppers.

Route 66 KIX 13 The Prince of the Blues

Savoy SJL 1146 Goin' Down Slow

Excellent selection of 14 sides recorded for Savoy between 1949–54, including five previously unissued titles. These sides feature a good variety of upbeat items and slow blues accompanied by various groups in New York and Atlanta.

BIG JIM WYNN

Whiskey, Women and . . . KM 703 Blow Wynn Blow

West Coast jump blues recorded between 1945–54 featuring bands led by fine and prolific tenor sax player Wynn. Most of the tracks are vocals, featuring vocalists Claude Trenier, Luther Luper, Jr., and Pee Wee Wiley. I particularly like the topical song "Shipyard Woman," sung by Wiley. There are also a couple of jazzy instrumental cuts. With excellent sound and interesting notes by George Moonoogian.

JIMMY YANCEY

Truly fine blues piano player who was active in the 30s and 40s and was an immense influence on the whole school of boogie piano players.

Oldie Blues 2802 Jimmy Yancey

Features a 1940 private party and 1943 session sides. Includes some vocals by Mama Estelle Yancey, and two tracks featuring organ.

Oldie Blues 2813 The Immortal Jimmy Yancey, Vol. 2

Features beautiful sides recorded for Solo Art in 1939.

Swaggie 824 The Piano Blues of Jimmy Yancey, 1939–40

Sixteen beautiful sides recorded for Victor, Bluebird, and Vocalion in 1939–40, including two vocals by Faber Smith and two by Yancey himself. Yancey was a warm, wistful, and moving singer, and it's a shame he didn't take the vocal spotlight more often. Although much of this material has been reissued elsewhere, the presentation here is exemplary and the sound, as remastered by John R. T. Davies, has an added sparkle. Includes two takes each of Yancey's "Bugle Call" and "35th and Dearborn."

COMPACT DISC

Solo Art SACD 1 In the Beginning

A beautiful collection of 12 piano blues and boogies recorded in 1939 for Dan Qualey's Solo Art label. These are Yancey's first recordings, and his playing is beautiful, sensitive, and fluid, and, compared to his contemporaries, is quite restrained, resulting in a different and unique texture to these performances. These tracks were originally issued some years ago on the long-out-of-print Jazzology LP JCE 51, and it is unfortunate that the producers didn't include the remaining five tracks from the session, which would have fit nicely on this CD. There are detailed notes by Rudi Blesh on the story of the Solo Art label. Sound quality is unexceptional, but the music is sensational!

JIMMY YANCEY and CRIPPLE CLARENCE LOFTON

Swaggie 1235 **Pitchin' Boogie**
Storyville 238 **The Yancey/Lofton Sessions, Vol. 1**
1943 recordings made for the Session label, some duplicated on Oldie Blues 2802. Beautiful music.

Storyville 239 **The Yancey/Lofton Sessions, Vol. 2**
More beautiful sides and, again, some duplication on Oldie Blues 2802.

MAMA ESTELLE YANCEY

Red Beans 001 **Maybe I'll Cry**
These recent recordings show that Mama Yancey, at 87 years old, is a powerful and moving singer. She performs excellent versions of original and traditional blues songs. The piano accompaniments by Erwin Helfer perfectly complement her vocals and bring the playing of Mama's late husband Jimmy to mind. Trouble in Mind/Monkey Man/Maybe I'll Cry/Weekly Blues/How Long.

MIGHTY JOE YOUNG

Excellent Chicago singer/guitarist who ventures into soul and R&B. All his albums are good, with the GNP Crescendo being the most down-home.

Delmark 629 **Blues with a Touch of Soul**
GNP Crescendo 10014 **Legacy of the Blues, Vol. 4**

COMPACT DISC
Black and Blue 59.521 2 **Bluesy Josephine**
Accompanied by a small band including Ken Sajdak (kybds) and Willie Mabon (pno). Recorded in 1976, five of the seven tracks here were previously on Black and Blue 33.521. Good performances but some of the songs go on a bit long. Does the world really need an eight-and-a-half minute version of "Sweet Home Chicago"?

JOHNNY YOUNG

Fine Chicago singer/guitarist and mandolin player. Although he never became very famous, Mississippi-born Young was an important active participant in the Chicago blues scene from the 40s until his death in 1974. All his recordings feature him in the company of top-notch sidemen and are all worthwhile.

Arhoolie 1029 **Johnny Young and His Chicago Blues Band**
With James Cotton and Otis Spann. Wild Wild Women/I'm Having A Ball/Doing Alright/Keep On Drinking.

Arhoolie 1037 **Chicago Blues**
With great harp by Walter Horton. Strange Girl/Sometimes I Cry/On the Road Again.

Testament 2226 **And His Friends**
This album presents him in a variety of settings recorded between 1962–66, accompanied by mostly small groups, featuring some of Chicago's finest sidemen: Otis Spann, John Wrencher, Walter Horton (listen to his inventive playing on "All My Money Gone"), Jimmy Walker, Little Walter, and Slim Willis. There is also one fine Mississippi-style country blues with Johnny accompanying himself on guitar only—"My Home Ain't Here." Very fine.

CASSETTE AND CD RELEASE ONLY
Arhoolie C/CD 325 **Chicago Blues**
All of Arhoolie 1029 and most of 1037.

COMPACT DISC
Arhoolie (Japan) PCD 2504 **Chicago Blues**
Combines his two Arhoolie albums 1029 and 1037 on one CD.

ZORAH YOUNG

Blue Sting 007 **Stumbling Blocks and Stepping Stones**
Good album of contemporary Chicago blues by this Chicago-based singer, with a hard-driving band, including excellent guitar and sax from Maurice John Vaughn, who helped produce the album. Other musicians featured include A. C. Reed and brilliant harmonica player Carey Bell. Zorah is a good singer, though her vocals are somewhat buried in the mix. Most of the songs are originals, including the title song, which is about the frustrations of trying to make a success as a blues singer, a theme which also appears in the one nonoriginal, "Fed Up with this Music" by A. C. Reed. The rest of the material is more standard blues fare, though well done. The album is a bit on the short side, being less than 19 minutes a side!

YOUNG JESSIE

Mr. R&B 1004 **Shuffle in the Gravel**
This collection follows through from the now out-of-print Kent 4005, picking up in '57 with the hard-driving title track recorded with The Sharps. Other standouts include the swampy "My Country Cousin," aided by The Rivingtons (Sharps), and two down-in-the-alley blues: "Too Fine for Cryin'," recorded with The Blossoms in 1962, and what must be his finest effort to date, "Make Me Feel a Little Good," which surfaced in 1962.

ZYDECO FORCE
Maison De Soul 1031
New group out of Opelousas, LA, led by accordionist Robby "Mann" Robinson.

PREWAR BLUES COLLECTIONS

ALABAMA

Mamlish 3812 **Barefoot Bill's Hard Luck Blues**
Superb LP of outstanding Alabama country blues artists, especially the music of singer/guitarist Ed Bell. Features five beautiful performances by Bell, three by Pillie Bolling, who was an associate of Bell's, and one each by May Armstrong and Sonny Scott. The sides are all from the late 20s and early 30s, but there are also four sides by tremendous singer/guitarist John Lee recorded in '51. All are exceptionally fine—his "Baby's Blues" is a masterpiece! There's also one cut by Lee from a previously unissued acetate featuring the rarely recorded pan-pipes. Sound quality is marvelous and there are lengthy interesting notes.

OJL 14 **Alabama Country**
Barefoot Bill, Jaybird Coleman, The Two Poor Boys, Ed Bell, Ollis Martin, Whistlin' Pete, and Daddy Stovepipe.

Yazoo 1006 **Alabama Blues**
George "Bullet" Williams, Edward Thompson, Ed Bell, Barefoot Bill, Jaybird Coleman, Marshall Owens.

Note: See also ED BELL, CLIFFORD GIBSON, BESSIE JACKSON, and WALTER ROLAND.

EAST COAST

Blues Documents 2002 **Georgia String Bands**
A lovely album of country blues, though there is a fair amount of duplication with currently available albums. The opening four cuts are superb duets by the North Carolina duo, Pink Anderson and Simmie Dooley, who belong on this album since they recorded in Atlanta. There are two superb sides by singer/banjo player Lonnie Coleman, including his classic "Rock Island Blues," and one previously unissued gospel side from 1930 by Brothers Wright and Williams featuring delightful violin, banjo, and guitar accompaniment. The bulk of the album features the superb fiddle player Eddie Anthony: two cuts with Henry Williams and eight with Tampa Joe, billed as Macon Ed and Tampa Joe. These are marvelous guitar/violin duets, some with vocals, but eight of these 10 tracks are currently available on OJL 22.

Blues Documents 2015 **Georgia Blues Guitars, 1928–33**
A fantastic collection, featuring the complete recordings of Willie Baker, Seth Richard, and Fred McMullen. There are nine tracks by Willie Baker, a wonderful singer and 12-string guitarist who often plays with a slide. Seth Richard is another fine 12-string guitarist, though his two sides pale in comparison to the fast company he has here. The remaining seven tracks are by Fred McMullen, a six-string guitarist who plays some lovely slide. Most of his tracks feature second guitar by Curley Weaver, and there are also accompaniments to Ruth Willis. Most of these tracks have been reissued before, and about half are still available, but it really is good to have all of these together.

Blues Documents 2038 **East Coast Blues in the Thirties (1934–39)**
Fine selection of late 30s rural blues, marred only by poor sound. Artists include Bob Campbell (whose classic "Starvation Farm Blues" has been unavailable on LP for decades), The Tampa Kid, the fine "Poor Bill," whose two sides from 1939 have not been reissued elsewhere, and eight cuts by the fine vocalist/slide guitarist Sam Montgomery, whose work has also been unavailable on LP for some 20 years.

Heritage 304 **Nobody Knows My Name**
Remarkable album of field recordings of blues recorded in South Carolina and Georgia between 1924–32 by Lawrence Gellert. Unlike the Gellert recordings on Rounder (4004 and 4013) that feature work songs, all these cuts are guitar-accompanied blues. The cuts from 1924 represent the first field recordings of country blues and may be the very first recordings of guitar-accompanied blues. Because much of the material Gellert recorded was political in nature, he didn't give the names of any of the performers that he recorded, but they are consistently fine. The sound quality is very poor on some cuts, but the music is so good that you will ignore the poor sound. This is a historically important and musically beautiful album.

HK 4005 **Georgia Blues, 1924–35**
Eighteen country blues sides. Quite a few have been reissued before, but very few are currently available elsewhere. The album opens with two tracks by the fine and mysterious Ed Andrews, recorded in April 1924; these are considered to be the first country blues vocals made. There are two tracks by brilliant guitarist Sylvester Weaver, complementing the reissues on Agram and Earl. The 12-string guitar was popular in Georgia and we hear it in the hands of

Emery Glen, George Carter, and in alternate takes by Blind Willie McTell and Barbecue Bob. The album winds up with some excellent country gospel from Blind Gussie Nesbit.

HK 4006 Carolina Blues, 1936–50
A lovely collection, featuring the complete recordings of Floyd "Dipper Boy" Council, Richard and Welly Trice, and Virgil Childers, plus tracks by Kid Price Moore and Carolina Slim. Many of these tracks have been reissued before, but most of these LPs have not been available for many years. Council and the Trices were associates of Blind Boy Fuller and play in the same fluid guitar style with excellent vocals. Childers sounds like an older musician with a style closer to medicine shows and the songster tradition. The fine "Pickin Low Cotton" by Kid Price Moore is a beautiful, previously unissued test which complements his recordings on Wolf 126. Carolina Slim was a splendid postwar artist who performed in the traditional style; these two tracks complement those on Travelin' Man 805.

JEMF 106 Atlanta Blues, 1933
Sixteen previously unissued or alternate takes of brilliant country blues by Blind Willie McTell, Curley Weaver, and Buddy Moss.

Matchbox 204 Ragtime Blues Guitar
Some wonderful singing and melodic guitar playing in the ragtime style popular on the East Coast. Recordings from 1928–30 featuring all the excellent sides by Virginia singer William Moore, South Carolina singer Willie Walker, Virginia duo Tarter and Gay, and the mysterious and possibly white guitar player Bayless Rose.

OJL 18 Let's Go Riding
Willie Walker, Will Bennet, Pink Anderson and Simmie Dooley, and Bill Moore.

OJL 25 The Black Country Music of Georgia, 1927–1936
A delightful album of rural blues and religious music recorded in Georgia. A variety of styles is featured on this set that includes Tampa Red, Lillie Mae, Sylvester Weaver, Charlie Lincoln, Eddie Head and Family, Georgia Tom, and Luther Magby (sensational!). Sound is excellent and there are extensive notes.

Old Tramp 1211 Carolina Blues Guitar, 1936–51
A delightful collection; most of these tracks have not been on LP before, and the few that have are not currently available. There are ten tracks from 1936 by the superb Cedar Creek Sheik (Philip McCutcheon), a fascinating artist whose style and repertoire seems to have a lot in common with white East Coast musicians like Frank Hutchison. He is an

excellent singer and flowing guitarist and tackles some fascinating material like the almost surrealistic "Watching the Fords Go By," the hokum "She's Totin' Something Good," and the outrageously obscene "Buy It from the Poultry Man." There are four tracks by "Roosevelt" Antrim from 1937, a powerful and intense singer and guitarist. There are four tracks from 1937 by Sonny Jones, a fine singer and guitarist in the style popularized by Blind Boy Fuller. The album is rounded out by two superb tracks from 1951 by Carolina Slim (aka Country Paul, aka Ed Harris) that have not been on LP before. Recommended.

Rounder 4004 Negro Songs of Protest
Documentary of work songs recorded in the field in the 30s by Lawrence Gellert.

Rounder 4013 Cap'n You're So Mean
Fine album of field recordings collected in North Carolina and Georgia in the late 20s and early 30s by Lawrence Gellert. Like Rounder 4004, this album is unique in that it features songs of social protest that were rarely collected by other researchers. The performances presented are mostly unaccompanied work songs with a couple of accompanied blues.

ESSENTIAL SELECTION

Yazoo 1012 (c) Georgia Blues 1927–1933
Superb. Includes Gitfiddle Jim's (Kokomo Arnold's) first recording, with some incredible slide guitar playing, plus tracks by Fred McMullen, Peg Leg Howell, Willie Baker, George Carter, and Barbecue Bob.

Yazoo 1013 (c) East Coast Blues
Great. William Moore, Willie Walker, Bayless Rose, Carl Martin, Bo Weavil Jackson, and Tarter and Gay.
Note: See also BARBECUE BOB, BLIND BOY FULLER, BLIND WILLIE MCTELL, PEG LEG HOWELL, and BUDDY MOSS.

MEMPHIS

Blues Documents 2006 The Sounds of Memphis
A lovely collection of country blues and jug-band music recorded between 1933–39. About two-thirds of the tracks have been reissued before, but some of these are not currently available; the album does include some tracks that have never been reissued. Side one features 10 tracks by the superb Jack Kelly and His South Memphis Jug Band, complementing Flyright 113. This is lovely jug-band music featuring the gruff vocals of Kelly, the guitars of Kelly and Dan Sane, and the lyrical violin of Will Batts. Side two features five tracks by Little Buddy Doyle with fine unknown harmonica. The album ends with four tracks by Charlie Pickett, a fine singer with an

expressive vibrato accompanied by his own guitar, Lee Brown on piano on two tracks, and Hammie Nixon (hca) on one.

Blues Documents 2029 Memphis Girls 1929–1935

The Memphis girls are: Leola Manning, whose six titles (including the incredibly raw "Laying in the Graveyard") feature fine singing and piano; the relatively uninteresting Madelyn James; the great Hattie Hart sides from 1934, with Allen Shaw and Willie Borum on guitars; and Minnie Wallace, with a jug-band-style group accompanying her, including Will Shade and Robert Wilkins. Little of this material is otherwise available, and on the whole this is a fine collection.

Blues Documents 2056 From Memphis to New Orleans

Four tracks by Charlie "Bozo" Nickerson, 13 by Tommy Griffin, and two by Oliver Brown of New Orleans. Only a couple of tracks have been reissued before.

HK 4002 Memphis Blues, 1927–37

Most of these tracks have been out before, but most of these reissues have been out of print for many years. Some of the best tracks here are on Yazoo 1002, including the fine "Goin' to Leave You Blues" by Big Boy Cleveland with some lovely slide guitar. Cleveland is also heard on a rare example of quill (panpipes) playing. There are four tracks by Tom Dickson, a fine expressive vocalist and fluid guitar player. There are two superb tracks by Allen Shaw, including the magnificent "Moanin' the Blues," with gorgeous churning slide guitar. Other artists include Walter Rhodes (featuring some weird accordion playing), Frank Stokes (an alternate take of "Downtown Blues"), Robert Wilkins (alternate take of "Rolling Stone, Part 2"), Sam Townsend, and George Torey. Marvelous.

Mamlish 3803 Lowdown Memphis Barrelhouse Blues

Fine collection, 1926–35. Hattie Hart, Robert Wilkins, South Memphis Jug Band, Kansas Joe and Memphis Minnie, John Estes, Mooch Richardson, Will Shade, Jack Kelly, and Jim Jackson.

Matchbox 213 Memphis Harmonica Kings

Seven sides recorded by Noah Lewis in 1929–30, some with his jug band. Lewis was a wonderful harmonica player who was featured on most of the recordings by Gus Cannon's Jug Stompers. The other 10 cuts are by another excellent Memphis harmonica player Jed Davenport, some with his Beale Street Jug Band. About two-thirds of these cuts have been reissued before, but it's nice to have

all the recordings of these two fine artists in one place.

OJL 21 The Blues in Memphis

Sleepy John Estes, Allen Shaw, Robert Wilkins, Yank Rachell, Furry Lewis, and the Beale Street Sheiks.

ESSENTIAL SELECTION

Yazoo 1002 (c) Ten Years in Memphis, 1927–37

After being out of print for almost 10 years, this magnificent collection is finally back in print. Although all of the tracks have since become available elsewhere, it still stands on its own as one of the great collections of prewar country blues with one classic performance after another. Familiar names include Furry Lewis, Kansas Joe, Frank Stokes, Gus Cannon (his truly amazing version of "Poor Boy" with bottleneck banjo accompaniment), and Robert Wilkins (his utterly magnificent "Falling Down Blues"). The other artists are obscure but do not pale at all in such fast company. George Torey is a tremendous singer and intricate guitar player and Allen Shaw accompanies his dark vocals with churning slide guitar. Sound is excellent and this reissue has an atmospheric new cover and musicological notes from Stephen Calt. Essential.

Yazoo 1008 Frank Stokes Dream

Utterly superb collection. Frank Stokes, Tom Dickson, Noah Lewis, Furry Lewis, Pearl Dickson, and Cannon's Jug Stompers.

Yazoo 1021 (c) Memphis Jamboree

Jim Jackson, Hattie Hart, Kansas Joe, Sam Townsend, Yank Rachell and Dan Smith, and the Two Charlies.

Note: See also JIM JACKSON, FURRY LEWIS, FRANK STOKES, ROBERT WILKINS, MEMPHIS MINNIE, and various jug bands.

MISSISSIPPI

Blues Documents 2014 Mississippi Blues Guitars, 1926–35

The complete recordings of bluesmen Mr. Freddie Spruell, Willie "Poor Boy" Lofton, and Chasey Collins. Almost all of these tracks have been reissued before, but many are not currently available. There are 10 tracks by Spruell (seven of them duplicated on Mamlish 3802), who was the first Mississippi Delta bluesman to record. Spruell was a fine, if not terribly exciting, singer and guitarist. On four of the tracks, he is teamed with the brilliant Carl Martin on second guitar. Most of the Willie Lofton tracks have not been available on LP for a long time, so it's great to have all of his eight recordings together. He was a superb performer, a powerful and expressive vocalist, and an intense and fluid guitarist. His material is varied and includes the hokum "It's Killing Me," the ferocious "Poor Boy Blues," and a superb rendition of Tommy Johnson's "Dark Road Blues." The album is rounded out with two songs by singer/violin player Chasey Collins accompanied by the great Big Joe Williams on guitar for a couple of beautiful performances.

Blues Documents 2018 Mississippi Girls, 1928–31

A truly wonderful collection. Many of these tracks have already been reissued, but there are several tracks that have never been on LP before. Side one features the complete recordings of Rosie Mae Moore and Mary Butler, who are probably the same person. She is accompanied in various combinations by Charlie McCoy (mdln, gtr), Ishman Bracey (gtr), and Bo Carter (vln). Side two features two tracks by the superb Mattie Delaney on a couple of stirring vocals, accompanying herself on guitar. Her playing on "Tallahatchie River Blues" is particularly lyrical. The remaining six tracks are by Geechie Wiley and Elvie Thomas, who perform singly and together, accompanying themselves on guitar. Both are moving singers and effective, if slightly chaotic, guitarists. Their selections include the moving "Motherless Child Blues" and the delightful and unusual "Pick Poor Robin Clean," a song also recorded by Virginia bluesman Luke Jordan. Sound on a few tracks is a bit rough but is generally listenable and the music is consistently superb.

Blues Documents 2043 Mississippi String Bands, 1928–36

A terrific collection of black string-band music. Although five different artists are featured, most tracks feature appearances by members of the Mississippi Sheiks, with most featuring fiddle or guitar by Bo Chatmon (aka Bo Carter) and guitar or mandolin by Charlie McCoy. McCoy is also featured on two vocals. There are five excellent tracks by Alec Johnson with Chatmon and McCoy, a lovely instrumental by Walter Jacobs (Vincson) with Bo on guitar and brother Lonnie on fiddle, and eight tracks by The Chatmon Brothers (Lonnie and Sam) giving us a chance to hear the delicious vocals of Sam. Those of us who had the privilege of seeing this delightful gentlemen in the 70s will realize how little his style had changed in almost 40 years. Some of these tracks have been reissued, but mostly on out-of-print collections. A few of the Chatmon Brothers tracks are from pretty worn 78s, but this set has generally good sound and is recommended.

Document 519 Mississippi Country Blues, 1935–51

All of the tracks here have been on LP before, but some have not been available for a while; if you don't already have these tracks, this is essential! Side one includes eight alternate takes by one of the very greatest of all Mississippi country bluesmen, the magnificent Robert Johnson. These are duplicated on the new Columbia set. There are six tracks by Johnson's "nephew," Robert Jr. Lockwood, including four magnificent 1941 sides which are very much in the Johnson vein and two from 1951 with Sunnyland Slim on piano, plus bass and drums. There are four superb tracks by the mysterious Otto Virgial, a magnificent and highly rhythmic performer. Excellent sound; fabulous!

Document 520 Mississippi Country Blues, Vol. 2

This excellent collection features eight tracks by the raucous and magnificent Tommy McClennan; these have all been on LP before but are scattered over several albums, many of which are out of print. Tommy was one of the most distinctive and exciting country-blues artists of the late 30s–early 40s. There are eight tracks by Willie "61" Blackwell. He was a distinctive vocalist and an interesting songwriter; unfortunately, all of his songs have the same tune and arrangements, so eight in a row becomes a little much! The album is rounded out with four tracks by the excellent John Henry Barbee accompanied on second guitar by Willie B. James. Two of these are from previously unissued test pressings and all are fine.

ESSENTIAL SELECTION

Document 532 Delta Blues, Vol. 1

This album represents the fruits of one of the greatest blues discoveries in recent years. As the story goes, a few years ago, a record collector moved into a house in Waukegan or Milwaukee supposedly owned by a former excutive for Paramount records. In the basement of the house, he found a stack of Paramount test pressings, including some 15 blues titles recorded in 1929 and 1930, including alternate takes and unissued songs by some of the greatest bluemen who ever lived. Eventually these records were purchased by Nick Perls of Yazoo Records with the intention of reissuing them on album. Following Nick's untimely death in 1987, the fate of the original tests and the planned album became uncertain. However, copies of the tests found their way to Document records, who in turn issued the Mississippi artists on this magnificent album. The album features three alternate takes by Charley Patton on

"Elder Greene Blues," "Some of These Days I'll Be Gone," and the magnificent "Hammer Blues." These are not terribly different from the issued versions. There is a superb previously unknown song by Son House called "Walkin' Blues," a magnificent performance which is lyrically similar to the song recorded by Son's protege Robert Johnson but musically different. This is the only Paramount track by Son featuring a second guitarist, probably Willie Brown. There are two unknown songs by Tommy Johnson—"Morning Prayer" and "Bogaloosa Woman"—both featuring some tremendous guitar by Tommy. There is an alternate take of Louise Johnson's "All Night Long Blues," featuring Louise's fine piano and spoken interjections by Son House and Willie Brown. The great Ishman Bracey is represented by a superb alternate take of "Woman Woman Blues." To round out the album, there are the four issued songs by Louise Johnson. Sound is generally excellent but it's unfortunate that such an important release didn't get better packaging and at least some notes. Still, the music speaks for itself and it is utterly magnificent.

Document 533 Delta Blues, Vol. 2
Country blues doesn't get any better than this! Although all but one of the tracks here have been reissued before, it's good to have them all together in one place. There are two cuts by the magnificent Kid Bailey with accompaniment by Willie Brown. Garfield Akers only knew one tune, which he features on his four tracks—but what a great tune it was! There are six tracks by Bukka White, four from his first session in 1930 and two from his 1939 Library of Congress recordings. The utterly obscure Jim Thompkins is featured on his only released track, the fantastic "Bedside Blues," featuring powerful vocals and unusual-sounding slide guitar. If the rest of his repertoire was this good, he would be up there with Patton, House, and Johnson—I kid you not! Rounding out the collection is the previously unreissued track from Sam Collins, "Graveyard Digger's Blues." A stunning release.

Herwin 214 Delta Blues Heavy Hitters
Incredibly rare sides by William Harris, Blind Joe Reynolds, and Skip James, though much duplication with other albums.

HK 4001 Mississippi Blues, 1927–37
A superb collection of Mississippi country blues, but a frustrating one for serious collectors, since most of the tracks have been reissued before (many are still available). However, it is good to have all seven tracks by Sam Collins that are not on OJL 10; Collins was a truly magnificent singer and guitarist. Two of the three tracks by the amazing Louis Lasky are

currently on Herwin, and the previously unissued test pressing "Caroline" is an unexceptional hokum song. There are two tracks by Uncle Bud Walker (available on Yazoo), two by the tremendous Lane Hardin (also on Mamlish), and two by Big Joe Williams, including the great "My Grey Pony," which does not seem to be available elswhere. There are two alternate takes by the great Robert Johnson: "Milkcow's Calf Blues" (on Yazoo) and a superb alternate of "Me and the Devil," which is available on the Columbia complete set. The album winds up with two tracks by the mysterious Mose Andrews.

Library of Congress AAFS L 59 Negro Blues and Hollers
Some great Mississippi country blues recorded by Alan Lomax in late 30s–early 40s, featuring David Edwards, Son House, William Brown, and Willie Blackwell, plus hollers by Charles Berry and spirituals.

Mamlish 3802 Mississippi Bottom Blues
Great Mississippi blues from 1926–35 including fabulous and rare sides by Otto Virgial, plus Charlie Patton, Freddie Spruell, Long Cleve Reed and Papa Harvey Hull, and Tommy Bradley.

OJL 5 The Mississippi Blues
Stupendous and pioneering set featuring some all-time classics. Bukka White, Willie Brown, Kid Bailey, Robert Wilkins, and Skip James.

OJL 11 The Mississippi Blues, Vol. 2
Son House, Louise Johnson, Charlie Patton, Jaydee Short, Blind Willie Reynolds, and Robert Wilkins.

OJL 17 Mississippi Blues, Vol. 3
Hambone Willie Newbern, Johnny Temple, Skip James, Big Joe Williams, Rosie Mae Moore, and Robert Johnson.

Wolf 116 Giants of Country Blues, Vol. 1
There's nothing here that hasn't been reissued before, but the music is absolutely superb, featuring some of the greatest Mississippi country blues recorded in the late 20s and early 30s. Bobby Grant, Rube Lacy, Willie Brown, King Solomon Hill, and Son House. Every track is a masterpiece.

Wolf 130 Central Mississippi Blues—The Jackson Area, 1926–35
The complete recordings of Willie Harris, Mississippi Cladwell Bracey, "Big Road" Webster Taylor, Arthur Petties, and The Mississippi Moaner.

ESSENTIAL SELECTION

Yazoo 1001 (c) Mississippi Blues, 1927–41
As always, Yazoo albums are noteworthy, not only for the music but for superb sound. William Harris,

Skip James, Son House, Charlie Patton, Henry Sims, and John Byrd.

Yazoo 1007 (c) **Jackson Blues, 1927–1938**
Beautiful sides by Tommy Johnson, Ishman Bracey, Charlie McCoy, Walter Vincson, and Bo Carter.

Yazoo 1009 **Mississippi Moaners**
Charlie Patton, Bobby Grant, The Mississippi Moaner, Rube Lacey, Washington White, and John Hurt.

Yazoo 1038 (c) **Lonesome Road Blues**
Skip James, The Mississippi Moaner, Sonny Boy Nelson, Freddy Spruell, Arthur Pettis, and Johnny Temple.

Note: See also BIG BILL BROONZY, BO CARTER, SON HOUSE, MISSISSIPPI JOHN HURT, SKIP JAMES, ROBERT JOHNSON, TOMMY JOHNSON, THE MISSISSIPPI SHEIKS, CHARLIE PATTON, and BIG JOE WILLIAMS.

ST. LOUIS

Blues Documents 2017 **The Blues from St. Louis, 1929–35**
A fine collection of 18 tracks from the musically fertile St. Louis scene that nicely fills in some gaps. There are three splendid tracks by Teddy Darby complementing the tracks on Earl 611, and six by the brilliant Clifford Gibson complementing the album on Yazoo 1027. The latter have all been reissued before, but it's good to have them together. Other tracks feature singer/piano player James "Stump" Johnson, Leroy Henderson (with marvelous accompaniment by Peetie Wheatstraw and Casey Bill Weldon), Dorothy Baker, and Pretty Boy Walker. An excellent collection.

Blues Documents 2055 **St. Louis Girls**
Nineteen tracks from Mae Bell Miller, Mary Johnson, Elizabeth Washington, Doretha Trowbridge, and Alice Moore. Mae Belle is a wonderful singer, and her four tracks probably feature Roosevelt Sykes on piano. Unfortunately, they are from very rare and worn originals, so the sound is poor. Johnson, Washington, and Trowbridge's selections are good, but have been reissued before on Magpie 4419. The last eight tracks are by Alice Moore, who is accompanied on piano by Henry Brown or Peetie Wheatstraw. Some of her sides feature guitar by Lonnie Johnson, and one track features the soulful blues trombone of Ike Rogers.

Document 582 **St. Louis Piano Styles**
Seventeen tracks recorded between 1925–37. Features Katherine McDavid, Barrelhouse Buck McFarland, Keghouse, and Arthur McKay. A few have been on LP before on mostly out-of-print collections.

Mamlish 3805 **Good Time Blues**
Splendid collection, 1926–32. Charley Jordan, Sylvester Palmer, Edith North, Jelly Roll Anderson, and Hi Henry Brown. Great music and exceptional sound!

Mamlish 3806 **Hard Time Blues**
Lane Hardin, Mary Harris, Henry Townsend, Walter Davis, Peetie Wheatstraw, and Charlie McFadden.

OJL 20 **The Blues in St. Louis**
Henry Townsend, Kokomo Arnold, Barrelhouse Buck, Peetie Wheatstraw, Henry Spaulding, and Bessie Mae Smith.

Yazoo 1003 (c) **St. Louis Town 1929–1933**
Henry Townsend, Joe Stone, Charley Jordan, and Teddy Darby.

Yazoo 1030 (c) **St. Louis Blues 1929–1935**
Henry Townsend, Joe Stone, Charley Jordan, Hi Henry Brown, and Peetie Wheatstraw.

Note: See also WALTER DAVIS and PEETIE WHEATSTRAW.

TEXAS

Blues Documents 2059 **Texas Piano Blues**
Twenty tracks by Nick Nichols, Perry Dixon, Big Boy Knox, Joe Pullum, and Whistlin' Alex Moore. About one-third were previously available on out-of-print issues.

Document 540 **Texas in the Thirties**
Excellent collection of Texas blues featuring the complete recordings of Carl Davis' Dallas Jamboree Jug Band, Black Ace, and Kitty Gray and Her Wampus Cats. The Dallas Jamboree Jug Band was, I believe, the only jug band from Texas to record, though there is actually no jug audible on the four tracks here. Nevertheless, they are excellent upbeat sides with fine vocals by Davis with guitar, swanee whistle, bass, and occasional washboard. Black Ace was a superb, rich-voiced singer who played excellent slide guitar. On his six tracks from 1937, he is joined by Smokey Hogg on rhythm guitar. These six tracks alone are worth the price of the album. The second side of the album features 10 tracks by hokum singer Kitty Gray. Most of the tracks are fairly undistinguished, though several feature the lovely slide guitar of Oscar Woods. Only a few of the tracks on this collection have been reissued before.

Fountain FB 305 **Texas Blues: Dallas, 1928**
Beautiful reissue of Texas blues singers that perfectly complements the series of Texas piano blues reissues on Magpie (see PIANO BLUES AND BOOGIE section). Some stunning vocals by Texas Tommy, Ollie Ross, Hattie Burleson, and Jewell Nelson with varied accompaniments, including

piano, banjo, trumpet, and clarinet. Wonderful clear sound and excellent notes by Paul Oliver.

Herwin 211 Jack of Diamonds
Lovely 30s recordings made for the Library of Congress of mostly unknown but very fine performers. Smith Casey, Ace Johnson, Pete Harris, and Tricky Sam.

HK 4003 Texas Blues, 1928–29
Nineteen great cuts, many of which have been reissued before, and quite a few currently available on Yazoo; this album does, however, gather together all of the prewar recordings by the eight artists here. There is a lot of lovely melodic yet rhythmic guitar from Will Day (his cuts also include some beautiful clarinet), Otis Harris, Willie Reed, and Sammy Hill. Jesse Thomas (who also recorded after the war) and Bo Jones favor more of a single-string approach to their playing. Two of the Thomas cuts do not appear to have been reissued before. Jake Jones is accompanied by a small group with guitar, clarinet, and banjo, and his two cuts have not been previously reissued. Will Head accompanied himself on guitar and kazoo on a two-part version of the traditional Texas tune "Fare Thee Blues."

ESSENTIAL SELECTION
Yazoo 1004 Tex-Arkana-Louisiana Country 1927–1932
Henry Thomas, Texas Alexander, Little Hat Jones, Blind Lemon Jefferson, and Sammy Hill.

Yazoo 1032 Blues from the Western States 1927–1949
Jesse Thomas, Will Day, Little Hat Jones, Willie Lane, Rabbit Brown, and Ramblin' Thomas.

Note: See also BLIND LEMON JEFFERSON, BLIND WILLIE JOHNSON, J. T. "FUNNY PAPA" SMITH, HENRY THOMAS, and RAMBLIN' THOMAS.

JUG BANDS
ESSENTIAL SELECTION
Blues Classics 2 Jug, Jook and Washboard Bands
Exhilarating collection featuring the Memphis Jug Band, Dixieland Jug Blowers, and Mississippi Jook Band. Great!

Blues Documents 2023 The Jug and Washboard Bands
Eighteen tracks featuring the complete recordings in chronological order of Whistler and His Jug Band (1924, 1927, and 1931), Chicken Wilson and Skeeter Hinton (1928), and The Two of Spades (1925). About one-third of these tracks have been reissued before, but only a few are currently available elsewhere.

Blues Documents 2024 The Jug and Washboard Bands, Vol. 2
A varied collection of obscurities featuring the complete recordings of four groups. There are four tracks by the Tub Jug Washboard Band, who, as you may gather from their name, feature both washboard and jug! They are a lively group, if not terribly memorable. Two tracks by Rev. E. S. "Shy" Moore are wonderful, sanctified sermons, with vocalists and a small jug-based band helping out at the close of each piece. Feathers and Frog are a dull hokum trio. The remaining eight tracks are by the Phillips Louisville Jug Band, a mostly instrumental group fronted by guitarist Phil Phillips. Their material is as much jazz as blues and is quite enjoyable. About half the tracks have been on LP before, but very few are currently available elsewhere.

Blues Documents 2028 Alabama Jug and String Bands, 1928–1932
This album is evenly split between the Birmingham Jug Band, whose eight sides make up Side one, and the one-man-band recordings of band member Ben Curry ("Blind Bogus Ben Covington"). Big Joe Williams claimed to have played on the Birmingham Jug Band session, but whoever it was, these are some of the wildest jug-band sides ever recorded! While most of these have been available on Roots and OJL, the whole session is presented here. Curry's solo sides are musically less interesting.

Historical 36 The Great Jug Bands
Jed Davenport's Beale Street Jug Band, Cannon's Jug Stompers, Phillips Louisville Jug Band, and Dixieland Jug Blowers.

OJL 4 The Great Jug Bands
Classic set. Memphis Minnie and Her Jug Band, Birmingham Jug Band, and Jack Kelly and His South Memphis Jug Band.

OJL 19 More of that Jug Band Sound
Memphis Jug Band, Noah Lewis' Carolina Peanut Boys, Vol. Stevens, and Jed Davenport.

Wolf 131 The Memphis Jug Band and Associates
Eighteen tracks in all: three alternates by The Memphis Jug Band, four previously released tunes by The Picaninny Jug Band (a rollickin' incarnation of Will Shade and company), and the remaining material features small groupings of The Memphis Jug Band, either under the leadership of Stevens or Shade, or backing Jenny Pope, Minnie Wallace, Hattie Hart, and Kaiser Clifton. With the exception of the Jenny Pope titles, I loved it all. Highlights include Will Weldon's guitar on the Memphis Jug

Band sides, Shade's "She Stabbed Me with an Ice-pick" and "You Got to Have That Thing," and "Tappin' That Thing" by the Picaninny Jug Band. A nice supplement to the "Memphis Girls" LP (Blues Document 2029), with no overlap with other Memphis Jug Band LPs. However, 14 of these tracks have been released elsewhere, though only five are currently avaiable.

CASSETTE ONLY RELEASE
MCA 1372 **Jazzy Jugs and Washboards**
Budget-priced album featuring 11 fine recordings made between 1928–34 by various groups that featured either a jug or washboard. Some of it is bluesy and some of it is more jazz-oriented but all of it is fine. Tampa Red's Hokum Jug Band, Beale Street Washboard Band, Alabama Jug Band, and Kansas Joe McCoy.

Note: See also THE MEMPHIS JUG BAND, CLIFFORD HAYES, and DIXIELAND JUG BLOWERS.

PIANO BLUES AND BOOGIE
Blues Documents 2033 **Barrelhouse, Blues and Boogie Piano (1927–30)**
Outstanding collection of late 20s piano blues but frustrating for the collector, since nearly every track here is available on scattered reissues, often with better sound. Still, for completists, there are, in the order recorded, the complete works of Raymond Barrow, Piano Kid Edwards, and the magnificent Bob Call (also heard accompanying "Boodle It" Wiggins, Blind Leroy Garnett, and James Wiggins). One classic track after the next, so dedicated piano blues devotees will have to cross-check the titles for duplication, but otherwise an excellent anthology.

Blues Documents 2034 **Piano Blues and Boogie Woogie**
This is a flawed and misleading collection, yet essential nonetheless, if only for compiling the eight sides recorded by "Jabo" Williams, a strong singer and an outstanding, romping pianist with a powerful left hand. "Jab Blues" is a masterpiece and "Pratt City Blues" is not far behind. The surface noise on four cuts dubbed from worn 78s makes listening difficult but rewarding. Charles Avery, the other pianist represented on the LP, appears in several settings. His accompaniments to Freddie "Redd" Nicholson and Lil Johnson are tasteful, if unspectacular. Avery does cut loose on his solo piece, "Dearborn St. Breakdown," and on his two duets with guitarist Red Nelson. This is not, as claimed, Avery's complete output. There are two other duets with Nelson and several tracks with Lucille Bogan (see Yazoo 1017 and Agram 2005) which have been

omitted. Half of these tracks have appeared elsewhere, mostly on the Magpie Piano Blues series.
Blues Documents 2051 **Piano Blues Rarities, Vol. 1**
Twenty rare piano blues sides recorded between 1926–40 by five utterly obscure performers. Nolan Walsh, aka Barrel House Welch, is featured on seven tracks, three featuring his own primitive but effective piano, and the rest featuring the plodding Richard M. Jones. Two of these cuts have fine cornet work by Louis Armstrong. Skeet Brown is an excellent and expressive singer backed with good piano by Troy Sapp. F. T. Thomas has fine piano by Lee Green and some rather incongrous sax. Four of the eight sides by Charlie Segar are fine flowing instrumentals, including versions of "Cow Cow Blues" and "Boogie Woogie." The other four are vocals and show Segar to be a decent singer, although these tracks are dragged down a bit by somewhat ponderous drumming. In all, a good collection that, with a few exceptions, features material that has never been reissued before. Some tracks are a bit noisy but most are listenable.

Blues Documents 2052 **Piano Blues Rarities, Vol. 2**
Includes the first two recordings by the excellent Red Nelson (with fine piano accompaniment), four tracks by the limited but outrageous Whistlin' Rufus, four by the obscure but good Earl Thomas, six by "Peg Leg" Ben Abney, and four by Curtis Henry, including his fascinating "G-Man Blues." Only a few of the cuts have been out before.

Blues Documents 2053 **Piano Blues Rarities, Vol. 3**
Features the complete recordings of Andy Chatmon, Little David, One Arm Slim, and George Davis. Chatmon is a decent, if unexceptional, singer and piano player. Little David is a fine piano player and an interesting singer, though I'm not sure if the world needs two versions of "Sweet Petunia." One Arm Slim is a vocalist, very much influenced by Peetie Wheatstraw. With accompaniments by Blind John Davis or Black Bob, his six tracks include two unissued alternate takes. George Davis is an extremely dull singer and piano player, though his "Radio Brown Blues" has interesting lyrics. Not an essential release!

Blues Documents 2070 **Rare Jazz and Blues Piano**
A lackluster set featuring the complete recordings in chronological order of Whistling Bob Howe and Frankie Griggs, Ike Smith, Billy Mitchell, Old Ced Odom and Lil "Diamonds" Hardaway, and Scott

Nesbitt recorded between 1935–37. Many of the recordings fall into the risque, hokum category that I find generally boring unless the performers show some enthusiasm, which is not the case here. Curiously enough, the most interesting tracks are by Scottie Nesbit; while not exceptional, his singing and playing are quite engaging.

Blues Documents 2073 Rural Blues Piano, 1927–35

Sixteen sides, including eight by Harry Chatmon and two by Leroy Carter that have not been on LP before, along with two fine tracks by Sugar Underwood that have been reissued several times, and four by Charley Taylor that have also been available before.

Blues Documents 2094 Piano Blues Rarities, Vol. 4

Twenty rare recordings made between 1923–29. Although these are very rare, their musical value is not terribly great. Most of the singers are dull and likewise the piano playing, with the exception of George Thomas' accompaniments to Tiny Franklin and the unknown piano player on the two Lucius Hardy sides. Other artists include Cry Baby Godfrey, Jack Erby, George Hannah, Guy Smith, and Freddie Brown.

Document 513 Piano Blues, Vol. 1—The Twenties

Eighteen tracks recorded between 1923–30, most not previously on LP and the remainder not available on LP for quite a while. It includes Clay Custer's lovely 1923 instrumental "The Rocks," which features, I believe, one of the first uses of the walking bass on record. There are a couple of fine instrumentals by Q. Roscoe Snowden, while the rest of the album features vocals with piano accompaniments, and includes Willie Jones, Jack Ranger, Blind Clyde Church, and the unexceptional vaudeville blues of L. C. Prigett and the mysterious track "Throw Me Down" from 1928, which is considered by some to actually be Skip James. Although there are some superficial similarities, the piano playing seems a little too smooth to be Skip. Still, whoever it is, it is a most enjoyable track.

Document 514 Piano Blues, Vol. 2—The Thirties

Eighteen tracks recorded between 1930–39. Some of these have been reissued before, but most are not currently available. Highlights of the album are the four tracks by Jesse James, a superb gruff-voiced singer and barrelhouse piano player. The album also includes the lovely "Policy Blues" by Albert Clemens, who is thought to be Cripple Clarence

Lofton and certainly sounds remarkably like him. It also includes tracks by Judson Brown, Pigmeat Terry, Harry "Freddie" Shayne (the fine "Original Mr. Freddie Blues"), Bob Robinson (generally unexciting hokum distinguished by the fine piano of Frank "Springback" James), Frank Busby, and James Carter.

Document 576 Deep South Blues Piano, 1935–37

A superb collection featuring almost all of the issued recordings of Blind Mack, Kid Stormy Weather, and the piano/guitar duo Mack Rhinehart and Brownie Stubblefield. All of the performers are obscure but truly fine. I particularly like Rhinehart and Stubblefield, who have the bulk of the recordings on this album (11 out of 14). The singer (no one knows which one) is very fine and overall they sound like a more rural version of Leroy Carr and Scrapper Blackwell. It's surprising that practically none of their recordings has been reissued before. Decent sound.

Document 599 Rare Piano Blues, 1925–35

Twenty rare sides, most of which have not been on LP before. There are two tracks by Ray Logan, a fine performer in spite of the poor recording and the presence of the kazoo. There are four sides by "Talking" Billy Anderson, who sounds like two different people. "Side Wheel" Sally Duffie is a fine singer, who is thought to be actually be Mae Glover; her four tracks have the brilliant piano of Will Ezell, but are from rather worn Paramounts. Jim Towel (accompanied by Cow Cow Davenport) is right out of the medicine show or vaudeville tradition on his two tracks. Davenport also accompanies the duo, The Southern Blues Singers. Also featured are Monroe Walker, James Bat Robinson, Kid Stormy Weather, and an alternate take of George Noble's "Sissy Man Blues."

Historical 29 Hot Pianos

Blues and jazz piano. Jelly Roll Morton, Montana Taylor, and Fats Waller.

HK 4010 Piano Blues, 1927–1930

An excellent collection of piano blues; however, most of these tracks have been reissued before and quite a few are currently available on Magpie's magnificent "Piano Blues" series. This set will be of most interest to those who would like to have together all of the recordings of the very fine Bert M. Mays and Kingfish Bill Tomlin (including the latter's remarkable "Army Blues," which has not been reissued before), and the few previously unreissued or currently unavailable tracks. Other artists include Sammy Brown, Ruby Paul, The

Southern Blues Singers, Dan Stewart, Jim Clarke, Rudy Foster, and the tremendous Joe Dean. Sound quality ranges from excellent to mediocre.

Magpie 4401 Piano Blues, Vol. 1—Paramount
First in a series of comprehensive reissues of prewar blues piano. Although there is some duplication with other reissues, sound quality is very good and all albums come with notes and full discographical information. Charlie Spand, Little Brother, Louise Johnson, Leroy Garnett, Charles Avery, and Will Ezell.

Magpie 4402 Piano Blues Vol. 2—Brunswick, 1928–1930
Lucille Bogan, John Oscar, Eddie Miller, Charles "Speck" Pertum, and Henry Brown.

Magpie 4403 Piano Blues, Vol. 3—Vocalion, 1928–1930
Cow Cow Davenport, Joe Dean, Jim Clarke, Romeo Nelson, Lil Johnson, Tampa Red, and Montana Taylor.

Magpie 4404 Piano Blues, Vol. 4—The Thomas Family
Hociel Thomas, Sippie Wallace, George Thomas, Moanin' Bernice, and Hersal Thomas.

Magpie 4405 Piano Blues, Vol. 5—Postscript, 1927–33
Little Brother, Roosevelt Sykes, James "Bat" Robinson, Sammy Brown, and Cow Cow Davenport.

Magpie 4406 Piano Blues, Vol. 6—Walter Roland
See Walter Roland.

Magpie 4407 Piano Blues, Vol. 7—Leroy Carr
See Leroy Carr.

Magpie 4408 Piano Blues, Vol. 8—Texas Seaport 1934–37
Fine set of 30s recordings. Rob Cooper, Andy Boy, Joe Pullum, and Walter "Cowboy" Washington.

Magpie 4409 Piano Blues, Vol. 9—Cripple Clarence Lofton/George Noble
See Cripple Clarence Lofton.

Magpie 4410 Piano Blues, Vol. 10—Territory Blues, 1934–41
Artists recorded in the South. Mississippi Jook Band, Big Boy Knox, Curtis Henry, and Peanut the Kidnapper. Great!

Magpie 4411 Piano Blues, Vol. 11—Texas Santa Fe, 1934–37
Features several fine Southeast Texas pianists. Son Becky, Black Boy Shine, Black Ivory King, Pinetop Burks, and Alfoncy Harris. Marvelous music, marvelous sound, great notes.

Magpie 4412 Piano Blues, Vol. 12—Big Four, 1933–41
Four cuts each by Little Brother, Walter Davis, Roosevelt Sykes, and Springback James. Superb music beautifully mastered. Excellent notes.

Magpie 4413 Piano Blues, Vol. 13—Central Highway
Sixteen great cuts, 1933–41, by a wide range of piano players/singers who recorded in the 30s. Georgia White, Lee Green, Black Bob, Pinetop, and Eddie Miller.

Magpie 4414 Piano Blues, Vol. 14—The Accompanist, 1933–41
Fine singers accompanied by a variety of piano players. Vocalists include Bumble Bee Slim, Lil Johnson, Bill Gaither, and Johnny Temple; accompanying piano players include Myrtle Jenkins, Pinetop Sparks, Black Bob, Roosevelt Sykes, Honey Hill, and Horace Malcolm.

Magpie 4415 Piano Blues, Vol. 15—Dallas, 1927–29
Sixteen beautiful sides by Texas Bill Day and Billiken Johnson, Whistlin' Alex Moore, Hattie Hudson (an all-time classic!), and Bobbie Cadillac. Usual superb sound and astute notes by Paul Oliver.

Magpie 4416 The Piano Blues, Vol. 16—Charlie Spand
See Charlie Spand.

Magpie 4417 The Piano Blues, Vol. 17—Paramount, Vol.. 2
Superb and incredibly rare recordings cut for Paramount between 1927–32. "Jabo" Williams, Freddie Brown, Raymond Barrow, Barrelhouse Welch, Louise Johnson, and Skip James. The sound is superb and the album comes with excellent notes by Bob Hall and Richard Noblett.

Magpie 4418 The Piano Blues, Vol. 18—Roosevelt Sykes/Lee Green
See Roosevelt Sykes.

Magpie 4419 The Piano Blues, Vol. 19—Barrelhouse Women
Focuses on female singers with piano accompaniments, including Doretha Trowbridge, Elzadie Robinson, Lucille Bogan, Lillian Miller, Evelyn Brickey, and Lil Johnson.

Magpie 4420 The Piano Blues, Vol. 20—Barrelhouse Years, 1928–33
A superb selection by some of the greatest pianists of the era. Although about two-thirds of these selections have been reissued before, many of them have not been around for a long time and the sound quality here is far superior to previous reissues. It's such a

pleasure to finally be able to properly hear "Fat Mama Blues" by the amazing Jabo Williams. Pinetop Smith, The Sparks Brothers (including the incredibly rare and very fine "Louisiana Bound"), "Boodle It" Wiggins, Lonnie Clark, and Speckled Red.

Magpie 4421 The Piano Blues, Vol. 21
The last album in this superb series features previously unissued recordings by the three giants of boogie woogie: Meade Lux Lewis, Albert Ammons, and Pete Johnson. These recordings were not even known to exist until recently! Eight of the performances are from the 1938–39 "Spirituals To Swing" concerts organized by John Hammond. Includes two duets by Ammons and Lewis and one cut with Johnson backing Joe Turner. Three of the remaining cuts are from 1944 film shorts and the last cut is from 1945. Wonderful music!

OJL 15 Rugged Piano Classics
Skip James, Jim Clark, Cripple Clarence Lofton, Henry Brown, Black Diamond Twins, Blythe and Burton, Blythe and Clark, and Cow Cow Davenport.

OJL 16 Ragged Piano Classics
Prewar ragtime by white and black performers. Sugar Underwood, Blind Leroy Garnett, and Rob Cooper.

Oldie Blues 2808 Piano Blues
James "Boodle It" Wiggins, Bob Call, Raymond Barrow, Spider Carter, and Ell-Zee Floyd.

RCA Bluebird 8334-1 (c,d) Barrelhouse Boogie
Piano blues and boogie by four of the greats, including two by Meade Lux Lewis, eight by Jimmy Yancey, and six incredible duets by Pete Johnson and Albert Ammons. The CD has two extra tracks by Yancey and three extra by Johnson and Ammons.

Rosetta 1303 Piano Singer's Blues
Recordings by blues women who accompany themselves on piano. Sixteen sides recorded between 1926–61 by Georgia White, Edith Johnson, Arizona Dranes, Cleo Brown, Julia Lee, Hazel Scott, and Una Mae Carlisle. There is some duplication with other reissues.

Rosetta 1309 Boogie Blues
Upbeat songs and tunes mostly in the boogie-woogie style. Sixteen recordings cut between 1930–61 by Lil Armstrong, Helen Humes, Hazel Scott, Sweet Georgia Brown, and Dorothy Donegan. With extensive notes and some great and rare photos.

Storyville 184 Boogie Woogie Trio
Three giants of boogie: Albert Ammons, Pete Johnson, and Meade Lux Lewis, from live broadcasts from the Sherman Hotel in Chicago in 1939. Some great performances: solos, duets, and one cut where all three play together. Most of these cuts are also available on Euphonic.

Swaggie 1326 Boogie Woogie Pianists
Recordings from 1928–30 by Pinetop Smith, Montana Taylor, Speckled Red, and Cow Cow Davenport.

Wolf 132 Texas Piano Blues, 1929–37
Excellent set featuring Texas Bill Day, Whistlin' Alex Moore, Blind Norris, Pinetop, Son Becky, Walter "Cowboy" Washington, Andy Boy, and Black Ivory King. About two-thirds of these have been reissued before, some on out-of-print collections.

Yazoo 1015 Country Blues Piano/Guitar Duets
Joe Evans, Leola Manning, Springback James, Roosevelt Sykes, Willie Harris, and Charlie Spand.

Yazoo 1028 Barrelhouse Piano, 1927–36
Bob Call, Lonnie Johnson, Raymond Barrow, Jabbo Williams, George Noble, Jesse James, and Cow Cow Davenport.

CASSETTE ONLY RELEASE

MCA 1332 Piano in Style, 1926–1930
Blues and jazz piano by Jelly Roll Morton, James P. Johnson, and "Pinetop" Smith.

CASSETTE AND CD RELEASE ONLY

ESSENTIAL SELECTION

CA 2098-2 Grinder Man Blues—Masters of the Blues Piano
Another superb collection prepared by Billy Altman for RCA's Heritage series. This one features three great piano players who recorded for Bluebind and Victor in the 30s and 40s: Little Brother Montgomery, Memphis Slim, and Big Maceo. All three are brilliant and very different performers. Montgomery's six cuts are from 1935 and '36 and reveal his lovely, subtle stride and ragtime-flavored piano. Memphis Slim's six cuts are from 1940 and '41; he is a more sophisticated performer, with his imaginative piano playing supported by the bass of Leroy Batchelor or Alfred Elkins. Big Maceo was one of the greatest of all piano bluesmen; his rich smokey voice and fluid and rhythmic playing are a joy to hear. On all six cuts, he is accompanied by Tampa Red, and the three from 1945 also include a drummer. Highlights include his definitive verison of "Worried Life Blues," the exquisite "Country Jail Blues," which is one of my favorites, and the storming instrumental "Chicago Breakdown." Sound is outstanding and the 12-page booklet has excellent notes by Altman and photos of all the performers. My only quibble is that I would have preferred to see individual CDs of all three performers. Still, this is unequivocally recommended.

COMPACT DISC

ESSENTIAL SELECTION

Magpie PY CD 01 The Piano Blues: Paramount, Vol. 1, 1928–32
Features all of Magpie 4401 plus four tracks from 4420. It's hard to be objective about this collection; every performance is a classic. Considering the recording and pressing quality of the original Paramounts, the sound here is outstanding. With detailed notes by Bob Hall and Richard Nobblett. Essential. (See reviews of albums above for more information on the contents.)

MISCELLANEOUS PREWAR

Agram 2011 Trouble Done Bore Me Down
Mostly previously unreissued prewar country blues by artists who have previously been featured on Agram LPs. This is, in a way, a sampler but one doesn't have to worry about duplication. The exceptions are the two tracks by Washington Phillips that were previously reissued by Agram, but the dubbings here are vastly superior. Includes Barbecue Bob, Walter Vinson, Lucille Bogan, James "Stump" Johnson, and Texas Alexander. Album comes in a fold-out jacket with booklet, extensive notes, song lyrics, tune analysis, and reproductions of old ads. The cover features a recently discovered photo of Washington Phillips complete with dulceola, and the notes give the first description of this unusual instrument. Excellent sound.

Blues Classics 5 Country Blues Classics, Vol. 1
Includes some postwar recordings. Willie Baker, Curley Weaver, Black Ivory King, and Monroe Mo Jackson (truly amazing!).

Blues Classics 6 Country Blues Classics, Vol. 2
Some postwar recordings. Bayless Rose, Joe Williams, Frank Stokes, Blind Norris, and Pinetop Slim.

Blues Classics 7 Country Blues Classics, Vol. 3
Some postwar recordings. Lonnie Coleman, Wright Holmes, Barbecue Bob, Willie McTell, and Casey Bill.

Blues Classics 14 Country Blues Classics, Vol. 4
Includes some postwar recordings. Leroy Dallas, Peter Warfield, John Henry Barbee, and Sonny Boy Johnson.

Blues Classics 26 When Women Sang The Blues
Lillian Glinn, Bobby Cadillac, Emma Wright, Chippie Hill, Bernice Edwards, and Bessie Tucker.

Blues Documents 2007 The Great Songsters, 1927–1929
A beautiful collection of 18 songs recorded by performers generally from the Eastern states. Many of these tracks have been reissued before but most are not currently available. Long-time collectors will welcome the inclusion of the two incredibly rare and fine tracks by Eli Farmer, which have never been reissued before: "God Didn't Make No Monkey Man" is a powerful, hard-driving performance with some lovely slide guitar, while "Farmer's Blues" is a more straight-ahead piece with fine singing and playing. The album features all eight discovered tracks by the fine Luke Jordan, with his distinctive vocals, including two takes each of his two most famous songs, "Church Bell Blues" and "Pick Poor Robin Blues," and his fine "Cocaine Blues." There are two tracks by Will Bennett, and four by the fine gospel singer Lonnie McIntorsh, with powerful singing and fine guitar. The album ends with two fairly unexciting gospel performances by Blind Willie Harris. A very good album.

Blues Documents 2015 Georgia Blues Guitars, 1928–33
A fantastic collection of Georgia country blues featuring the complete recordings of Willie Baker, Seth Richard, and Fred McMullen. There are nine tracks by Baker, a wonderful singer and 12-string guitarist who often plays with a slide. Seth Richard is another fine 12-string guitarist, though his two sides pale in the fast company he has here. The remaining seven tracks are by McMullen, a six-string guitarist who plays some lovely slide. Most of his tracks feature second guitar by Curley Weaver, and there are also accompaniments to Ruth Willis. Most of these tracks have been reissued before and about half are still available, but this release brings them together in one place.

Blues Documents 2016 Bluesmen and Songsters, 1926–36
An excellent collection of artists whose music straddles the line between blues and an earlier preblues tradition. With the exception of the awful "Beans" Hambone, the music is consistently fine, and includes the complete recordings of the very fine "Mooch" Richardson and Hambone Willie Newbern. The latter's 1929 "Roll and Tumble Blues" is possibly the first recording of this Mississippi standard. Also included are "Big Boy" George Owens, Freezone, and Charlie Manson. Most of these tracks have been out before but only a few are currently available.

Blues Documents 2021 Cincinnati Blues, 1928–36
This fine album of country blues features the complete recordings of Bob Coleman, Kid Cole, and Walter Coleman, who are thought to all be the same

man! Whatever his real name, he is a fine singer and guitar player, with some distinctive vocal trademarks. Four of the tracks feature Coleman with The Cincinnati Jug Band, including the magnificent "Tear It Down" and "Cincinnati Underworld Woman." Other gems include "Niagra Fall Blues" and the fascinating "I'm Going to Cincinnati," with its evocation of Cincinnati locations in the 30s. Several of the tracks have been on album before, but many are on album for the first time. Sound is generally good, and this is definitely recommended.

Blues Documents 2040 Female Country Blues, Vol. 1: The Twenties

Eighteen tracks recorded between 1924–28, featuring the complete recordings of five singers: Anna Lee Chisholm, Virginia Childs, Eva Parker, Cora Perkins, and Lulu Jackson. Only a few of these tracks have been reissued before.

Blues Documents 2041 Rare Paramount Country Blues

The Paramount label was responsible for discovering and recording some of the greatest country blues singers of the prewar era, including Blind Blake, Blind Lemon Jefferson, Charlie Patton, and Son House. However, in among the giants, were a fair number of second- and third-rate performers, and a selection of these is presented here, most of them not reissued before. Sweet Papa Stovepipe and Jack of Diamonds are fairly undistinguished hokum singers. Charlie "Dad" Nelson is a moderately interesting singer and guitarist, but his songs are ruined for me by the omnipresent kazoo. Singer/piano player Lonnie Clark is the most exciting performer here, but his two tracks have been reissued several times before. Smokey Harrison is a relatively unexciting singer and guitarist, but his songs, including "Hop Head Blues" and "Iggly Oggly Blues," are a bit out of the ordinary. The album is rounded out by the fascinating "Hometown Skiffle, Parts 1 and 2," which was a 1929 sampler from the Paramount label, featuring snippets by Blind Lemon, Charlie Spand, The Hokum Boys, and others, with introductions by Alex Hill. Sound varies from good to mediocre. A release for Paramount or Blues Documents completists.

Blues Documents 2057 Country Blues Collector Items, Vol. 2

The 10 tracks on Side one feature the entire recorded output of Spark Plug Smith. The most interesting thing about him is his name (not to be confused with Six Cylinder Smith—as if we would do such a thing!). He is a dull singer and an even duller guitarist, though his repertoire is somewhat interesting. Side two starts off with two fine rarities from

Teddy Darby under the pseudonym of Blind Squire Turner. Things take a nosedive with Sophisticated Jimmy LaRue who, as you might expect from his name, is not at all a country blues artist but a rather urbane and excrutiatingly dull hokum singer. The rest of the album is all prime stuff, featuring Charlie McCoy's very rare and fine "Times Ain't What They Used to Be," the two prewar recordings of Andrew "Smokey" Hogg, and white country pioneer Jimmie Rodgers accompanied by the brilliant St. Louis guitarist Clifford Gibson.

ESSENTIAL SELECTION

Blues Documents BOX BD 01 The Greatest in Country Blues, 1927–56

That indefatigable Austrian chronicler of prewar blues, Johnny Parth, has come up with a new idea. This three-LP box set features 60 of the greatest country blues recordings as selected by Johnny together with a 24-page illustrated booklet with notes by Paul Oliver. Although long-time collectors will have most of these recordings, this is a perfect introduction for the beginning collector. Even if you have all these tracks, it's nice to be able to put on a record and know that every track is a gem! Includes Charley Patton, Richard "Rabbit" Brown, Tommy Johnson, Blind Willie Reynolds, Blind Willie Johnson, Mississippi John Hurt, Willie Brown, Sam Collins, "Hi" Henry Brown, The Memphis Jug Band, Furry Lewis, Memphis Minnie, Palmer McAbee, Smith Casey, Big Bill Broonzy, Lane Hardin, Leroy Carr, Kid Bailey, Dan Pickett, Howlin' Wolf, and many more. A few minor criticisms are in order, though. The selection is overwhelmingly slanted towards Mississippi, Tennessee, and Louisiana blues, with very little representation of the Eastern states (no Blind Boy Fuller!), and the presentation of postwar blues is very cursory; these titles should have either been left off entirely or, at least, be expanded to a whole LP's worth. Still, a most worthwhile collection, particularly for the neophyte.

Bluetime 2015 Roots of the Postwar Blues

Sixteen songs recorded in the 20s, 30s, and early 40s that were later covered by postwar artists or inspired songs by them. For instance we have "Crawling Kingsnake" by Tony Hollins (redone by John Lee Hooker), "Beer Drinking Woman" by Memphis Slim (covered by Jimmy McCracklin), "Mattie Mae Blues" (first verse inspired Baby Boy Warren's "Hello Stranger"), and "She Fooled Me" by Washboard Sam (recorded by the obscure Harvey Hill, Jr.). Although the idea is a good one, the cursory notes do not go into enough depth; therefore, the connections may be obscure for all but the most knowledgeable collector. Couple this with the fact that all of these tracks have been reissued before, some more than once, making this a fairly dispensable acquisition.

Bluetime 2016 Show Me What You Got

Even if you have a lot of dirty blues collections, I think you'll find more than a few dirty ditties here that you don't have; there's also the beautiful vintage erotic cover to further entice you. There's a lot of bacon frying in the grooves of these griddle cakes, but what can you expect when you're dealing with scarce vintage filth like Carl Rafferty ("Dresser with the Drawers"), Little David ("New Sweet Patunia"), Lizzie Miles ("My Man o' War"), Napoleon Fletcher ("She Showed It All"), Blind Squire Turner ("Don't Like the Way You Do"), and Georgia Pine Boy ("One More Greasing"). A real stocking stuffer, this one.

Columbia 46215 (c,d) Legends of the Blues, Vol. 1

Sampler of the many magnificent blues artists that recorded for Columbia and its various predecessors, Vocalion, ARC, and OKeh. Although most of the tracks have been reissued before, the sound here is superior, and the set does include two previously unissued gems: Lonnie Johnson's incredible "Low Down St. Louis Blues," in which he catalogs the violent tendencies of his St. Louis girlfriends, and a fine 1939 Big Bill Broonzy cut, "Spreadin' Snake Blues." The rest of the set includes Bessie Smith, Blind Lemon Jefferson, Mississippi John Hurt, Blind Willie Johnson, Bo Carter, Blind Willie McTell, Charley Patton, Leroy Carr, Josh White, Leadbelly, Peetie Wheatstraw, Robert Johnson, Blind Boy Fuller, Bukka White, Muddy Waters, Big Joe Williams, and Son House. Whew! Fine notes by Paul Oliver.

Columbia 46217 (c,d) News and the Blues: Telling It Like It Is

Twenty fine examples of blues that comment on external events. Among the subjects covered are disasters ("Black Water Blues" by Bessie Smith and "God Moves on the Water" by Blind Willie Johnson), vice ("Dope Head Blues" by Victoria Spivey and "Gambling Man Blues" by Sister O. M. Tarrell), real and mythical heroes and villains ("Frankie" by Mississippi John Hurt, "Joe Louis Special" by Jack Kelly, and "Ma Rainey" by Memphis Minnie), poverty and unemployment ("'34 Blues" by Charley Patton, "Unemployment Stomp" by Big Bill Broonzy, and "Homeless Blues" by Willie "Long Time" Smith), and others ("Parchman Farm Blues" by Bukka White and "Atomic Bomb Blues" by Homer Harris). Although most of these tracks have been reissued before, there are a couple of otherwise unavailable tracks and informative notes by Pete Welding.

Columbia 46218 (c,d) The Slide Guitar: Bottles, Knives, and Steel

This collection features some of the finest exponents of the slide style. There are two tracks by the wonderful Sylvester Weaver and Walter Beasley, including their lovely slide-guitar duet, "Bottleneck Blues." Weaver also does a solo on "Guitar Rag" that was later adapted by country steel guitarist Leon McAuliffe into the most popular slide guitar tune of all time, "Steel Guitar Rag." There are two cuts by the magnificent gospel singer/guitarist Blind Willie Johnson, including his spine-tingling "Dark Was the Night." Also included are Barbecue Bob, Ruth Willis with Blind Willie McTell, Tampa Red and Georgia Tom, Charlie Patton, Robert Johnson, Casey Bill Weldon (a previously unissued track), Bukka White, and rare slide guitar outings by Blind Boy Fuller and Leadbelly. From the postwar era, there is the lovely 1953 recording of gospel singer/guitarist Sister O. M. Terrell and a track from Son House's 1965 Columbia LP. Detailed and interesting notes by Richard Spottswood.

Document DLP 503/504 Harmonicas Unlimited, Vols. 1 and 2

Two-LP set of 36 harmonica blues recordings, mostly from the 20s and 30s but featuring one session from 1949 by Elder R. Wilson and family. This incredible session of six tracks features gospel singing accompanied by three harmonicas! The rest of the album features mostly previously unreissued material and includes the complete recordings of Eddie Mapp, James Moore, Ellis Williams, William McCoy, and Blind Roger Hays, and all the tracks by Daddy Stovepipe (Johnny Watson) that have been found. Many of the tracks here are instrumental—usually harmonica/guitar duets. The harmonica duets of Eddie Mapp and James Moore are very fine, as are the William McCoy tracks. McCoy is a fine harmonica player and an engaging singer; the addition of clarinet on his "Out of Doors Blues" is very effective. Sound is generally good though a few tracks are from heavily worn 78s. No notes but full discographical information.

Document 573 Chicago Blues Roots, Vol. 1
Twenty tracks recorded in 1937–38 featuring John D. Twitty (aka Black Spider Dumplin'), Little Bill, Charley West, the Midnight Ramblers, James Hall, and George Curry. Most tracks not previously issued on LP.

Document 574 Chicago Blues Roots, Vol. 2
Sixteen tracks recorded between 1938–40, two by George Jefferson, two by Lulu Scott, and 12 by Roosevelt Scott. Most are new to LP.

Document 578 Chicago Blues Roots, Vol. 3
Recordings from 1934–36. Ten by Louisiana Johnny and Kid Beecher, six by Arkansas Shorty, and two by Willie Hatcher, most new to LP.

Document 579 Blue Ladies
Twenty tracks recorded between 1934–37, featuring Irene Sanders, Trixie Butler, The Za Zu Girl, and Billie (Willie Mae) McKenzie. Mostly new to LP.

Document 586 Female Country Blues Singers, 1929–31
Nineteen mostly vaudeville rather than country-blues sides. Alura Mack, who has 13 of the 19 tracks here, has an unusual voice and her lyrics are often out of the ordinary. Many of her cuts have a lovely ragtimey rolling piano on them. There are two tracks by Lena Matlock, which are generally unexceptional. The four tracks by Lillie Mae are the high points of this collection. She is a wonderfully intense singer accompanied by solid piano and guitar (possibly Barbecue Bob or Curley Weaver). Most of the tracks here have never been on LP before.

Document 591 Cornet Blues, 1924–30
Twenty tracks featuring the sound of the cornet. It opens with two instrumentals from Johnny Dunn, but the rest are vocals with cornet accompaniments, including Sadie McKinney (with Charley Williamson), Araha "Baby" Moore (with Williamson), Cleo Gibson (with Henry Mason), David Pearson (with Mason), Elizabeth Johnson (the most interesting artist here by far, with a two-part "Empty Bed Blues" with King Oliver, and the very rural-sounding "Be My Kid Blues" and "Sobbin' Woman Blues" with an unknown and very fine cornet player), Oliver Cobb (with his own cornet), and Bee Turner (with Cobb). Except for the very fine Elizabeth Johnson sides, the rest of this collection is relatively nondescript. About two-thirds of these tracks have been reissued

before, but most are not currently available elsewhere.

Document 600 The Deep South, 1927–37
Document's 100th album (!) is a collection of extremely rare country blues recordings. Highlights are the recently-discovered third Paramounts of Edward Thompson and Tommy Johnson. These are as fine as their other recordings, though both are in rather rough shape. This set also features alternate takes of songs by Frank Stokes and Bessie Tucker, and a fine rare instrumental from the Black Patti label by Al Miller's String Band. The eight tracks on Side two feature all the discovered recordings of Tommy Settlers—a rather bizarre performer who sings and accompanies himself on kazoo—sometimes singing through the kazoo to produce an interesting, if somewhat irritating, effect. The first four tracks from 1930 are solo recordings, while the remainder, from 1937, include piano and guitar and are somewhat more appealing.

Flyright 542 I'm the Highway Man
Fine reissues from the Library of Congress. 1938 recordings from Detroit featuring Calvin Frazier and Sampson Pittman. Some beautiful singing and guitar playing, though sound from very worn acetates is rough.

HK 4007 Chicago Blues
Splendid collection featuring two tracks by singer/piano player Perry Weston from 1937, eight by singer Alfred Fields (with Josh Altheimer, Big Bill Broonzy, and Washboard Sam) from 1939, four by the splendid singer/guitarist/harmonica player Frank Edwards from 1941, and six by the brilliant singer/guitarist Tony Hollins (one of the few bluesmen to have strongly influenced John Lee Hooker) from 1941. About eight of these tracks have been reissued before, but most of those were on a long-out-of-print Kokomo album.

HK 4009 String Bands, 1927–29
A fascinating and delightful collection featuring black string bands. There are four tracks by Taylor's Kentucky Boys and one by The Booker Orchestra, overlapping groups that included both white and black musicians, and whose approach and repertoires were similar to those of the many white string bands of the era. Ki Ki Johnson's music seems to come out of the minstrel tradition, with his songs accompanied by violin, banjo, and guitar. There are seven tracks by the excellent North Georgia duo Andrew and Jim Baxter, who accompany themselves with violin and guitar. Their music ranges from straight blues to hillbilly breakdowns. As a solo performer, Joe Linthecombe can hardly be con-

sidered a string band, but his music fits in well here. He accompanies himself on ukelele and does some trumpet-like vocal effects. About half of the tracks here have been reissued before, but most are not currently available elsewhere.

Jass 3 (c) Copulatin' Rhythm

Blues and jazz songs relating to sex, including such items as "Candy Man" by Rosetta Crawford, "You've Got to Save That Thing" by Ora Alexander, "Don't Tear My Clothes" by the Chicago Black Swans (a spirited group featuring lead vocals by Big Bill Broonzy), "If You Don't Give Me What I Want" by Lil Johnson, and "If You See My Rooster" by Memphis Minnie. Some tracks are available elsewhere. Sound is good and there is discographical information.

Jass 4 (c) Viper Mad Blues

"Sixteen songs of dope and depravity," featuring both blues and jazz performances. Includes "Kicking the Gong Around" by Cab Calloway, "Smoking Reefers" by Larry Adler, "The Stuff Is Here and It's Mellow" by Cleo Brown, "Junker's Blues" by Champion Jack Dupree, and the incredible "Dope Head Blues" by Victoria Spivey (with great guitar by Lonnie Johnson). Great stuff with excellent sound, discographical details, lyric transcripts, and a delightful cover.

Jass 5 (c) Copulatin' Rhythm, Vol. 2

Not as strong as the first volume, with much more duplication with other albums. Tracks include "Get Them from the Peanut Man" by Georgia White, "Six or Seven Times" by The Chocolate Dandies, "What's That Smell Like Fish" by Blind Boy Fuller, and "All Around Man" by Bo Carter.

Library of Congress AAFS L 3 Afro-American Spirituals, Work Songs and Ballads

Wonderful, mostly unaccompanied field recordings from 1933–39, with annotated booklet. Doc and Henry Reed, Vera Hall, and Willie Williams.

Library of Congress AAFS L 4 Afro-American Blues and Game Songs

1933–40 field recordings including 1938 recordings by Sonny Terry, plus Smith Casey, Jim Henry, and Vera Hall.

Library of Congress AAFS L 8 Negro Work Songs and Calls

1933–40 field recordings of songs to accompany unloading rail cars and tamping ties, arwhoolies (cornfield hollers), and more.

Mamlish 3801 New Deal Blues

Very fine collection of sides from the mid-30s. Joe McCoy, Black Ace, Bo Carter, the Chatmon Brothers, Memphis Minnie, Bumble Bee Slim, Sonny Scott, and One Arm Slim.

Mamlish 3809 Bullfrog Blues

Incredible country blues. Sam Butler, Buddy Boy Hawkins, William Harris, and Bo Weavil Jackson.

Matchbox 201 Country Blues—The First Generation

Eleven wonderful sides from 1927, including six songs recorded by the fabulous and mysterious duo from Mississippi, Long Cleve Reed and Harvey Hull, and all five recordings by the superb New Orleans street singer Richard "Rabbit" Brown, who sang some wonderful blues, ballads, and minstrel-type songs.

Matchbox 209 Great Harp Players, 1927–1930

Early and rare recordings of blues harmonica playing by William Frances and Richard Sowell, El Watson, Palmer McAbee, Freeman Stowers, Blues Birdhead, and Alfred Lewis. I'm not sure that all these artists could be considered "great," but there are some great performances. Alfred Lewis is particularly fine, Freeman Stowers does some astonishing train and animal impressions on the harmonica, and Blues Birdhead's playing is remarkably sophisticated for the era. Very few of these titles have been reissued before.

Matchbox 216 Country Girls, 1926–29

Features the complete recordings of Lillian Miller, Hattie Hudson, Gertrude Perkins, Pearl Dickson, Laura Henton, and Bobbie Cadillac.

Matchbox 2001/2 Songster and Saints

This excellent two-LP set of 36 songs is the first of two that are being issued to coincide with the publication of the Paul Oliver book with the same title. Each of the four sides in this set focuses on a different aspect of prewar black vocal traditions other than blues. Side one covers Dances and Travelling Shows; Side two: Comment, Parodies and Ballad Heroes; Side three: Baptist and Sanctified Preachers; and Side four: Gospel Soloists and Evangelists. Although many of the cuts have been reissued before, the purpose here is to put the recordings into perspective. Sound is excellent and the fascinating notes by Oliver will inspire one to read the book.

Matchbox 2003/4 Songsters and Saints, Vol. 2

Thirty-six titles sampling some of the vast wealth of prewar black vocal traditions that have been somewhat neglected in the past. Side one features medicine show singers like Papa Charlie Jackson, Gus Cannon, and The Beale Street Sheiks. Side two features "songsters" like Stovepipe No. 1, David Crockett, and Luke Jordan. Side three features "straining preachers," like Rev. J. C. Burnett and Rev. F. W. McGee., and Side four presents sacred vocalists/instrumentalists, including Arizona Dranes, Blind Willie Johnson, and the Memphis Sanctified Singers. Many of these cuts have been reissued before. Good sound and notes by Oliver.

Milestone 2016 The Blues Tradition
Great collection but much duplication with other sets. Big Bill, King Solomon Hill, Bumble Bee Slim, and Willie Brown.

New World NW 290 Let's Get Loose
A real gem, featuring 16 recordings cut between 1916–42, most never reissued before. Features two performances by white artists, a 1928 string band and a 1916 vaudeville singer, plus some great tracks by Yank Rachell, The Johnson Boys, Hattie Hudson, Tyus and Tyus, and Leroy Carr. With detailed notes by David Evans.

Nighthawk 105 Lake Michigan Blues, 1934–41
Beautiful reissue of Chicago and St. Louis-based blues performers, including six great sides from 1937–40 by Robert Nighthawk. Yank Rachell, Tampa Red, Elijah Jones, Sonny Boy Williamson, Tampa Kid, Milton Sparks, and Robert Jr. Lockwood.

OJL 2 Really the Country Blues
One of the greatest-ever prewar country blues collections. Most of these tracks are available elsewhere with better sound, but this is the collection that started it all. Tommy Johnson, Son House, Skip James, Sam Collins, Sonny Boy and His Pals, and William Moore.

OJL 6 The Country Girls
Fabulous collection of women country blues singers. Lottie Kimbrough, Geeshie Wiley, Rosie Mae Moore, Lulu Jackson, Lillian Miller, and Lucille Bogan.

OJL 8 Country Blues Encores
Superb collection of mostly Mississippi artists. Garfield Akers, Big Bill and Thomps, John Byrd, Skip James, Charlie Jordan, and William Moore.

Retrieval FB 306 Thomas Morris and the Blues Singers: Goin' Crazy with the Blues
Excellent collection of 16 sides from 1926–27 featuring the fine New York-based cornet player Thomas Morris accompanying four blues singers, with Bob Fuller on clarinet or soprano sax and usually Mike Johnson on piano and Charlie Ivis on trombone. Features four sides by the powerful and prolific Mamie Smith, two by the rather light-voiced Elizabeth Smith, two by the excellent Margaret Smith, and eight sides by Edna Wilson, who is generally unexceptional though the ensemble in-

strumental work is some of the best here. Remastering by John R. T. Davies is exceptional. There is full discographical information and pedantic notes by Richard Reins.

ESSENTIAL SELECTION

Rosetta 1300 (c,d) Mean Mothers
Excellent reissues of women blues singers recorded 1927–49, only a few of which have been reissued before. Excellent mastering and handsome packaging. Martha Copeland, Bessie Brown, Maggie Jones, Susie Edwards, Gladys Bentley, Ida Cox, and Lil Green.

Rosetta 1301 Women's Railroad Blues
Trixie Smith, Bessie Smith, Clara Smith, Ada Brown, Martha Copeland, and Lucille Bogan singing blues songs about trains.

Rosetta 1302 Red White and Blues Women
Blues songs about various parts of the US, featuring recordings from 1928–52 by Billie Holiday, Lillian Glinn, Victoria Spivey, Mildred Bailey, and Blue Lou Barker.

Rosetta 1306 (c) Big Mamas
Sixteen recordings cut between 1925–53 by Ethel Waters, Viola McCoy, Issie Ringgold, Clara Smith, and Julia Lee. Excellent sound and packaging.

Rosetta 1308 (c) Super Sisters
Sixteen cuts recorded between 1927–55 by Ida Cox, Helen Humes, Mildred Bailey, Lil Johnson, Susie Edwards, and Ella Fitzgerald. Excellent sound quality as usual and informative notes.

Rosetta 1311 (c) Sweet Petunias
This collection ranges from the 20s (the wonderful "All Around Mama" by Mary Dixon) to the 50s (powerful R&B sounds from Annisteen Allen and Big Mama Thornton). Along the way, we hear such fine artists as June Richmond (with Andy Kirk and His Clouds of Joy), Monette Moore, Stella Johnson, Bea Foote, Bertha "Chippie" Hill, Victoria Spivey, Betty Hall Jones, Helen Humes, and a surprise appearance by Mae West with her 1933 recording of "My Man Friday." Good sound, full discographical info, and the usual extensive notes from Rosetta Reitz.

Rosetta 1316 Jailhouse Blues
A remarkable, beautiful, and moving collection of unaccompanied songs performed by women and recorded in 1936 and 1939 at Parchman Penitentiary. Although there are numerous collections featuring male prisoners, this is the only extended selection by women prisoners. The material covers the whole spectrum of black rural folksong: blues, spirituals, game songs, and pre-blues songs, with both solo and group performances. There are some

superb performances here, most notably the splendid Mattie Mae Thomas and Beatrice Parry, who perform some lovely blues. The album features detailed notes by Beatrice Reagan Johnson and album producer Rosetta Reitz, and some atmospheric photos. An exciting and important issue.

Rounder 0238 (c,d) Altamount: Black Stringband Music

Library of Congress recordings of two wonderful Black Tennessee string bands of the '40s who never recorded commercially. Both groups play high-energy dance music, not all that different from their white counterparts, although it's rare to hear the music played with such zest and verve. Side one is given to banjoist and vocalist Nathan Frazier, with Frank Patterson on fiddle (recorded in 1942). Side two spotlights John Lusk on fiddle, with Murph Gribble on banjo and Albert York on guitar (recorded 1946, except one cut from '49). Sound quality isn't that great, but after all these are field recordings from the '40s, and the music is exceptional. With notes by producer Bob Carlin.

Rounder 4007 Hard Times

A marvelous collection of blues of social commentary recorded between 1916–52 featuring such recordings as "We Sure Got Hard Times" by Barbecue Bob, "Warehouse Man Blues" by Champion Jack Dupree, "When the Soldier's Get Their Bonus" by Red Nelson, "Silicosis Is Killing Me" by Pinewood Tom, and "Sadie's Servant Room Blues" by Hattie Burleson. Excellent sound and informative notes by Archie Green.

Stash 100 (c) Copulatin' Blues

Blues on the subject of sex including some unexpurgated classics. Sidney Bechet, Bessie Smith, Lil Johnson, Merline Johnson, and Grant and Wilson.

Stash 101 (c) Reefer Songs

Blues and jazz songs on the subject of marijuana. Harlen Lattimore, Stuff Smith, Benny Goodman, Trixie Smith, The Harlem Hamfats, Georgia White, and Cab Calloway.

Stash 102 Pipe, Spoon, Pot, and Jug

Blues and jazz about dope. Cab Calloway, Jack Dupree, Slim and Slam, Lil Green, The Memphis Jug Band, Sam Price, Hazel Myers, Blue Lu Barker, and McKinney's Cotton Pickers.

Stash 106 AC-DC Blues

Blues and jazz songs about being gay. Ruby Smith, Bessie Smith, Tampa Red's Hokum Jug Band, Kokomo Arnold, and George Hannah.

Stash 107 Weed: A Rare Batch

More blues and jazz on dope. Chick Webb, Tampa Red, Carl Martin, Julia Lee, Cootie Williams, and Lorraine Walton.

Stash 110 Jake Walk Blues

Wonderful collection of songs by blues and white country artists on the ills of consuming "jake" liquor. Allen Brothers, Byrd Moore, Willie Lofton, Asa Martin, and Gene Autry.

Stash 117 Street Walking Blues

Songs about prostitution. Some great performances, but a lot of duplication with other albums. Memphis Minnie, Lucille Bogan, Maggie Jones, and Virginia Liston.

Stash 118 Straight and Gay

Extensive duplication with other reissues. Victoria Spivey, Maggie Jones, and Lil Johnson.

Stash 119 (c) Reefer Madness

Bea Foote, Ernest Rodgers, Cow Cow Davenport, and Frankie "Half Pint" Jaxon.

Stash 122 (c) Copulatin' Blues, Vol. 2

Black blues, country songs, and jazz, including several amazingly explicit items from the 30s including "I'm Gonna Shave You Dry" by Walter Roland, obscene parodies of "Frankie and Johnny" and "Bye Bye Blackbird" by a 30s cowboy singer, and the infamous parody of "Darktown Strutters Ball" recorded in the 50s by the Clovers. Also includes less explicit items by Eddie Johnson and His Crackerjacks, Cliff Edwards, The Hokum Boys, and Harry Roy and His Bat Club Boys.

Travelin' Man 809 Going Back on the Farm

Excellent collection of blues recorded in Chicago between 1940–42 documenting the transition from rural to urban culture of blacks arriving from the South. Includes country-flavored blues with rural themes like "I'm Gonna Walk Your Dog" by Leonard "Baby Doo" Caston and "Three Women Blues" by Frank Edwards. There are urban-flavored blues with urban themes like "Let The Black Have His Way" by Roosevelt Sykes and "99 Blues" by Lil Green. Linking these are the rural-flavored items with urban themes like the wonderful "Machine Gun Blues" by Willie "61" Blackwell. Finally, there are urban-sounding blues with rural themes like "I'm Going Back On The Farm" by The Florida Kid and "Good Old Cabbage Greens" by Washboard Sam. There are also tracks by Big Bill Broonzy, Bill Gaither, and Memphis Slim. Includes illuminating notes by John Cowley. Regardless of whether you pay attention to the "theme" of the album or not, this is an excellent collection of early 40s blues.

Travelin' Man 8811 Any Kind of Man
Fourteen women's blues recorded between 1934–38, all alternate or previously unissued takes. Includes Lil Johnson, Victoria Spivey, Barrelhouse Annie, and Memphis Minnie.

Travelin' Man 8812 Down in the Alley
Fourteen tracks recorded between 1934–42, all previously unissued. Includes the Midnight Ramblers, Kid Beecher, Monkey Joe, Big Bill Broonzy, Louisiana Johnny, and One Arm Slim.

Wolf WBJ 003 Down South Blues
Interesting anthology of previously unreissued piano blues recorded in Chicago in 1940. Bob White went on to later fame as "Detroit Count"; here he has two sides under his own name, and provides fine accompaniment to Ernest Blunt, the "Florida Kid," whose eight sides are fine blues when taken one at a time, but tend to sound familiar when taken in one dose! The album is filled out with six titles by the fine Willie Right, accompanied on piano by the always excellent Joshua Altheimer. Good, if undistinguished, samples of Chicago blues.

Wolf 109 Harmonica Blues
A diverse collection of blues recorded between 1936–40 featuring harmonica, only a few of which have been reissued before. Features the complete recordings of Smith and Harper, George Clarke, Rhythm Willie, and Eddy Kelly.

Yazoo 1016 (c) Guitar Wizards 1926–1935
Blues by spectacular guitarists like Blind Blake, Carl Martin, Tampa Red, Billy Bird, William Moore, and Sam Butler.

Yazoo 1018 Going Away Blues 1926–1935
Lottie Beaman, George "Big Boy" Owens, Henry Thomas, Charlie Jordan, Robert Wilkins, and George "Bullet" Williams.

Yazoo 1026 (c) Country Blues Bottleneck Guitar Classics 1926–1937
Bo Weavil Jackson, Ruth Willis, King Solomon Hill, Ramblin Thomas, and Irene Scrugs.

Yazoo 1040 Mama, Let Me Lay It on You 1926–1936
Blind Blake, Blind Boy Fuller, Leecan and Cooksey, Smith and Harper, Pink Anderson, and Simmie Dooley.

Yazoo 1042 Uptown Blues 1927–1931: A Decade of Guitar-Piano Duets
Big Bill Broonzy, Bo Carter, Teddy Darby, Leola Manning, and Cripple Clarence Lofton.

Yazoo 1043 Please Warm My Wiener
All hokum material, with sexually explicit lyrics. Georgia Tom and Tampa Red, The Hokum Boys, Butterbeans and Susie, and The Paramount All Stars.

Yazoo 1045 String Ragtime
White and black ragtime performers on a variety of string instruments.

Yazoo 1046 (c) The Voice of the Blues: Bottleneck Guitar Masterpieces
White and black bottleneck guitarists. Barbecue Bob, Georgia Brown, Ramblin' Thomas, Tampa Kid, The Hokum Boys, and The Too Bad Boys.

Yazoo 1053 (c) Harmonica Blues
Great collection. Chuck Darling, Jaybird Coleman, Carver Boys, Leecan and Cooksey, Alfred Lewis, and Jazz Gillum.

ESSENTIAL SELECTION

Yazoo 1063 (c) Roots of Rock
Prewar country blues that were later covered by rock artists. Includes "When The Levee Breaks" by Kansas Joe and Memphis Minnie, "Shake Em On Down" by Bukka White, "Corrine Corrina" by Bo Carter, "Statesboro Blues" by Blind Willie McTell, "Big Road Blues" by Tommy Johnson, and nine others. Outstanding sound.

Yazoo 1073 (c) The Roots of Robert Johnson
Although Johnson was one of the greatest and most influential Mississippi blues artists, it is sometimes forgotten that he was influenced by other artists. This album presents some of the recordings that may have influenced Johnson. Includes Skip James's "Devil Got My Woman" (a possible influence on "Hellhound On My Trail"), the lovely "When the Sun Goes Down" by Leroy Carr (a possible influence on "Love In Vain"), "Life Saver Blues" by Lonnie Johnson (Lonnie's style did influence Robert on a couple of songs), Charlie Patton's "Revenue Man Blues" (features Patton's trademark descending bass riff, which Johnson would later rework as his distinctive walking bass), plus tracks by Son House, Hambone Willie Newbern, and Scrapper Blackwell. Many of the tracks have been reissued before, but the sound is exceptionally good. Stephen Calt's liner notes are awful; you should buy this album for the great music, avoid reading the notes, and draw your own conclusions!

CASSETTE ONLY RELEASE
MCA 1352 Out Came the Blues
Budget-priced reissue of long-out-of-print album with four fewer cuts. Excellent selection of country and urban blues from the 30s. Memphis Minnie, Georgia White, Red Nelson, Johnnie Temple, Rosetta Crawford, Oscar Woods, Kokomo Arnold, and Trixie Smith.

MCA 1353 Blues and All That Jazz
Fine set of 30s and 40s Decca recordings. Rosetta Howard, Georgia White, Blue Lu Barker, and Joe Turner and Cousin Joe.

COMPACT DISC
Buda 82462-2 Great Classic Blues Singers
An excellent collection from the period of 1927–41, featuring five tracks apiece by five of the finest performers: Blind Blake (including his classic collaboration with Charlie Spand on "Hastings Street"), Blind Lemon Jefferson, Georgia Tom (including tracks with The Hokum Boys and Jane Lucas), Tampa Red (including tracks with the outrageous Frankie Jaxon and a fine accompaniment to Lil Johnson), and Big Bill Broonzy. Music is superb and sound is excellent. There is discographical data but the typesetter seems to have shifted personnel and dates and so unravelling it is a bit of a challenge. There are no surprises, but I think this is the first time most of these tracks have appeared on CD.

Jass CD 1 The Copulatin' Blues Compact Disc
Dirty ditties for the high-tech set. Twenty-two classics and favorites for over an hour of classic blues, jazz, and hokum. Sound quality is as good as you can get from worn 78s. Includes Jelly Roll Morton's unexpurgated version of "Winin' Boy" from The Library of Congress recordings, along with such greats as Lucille Bogan and Walter Roland ("Shave 'Em Dry"), Clara Smith ("It's Tight Like That"), Frankie "Half Pint" Jaxon ("Wet It!"), Tampa Red's Hokum Jazz Band ("My Daddy Rocks Me with One Steady Roll"), and Merline Johnson ("The Yas Yas Girl").

Jass CD 13 Sissyman Blues—25 Authentic Straight and Gay Vocals
Blues and jazz sides by The Harlem Hamfats, Tampa Red, Ma Rainey, Peg Leg Howell, Sippie Wallace, The Hokum Boys, and Josh White from Stash's/Jass' vast archives of risque recordings. A generous selection, most of which have been released previously on LP, oriented towards campy songs of same-sex preference.

POSTWAR COLLECTIONS
CHICAGO

Alligator 101 (c) Genuine House Rockin' Music
Sampler from the Alligator catalog featuring Koko Taylor, Johnny Winter, Albert Collins, and Son Seals.

Alligator 102 (c,d) Genuine House Rockin' Music, 2
More living blues legends, plus 80s discoveries Lil' Ed, The Kinsey Report, Little Charlie, and more from recent Alligator releases. Budget-priced and packed with 16 tunes.

Alligator 103 (c,d) Genuine House Rockin' Music, 3
Twelve-track sampler drawn from issues on Alligator. Includes Elvin Bishop, Katie Webster, A. C. Reed, Lonnie Brooks, Little Charlie and The Nightcats, Maurice John Vaughn, and The Siegel-Schwall Band.

Alligator 104 (c,d) Genuine House Rockin' Music, 4
Sampler with Carey Bell, William Clarke, and Junior Wells.

Alligator 7701 (c) Living Chicago Blues, Vol. 1
First in a six-volume set featuring some of the best bands active in Chicago in the early 70s; an excellent series. Includes Jimmy Johnson, Eddie Shaw, and Left Hand Frank.

Alligator 7702 (c) Living Chicago Blues, Vol. 2
Carey Bell, Magic Slim, Big Moose Walker.

Alligator 7703 (c) Living Chicago Blues, Vol. 3
Lonnie Brooks, Pinetop Perkins, S.O.B. Band.

Alligator 7704 (c) Living Chicago Blues, Vol. 4
A. C. Reed and The Spark Plugs with Larry Burton (gtr); Scotty and The Rib Tips; Lovey Lee with Carey Bell (hca) and Lurrie Bell (gtr).

Alligator 7705 (c) Living Chicago Blues, Vol. 5
Lacey Gibson with the Chicago Fire Band; Big Leon Brooks Blues Harp Band with Louis Myers (gtr) and Pinetop Perkins (pno); Andrew Brown.

Alligator 7706 (c) Living Chicago Blues, Vol. 6
Detroit Junior, Luther Guitar Junior Johnson, Queen Sylvia Embry.

Alligator 7707 (c,d) The New Bluebloods
Sampler featuring some of the up-and-coming younger blues singers and musicians in Chicago. The general feel is high-energy, with lots of flashy

guitar and declamatory vocals. Includes Donald Kinsey and the Kinsey Report, Valerie Wellington (the blues-singing opera singer), Dion Payton and The 43rd Street Blues Band (soul-flavored track), The Sons Of The Blues, Professor's Blues Review featuring Gloria Hardman (one of the best singers here, with an Aretha Franklin quality to her voice), and John Watkins.

Alligator/XRT 9301 (c,d) Blues Deluxe
Recorded live at the 1980 Chicagofest, this album features a selection of popular Chicago blues artists in a mostly high-energy set of performances. Lonnie Brooks, Son Seals, Mighty Joe Young, and Muddy Waters.

Blues Classics 8 Chicago Blues—The Early 50s
Some real classics by Homesick James, Baby Face Leroy, Little Walter, J. B. Hutto, and Eddie Boyd.

Chess 9168 (c) Super Blues
Reissue of Checker 3008 from 1967 featuring a studio jam with Muddy Waters, Bo Diddley, and Little Walter accompanied by Otis Spann and Sammy Lawhorn. There's a lot of good-natured banter and shared vocals on versions of some of the artists' old favorites. Musically it's quite chaotic, and Walter, who died a few months later, was not in his best form, but it's a lot of fun.

Chess 9169 (c) Super Super Blues Band
Reissue of Checker 3010 from 1968. A similar idea to the above with Little Walter replaced by Howlin' Wolf and Hubert Sumlin replacing Lawhorn. Again, a chaotic but fun collection. Ooh Baby/Wrecking My Love Life/Spoonful/Diddley Daddy.

Chess 9253 (c) The Blues
CD issue: Chess CHD 31262 (CP)
Reissue of Argo 4026, originally issued in 1963. This is a sampler of some of the great blues artists that recorded for Chess and Checker. Most of the

tracks here are available elsewhere. It includes "Don't Start Me to Talkin'" by Sonny Boy Williamson, "First Time I Met the Blues" by Buddy Guy, "Hoochie Coochie Man" by Muddy Waters, and "My Babe" by Little Walter.

Chess 9267 (c) The Blues, Vol. 2
CD issue: Chess CHD 31263 (CP)
Reissue of Argo 4027 from 1963. A marvelous sampler of tracks from the Chess/Checker catalog. Most tracks are available elswhere but this is a perfect introductory collection, featuring such great items as "Thirty Days" by Chuck Berry, "Evil" by Howlin' Wolf, "I'm a Man" by Bo Diddley, "Key to the Highway" by Little Walter (my all-time favorite version of this great song—this should be in every blues lover's collection!), "It Ain't No Secret" by Jimmy Witherspoon (not readily available elswhere, this is a nice secular version of an old gospel song), "Ten Years Ago" by Buddy Guy, and Otis Rush's masterpiece "So Many Roads." Excellent sound.

Chess CH 9276 (c,d) The Blues, Volume 3
Reissue of Argo 4034 from 1964. A great collection of 12 tracks from the Chess/Checker catalog. Most of the tracks are available on other LPs, but this does include an alternate version of Elmore James' magnificent "The Sun Is Shining," which is not on Chess 9114. Other tracks includes Washboard Sam's lively "Diggin' My Potatoes," Little Milton's "Lonely No More," Little Walter's "Off the Wall," the 1960 Newport Jazz Festival version of "Baby Please Don't Go" by Muddy Waters, Jimmy Witherspoon's "Time Brings About a Change," and Jimmy Rogers' "The World Is in a Tangle." Excellent sound, new notes, a reprint of the original notes, and full discographical information.

Chess CH 9293 (c,d) Wrinkles—Classic And Rare Chess Instrumentals
Jody Williams (who played on Howlin' Wolf and Bo Diddley sessions) kicks things off with a dynamic guitar instrumental called "Lucky Lou," Lafayette Leake tickles the ivories, and Harold Ashby takes a lively sax solo. Leake does the title tune in a trio setting, and Little Walter is represented by an alternate take of "Blue Midnight." Chuck Berry does a wild version of the Les Paul signature tune "How High the Moon" and Paul Gayten closes out the side with his Argo (5263) single "Driving Home, Part 2," powered by the great Lee Allen on sax. Side two opens with Otis Spann's "Five Spot" (Checker 807), actually more of a showcase for the unknown but fabulous guitarist on the session. Lloyd Glenn is joined by Lowell Fulson on the previously-unreleased "Little Eva." Gene The Hat does a spirited

version of Bill Doggett's "Ram-Bunk-Shush," J. C. Davis chills out on "Coolin' Out," and Bo Diddley does his thing on "Mess Around." If you like instrumentals, there's something here for everyone.

Chess 9320 (c,d) The Blues, Vol. 5
Twelve-track sampler originally issued in the early 60s includes Jimmy Rogers, Howlin' Wolf, Jimmy Nelson, Willie Mabon, Sonny Boy Williamson, and Little Walter.

Chess 2-92518 (c) Blues/Rock—Avalanche
Two-LP set, reissuing Chess 60015 with 2 fewer cuts. This set features live recordings cut at the Montreux Jazz Festival in 1972 by Bo Diddley, Louis Myers, Koko Taylor, Lafayette Leake, Muddy Waters, and T-Bone Walker with The Aces. The performances are, for the most part, not terribly exciting, though the duets by Muddy and T-Bone are interesting.

Chess 2-92519 (c) Blues Rarities
Two-LP set featuring a selection of unissued or rarely reissued sides from the Chess archives by B. B. King (four songs), Howlin' Wolf (nine), Buddy Guy (seven), Hound Dog Taylor (five), and Sonny Boy Williamson (two). Quite a few of these have appeared on various out-of-print bootlegs. Performances vary from the very good to the not-so-good.

ESSENTIAL SELECTION

Chess 93002 (c,d) Drop Down Mama
Excellent collection of 14 selections displaying the country roots of Chicago blues. Early (1949–53) Chess recordings by Johnny Shines, Robert "Nighthawk" McCullum, Big Boy Spires, David "Honey Boy" Edwards, Floyd Jones, and C. "Blue Smitty" Smith, with backup by Little Walter, Jimmy Rogers, and Willie Dixon. All selections were originally unreleased or on 78s. Previously available as a Japanese import.

Chess 2-6023 (c) The Best of Chess Blues
Though not the only label in town, Chess has grown to be synonymous with Chicago blues. The stars, the tunes, and even the sidemen are legendary. The material on this two-LP set ranges from the rural Mississippi sound of "Rollin' Stone," by Muddy Waters from 1950, to Koko Taylor's raucous big-band sound on "Wang Dang Doodle," Chess' last big blues hit before the tunes were recycled by the white rock market. Although there are no surprises here for the seasoned collector, this collection of 20 tunes is the best collection on Chess I've ever seen, with excellent sound and not a loser in the bunch. Includes "Hoochie Coochie Man" by Muddy, "Smokestack Lightnin'" and "Back Door Man" by Howlin' Wolf, "Juke" by Little Walter, "Bring It on Home"

and "Your Funeral, My Trial" by Sonny Boy Williamson, "Madison Blues" by Elmore James, Robert Nighthawk's "Black Angel Blues," plus tracks by Otis Rush, Jimmy Rogers, Buddy Guy, J. B. Lenoir, and Willie Mabon.

Chess CH3 16500 (c,d) Willie Dixon: The Chess Box

A tribute to one of the most important blues songwriters, whose songs have been recorded by hundreds of performers. This three-LP box set (or two cassettes or CDs) features 36 songs written by Willie. Six of the songs are performed by Willie himself (one previously unissued), plus recordings by great Chess and Checker performers like Muddy Waters, Howlin' Wolf, Little Walter, Bo Diddley, Lowell Fulson, Koko Taylor, and Sonny Boy Williamson. Includes 12-page booklet with extensive liner notes and rare photos. My Babe/Hoochie Coochie Man/Mellow Down Easy/I Just Want to Make Love to You/You Can't Judge a Book by Its Cover/You Need Love/Back Door Man/Wang Dang Doodle.

Chess (France) 515.005 Heavy Heads

A miscellaneous collection of 12 sides mostly available on other albums, including Muddy Waters, Sonny Boy Williamson, Howlin' Wolf, and Little Walter.

Delmark 624 Chicago Ain't Nothin' but a Blues Band

Reissue of 60s recordings from the Atomic H label. Features Sunnyland Slim, J. T. Brown, and Jo Jo Williams.

ESSENTIAL SELECTION

Delmark 648 The Blues World of Little Walter: The Parkway Sessions

Previously available as a Japanese import (P-Vine PLP 9038). Features the entire session of eight songs recorded for the Chicago label Parkway in 1950, one of the greatest blues sessions of all time, featuring Baby Face Leroy (vcl, drm), Little Walter (hca, vcl, gtr), and Muddy Waters (gtr). All of these cuts have been reissued before, but this issue has superior sound quality. Also includes three J.O.B. sides by J. B. Lenoir (also available on Flyright), and two cuts by Sunnyland Slim from 1950 that were previously unissued.

Echo Blues 803 Blues Anthology, Vol. 3—Real Chicago Blues

Originally one half of a double set called "Really the Chicago Blues" (Adelphi 1005), this features an informal gathering in 1969 of various Chicago blues artists, including Johnny Shines, John Lee Granderson, Sunnyland Slim, David "Honeyboy" Edwards,

Big Joe Williams, and Big Walter along with white blues interpreter Backwards Sam Firk. They perform a selection of 12 mostly familiar songs. The performances are OK, but all of these artists have done much better elsewhere and the informal nature is more of a nuisance than a stimulus for creativity.

Echo Blues 804 Blues Anthology, Vol. 4

The other half of the Adelphi 1005 set, with the same group of artists.

Flyright 549 Chicago Blues Live at the Fickle Pickle

1963 recordings from a famous Chicago club by Johnny Jones, Maxwell Street Jimmy, John Henry Barbee, Billy Boy Arnold, and Blind James Brewer.

Flyright 567 King Cobras: Chicago Kings of the Harmonica

A great reissue from the Cobra label, this features the playing of Sonny Boy Williamson, Little Willie Foster, Walter Horton, Louis Myers, with vocals by Charles Clark, Sonny Boy, and Sunnyland Slim. Five sides were never issued before. Classic stuff!

Flyright 582 Fishin' in My Pond

Fourteen fine sides reissued from the Chicago labels Cobra and Artistic, featuring Buddy Guy, Arbee Stidham, Lee Jackson, and Guitar Shorty, with superb bands including sidemen like Otis Rush, Willie Dixon, Wayne Bennett, Walter Horton, and Lafayette Leake.

Flyright 585 World of Trouble

Another splendid collection drawn from Chicago's J.O.B. label featuring mostly previously unissued recordings made between 1953–58 by John Lee Henley, Snooky Pryor, Eddie Boyd, Memphis Minnie, Little Son Joe, Harry Brooks, and J. T. Brown. Excellent Chicago blues with fine notes by Mike Rowe.

Flyright 590 Out of Bad Luck

Sixteen sides of Chicago blues recorded between 1961–66, including Magic Sam, Jesse Fortune, Homesick James, and J. B. Lenoir, along with some less interesting sides by Koko Taylor, Ricky Allen, and A. C. Reed. There is also an overabundance of alternate takes. A good album, though it could have been better if some of the weaker cuts and alternates had been replaced by stronger material.

Flyright 594 The Final Takes

A record for completists. This album presents alternate takes from Cobra and J.O.B. by Otis Rush, Buddy Guy, Charles Clark, Sunnyland Slim, and John Brim that are not featured on the previous reissues on Flyright. It also includes tracks not previously issued by Eddie Boyd, Freddie Hall and The Aces, and an unknown and quite good performer.

There are some exciting moments here, but I'm not sure if these alternates are different enough to warrant having a whole album devoted to them.

Flyright 602 Chicago Blues of the Sixties
Excellent collection recorded in Chicago for the U.S.A., The Blues, and Jewel labels between 1962–74, documenting the changing Chicago blues sounds of the 60s. Most of the tracks here find the down-home sound gone, replaced by a more urbane one with larger bands and effective use of brass. There are two superb sides by Fenton Robinson with tremendous guitar. Other fine sides are by Mighty Joe Young, Andrew Brown, Big Moose, and Bobby Rush.

L+R 42.004 Blues Anytime
Chicago blues set recorded in Europe in 1964 and only issued in its entirety in East Germany though parts were issued on the Scout label. Hubert Sumlin, Willie Dixon, Sunnyland Slim, and Clifton James in various combinations.

Nighthawk 101 Windy City Blues, 1935–1953
Great sides, including some prewar recordings. Pinetop, Washboard Sam, Sonny Boy Williamson #1, Pete Franklin, Tony Hollins, and Robert Jr. Lockwood.

Nighthawk 102 Chicago Slickers, 1948–53
Little Walter, Forest City Joe, Earl Hooker, Homesick James, and Big Boy Spires.

Nighthawk 107 Chicago Slickers, Vol. 2
Sixteen great and rare Chicago blues recordings from 1948–55. Little Walter (rare 1948 side), Man Young (Johnny Young), Robert Nighthawk, Grace Brim, Johnny Shines, Willie Nix (with Snooky Pryor and Eddie Taylor), and other great ones!

Oldie Blues 8014 Hot Screamin' Saxes from Chicago, 1947–51
This album is not outstanding in the hot screaming saxes department but excels in other ways. Approximately half of the 16 rare blues are swing and jump boogie sides. Side one includes two fine Van-Walls-type blues items from The Dick Davis Orchestra, featuring Sonny Thompson on vocals and ivories and Sugar Man Penigar (who sounds like Ivory Joe Hunter) belting out the lyrics to "I Love You Mama," driven along by Oett "Sax" Mallard and The Chicago All Stars. Side two includes the hot and sexy "Not Now Baby" by Benny Kelly. Also includes Grant "Mr. Blues" Jones and Jack Cooley, and Buster Bennett and The Jump Jackson Orchestra.

Pearl 12 Harmonica Blues Kings
Marvelous album of harmonica blues recorded for the States and United labels in 1954. The first side features the brilliant Walter Horton in his prime—two tracks under his name and four accompanying urban blues singer Tommy Brown, including the classic "Southern Woman" that features some of Walter's best playing. There are two previously unissued cuts from the Brown session. Side two has seven sides featuring the brilliant but mysterious Alfred Harris, a fine rural sounding harmonica player accompanied by a lovely down-home group. Only two tracks from this session were ever issued: the superb "Gold Digger" and "Blues and Trouble," featuring vocals by drummer James Bannister. The other five tracks feature vocals by Harris, an excellent country blues singer.

Pearl 16 (c) Wrapped in My Baby
1954–55 recordings cut in producer Al Smith's basement by Morris Pejoe, Arthur "Big Boy" Spires, and Willy "Big Eyes" Smith. Previously available on the Japanese P-Vine label.

Pearl 17 (c) Long Man Blues
United recordings cut between 1952–57 of Jack Cooley, Harold Burrage, Dennis "Long Man" Binder, Cliff Butler, Edward "Gates" White, and Arbee Stidham.

Red Lightnin' 005 Blues in D Natural
Fine reissue of mostly 50s Chicago sides. Much of this is available elsewhere with better sound. Robert Nighthawk, Elmore James, Charles Clark, and Homesick James.

Red Lightnin' 0017 Guitar Stars
Sixties recordings by fine Chicago guitarists. Mighty Joe Young, Big Moose, and Fenton Robinson.

Red Lightnin' 0019 Meat and Gravy from Cadillac Baby, Vol. 1
Issued and unissued 60s/70s sides from Bea and Baby labels. Homesick James, Willie Williams, Andrew McMahon, and Little Mac.

Red Lightnin' 0020 Meat and Gravy from Cadillac Baby, Vol. 2
Sunnyland Slim, Andrew McMahon, Homesick James, Jimmy Cotton, Eddie Boyd, and Little Mac.

Red Lightnin' 0027 Superharps
Seven-inch EP featuring two previously unissued 1967 recordings by Little Walter with Muddy Waters and Bo Diddley, and two 1977 recordings by Billy Boy Arnold.

Red Lightnin' 0050 The Ralph Bass Sessions, Vol. 1: Lacy Gibson/Joe Carter
This LP and the following series of four Red Lightnin' LPs feature recordings of various Chicago blues performers cut in Chicago in 1977 and

produced by veteran blues producer Ralph Bass. These are consistently good performances though none are exceptional, perhaps the fault of hasty production and sparse accompaniments. This LP features five songs by Gibson and Carter, accompanied by Sunnyland Slim (pno), Willie Black (bar sax), and Fred Below (drm). Gibson is a good, solid modern-styled singer and guitar player who performs five original songs. Carter is a slide guitar player who is strongly influenced by Elmore James.

Red Lightnin' 0051 The Ralph Bass Sessions, Vol. 2: Jimmy Johnson/Eddie Clearwater

One of the best albums in the series. Johnson is one of the finest of the younger generation of Chicago blues singer/guitarists. Eddie Clearwater is also in good form and his sides have a richer sound quality, thanks to the use of second guitar and harmonica (Little Mac).

Red Lightnin' 0052 The Ralph Bass Sessions, Vol. 3: Willie Williams with Carey Bell/Magic Slim

Williams is a solid drummer but only an average singer; however, on his tracks, Carey Bell provides some great harp. Magic Slim is accompanied by his usual band, The Teardrops, and his performances are good, though his usual stinging guitar tone is absent.

Red Lightnin' 0056 The Ralph Bass Sessions, Vol. 4

Features recordings by Willie Williams (vcl, drm) with Carey Bell (hca), Sunnyland Slim (pno), Lacy Gibson (gtr), and Willie Black (bar sax), Sunnyland Slim (with Gibson, Black, Lee Jackson [gtr], and Fred Below [drm]), Lee Jackson (with Slim, Black, Gibson, and Below), Eddie Clearwater (with Little Mac [hca], Aaron Burton [bar sax], Thomas Eckert [gtr], Bob Riedy [pno], and Sam Lay [drm]), Jimmy Johnson (with his regular band), and Magic Slim (with his band, The Teardrops). Some decent, if unexceptional, performances.

Red Lightnin' 0057 The Ralph Bass Sessions, Vol. 5

Similar lineup to 0056, with tracks by Lee Jackson, Lacy Gibson, Magic Slim, Sunnyland Slim, Eddie Clearwater, and Joe Carter.

Red Lightnin' 055 Chicago Blues

Two-LP set featuring 19 performances recorded in 1970 for use in a film about Chicago blues made by documentary filmmaker Harley Cokliss. Artists featured are Buddy Guy, Junior Wells, Johnny Young, Muddy Waters, Mighty Joe Young, Koko Taylor, J. B. Hutto, and Johnny Lewis. Buddy and Junior have six tracks between them, four are fine down-home Chicago blues. The Young cuts are OK though his

electric mandolin is overamplified. Muddy does a good job on his three songs, a very nice "19 Years Old" and the expected "Hoochie Coochie Man" and "Mojo." Young, Taylor, and Hutto turn in some good, if not exceptional, performances.

Red Lightnin' (12" 45 rpm) RLEP 120045 It's Great To Be Rich

Five examples of solid Chicago-style blues by Billy Boy Arnold (with Tony McPhee and Lester Davenport), Good Rockin' Charles, Bo Diddley (with Simon Hickling [hca]), and Big John Tric (with Lester Davenport [hca]).

Redita 108 Chicago Rock

In spite of the title, this is mostly a set of jumping blues recorded for Jump Jackson between 1959–70, featuring Eddie Clearwater, Little Mack, Sy Perry, Wilbur "Hi Fi" White, Sunnyland Slim, and Eddie Boyd.

Relic 8024 Parrot/Blue Lake 1—Hand Me Down Blues

An excellent collection of down-home Chicago blues drawn from Al Benson's Parrot and Blue Lake labels recorded in the mid-50s. The album starts with a previously unissued session by brilliant piano player Henry Gray, including four fine songs accompanied by a fine band with a harmonica player whose identity is the cause of much speculation in Dick Shurman's detailed notes. Gray also accompanies singer/harmonica player Dusty Brown on four tracks, two previously unissued. There are also two fine early tracks by Albert King, before he had perfected his readily identifiable style; there are two by Sunnyland Slim, including his wonderful "Going Back to Memphis," based on the traditional "Minglewood Blues" theme, with a wonderful harmonica player whose identity is also uncertain! The set is rounded out by tracks from John Brim, Snooky Pryor, and Little Willie Foster. Excellent sound and informative notes. All in all, a terrific set of Chicago blues from its heyday.

Relic 8025 Parrot/Blue Lake 2—Cool Playing Blues

Another excursion into the vaults of the Parrot and Blue Lake labels, focusing on more urban stylings and including a healthy dose of previously unissued material. There are four tracks by the brilliant Jody Williams—a fine singer and outstanding guitarist—who, though little-known, was an influential figure on the Chicago scene in the 50s. His previously unissued "Groan My Blues Away" is the only known time he played slide guitar on record. There are two tracks by the excellent T-Bone Walker-flavored singer/guitarist, L. C. McKinley, who also accompanies Curtis Jones on his last commercial recordings. St. Louis Jimmy is represented here by his last commercial recordings, including a version of his most famous song, "Going Down Slow." Jazzy blues shouter JoJo Adams has two tracks, and the collection is rounded out by three previously unissued tracks from the dean of Chicago sax players, J. T. Brown. Excellent sound and informative notes by the indefatigable Dick Shurman.

Spivey 1003 Chicago Blues
1960s recordings of Sunnyland Slim, John Henry Barbee, and St. Louis Jimmy.

Spivey 1009 Encore for Chicago Blues
Sixties recordings of the Muddy Waters Blues Band, Harvey Hill, Koko Taylor, Memphis Slim, Babe Stovall, and J. B. Lenoir.

Syndicate Chapter 005 We Three Kings
Fine sides by Muddy Waters, Howlin' Wolf, and Little Walter. Most available elsewhere with much better sound.

Testament 2203 Modern Chicago Blues
An exciting, pioneering album from 1965 featuring a cross-section of the excellent Chicago blues artists who were then working on the club circuit. Outstanding performances by Johnny Young (with Otis Spann [pno], Slim Willis [hca], and Robert Whitehead [drm]), Maxwell Street Jimmy (lovely country blues with acoustic guitar), and Big Walter Horton (with Johnny Young and John Wrencher).

ESSENTIAL SELECTION

Testament 2207 Chicago Blues: The Beginning
A classic Testament album available again. This album features 12 mostly unissued tracks from 1946, including the first Chicago recordings of Muddy Waters and Johnny Shines, plus the lesser-known but very fine James Clark and Homer Harris. Waters, Harris, and Clark are accompanied by a small group with great piano by Sunnyland Slim and unknown bass and drums, while Shines is accompanied by bass and drums only. Curiously, although Muddy and Johnny are masters of the slide, neither plays slide here but are superb nonetheless. James "Beale" Street was a fine singer who recorded a dozen or so sides in the 40s; his tracks here are the only ones that were originally issued. Homer Harris is a complete mystery; his three songs here are excellent, including the then-topical "Atomic Bomb Blues." Some of these tracks were reissued a few years ago on the "Okeh Chicago Blues" album on Epic, which was in print for about five minutes. Essential recordings!

Testament 2218 Goin' to Chicago
Reissue of long-unavailable LP made c. 1968. In-cludes three frenetic sides by Sam Lay, who abandons his usual role as drummer to sing three Chicago blues standards accompanied by an unexceptional band. Vocalist/harmonica player Billy Boy Arnold turns in three nice performances with good guitar backup from Mighty Joe Young. J. B. Hutto performs two songs accompanied by Johnny Young and Big Walter Horton, and The Floyd Jones/Eddie Taylor Band (with Horton and Otis Spann) plays three numbers. Sound is poor.

Vanguard VSD 1/2 The Best of Chicago
Two-volume distillation of three fine out-of-print albums presenting some of the fine blues artists active in Chicago in the mid-60s: Jimmy Cotton, Junior Wells, Otis Spann, Buddy Guy, J. B. Hutto, Homesick James, and Johnny Shines.

Vee Jay VJLP 1074 (c) Soul Meeting Saturday Night
Jimmy Reed, John Lee Hooker, and Memphis Slim.

Wolf 120 287 Chicago Blues Live
Recorded in Austria in 1977 and 1978. Homesick James, Detroit Junior, Brewer Phillips, and J. B. Hutto are included, but they are not at their best.

Wolf 120 847 Chicago Blues Sessions, Vol. 1
Eight tracks were recorded in 1984 by a band including Willie Kent (b), Eddie Taylor (gtr), Johnny B. Moore (gtr), and Timothy Taylor (drm). Four of the tracks feature vocals by Kent, while the other four feature vocals and harmonica by Birmingham Jones. Good solid Chicago blues with particularly nice guitar by Taylor and Moore. Jones is a pretty good harp player, but his vocals emulate Jimmy Reed a bit too much. There are two tracks by Snooky Pryor with Homesick James, featuring good singing and playing by Snooky but mediocre guitar by Homesick. The album is rounded out by two nice tracks by barrelhouse piano player Jimmy Walker.

Wolf 120 848 Chicago Blues Sessions, Vol. 2
Most of the tracks on this album appear to be from the same 1984 sessions as on Vol. 1 with various musicians taking the vocal spotlight. There are four nice, relaxed sides by Smokey Smothers, a couple of unexceptional songs by Eddie Taylor's wife Vera, and two nice ones by Eddie Taylor. The fine Johnny B. Moore takes the lead on two tracks, and the album is rounded out by a pretty good solo side by Homesick James from 1977 and an unexceptional acoustic version of "Take a Little Walk with Me" by Floyd Jones.

Wolf 120 850 Chicago Blues Session, Vol. 4
This album, recorded in 1987, focuses on Alabama Jr. Pettis and his band with vocals by Pettis himself, John Primer, and a guest appearance by Magic Slim.

Pettis backed Slim for many years in the 70s and early 80s and some of Slim's intense funky style seems to have rubbed off on him. Joining the band are bassist Nick Holt, drummer Timothy Taylor, and occasional piano from Christian Dozier. The resulting album is a hard-driving collection of no-nonsense Chicago blues with tough vocals and powerful guitar. Both Pettis and Primer are fine vocalists and guitarists, with Primer being the slightly flashier of the two. Magic Slim does a guest vocal on Eddie Boyd's "Third Degree" and, as always, is a joy to listen to.

Wolf 120 853 West Side Blues Singers

Some West Side Chicago blues by four fairly obscure singers, accompanied by a solid Chicago band featuring the excellent guitars of Johnny B. Moore and John Primer. There are four tracks by Bonnie "Bombshell" Lee, a fairly good singer who overdoes the Koko Taylor-style growls. Eddie Taylor's son Larry is featured on two songs, including a version of his dad's "Bad Boy." He is a warm and effective vocalist. Mississippi-born Barkin' Bill has a catch in his voice, a bit reminiscent of Eddie Vinson, but is generally unexceptional. Mary Lane from Arkansas is the most impressive performer. She is a powerful and expressive singer, performing three fine songs, including the hard-driving "Ride My Automobile" with nice slide guitar, and the slow, intense "You Can't Take Out."

Wolf 120 855 Chicago Blues Session, Vol. 9: Teardrops Blues Jam

Three songs by Magic Slim, two by Nick Holt, one by John Primer, and three by Jr. Pettis.

CASSETTE ONLY RELEASE

Atlantic 81697-1 Atlantic Blues: Chicago

Since Atlantic recorded very little Chicago blues during its heyday in the 50s, most of the recordings on this cassette are from the late 60s through the early 80s. The first half is most worthwhile, featuring two utterly superb tracks by Johnny Jones, one with lovely slide guitar by Elmore James. There are a couple of tracks from 1955 by T-Bone Walker, who, though not a Chicago blues artist, is featured with a Chicago blues group including Junior Wells on harp and Jimmy Rogers on guitar. There are also some fine tracks from the Cotillion LPs of Freddy King and Otis Rush and some OK cuts by Buddy Guy and Junior Wells. The second part features live recordings from the 1972 Ann Arbor Blues Festival and the 1982 Montreux Jazz Festival by Howlin' Wolf, Muddy Waters, and Johnny Shines. These cuts are rather dull.

Chess 9102 Wizards from the Southside

Excellent sampler of 14 tracks from the 50s and early 60s by Chicago blues giants: Wolf, Muddy, Sonny Boy, Bo Diddley, Little Walter, and John Lee Hooker. Good mono sound but stupid notes by Michael Lydon.

Chess 9113 Folk Festival of the Blues

Originally issued in 1969 on Chess 1533 as "Blues from Big Bill's Copa Cabana," this cassette features mostly live recordings from 1963 by Muddy Waters, Buddy Guy, Sonny Boy Williamson, Howlin' Wolf, and Willie Dixon, with backup including Jarrett Gibson (ten sax), Otis Spann (pno), and Jack Myers (b). Some nice performances.

Chess 2-92520 Chicago Blues Anthology

Superb and diverse collection, featuring Robert Nighthawk, John Brim, Jimmy Rogers, Eddie Boyd, and Buddy Guy.

COMPACT DISC

Chess CHD 31315 (CP) The Best of Chess Blues, Vol. 1

The first album from the "The Best of Chess Blues" double set plus two extra tracks, one each by Sonny Boy Williamson and Little Walter.

Chess CHD 31316 (CP) The Best of Chess Blues, Vol. 2

The second album of "The Best of Chess Blues," plus one extra track each by Muddy Waters and Howlin' Wolf.

Chess (UK) CD RED 9 Vintage Blues

Great collection featuring eight tracks by Albert King, six by Otis Rush, four by Otis Spann, and five by John Brim.

Chess (UK) CD RED 11 First Time I Met the Blues

A perfect sampler drawn from two of the greatest blues labels, Chess and Checker. This 67-minute, 24-track collection includes "Don't Start Me to Talkin'" and "Fattening Frogs for Snakes" by Sonny Boy Williamson, "Hoochie Coochie Man" by Muddy Waters, "Smokestack Lightnin'" by Howlin' Wolf, "So Many Roads, So Many Trains" by Otis Rush, "Wee Wee Hours" by Chuck Berry, "First Time I Met the Blues" and "Third Degree" by Buddy Guy, "The Sun Is Shining" by Elmore James, "I Don't Know" by Willie Mabon, "Be Careful" by John Brim, "Walking the Blues" by Willie Dixon, and "Guess I'm a Fool" by Memphis Slim. Sound, as usual for English Chess, is unexceptional and there are no real surprises, but this is a great set to just slip in your CD player and enjoy from beginning to end; a perfect introduction to the music for a neophyte collector!

Chess (UK) CD RED 12 Second Time I Met the Blues

Another tremendous collection, including "Talk to Me Baby" by Elmore James, "Chicago Bound" and "The World Is in a Tangle" by Jimmy Rogers, "Ten Years Ago" by Buddy Guy, "Help Me" by Sonny Boy Williamson, "I'm a Man" by Bo Diddley, "Trouble Trouble" by Lowell Fulson, "I'm In Love with You Baby" by Otis Spann, "Billy's Blues, Part 2" by Billy Stewart, "She's 19 Years Old" by Muddy Waters, "Leave My Wife Alone" by John Lee Hooker, "I Asked for Water" by Howlin' Wolf, "Thirty Days" by Chuck Berry, and 11 more!

Chess (France) 600048 The Golden Age of Chicago Blues

A great introduction to the Chess catalog featuring 18 classic recordings cut between 1950–61 for the Chess and Checker labels. Includes Muddy Waters, John Lee Hooker, Little Walter, Elmore James, Albert King, Howlin' Wolf, J. B. Lenoir, Sonny Boy Williamson, Buddy Guy, and Otis Rush. The sound quality is very good, though Vogue (who release Chess material in France) still doesn't achieve the state-of-the-art sound that is possible. Booklet features short notes on each title in French and English and discographical details.

Flyright FLYCD 11 Chicago Blues Harmonicas

A tremendous collection drawn from various Flyright albums and originally recorded for the J.O.B., Cobra, Artistic, and Abco labels. The set starts with one of my all-time favorites, Baby Face Leroy's magnificent "My Head Can't Rest More" and "Take a Little Walk with Me," with lyrical harp by Snooky Pryor. Pryor himself has four vocals, including two with great guitar by Eddie Taylor. There are two tracks each by the obscure John Lee Henley and Little Willie Foster, and two fine instrumentals by Louis Myers. There are two great tracks by Sonny Boy Williamson from 1958, which were unissued until they appeared on Flyright 567. Sonny Boy also accompanies the relatively undistinguished Charles Clark, along with Otis Rush, Louis Myers, and Willie Dixon! There are two fine Cobra sides by Walter Horton, who also appears here on songs by Arbee Stidham and Sunnyland Slim. Although the sound is unexceptional, this is certainly a fabulous collection.

Flyright FLYCD 18 Chicago Boss Guitars

Twenty fine sides recorded for Artistic and Cobra between 1956–58. Includes all four songs recorded by Buddy Guy for Artistic (with two takes each of "You Sure Can't Do" and the intense "This Is the End"). There are six tracks by Otis Rush and six by Magic Sam.

P-Vine PCD 2130-32 Chicago Blues: A Quarter Century

Three-CD box set drawn from recordings made from the early 50s through the 70s for J.O.B., Cobra, U.S.A., Age, Ronn, and affiliated labels. Almost every track is a gem. Features a who's who of Chicago blues greats: Johnny Shines, Floyd Jones, Eddie Boyd, Memphis Minnie, Little Brother Montgomery, Baby Face Leroy, J. B. Lenoir, Louis Myers, Walter Horton, Little Willie Foster, Junior Wells and Earl Hooker, Robert Jr. Lockwood, Homesick James, Otis Rush, Buddy Guy, Magic Sam, Willie Mabon, Fenton Robinson, Earl Hooker, Lonnie Brooks, Andrew Brown, Koko Taylor, Big Mac, Buster Benton, and many more. A few tracks are available on CD elsewhere, most notably on Flyright. Sound is generally very good.

Vanguard VMD 79216 Chicago/The Blues/ Today! Vol. 1

Vanguard VMD 79217 Chicago/The Blues/ Today! Vol. 2

Vanguard VMD 79218 Chicago/The Blues/ Today! Vol. 3

DETROIT

Blues Classics 12 Detroit Blues, The Early 50s

"Baby Boy" Warren, Dr. Ross, Bobo Jenkins, Eddie Kirkland, Detroit Count, and L. C. Green.

Blues Factory 1000 Detroit Blues Factory, Vol. 1

Excellent collection of tough blues by seven different performers. With the exception of Eddie "Guitar" Burns, the rest are obscurities but all are good. Harmonica Shaw is a fine singer and effective harmonica player in the squeaky vein, who turns in his own unique treatment of the Johnny Jones/Eddie Taylor "Bigtown Playboy," here called "Detroit Playboy." He is accompanied by a tough, churning band with fine slide guitar from Robert Noll, who also has a couple of his own tracks. Willie D. Warren is a good, solid singer and guitar player who does a fine job on "Door Lock Blues." Johnny "Yard-Dog" Taylor is probably the best singer here, a wonderful soulful vocalist who also plays some effective harmonica. Rounding out the collection are fine tracks by The Butler Twins and Billy Davis (the latter's "Troubled Shoes" is particularly good). Well worth a listen.

Flyright 542 I'm the Highway Man

Fine reissues from 1938 Library of Congress recordings, featuring Calvin Frazier and Sampson Pittman. Some lovely vocals and guitar.

Nighthawk 104 **Detroit Ghetto Blues**

Fine 50s sides, featuring Slim Pickens, Walter Mitchell, L. C. Green (magnificent!), Sam Kelly, and Playboy Fuller (amazing early recording by Louisiana Red, who plays stunning slide guitar).

Relic 8003 **Three Shades of the Blues**

Mostly previously unissued recordings cut for the Detroit Lupine label between 1959–61. There are eight sides by singer/guitarist Eddie Kirkland, including several with the vocal group The Falcons, giving some powerful and intense performances. There are four cuts by Mr. Bo, a fine singer and guitarist who, vocally, is very much influenced by B. B. King. He performs a fine version of Floyd Jones' "Hard Times." There are four fine sides by The Ohio Untouchables, featuring soul-flavored vocals by Benny McCain and nice guitar by Robert Ward.

MEMPHIS

Ace CHAD 265 **The Original Memphis Blues Brothers**

Seventeen tracks recorded for Modern in the early 50s by Bobby Bland, Junior Parker, Earl Forest, and Johnny Ace, including some previously unissued material.

Arhoolie 1084 **Kings of Country Blues**

Lovely country blues recordings. Memphis Piano Red, Bukka White (possibly his best postwar recordings), Sleepy John Estes, and the incredible Nathan Beauregard, who was reportedly over 100 at the time of these recordings.

Arhoolie 1085 **Kings of Country Blues: Vol. 2**

Napoleon Strickland and The Como Drum Band, Fred McDowell (fabulous sides with harmonica player Johnny Woods), Other Turner, Furry Lewis, and the mysterious R. L. Watson and Josiah Jones.

Blues Classics 15 **Memphis and the Delta**

Splendid collection. Houston Boines, Junior Brooks, Forest City Joe, Joe Hill Louis, Boyd Gilmore, Willie Love, and Baby Face Turner.

Echo Blues 801 **Blues Anthology, Vol. 1 Memphis Blues**

Originally issued as "Memphis Blues Again, Vol. 1" (Adelphi 1009), this is an enjoyable collection of Memphis country blues recorded in 1969–70. It includes two tracks by the amazing Nathan Beauregard; his two tracks are not merely of novelty interest but are powerful and intense blues. Also includes Earl Bell, the fine singer and piano player Mose Vinson, the great Furry Lewis, who is in good form on "Natural Born Eastman #2" and "New Turn Your Money Green," singer/piano player Joe Dobbins, Gus Cannon, Dewey Corley, and Sam Clark.

Not all of the music is that exceptional but there are a lot of good moments here.

Echo Blues 802 **Blues Anthology, Vol. 2 More Memphis Blues**

Originally "Memphis Blues Again, Vol. 2" (Adelphi 1005), this features one track by Bukka White, two instrumental tracks by the splendid and too infrequently recorded Richard "Hacksaw" Harney, plus tracks by Willie Morris (including a fine version of "Stop and Listen"), Walter Miller, John "Memphis Piano Red" Williams, Sleepy John Estes, and Van Hunt, whose career stretches back to before 1920!

Krazy Kat 7427 **Memphis Blues: Unissued Titles from the 1950s**

Amazing album of all previously unissued songs mostly recorded in the Sun studios. Most cuts feature that unique blend of rural and urban sounds that was so distinctive in Memphis. Side one features straight-ahead country blues from singer/guitarist William Stewart and singer/harmonica player Willie Carr. There are two cuts by Dr. Ross and Henry Hill and some great sounds by Woodrow Adams featuring excellent harp by Sylvester Hayes. Side two is more urban with a sax on most tracks, though the tracks still have a rural feel. This is generally less interesting than the first side. Includes cuts by Johnny O'Neal with piano by Ike Turner and Eddie Snow.

L+R 42.034 **Living Country Blues: Vol. 4— Tennessee Blues**

1980 recordings of Hammie Nixon, Memphis Piano Red, Lottie Murrel, and Charlie Sangster. Except for Murrel, most of the performances are mediocre.

Nighthawk 103 **Lowdown Memphis Harmonica Jam**

Great 1950–55 cuts including some incredibly rare titles by Hot Shot Love, Joe Hill Louis, J. D. Horton, Walter Horton, and Willie Nix.

Rounder SS 29 (c,d) **Sun Records Harmonica Classics**

A wonderful selection of harmonica blues recorded for Sam Phillips' legendary Sun label between 1951–55. Though there is some duplication with the great nine-LP Sun Blues Box (now out of print), this does include some alternate takes, a few tracks not issued on LP before, and some unissued titles. There are three tracks by the magnificent Walter Horton, including his classic "Easy," a track which has been reissued several times before but is always worth hearing again; it's one of the greatest blues instrumentals ever! There are four tracks by Doctor Ross including his lovely "Country Clown," which has not been available on LP for a long time, and the previously unissued and very fine "Downtown Boogie." Accompanied by the stirring guitar of Pat Hare and the raggedy piano of Mose Vinson, Arkansas singer and harmonica player Coy "Hot Shot" Love works out on three songs, including an alternate take of his best-known song, "Wolf Call Boogie." The album is rounded out with three songs by the superb one-man band Joe Hill Louis, who recorded prolifically for Phillips (only a handful of songs were issued originally). Included is the previously unissued "Got Me a New Woman," which is every bit as good as his issued material. Sound throughout is excellent, even on the tracks which had to be dubbed from 78s, and there are full discographical details and informative notes by Sun maven Colin Escott. Even if you have some of the material here, this album is still well worth getting— and it's on compact disc, too!

Rounder SS 38 (c,d) Mystery Train
If you already have the Sun BOX 105 and Charly 30105, then you have 11 of the 14 performances here. This collection adds a previously unissued take of Junior Parker's "Love My Baby" and previously unissued alternates of Pat Hare's "I'm Gonna Murder My Baby." Additionally, you get eight others by Junior Parker and three by James Cotton, including his fantastic "Cotton Crop Blues," with blistering guitar by Pat Hare. Good notes from Colin Escott, who is the leading world authority on Sun records, excellent sound, full discographical information, and a couple of nice photos.

Rounder 2006 Beale Street Mess Around
Informal recordings of Furry Lewis, Dewey Corley, and Will Shade.

Southland SLP 14 Tennessee Legends
Nice album of country blues recorded in Memphis in 1962. Includes Sleepy John Estes, who had only been rediscovered a few months earlier and was in particulary good form on some familiar songs. Furry Lewis was also in great form, and his "Fare-Thee-Well, Old Tennessee" is especially good. There are four tracks by Memphis Jug Band veteran Will Shade, who accompanies himself on guitar or harmonica. There are also tracks by Gus Cannon, Charlie Burse, and Jenny Mae Clayton. Not all of the album is that good but most is of interest.

Tennessee Folklore Society TFS 102
Tennessee: The Folk Heritage, Vol. 1—The Delta
A rather unexceptional selection of blues and gospel recorded in the Memphis area in the 60s and 70s plus a reissue of Memphis Minnie's "Nothin' In Ramblin'." Includes Little Laura Dukes, Mose Vinson, Big Sam Clark, Memphis Slim, Furry Lewis, Red Williams and Dewey Corley, and the Choir of the Lambert Church of God in Christ.

Tennessee Folklore Society TFS 106 Free Hill: A Sound Portrait of a Rural Afro-American Community
1981–83 field recordings featuring narration, songs, and preaching.
COMPACT DISC

ESSENTIAL SELECTION

Charly CD 67 The Blues Came Down from Memphis
An hour's worth of the best of the "Sun Blues Box." Twenty-two sides by a dozen artists, all produced by Sam Phillips. Plenty of country and city blues, even one-man bands (Dr. Ross, Joe Hill Louis), almost all uptempo or shuffle tunes. Includes Rufus Thomas ("Bear Cat," "Tiger Man"), Walter Horton ("West Winds Are Blowing," "Walter's Instrumental"), Little Junior's Blue Flames ("Mystery Train," "Love My Baby"), Hot Shot Love ("Wolf Call Boogie"), and more from Jimmy DeBerry, James Cotton, Willie Nix, and Sammy Lewis.

Sun (UK) CD 1 The Sun CD Collection: Black Music Originals, Vol. 1
Twenty-two great Sun blues tracks, featuring both sides of 11 Sun blues singles, including "Gotta Let You Go" by Joe Hill Louis, "Got My Application Baby" by Handy Jackson, "Baker Shop Boogie" by Willie Nix, "Bearcat" by Rufus Thomas, "Greyhound Blues" by D. A. Hunt, and "Take a Little Chance" by Jimmy DeBerry. With illustrated booklet including notes by Sun expert Martin Hawkins.

Sun (UK) CD 4 Black Music Originals, Vol. 2
This is the second CD in an ongoing series designed to reissue all the blues, R&B, and gospel recordings issued on Sun and associated labels between 1950–57. This one features 20 songs issued between June 1953 and February 1954. It opens with two songs by the Prisonaires, including their beautiful "Just Walkin' in the Rain," followed by Junior Parker with his classic "Feelin' Good," and Rufus Thomas and his thundering "Tiger Man," with incredible funky guitar by Joe Hill Louis. Also on this disc are great tracks by Dr. Ross, Little Milton, Billy "The Kid" Emerson, and primitive harmonica player Hot Shot Love. Marvelous stuff.

Sun (UK) CD 7 Black Music Originals, Vol. 3
Features both sides of 11 records issued between April 1954 and June 1955. Includes songs by James Cotton (including his classic "Cotton Crop Blues," with stunning guitar by Pat Hare), Little Milton, Billy "The Kid" Emerson, Raymond Hill (fine sax

player from Jackie Brenston's band), The Prisonaires, Dr. Ross (including his wonderful "Boogie Disease"), The Jones Brothers (one of the few gospel groups who recorded for Sun), and the superb Sammy Lewis-Willie Johnson Combo.

Sun (UK) CD 10 Black Music Originals, Vol. 4
The last CD in this series. This one features both sides of 10 singles issued between 1955–57. It is dominated by the unique stylings of Roscoe Gordon, who is featured on eight tracks, including "The Chicken," the weird "Cheese and Crackers," and "Sally Jo." Also includes Little Milton's terrific "Lookin' for My Baby," with some shattering electric guitar, doo-wop from The Five Tinos, black rock 'n' roll from Bill Pinkey, plus tracks by Eddie Snow and Billy Emerson. As usual for Sun CDs, the sound is adequate, and it comes with a booklet giving notes on all the performances by Martin Hawkins.

Sun (UK) CD 27 Blow It 'Til You Like It
Twenty-four fine tracks of harmonica blues, most of which were not originally issued, though many have subsequently appeared on LP, most recently on the out-of-print Sun BOX 105 and Rounder SS 27. However, there are still several treasures that have never been issued before, including three by Walter Horton, three by Joe Hill Louis, one by Woodrow Adams, and four by Dr. Ross, along with previously reissued sides by these artists plus tracks by Houston Boines, Hot Shot Love, and Willie Nix. The music is consistently fine, sound is good, and there are full discographical details and informative notes by Neil Slaven.

Sun (UK) CD 28 Let's Drink Some Juice and All Get Loose
A diverse collection of 28 urban-flavored blues recorded for Sun in the mid-50s, including tracks previously on Sun BOX 105 and various Charly LPs, along with previously unissued and alternate takes. Includes Kenneth Banks, Jackie Brenston (his classic "Rocket 88" again!), Billy Emerson, Pat Hare, Earl Hooker, Billy Love, Junior Parker, Eddie Snow, and Albert Williams.

MISSISSIPPI and LOUISIANA

Ace (US) 2028 Genuine Mississippi Blues
Odd little album featuring recordings made for the most part in the 70s. Fine Jackson singer/harmonica player Sam Myers is featured on four good cuts under his own name and also plays on the three cuts by John Littlejohn and two by King Edward. Bad Smitty does tough versions of a couple of Howlin' Wolf songs and Elmore James, Jr. (who sounds nothing like his namesake) performs three songs.

Surprise of the album is one cut by the late great Fred McDowell, performing a fine version of "Baby Please Don't Go" with some good harp. Not a great set but some interesting moments.

Arhoolie 1005 I Have to Paint My Face
Mississippi field recordings of Sam Chatmon, K. C. Douglas, Big Joe Williams, Wade Walton, R. C. Smith, Bukka White, and Wade Walton.

Arhoolie 1041 Mississippi Delta Blues, Vol. 1
Fine field recordings of Napoleon Strickland, Johnny Woods and Fred McDowell, and Tom Turner. Recorded in the 60s by George Mitchell.

Arhoolie 1042 Mississippi Delta Blues, Vol. 2
More excellent recordings from George Mitchell of R. L. Burnside (probably his best recordings), Rosa Lee Hill, and Joe Calicott.

Arhoolie 1054 Louisiana Blues
Fine 60s recordings of Henry Gray, Guitar Kelley, Silas Hogan, Clarence Edwards, and Whispering Smith.

Arhoolie 2012 Prison Work Songs
Fine recordings cut at the Louisiana State Penitentiary of Rodney Mason, Roosevelt Charles, Hogman Maxey, and Rev. Rogers.

Arhoolie 2018 Country Negro Jam Session
Great country blues by Butch Cage and Willie Thomas, Clarence Edwards, Sally Dotson, and Smokey Babe. Some tremendously exciting performances.

Blues Classics 15 Memphis and the Delta
Fine 50s recordings of Houston Boines, Junior Brooks, Forest City Joe, Joe Hill Louis, Boyd Gilmore, Willie Love, and Baby Face Turner.

Excello 8021 Blues Live in Baton Rouge
A rather unexceptional set of performances supposedly recorded at the Speak-Easy club in Baton Rouge in the early 70s. Artists include Silas Hogan, "Guitar" Kelly, Whispering Smith, and Clarence Edwards. These are all fine artists in their own right, but all are lacking in spirit here.

Flyright 517 Gonna Head for Home
Fine, unissued Jay Miller recordings of Sylvester Buckley, Mr. Calhoun, Blue Boy Dorsey, and Joe Johnson.

Flyright 518 Rooster Crowed for Day
More Jay Miller unissued recordings of Mr. Calhoun, Silas Hogan, Whispering Smith, Blue Charlie, and Jimmie Dotson.

Flyright 540 Rockin' Fever
Upbeat blues and R&B from the Jay Miller archives. Includes Pee Wee Trahan, Rocket Morgan, Doug Charles, Slim Harpo, Clifton Chenier, and Al Harris.

Flyright 606 Rock Me All Night Long

More unissued treasures from the Jay Miller vaults; Volume 41 in "The Legendary Jay Miller Series." This album features 14 R&B sides recorded around 1960, eight never before issued, four alternate takes of tracks on other Flyright albums, and two (by Jay Nelson) previously issued as singles on Excello. There are four tracks by the excellent singer/guitarist Travis Phillips. There is a previously unissued alternate take of Katie Webster's soulful "I Feel So Low," a fine previously unissued cut by Leroy Washington, "Love Me Now Or Never," plus tracks by Tal Miller, Honey Boy Allen (nice down-home cut with Lazy Lester probably on harmonica), Cassie Ballou, and an unknown artist. Not the best album in the series but an enjoyable selection.

Flyright 607 Baton Rouge Blues

Late 50s–early 60s down-home blues from the archives of Jay Miller (this is volume 42 in the series!). Features 14 fine sides recorded by bluesmen based in the Baton Rouge area and, like other albums in the series, includes unissued songs and alternate takes. The three most popular Baton Rouge artists, Slim Harpo, Lightnin' Slim, and Lazy Lester, are represented by one track each, and there are also excellent sides by Jimmy Anderson, Silas Hogan (great lowdown track with fine Katie Webster piano), Tabby Thomas, and Boogie Jake.

Flyright 608 It's Your Voodoo Working

Volume 43 in "The Legendary Jay Miller Series" features 14 fine blues and R&B sides recorded between 1961–63 with a great six-piece studio band that included Lionel Prevost (tenor sax), Katie Webster (pno), and Warren Storm (drm). Vocalists include Charles Sheffield, Tabby Thomas, Sonny Martin, Bobby Jay, Rocket Morgan, Leroy Washington, and Lionel Torrance. All are fine, and the instrumental work is superb, much of it with a New Orleans feel. There are some great sax solos by Prevost.

Flyright 614 Baton Rouge Harmonica

Another fine collection of rare songs, unissued tracks, and alternate takes from the Jay Miller archives. This LP focuses on harmonica bluesmen who worked the clubs in Baton Rouge in the late 50s and early 60s. The album is dominated by Jimmy Anderson, a Jimmy Reed clone; his six tracks, though very derivative, have a nice rolling Louisiana feel to them. Highlights of the album are the four tracks by Lazy Lester, including the loping "Tell Me Pretty Baby," and two wonderfully doomy minor key blues: "Sad City Blues" and "Courtroom Blues." The album is rounded out by an alternate take of Slim Harpo's "One More Day," the obscure but excellent Sylvester Buckley on "I'm Getting Tired," and two tracks by Jimmy Dotson, both featuring Jay Miller's penchant for odd percussion sounds. Excellent sound and good notes by John Broven, though the absence of discographical data is to be regretted.

Flyright 620 I Ain't Got No Money

More treasures from the Jay Miller vaults, including more unissued songs and alternate takes. The album opens with the controversial "I Hope You Come Back Home," which is claimed to be a Buddy Guy track, who returned to his home in Louisiana from time to time. Although it doesn't really sound a whole lot like Buddy to me, there are a few Guyish vocal and instrumental mannerisms. Whether it is Guy or not is unimportant, since it is an excellent performance with that typical "Miller" sound. Blue Charlie Morris is represented by three tracks, including an alternate of his most well-known songs "I'm Gonna Kill That Hen" and the unissued and similar "Watch That Crow" (a bird fetishist?). The album's title song is a rare acoustic blues performed by the obscure and chaotic Clarence Locksley, who is featured on three other tracks here, including the dreadful instrumental "Crowley Blues." Other artists include the B. B. King-inspired Joe Johnson, the very fine Ramblin' Hi Harris, Jake Johnson, Joseph Bob (a primitive solo harmonica blues with a vocal that harks back to field hollers), Jake Jackson, and harmonica player Wild Bill Phillips, with a brilliant version of the Zydeco song, "Paper in My Shoe." An excellent collection.

L+R 42.032 Living Country Blues, Vol. 2: Blues on Highway 61

Nice recent field recordings of Mississippi country bluesmen: James "Son" Thomas, Sam Chatmon, Walter Brown, and Joe Cooper.

L+R 42.035 Mississippi Delta Blues

Vol. 5 in L+R's "Living Country Blues" series, featuring recent field recordings of James "Son" Thomas, CeDell Davis, Othar Turner, Walter Brown, and Stonewall Mays.

L+R 42.037 Afro-American Blues Roots

Vol. 7 of the "Living Country Blues" series is a fine set of field recordings made in Mississippi and Louisiana in 1980 of music that is the well-spring of the blues: one-string guitar, field hollers, fife and drum bands, plus elemental guitar and harmonica accompaniments. Some powerful music by Sam "Stretch" Shields, Lonnie Pitchford, Cora Fluker, Othar Turner, Napoleon Strickland, and Arzo Youngblood.

L+R 42.039 Mississippi Moan
Vol. 9 in the "Living Country Blues" series is an
excellent collection of Mississippi country blues
singers recorded in 1980: the Tommy Johnson-in-
fluenced Boogie Bill Webb and Arzo Youngblood,
the fascinating sound of Lonnie Pitchford and his
one-string guitar, blueswoman Cora Fluker, harmonica player Sam "Stretch" Shields, unaccompanied vocals by Joe Savage and Walter Brown, and
fine singing and guitar by James "Son" Thomas.

**Library of Congress AAFS L 67 Afro-American
Folk Music from Tate and Panola Counties,
Mississippi**
Blues and religious music recorded by David Evans,
1969–72, with several cuts from 1942. Includes
Napoleon Strickland, Sid Hemphill's Fife and Drum
Band, Compton Jones, and Ranie Burnette. Comes
with an extensively annotated booklet.

**Maison De Soul 1006 Louisiana Explosive
Blues**
Texas and Louisiana blues recorded between 1958–
75, and originally issued on Jin and Maison De Soul.
Features Li'l Joe Gordon, Rockin' Dopsie, Margo
White, Donnie Jacobs, The Vel-Tones, Junior Cole
(with excellent guitar by Johnny Winter), and Clif-
ton Chenier.

Red Pepper RP 702 Louisiana R&B from Lanor
Fourteen blues and R&B sides recorded for the
Louisiana label Lanor between 1961–63. Fine sides
bearing that distinctive relaxed Louisiana feel by
Elton Anderson, Duke Stevens, Little Victor, Char-
les Tyler, and Drifting Charles. With notes by
Louisiana music expert John Broven.

Rounder 2009 (c) South Mississippi Blues
Fine field recordings by Dave Evans. Features Babe
Stovall, Herb Quinn, and Eli Owens.

Rounder 2012 Goin' Up the Country
More great Dave Evans field recordings, originally
issued in the 60s on Decca, featuring Roosevelt
Holts, Isaiah Chatman, Arzo Youngblood, and Jack
Owens.

Southern Culture 1700 Mississippi Folk Voices
A collection of music by black and white performers, this album features fife and drum music and
harmonica playing from Napoleon Strickland, traditional fiddle music by Bill Mitchess, blues singing
and guitar by James Thomas, and Jimmie Rodgers-
style white blues by John Arnold

Southern Culture 1703 Bothered all the Times
Excellent collection of Mississippi blues artists. In
addition to the singing and playing, there are several
spoken reminiscences and tales. Features Lovey

Williams, Louis Dotson, Parchman work gang, and
Lee Kizart.

White Label 9955 Going Down to Louisiana
Nice collection of previously unissued 50s down-
home blues recordings by Joe Hill Louis, Schoolboy
Cleve, and Big Boy Crudup.
COMPACT DISC

Flyright FLYCD 09 Louisiana Swamp Blues
Tremendous 20-song collection of Louisiana blues
recorded by the redoubtable Jay Miller. The collec-
tion is a mixture of recordings originally issued on
Excello, along with unissued songs and alternate
takes released in the 70s and 80s on Flyright. The set
opens with Slim Harpo's all-time classic "I'm a King
Bee" and ends with his "Little Queen Bee." Along
the way we have such gems as "I'm Warning You
Baby" by Lightnin' Slim, "Gonna Stick to You
Baby" by Lonesome Sundown, "Sugar Coated
Love" by Lazy Lester, the fantastic "Baby Baby" by
Katie Webster and Ashton Savoy, "Alimonia Blues"
by Joe Johnson, "Mumblin Blues" by Sylvester
Buckley, "Early in the Morning" by Boogie Jake,
and "Baby Left Me This Morning" by Whispering
Smith. Sound quality is excellent. Highly recom-
mended.

NEW ORLEANS
Flyright 601 Going to New Orleans
Volume 38 of rare and unissued recordings from the
vaults of famed Crowley, LA, record producer Jay
Miller is another excellent collection. Although not
all the artists here are from New Orleans, most of
them worked in New Orleans at one time or another,
and the music in general has a Crescent City sound.
Most of the artists are unknown, except for Lester
Robertson, Rockin' Sidney, and Tabby Thomas, but
their music is very good, featuring such fine performers as Billy Tate, Eddie Hudson, Skinny
Dynamo (!), and Ernie Holland.

**Krazy Kat 7403 New Orleans Rhythm 'n Blues,
1949–1967**
Sixteen great sides drawn from two long out-of-print
albums on Flyright. Lloyd Price, Jivin' Gene, Allen
Toussaint, Professor Longhair, Joe Barry, and Eddie
Bo.

Mardi Gras 1001 Mardi Gras in New Orleans
Mostly 60s R&B songs about the Mardi Gras by Bo
Dollis and The Wild Magnolia Mardi Gras Band
(two tracks), The Hawketts, Al Johnson, Earl King,
and two by Professor Longhair.

Moonshine 116 **Bourbon Street Boogie**
Sixteen recordings from the Crescent City made between 1957–62. Features Tommy Ridgley, "Mr. Google Eyes" August, Paul Gayten, Bobby Charles, and Little Jimmy Merritt.

Pearl 15 (c) **Jump and Shout**
Twelve New Orleans R&B sides from the late 40s– early 50s. Features Dave Bartholomew, Erline Harris, Joseph "Mr. Google Eyes" August, Chubby Newsome, and James "Blazer Boy" Locks. Previously on Japanese P-Vine.

Rounder 2080 (c,d) **Troubles, Troubles—New Orleans Blues from Ric and Ron**
Excellent continuation of Rounder's exploration of Joe Ruffino's Ric and Ron labels, focusing on its blues output. The chief New Orleans exponent was the tough guitarist Eddie Lang, whose five hot Guitar Slim-styled bluesrockers from 1958 highlight this LP. Edgar Blanchard and His Gondoliers and Jimmy Rivers contribute several fine instrumentals, while the rest are performed by non-New Orleanians. Mississippi-based Mercy Baby, who was Frankie Lee Sims' drummer, adds two raunchy Excello-flavored sides, and the LP is rounded out by Jerry Morris of Lafayette, backed by some burning guitar from Clarence Garlow, on four raucous tunes. Seven of the 14 songs here are previously unissued.
CASSETTE ONLY RELEASE

Chess 9174 **New Orleans R&B**
Fine selection and very little duplication with other sets. Features Myles and Dupont, Sugarboy Crawford, Clarence Henry, Allen Brooks, Charles Williams, Eddie Bo, Rod Bernard, and Clifton Chenier.
COMPACT DISC

P-Vine PCD 1613 **Gumbo Ya Ya**
A fine collection of 28 New Orleans blues and R&B songs from the 50s and 60s. Includes Jessie Hill, Ernie K. Doe, Chris Kenner, The Showmen, Chick Carbo, Eskew Reeder, Raymond Lewis, Irma Thomas, Alvin Robinson, Robert Parker, Huey Smith and The Pitter Pats, Betty Harris, Cyril Neville, and The Meters.

TEXAS

Arhoolie 1017 **Texas Blues, Vol. 2**
Reissues and field recordings of superb Texas country blues by Manny Nichols, Mance Lipscomb, Black Ace, Rattlesnake Cooper, Isam Hisam (with great guitar by Lightnin' Hopkins), Mercy Dee, Billy Bizor, Alex Moore, and Smokey Hogg.

Arhoolie 2006 **Texas Blues**
Great 40s Gold Star reissues of Lil Son Jackson, L. C. Williams, Lightnin' Hopkins, Thunder Smith, and Lee Hunter.

Blues Classics 16 **Texas Blues**
Great reissue of 40s and 50s recordings of Smokey Hogg, John Hogg, Mercy Dee, L. C. Williams, Frankie Lee Sims, and Buddy Chiles.

Catfish 1002 **Texas Piano Professors**
1988 recordings of three veteran pianists—R. T. Williams (aka Grey Ghost), Lavada Durst (aka Dr. Hepcat), and Erbie Bowser.

Home Cooking 106 **Blues as Big as Texas**
This fine album is the first in a series to reissue recordings from the vaults of Houston record producer Roy Ames, featuring all previously unissued sides recorded between 1958–71. There are some fine sides here, though some of them are rather sparse and sound like demos. Artists include Johnny Copeland (fine versions of "Rock Me Baby" and "Baby, Please Don't Go"), Jimmy Nelson, Gatemouth Brown (not at his best here), Juke Boy Bonner (the fine and fascinating "Carried to the Cleaners and Hung Out to Dry"), Joe Medwick (the sparse but fine "You Bit the Hand That Fed You"), Percy Mayfield (also not at his best), Joe Hughes, Big Walter Price (his brilliant version of the ominous "Bloodstains on the Wall" is probably the best track here), Calvin "Loudmouth" Johnson, and Clarence "Bon Ton" Garlow.

Home Cooking 109 **Texas Guitar Greats**
A diverse but not terribly consistent selection recorded by Houston producer Roy Ames. Most of the tracks are instrumental, and although there are some good performances by Clarence Green, Johnny Copeland, Johnny Winter, and James Bolden, the performances generally have an anonymous feel to them, and such performers as Ted Hawley and Rockola are genrally forgettable. Is it really "Gatemouth" Brown playing on the second track on Side one? It could be anybody! For completists only.

Krazy Kat 7407 **Houston Jump**
Sixteen excellent sides of Texas urban blues, an area that has rarely been explored in blues reissues. Fine jumping blues and boogie by Lonnie Lyons, Connie McBooker, Elmore Nixon, Jesse Thomas, Henry Hayes, and Willie Johnson.

Krazy Kat 7418 **Down in the Groovy**
Another fine collection of postwar Texas urban blues. This one has lots of riffing saxes, plummy vocals, and some nice boogie piano and stinging guitar on some cuts. Four of the cuts are by Dallas bluesman Zuzu Bollin, while the rest of the artists are from Houston, including Lonnie Lyons, Goree Carter, James "Widemouth" Brown (brother of "Gatemouth" Brown), and Carl Campbell. Good notes and fine sound.

Krazy Kat 7425 **Houston Shuffle**
Fourteen sides recorded in Houston between 1955–58, including Albert Collins's first two sides from 1958. Other great hot guitarists include Clarence Green, Pete Mays (fine T-Bone-styled blues), and Joe Hughes (two by himself and two accompanying Earl Gilliam), along with some fine unknown guitarists accompanying Gene Vell and Tommy and The Derbys.

Krazy Kat 7426 **Fort Worth Shuffle**
Fourteen sides from 1958–64 featuring some great hot guitar by Cornell Dupree (with Louis Howard and The Red Hearts), Cal Valentine, Ray Sharpe, Sonny Rhodes (with The Daylighters), Earl Bell (with Royal Earl and The Swinging' Kools), and Travis Phillips, along with some fine unknown artists. Excellent music, fine sound, and informative notes.

Krazy Kat 7434 **Texas Country Blues, 1948–53**
A lovely collection of country blues. Only one of these tracks has ever been on LP and five have never been issued before. Includes three tracks by the superb Willie Lane, a rich-voiced singer and guitar player whose performances hark back to the influential Texas singer J. T. "Funny Papa" Smith. Singer/guitarist Rattlesnake Cooper's style also harks back to Smith, and, although he is a little out of tune, his performances are lovely. Cooper's playing partner, Sonny Boy Davis, is featured on two fine solo performances. Two magnificent tracks by Rosenberg, TX, bluesman Manny Nichols, an intense singer and a fluid guitarist, are included, along with three somewhat chaotic tracks by Big Son Tillis and D. C. Bender, who were strongly influenced by Lightnin' Hopkins. The album winds up with the brilliant Frankie Lee Sims, a magnificent singer and fine guitarist who is the only artist here who has made a long-term career out of his music. Fine sound, excellent notes by Chris Bentley, and full discographical details.

ESSENTIAL SELECTION

Krazy Kat 7445 **Water Coast Blues**
Sixteen country-blues tunes from Texas, recorded in the late 40s and early 50s. Thirteen of these were on the now-out-of-print Flyright 4704, so if you missed that one you have another chance to pick up on some obscure but fine Texas blues. We start off with The Sugarman, a one-record wonder, who recorded the fabulous "She's Gone with the Wind" backed with "Which Woman Do I Love," for the Sittin' In With label in 1951. He's a good singer and a great guitarist with an amazing sense of dynamics. James Tisdom does six tunes, half raucous boogies and half rollin' country blues, and all are excellent, including "Throw This Poor Dog a Bone," "Model T Boogie," and "Winehead Swing." Lightnin' Hopkins, the king of postwar Texas country blues, is a strong influence on both of these bluesmen, as well as on the five artists on Side two: Leroy "Country" Johnson, Luther Stoneham, Sunny James (aka Jessie James), Sonny Boy Holmes, and Mr. Honey. Classic stuff.

Moonshine 104 **Guitar in My Hands**
Complementing the albums of Texas blues on Krazy Kat, this set features 18 sides of Texas blues guitar recorded between 1949–66. Includes some well-known names like T-Bone Walker, Albert Collins, Johnny Copeland, and Ray Sharpe, along with more obscure performers like Texas Johnnie Brown, Long John Hunter, Travis Phillips, and Clarence Green. Some nice stuff!

Moonshine 110 **Guitar in My Hands, Vol. 2**
Eighteen tracks recorded between 1947 and the mid-60s. Besides Texas-based musicians, the LP also features some who made their home on the West Coast, including Pee Wee Crayton, who is represented here by his first recording from 1947, "After Hours Boogie," and the brilliant Lafayette Thomas, who is featured on one of his few solo recordings, "The Thing." Other performers include Lightnin' Hopkins, Lester Williams, Clarence Garlow, Cal Green (the splendid, soulful "I Can Hear My Baby Talking"), Albert Collins, Ray Sharpe, Roy Gaines, T. B. Fisher, and the Chicano band Charlie and The Jives. Decent sound, detailed notes, and some rare photos.

Nighthawk 106 **Down Behind the Rise, 1947–1953**
Rare Texas and West Coast country blues recordings including six sides by the fine and previously unreissued Jesse Thomas, plus Frankie Lee Sims, Lightnin' Hopkins (his rarest!), Beverly Scott, Willie Lane, Wright Holmes, and Johnny Beck.

ESSENTIAL SELECTION

Rounder 2031 (c) **Angels in Houston**
Excellent set of late 50s/early 60s recordings drawn from the Duke label featuring Bobby Bland, James Davis, Larry Davis, and Fenton Robinson. Davis and Fenton are particularly fine, with tough vocals and stunning guitar by Fenton. James Davis is a little-known but very fine performer and it's good to hear his original recordings of "Blue Monday" and "Your Turn to Cry." Bland, as always, is fine. The album has excellent and extensive notes by Dick Shurman.

Documentary Arts **Deep Ellum Blues**
Eighties recordings of Texas blues and R&B, featuring Bill Neely, Heat Wave Of Swing, Robert Shaw, Alex Moore, and Lavada Durst (Dr. Hepcat).

COMPACT DISC
Arhoolie (Japan) PCD 2519 **Texas Blues**
Twenty-five country blues drawn from Arhoolie 1017 and 2006. About two-thirds are recordings from the late 40s–early 50s, many of them from Bill Quinn's legendary Gold Star label. Includes Lil Son Jackson, Lee Hunter, Leroy Ervin, Lightnin' Hopkins, Thunder Smith, L. C. Williams, Manny Nichols, and Rattlesnake Cooper. The remaining tracks are fine field recordings made in the early 60s by Chris Strachwitz of Mercy Dee, Robert Shaw, Alex Moore, and Billy Bizor. A wonderful collection!

P-Vine PCD 2514 **Houston Deep Throat—Blues**
Eighteen tracks featuring Earl Gilliam, Clarence Garlow, Junior Cole, Lonnie Mitchell, Piano Slim, Calvin "Loudmouth" Johnson, Juke Boy Bonner, and Joe Medwick.

WEST COAST
Ace CHD 258 (c,d) **R&B Confidential No. 1: The Flair Label**
A great collection of 18 blues and R&B tracks recorded for Modern's subsidiary, Flair. The emphasis is on the West Coast sound, including hard-driving jump blues from Robbie Robinson, Big Duke Henderson (including his witty "Hey Dr. Kinsey"), James Reed, and Richard Berry (his great takeoff on Willie Mabon's "I Don't Know" called "Next Time"). There's doo-wop from Shirley Gunter and The Queens and the label's most popular group, The Flairs, and hard blues from Mercy Dee and Johnny Fuller. Non-West Coast artists include Elmore James, Ike Turner, and Turner sideman Billy Gale. The CD adds four more tracks: the obscure down-home group The Dixie Blues Boys, Baby "Pee Wee" Parham, Matt Cockrell, and Saunders King. Sound is superb and there are informative notes by Jim Dawson.

ESSENTIAL SELECTION
Arhoolie 2008 **Oakland Blues**
Fine reissue of early 50s Bob Geddins recordings of K. C. Douglas, Willie B. Huff (lovely vocals with great doomy guitar by Johnny Fuller), Mercy Dee, Johnny Fuller, and Sidney Maiden.

Blue Moon BMLP 1.029 **Live at Small's Paradise**
A generally undistinguished set of live performances recorded at the Los Angeles club Small's Paradise in 1969. It features two tracks by George Smith, three by Rod Piazza with Bacon Fat, one by J. D. Nicholson, and three by Pee Wee Crayton. Crayton's tracks are the highlight and feature some tough, though somewhat out of tune, guitar.

Collectables 5050 (c,d) **Blame It on the Blues**
Mid-to-late 50s recordings for Dootsie Williams' Dootoo label. There are four tracks by the powerful Willie Headen, ranging from the intense "You Can Be Replaced" to the novelty "I Love You Bobby Sox." There are four sides of smooth big-band blues from the consistently fine Roy Milton, four varied sides by Chuck Higgins, and two forgettable tracks by Filmore Slim. There are no notes or discographical data and the sound is unexceptional. Still, a nice cross-section of West Coast blues.

Diving Duck 4312 **Jericho Alley Blues Flash! Vol. 1**
Diving Duck 4313 **Jericho Alley Blues Flash! Vol. 2**
Two albums featuring all the blues recordings cut for the Los Angeles-based Flash label between 1955–59. These were previously issued as a double set on the Japanese P-Vine label some years ago. Volume 1 has four tracks featuring singer/guitarist Haskell Sadler and singer/harmonica player Sidney Maiden, two in a more traditional acoustic style and two in an intense electric style, with fine guitar by Sadler. There are also two very low-down tracks by singer/guitarist Slim Green. Volume 1 also features tracks by B. Brown, Paul Clifton, Sheryl Crowley, Sweet Pea Walker, and Frank Patt, who recorded the classic "Bloodstains on the Wall" for Specialty under the pseudonym of Honeyboy. Volume 2 focuses mostly on the work of two performers, the singer/guitarist Guitar Shorty and singer/piano player Gus Jenkins. Shorty is a powerful singer and player, and his minor key "Hard Life" is particularly fine. Jenkins' performances are varied and consistently interesting. Rounding out Volume 2 is another track by Frank Patt. Although the recordings for Flash and its subsidiaries are not earthshaking and were commercially unsuccessful, they are an interesting musical footnote and a look at the blues scene in LA in the 50s.

Diving Duck 4314 **Mr. Fullbright's Blues, Vol. 1**
Diving Duck 4315 **Mr. Fullbright's Blues, Vol. 2**
Recordings made in the 50s for eccentric West Coast producer J. R. Fullbright and issued on his Elko label, plus some from his vaults that were never originally issued. Originally issued on the Japanese P-Vine label, these 2 LPs are also available on a

single CD on P-Vine (minus one track due to space limitations). The first volume features the first recordings of singer/guitarist Phillip Walker, the fine Jimmy Nolen (with superb guitar by Lafayette Thomas), Arkansas singer/harmonica player Elmon Mickle, the obscure but excellent singer/piano player Mac Willis, plus West Coast stalwarts Smokey Hogg and Jesse Fuller. Full discographical details and informative notes by Chris Bentley. The second volume features generally more obscure artists, including three dubbed from unidentified acetates, four chaotic country blues by Big Son Tillis and D. C. Bender, one by Jesse Thomas, an early George Smith side, plus tracks by J. D. Nicholson, Jimmy Nolen, and Willie Egans.

Moonshine 103 West Coast Winners
A fine collection of West Coast blues and R&B recorded between 1953–67. A few cuts have been issued before, including "On My Way" by Alvin Smith, which was reissued on Blues Classics, but most of the tracks have not been previously reissued. Nice small bands, tough vocals, and lots of hot guitar by Little Joe Blue, Al King, Johnny Morisette, Haskell Sadler, Tiny Powell, Bob Reed, and T-Bone Walker Jr. Good sound and detailed notes.

Moonshine 108 West Coast Guitar Greats
Eighteen sides recorded between 1948–59, featuring six sides by the excellent Jimmy Nolen from 1955–56. Also includes Pee Wee Crayton, the great Bay Area guitarist Lafayette Thomas, Chuck Norris (like Thomas a brilliant musician best known for his accompaniment of others), Jimmie Toliver, Lowell Fulson, Gene Phillips, and Pete "Guitar" Lewis. Fine performances.

Moonshine 115 More West Coast Winners
Eighteen tracks—mostly from the 60s—feature Larry Evans, Big Mama Thornton, Al King, J. J. Malone, Arthur H. Adams, Percy Mayfield, Jessie James, Little Joe Blue, and King Solomon.

Oldie Blues 2832 Hollywood Boogie: Obscure Piano Blues and Boogie from LA, 1945–52
An interesting collection of rare numbers including two standouts from "Poison" Gardner, a frantic R&B pacer; "Central Ave. Blues" from Al Winter; a tasty torcher from Lillette Thomas, "Old Time Daddy Blues"; the nifty novelty, "I Don't Know Boogie" from Elliot Carpenter; and, best of all, Willard McDaniel's skillfully played "Blues For Mimi." Also Don Miles, Buddy Collette, and a gem by Red Miller. A fine set.

Oldie Blues 8012 Tornado—Hot Screamin' Saxes From LA, 1945–47
A mix of boogie, jump, and blues, the most noteworthy being the bouncing "Banks Bang Boogie" by The Buddy Banks Sextet with warbling from Fluffy Hunter (who later fronted Jesse Powell's Band), a rubber-fingered rendition of the title track by the great "Poison" Gardner and His All Stars, plus seven amazing jump and blues numbers from Luke Jones with Joe Alexander's Highlanders. Also includes Dick Lewis and His Harlem Rhythm Boys. Outstanding vintage collection.

Relic 8002 The Rockin' Blues
Excellent album of rockin' West Coast blues recorded in the mid-50s for the Vita and Mambo labels, including eight sides by the very fine Willie Egans (these were also issued a while back on Krazy Kat), one by Jimmy Thomasson, two by Ervin "Big Boy" Groves (includes the great stop-time number "You Can't Beat The Horses"), four by Harmonica Slim (with a fine unnamed guitar player), and three by Effie Smith. A very good set.

Route 66 KIX 1200 Hunter Hancock Presents Blues and Rhythm Midnight Matinee 1951
Recorded live (!) at the Olympia Auditorium in LA on two separate dates in 1951, famed R&B deejays Jay Hancock and Roy Robinson present a hit-parade set featuring the wild honking tenor sax of Big Jay McNeely, jumping, shouting Duke Henderson, the silver voice of Betty Jean Washington, the crooning Ernie Andrews, the rocking Madelyn Perkins, the boogie madness of Floyd Dixon, backed by some riveting guitar from Chuck Norris, plus shouter Smilin' Smokey Lynn, a smoldering Bixie Crawford, Peppermint Harris, and the fine close-gospel harmonies of the Golden Keys of Oakland. An enjoyable blast from the past.

NEW YORK
ESSENTIAL SELECTION

Detour 33-003 Groove Jumping
Fourteen rockin' blues and R&B cuts recorded for the RCA subsidiary Groove between 1953–55. New York guitarist Mickey Baker is extensively featured on cuts by Mickey and Sylvia, Tiny Kennedy, and two hilarious cuts by Mr. Bear. Includes other fine cuts by Sonny Terry, The Dudroppers, The Five Keys (previously unissued), Big John Greer, and Roy Gaines (great guitar!). Absolutely incredible sound, informative notes, full discographical information, and excellent packaging.

Fire (Japan) PLP 6008 Bobby's Harlem Rock, Vol. 1: NY Wild Guitars
A great collection drawn from Bobby Robinson's Fire and Fury labels in the late 50s and early 60s. About half of the tracks here have been reissued before on Krazy Kat, but this collection appears to

have been made from master tapes, so the sound is a little better. Features four instrumentals by the fabulous guitarist Wild Jimmy Spruill, and two tracks by Charles Walker with Spruill on guitar. There are two fine cuts by Titus Lee Turner, not reissued elsewhere, that also feature Spruill on guitar, as does Wilbert Harrison's classic "Kansas City." There are three tracks by Riff Ruffin and one by the Charlie Lucas Combo. The Ruffin tracks are good though they don't feature much guitar; Spruill may be present on the Lucas tracks. The album is rounded out with three tracks by Tarheel Slim, one with Little Ann.

Fire (Japan) PLP 6101/2 **New York on Fire**
Splendid two-LP set of mostly tough city blues recorded for Bobby Robinson's Fire, Fury, Enjoy, and other affiliated labels in the late 50s and early 60s. The highlight of this set is the opening cut: a previously unissued track by fine Mississippi singer and harmonica player Sammy Myers that includes some lovely slide guitar by Elmore James. Most of the artists on this collection are obscure, including Johnny Acey (some nice harp), Mighty Joe Young (powerful West-Side Chicago blues), B. Brown and His Rockin' McVouts (B. Brown may be Buster Brown, because some of these tracks feature harp), Hal Paige and His Whalers, Dr. Horse (some unique talking blues), Noble Watts and The Possum Bellys (featuring June Bateman), Billy Lewis (the terrific "Heart Trouble"), Tommy Tucker, and Bobby Porter. Some of the tracks sound as though they have been dubbed from 45s, but, on the whole, the sound is very good.

Krazy Kat 778 **Thunderbolt**
Enjoyable album of honking-sax R&B instrumentals recorded in New York between 1952–56, including Al King and His Royal Crowns, Warren Lucky and His Combo, Haywood Henry, and Al King and His Kingsmen.

Krazy Kat 780 **Listen to Jr. Jive**
Fourteen rare and unissued urban blues and R&B recordings cut between 1953–56 in New York by veteran record producer Joe Davis. Features Warren Lucky, Danny Run, Joe Taylor, Otis Blackwell, and Dean Barlow. Album has a great cover photo of Dean Barlow with Alan Freed.

Krazy Kat 795 **R&B from Joe Davis**
The seventh Krazy Kat album in a series devoted to Joe Davis's stable of labels and many leasings. Features sultry blues sides by Miss Basil Spears, excellent novelty R&B items by Stump and Stumpy, fine raspy renderings from Paula Watson, low-down blues by Nat Foster, plus the fine unissued blues

ballad "I Got A Letter" by Lizzie Baker, backed by an extraordinary mystery pianist (Harry Van Walls?). Other artists include Lem Johnson and Teddy Williams. Rare cover pics and complex, yet concise, sleeve notes by Bruce Bastin.

Moonshine 105 **New York Notables**
The first in a series of five albums to explore the blues and R&B scene in New York in the 50s and early 60s, featuring 18 sides recorded between 1951–60. Roy Gaines provides some hot black rock 'n' roll on five fine tracks, including "Skippy Is a Sissy," featuring a nice taste of his hot guitar playing. There are three fine R&B-flavored sides by Brownie McGhee and one by Jack Dupree, but the rest of the artists are mostly obscure. Drummer Curley Hamner has a fine instrumental, "Air-Raid," with hot sax by King Curtis, and Dossie Terry turns in a down-home-flavored "Didn't Satisfy You." Also includes H-Bomb Ferguson, Billy Hope, and Mike Gordon.

Moonshine 107 **Harlem Heavies**
This second volume of New York blues and R&B features 18 sides, most with a rocking upbeat flavor. Includes the underrated but excellent singer/guitarist Larry Dale and tracks by Brownie McGhee and Jack Dupree, working in an R&B setting. There are a couple of excellent Wilbert Harrison tracks including "Off to School Again," with sax by King Curtis. Other artists include Cousin Leroy (with fine harp), Teddy "Mr. Bear" McRae, James Wayne (not the Texas singer), and Mickey Baker. Sound is good and there are interesting notes.

Moonshine 111 **New York Knockouts—R&B 1951–62**
This album cooks with hot sounds from some of R&B's strongest exponents. The leading contenders are Sylvia Robinson and her sultry rendition of "Little Boy" from Savoy, Big John Greer's followup to Chuck Berry's "Maybelline," entitled "Come Back Maybelline," recorded for Groove, Pearl Reaves and The Concords belting out "You Can't Stay Here" from the Harlem label, plus 15 bouncers and scorchers of equal merit. Recommended.

Moonshine 112 **Big Apple Boogie**
Jumping R&B, featuring shouters and honkers like Jimmy Griffin, Linda Hopkins, Bob Oakes, Ella Johnson, Walter Sandman Howard, Freddie Mitchell, and Mr. Bear. The more bluesy end of things is featured on two excellent cuts by Wilbert Harrison, and the wonderful down-home "Help Me Find My Love" by Betty James.

Moonshine 114 **Leapin' on Lenox**
Another collection of upbeat blues and R&B from New York featuring a diverse mixture of 18 tracks

recorded between 1947–60. Among the artists included are Titus Turner, Red Saunders (a bandleader whose group features the vocals of Joe Williams, generally associated with a smoother style but who reveals himself to be a pretty good blues shouter here), Big John Greer, Sil Austin (some pretty boring honking), Teddy Brannon, Faye Adams, and H-Bomb Ferguson. Although there is some good stuff here, very little really stands out.

Oldie Blues 8013 Back Bay Boogie—Hot Screamin' Saxes from New York, 1941–51
Straddles the thin line between swing/jump and R&B with a handful of honkers and jivers featuring the talents of Benny Carter, Al Killian, Ray Abrams, Flip Phillips, and Harry Dial. Notable cuts include "Doby's Boogie," with Joe Black at the piano, a mean and dirty "Blues Stay Away From Me" by Fat Man Robinson, and "Sleepy Time Creep," with swoon-tenor clefs from Freddie Mitchell.

PIANO BLUES AND BOOGIE

Euphonic 1204 Barrelhouse Blues and Stomps, Vol. 5
White and black performers are included: Speckled Red, Charlie Rasch, James Crutchfield, and John Bently.

Euphonic 1205 Barrelhouse Blues and Stomps, Vol. 4
Lawrence Henry, Henry Brown, James Crutchfield, James Stump Johnson, and Dink Johnson.

Euphonic 1209 Boogie Woogie Kings
Albert Ammons, Meade Lux Lewis, and Pete Johnson in various combinations.

Krazy Kat 802 Piano Boogie and the Blues
More tracks from the vaults of New York entrepeneur Joe Davis. This one features a diverse selection of piano blues and boogie, from Rene Faure's exuberant rendering of Meade Lux Lewis' "Honky Tonk Train Blues" (from 1940) to Laverne Holt's fascinating "Mr. Black Man," with unknown piano accompaniment. There are six fine tracks by teenage player Deryck Sampson complementing the previously-issued album on Harlequin 2006, and three by Gene Rodgers, a flamboyant and skillful, but occasionally tasteless, player. There are two tracks by fine vocalist Beverly White with Willie "The Lion" Smith doing the piano honors and Al Casey on guitar, two by Billie Hayes with the mysterious "Peter Pan" on piano, and one previously unissued track by the mediocre Lizzie Baker with Van Walls. Not a consistently good album but one with some very good moments.

Muskadine 104 Unfinished Boogie
Wonderful album of blues and boogie piano

recorded in Texas and California in the 40s and early 50s, featuring Thunder Smith, Little Son Willis, Little Willie Littlefield, and Jimmy McCracklin.

Official 3031 (d) Boogie Woogie Masterpieces
Sixteen classic boogie recordings covering the period 1928–44; most have been on LP before. Includes Cow Cow Davenport, Montana Taylor, Romeo Nelson, Meade Lux Lewis, Albert Ammons, Jimmy Yancey, Joe Hunter, and Pete Johnson. CD includes four extra tracks by Pete Johnson, Lionel Hampton, and Amos Milburn.

Storyville 213 Barrel-House Blues and Boogie, Vol. 3
Twelve fine sides of piano blues and boogie recorded in the early and mid-60s, mostly in Europe, featuring Roosevelt Sykes, Champion Jack Dupree, Memphis Slim, Sunnyland Slim, and Henry Brown. Vols. 1 and 2 in this series are not currently available.

Storyville 229 The Boogie Woogie Boys
A diverse selection featuring the talents of the three great boogie-woogie piano players, Albert Ammons, Pete Johnson, and Meade Lux Lewis, drawn from live broadcasts recorded between 1939–53. Includes several duets and some vocals by Joe Turner. Yancey Special/Boogie Woogie/Roll 'Em/Foot Pedal Boogie/Turner's Blues.

Storyville 4006 Boogie Woogie Trio
Live recordings from 1939 and 1953–54 by Meade Lux Lewis, Pete Johnson, and Albert Ammons. Mostly solos plus a couple of duets and a few with rhythm section.

Zeta 717 Piano in Blues
A fine collection of piano blues and boogies featuring various veteran performers mostly recorded in France in the late 70s and early 80s, originally issued on the Blue Silver and Paris Album labels. The music ranges from solo piano to tracks with small bands, and the artists included are Booker T. Laury, Roosevelt Sykes (includes an excellent version of "Mistake in Life"), Champion Jack Dupree (good performances marred by a wretched organ), Little Willie Littlefield (lovely solo piano performances), Screamin' Jay Hawkins (the unforgettable and unforgiveable "Constipation Blues"), Eddie Boyd, Memphis Slim, Lafayette Leake, and J. J. Malone (with a tough band). Sound is excellent.

CASSETTE ONLY RELEASE

Atlantic 81694-1 Atlantic Blues: Piano
Twenty-nine fine examples of piano blues, mostly from the 40s and 50s but with a few from the 70s. Three of the legendary veterans of piano blues—Jimmy Yancey, Little Brother Montgomery, and Meade Lux Lewis—are represented by three or four

tracks from 1951. There are three superb tracks by Champion Jack Dupree from his brilliant (and out-of-print) "Blues From the Gutter" album and two by Professor Longhair from his "New Orleans Piano" set. There are three fine instrumental cuts by Ray Charles, including a delightful solo piece, "Low Society," from a previously unissued rehearsal session. There are two low-key jazzy blues from Vann "Piano Man" Walls, a fine and important New York piano player who is under-represented on reissues. Other featured artists include Joe Turner (with Pete Johnson on piano), Jay McShann (one vocal and one instrumental from 1977), Floyd Dixon, Texas Johnny Brown (a previously unissued 1949 track with lovely relaxed piano by Amos Milburn), Dr. John (a track from his classic "Gumbo" album), and Willie Mabon (an undistinguished previously unissued recording from 1976).

ZYDECO

Arhoolie 1009 **Zydeco**
Fine black French music from the 40s to the 60s, including Paul McZeal, Sydney Babineaux, Albert Chevalier, Herbert Sam, Amadé Ardoin, and Leadbelly.

Arhoolie 1090 **Zydeco, Vol. 2**
This album, issued 22 years after Volume 1 (!), presents two groups: Preston Frank's Swallow Band and Ambrose Sam's Old Time Zydeco. Frank's band is a six-piece band that, besides Preston's vocal and accordion, includes his uncle Carlton on fiddle and Leo Thomas on vocals and drums. They are an exciting and lively group and the fiddle gives them a different sound. Ambrose Sam plays accordion and sings in an older, blues-based style. His sound is very basic, with only rubboard and drums accompaniment. Both groups are fine and well worth a listen.

Flyright 539 **Zydeco Blues**
Great material from the Jay Miller archives, including late 50s recordings by Clifton Chenier, Fernest and The Thunders, Rockin' Dopsie, and Marcel Dugas.

Flyright 600 **Zydeco Blues, Vol. 2**
Includes Clifton Chenier (four sides including the fine "Worried Life Blues," with shattering guitar by Travis Phillips), Rockin' Dopsie (three songs, one previously unissued), Marcel Dugas and the Entertainers, Fernest and the Thunders, and the fascinating Joseph Bob, who plays Zydeco on the harmonica.

Maison De Soul 1004 **La La—Lousiana Black French Music**
Superb album produced by folklorist Nick Spitzer in the 70s, presenting on Side one fiddler Bebe Carriere and his brother, accordionist Eraste. They have a raw Zydeco style that is captivating. Side two gives us the Lawtell Playboys, with accordionist Delton Broussard and Bebe's nephew Calvin on fiddle.

Maison De Soul 1024 (c) **Zydeco Festival**
CD issue: Maison de Soul CD 101
Zydeco selections from various Maison de Soul albums by Buckwheat Zydeco, The Carriere Brothers, Terrence Simien, Rockin' Dopsie, Chuck Martin, Morris Francis, Clifon Chenier, and Rockin' Sidney.

Maison De Soul 1030 (c,d) **101 Proof Zydeco**
A rockin' collection of young, old, famous, and not-so-famous names from the Zydeco scene. As many as half of the selections are either previously unreleased or licensed from other record companies. It's no surprise that the strongest, purest cuts come from the best-known names: Boozoo Chavis' "Zydeco Hee Haw," Rockin' Sidney's "Jalapeno Lena," and the legendary Clifton Chenier's "Johnny Can't Dance." There are also some promising newcomers here; highlights include a feverish live rendition of "Turn On Your Lovelight" by Terrance Simien, the slow and soulful sound of the Sam Brothers Five, and the raw Chuck Berry-style energy of 19-year-old accordionist Jo Jo Reed and his band.

Rounder 6009 (c) **Zodico**
Fine album of black Cajun-style music by various groups from Louisiana, with an extensively annotated booklet.
COMPACT DISC

ESSENTIAL SELECTION

Arhoolie CD 307 **Zydeco—The Early Years**
Some of this material is also available on LP 1009. Includes McZiel and Gerner, Sidney Babineaux, Albert Chevalier, George Alberta, Peter King and L. Hebert, Willie Green, Herbert Sam, Clifton Chenier, and Clarence Garlow.

Rhino 70946-2 (21S) **Alligator Stomp: Cajun and Zydeco Classics**

Ten Zydeco players, including Clifton Chenier, Rockin' Sidney, Queen Ida, Boozoo Chavis, and Rockin' Dopsie, and eight stompers from Cajun country by D. L. Menard, Cleveland Crochet, Bruce Daigrepont, Johnnie Allan, Jo-El Sonnier, Rusty and Doug Kershaw, and Beausoleil. No real obscurities here, as all are familiar names and most of these cuts are still in print on the original labels.

MISCELLANEOUS COUNTRY BLUES

Ace CH 247 (c,d) **Bluesville, Vol. 1: Folk Blues**

Sixteen fine country blues sides recorded for the Bluesville label in the early 60s. Includes Furry Lewis, K. C. Douglas, Robert Curtis Smith, Wade Walton, Lightnin' Hopkins, Blind Willie McTell, Scrapper Blackwell, and Snooks Eaglin. CD includes extra tracks by Furry Lewis, Memphis Willie B., and others, though it leaves off the Lightnin' Hopkins track on the LP!

Arhoolie 1006 **Blues 'n' Trouble**

Fine and varied country blues set, featuring Big Joe Williams, Lowell Fulson, Jasper Love, Willie Thomas, Alex Moore, Robert Curtis Smith, Lil Son Jackson, and Mance Lipscomb.

Arhoolie 1012 **Blues 'n' Trouble, Vol. 2**

Lightnin' Hopkins, Little Son Willis, Lil Son Jackson, Joe Turner, Big Joe Williams, Mercy Dee, Blind James Phillips, and Guitar Slim and Jelly Belly.

Arhoolie 1018 **Bad Luck 'n' Trouble**

Excellent anthology, featuring Clifton Chenier, R. C. Smith, Mercy Dee, Lightnin' Hopkins, James Phillips, Little Son Willis (beautiful West Coast singer and piano player), K. C. Douglas, and Fred McDowell.

Arhoolie 1030 **Berkeley Blues Festival**

Mance Lipscomb, Clifton Chenier, and Lightnin' Hopkins.

Arhoolie 1094 **Louie Bluie**

Delightful album of black string-band music from the Terry Zwigoff movie "Louie Bluie" about vocalist/multi-instrumentalist Howard Armstrong, who is best known as one-third of Martin, Bogan, and Armstrong. He plays mandolin, guitar, and violin, and on many cuts is joined by his long-time playing partner Ted Bogan on vocals and guitar. Also includes "Banjo" Ikey Robinson (vcl, bjo) and Yank Rachell (vcl, mdln). There is a wide variety of music here—pop songs, jazz, country, blues, and even a Polish tune! Most of the tracks were recorded recently, but the album includes both sides of Bogan and Armstrong's 1934 recordings.

BRI 003 **Virginia Traditions: Western Piedmont Blues**

Delightful album of country blues from Virginia featuring mostly recent recordings plus a couple of 20s reissues by Luke Jordan. A few cuts have previously appeared on albums on the Outlet label. Includes Clayton Horsley, John Tinsley, James Lowery, Marvin Foddrell.

BRI 006 **Tidewater Blues**

Country blues recordings featuring commercial recordings from the 20s and the 50s, field recordings from the 70s, and one superb field recording from 1940. Also includes a wonderful gospel performance from 1929 by the Monarch Jazz Quartet. Some lovely music, beautifully annotated in an extensive booklet. Includes Carl Hodges, The Virginia Four, William Moore, John Cephas, The Back Porch Boys, and Pernell Charity.

BRI 007 **Work Songs**

BRI 008 **Virginia Traditions: Southwest Virginia Blues**

This LP, compiled by Vaughan Webb, is another magnificent collection, featuring both black and white performers, and shows the musical interchange between them. From commercial recordings we have artists like Tarter and Gay, The Carter Family (the superb "Bear Creek Blues" from 1940), Carl Martin (his stunning "Old Time Blues" from 1935), Dock Bogg (recorded in 1929 for the rare Lonesome Ace label), and Byrd Moore. The field recordings cover the period 1962–83, and include such obscure but talented performers as Fred Galliher, John Henry Diggs, Earl Gilmore (wonderfully intense piano blues), Josh Thomas (doing Barbecue Bob's "Mississippi Heavy Water Blues" with his own banjo accompaniment), Howard Twine, and Malcolm Johnson (a remarkably intense white singer and guitarist who appears to have been inspired by Blind Lemon Jefferson). The music is consistently outstanding and the sound is superb. There is a large 24-page booklet with extensive notes, great photos, full discographical information, information on songs, performers, and lyrics.

Echo Blues 805 **Blues Anthology, Vol. 5: Blues from St. Louis**

Some lovely performances by St. Louis country blues performers, including the superb Henry Townsend and the powerful Arthur "Big A" Weston, who has a tough expressive voice, plays some exciting percussive guitar, and is accompanied in fine style by harmonica player George Robertson. There are two tracks by George McCoy, who has one of the most mournful voices I have ever heard!

George's sister Ethel is another expressive singer; she performs a version of their aunt Memphis Minnie's classic, "Bumble Bee." Also includes Jimmie Brown, Henry Brown, and Clarence Johnson.

Florida Folklife 102/103 **Drop on Down in Florida**
Interesting two-LP set featuring the rarely documented Afro-American traditional music of Florida. One album features secular music: blues, folk songs, and music with one-string accompaniment. The other album features religious music, including church services, gospel singing with guitar, and sacred harp singing. There are several exciting performances, but there is quite a bit that might be interesting from an academic point of view but is not as interesting musically! Comes with a large-format 24-page booklet.

Flyright 528 **Another Man Done Gone**
Superb album of country blues artists from the Southeast recorded in the 60s and 70s. They are all now dead or have disappeared, including Baby Tate, Jack Harp, and Guitar Shorty; with excellently annotated booklet.

Krazy Kat 824 **East Coast Blues**
Gotham and its affiliated 20th Century label didn't record a lot of country blues, but that which it did is of a very high standard. This album complements the Sonny Terry album on Krazy Kat 807 and the utterly magnificent Dan Pickett album on Krazy Kat 811, with some more great country blues from East Coast guitarists. The album features three alternate takes of songs by Pickett, plus the superb, previously unavailable "I Can Shake It." There is also a previously unissued alternate of "No Love Blues" by Sonny Terry with fine slide guitar. There are three tracks by the very fine Doug Quattlebaum from 1953, including the beautiful, previously unissued "Foolin' Me," and the remarkable five minute, 18 second "Don't Be Funny Baby," which was edited down to two-and-a-half minutes when it was issued on a single. There are two recently discovered tracks by Tarheel Slim on which his melodic vocals and guitar are accompanied by a fine second guitarist— marvelous! There are six tracks by fine Alabama singer/guitarist Ralph Willis with second guitar and bass. These are fine performances though they pale compared to most of the other artists here. Interesting notes by Chris Smith. Unreservedly recommended.

L+R 42.030 **The Introduction to the Living Country Blues**
Two-LP set, the first in a series on L+R featuring recent field recordings of country blues artists from

various parts of the South. This sampler of the artists featured in the series includes some very nice performances by Guitar Frank, Flora Molton and The Truth Band, Sam Chatmon, Archie Edwards, Lonnie Pitchford, CeDell Davis, and Boyd Rivers. None of these selections are duplicated on the other albums in the series.

L+R 42.038 **Lonesome Home Blues**
Six cuts each by Guitar Slim (who actually plays piano on half his cuts) from South Carolina and Guitar Frank from Delaware. Enjoyable set of country blues.

L+R 42.040 **Country Boogie**
Vol. 10 of the "Living Country Blues" series is an enjoyable collection of boogies and uptempo blues performed by country blues artists from Mississipi, Virginia, and North Carolina. Includes Lottie Murrel, Guitar Slim (playing piano), Othar Turner and The Rising Star Fife and Drum Band, Lonnie Pitchford (playing one-string guitar), and Memphis Piano Red.

Longleaf 001 **Eight Hand Sets and Holy Steps**
Reissue of collection of field recordings of traditional black music from North Carolina recorded in the late 70s. One side features secular dance tunes, while the other features spirituals and songs of praise. This new edition has an extensively annotated 28-page booklet.

Matchbox MB 904 **Rural Blues**
Reissue of long-out-of-print LP featuring 14 great sides from the late 40s-early 50s by Papa Lightfoot, Boogie Bill Webb, J. D. Edwards, Lowell Fulson, Roosevelt Sykes, Manny Nichols, Country Jim, and Little Son Jackson.

Muse 5212 **Cryin' in the Morning**
Reissue of fine down-home blues from the vaults of Savoy/Regal. Most of these tracks are available elsewhere. Includes Frank Edwards, Blind Willie McTell, Curley Weaver, Dennis McMillan, and David Wylie.

New World 252 **Roots of the Blues**
Excellent selection of field recordings collected by Alan Lomax in the South in 1959–60 featuring a wide range of blues and pre-blues performances. Much of this has appeared before on now-out-of-print albums on Atlantic and Prestige. Includes John Dudley (incredible!), Leroy Miller, Ed and Lonnie Young, Miles and Bob Pratcher, and Fred McDowell.

Nighthawk 109 **Downhome Delta Blues**
Sixteen great and rare sides from Memphis and Mississippi recorded between 1949–52. A couple of unnecessary duplications with Mamlish 3799, but

otherwise a great album. Includes Big Joe Williams' incredibly rare 1949 sides for Bullet, plus Pee Wee Hughes, Little Sam Davis, Earl Hooker, Joe Hill Louis, Sunny Blair, Baby Face Turner, and Junior Brooks.

Rooster Blues 7605 Keep It to Yourself

Field recordings made in Arkansas in the mid-70s by Louis Guida. Features solo country blues performances (mostly with guitar) by W. C. Clay, Mack White, Willie Moore, Trenton Cooper (with piano), and CeDell Davis. There are some fine and interesting performances but, in general, the musical standard is not very high, with many "bum" notes. Much of the material is derivative.

Rounder 2008 Georgia Blues

Nice country-blues field recordings of Jessie Clarence Gorman, George Hollis, Bud Grant, and Willie Rockomo.

Rounder 2013 Wake Up Dead Man

Black worksongs from Texas prisons recorded in the 60s.

Rounder 2014 Get Your Ass in the Water and Swim Like Me

Unexpurgated album of black toasts and street and prison rhymes; not for the squeamish.

Rounder 2016 Ain't Gonna Rain No More

1970s recordings of preblues and blues recorded in Piedmont, North Carolina, featuring John Snipes, Dink Robert, and Jamie Alston.

Southland SLP 21 National Downhome Blues Festival, Vol. 1

Features only two artists: Mississippi bluesman Lonnie Pitchford and Georgia singer/guitarist Precious Bryant. Pitchford, one of the youngest at the festival, plays in the most archaic style. He accompanies his singing with a homemade electric one-string guitar, an instrument that is descended from African one-string instruments. Lonnie both picks and uses slide on the instrument, and is very adept at overcoming its limitations. Bryant is an enthusiastic singer and adequate guitarist who sticks mostly to overly familiar songs ("Ain't That Loving You Baby," "Black Rat Swing"), although there is one good autobiographical original, "Precious Bryant Staggering Blues."

Southland SLP 22 National Downhome Blues Festival, Vol. 2

Features a half-dozen performers, including the excellent old-time North Carolina singer/guitarist Thomas Burt, who performs three relaxed traditional pieces. Jessie Mae Hemphill turns in a driving, hypnotic number, as does Junior Kimbrough. Sunnyland Slim is in good form and Frank Edwards,

whose recording career dates back to the early 40s, turns in a nice version of "Chicken Raid." The album closes with two sides by those excellent young traditionalists, John Cephas and Phil Wiggins.

Southland SLP 23 National Downhome Blues Festival, Vol. 3

This one is a bit of a mixed bag. John Jackson, as always, turns in a fine performance, and Alabama country blues duo Albert Macon and Robert Thomas are enjoyable. Piano Red does a couple of his old favorites in his spirited fashion. Electric bluesmen Robert Jr. Lockwood and Eddie Kirkland turn in competent though unexciting performances. The two tracks by Snooky Pryor and Homesick James should never have been issued. Snooky sings and plays harmonica well, but Homesick James is so badly out of tune that listening is painful!

Southland SLP 24 National Downhome Blues Festival, Vol. 4

Features the brilliant Dr. Ross, who, as always, is fine and exciting. Although his songs are very familiar, he brings his own unique touch to them. Booker T. Laury is a decent piano player, though his vocals are a bit hard to take. Son Thomas is in typical form: good, though not exciting. Henry Townsend does a couple of fine numbers, one featuring his wife Vernell. Larry Johnson turns in some nice East Coast blues, and the bizarre Hezekiah and The Houserockers (a trombone-led group) perform the popular "Down Home Blues."

Specialty 2149 (c) Dark Muddy Bottom

Great collection of down-home blues recorded in the early 50s, featuring John Lee Hooker, Pinebluff Pete, Big Joe Williams, Lightnin' Hopkins, and Clarence London.

Storyville 842 Blues All Around My Bed

Fine and diverse selection of country blues recorded in early 60s by Pete Welding. Includes Carl Hodges, Big Joe Williams, John Lee Granderson, Johnny Young, and James Robinson.

Testament 2223 Traveling Through the Jungle: Negro Fife and Drum Music from the Deep South

A fascinating album of field recordings of black fife and drum groups that were once popular in the South. This album features Sid Hemphill and his group recorded in Sledge, MS, in 1942 by the Library of Congress, along with 1970 recordings made in Senatobia and Como, MS, and Waverly Hall, GA, by David Evans featuring Ephram Carter and group, J. W. Jones and group, and Napoleon Strickland and group. Amazing stuff.

Wolf 120.911 Giants of Country Blues Guitar, 1967–81

A mixed bag featuring Mississippi country blues artists recorded mostly in their homes. The tracks by the great Son House and Furry Lewis are weak performances, poorly recorded; both artists are much better represented elsewhere. The three tracks by Sam Chatmon are fine but poorly recorded. Eugene Powell (aka Sonny Boy Nelson) was a fine artist but his performances here are a bit erratic. Jack Owens is the most impressive artist here. He gives four magnificent performances, which are among the best recorded, though a couple of the songs are also on Testament 2222. Tommy Johnson's brother Mager is represented on a fine vocal on "Traveling Blues," but the chaotic electric guitar mars the performance. The album winds up with three unexceptional performances by Matt Willis.

Trumpet AA 702 (c,d) Delta Blues—1951

More gems from the Trumpet archives. This one features eight superb tracks by Big Joe Williams (two previously unissued), four by the outstanding Luther Huff, and six by Willie Love.

Vanguard VSD 25/26 (c,d) Great Bluesmen
Vanguard VSD 77/78 (c,d) Great Bluesmen At Newport

Live recordings from Newport, 1959–65. Includes Robert Pete Williams, John Lee Hooker, Sleepy John Estes, Mississippi John Hurt, and Skip James.

COMPACT DISC

Biograph BCD 107 Three Shades of Blues

A beautiful collection of country blues by three of the greatest country blues performers. There are five tracks by Bukka White recorded in 1974 and originally issued on Biograph 12049. Bukka was in great form, with powerful, raspy vocals and slashing slide work on his steel-bodied National guitar. In complete contrast are three performances by fellow Mississippian Skip James from 1964 (originally on Biograph 12016). Unlike Bukka's ferocious approach, Skip's is a more gentle melodic approach with lovely flowing guitar on remakes of three songs he had originally recorded in 1931. A third contrast is provided by Georgia singer and 12-string guitarist Blind Willie McTell, with six songs recorded for Regal in 1949 with Curley Weaver on second guitar (and vocal on one track). Willie was in tremendous form on these recordings and the interplay between the guitars is stunning. All tracks have been remastered from original master tapes and sound is exceptionally fine. There are very few country blues recordings available on CD and this is certainly one of the best.

P-Vine PCD 2104 Sorrow Come Pass Me Around

Reissue of Advent 2805, a great collection of rural gospel music recorded by David Evans in the 60s and early 70s, mostly in Louisiana and Mississippi. Features Ephram Carter and his Fife and Drum Band, Babe Stovall, Rev. Rubin Lacy, Robert "Nighthawk" Johnson, Furry Lewis, Willard Artis, and "Blind Pete" Burrell.

Rykodisc RCD 90155 Blues in the Mississippi Night

An extraordinary documentary collection that has been unavailable for some 30 years. Features a conversation held in New York in 1947 between Sonny Boy Williamson, Big Bill Broonzy, and Memphis Slim, recorded by Alan Lomax. Because of the brtually frank nature of the discussion (for the time), Lomax originally disguised the performers identities under the names of "Sib," "Natchez," and "Leroy." They talk about the blues and about life on the plantation and the horrific repression of the black plantation workers. The conversation is full of anecdotes, ranging from the appalling to the hilarious. There are musical performances interspersed, mostly by Slim, along with several field recordings of work songs, field hollers, and church singing. The original recordings have been cleaned up for CD using the CEDAR system and there are informative and interesting notes by Chris Smith. Also available in Britain as Sequel NEX CD 122.

ESSENTIAL SELECTION

Sequel NEX CD 121 Murderers' Home

A remarkable collection of field recordings made at the infamous Parchman Farm Penitentiary in Mississippi in 1947. Mostly features unaccompanied work songs performed solo or as duos, trios, and, in one case, as a quartet singing to the rhythm of cutting down a tree. It also includes a few accompanied blues; one harmonica-accompanied item by "Alex" and two with vocals and guitars by Bob and Leroy. Excellent sound and informative notes by Chris Smith.

Tomato 2690619-2 A Tribute to Leadbelly: His Songs Sung by His Friends

Live recording of Leadbelly memorial concert, with Arlo Guthrie, Pete Seeger, Sonny Terry and Brownie McGhee, and the Lunenberg Travelers. Twenty-two selections including Leadbelly's best-known songs.

Vanguard VCD 115/6 Blues at Newport

Early 60s recordings of Newport Blues Festivals including old-timers and revivalists.

Zeta 718-2 Rural Blues

Live recordings of Robert Pete Williams, J. C. Burris, Brownie McGhee, Robert Jr. Lockwood, Johnny Shines, Sonny Terry, Dave Van Ronk, Mickey Baker, and Lightnin' Hopkins made between 1974–83. Also includes a 1956 Big Bill Broonzy cut.

MISCELLANEOUS URBAN BLUES

Ace CH 235 (c,d) **Blues Around Midnight**

Eighteen sides recorded for Kent, Modern, and affiliated labels between 1949–72. The emphasis here is on slow and mid-tempo blues, and the album includes quite a few previously unissued recordings. There are two fine previously unissued tracks by Larry Davis, including the fine minor key "Something About You," there's a previously unissued T-Bone Walker track, two fine sides by Lowell Fulson, plus tracks by B. B. King, Jimmy Nelson, Franie Ervin (including the witty "Dragnet Blues"), and previously unissued tracks by Mari Jones and Jimmy Witherspoon. Probably my favorite here is the moving minor-key "Old Man Blues," recorded by Johnny Copeland in 1972 with The Jazz Crusaders. A highly recommended set. CD has two additional songs, one each by Jimmy Nelson and Ray Charles.

Ace CH 250 (c,d) **Bluesville, Vol. 2: Electric Blues**

Complementing Ace CH 247 which focused on the acoustic blues recorded for Bluesville, this one features some more urban-sounding material and also draws on material from the parent Prestige label and the short-lived Tru-Sound label. Included among the 14 tracks are the raucous stylings of Eddie Kirkland, the electric Chicago slide of Homesick James, the sophisticated sound of Memphis Slim, a rare vocal outing by King Curtis, the smooth tenor sax of Buddy Lucas, city blues shouting of Jimmy Witherspoon, plus tracks by Lightnin' Hopkins, Sonny Terry, Roosevelt Sykes, and Billy Boy Arnold. The CD features 4 extra tracks by some of the same artists.

Ace CH 276 (c,d) **Kings of the Blues**

A terrific, diverse collection of blues from the archives of Los Angeles' Modern, Specialty, and Combo labels reproduced with crystal clear clarity that makes it hard to believe that some of these recordings are almost 40 years old! Included are B. B. King (the rare 45-rpm version of "Sweet Little Angel"), Guitar Slim, Frankie Lee Sims (the previously unissued "I'll Get Along Somehow"), Flash Terry (fine Oklahoma singer/guitarist), T-Bone Walker, Howlin' Wolf, Smokey Hogg, Clifton Chenier, Johnny Fuller, and Elmore James. The CD and cassette versions have four extra tracks (Bumble Bee Slim, Gus Jenkins, Chuck Higgins, and a pre-

viously unissued track by Pee Wee Crayton). Brief but enthusiastic notes by Ted Carroll.

Ace CHA 216 (c,d) **The Fifties—Juke Joint Blues**

Twenty great blues sides from the Modern, RPM, and Flair labels. Although some of these tracks are currently available on other Ace LPs and many were issued some years back on Kent, this beautifully remastered collection is a joy to listen to. Includes such great tracks as "Three O'Clock Blues" by B. B. King, a dynamite version of Robert Johnson's "Rambling on My Mind" by Boyd Gilmore, a duet by Junior Parker and Bobby Bland on "Love My Baby," the doomy "This Is the End" by James Reed, the dynamic "Jake Head Boogie" by Lightnin' Hopkins, the mysterious Dixie Blues Boys doing "Monte Carlo" with two harmonicas, and a marvelous previously unissued Joe Hill Louis track, "Good Morning Little Angel." Other artists include Elmore James, Howlin' Wolf, George Smith, Floyd Dixon, and Mercy Dee. CD has two additional tracks. No discographical information but interesting notes by Mike Rowe.

Ace CHA 232 (c,d) **Blues Guitar Blasters**

A great collection of electric blues guitar from Modern, Kent, RPM, Specialty, and Stax, featuring 20 tracks from the 50s and 60s. However, this set is a bit frustrating for the collector, as many of the cuts here have been out before on Ace. As a teaser, the album includes the splendid previously unissued "After Hours" by Jimmy Nolen and the wild "Twisting the Strings" by Ike Turner. Other artists include Albert King, Lowell Fulson, B. B. King, Elmore James, Lafayette Thomas, Guitar Slim, Johnny "Guitar" Watson, Pee Wee Crayton, T-Bone Walker, and John Lee Hooker. Excellent sound and interesting notes by Neil Slaven.

Antones 004 (c,d) **Tenth Anniversary Anthology, Vol. 1**

Ten tracks recorded live at the famous Antones Club in Austin, Texas, in July 1985. Except for Albert Collins, this is a Chicago blues album, featuring Snooky Eddie Taylor, James Cotton, Sunnyland Slim, Buddy Guy, Pinetop Perkins, Otis Rush, and Jimmy Rogers. The late, great Eddie Taylor turns in a hard-driving "If You Don't Want Me Baby," accompanied by Pryor, Rogers, Slim, Bob Strogher (b), and Timothy Taylor (drm). This group of musicians is also featured on Pryor's "How'd You Learn To Shake It Like That." Guy turns in excellent versions of "Look On Yonder's Wall" and "Things I Used To Do." Rush does a chilling version of his classic "Double Trouble," and Collins does a good job on "Cold Cold Feeling." Though recorded live, the sound is excellent. There are no surprises here, just some solid blues singing and playing. CD has three extra tracks.

Arhoolie 1030 Berkeley Blues Festival
Mance Lipscomb, Clifton Chenier, and Lightnin' Hopkins.

Atlantic 81695-1 (c,d) Atlantic Blues: Guitar
Twenty-four tracks by 17 different artists including one track from Blind Willie McTell's brilliant 1949 session for Atlantic and one by Fred McDowell recorded by Alan Lomax in 1959. There is a nice previously unissued Sticks McGhee cut from 1949 with guitar by brother Brownie, and three tracks featuring fine, though obscure, Houston guitarist Texas Johnny Brown. There are two tracks from T-Bone Walker's brilliant 1957 session for Atlantic; he is followed by LA guitarist Chuck Norris, who was very strongly influenced by him, both vocally and instrumentally. The king of slide guitar, Elmore James, is featured on Big Joe Turner's classic recording of "T.V. Mama," and the brilliant New York guitarist Mickey Baker is heard on the splendid "Midnight Midnight." Also includes John Lee Hooker, Guitar Slim, Cornell Dupree, Al King (with great guitar by Johnny Heartsman), Ike and Tina Turner, B. B. King (recorded live in Puerto Rico in 1972), Albert King (two classic Stax sides), John Hammond Jr., and Stevie Ray Vaughan. CD has fewer tracks.

Austin 8301 An Austin Rhythm and Blues Christmas
Featuring The Fabulous Thunderbirds, Lou Ann Barton, and Paul Ray.

Bellaphon BID 8026 Risky Blues
Fine collection of blues and R&B recordings from the 50s recorded for King and Federal, featuring risque lyrics. Includes such classics as "Big Ten Inch Record" by Bull Moose Jackson, "It Ain't The Meat" by the Swallows, "Lovin' Machine" by Wynonie Harris, and 11 others.

Black Top 1044 Black Top Blues-Arama Live. . .
Black Top label blues artists recorded live at Tipitina's in New Orleans. Includes Anson Funderburgh and The Rockets with Sam Myers, Ron Levy, and Grady Gaines.

Black Top 1045 Black Top Blues Arama Live— Vol. 2
More live recordings from Tipitina's, featuring Nappy Brown, Earl King, Ronnie Earl, and James "Thunderbird" Davis.

Blues Classics 23 Juke Joint Blues
Great down-home blues from the 50s, including Eddie Burns, Harvey Hill, L. C. Williams, Alvin Smith, and Sonny Boy Holmes.

Cascade DROP 1001 (c) Twenty Great R&B Hits of the 50s
Excellent budget-priced collection of blues and R&B cuts mostly from the Ace and Modern group of labels, many previously issued on individual albums on the English Ace label. Includes Huey Piano Smith, B. B. King, John Lee Hooker, Pee Wee Crayton, The Queens, Jimmy Witherspoon, Howlin' Wolf, The Cadets, Roscoe Gordon, Joe and Ann, and Little Willie Littlefield.

Cascade DROP 1005 (c) Twenty Great Blues Recordings of the 50s and 60s
A marvelous budget-priced collection of recordings mostly from the Modern group of labels. Includes Lightnin' Hopkins, Roosevelt Sykes, Jimmy Witherspoon, John Lee Hooker, Lonnie the Cat, Johnny "Guitar" Watson, and Little Willie Littlefield.

Cascade DROP 1010 (c) Twenty Great Blues Recordings of the 50s and 60, Vol. 2
Twenty more great sides drawn from the Modern group of labels: Ace, Combo, and Specialty. Although most of these cuts have been issued on other Ace albums, this is a great collection. Includes Elmore James, Roy Hawkins, Johnny "Guitar" Watson, Frankie Lee Sims, Earl King, Little Willie Littlefield, Pee Wee Crayton, Bumble Bee Slim, and Joe Hill Louis.

Chicago 202 Collector's Blues Series, Vol. 1
This LP and the four following albums on the Chicago label have minimal packaging and no notes, but do feature some nice reissues of 50s urban blues sides that are not available elsewhere. Volume 1 includes Rocky Fuller, Barrelhouse Blott, Square Walton, Carl Campbell, Camille Howard, and George Vann.

Chicago 205 Collector's Blues Series, Vol. 2
Sticks McGhee, Carolyn Hayes, Zilla Mays, Bobby Prince, Danny Taylor, Camille Howard, and Red Mack.

Chicago 210 Collector's Blues Series, Vol. 3
Joe "Mr. G" August, Tulsa Red, Elmon Mickle, Lee Richardson, and Little Willie Littlefield.

Chicago 212 Collector's Blues Series, Vol. 4
Sunnyland Slim, Jackie Brenston, Galveston Green, Luther Huff, Rudy Green, and Great Gates.

Chicago 213 Collector's Blues Series, Vol. 5
Camille Howard, Max Bailey, Scat Man Bailey, Annisteen Allen, Eddie Gorman, Eddie Chamblee, and Todd Rhodes and His Toddlers.

Collectables 5127 (c,d) **The Collectables Blues Collection, Vol. 1**

Collectables 5128 (c,d) **The Collectables Blues Collection, Vol. 2**

Collectables 5129 (c,d) **The Collectables Blues Collection, Vol. 3**

Each disc carries a generous 16-song selection with three or four rare nuggets by artists who are, as far as I know, making their first CD appearance: Thelma Cooper, George Grant and The Rockin' Highlanders, Daisy Mae and The Hepcats, James Crawford, J. B. Summers, and many more really up the ante for you collectors. The drawbacks are minimal packaging, inattention to remastering details, resulting in merely average sound quality, and no liner notes. The inclusion of well-known tracks by Howlin' Wolf, Muddy Waters, and Little Walter from Chess and an abundance of Jimmy Reed hits, presumably from the Vee Jay label, is irritating; why don't they reissue classic material that languishes in the vaults, rather than padding out the lineup with the most commonly heard standards from other labels? Beats me. Anyway, get these for a great selection of hits and obscurities from Lightnin' Hopkins, Elmore James, Sonny Terry, Buster Brown, Screamin' Jay Hawkins with Tiny Grimes, and Champion Jack Dupree.

Collector CCSLP 103 (d) White Boy Blues

Two-LP set of late 60s recordings featuring Eric Clapton, Clapton and Jimmy Page, John Mayall and The Bluesbreakers, The All Stars (featuring Page, Jeff Beck, and Nicky Hopkins), Santa Barbara Machine Head (with Ron Wood), and Jeremy Spencer.

Collector CCSLP 142 (d) White Boy Blues, Vol. 2

Another 2-LP set of early British Blues, mostly from the Immediate and Decca labels. Main groups and performers here are Tony "T. S." McPhee, Savoy Brown Blues Band (1967 Purdah singles with Bob Hall on piano), current country guitar hero Albert Lee (three 1968 sides), and John Mayall, heard doing "Hideaway" and "On Top Of The World" with Eric Clapton and "The Supernatural" with Peter Green, along with early Ten Years After doing "Crossroads," Rod Stewart, Dharma Blues Band (with future Hawkwind leader Dave Brock), and The Cyril Davies All Stars in an unissued version of "Not Fade Away."

Detour 33-006 Still Groove Jumping

A great collection of hard-driving blues recorded in New York for RCA's Groove subsidiary between 1954–56. This album features lots of great guitar by Mickey Baker, plus other great New York studio musicians like King Curtis, Sam "The Man" Taylor, Al Lucas, and Panama Francis. Highlights for me are the three previously unissued tracks by guitarist Larry Dale, who lays down his guitar to do some fine singing and leaves the fretwork to Baker, who does some devastating playing on "Midnight Hours." Baker is also much in evidence on the powerful "Country Boy," by Big Tiny Kennedy. There are three novelty vocal tracks by gravel-voiced Mr. Bear, plus one instrumental under his name, featuring hot sax by King Curtis and Sam Taylor. Other tracks include Roy Gaines, The Du-Droppers (a previously unissued take), Piano Red (including his classic "Rockin' with Red"), Buddy Lucas, Champion Jack Dupree, and Arthur "Big Boy" Crudup. Since this label is run by mastering engineer Bob Jones, the sound is superb, there are full discographical details, and informative notes by Bez Turner.

Gusto 5018 (c,d) Merry Christmas Baby

Fifteen sides by Charles Brown, Mabel Scott, Johnny Moore's Blazers, Freddy King, Lowell Fulson, Lloyd Glenn, and Jimmy Witherspoon.

Hi (UK) DHIUKLP 427 Hi Records—The Blues Sessions

This splendid 2-LP set features all the blues recordings cut for Memphis's Hi label and its MOC subsidiary in the 60s and early 70s, and are among the last commercial recordings of blues made in Memphis by a relatively good-sized label. Many of the recordings were produced by the multi-talented Willie Mitchell. There are six tracks by the fine soul-flavored Don Hines, including a fine version of "Stormy Monday Blues" and the intense "Trouble Is My Name." Big Amos Patton and Big Lucky Carter are more down-home-flavored performers and have six tracks each. There are four tracks by the very fine Detroit singer Joe L. Carter, including his topical "Please Mr. Foreman," and a searing version of "As the Years Go Passing By." The rest of the set features the more blues-oriented recordings of R&B/soul artists Don Bryant, Willie Mitchell, Gene Miller, and George Jackson. Some fine stuff.

Kent (UK) 069 Blues And Soul Power

Unlike most albums in this series, this collection is as much blues as soul, featuring 16 sides recorded for the Kent and Modern labels between 1963-70. The album opens up with Johnny Otis and his gang on the X-rated "Signifying Monkey." There is more fine blues from B. B. King, Lowell Fulson, and Al King, while for R&B and soul we have Z.Z. Hill, Ike and Tina Turner, Vernon Garett, and Tommy Youngblood. A fine collection.

King 528 (c,d) After Hours

It's 3 A.M., and there you are at the Dew Drop Inn, too broke, too drunk, or just too blue to go out and hit that long highway home. Life just wouldn't be worth livin' if it weren't for the cool after-hours sounds these cats are puttin' down: Sonny Thompson, Earl Bostic, Todd Rhodes, guitarists Bill Jennings, Pete Lewis, and Jimmy Nolen, all blowing soft, sweet, and reet in a solid nocturnal groove. Lots of slinky sax, laid-back ivories, and dreamy guitar on 10 all-instrumental cuts, with the original King cover. Take it from me, you can't get anything this mellow anymore without a prescription.

King 668 (c,d) Battle Of The Blues, Vol. 4

Features Roy Brown, Cleanhead Vinson, and Wynonie Harris.

King 859 Turn Back the Clock

Reissue of long-out-of-print collection of 12 tracks from the 40s and early 50s drawn from the vast archives of King Records. Although it includes tracks that are readily available elsewhere (of Memphis Slim, Lonnie Johnson, and Eddie "Cleanhead" Vinson), it also includes rare tracks like postwar recordings by prewar favorites Johnny Temple and Jimmy Gordon, a 1945 recording of Walter Brown's "Confessin' the Blues," and a harmonica solo by Pete "Guitar" Lewis (!). The track labelled "Flub" by Memphis Slim is really "Stomp Boogie" by John Lee Hooker. Good stuff!

King 875 (c,d) Everybody's Favorite Blues

Welcome reissue of a collection taken from King's vast recorded legacy. An even dozen blues and R&B tunes, including some hard-to-come-by items along with the better-known tunes. How about Ralph Willis' "Door Bell Blues," Johnny O'Neal's "Ruth Ann," Harold Tinsley's "Bad News Blues," and Robert Richard's "Root Hog," just for starters. Some real good ones here.

ESSENTIAL SELECTION

Krazy Kat 783 Nashville Jumps

A wonderful selection of urban blues recorded for the Nashville-based Bullet and J-B labels between 1946–53. Includes both sides of B. B. King's first two records, plus excellent cuts by Cecil Gant, Wynonie Harris, Rudy Greene, St. Louis Jimmy, The Red Miller Trio, and Guitar Slim.

Krazy Kat 793 Blues Women

With Taft Jordan.

Krazy Kat 803 Gotham House Party

This album kicks off an ongoing series of reissues from the Gotham label. It's a sampler of material recorded from 1949–53, including the rocking "Roly Poly Mama" by Harry Crafton, with a fine wailing sax break, the mellow Eddie Cole on "That's Right," Charlie Gonzales sounding like Calvin Boze on the jumping "I'm Free," and a down-in-the-alley T. N. T. Tribble on "House Party." Other jive cats include J. B. Summers with Tiny Grimes, Bill Jennings, Sax Gill, Frank Motley, Jimmy Preston, The Jones Boys, Johnny Sparrow, Danny Turner, and Daisy Mae and The Hepcats. Sleeve notes by Bruce Bastin trace the birth and growth of the Gotham label.

Krazy Kat 808 Brown Gal—Camille Howard, Dorothy Donnegan, Lil Armstrong

This volume of Gotham masters features female boogie pianists. Side one features six 1946 Miltone recordings by Roy Milton and His Solid Senders with Camille Howard on piano and a few vocals. Also includes Milton's re-recordings of "RM Blues" and "Milton's Boogie," plus Camille's own vocals on "Mr. Fine," "Groovy Blues," and "If I Had You." Lil Hardin Armstrong, Louis's wife and pianist during the 20s, is heard on fine R&B sides from 1950 with unknown backing featuring a fine bluesy guitar. She performs the title tune (later a hit for The Jive Bombers as "Bad Boy"), plus previously unissued takes of "Baby Daddy" and "Rock It." Finally there are two fine boogie instrumentals from Donnegan.

Krazy Kat 814 Big Band Blues—Tiny Tim, Jimmy Rushing, and Ernie Fields

Fourteen tunes from the Gotham vaults recorded in the early 50s. Mostly Jimmy Rushing and Ernie Fields, with a cut by J. B. Summers and three by Tiny Tim (no, not that one!). Rushing does "Lotsa Poppa," "Fool's Blues," plus three others.

Krazy Kat 820 Alley Special

Great collection of down-home blues from the Gotham and 20th Century labels, though most of it was leased from elsewhere. The most interesting track historically is "Mean Red Spider," which was issued by James "Sweet Lucy" Carter on 20th Century in 1946 but turns out to be Muddy Waters performing his first commercial recording, one of the staples of his repertoire, accompanied by an urban band with a truly appalling soprano sax. The rest of the album is not as interesting historically but is far superior musically, and includes three tracks by the amazing Texas singer/guitarist Wright Holmes, featuring some amazing jagged guitar and intense vocals. There are two tracks each by splendid Louisiana bluesmen David Pete McKinley and Stick Horse Hammond, one by California singer/harmonica player Sonny Boy Johnson, two by the wonderful Detroit singer/guitarist Baby Boy Warren, two previously unissued sides by the mysterious

W. H. Harris (a fine gruff-voiced singer accompanied by guitar, bass, and drums), and a previously unissued cut by Eddie Burns. Excellent sound and informative notes by Chris Smith.

Krazy Kat 834 Philadelphia Boogie
Although reissued from Philadelphia's Gotham label, this features recordings cut primarily in Chicago and California, the former from the legendary J. Mayo Williams and the latter from Roy Milton's Miltone label. The Chicago recordings, with the exception of veteran prewar piano player Lee Brown's "Bobbie Town Boogie," are generally undistinguished. Duke Groner's plummy version of the Dinah Washington hit "Blow Top Blues" is pretty mediocre. The West Coast recordings are more lively, with interesting material from veteran West Coast drummer Jesse Price (the unsung hero of West Coast blues), Maxwell Davis, and powerful blues shouter Ed "The Great Gates" White.

ESSENTIAL SELECTION

Krazy Kat 7431 Nashville R&B, Vol. 1
Documents Nashville's R&B in 1951–56. The emphasis is on jumping blues, boogie, and shuffles with honking saxes and shouted vocals. There are four fine instrumentals by bands led by sax player Louis Brooks. Brooks' band also accompanies singers Helen Foster and Earl Gaines. Kid King's Combo has one instrumental cut with fine piano by Skippy Brooks and hot sax; this band also accompanies down-home vocalist Good Rockin' Sam. Also includes Charles Ruckles and His Orchestra, Tommy McGhee (some very jazz-oriented sax), and The Blue Flamers. Fine and obscure material, well-programmed, with interesting notes by Martin Hawkins and Hank Davis putting the music into perspective.

Krazy Kat 7442 New Jersey Burners
A rug-cutting set of jumpers and stompers culled from a slew of small New Jersey labels, including On The Square, De Luxe, and Alton. Featured artists are Johnny "Rockhouse" Green, Bird Rollins, Eddie "Big Blues" Carson, Little Luther, Buddy Love and His Blue Flames, Joe "Guitar" Tubbs, Gene Franklin and His House Rockin' Spacemen, Terry Orlon, and Dave "Baby" Cortez. These performances give us a frantic insight into the frenzied late 50s and early 60s. Great cover picture.

Krazy Kat 7448 Tough Mamas
Hot blues and R&B from female singers recorded in the 50s. Includes Big Mama Thornton, Honey Brown, Joe Evans, Gladys Bentley, and Sheri Washington.

L+R42.006 The Blues Sampler
One track from each of the first 12 L+R albums.

L+R42.010 Early Morning Blues
Washboard Doc (whbd), Lucky (gtr, vcl), and Flash (b, humazoo, vcl), with Louisiana Red.

L+R42.013 American Folk Blues Festival, 1980
Two-LP set recorded live during the 1980 blues tour of Europe featuring Louisiana Red, Sunnyland Slim, Willie Mabon, Carey Bell, Hubert Sumlin, Eddie Taylor, and Bob Stroger. Not a great set of performances but some very good moments, and Carey Bell's harp playing is exceptionally fine.

L+R42.017 American Folk Blues Festival, 1962
CD issue: L+R CD 2017
Recordings of the first blues tour of Europe. Excellent performances by T-Bone Walker, Sonny Terry, John Lee Hooker, and Shakey Jake. This album has been reissued many times before so check your collection!

L+R42.018 American Folk Blues Festival, 1972
CD issue: L+R CD 2018
Two-LP set featuring live recordings cut in Germany, one album of country blues and the other of urban blues. Decent performances by Bukka White, Big Joe Williams, Robert Pete Williams, Memphis Slim, Big Mama Thornton, T-Bone Walker, Jimmy Rogers, and Jimmy Dawkins.

L+R42.021 American Folk Blues Festival, 1970
CD issue: L+R CD 2021
Two-LP set recorded live in Germany, featuring the Chicago Blues All Stars, Shakey Horton, Bukka White, Champion Jack Dupree, and Sonny Terry and Brownie McGhee.

L+R42.022 American Folk Blues Festival, 1981
Two-LP set featuring a mixture of country and urban blues artists, including Louisiana Red, Margie Evans, Bowling Green John and Phil Wiggins, Lurrie Bell, Bob Stroger, and Hubert Sumlin.

L+R42.023 American Folk Blues Festival, 1963
CD issue: L+R CD 2023-2
Recorded live in Germany and previously issued on European Fontana. Excellent selections by Memphis Slim, Victoria Spivey, Sonny Boy Williamson, Otis Spann, and Muddy Waters.

L+R42.024 American Folk Blues Festival, 1964
CD issue: L+R CD 2024
Reissue of live recording cut in Germany documenting one of the most exciting blues tours of Europe in the 60s, featuring Sonny Boy Williamson, Lightnin' Hopkins, Sleepy John Estes, John Henry Barbee, Sugar Pie Desanto, and Howlin' Wolf, with

Hubert Sumlin, Willie Dixon, Sunnyland Slim, and Clifton James as backup!

L+R42.025 American Folk Blues Festival, 1965
CD issue: L+R CD 2025

Very fine recordings cut in Germany, previously available on Fontana but out of print for many years. Includes Fred McDowell, J. B. Lenoir (with Walter Horton [harp]), Walter Horton (with Buddy Guy, Jimmy Lee, and Fred Below), Roosevelt Sykes (With Guy, Lee, and Below), Eddie Boyd (also backed by Guy, Lee, and Below), John Lee Hooker (with Guy and Below), and Doctor Ross.

L+R42.052 Blues Live '82

Two-LP set featuring live recordings cut in Germany, half country blues and the rest urban blues. Features James Son Thomas (quite good), Archie Edwards (fine East Coast country blues), Lurrie Bell and Billy Branch, Blues Harp Meeting (unaccompanied blues harmonica trio), and Margie Evans.

L+R 42.063 American Folk Blues Festival, Live '83

Two-LP set recorded live in Germany, featuring folky Tennessee bluesman James "Sparky" Rucker, Louisiana Red and His Chicago Blues Friends (Jimmy Rogers, Lovie Lee, Carey Bell), New York country bluesman Larry Johnson, remarkable Mississippi bluesman Lonnie Pitchford, who plays some extraordinary one-string guitar on a couple of cuts, Louisiana Red and Carey Bell, Lovie Lee and band, and Queen Sylvia Embry and band. Some good material here but the best could have been condensed into one very strong album!

L+R 50.002 American Folk Blues Festival

Documents the 1983 Folk Blues Festival Tour. A few cuts are from previously issued L+R albums but most have not been issued before. Includes Louisiana Red, Sparkey Rucker, Larry Johnson, Lonnie Pitchford, Lovey Lee, and Queen Sylvia. Unexceptional.

Malaco 7430 (c) The Blues Is Alright

A sampler of 10 songs, mostly drawn from various Malaco albums. It naturally includes Z. Z. Hill's big hit, "Down Home Blues," plus Denise LaSalle's X-rated version of the same song, along with songs by Little Milton, McKinley Mitchell (the soulful "The End Of The Rainbow" from a Chimneyville album), Dorothy Moore, Johnnie Taylor, Bobby Bland, and Latimore.

Malaco 7438 (c) The Blues Is Alright, Vol. 2

Sampler mostly drawn from various Malaco LPs. Includes "Members Only" by Bobby Bland, "Don't Mess With My Tu Tu" by Denise LaSalle, "Let's Straighten It Out" by Latimore, "St. James Infir-

mary" by Bobby Bland, "Sweet Sixteen" by B. B. King, and "Part Time Lover, Full Time Fool" by Formula IV.

Malaco 7449 The Blues Is Alright, Vol. III

An odd collection including recent Malaco recordings along with 30-year-old titles from Kent and Vee Jay. Includes tracks by Bobby "Blue" Bland, Latimore, Little Milton, Johnnie Taylor, Jimmy Reed, and B. B. King.

Mamlish 3799 Home Again Blues

A tremendous album featuring some of the rarest postwar blues records, most of which have never appeared on album before. Some beautiful down-home and country blues performances by Luther Huff, Sonny Boy Johnson, Bluesboy Bill, Sunnyland Slim, Hot Rod Happy, Hank Kilroy, Baby Face Leroy, and Brother Willie Eason. A classic album!

Mamlish 3800 Black Cat Trail

Great, diverse collection of postwar blues, featuring Elmore James, Johnny Howard, Robert Nighthawk, and Willie Lane.

Moonshine 102 A Taste of Harp

Postwar blues harmonica, featuring 14 rare sides from the 60s and early 70s by The Right Kind, Big John Wrencher, Tommy Louis, Big Jay McNeely, and Ace Holder. Although there are some very good performances, there is quite a bit of material that can best be described as filler.

Moonshine 117 Take a Greyhound Bus and Ride

Fabulous collection of front porch rockin' blues taken from hither and yon: Mississippi, Tennessee, Texas, and Chicago. Four of Jerry McCain's best recordings are here, including "Trying to Please," and "My Next Door Neighbor." Betty James is just sensational on her two cuts, especially the hypnotic "I'm a Little Mixed Up." Woodrow Adams' deep vocals and exciting harp playing, backed by a tough little band, enliven the proceedings. Also featured are juke-joint heroes McKinley James, John Hogg, Juke Boy Bonner, Model T. Slim, G. L. Crockett, and Little Eddie, each one with a tough tale or two to tell.

Muse 5212 Cryin' in the Morning

Reissue of fine down-home blues from the vaults of Savoy/Regal. Most of these tracks are available elsewhere. Includes Frank Edwards, Blind Willie McTell, Curley Weaver, Dennis McMillan, and David Wylie.

New World 261 Straighten Up and Fly Right

A fine collection of blues and R&B from the end of the swing era to the birth of rock 'n' roll. Fourteen tracks by Tiny Bradshaw, The Clovers, Cecil Gant, Lionel Hampton, Lightnin' Hopkins, The Ravens, Joe Turner, and Muddy Waters.

O.B.C. 508 South Side Blues
Reissue of Riverside 9403 from 1961, featuring Mama Yancey, Walter Vinson, and Little Brother Montgomery.

O.B.C. 520 (c) Songs We Taught Your Mother
Reissue of Bluesville 1052 from 1961. Fine set of jazz/blues from three popular artists who originally recorded in the 20s and 30s: Alberta Hunter, Lucille Hegamin, and Victoria Spivey, accompanied by excellent small jazz bands. Hunter and Spivey are accompanied by the splendid Buster Bailey (clr), J. C. Higginbotham (trb), and Cliff Jackson, while Hegamin is accompanied by a smaller group with Willie "The Lion" Smith (pno) and Henry Goodwin (tpt). Hunter and Spivey sound great; Spivey sounded very little changed in 1961 from her recordings 30 years earlier and is in better form than on the recordings on her own label. Although Alberta wasn't as strong as on her earlier sides, she was fine and continued that way for another 25 years! Lucille Hegamin is the least interesting artist here; her singing is much more in the pop vaudeville style.

O.B.C. 1202 (c) Original Blues Classics
A budget-priced, 15-track sampler of recordings drawn from the various Original Blues Classics albums, featuring reissues from Bluesville, Prestige, Riverside, and affiliated labels. Includes Jimmy Witherspoon, Memphis Slim, Eddie Kirkland, Pink Anderson, Blind Willie McTell, Alberta Hunter, Reverend Gary Davis, and Sonny Terry.

ESSENTIAL SELECTION

CA 6279 (c) The RCA Victor Blues and Rhythm Revue
Here are 28 choice examples of the history of R&B (1940–59) hand-picked by the man who coined the term, Jerry Wexler; his straightforward sleeve notes guide one through the changes exemplified by major big bands and soloists, vocal groups, and jump-blues outfits. This outstanding gatefold double set includes Erskine Hawkins ("After Hours"), two excellent Earl Hines cuts featuring Billy Eckstine, Rene Hall's "Two Guitar Boogie" with Van Walls on piano, Cab Calloway's jumpin' "Rooming House Boogie," Lucky Millinder with the pipes of Annisteen Allen, Count Basie, Jesse Stone, Mr. Sad Head, Blow Top Lynn, previously reissued Little Richard, The Heartbreakers, stompin' Du Droppers, The Isley Brothers, and more. Highly recommended.

RCA Bluebird 6758 (c,d) How Blue Can You Get?
Subtitled "Great Blues Vocals in the Jazz Tradition," this fine collection starts with Leadbelly's famous 12-string "Good Morning Blues," and contines with Satchmo's humorous 1947 live recording of "Back o' Town Blues," Jack Teagarden's "St. Louis Blues," Mildred Bailey's perky "That Ain't Right," Lonnie Johnson's excellent "Crowing Rooster Blues," with Lil Armstrong on piano, Teddy Bunn's "Evil Man's Blues," with Hot Lips Page playing some righteous trumpet, Lil Green's classic "Why Don't You Do Right," with Broonzy on guitar, and Wingy Manone's jumpin' "Corrine Corrina Blues." Side two opens with Fats Waller's hilarious "Bessie, Bessie," followed by the mellow Three Blazers on "How Blue Can You Get," Billy Eckstine crooning "Stormy Monday Blues" with Earl Hines, Little Richard's jumpin' "Taxi Blues" from 1951, Jimmy Rushing's "Brand New Wagon" with Basie, Tiny Davis' impressive "Tiny Boogie," supported by the all-female Sweethearts of Rhythm, Joe Williams "Rocks in My Bed," and "Just Another Woman," by Hot Lips Page. CD has three extra cuts by Maxine Sullivan, Helen Humes, and Ruby Smith. An impressive collection.

Red Lightnin' 006 When Girls Do It
Two-LP set, featuring a diverse selection of 50s and 60s reissues of Bobby "Guitar" Bennett, Little Oscar, Magic Slim, Sam Baker, and Driftin' Charles.

Red Lightnin' 0033 The Devil's Music
From the soundtrack of a British TV series.

Red Lightnin' 0038 More Devil's Music
More selections from the soundtrack of the British TV program "The Devil's Music," which, alas, has not been shown in the US. Side one of the album features six excellent live sides recorded by tough St. Louis blues singer/guitarist James De Shay, accompanied by a small group. Sound is not great but the performances of some familiar songs are very good. The second side features some nice performances by Big Joe Williams, Henry Townsend, and Victoria Spivey.

Red Lighnin 0060 The Unissued 1963 Blues Festival
The blues package that toured Europe in 1963 featuring Memphis Slim, Big Joe Williams, Willie Dixon, Victoria Spivey, and Matt Murphy was recorded several times, but, up to now, only one set of recordings has been issued on LP—the October 13 concert in Bremen, and those recordings have been reissued several times. This album features previously unissued recordings made in Ober-

hausen, Germany, and features recordings by Memphis Slim (four songs), Sonny Boy Williamson (five songs), and two instrumentals by Matt "Guitar" Murphy. Accompaniments are provided by Willie Dixon (b) and Billy Stepney (drm). There are some decent performances here, particularly by Sonny Boy Williamson. The reason that this set was not issued before is probably due to the annoying 60-cycle hum that exists all the way through the recordings and makes extended listening uncomfortable!

Red Lightnin' 0064 **Down on Broadway and Main**

Complementing Red Lightnin' 0047, this is an excellent selection of blues and R&B recorded in St. Louis between 1956–66. Includes Billy Gayles with the Ike Turner Band, Little Aaron (Andrew Odum, with fine guitar by Willie Kizart), Benny Sharp and His Band, and the instrumental group The Earthworms, which included Little Milton on guitar and Oliver Sain on tenor sax. Excellent notes by St. Louis researcher Bill Greensmith.

RR Esoldun 2020 **Jump the Boogie**

A nice selection of upbeat boogie recorded by various artists, mostly West Coast, in the late 40s and early 50s. Some of these tracks have been reissued elsewhere, but there is a lot of stuff that has not been on LP before. Highlights are two jumping tracks by Luke Jones, James Wayne's "Please Baby Please," Dennis "Long Man" Binder's hot "I'm a Lover" (with hot guitar by Vincent Dulong), and Joe Brown's jumping Detroit effort "Leroy Sent Me." Also included are Rufus Beacham, Junior Blues, Jimmy Wilson, and Percy Mayfield.

RR Esoldun 2021 **I Want to Boogie Woogie**

Fourteen solid senders featuring piledriving eight-to-the-bar rhythm. Another solid RR Esoldun anthology, this time with black boogie and blues, mostly from the late 40s through early 50s, most never before on microgroove. Includes Marvin Phillips and His Men from Mars ("Wine Woogie"), Ray Agee ("Wobble Loo"), Cousin Joe with Dickie Welle's Blue Seven ("Come Down Baby," "Don't Pay No Mind"), Roosevelt Sykes ("Walkin' the Boogie"), and The Buster Bennett Trio performing the title tune. Rompin', stompin' piano and booting sax. Highest recommendations.

RR Esoldun 2022 **Rockin' the Blues**

A diverse mixture of postwar blues from the 50s, mostly uptempo and with harmonica. Some of these tracks are available elswhere, but this is an enjoyable collection, including two fine and very rare cuts from the Delta label by Little Milton (not the same Little Milton as Little Milton Campbell). The album also includes Freddy King's rare first recordings for El+Beein made in 1956, nice but not typical of his later work. It also includes Eddie Hope's great "A Fool No More," the fine country blues of McKinley James, plus tracks by Tender Slim and Willie King (with the Ike Turner Band).

Rogue FMSL 2016 **Matchbox Days**

A fun and nostalgic collection of acoustic country blues as recorded by various English blues interpreters for the Matchbox label between 1967–70. In most cases the performers have tried to remain faithful to the spirit of the black artists of the 20s and 30s, and we have some fine guitar playing here from Mike Cooper, Dave Kelly, and Al Jones. However, the vocals are far less convincing and Al Jones' prim English enunciation of Blind Willie McTell's "Searching the Desert" is very silly indeed. On the other hand, Jo Ann Kelly's interpretation of Memphis Minnie's "Northin' in Ramblin'" is really quite convincing. Other artists here include John James, The Panama Limited Jug Band, and Ian Anderson (no, not that Ian Anderson!). There's nothing here for the serious blues enthusiast but it certainly is fun!

Savoy 2233 (c) **Ladies Sing the Blues**

Two-LP set featuring female blues and R&B singers recorded by Savoy in the late 40s and early 50s. Thirty songs by Miss Rhapsody, Albinia Jones, Linda Hopkins, Little Esther, and Big Maybelle.

Savoy 2234 **Honkers and Screamers**

Featuring Lee Allen, Big Jay McNeely, and Hal Singer.

Savoy 2244 **The Shouters**

Two-LP set of fine blues and R&B shouters from the late 40s and early 50s, including Gatemouth Moore, Chicago Carl Davis, Eddie Mack, H-Bomb Ferguson, and Nappy Brown.

Savoy 2255 **Southern Blues**

Volume 11 in the series of double albums drawn from the Savoy catalogue featuring recordings of blues singers living in the South or who had recently moved from the South. Most of this material has never been issued on album and quite a bit has never been issued in any form. Includes seven superb 1948 cuts by John Lee Hooker, plus country blues by Little Boy Fuller and Ralph Willis, New Orleans blues by Billy Tate and Earl King, and Georgia recordings by Billy Wright.

Savoy 2256 **Ladies Sing the Blues, Vol. 2**

Thirty-two sides by seven fine female blues singers who recorded for Savoy between 1944–57. Features Albinia Jones, Little Miss Sharecropper, Annie Laurie, Big Maybelle, and Varetta Dillard. Beautifully produced with excellent notes by Bob Porter.

Specialty 2117 (c) This Is How It All Began, Vol. 1
Superb album drawing on the Specialty vaults. Fourteen great recordings of gospel, country blues, city blues, blues ballads, and jump and boogie recorded between 1945–55. Includes Chosen Gospel Singers, Alex Bradford, John Lee Hooker, Mercy Dee, Joe Liggins, The Four Flames, and Roy Milton. With extensive notes by Barry "Dr. Demento" Hansen.

Spivey 1001 Basket of Blues
70s recordings of Lucille Hegamin, Hannah Sylvester, and Victoria Spivey, accompanied by Buddy Tate and Eddie Barefield.

Spivey 1004 Three Kings and a Queen
Features Roosevelt Sykes, Big Joe Williams (with a young Bob Dylan!), Lonnie Johnson, and Victoria Spivey.

Spivey 1006 The Queen and Her Knights
Victoria Spivey with Memphis Slim, Little Brother Montgomery, and Lonnie Johnson.

Spivey 1011 The All Star Blues World of Spivey Records
Roosevelt Sykes, Willie Dixon, including a bogus track purportedly by Smokey Hogg!

Spivey 1012 Spivey's Blues Parade
Sonny Boy Williamson, Sippie Wallace, Lonnie Johnson, and Walter Horton.

Spivey 1014 Kings and the Queen
Victoria Spivey, Memphis Slim, Lonnie Johnson, Roosevelt Sykes, and Bob Dylan.

Spivey 1015 Spivey's Blues Cavalcade
Larry Johnson, Danny Russo, Homesick James, and Bukka White.

Spivey 1017 Spivey's Blues Showcase
Lefty Dizz, Sparkey Rucker, Otis Spann, and Victoria Spivey.

Spivey 1018 New York Really Has the Blues
Paul Oscher, Sugar Blue, Dicey-Ross Blues Band, and Washboard Doc.

Stax 8528 Blue Monday
An excellent collection of 60s and early 70s blues recordings from the Stax vaults, most previously unissued. Includes Albert King, Little Milton, the fine singer and brilliant guitarist Freddy Robinson, and Detroit singer/harmonica player Little Sonny.

Stax 8547 (c) The Stax Blues Brothers
Includes Albert King, John Lee Hooker, and Johnny Taylor.

Storyville 214 A Festival of Blues
Enjoyable collection of blues artists recorded in Europe in early/mid 60s, including Champion Jack Dupree, Memphis Slim, John Henry Barbee, Sippie Wallace, Roosevelt Sykes, and Speckled Red.

Storyville 4008 The Harmonica Blues
Recorded in Europe in the 60s. Features Sonny Terry, Doctor Ross, Hammie Nixon, and Sonny Boy Williamson.

Storyville 4023 The Best of the Blues
Sundown 709-01 Blow by Blow
Fine postwar harmonica blues records, featuring rare sides by Junior Wells, Jerry McCain, Andy Belvin, Sammy Lewis, Eddie Hope, and Charles Walker.

Sundown 709-03 Suckin' and Blowin'
Second album of postwar harmonica blues, featuring 16 excellent and rare recordings by George Smith, Jerry McCain, Papa Lightfoot, Cousin Leroy, Long Gone Miles, John Lee "Sonny Boy" Williamson, Old Sonny Boy, and Sonny Terry.

Sundown 709-06 Juicy Harmonica
Third album of postwar harmonica blues, presenting 16 sides recorded between 1947–66 by Eddie Burns, Jerry McCain, Chicago Sunny Boy (Joe Hill Louis), Sonny Boy Williamson, Sonny Terry, Model T. Slim, Mule Thomas (Jesse Thomas), and Sir Arthur.

Swing House SWH 8 R&B and Boogie Woogie
Excellent collection of live recordings of blues and R&B from 1943–49, including Four Joes and A Jane, Meade Lux Lewis, Four Blazes, and the Ray McKinley Quartet.

Swinghouse SWH 30 Hey Lawdy
Big-band blues and boogie from 1943–48 radio transcriptions, featuring recordings by Count Basie, June Richmond with Andy Kirk's Orchestra, Saunders King, Meade Lux Lewis, and T-Bone Walker. Excellent sound quality.

Swinghouse SWH 43 Rhythm and Blues and Boogie Woogie
Fifteen sides taken from rare 1940–45 radio transcriptions. Highlights are two superb cuts by Joe Turner and Pete Johnson and a very fine side by Leadbelly. Also includes Woody Herman, Will Bradley, Joe Marsala, and Conny Jordan Quartet.

Trumpet AA 701 (c,d) Strange Kind of Feeling
Features Tiny Kennedy, a big, bad blues shouter who was sent by Trumpet to Sam Phillips' Memphis Recording Service in 1952 to cut a session with Calvin Newborn on guitar. All five tracks that they recorded are here, three previously unissued on LP. Clayton Love was recorded in 1951 doing "Shufflin' with Love" and "Susie" but cut out shortly thereafter to hook up with Ike Turner's Kings of Rhythm. Jerry "Boogie" McCain brought his bag of harps to Trum-

pet in '53, cutting a couple of blues tunes, but back in the studio the next year he really cut loose with some jumping juke tunes like "Stay Out of Automobiles" and "Crazy 'Bout That Mess." Fourteen tunes in all, about half previously unissued.

Wolf 120 854 From Helena to Chicago!
Informal and mostly acoustic recordings cut in Chicago in 1988. Features Honeyboy Edwards, Eddie C. Campbell, and Johnny B. Moore. Mostly fairly nondescript performances.
CASSETTE ONLY RELEASE

Atlantic 81666 Atlantic Honkers: An R&B Saxophone Anthology
Two-LP reissue contains important work by early R&B saxmen Frank Culley, Willis Jackson, Hal Singer, Sam "The Man" Taylor, and Arnett Cobb. Standouts include "Love Groovin'" by The Joe Morris Orchestra, "C. C. Rider" by Tiny Grimes, "Barrel House" by Jesse Stone, and the powerhouse "Just Smoochin'" by King Curtis. Intelligent sleeve notes by Bob Porter. Much of this material is reissued for the first time in 35 years.
CASSETTE AND CD RELEASE ONLY

Atlantic 81696-1 Atlantic Blues: Vocalists
Twenty-nine tracks by 20 artists. The first album is mostly from the 40s and 50s and includes some lovely sides by Mama Yancey, Lavern Baker (a fine version of Bessie Smith's "Gimme A Pigfoot"), Joe Turner, Lil Green (her only 50s recordings), the rare Atlantic sides by Wynonie Harris, and two by Ruth Brown, including the previously unissued "Rain Is A Bringdown" from 1949, with Amos Milburn on piano. The second album is mostly from 45s issued on Atlantic and subsidiary labels in the 60s and 70s. There are fine sides by Percy Mayfield (from 1974 with fine guitar by Johnny "Guitar" Watson), Ted Taylor, Esther Phillips, Johnny Copeland (the brilliant "It's My Own Tears That's Being Wasted"), Eldridge Holmes (New Orleans singer, with Art Neville and Leo Nocentelli), Johnny Taylor, a surprisingly blues-flavored cut by Aretha Franklin, and Z. Z. Hill. CD has fewer tracks.

Atlantic 80149 Blues Explosion
Live from 1982 Montreux Jazz Festival, featuring John Hammond, Stevie Ray Vaughan, Sugar Blue, Koko Taylor, Luther Johnson, and J. B. Hutto.
COMPACT DISC

Ace CDCHD 941 Jumpin' the Blues
A high-octane compilation of four-to-the bar blues and boogie, taken from the R&B divisions of Decca, Coral, and Brunswick, and previously available some years ago on a series of now-out-of-print LPs. Twenty-two song compiliation featuring a wealth of

seldom-heard singers like Stomp Gordon, whose excellent "Damp Rag" opens the proceedings, plus lively tracks led by Dole Dickens of The Redcaps fame, Big Bob Dougherty, trumpeter Tiny Davis and her orchestra (on the surprisingly racy "Race Horse"), Willie Brown (not the Delta bluesman), and Connie Jordan. We also hear from pianoman Cecil Gant, Texas guitar slingers Goree Carter and Johnnie Brown, the sassy Margie Day, with her bizarre "Take Out Your False Teeth Daddy," Johnny Otis sideman James Von Streeter, and songbirds Zilla Mays and Eunice Davis.

Antones ANT 9001 Bringing You the Best in Blues
Sixteen-track sampler from Antones' releases.

Charly CD 26 Blues Upside Your Head
Twenty-two tracks drawn from Charly's catalog of material from Vee Jay, Duke, King, Jewel, and Sun, including Jimmy Reed, Bobby Bland, Elmore James, Freddy King, Billy Boy Arnold, Eddie Taylor, The Carter Brothers, Memphis Slim, George and "Wild Child" Butler. Some fine music here though the sound quality doesn't do justice to the compact disc format and the choice of material is a little odd. There are two Elmore James cuts but neither has slide, and the tracks by Jimmy Reed, John Lee Hooker, and Bobby Bland don't represent them at their best.

Conifer CDRR 301 Blues Experience, Vol. 1
Hour-long CD, reissuing 15 recordings from the JSP label by Buddy Guy, John Lee Hooker, Prof. Longhair, Eddie Vinson, Jimmy Witherspoon, and Lowell Fulson.

DCC Compact Classics DZS 026 The Real Blues Blues Brothers
In spite of the silly title, this is an excellent collection of 19 sides recorded in the 50s and early 60s for Vee Jay. Included are five of John Lee Hooker's best-known Vee Jay sides, including "Boom Boom" and "Whiskey and Women," four by Jimmy Reed including "Baby What You Want Me to Do" and "Honest I Do," two by Pee Wee Crayton including his classic "The Telephone Ringing," two by Memphis Slim including "Messin' Around with the Blues," with a great guitar solo by Matt Murphy, plus tracks by Brownie McGhee and Sonny Terry, Eddie Taylor, Roscoe Gordon, Billy Boy Arnold, and Lightnin' Hopkins. An excellent selection with crisp, clear, and dynamic sound.

EPM Musique FDC 5503 Welcome to the Blues
Sixteen-track sampler drawn from mostly out-of-print albums on the Paris Album and Blue Silver labels. Mostly mediocre performances by Booker T.

Laury, Memphis Slim, Clifton Chenier, Zora Young, Mississippi Johnny Waters, Big Time Sarah, Hubert Sumlin, and Brownie McGhee. 68 minutes of music.

EPM Musique FDC 5507 San Francisco Blues Festival: European Sessions

EPM Musique FDC 5508 Blues with the Girls

1982 recording done in France by little-known blues singers Zora Young, Bonnie Lee, and Big Time Sarah, with a European band featuring Hubert Sumlin. Each singer gets five or six songs and does a mixture of blues standards and originals.

EPM Musique FDC 5513 American Livin' Blues Festival 1982

Festival recording from France, with Smokey Smothers, Lester Davenport, Lafayette Leake, Queen Sylvia Embry, and Jimmy Dawkins, culminating in a nine-minute jam session. Lots of original material, not the usual overdone live fare.

EPM Musique FDC 5519 Life in Blues

Eleven tracks mostly from the 70s and early 80s and previously available on albums on the Blue Silver and Paris Album labels. Includes Lightnin' Hopkins, Queen Sylvia Embry, Big Bill Broonzy, Mickey Baker, Booker T. Laury, and Jimmy Dawkins.

EPM Musique FDC 5523 100% Blues

A real mixture of some acoustic and some electric blues, some classic studio cuts and some expendable contemporary live recordings. In spite of the lack of focus, it's still good listening, with memorable cuts by John Lee Hooker, Otis Rush, Brownie McGhee, Billy Boy Arnold, Little Johnny Taylor, Clifton Chenier, Lightnin' Hopkins, and Robert Pete Williams.

Instant CD 5016 Stoned Alchemy—Hits That Inspired The Rolling Stones

Same idea as the P-Vine "Rolling Stones Classics" CD: Go back to the vaults and present the original versions of great old blues/R&B tunes covered by Jagger and Co. in their formative years. CD contains 27 cuts (3 less than double-LP version) at a special budget price!

JSP CD 210 The Paul Jones Rhythm and Blues Show

Radio recordings featuring Phil Guy, Lowell Fulson, Little Willie Littlefield, and Louisiana Red.

JSP CD 221 The Paul Jones Rhythm and Blues Show, Vol. 2

New studio recordings by Rockin' Sidney, Carey Bell, Katie Webster, and Bill Dicey from English DJ Paul Jones' show.

JSP CD 228 The Burnley National Blues Festival 1989

Live performances from British blues festival, featuring Fenton Robinson, Champion Jack Dupree, Little Willie Littlefield, Big Town Playboys, Otis Grand and The Dance Kings, and more. 14 cuts.

JSP CD 235 The Paul Jones Rhythm and Blues Show—The American Guests, Vol. 3

Four American bluesmen recorded in the BBC studios for the only British national radio program devoted to blues and R&B. Lurrie Bell is in good form accompanied by dad Carey on harp and The Norman Beaker Band. Mojo Buford turns in some energetic harp blowing and hoarse vocals on four songs with The Richard Studholme Blues Connection. Fenton Robinson is also featured with the Beaker band but his sides don't really click; part of the problem is his under-amplified guitar. Louisiana Red winds up the proceedings (also with the Beaker band) with an uncharacteristically urban-flavored trio of songs, which are very effective.

JSP CD 238 The Second Burnley National Blues Festival

Recorded live in the North of England in April 1990, this set features Louisiana Red, Lucky Lopez Evans, Buddy Guy, Angela Brown (accompanied by pianist Christian Christ!), and Carey and Lurrie Bell.

L+R CDLR 42066 American Folk Blues Festival, 1963–67

An excellent cross-section of live recordings by some of the great blues artists who toured Europe as part of the American Folk Blues Festivals. The music is varied and consistently fine, with performances by Sleepy John Estes and Hammie Nixon, Buddy Guy, Big Mama Thornton (with Guy and Fred Below), Muddy Waters, Howlin' Wolf, John Lee Hooker, Sonny Boy Williamson (with Hubert Sumlin), Sonny Terry and Brownie McGhee, Roosevelt Sykes, Junior Wells (with Otis Rush), Bukka White, and Lightnin' Hopkins. It's sad to think that most of these artists have now passed on, but this one will bring back many wonderful memories. Sound quality is excellent.

Line CD 9.00680 Blues Anytime, Vols. 1–4

Twenty-four mid-60s selections on both of these CDs reissued from the British Immediate label. Volumes 1 and 2 feature early Eric Clapton, Savoy Brown, Tony McPhee, John Mayall, and Fleetwood Mac's Jeremy Spencer. Volumes 3 and 4 include Albert Lee, Rod Stewart, Jeff Beck, and Stuff Smith. Eric Clapton and Jo Ann Kelly are represented on both discs, which constitute a veritable encyclopedia of early British blues.

Mobile Fidelity MFCD 874-2 A Riot in the Blues

This one isn't exactly going to bring out the riot squad, but is an interesting collection of surprisingly well-produced sides recorded by Bob Shad (in what are referred to as "highly informal settings") for the Mainstream/Time labels. Of particular appeal to collectors are three early Ray Charles cuts (a hard-edged "Why Did You Go," the Charles Brown-styled "I Found My Baby There," and the romping instrumental "Guitar Blues"), plus selections by the rarely heard James Wayne, a real down-home singer from the Texas-Louisiana area. Arbee Stidham lays down some solid sounds, particularly on the rockin' double-sax arrangement on "I'm in the Mood." The Lightnin' Hopkins tracks are fine as always, and the remaining 10 cuts by Sonny Terry and Brownie McGhee are sure to satisfy any folk blues fan. Twenty-three selections in all.

Motown MOTD 5463 Switched on Blues

Ten sides from the mid-to-late 60s. Although most of the tracks are more in the deep-soul vein than straight 12-bar blues, there are some fine performances from Sammy Ward, Gino Parks, and Mable John. Also includes one of Amos Milburn's rare Motown recordings, plus Stevie Wonder's "I Call It Pretty Music but the Old People Call It the Blues," the least successful track here.

P-Vine PCD 2005 Rollin' Stone Classics

The premise on this disc is to put together the original versions of tunes covered by the Rolling Stones. Since they were heavily influenced by Chicago blues and Chess records, there's some great Chuck Berry ("Around and Around," "Come On"), Bo Diddley ("Mona," "Crackin' Up," "I'm Alright"), and Muddy Waters, including his song, "Rolling Stone," which gave the group their name. There is also "Time is One My Side" by Irma Thomas, "Harlem Shuffle" by Bob and Earl, "Little Red Rooster" by Howlin' Wolf, and the first-ever reissue of "It's All Over Now" by The Valentinos (with Bobby Womack). This was also the first CD appearance of Robert Johnson's "Love in Vain." Also "Prodigal Son" by Robert Wilkins and "Susie Q" by Dale Hawkins. Twenty-six tracks in all; Seventy minutes of great music.

Pair PCD2 1205 Best of the Blues—A Summit Meeting

Reissue of Buddah label 2-LP set of live recordings from the 1973 Newport in New York show (recently released in its entirety on vinyl by Charly). Apparently time restrictions did not allow the inclusion of the Lloyd Glenn set, and one Gatemouth Brown song is also left out, making the total time on disc one hour and nine minutes. With B. B. King, Muddy Waters, Big Mama Thornton, Jay McShann, Cleanhead Vinson, Big Boy Crudup, and Gatemouth Brown.

Polydor 839 393-2 (GM) Best of Blues

Fourteen tracks drawn from various albums recorded for the French Barclay label in the 70s. A mixture of good and indifferent material from Furry Lewis, Clifton Chenier, Clarence "Gatemouth" Brown, Memphis Slim and Buddy Guy, Memphis Slim and Roosevelt Sykes, Mickey Baker, and Prof. Longhair.

Rhino 75758-2 (21S) Soul Shots Vol. 4—Urban Blues

A nice collection of tough electric blues by B. B. King, Buddy Guy, Otis Rush, Bobby Bland, Junior Wells, Lowell Fulsom, Little Milton, Albert Collins, and Little Richard. Blues enthusiasts will probably own most of these 16 relatively common tracks already, but hey, they're great tunes. Highly recommended for casual blues listeners and anyone who likes that gritty city sound. Driving Wheel/Stormy Monday/Feel So Band/High-Heel Sneakers/Sweet Sixteen/Messin' With the Kid/Tramp.

Vogue 600171 Blues Jubilee

Live recordings from concerts organized in California by Frank Bull and Gene Norman. Features Dinah Washington, Jimmy Witherspoon, Helen Humes, and Joe Turner. Includes some previously unissued tracks.

Vogue 670032 Blue Guitar Album

52-minute collection of blues drawn from various Vogue albums (many now out of print), which come from a variety of sources. Artists include Big Bill Broonzy, Lightnin' Hopkins, Jimmy Reed, Hubert Sumlin, The Aces, Louisiana Red, John Lee Hooker, Jimmy Dawkins, Brownie McGhee, and Jimi Hendrix(!). Enjoyable selection and decent sound.

Zeta 715 Back to the Blues

A collection of 16 tracks released in the 70s and early 80s on the Blue Silver and Paris Album labels. Included are Otis Rush (from his 1971 recordings originally on Bullfrog and now on Hightone), Johnny Shines, Robert Jr. Lockwood (both with same band), Ron Thompson (lively version of Hop Wilson's "Rockin' at the Cocoanut Top"), Brownie McGhee, Hubert Sumlin, Sugar Blue (weird!), Jack Dupree (with horrible organ), Clifton Chenier (recorded live in France), Screamin' Jay Hawkins (awful!), Luther Tucker, and Sonny Terry. Mostly unmemorable. Sound, however, is very good.

Illustration Credits

Kokomo Arnold: Courtesy Yazoo Records

Big Three Trio: Courtesy Columbia Records

Elvin Bishop: Photo by Pat Johnson, courtesy Alligator Records

Blind Blake: Courtesy Yazoo Records

Bobby Bland: Courtesy MCA Records

Big Bill Broonzy: Courtesy Yazoo Records

Charles Brown: Photo by Kelly Bryant, courtesy Alligator Records

Clarence "Gatemouth" Brown: Photo by Robert Barclay, courtesy Alligator Records

Leroy Carr and Scrapper Blackwell: Courtesy Yazoo Records

Bo Carter: Courtesy Yazoo Records

Clifton Chenier: Photo by Edmund Shea, courtesy Arhoolie Records

Albert Collins: Photo by Paul Natkin, courtesy Alligator Records

Elizabeth Cotten: Courtesy Smithsonian/Folkways Records

James Cotton: Photo by Susan Mattes, courtesy Alligator Records

Robert Cray Band: Courtesy PolyGram Records

Reverend Gary Davis: Photo by/Courtesy Richard Carlin

Dr. John: Courtesy Alligator Records

Buddy Guy: Courtesy MCA/Chess Records

Earl Hooker: Photo by Chris Strachwitz, courtesy Arhoolie Records

Howlin' Wolf: Courtesy MCA/Chess Records

Alberta Hunter: Courtesy Columbia Records

Mississippi John Hurt: Courtesy Yazoo Records

John Jackson: Photo by Chris Strachwitz, courtesy Arhoolie Records

Skip James: Courtesy Yazoo Records

Lonnie Johnson: Courtesy Columbia Records

Robert Johnson: Courtesy Columbia Records

B. B. King: Photo by Keith Perry, courtesy Sidney A. Seidenberg Inc.

The Kinsey Report: Photo by Paul Natkin, courtesy Alligator Records

Lazy Lester: Photo by Steve Koress, courtesy Alligator Records

Leadbelly: Courtesy Smithsonian/Folkways Records

Mance Lipscomb: Photo by Chris Strachwitz, courtesy Arhoolie Records

Little Milton: Courtesy MCA/Chess Records

Little Walter: Courtesy MCA/Chess Records

Magic Sam: Photo by Ray Flerlage, courtesy Delmark Records

Magic Slim: Photo by D. Shigley, courtesy Alligator Records

Martin, Bogan, and Armstrong: Courtesy Flying Fish Records

Fred McDowell: Courtesy Arhoolie Records

Brownie McGhee: Courtesy Fantasy Records

Blind Willie McTell: Courtesy Yazoo Records

Muddy Waters: Courtesy MCA/Chess Records

Charlie Musselwhite: Photo by Gregg Toland, courtesy Arhoolie Records

Ma Rainey: Courtesy Yazoo Records

A. C. Reed: Courtesy Alligator Records

Jimmy Rogers: Courtesy MCA/Chess Records

Otis Rush: Photo by Amy van Singel, courtesy Delmark Records

Bessie Smith: Courtesy Columbia Records

Frank Stokes: Courtesy Yazoo Records

Roosevelt Sykes: Courtesy Yazoo Records

Tampa Red: Courtesy Yazoo Records

Koko Taylor: Photo by Sandra Miller, courtesy Alligator Records

Sonny Terry: Courtesy Fantasy Records

Stevie Ray Vaughan: Courtesy Epic/Columbia Records

Katie Webster: Photo by Peter Amft, courtesy Alligator Records

Junior Wells: Photo by Ray Flerlage, courtesy Delmark Records

Sonny Boy Williamson: Photo by Chris Strachwitz, Courtesy Arhoolie Records

Johnny Winter: Photo by Paul Natkin, courtesy Alligator Records

Legends of the Blues: Courtesy Columbia Records

Altamount: Courtesy Rounder Records

Sons of the Blues: Courtesy Alligator Records

Lawrence "Black" Ardoin: Photo by Chris Strachwitz, Courtesy Arhoolie Records

About the Author

Frank Scott was born in London, England in 1942 and has been collecting blues since the early 60s when he was first introduced to the music in London's flourishing club scene. Trained as an aerospace engineer, he moved to Southern California in 1966 to pursue his career and to be closer to the music he loves. In the early 70s, he and a friend started a small mail-order business for blues recordings that became a full-time occupation when he quit engineering in 1974.

In 1978 he moved to Northern California, where he joined Chris Strachwitz of the internationally renowned Arhoolie Records to form a mail-order operation as an adjunct to Chris' retail store, Down Home Music. Over the years this company has acquired a reputation for having the most comprehensive stock of blues and other specialty music. In 1990, Frank and his wife Nancy spun off the mail-order operation into a separate business, which continues to serve some 13,000 customers worldwide.

In the 70s and early 80s, Frank also ran a small record company, Advent, that produced a handful of critically acclaimed blues and folk recordings. Besides his contributions to Down Home newsletters and catalogs, he has written album liner notes and articles for specialty magazines, and has hosted several radio programs over listener-sponsored radio stations.

He currently lives in El Cerrito, California with Nancy and their two-year-old son, Benjamin.

- -

Keep Up to Date with the Blues!

All the records, cassettes and compact discs listed in this book are available through Down Home Music, America's leading specialty music mail order company. If you would like to receive regular newsletters with information on all new blues releases (and lots of other music, too!) please fill out the coupon below.

You will also receive a price list for the releases in this book along with a 15% discount certificate good for your first order with us.

NAME:_____

ADDRESS:_____

CITY:_____**STATE:**_____**ZIP CODE:**_____

MUSICAL INTERESTS:_____

_____

Mail coupon to:
DOWN HOME MUSIC
6921 Stockton Ave.
El Cerrito, CA 94530

You may also phone (415) 525-1494, or fax us, (415) 525-2904.